# Development and Disorder

# Development and Disorder

## A History of the Third World since 1945

Mike Mason

Between The Lines
Toronto, Canada

Published by
Between The Lines
720 Bathurst Street, #404
Toronto, Ontario
M5S 2R4

Cover design by Gordon Robertson
Interior Design by Steve Izma
Maps by Kent Benson
Printed in Canada

Between The Lines gratefully acknowledges the support of the Ontario Arts Council, the Canadian Heritage Ministry, and the Canada Council for the Arts for our publishing program.

## Canadian Cataloguing in Publication Data

Mason, Mike, 1938-
  Development and disorder : a history of the Third
World since 1945

Includes bibliographical references and index.
ISBN 1-896357-08-3

1. Developing countries—Economic conditions.
2. Developing countries—Economic policy.  3. Developing countries—History.  4. Economic development.  I. Title.

HC59.7.M368 1997      330.9172'40825      C97-930267-6

# Contents

# Acknowledgements

In the process of writing this book, I have incurred immense debts, all of which I would like to warmly acknowledge. Most of these are to friends, some to colleagues, others to students, and some to institutions. In some cases, friends, colleagues, and students are one in the same. Let me begin with just a few of the friends. More than a decade ago, Kent Benson patiently showed me how to use a computer. In the years that followed, Bob Shenton suggested to me that development had a history and later let me read his history of development in manuscript form. Dan O'Meara, Steve Soroka, and the editors at Between The Lines all suggested that I might be on the road to writing such a history. Other friends along the way provided me with suggestions and encouragement; in particular, Bruce Berman, Myron Echenberg, Linda Freeman and Edward Kissi, Tim Brook, Robin Porter, Micheline Lessard, Keith Meadowcroft, Jamie Swift, and Brian Tomlinson all made invaluable suggestions. Kent Benson prepared the maps. Maggie Cahill provided me with limitless friendship and hospitality in London, England, and Ms. Givings read the whole manuscript painstakingly and offered, as usual, a perfect blend of sympathy and criticism.

Students in my introductory course on the Third World, for which I wrote this book, were most helpful, offering suggestions and providing criticism of all kinds. Since this course is large and I have taught it several times, I cannot thank them all individually. I would also like to acknowledge my debt to my graduate students, past and present, for the stimulation and pleasure that their enthusiasms and fresh insights afforded me.

I have researched this study in the libraries of Concordia, McGill, and Queen's universities in Canada, and in those of the University of North London and the School of Oriental and African Studies in Britain. To all these institutions and to the Public Record Office in London I am indebted. I would also like to thank Judy Appleby and Wendy Knechtel of the Concordia libraries, and, in particular, the reference librarians at McGill and Queen's. Of all my obligations, my greatest is to another librarian, my wife, Mary Mason, of McGill and Queen's, for three decades of companionship and encouragement.

Finally, Shahan and Arshak Markaryan of Papeterie Harvard have been the best photocopiers a writer could ask for, as well as perceptive critics of my account of the contemporary history of Turkey.

This book is for Lucia and Catherine Mason, and dedicated to the memory of John E. Lavers of London and Kano and Alfie Roberts of St. Vincent and Montreal.

# Chapter 1

# The Third World: From Western Perspectives

## Genesis

The "Third World" emerged from the dying body of colonialism. Named in 1952, this general group of nations has come to include almost all of the countries of Latin America, the Caribbean, Africa, the Middle East, South, Southeast, and East Asia, and Oceania—that is, most of the peoples and states of the world with the exception of the 26 members of the Organization for Economic Co-operation and Development (OECD).*

In 1950, out of a total world population of 2.5 billion, the Third World population comprised 1.6 billion, or just under 65 per cent of the total. By 1992, out of a world population of 5.5 billion, the Third World population made up 4.25 billion, or around 70 per cent.

It seems fair to insist, then, that when we speak of "the world" we are speaking mainly of the Third World. Indeed, because much of what has been known as the "Second World"—the formerly Eastern European countries that had socialist economies—seems to be now on its way to joining the Third World, it is also the case that contemporary world history, that is, the history of the women and men who make up most of the planet, has become more and more the history of the Third World.

---

* The OECD bloc comprises the 26 richest countries in the world: Australia, Austria, Belgium, Canada, Czech Republic, Denmark, Finland, France, Germany, Greece, Ireland, Iceland, Italy, Japan, Luxembourg, Netherlands, New Zealand, Norway, Portugal, Spain, Sweden, Switzerland, United Kingdom, United States, Turkey, and, since April 1994, Mexico. These countries contain around 16 per cent of the world's population but control two-thirds of its merchandise (or tradeable goods). They produce three-fifths of the world's exports and supply four-fifths of the world's aid, enjoying a mean per capita Gross National Product (GNP) of over $18,000.

## The Imaginary and the Real

The idea that the term "Third World" carries a clear meaning and has utility—that there really is such a thing as a coherent Third World—was born in the West, and remains largely a Western concept. The unity and most of the qualities assigned to the Third World have also been largely Western.

In *Iran and the Muslim World* Nikki Keddie makes much this same argument: "'Third Worldism' ... is a term used by outside students of this trend and not by those who adhere to it. Hardly anyone refers to himself as a third worldist. ... Without some such term, however, it is impossible to draw significant comparative conclusions about a variety of related though non-identical movements that have great importance in today's ideological universe."[1]

The very idea of a Third World falls into the same category as the older, equally well-established idea of the "Orient." For example, various terms have been used to describe the people from these nations as a whole—"Third World people," "people from developing countries," or "people from the South"—as well as separately—"Africans," or "indigenous peoples of (say) the Andes," or even "peasants." But these terms tend to be simply revised and more palatable forms of older, European, words such as "savages," "natives," "Orientals," or *autochthones*.

Many, perhaps most, of the terms used to refer to the peoples of the Third World—for instance, as members of (ethnic) "tribes" or (religious) "communities"—emerged in the 19th century. In some cases, as in India, people had earlier on identified themselves more with labels that reflected social standing than with ethnic or communal labels; only from the 19th century did the idea of ethnicity *above all else*, that is, the idea of fundamental and irrevocable ethnic identity, become widely accepted. Yet in spite of these neologisms, many of the archaic terms that have governed the identities of non-Westerners remain in place. People in Canada, to the amazement of foreigners, still often use the colonial pejorative "natives" to refer to the original inhabitants of the country.

The central assumption of "otherness" and "essentialness" is invariably woven within all these terms. "We" and "they," it is assumed, both have special qualities (moral, intellectual, physical). "We" (North Americans, Western Europeans, Australians, New Zealanders) have one essence, and "they" (Muslims, Africans, Asians) have another. All of us know, or think we know, what "white" North Americans and Western Europeans have in common. "We" also think we know what qualities various Third World peoples share. Although Zulus are in large part urban dwellers, industrial workers, and Christians, and Somalis are, or were, pastoralists and Muslims, both groups of people are, we know, *essentially*

"African." People from East and Southeast Asia—whether they are boat people, factory workers, guerrillas, millionaires, or molecular biologists—are often still referred to as "Orientals."

Many of these terms, though ambiguous and deeply problematic, are to a large extent inescapable. In this book I am sticking with some of them ("peasants" and "Third World," for instance) because of their familiarity and convenience, but I do have misgivings about these words. By using them with appropriate disclaimers, I hope to avoid perpetuating mischievous illusions or ideologies; for I think both the "Third World" and "the West" have existed in one form and do exist in another—if neither precisely in the way in which we have conceived them, then in some approximation of this way.

For instance, most of the overwhelming part of the globe that we call the Third World has had a common history. Most of it has been colonized, politically and economically. Much of it was colonized in relatively recent times and by the countries of the West. The most decisive result of this colonization has been Western European domination over people of other identities. In even more recent times the forms of this domination have changed, in most cases, but the domination itself has not ended. A quick example: in October 1995, Guatemalan government soldiers killed a number of "Indians." These "Indians"—in actuality, Mayas—had just returned to their homeland from Mexico, where they had fled to escape earlier massacres. The government of Guatemala is almost exclusively made up of people of European descent, and it is a government that could not exist without the support of Washington. About 70 per cent of the population are of Maya descent. The word "domination," together with terms such as "colonization" and "terror," have existed side by side in Guatemala for four centuries; colonization and its corollary, domination, are clearly alive and well there.

The one overwhelming fact about the Third World, then, is that it has been, in part or whole, then and even to some extent now, ruled over by Europeans and Americans (and their descendants such as white South Africans and white Latin Americans).

There are exceptions to the rule of a common colonial history involving Western dominance. Neither Iran nor Thailand, for instance, was ever colonized. The mammoth exception to the rule is China. The formal colonization of China itself was limited to a few offshore islands—notably, Hong Kong and Taiwan—and the peninsula of Macao. The largest of these islands, Taiwan, remained in foreign possession for only half a century, until 1945. Furthermore, the conquest of China and Manchuria in the 1930s was carried out not by the West, but by Japan.

Yet China, the world's most populous country, Iran, and Thailand are unusual. China's history of independence from the West differs markedly from that of India, the world's second most populous country, or Indonesia, in third place. In India, European rule, direct and indirect, lasted for almost two centuries. Contemporary India was forced into the school of Western modernity by British colonialism, just as Indonesia was schooled by Dutch colonialism. This colonial conditioning is also a necessary factor in considering the economic and social histories of Latin America, the Caribbean, Africa, the Middle East, and the rest of Asia or Oceania.

Most of the Third World also has another element in common: poverty. And much of it is getting poorer. Most of it is also, in Western eyes, disorderly—including China, given the famous events in Tiananmen Square in June 1989—as well as threatening.

In the early days of the concept of the Third World, Western theorists tended to explain poverty and disorderliness in terms of history. They said the Third World had always been that way due to either lack of technique or unfortunate approaches to life, which included unhelpful and irrational sentiments and practices (superstitions, bad hygiene, fatalism, laziness, deviousness, cruelty, factiousness, venality), which were often said to be "traditional." Tradition was the enemy of Progress. The writers' tendency to capitalize the "p" in "progress" suggested not just that the word was a proper rather than a common noun but also that it was a spiritual concept, like God and Civilization. The forward march of Progress was, and still is, called "modernization."

So this "Third World" and the senses of "development" and "modernization" that have transformed or at least distorted that world are both imaginary and real. This Third World is an imaginary place inhabited by "Africans" and "Orientals" whose distinctive "otherness" is largely a product of Western exaggerations. It is also an imaginary place to the extent that it is homogeneous; it is not. Contemporary East Asia has little in common, culturally or politically, with contemporary Africa; even the different parts of Africa share only a tenuous commonality. The "development" and "modernization" that were supposed to have taken place in the 1960s and early 1970s turned out to be largely part of a long-lasting Cold War magic lantern show—for the most part they too were only illusory.

What is real then? A large part of what we call the Third World is more or less like we perceive it (although the reasons for this are often not as we are told). This real Third World is dominated by and dependent upon Western governments and institutions, with other kinds of governments and institutions, communist or Eastern, having failed in their interventions.

To understand this Third World, illusory and real, we must also consider the makeup of the First World, that is, the world encompassed within the boundaries of what is generally, especially in North America, called "Western civilization." The Third World, as the descendant of the historical Orient, is the antipode of this Western civilization.

## Unstable Certainties: Western Civilization and Its Obligations

"Civilization" as we know it in the West is just over two centuries old. The English diarist James Boswell explained to Samuel Johnson in 1772 that it was the opposite of barbarity. Behind the idea of "civilization," Raymond Williams suggests, was the general spirit of the Enlightenment "with its emphasis on secular and progressive human self-development."[2]

The word was later used in both England and France to explain superiority and justify imperialism. Imperialists had a duty to carry civilization to those parts of the world in which savagery or barbarism prevailed. Propagandists and politicians in both countries accepted that in the past certain other countries had established civilization—the Chinese and the Egyptians were examples—but they also believed that these civilizations had, due to the innate weaknesses of their rulers, become ramshackle and ruinous. They also accepted that some countries were "half-civilized." China was a perfect example here, too. In 1850 the British prime minister, Lord Palmerston, wrote of such countries: "These half civilized Governments, such as those of China Portugal Spanish America require a Dressing every eight or Ten years to keep them in order [sic]." By "a Dressing," he meant that force had to be used to make them conform to British requirements. Still, even with such stern remedies as the British were willing to apply to ensure some form of order, the thinkers of the time assumed that by the end of the century chaos would reign supreme and China would effectively disintegrate.[3]

The idea of order as connected to "development," sometimes with, and sometimes without civilization, congealed in the 19th century and became one of the central preoccupations of the 20th. At first meaning something like a general unfolding or unrolling, the word came to be applied in the 19th century to certain ideas relating to economic change and then more specifically "for the processes of an *industrial* and trading economy."[4] You couldn't be developed, or be developing, if you didn't have industry and proper trade. Communists poring over five-year plans and fascists boasting of trains running on time were alike concerned with orderly development. Not everyone who was fond of order and development was enthusiastic about civilization; rightists and especially militarists often saw it as being a little corrupt, that is, bourgeois and somewhat effeminate (for order is, above all, a manly value). In times of crisis, governments and state elites would put aside the question of development and become preoccupied largely with order.

The civilized, orderly, world has always included Western Europe and North America as well as ex-colonies in which white settlers dominated, such as Australia, New Zealand, and, for a brief time at least, South Africa, Southern Rhodesia, Algeria, and Israel. Other non-Western or partially Western countries such as Japan, Turkey, and Brazil (with its national motto of "Order and Progress") that believed in progress and were orderly only in parts, or some of the time, were often regarded as existing in the shadowlands of civilization. Some Westerners believed that these countries were civilized—or that at least some of them were civilized— and others thought not. In general, those people who were not possessed of civilization were thought to be "barbarians" or "savages" (or "natives"). Although they lacked civilization, such peoples might, at best, have cultures. Exotic peoples with cultures were "anthropologized," that is, probed by Westerners who sought to explain how the universal laws and truths of humankind were either absent or at least present in peculiar forms. The laws and truths that governed the West were thought to be more or less normal.

Sometimes there were exceptions to the general rule that the normal abode of civilization was in the West. One of these was the orderly and energetic, but enigmatic, Japan. General Douglas MacArthur himself explained Western superiority in these terms: "If the Anglo-Saxon was say forty-five years of age in development in the sciences, the arts, divinity, culture, the Germans were quite as mature. The Japanese, however, in spite of their antiquity . . . were in a very tuitionary condition. Measured by the standards of modern civilization, they would be like a boy of twelve compared with our development of forty-five years."[5] MacArthur, who governed Japan after its surrender in August 1945, did not believe that the Japanese were at a par with the Anglo-Saxons and Germans in terms of civilization. The dour banker and sometime state envoy John Foster Dulles had a different idea. In 1951, when he was the special consultant to the U.S. secretary of state, Dulles entertained the idea of inviting Japan to join what he called an "elite Anglo-Saxon club." On the basis of a few days' experience in Japan, where he talked mainly with fellow Americans, he wrote confidently, "I have a feeling that the Japanese people have felt a certain superiority as against the Asiatic masses." His hope was that Japan might tie itself to the United States.[6] Later, in 1954, when he had become secretary of state himself, he poured out his views on Western civilization and the glories of European and American colonialism.

> We can be grateful for the wise statesmanship that, on the whole, has guided the post-war policies of the Western colonial powers. . . . It was the religion of the West that made the colonial system of the West profoundly different from the empires of the past. Those empires were wholly based on a material concept. When the rules weakened, the ruled fought themselves free. They turned on their masters and destroyed them. That is the way in which civilizations of the past have gone down in ruins. Western civilization may perhaps escape this fate.[7]

But orderliness and industry were not by themselves enough. To count as civilized, the affairs of a country had to be built up in a certain way and in the right order—and have the right look. After all, some "Orientals," like the Japanese, were orderly and successful in economic matters, were they not? But could they be called "civilized," like us? There was room for some doubt here. Edith Cresson, the outspoken prime minister of France (1991-92), exercised by the trade imbalance between the European Community and Japan, infamously let it slip that she thought the Japanese were "short yellow people who stay up all night thinking of ways to screw the Americans and the Europeans" and that Japan had "an absolute determination to conquer the world."[8] This seemed to suggest a serious shortage of civilized behaviour.*

There have always been optimists who believe that progress towards civilization is inevitable even among the most benighted peoples in the most backward corners of the globe. This belief has even been shared by some members of the "backward races" themselves: "It is idle and fruitless to resist the onward march and insidious influences of Civilization and Progress" wrote a West African commentator in the *Lagos Weekly Record* of March 6, 1915. Others were less hopeful. The late 19th-century French thinker Ernest Renan explained bluntly in 1890 that "the equality of races is a dream." That is, some races are civilized, and others might never be.[9]

The optimists argued that it was the *duty* of those who had enjoyed progress to instruct and guide those who had not. This was not to be the help given by one equal to another, but the help offered by a superior to an inferior. The task carried with it the will to dominate, to confer superior

---

* This representation of Japan cannot be put down merely to Gaulic peevishness, but rather should be seen in the light of a generalized Western reaction to the economic threat posed by Japan. Mikiso Hane cites a report written by the CIA for a conference in 1991 in which Japan is described as being non-democratic and racist as well as "immoral, manipulative and controlling." See Hane, *Eastern Phoenix*, 1996, p.83.

values, and ultimately even to govern. In contemporary terms, we see Western countries aiding and advising Third World countries on how to govern and, particularly, how to maintain, or regain, political and economic order. The "White Man's Burden" in contemporary times came to fall under the rubric of "aid," "assistance," or *coopération*." Earlier on this relationship was accepted as being especially incumbent on the colonial countries towards the nations that they had colonized. In 1906, a speaker at a colonial banquet explained: "France has not wanted to see in the creation of her colonies a simple extension of political domination, still less of her commercial exploitation. She has seen a means of making penetrate, among the peoples outside the general movement of civilization, those of her ideas which have placed her at the head of the civilization of the world."[10]

The French idea of civilization differed from the English idea, for reasons that are not surprising. The French were more interested in the extension of their national culture, which they felt was superior. The British, more businesslike, were concerned not so much with culture as with commerce. The great British missionary to Africa, David Livingstone, spoke of "Commerce, Christianity and Civilization" marching together into the "Dark Continent."

There was a major difference between commerce and civilization. While commerce could redeem, it could never transform. But an African with enough French culture could become an assimilated Frenchman; and not only the French thought this. The Martinican poet Aimé Césaire, whose ancestors were taken from Africa and who was himself educated in France, became a *Deputé* in the National Assembly in Paris after World War II. He declared, "I am . . . French, my mind is French."[11] This seems to suggest that the assimilation was more than a vain, imperial claim. Although the chances of becoming French were infinitesimally small, they did exist. By the end of World War I, one African, Blaise Diagne, already sat in the National Assembly in Paris. Just before the outbreak of World War II another man of African descent, Félix Eboué, who came from the colony of French Guiana, became a colonial governor. During the war he was promoted to the governor-generalship of a federation of French African colonies. By contrast, no matter how much money he had, or how brilliantly he played cricket, no African or West Indian or even Indian maharajah could become an Englishman. And practically no one, French or English, even dreamed, before 1945, of an African woman being transformed like Eliza Doolittle into a "gentlewoman." Indigenous women could, on the other hand, be protected from their own menfolk. The "Committee for the Protection of Coloured Women in the Colonies," formed in London in the 1920s, sought to do just that.

By the early 20th century, expansionism had convinced the Americans, too, that they were enrolled in civilization's mission by pushing back frontiers. Early in the previous century Thomas Jefferson had a vision of "civilization" moving across the American continent, imposing itself on "savages" who were "living under no law but that of nature, subsisting and covering themselves with the flesh and skins of wild beasts." In 1828 another American provided Washington's version of the *mission civilatrice* by proclaiming that the young country had been "destined by Providence to carry westward . . . the blessings of civilization and liberty." By the end of the century one of his countrymen could assert with confidence:

> There is no more interesting question of the present day than that of what is to be done with the world's land which is laying unimproved; whether it shall go to the great power that is willing to turn it to account, or remain with its original owner, who fails to understand its value. The Central Americans are like a gang of semi-barbarians in a beautifully furnished house, of which they can understand neither its possibilities of comfort nor its use.[12]

Obviously, Central America needed Uncle Sam. A series of headlines over an article by Frederick Palmer, a journalist writing on Central America for the *Chicago Tribune* (March 1, 1909), put this plainly: "Honduras Wants Uncle Sam's Aid . . . Lack of Good Government Alone Keeps Davilla's Country from Being a Second California." Three years later Miguel Dávila was forced to resign when Honduras was invaded by mercenaries financed by a precursor of the United Fruit Company.

Often the problems thrust upon the civilized required rough and apparently arbitrary solutions; it was necessary to be cruel to be kind. Joseph Conrad, the Polish-English novelist, had seen this in the Belgian Congo, where, in his novel *Heart of Darkness*, his character Kurtz uttered the refrain that best serves as the motto of early colonialism: "the horror, the horror." In another of Conrad's novels, *Nostromo* (published in 1904, only a year after J.A. Hobson published his classic study of imperialism), a U.S. financier who had put his money into a mine in Central America warned: "We can sit and watch. Of course, some day we shall step in. We are bound to. . . . We shall run the world's business whether the world likes it or not."[13]

President Theodore Roosevelt's ideas followed the same lines; he thought that to ensure order the United States would have to become the policeman of the hemisphere. Perhaps his successor, William Howard Taft, had been inspired by Conrad. Taft claimed, regarding the governments of Central America: "[We] have the right to knock their heads together until they should maintain peace between them."[14] Towards the end of the 20th century another president would talk manfully about "kicking butt."

Non-Western people were likened sometimes to a species of schoolchildren—human, certainly, but immature and needing discipline if they were to become civilized. Spare the rod and spoil the native. Half a world away from Central America but only a couple of decades later, in 1941, a white settler member of the Kenya Legislative Council reiterated the message: "I always treat my natives the same way as I treat children. I try to be kind to them, and to advise them and direct them, but when kindness has no effect you have to do the same as they do in the public schools at home and throughout the empire—use the cane."[15]

In some Western eyes, Egyptians were in much the same boat as Kenyans. The British ambassador to Egypt at the end of World War II, who had previously served in the embassy in China, made the connection between the childishness of the "natives" of East Asia and those of the Middle East when he wrote: "The Egyptians are essentially a docile and friendly people, but they are like children in many respects. They need a strong but essentially a fair and helpful hand to guide them: 'firmness and justice' is the motto for Egypt, just as it used to be for the Chinese."[16]

The idea of tuition and firmness requiring the cane wasn't merely a metaphor. "Natives" were regularly flogged. In Kenya in the 1950s, when some of them threatened to destroy colonial rule over 1,000 were hanged. In French Vietnam and Algeria (and even in France in the 1950s) they were guillotined. And on the streets of Paris in October 1962, in a law and order frenzy orchestrated by the Prefect of Police, a former Vichyite, over 200 Algerians were killed by shooting, beating, or drowning.* There was no Amnesty International or Middle East Watch to monitor human rights in the colonies, although reports of the more monstrous excesses of the colonialists did frequently seep out.

By the postwar period the truths about Western civilization had become canonical; that is, like the words and stories of the Bible in the minds of fundamentalist Christians, they were considered to be absolute truth, free of error. Just as the study of Quranic exegesis was central to the curricula of the Muslim theological schools of the Middle East, from

---

* The Prefect of Police, Maurice Papon, who ordered the massacre of the Algerians, had during World War II been instrumental in the deportation of Jews from Bordeaux. In March 1996, representatives of the Jewish victims demanded that he be tried for crimes against humanity—crimes that apparently did not include killing Algerians. Perhaps this was because so many Frenchmen had done the same thing—in the late 1950s, during the war in Algeria, the term *ratonnade*, "rat hunt," had regularly been employed for the hunting, and often killing, of Algerians by French forces of law and order. Thousands of Frenchmen were involved, thousands more implicated.

the end of World War I exegetic studies of Western civilization had entered the curricula of colleges in the United States, and by the end of World War II they had become more widely taught than any other courses in history. The anthropologist Eric Wolf, in providing a testament of the teachings in his youth of "Western Civ." (as it became known), says that many of his generation grew up believing that the West had "a genealogy, according to which ancient Greece begat Rome, Rome begat Christian Europe, Christian Europe begat the Renaissance, the Renaissance the Enlightenment, the Enlightenment political democracy and the industrial revolution. Industry, crossed with democracy, in turn yielded the United States, embodying the rights to life, liberty, and the pursuit of happiness."[17]

This conception of "Western Civ." remained at the centre of the American approach to world historical development, at least until the 1960s when the universalist and triumphalist claims were challenged by those who argued that their truths were partial at best. But, however battered, "Western Civ." even as late as the 1990s remained unapologetically alive in the history departments of most North American universities.[18]

## East and West: Them and Us

Long before the invention of "Western civilization," the main focus of the Western view of the non-Western world had been "the Orient," that is, the ancient world that lay on Europe's doorstep in the Eastern Mediterranean and beyond. But this "Orient" of the European mind, invoked and then dismissed in chapters in "Western Civ." texts with headings like "Cradles of Civilization" and "the Ancient East," has always been in large part a mirage, produced first of all by a mixture of Western apprehension and curiosity, and later, from the early 19th century, by Western attempts at domination (as often expressed in art and literature using sexual imagery).

The way in which this "Orient" has been caricatured and our relationship to it legitimated has been summed up in the term "Orientalism." The literary critic Edward Said made this important argument most forcefully in his book *Orientalism: Western Conceptions of the Orient* (1978). The suffix "ism" in "Orientalism" suggests that it is an ideology, like "capitalism" or "Stalinism," and that many of its essential qualities have been determined not by the subject in question, but by the Western viewer: that is, they have been constructed. This construction was the accomplishment of layer after layer of claims about the Orient, with each claim, in its own time, regarded as being generally authoritative. Thus the most important statements of Orientalism have always been made by

Westerners, not by Easterners (who could not be trusted to explain themselves). These statements or ideas formed a "canon"—an authoritative but partisan body of testimony.

The Orientalist canon was utterly panoramic, including everything from arguments about the authorship of biblical narratives to prurient peeps into harems. All of its parts taken together formed a kind of archive, that is, a collection of views, reports, testimonies, and opinions that, while increasingly refined and complex, tended to remain locked within the perspective of a particular, and narrow, worldview. The earliest elements in this archive were deposited as long ago as the 13th century; the archive has continued to grow right up to the present. This is not to say that contemporary Western views are precisely the same as those held, for instance, at the time of Napoleon's invasion of Egypt at the end of the 18th century, but they are part of the same spectrum.

What is the essence of this archive? Most important of all, the canon emphasizes the fundamental (that is, ontological) difference between the Third World "them" and the Western "us," a difference that has mutated little over time and that allows us to believe that the nature of the West is essentially (and ineradicably) different from that of the Orient. What is particularly important about this essentialism is that "they," even when they are enchanting, are unchanging. This permits us to think about "them," in part or whole, as being "traditional." They have "traditional" views regarding women, or concerning time, or towards work. In some authoritative Western views, "they" (if they are male, at least) are quite openly viewed as being irremediably repulsive: ugly, lazy, unfeeling, lecherous, fanatical—in short, bestial. Lord Soames, son-in-law of the British prime minister Winston Churchill, expressed this point of view perfectly on his arrival in Salisbury in 1979 to negotiate, on behalf of the British government, the end of white rule in Rhodesia: "I want to see the freest, fairest elections possible in this country . . . but intimidation [and] violence [are] rife. . . . You must remember this is Africa. This isn't Little-Puddleton-on-the-Marsh, and they behave differently here. They think nothing of sticking tent poles up each other's whatnot, and doing filthy, beastly things to each other. It does happen, I'm afraid."[19]

Said suggests, like others before him, that history is written by those who win and those who dominate. It has always been one of the tasks of historians to make hegemony seem natural and moral. "Was there ever any domination that did not appear natural to those who possessed it?" asked John Stuart Mill in the mid-19th century. A century later the political philosopher Barrington Moore made the same argument:

In any society the dominant groups are the ones with the most to hide about the way society works. Very often therefore truthful analyses are bound to have a critical ring, to seem like postures rather than objective statements. . . . For all students of human society sympathy with the victims of historical processes and scepticism about the victors' claims provide essential safeguards against being taken in by the dominant mythology. A scholar who tries to be objective needs these feelings as part of his working equipment.[20]

Despite sometimes harsh criticisms of Said's view, the idea of "Orientalism" has not only stuck with us but also continues to penetrate. It is now almost impossible to read or write about Africa or Asia, or even to read or write about writers about Africa or Asia, without considering the obstacles to understanding that are implicit in the "Orientalist" outlook. But this is not to say that our view of the Third World is now unobstructed by preconception and prejudice.

A few years after Said published *Orientalism*, Eric Wolf published a book that complemented Said's work inasmuch as it sought to challenge the conventional Western interpretation of the non-Western world. At the height of the Cold War, Wolf wrote, anthropologists had been forced to wear the leper's bell because of their dubious loyalties. Their besetting sin was known as "cultural relativism," an approach that was unacceptable during a time when moral certainties were demanded. One moral certainty was the superiority of American modernism.

But the 1960s and 1970s wounded moral certainty, although not mortally. This is reflected in Wolf's *Europe and the People without History* (1982), which stresses the interconnectedness of earthly matters: not the superiority and dominance of one history, such of that of the West, and the dependency and subordination of other histories, but the mutual relationship of peoples connected by diseases, plants, human migration, and even culture. As Wolf put it, "If there are connections everywhere, why do we persist in turning dynamic, interconnected phenomena into static, disconnected things?" His answer was that we owed some of this tendency "to the way we have learned our own history. We have been taught, inside the classroom and outside of it, that there exists an entity called the West, and that one can think of this West as a society and civilization independent of and in opposition to other societies and civilizations."[21]

In his book Wolf strives to discredit the idea that there exists a timeless "West," distinctive and largely homogeneous, and separate from an "East." He begins by showing how from the early 15th century the world became connected and interdependent, a "world system" in fact. "Western civilization," Wolf seems to argue, is not a particularly useful concept, except perhaps to those who persist in believing in Western superiority.

A year later another study appeared that would forever cast doubt on the idea of "tradition." This was *The Invention of Tradition*, edited by Eric Hobsbawm and Terence Ranger. Hobsbawm was by 1983 the most widely read historian writing on the long and golden 19th-century age of capitalism. He was a Marxist, an important element because it led him to have a view of the triumph of this golden age of capitalism with a certain scepticism. Indeed, when he wrote about the fall of this 19th-century capitalist age in 1914 and the rise of communist civilization a few years later, he betrayed a certain satisfaction. His co-editor, Terence Ranger, was a historian of Africa whose studies emphasized the role of resistance against colonialism.

*The Invention of Tradition* stressed the mutability of the human condition and the normal willingness of men and women to invent their pasts. The pasts of neither Western civilization nor the non-Western world were miraculous machines that either rose ever upward (as was claimed for the West) or went around in circles, as was thought to be the case of the non-West. The past, therefore, is continually being reinvented—all of its most sacred institutions and its most precious identities, political rituals, peoples, authorities, and institutions. Even before *Invention* was published we knew that many African tribes had been invented; now it was clear that the Welsh and the Scots, at least as they became normally characterized, were no less fabrications. Later, other studies were to show not only how Britons invented themselves but also when. In sum, then, it became evident not only that the Orient was constructed by the West, but also that an essential part of the West, far from being natural and stable, was itself constructed.

A further formidable attack on the idea of a distinctive and separate "Western civilization," a civilization with its own roots sustained by little non-Western nourishment, came in 1987, launched by historian Martin Bernal. Bernal's earliest renown came in his book *Chinese Socialism to 1908*, in which he concerned himself with the influence of the West on Chinese political ideas. Unlike most Western observers of Asia and Africa, Bernal showed himself to be sceptical about the benefits of Western intervention. As he explained at the beginning of his study, "*Chinese Socialism to 1908* is concerned with one of the very few areas where foreign influence on China has been beneficial."[22]

If Said asked the question "Just how did the Western view of the East come to be so malign?" Bernal asked, "Just how did the Western view of the West come to be so exalted?" The West referred to here is the Mother of All Wests, Classical Greece, subject of a thousand books on the origins of Western civilization. Bernal argued that the historical development of classical Greece was inextricably linked and deeply indebted to the civilizations of West Asia and Northeast Africa, Egypt especially. The Mother of the West is therefore herself of mixed antecedents; worse still, perhaps her civilization is mainly Afro-Asiatic. The title of Bernal's thesis, *Black Athena*, hardly sought to avoid controversy. Oddly enough, initially at least, Bernal's main arguments were generally greeted by a sympathetic reception from critics. This is not to say that either his evidence, which is based on translations of texts and inscriptions that only a handful of people can read, was compelling, or that his synthesis was not polemical.

What is most disturbing among Bernal's many arguments is the claim that the ideology of "Western civilization," which traces the origins of Western European and North American civilization to Classical Greece, has the same roots as modern race theory. These roots are not particularly deep in the West; they go no further than the late 18th century. What both the ideology of "White Athena" and race theory arguments have in common, it seems, is their equation of "civilization" with "Western civilization."

A final perturbation overlapped Bernal's researches. It came with the publication, also in 1987, of Paul Kennedy's book *The Rise and Fall of the Great Powers*. Unlike Wolf and Bernal, Kennedy showed no particular interest in the Third World; he is a historian interested in forms of Western power: naval power, imperial power, industrial power. The cover of Kennedy's book shows a mustachioed John Bull (a caricatural Englishman in Edwardian dress) stepping down from the top of the world and looking over his shoulder; behind him, still on top of the world but in a posture of descent, is Uncle Sam, also wearing an archaic costume and sporting his usual goatee. Climbing up to the top, to take Uncle Sam's place, is a clean-shaven contemporary businessman wearing horn-rimmed glasses and a smart suit and carrying a Japanese flag.

On one of the last pages of the book, under the heading "The United States: The Problem of Number One in Relative Decline," Kennedy summarizes his message: "To be a Great Power . . . demands a flourishing economic base. . . . Yet by going to war, by diverting a large share of the nation's 'manufacturing power' to expenditures upon 'unproductive' armaments, one runs the risk of eroding the national economic base, especially vis à vis states which are concentrating a greater share of their income upon productive investments for long term growth."[23]

Unlike the work of Said or Bernal, Kennedy's book attained "Book of the Month Club" status, its message spilling into the sitting rooms of educated America. By 1989, half of the U.S. public believed that their nation was in decline.[24]

In 1993 Kennedy returned with a new book, *Preparing for the Twenty-First Century*. In it, he tentatively suggested two main things. First, the Pacific was going to replace the Atlantic as the centre of history, and the economies of East Asia would be its driving force. Second, the Third World was going to become enormously overpopulated—the neo-Malthusian spectre. This concern, recycled from the 19th century, had again become popular, with its attractiveness resting in its reminder of something we have apparently known all along, that the people of the Third World have too many children and are improvident. Africa's population, in 1950 half that of Europe, was now its equal. In 30 years it would be three times greater. It doesn't take much imagination to see masses of Africans skiffing across the Straits of Gibraltar and crowds of "Latinos" wading across the Rio Grande and burrowing under the Tex-Mex frontier. Will the West then be flattened under a million immigrant feet?

By 1993, fear of Western decline (the ideology of "declinism") and especially of the United States trading places with Japan had reached epidemic proportions. "My enemies say that America is a nation in decline," ex-President Bush admitted.

There is nothing new about these ideas about the West or the concern about its rivals. Gloomy prophecies have been part of the political baggage of the West since the Trojan wars. In his *Capitalism, Socialism and Democracy*, published in 1942 (the year the publisher of *Time* and *Life* magazines, Henry Luce, claimed the future for the United States) the Harvard economist Joseph Schumpeter asked "Can Capitalism survive?" His answer: "No. I do not think it can."

Still, few believed Schumpeter then and few believe now that there is anything other than a Western future for the world. It must also be said that despite the influence that Said, Hobsbawm, Bernal, Wolf, and others have had on historians and some social scientists, Western triumphalism and self-satisfaction lives on without many serious misgivings in the main centres of power in the West: the great corporations, banks, conservative think tanks, and universities.

## The Image of the Future: Recipes for Westernization

Contemporary self-confidence in Western civilization has been bolstered by a single fibre called "development." The idea of development is an entirely Western concept, traceable to the French philosopher Henri de Saint-Simon (1760-1825) and beyond him to the debates of the classical political economists of the late 18th and 19th centuries—Adam Smith, Adam Ferguson, and David Ricardo.[25] By "development" the political economists meant orderly economic growth, that is, the steady rise in output in an environment of political stability; and they believed in trade as the main engine of growth both nationally and internationally. They thought that trade should not be fettered by any kind of governmental laws; this would only hamper its natural functions. Their views about trade and markets bordered on the metaphysical—that is, on the basis of signs rather than science—yet they held strongly to them.

The classical political economists were attempting to account for the coming of an absolutely new phenomenon, industrial capitalism, which they knew was stimulated by this trade. But they were not particularly concerned with non-Western economic activity, and certainly could not conceive of it as taking place according to rules that were different from those applying to the world they knew.

Like modern economists, the classical (or "liberal") economists were worried men. The growth of population and the disorder that was inherent in the transition from agricultural economies to industrial ones concerned them. Contemporary moralists feared what they called "corrupt" development. In the late 1950s and 1960s some of the same problems of capitalist development tormented economists and others concerned about the emerging Third World. How would this world develop in the future? How could it be kept under control? In the late 1980s these questions took on a different twist. Could this other world be sustainable, and would its overpopulation threaten us in the West?

In answer to questions about the fate of the non-Western world, political economists surmised that it should follow roughly along the lines taken up in the past by Western Europe and North America. "The country that is more developed industrially only shows, to the less developed, the image of its own future," predicted one of their number, Karl Marx, in the middle of the 19th century.

A hundred years later this view had become dogma. From the late 1940s through the early 1960s, an increasing number of previously colonized states became independent. All these states sought the same thing: *development*. This goal broke down into three elements: economic growth (or industrialization); political restructuring (stable and, if possible, democratic political systems by sovereign states); and modernization (the building of institutions and standards that were more or less based on a Western model). These three elements were usually viewed as aspects of the same phenomenon; in fact, the buzzwords development and modernization were often used interchangeably. The United States was seen as the leading developed and modern state. That the modern ideal was the U.S. ideal was no less true in the Third World than it was everywhere else. Virtually all roads from the Third World, excepting for communist countries, led to the U.S. model.

The transition from pre-capitalism to capitalism was a jungle, and modernizers had to hack a path through it on their way to the eventual goal. There were some nasty things lurking in this jungle, including communism, nationalism, and neutralism. Later there would be fundamentalism and later still the ideologically eclectic antidevelopment that would manifest itself in the forests of southern Mexico. These "isms" were the modern manifestations of the "corrupt" development that 19th-century moralists feared—that is, of *disorderly development*. Sometimes such development was characterized as threatening "international security," a concept that demanded a certain kind of world order and the primacy of some nations over others.

In the second half of the 20th century it was economic nationalism, not communism, that was seen as the most potent threat to the security of world development. The blackest sin of economic nationalists was the "autarky" that often seemed to entrance them. Autarky—the ideal of national economic self-sufficiency and independence—suggested the backwardness of aboriginal self-sufficiency; it was deplored because countries where it was practised closed their doors to the truths of globalism. The economic nationalists suffered damnably and still do. An account in the *Far Eastern Economic Review* testifies to the torments of India, for instance, noting that its economy "is less sprightly" than China's, but pointing out the "potential for big gains" if India were to adopt more liberal economic policies: "Forty years of trade autarky has reduced its share in world exports to a measly 0.5 percent compared with 19 percent in 1950 and China's 2.3 percent now."[26]

Iran shared the same inferno, and because of the theocratic nature of its regime it was described even more demonologically. *Time* magazine, for instance, denounced the Ayatollah Khomeini, a self-confessed proponent of "Islamic economics," as an "ascetic despot" and a "mystic."[27] "Ascetic" and "mystic" suggested non-rational, that is, non-Western.

There were few second thoughts about the costs of this push towards development. If there had been, there might have been a sharper awareness that the jungle of transition from non-developed to developing nations contained smouldering settlements and mounds of corpses: the products of transformations, revolutions, civil wars, pogroms, genocides, ethnic cleansings, population transfers, forced famines, and invasions; in short, the victims of capitalist development and its communist antithesis, as well as all of their mutant forms, such as Nazism and Maoism. Not surprisingly, many people were reluctant to enter this transitional zone, and of those who did, many regretted it. As Barrington Moore observed: "There is no evidence that the mass of the population has wanted an industrial society, and plenty of evidence that they did not."[28]

Even the early development specialists working for the United Nations recognized this. Writing in 1951, in a document called *Measures for the Economic Development of Underdeveloped Countries*, they explained: "There is a sense in which rapid economic progress is impossible without painful adjustments. Ancient philosophies have to be scrapped; old social institutions have to disintegrate; bonds of cast, creed and race have to burst; and large numbers of persons who cannot keep up with progress have to have their expectations of a comfortable life frustrated. Very few communities are willing to pay the full price of economic progress."[29]

Still, development seemed as inevitable as the future itself; no Nostradamus, in the modern robes of an economist or a political scientist, ever envisioned a non-development future. Thus Daniel Lerner, a 1950s expert on modernizing the Middle East, could write confidently: "No area of the world has resisted the attractions, despite the increasingly evident risks, of modernization."[30]

Lerner can be cast among a group of researchers called the "developmentalists," the scientists of the contemporary discipline known as "development studies." Practically all of the dominant ideas about development and modernization, indeed most ideas about the modern world within the social sciences were, and are, American, if not in conception then in amplification. This is particularly the case in the fields of political science and economics. Until the 1980s, at least, writers in the West and the Third World mostly took their cues from the Americans. (Though, according to Arturo Escobar, this tendency changed in the mid-1980s to late 1980s, when there emerged a coherent body of criticism of the developmentalist idea connected with grassroots movements in the Third World.)[31]

American ideas on the subject of development have tended to be homogeneous—although there were breaks in this pattern in the late 1960s and 1970s and again after the mid-1980s. The reasons for this are, at one level, simple: the United States is the world's richest nation. Money to conduct research in all fields often comes from the major corporations and has been channelled through the hands of the assenting few. These few became the bards of the development discourse in the 1950s and 1960s. Another reason is that the means of popularizing ideas, the media, have been tightly, if by no means completely, controlled.

Which specific pathways did the developmentalists actually foresee for the world after World War II, and how did they hope to arrive at what they foresaw? Let us consider the views of two of them, towering figures whose opinions prevailed in their times.

## The Bards of Development

Walt Whitman Rostow, whose writings were universally admired in the 1960s, was a professor of economic history, specifically the history of English industrialization, at the Massachusetts Institute of Technology. England, as most educated people knew, was the first country to be industrialized; the modern world was born under the smokestacks of Lancashire, the heartland of industrial England. If the conditions of English industrialization could be understood, Rostow and others thought, the experience might be duplicated elsewhere. England thus became the comparative model for global industrialization.

Based on his assumptions about England, in 1959 Rostow published a book, *The Stages of Economic Growth*, in which he made no bones about his objectives: his subtitle was *A Non-Communist Manifesto*. He made it obvious that he was writing a guide to explain how India might do what Karl Marx said it would have to—follow Britain or Japan into an industrialized future—but without the revolution that Marx predicted would ensue once the peasants became workers. The book outlined the five stages of non-revolutionary, that is, evolutionary, growth that Rostow expected to take place among the unindustrialized nations. In this plan Rostow gave an exalted place to the "entrepreneurial elite."

With the publication of *Stages of Economic Growth*, Rostow achieved immediate renown. He was viewed as being the Wernher von Braun of developmentalism, a reference to the rocket scientist who understood how to escape the gravitational force of the preindustrial world in safety. From the moment of its publication until well into the early years of the "development decade," as the 1960s became known, despite the adverse comments of a few critics who considered Rostow's ideas completely ahistorical and utterly misconceived, *Stages of Economic Growth* was received with enthusiasm. Practically everyone studying the exciting new discipline called "development studies" read Rostow's "Non-Communist Manifesto" and memorized its central tenets. Among his keenest supporters was the conservative but increasingly influential British business weekly, *The Economist*, which pronounced Rostow's ideas to be among "the most stimulating contributions made to economic and political thought since the war."[32]

As a theoretician concerned with the export of U.S. modernism, Rostow did not soldier on alone. Whereas he had focused on economic development, his colleagues in political science were preoccupied with political modernization. Like him, they were concerned with the problems inherent in the transition from "traditional," that is precapitalist and often colonial, societies, to the more modern structures of the postcolonial world. The 1960s were the beginning of the age of Third World "nation-building," and these political scientists wanted to ensure that new nations developed in certain ways. As Thomas J. McCormick explains, "Out of fragments of broken colonial empires," the United States "sought to create new nations that would be sufficiently autonomous to be credible and yet would be politically stable market economies, integrated into global multilateralism." These new states would be "showcases" that would convince others in the Third World "of the material rewards of development via the world market rather than development by state planning."[33]

The biggest problem for this new-nation modernization was communism, which until the late 1960s, it was assumed, fed on poverty. Crudely put, the idea was that if poverty were banished, communism would be starved.

In 1968 a second major work, this one by the U.S. political scientist Samuel P. Huntington (b.1927) and called *Political Order in Changing Societies*, argued that the problem of developing societies was political, not economic; that is, developing societies lacked the political structures and practices to be stable. Without political stability, economic development was impossible. Huntington expressed this as a simple paradox: "Modernity produces stability and modernization instability."[34] The model of stability was, as usual, the United States, and all of the *desirata* of political modernity were American. Huntington, too, shared the view that the United States was the promise to be found at the end of civilization's rainbow.

Huntington's writings were buttressed by a breathtaking grasp of comparative political history. He seemed to be as familiar with arguments about the Tudor constitution in 16th-century England as with details concerning Nigerian nationalism in the 1960s. His work was given further credibility because, in an epoch when the air was full of obfuscating social science jargon, he wrote in an English that was bold and direct.

His meditation on political order in developing societies led Huntington to support the military in the Third World as a stabilizing institution. Rostow's entrepreneurial elites were replaced by military elites known as "praetorians." His preferred models of political order were such modernizing dictators as the prototypical Mustafa Kemal in Turkey and those who emulated Kemal, such as Reza Shah in Iran, Ayub Khan in Pakistan, and Gamal Abdul Nasser in Egypt. The idea that parliamentary democracy was a luxury that developing states could not afford, an idea held dearly by several of the uniformed dictators of the Third World, was one to which Huntington seemed to subscribe.

What developing societies needed was the consolidation of power around an effective state bureaucracy. The central element in this bureaucracy was the military officer corps. "The prerequisite of reform . . . is the consolidation of power. Hence, first attention is given to the creation of an efficient, loyal rationalized and centralized army."[35] The leaders of this army, the praetorians, would guarantee the order necessary for development to take place. Only later was it shown that this assumption of Huntington's was untenable—that there is no causal link between authoritarian regimes and economic development. As Alan Richards and John Waterbury explain: "It is difficult in the 1980s to unearth anyone who finds merits in military or quasi-military rule."[36]

By the end of the 1960s, then, options had narrowed. In the arguments of leading political scientists writing about the Third World (not only conservatives, but neo-Marxists), economic growth was not likely to take place without political order.\* Order was perceived as requiring strong and committed, but not necessarily democratically elected, leaders. If the "free world" needed allies who were despots in the short term, this was an acceptable price at least until the modernizing states were able to develop solid institutions. Thus the shah of Iran, the generals who dictated policy in Argentina, Brazil, Pakistan, Indonesia, and later in Chile, and the securocrats who ruled South Africa were given legitimacy by the leading figures of the political and economic development schools. And, more vitally, they received the support of succeeding U.S. administrations, which were advised by the developmentalists. Nor did they suffer from the indifference of the United States people at large—for the modernizing dictators generally received the support of the Western media. News coverage of the shah provides one example of this tendency. As Noam Chomsky has argued regarding the coverage by *The New York Times*, the United States' most influential newspaper: "The shah was virtually never described in [dictatorial] terms despite being identified by Amnesty International as one of the worst human rights violators in the world."[37]

Rostow, Huntington, and their colleagues did not merely research and write, but also advised. They wrote prescriptions and offered solutions,

---

\* Ellen Kay Trimberger explains the possibilities of military authoritarianism or praetorianism from a neo-Marxist point of view; and Guillermo O'Donnell applies it to Latin America, calling it "bureaucratic authoritarianism" (BA). Like the theory of praetorianism as applied to the Middle East, the theory of "bureaucratic authoritarianism" was judged and found to be wanting. See Trimberger, *Revolution from Above*, 1978; and O'Donnell, "Reflections on the Patterns of Change in the Bureaucratic-Authoritarian State," 1978.

which they showered on the State Department, the military, the CIA, and even foreign dictatorships. Indeed, they and their universities competed clamorously for government contracts to do research on weapons that would cause ever more serious mutilation, on the subversion of the media, and on techniques of interrogation. Rostow himself became quite celebrated as one of the "best and the brightest," as the enthusiasts for the U.S. intervention in Vietnam were called. Huntington advised the U.S. government's Agency for International Development (USAID) on Vietnam and went to Saigon for the State Department. And many others had a share in the pie. Michigan State University trained Saigon's policemen, the University of California at Berkeley provided the "Berkeley boys" (economists who advised the Suharto dictatorship in Indonesia), and the University of Chicago supplied the "Chicago boys" (who assisted Chile's Pinochet dictatorship in installing its monetarist policies). In the unusual case of Dean Rusk, who had been a partner with Rostow in the United States' monumental miscalculation in Vietnam, a university professor became successively a civil servant, the head of the Rockefeller Institute, a secretary of state, and, finally, a professor again.

## The Dissidents of Dependency Theory

The theories of modernization and political and economic development, underpinned by a modernized version of Adam Smith's "classical" economic theories (known as "neoclassical theory"), dominated the thinking of a whole generation of Western social scientists who wrote about the Third World. But they eventually came under devastating attack in the form of "dependency theory." The most voluble and persistent exponent of dependency theory was André Gunder Frank, a U.S. academic whose most powerful work was *Capitalism and Underdevelopment in Latin America: Historical Studies of Chile and Brazil* (1967).

If Huntington's book represented the highest point of what we might qualify as the neo-Enlightenment thinking of the golden age of U.S. development studies and, not coincidentally, U.S. power, Frank's book was like the Tet offensive in Vietnam: the unacknowledged beginning of the end—not an outright victory, but a defeat foretold. Frank's ideas "caught on like wildfire," in the words of David Lehmann, a British writer on development issues.[38] Why? Cuba and Vietnam were the answers; both demonstrated the vulnerability of U.S. power and therefore of U.S. assumptions.

Frank did not invent what was known as "dependency theory." It had roots going back for more than a century to the debates about the British exploitation of India. Its modern form had emerged in the 1930s and was propounded by a school of Latin American economists, known as *dependentistas*, who were sceptical about contemporary ideas concerning development and order. Then, in the 1950s, a U.S. Marxist, Paul Baran, had relaunched the critique of liberal development theories with his book *The Political Economy of Growth* (1957). Baran's main argument was that the major effect on the Third World of capitalist development in the West was to slow it down and bring it under control. The penetration of the Third World by Western capitalism, thought Baran, led to stagnation, not development. When Baran and the English historian Eric Hobsbawm joined together to write about Rostow's theory of growth, his "anti-communist manifesto," they minced no words. Rostow's ideas, they decided, were hopelessly confused and banal.[39]

The central question that the *dependentistas* had asked was the essential question of economic development. Do all countries go through the same stages? Neoclassical orthodoxy, represented by Rostow, said "yes." Trade spread the benefits of capitalist development to all. Theoretically, at least, any country, or at least any major country, could develop if it followed the rules. Baran, and after him Frank, disagreed. They argued that the countries of the West that were the first to develop had gone from "undevelopment" to "development." In the 16th century, in the process of the development of their capitalist economies, they began to gain control of the economies of what was to become the Third World. By means of this control they simultaneously accelerated their own development and *underdeveloped* the economies of the Third World. The Western countries had themselves been *un*developed but had never been *under*developed; that is, no more developed countries existed to actively manipulate and therefore distort their economic growth.

Underdevelopment was thus a condition created by, and a part of, capitalism, not one that preceded development. It was thus in no way a stage that would be superseded. Capitalism could not stimulate the development of a world overseas in its own image, because with its advent it destroyed or at least dislocated the local nurseries of capitalist development. So, for example, the kind of early capitalist centre that emerged in Flanders in the 16th century could not develop in India once the Europeans had arrived, because they, the Europeans, not the Indians, dominated the trade of the adjacent oceans and the trading ports on either side of them. As Amiya Kumar Bagchi explains: "The typical paths of development in the past have needed some countries to stay retarded, transferring capital, providing cheap raw materials and markets for manufactures . . . acting as reservoirs of cheap labour and sometimes . . . functioning as easy new frontiers to be conquered through very private (and often socially reprehensible) enterprise (as in Brazil today)."[40]

In Latin America, which provided the examples for Frank's argument, mercantile capitalism had not stimulated modernization. Instead it had created a kind of local feudalism and a general backwardness. The *latifundia* (large rural estates on which peasants laboured in precapitalist conditions), which were seen as being an obstacle to capitalist agrarian development, were the creations of this capitalism; they were not the residues of precapitalist ("feudal") systems. Contrary to what the liberal economists had supposed, according to Frank the masses of people in the Third World were not wretched because they were shut out from capitalism, they were wretched because they had been locked in by it. Capitalism in the Third World, therefore, did not promote development; capitalism guaranteed underdevelopment. Rostow talked about capitalism "taking off" as a phenomenon that might happen in places outside the West. Frank argued that in these places capitalism had about the same possibility of flight as a penguin.

Finally, Frank issued a challenge to the elites of Latin America, those who were responsible for political order, such as it was. According to Lehmann he accused them of being:

> an integral and supportive part of the metropolis-satellite system. Their way of life and their economic interests were dependent on the continual exploitation of the poor, they were mere links, agents or intermediaries in long macro-historical chains of exploitation linking successive metropolitan centres to successive satellites from the great financial and industrial centres of the world down to the last syllable of exploited peasantry, and sucking 'surplus' back into the opposite direction. They would therefore resist any change.[41]

The only way, therefore, of escaping from the dead hand of such local elites and of dependency was revolution; and "revolution," often personified in the Christlike figure of a youthful and lonely guerrilla in the mountains, became a prominent word in the young person's political vocabulary of the 1960s and early 1970s. "Solidarity" was the bridge that linked the guerrillas in the mountains and jungles with young people in the West who identified as far as possible with the struggles against neocolonialism and capitalism.

With his arguments against capitalism and bogus developmentalism, Frank became what Lehmann has called a "phenomenon," not just an invisible author of an inaccessible theory of economic history but an unavoidable reality and a constant reference. He was the antidote to Rostow, whose exile from public life, in some ignominy, coincided quite perfectly with the defeat of the U.S. intervention in Vietnam.

Yet by the 1970s, the shelf life of theories meant to explain the contemporary world had become unusually short. Thousands of political flowers bloomed, but few survived the wintry tempests of the changing world economy. So dependency theory, too, had its decade. Within a few years of being launched it had come under attack. By 1977 Colin Leys, a political scientist who studied Kenya and was himself once a dependency theorist, wrote: "It is becoming clear that 'underdevelopment' and 'dependency' theory is no longer serviceable and must now be transcended."[42] Many agreed, although some remained impressed not so much by the theory itself but by the questions it had asked.

Many of the dependency theorists' questions were tackled in a final theoretical attempt to explain not only development in the contemporary Third World but also the development of the entire capitalist system in the modern period, that is, from its origins in the 14th century. This novel theoretical enterprise, which became known as "world-systems theory," was based on several arguments made by the French historian Fernand Braudel and then popularized, embellished, and baptized by the U.S. sociologist Immanuel Wallerstein.

World-systems theory considered capitalism, which it identified as a system of trade and finance, as an expanding and unifying set of mercantile networks, emanating first from the city-states of Genoa and Venice. Like dependency theory, this theory explained how the expansion of this system affected the non-development of capitalism in the non-West. World-systems theory considered the world as being in the process of becoming a unified whole (that is, "globalized") over the long term (some six centuries). It thus envisioned development as having both spatial and temporal centres, at first manifest in Italy, later moving northwards to France and England, then across the Atlantic to North America, and, finally, perhaps, across the Pacific to the new capitalist archipelago that includes Japan, South Korea, Taiwan, and Singapore.

This was one of the theory's greatest strengths: it did not hold that development is a synonym for "Western civilization," nor did it argue that the underdevelopment of the non-Western was inevitable. It did, however, stress that there was only one road to development: the capitalist road. It also tended to be somewhat monocausal, that is, it tended to suggest that world history had only a single driving force: the development of the world market. It tended to discount independent internal development in the West or the Third World. Development in anticapitalist states, in socialist Cuba, or in the Islamic Republic of Iran, for instance, is therefore inconceivable. The rules of the game were the rules of advanced capitalism;

revolutions against capitalism, that is, against capitalist development, were therefore doomed.*

## The Revenge of the Neoliberals

Eclipsing the dependency theories of the 1960s and 1970s, and thus roughly paralleling the development of world-systems theory, were the "neoliberals," whose credibility had risen from the mid-1970s due to two phenomena: the growing problems of the Western capitalist economies; and, arising from the first, the electoral successes of rightist governments. Neoliberal ideas had two parents and were conceived during the lunchtime meetings of a private club of conservative economists bankrolled by businessmen. Their godfather was an Austrian economist named Friedrich von Hayek, who passionately detested the intervention of the state in the economy, that is, the philosophy and practice known as "Keynesianism." Arguing that state involvement in people's lives turned them into serfs, Hayek insisted that it was in everyone's interest to render more unto Caesar, or at least unto Mammon, and less to governments. In 1974 Hayek was awarded a Nobel Prize in economics for his "free-market" theories. He was at this time at the University of Chicago, a university that was to become the Vatican of the new neoliberal economic theories. Over the next two decades (1974-95) economists at the University of Chicago were to win nine Nobel Prizes.

A second, and necessary, parent of neoliberalism was crisis— particularly the decline in the rate of profit faced by Western firms and their owners. The main culprit in this decline, thought the neoliberals, was the giveaway state, which taxed and borrowed too heavily and gave too much away to the working class and the indigent (and not enough to the owners). The main solution to decline was the liberation of the market. The neoliberals were determined to put an end to decline by

---

* Fernand Braudel's great trilogy, *Material Civilization and Capitalism: Fifteenth to Eighteenth Centuries*, appeared in the early 1970s. Wallerstein's earliest expansion and elaboration of Braudel's ideas are found in *The Modern World System*, 1974. A recent world-systems synthesis by Giovanni Arrighi, in *The Long Twentieth Century*, 1994, charts the movement of the centres of capitalism from the Italian city-states in the late 14th century westwards across the world. Arrighi also discusses how capitalism has been recentralized in recent decades (since around 1970). He argues (p.21) that the three worlds—the West (including Japan), the Communist bloc, and the non-West—rose in the aftermath of the Bolshevik revolution (1917) and lasted until just after the Vietnamese revolution (1975). In the late 1970s it seemed as if there might be some equality between the three worlds, but by the mid-1980s it was clear this was not to be. The triumph of the First World guaranteed that the old hierarchical order of wealth and power would survive, though perhaps not forever. Arrighi suggests (pp.354-55), "East Asian capital may come to occupy a commanding position in the systemic processes of capital accumulation," that is, become the home of the dominant capitalist states.

smashing the state-forged chains of regulation and protection, which would free the market to assume its natural "Smithian" role—to rule the universe. A free market would permit a return to Promethean economic growth, they argued. Profits would return, which would benefit everyone (though not equally, and not immediately). Neoliberal doctrine insisted that national governments would have to move on deregulation and denationalization. They would have to guarantee international trade access to all national markets. The organs of neoliberalism attacked their foes on all fronts, including those in the crumbling Communist regimes of Eastern Europe, and using any ammunition at hand. *The Times* (London), for instance, made it clear that Keynesian economics, homosexuality, and treachery to one's country were all part of the same syndrome.[43]

Thus tolled the bell for protectionism and self-reliance, both of which had been widely accepted by development economists as the main means for achieving economic growth and stability in the Third World. Yet problems remained. Brought to the bedside of the already sickly Third World economies, "free-market" prescriptions, some said, had the same effects on their health as leeching; their condition for the most part went from dangerous to critical. According to Cristóbal Kay, in Latin America free-market policies had only increased foreign debt, which then more than cancelled out the rise in exports:

> The net effect has thereby been a marked deterioration in the foreign exchange balance to the extent that the debt problem has become the central economic problem in most Latin American countries today.
>
> More importantly, neo-conservative policies have led to deindustrialization, unemployment, income inequalities and poverty. There have been brief spurts of economic growth but as a result of greater income inequalities poverty has risen. Whatever has taken place has benefitted only a minority of the population.[44]

In early 1996, a study by the UN Economic Commission for Latin America and the Caribbean showed that in spite of greater macroeconomic stability engendered by the "free-market" prescriptions of the 1980s, in many cases poverty in the region had worsened.[45]

One form of the neoliberal prescriptions for ailing economies had been the Structural Adjustment Programs (SAPs). From the early 1980s, these SAPs were imposed on Third World countries by the World Bank and the IMF as a condition of loans. They sought to dismantle many of the institutions of the state, to allow the free market unhampered movement. Yards of discussion have been produced detailing how the SAPs have

created economic and social havoc in the Third World and particularly
Africa. (See chapter 10.)

By the time Kay wrote his condemnation of the free market, at the
end of the 1980s, the Third World was enduring what has been called its
"lost decade," and Western commitment to Third World development had
gone into a nose dive. There were still debates about capitalist development, however, and in particular speculations about the Newly Industrialized Countries (NICs) of East Asia. How had these nations managed to
develop? The neoliberals, now in power in most Western governments
and in control of most serious newspapers and business magazines, said
that this group of countries had industrialized by adopting neoclassical
principles, particularly those of limited government intervention, and promoting export-oriented strategies. University economics departments,
often uncomfortable with the heterodoxies of development economics,
offered their confirmation. The World Bank, the world's largest development agency, and the IMF, which had since the mid-1970s grown colossally
in influence, not only supported but also adopted this view. Only a minority dissented.

Yet while many Third World economies went into deep decline, at the
official level came an earnest reassurance that development still mattered.
The plea of the 1987 Brundtland Report, produced by the World Commission on Environment and Development (WCED) and chaired by Gro
Harlem Brundtland, the Norwegian prime minister, was that all of the people of the world have a common future, which can only be guaranteed by
"sustainable development." This was a new developmentalist catch-
phrase intended to place the degradation of the global environment alongside the eradication of poverty. "Sustainable development is development
that meets the needs of the present without compromising the ability of
future generations to meet their own needs," the report affirmed.[46] But
some critics had reservations. The anthropologist Arturo Escobar comments that the report "still assumed that the benevolent (white) hand of
the West will save the Earth; it is up to the fathers of the World Bank,
mediated by Gro Harlem Brundtland, the matriarch scientist, and a few
cosmopolitan Third Worlders who make it to the World Commission, to
reconcile 'humankind' with 'nature.' The Western scientist continues to
speak for the Earth. God forbid that a Peruvian peasant, an African nomad,
or a rubber tapper of the Amazons should have something to say in this
regard."[47]

# Solitudes: The Invention and Relegation of the Third World

I have taken what might seem a long detour in order to examine, first, how the Third World must be seen in relation to Western civilization and, second, how theories of development originated and mutated to outline what the Third World would have to be in order to be more like the West. But where had the idea that such a place as the Third World existed come from in the first place? Surely it is recent. When I was an undergraduate studying East Asia in the 1950s, for instance, the term did not exist.

Like other locations—or even periods of history—the concept of a "Third World" has been since its inception inexact and even contentious. It seems to have been invented in 1952 by the French demographer Alfred Sauvy, who wrote, in an article in *L'Observateur* (August 14, 1952), that both of the two main blocs of power, those of the West and the Soviets, were "struggling for the possession of the Third World, that is, the collectivity of those that were called in the language of the United Nations 'underdeveloped.'" Sauvy regretted this situation, finishing his article with the observation that the Third World was like the Third Estate at the time of the French Revolution: ignored, exploited, and misunderstood.

What must be underlined is that the term "Third World" was coined in the West, in France, and that it was invoked at a particular historical moment. That it was coined to describe the non-West indicates that it is necessarily an outsider's view, one most probably anchored in other long-rooted assumptions such as those about "Western civilization" and the "Orient." Another key is the birth date of "Third World" as a term: August 1952. This was a time of both optimism and emergency: "optimism" because Western leaders had recently discovered the "underdeveloped" world and were confident that it could be developed;* "emergency" because it was a period in which the Western European empires—the British, French, Belgian, and Dutch—had reached or were approaching the end of their leases. Alfred Sauvy must have been aware that things were going badly for the French in Tunisia and Vietnam and that the British had only recently scuttled in South Asia, Greece, and Palestine. On the other side of Asia, the Western armies of the United Nations had been hurled out of North Korea by the Chinese in early 1951, and by the end of the

---

* Briefly, as we shall see in subsequent chapters, the British had appropriated the word "development" immediately before World War II as a means of regulating and guaranteeing political and social change in their colonies and dependencies. The French picked up the idea and promoted it in early 1944, and the Americans began to take it seriously, according to Escobar, around 1950.

year the war there had reached a stalemate. Finally, on July 20, 1952, just before Sauvy published his article, the Egyptian Revolution had taken place. This was an event of epochal significance. For the first time since Alexander the Great, the country that had held the Western imagination in thrall for centuries, had Egyptian, as opposed to foreign, rulers. This rapidly changing situation in the Near East left the French alarmed and the British vexed. And worse was to follow from the point of view of the old colonial countries.

The existence of Sauvy's "Third World" seemed to be confirmed when, on April 17-24, 1955, delegates from 29 Asian and African countries met at Bandung in Indonesia. The stars of the Bandung Conference were Achmed Sukarno from the host country, Jawaharlal Nehru, the Indian prime minister, Zhou Enlai, the Chinese foreign minister, and Gamal Abdul Nasser, the leader of Egypt's "Free Officers," who had brought about the Egyptian Revolution. The main preoccupations of the conference were the struggle for emancipation from colonial rule, which most of the leaders had experienced, and détente vis-à-vis the two main blocs or worlds, those of democracy and communism. "Solidarity" on the basis of anticolonialism, geographical location, and the struggle against underdevelopment was invoked and principles of non-intervention and peaceful co-existence, inspired by Buddhism, embraced. The conference proposed the creation of a United Nations fund for development and gave birth to an ideology, promoted in particular by Nasser and President Tito of Yugoslavia, that in the West, at least, was regarded as quite heretical: "non-alignment." Conferences of "non-aligned" states appeared thereafter with regularity, although with declining influence. For instance, Asian Games and Afro-Asian Games continued to be played into the 1980s, though they attracted disappointingly little attention.

Euphoria encouraged a kind of political amnesia regarding the actually existing political alignments of many of the states at Bandung. For instance, the ties between China and the Soviet Union and between Turkey, the Philippines, Pakistan, and the United States. Thus the detachment of the non-aligned group and the political unanimity of its members were more apparent than real. Still, Léopold Senghor of Senegal (not yet independent) declared the conference the most important event since the Renaissance. By the end of 1960 Senegal, in common with most of Africa and much of the Third World, was independent. It was in the new decade, the 1960s, that the concept of a "Third World" came to maturation.

Besides amnesia concerning actually existing political arrangements, the leaders at Bandung were also neglectful of another consideration: class. Did Léopold Senghor and Achmed Sukarno really have identical interests with the mass of their countrymen and women? Of course not, but this was overlooked. At the time of struggles of nations, the struggles of classes had to be put aside.

The Third World was a world being born as it was being named, with a name that referred to a particular and dated set of expectations. It was received into a world of classrooms and newsrooms with varying degrees of solicitude, in some cases verging on rapture. Why was this? The simple answer is "the sixties." That is, in the United States, France, Britain, and Canada many people had become disillusioned with the recent political past—the suffocating social norms and political practices of the old political leaders and parties and the accompanying conformist culture and morality that had developed since 1945. Furthermore, entirely new political and social constituencies had been born—in the United States, for instance, African Americans, and there and elsewhere, students. A sense of idealism surrounding these constituencies sustained the hope for change that was central to the idea of the creation of a Third World.

This hope for change was inflated by two tides, one political and one intellectual. The political tide, which manifested itself in the Third World, took the form of struggles for liberation, usually guerrilla wars. The guerrilla war of the Front de libération nationale (FLN) in Algeria, celebrated in the writings of Franz Fanon, attracted French intellectuals right across the board, from Catholics to communists. English writers soon picked up on these struggles. Then there was Cuba. A recent writer suggests that the guerrillas in Cuba's Sierra Maestre attracted, indeed, rejuvenated, the U.S. left.[48] Everywhere in the Western world, then, between the mid-1950s and the end of the 1970s, young people and those who still thought of themselves as young came to support the idea of guerrilla action against the established oppressive order.*

The second stimulus to this Third Worldism was less cultural and political and more literary and intellectual. It was also entirely Western. In 1960, in Paris, the journal *Tiers Monde* (later to become *Revue Tiers-Monde*) was founded, and the popularization of the term "Third World" in English followed a few years later. This popularization was guaranteed by a single literary event, the publication of Peter Worsley's *The Third World* (1964), a book about imperialism and non-Western societies, written from a socialist viewpoint. Even before Worsley, Keith Buchanan, a British

---

* While my point here concerns Western "Third Worldism" it should not obscure the fact that the Cuban revolution also inspired young people in the Third World. As Mohsen M. Milani points out, both of the guerrilla movements that opposed the shah in Iran—the Mojahedin and the Fedayan—"were inspired by Castro's victory in Cuba in 1959." See Milani, *The Making of Iran's Islamic Revolution*, 1994, p.83.

geographer, had published an article on "The Third World" in one of the first issues of what was to become the pre-eminent vehicle for neo-Marxist (and particularly French) ideas in the anglophone world, the still-obscure *New Left Review*. This article bears the Gallic imprint of Franz Fanon's *Les damnés de la terre* (*The Wretched of the Earth*), which had been released in Paris two years previously by the radical publishing house Maspéro, complete with a "Preface" by Jean-Paul Sartre. Sartre's blessing guaranteed the lift-off of *The Wretched*, because he was certainly the most influential and modish philosopher in the West in the postwar decades. In the pages of the *New Left Review* Buchanan remarked:

> The most striking political development of the last two decades has been the emergence of what French geographers and social scientists term the Tiers Monde—the Third World. This term applies to a great bloc of countries stretching from the Andean republics of South America, across Africa and the Middle East, to Indonesia and the islands of the tropical Pacific. . . . All are poor, most are backward, all are either crippled by lack of development or deformed by exploitative development. They contain an aggregate population of almost two thousand million people—two-thirds of the world total.[49]

The people in the countries Buchanan described were mainly peasants and, he thought, would form the combustible fuel for a global revolution. He was not alone; others would write about a revolutionary axis of workers and peasants.

Asia, Africa, and Latin America did, of course, have an existence in the West independent of the revelations of the "Third Worldists" in the early 1960s. Even before the 1960s there had been, in Western capitals, universities, business centres, and churches, a well-established interest in Asia and Latin America. But these exotic places were viewed separately, or united as components of larger empires, when they were viewed at all. They were wired to either the old imperial capitals or (like China) to Moscow. Most of those interested did not think that China shared any circuits with Cuba, or even that Nicaragua was on the same board as Chile. In North America the existence of Africa, for instance, had largely been ignored, except by missionaries, big game hunters, and the most underemployed of journalists. As late as 1957, as Martin Staniland points out, there were more U.S. foreign service officers in Germany than there were in the whole of Africa. U.S. investment in Canada was eight times greater than in the whole of Africa, where 50 per cent of U.S. investment was in one country, South Africa.[50]

In the 1960s this perception of the Third World woke up to one reality, but remained asleep to another. The first reality was that parts of the Third World were attempting to break away from the political, economic, and cultural domination of the West. For most of the decade, as seen from the outside, the heroism associated with the struggles against imperialism and what was to become known as "underdevelopment" continued to give the Third World an attractive and generally unified image. At a time when the existence of Western civilization had become a matter of controversy, the existence of the Third World was unarguable. "For many," wrote the South Commission, "there was the hope born of success in their liberation struggles. Everywhere there was talk of equality and progress. . . . It is important to remember this period of progress and its atmosphere of hope now, when there is deep pessimism in much of the Third World about the prospects of economic development."[51]

## Collapse

Beyond this image of a Third World, which was personified in the generation of leaders of liberation such as Jawaharlal Nehru, Achmed Sukarno, Mao Zedong, Fidel Castro, Gamal Abdul Nasser, and Kwame Nkrumah, there was an actually existing Third World that had forgotten the invocations to unity at Bandung and was rapidly breaking down. This happened in two ways. First of all, non-alignment was destroyed as an option. Second, the economic growth that did occur in the Third World was producing two or more Third Worlds, only one of which was actually improving its position.

In less than a decade after Bandung, the great defenders of non-alignment had all been defeated. In November 1962, fearing a Chinese invasion from across the Himalayas, Nehru abjectly invited U.S. military intervention to save India. At exactly the same time the Cuban missile crisis was gluing Castro to the arms of Moscow. By 1971, to the dismay of Western "Third Worldists," Castro had gone so far as to arrest the poet and novelist Heberto Padilla, which was seen by many as a breach of faith and a gross abuse of the emancipationist promise of the Cuban Revolution. More importantly, here was confirmation that the practices of the Kremlin had been exported to Havana. In October 1965 in Indonesia, Sukarno's Communist-supported government was overthrown by a military group. A few months later, in early 1966, Ghana's Kwame Nkrumah was ousted. In 1970 Nasser died. His death and the destruction of the Allende regime in Chile three years later drove all but the last nails into the coffin of the non-aligned or "Third Way" era. A further nail was the failure of a prominent plan for a New International Economic Order (NIEO), strongly supported by all Third World countries but rejected by Western members at the United Nations in December 1974.* Oddly, perhaps, 1974 was the year that Friedrich von Hayek was awarded the Nobel Prize for economics and the free-market school of economic development began its roll towards global renown. At any rate, by 1980 the last page had been turned on the Third World attempts to find new paths of development.

In terms of actual development, by the mid-1970s, while one corner of the Third World was experiencing rapid capitalist growth, the rest had begun to slow down. Both emulating, and stimulated by, Japan, from the 1960s parts of East and Southeast Asia, under regimes that were dictatorial to the extent of tolerating practically no political competitors, had begun to move in the direction of capitalist modernism. Quite remarkably, within a mere 30 years and sometimes much less, a large part of the former Japanese Co-Prosperity Sphere—Japan itself, South Korea, the southern coast of China, plus Vietnam, Malaysia, Thailand, and Indonesia—had moved themselves out of the Third World in the sense that they were becoming rapidly industrialized. Nor were they Third World in the political sense of being disorderly; on the contrary, they were often pilloried in the West for being Kafkaesque in their repressive orderliness. These states were Third World in only two ways: they were ineradicably "foreign" and, in common with the original Orient, they were menacing. It was not clear whether we should join them, in some sort of "Pacific Rim" kingdom in which capitalist lion would lie down with capitalist lamb, or whether we would have to fight them, face to face, civilization against civilization.

For the rest of the Third World the development story was different, and complicated. Between 1960 and 1984 the Third World as a whole had seen economic growth. The average annual increase in Gross Domestic Product (GDP) per capita was a respectable 2.8 per cent (excluding China and the oil-producing countries). Latin America and the Far East had grown at even higher rates. But between the hares and the tortoises there were striking differences, one of which was the possession of oil. Of the 27 countries that more than doubled their per capita GDP between

---

* The NIEO Declaration contained a list of 20 principles calling for the establishment of a world order based on "equity, sovereign equality, independence, common interest and cooperation among all states." On December 12, 1974, 120 states voted in favour of the Charter of Economic Rights and Duties of States, with 6 against and 10 abstaining. The abstainers were Austria, Canada, France, Ireland, Israel, Italy, Japan, the Netherlands, Norway, and Spain. Belgium, Denmark, the Federal Republic of Germany, Luxembourg, the United Kingdom, and the United States voted against it. Those who voted for it represented 70 per cent of the world's population, while those who voted against it contributed 95 per cent to the UN budget. In rejecting the outcome of the vote, the U.S. representative stated: "When the rule of the majority becomes the tyranny of the majority, the minority will cease to respect or obey it."

1960 and 1982, ten were oil producers (Algeria, Ecuador, Egypt, Indonesia, Iraq, Libya, Mexico, Nigeria, Saudi Arabia and Syria).

By the mid-1980s, however, a generalized crisis was in place throughout the Third World. Many countries both in Africa and in parts of Asia were experiencing at best tepid growth, and at worst were stagnating economically. In many countries, some economic growth continued, but the gap between the rich and the poor widened; in some cases this was a function of population increase. Simultaneously, when a country developed, a minority got richer, and the majority got even poorer.

## Relegation

By the end of the 1980s, the postwar Western conception of a Third World that was to be a locus of orderly liberation and emancipation had been all but buried. Continuous and high levels of economic growth had been witnessed only on the coasts of Pacific Asia. In most of Latin America, where the idea of development was first formulated, there was stagnation. Indeed, in that decade, according to Escobar, "Latin American countries experienced the harshest social and economic conditions since the conquest."[52] By 1993 average real per capita income in the continent was 5 per cent below the 1980 level. Conditions in Africa were worse. Indeed, much of Africa, at least as represented in the dominant Western media, had simply not developed, but instead retrogressed into the barbarisms of despotism and genocide.*

Now there were at least two "Third Worlds." One of these worlds was "developed," "modern," and even, perhaps, "civilized." The second was a new Bedlam—simultaneously a poor house and a lunatic asylum. The signs "liberation" and "emancipation" had been put aside, replaced in one world by "emerging markets" and "GDP growth" and in the other by "danger" and "debt." The term "Third World" was generally retained for the second of these worlds.

The use of the term in the feverish period of the 1992 U.S. presidential election campaign was especially revealing. The election was taking place at the end of a major recession, and as it reached its climax several doom-laden voices were raised warning that the legacy of Reagan and Bush would have to be abandoned and America put on a new course. Various spokespersons argued that the policies of the previous decade had

---

* Barbarisms not unconnected, of course, with the new economic order. As Leys points out: "It can hardly be irrelevant that before the outbreak of genocide in Rwanda in 1994, per capita incomes, already among the lowest in the world, had fallen by 50% in one year as a result of a collapse in coffee prices, followed by a drastic rise in food prices imposed by an IMF/World Bank structural adjustment programme." (1996, p.25, fn.57)

been disastrous for the United States at home and abroad; the nation was in palpable decline. One writer, asking rhetorically at what date the United States would reach the level of the Third World, decided the answer was, "in 2020." But perhaps this was an optimistic estimate. According to Mike Davis, "Los Angeles now has most of the vices of a third-world city [but] few of the virtues."[53]

The meaning behind these warnings was obvious. The analogy with the Third World would give us to assume that the U.S. economy would continue to decline in vital areas. The country would become deeply indebted to the financial institutions of the richer countries (the point being stressed by Ross Perot in the 1992 presidential elections). *Foreigners* would own America, its viable industries, valuable resources, profitable properties. U.S. cities would become festering slums. Jobs would disappear southwards amid a swooshing sound. And worse: the peoples of the Third World—Maghrebians, Turks, Africans, and Hong Kong Chinese in the case of Western Europe, Mexicans and other Latinos and Haitians in the case of the United States—would actually invade. As Jean-Marie Le Pen, the leading French far-rightist put it, "I don't want the French to become like the Red Indians—annihilated by immigration."

Underlying this dystopian promise was the "common knowledge" of the Third World—a common knowledge quite different from that of the 1960s. In the intervening decades the Third World had gone from being a utopia, to which many Westerners had travelled in hope, to a dystopia—an alien and blighted world, disordered, often out of control (like Somalia or Burundi or, closer to home, Haiti). Visiting Westerners often suggested that this was a land blinded by irrationality, a condition propounded, for instance, in the standard media representation of Haiti—violence and voodoo—or of the Middle East—fanaticism and fatalism. The contagions were liable to spread if these peoples were not properly treated, or at least quarantined. Perhaps the West would have to go to war with them. Samuel P. Huntington, by now director of the Olin Institute for Strategic Studies at Harvard, wrote in *Foreign Affairs* that in the "dawning era" that lies ahead we might expect to see a conflict between the West and the Rest. In this conflict "the fault lines between civilizations will be the battle lines of the future. . . . The core of global politics will be the interaction between the West and the non-Western cultures. . . . The next world war, if there is one, will be a war between civilizations."[54]

After 1992 the situation only worsened. In a widely admired treatise in *The Atlantic Monthly* Robert Kaplan warned of the threat of the contagion of Third World chaos. Steven David, professor of political science at Johns Hopkins University, proclaimed that non-Western civilizations had social and religious systems that led them to war. "The ideologies of many Third World states are more supportive of war than ideological beliefs held elsewhere.... [Western] countries have assimilated the social ideas and attitudes of peace.... Third World states openly seek the destruction of their neighbours."[55]

Although they may have been the first, U.S. writers were not alone in formulating this astonishing reinterpretation of history, in arguing that the blight of the Third World was spreading throughout the United States. The model here, and the metaphors, are epidemiological. Disorder, poverty, overpopulation, and disease are all assumed to be contagions that travel from the Third World to our world. A series of articles in *Le Monde* on "America" (timed to coincide with the 1992 U.S. presidential election) followed this same tack. Here Alain Franchon discussed the question of poverty, which he called "the 51st State of the Union." He talked about the urban ghettos of the United States as "islets of the Third World." Another writer in *Le Monde Diplomatique*, Michel Chossudovsky of the University of Ottawa, made the same point: "In the ghettos of certain American cities poverty can be compared to that of the countries of the Third World." Edward Luttwak, on the road to becoming one of the most widely quoted pundits in the field of global trends, was less equivocal: "America may be undergoing Thirdworldization but it cannot catch up with Britain's faster progress." If Britain and America, can Canada be far behind? "We Have Joined the Third World" asserted the headlines of Montreal's *La Presse*. Here was an idea, or at least half an idea, whose time, apparently, had come.[56]

A large part of this "Third World" labelling is nonsensical, the product of a journalistic fad of the early 1990s. Housing estates, urban ghettos, provinces, and even regions within rich or relatively rich Western countries can "become Third World," but only in the restricted sense of being poor and perhaps full of people whom journalists themselves deem to be alien to their own standards. Nevertheless, in quite quantifiable ways the United States has become like parts of the Third World. As Walden Bello points out, "By the end of the Republican era, the United States, a Congressional study asserted, had become 'the most unequal of modern nations.'" According to Bello, the Republican Party's brand of structural adjustment had begun "to give the U.S. a Third World appearance: rising poverty, widespread homelessness, greater inequality, social polarization."[57]

Hunger had become a constant fact of life for at least 29 million Americans, and 25 million—one in every ten—were receiving federal food stamps. Almost 50 per cent of children in minority groups were considered to be living in poverty, and the U.S. child poverty rate in general was the highest in the industrialized countries. Perhaps the most stark statistic was the infant mortality rate for African-Americans, which at 17.7 deaths per 1,000 live births was in roughly the same league as figures for "poor" Caribbean nations, such as Jamaica (17.2 per 1,000), Trinidad (16.3), and Cuba (16).[58]

By the 1990s, then, the "Third World" had come to refer not just to countries but to conditions as well, especially conditions of destitution and disorder. These conditions, like the new plagues of the late 20th century, were universal and spreading, even to the hitherto most secure and healthy. On April 5, 1995, Canada's National Council of Welfare reported that poverty rates in the country had grown "dramatically in 1993 despite the beginnings of an economic recovery." Of 29.4 million Canadians, 4.8 lived in poverty.[59]

# Conclusion

The idea of a "Third World," a world in which at least 70 per cent of the people of the world now live, was conceived during the dusk of a colonialism that had been in existence since the 16th century. The first decades of its existence, sometimes referred to as the "postcolonial" period, began with the independence of India in 1947.

In the 1950s, when the term was invented, and the 1960s, when it was popularized, the "Third World" had two locations. First was a location that was political and ideological. The Third World was "Non-Aligned," that is, it was notionally suspended in a space *between* the First (Washington-led, capitalist) World and the Second (Moscow-led, Communist) World, sharing some features of both but belonging to neither. In this period the Third World was, at least in theory, united. The second location of the Third World was not to be found on maps but on economic graphs, where it was seen to be arching upward towards development and modernization. Certainly most of it was following the West.

In the 1970s and early 1980s the idea of the political aspect of the "Third World" (non-aligned and united) was increasingly abandoned when it became apparent that the space between that world and the First World had existed only polemically, that is, in speeches and political texts. A politically independent Third World didn't really exist, or existed only delinquently, as in the "rogue states" outside the "community of nations"—in such places as Libya, Iran, and North Korea. Other nations run by homicidal maniacs or delusives, however bloodthirsty—so long as they conformed to the policy requirements of the West and thus did not threaten "international security"—were within the community.

More significantly, the Third World no longer had any unity; one part of it had split off. This part, the capitalist archipelago of Pacific Asia, was achieving economic growth and social improvement for the majority of its people. Many parts of the trunk of the Third World, from the shores of the Indian Ocean to the banks of the Rio Grande, were economically faltering, increasingly chaotic, and politically dangerous. Although no official announcement had yet been made, those areas had been in effect joined by much of what had been the Second World. The Chechens and the Bosnian Muslims were among the first casualties of this move: they were on their way to becoming Mexicans and Tutsis.

By the early 1980s, fewer Westerners talked about development with confidence. Some went so far as to note that unnerving signs could be seen even in the previously industrialized world. Prosperity and order were no longer flowing from the West outward; poverty and disorder now seemed to be flowing from the Third World inward.

Yet the Third World itself presented evidence of change and of attempts at reidentification. This change included the abandonment of the Western notion of "development" altogether. Development, as Arturo Escobar explains, had become the main "discourse" or analytical convention for describing the history of the Third World in the half-century after World War II, and attempts to overthrow, or at least renegotiate, the Western developmentalist idea were evident throughout the Third World from the 1950s.[60] The non-alignment attempts at Bandung in 1955 represented the earliest collective attempt to establish a bloc of Afro-Asian nations outside the magnetic field of the West.

The most important surviving model for an alternative approach is Cuba, an example that has influenced attempts at alternative development in nearby Jamaica, Grenada, and Nicaragua and as far away as Algeria and Iran. But the reaction to dissident development has been massive and relentless. Attempts have been made to crush it wherever it has manifest itself, from Guatemala in 1953 to Chile in 1973, through Grenada in 1982 and Nicaragua in the 1980s, to the Gulf in 1991. Most Western writers, however critical they may be of developmentalism, have been led to the conclusion that there is only one door marked "modernity," and the keys to that door were cut in the West (although they remain no longer, perhaps, confined solely to Western pockets).

Modernity, it is usually argued, means inescapable globalization and homogeneity. It connotes the inevitability of "McWorld," to take a word from the title of a recent book.[61] It also means endless, hypothetically sustainable, economic growth; for instance, the doubling of China's automobile population every three or four years. All alternative or even modified dreams to the contrary are bound to be dismissed as being utopian, Luddite, and disastrous. Their reality is represented as being the failed, fragmented, and near-forgotten worlds that have given up or been bypassed by development—the worlds conjured up by words such as "Liberia" and "Kampuchea"—worlds that are marginalized but still a threat to world order.

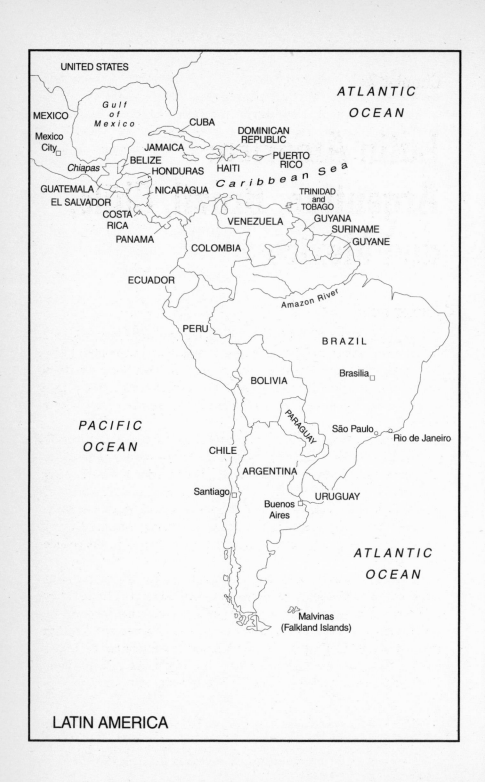

LATIN AMERICA

# Chapter 2

# Latin America: Argentina, Brazil, Chile, and Mexico

## Background

Over a period lasting from the early 16th to the early 19th centuries, Latin America was transformed by colonialism. Brazil was ruled from Lisbon and settled by African slaves and Portugal settlers; Saint Domingue (Haiti) was ruled by the French; and the rest of the continent, with the exception of small enclaves on the Caribbean coast (British Guiana, French Guiana, Dutch Suriname), was under Spanish rule.*

Then, in a process completed by the late 1820s, the great colonial viceroyalties of Spanish and Portuguese America were transformed into independent countries. In contrast to the case of most of the rest of the colonized non-Western world—the West Indies or Caribbean, Africa, the Middle East, India, Indochina, and Indonesia—the Latin American experience of rule by foreigners from overseas was mainly a memory by the beginning of the 20th century—although the question of economic independence remained.

In the first decades of the 20th century, for most of Latin America the prospects for successful economic growth were impressive. All the states on the continent were independent, and most of them were well-endowed with resources and had populations that would become increasingly urbanized and educated. Argentina, for instance, was prosperous and democratic and had every reason to look forward to a bright and modern future. Brazil, larger, richer, and more volatile, was bursting with potential. It had

---

* *Latin America*, like most regional terms, is inexact. The term usually refers to all of the mainland states in the Western hemisphere from Mexico southwards, even Belize and Guyana. The *Cambridge History of Latin America* includes the Spanish- and French-speaking states of the Caribbean, but not the English-speaking ones. (Here I treat the Caribbean in a separate chapter.)

the greatest reserves of iron in the world. Chile and Uruguay were smaller but viable because of stable political regimes and considerable natural wealth. Chile had great mineral wealth, while Uruguay was sometimes characterized as being the New Zealand of South America, able to build a prosperous society around the livestock industry. As early as 1923 it was suspected that Venezuela was floating on oil. By 1930 Colombia had already become the fourth most industrialized country on the continent. Mexico had been through a revolution that had destroyed the system of colonial landholdings and was on the verge of modernizing its economy based on oil and agriculture. It seemed that poor, mined-out Bolivia and the grassy backwater that was Paraguay were the only Latin American republics that entered the century with unexciting economic futures.

Until the Depression years of the 1930s most of the economies of Latin America were externally oriented, dependent on the export of a few staples. This approach, known as *desarrollo hacia afuera* ("export-led development"), was in itself unremarkable. The same approach not only governed most of Africa and Asia but also ruled the trade of Canada, Australia, and New Zealand as well as Iceland, Ireland, and a number of other European countries. To modernize their economies and increase their exports, the governments of most Latin American states borrowed heavily from U.S. bankers.

From the beginning of the Great Depression, in common with most of the world, the Latin American economies came under an unbearable pressure. The market for all their products, manufactured and raw, went into sharp decline. In two years (1929-31) the price of wheat fell by two-thirds and coffee prices tumbled from 22 cents to 8 cents a pound. The decline in exports led to a decline in imports: the earnings to pay for manufactured goods and to service the loans from the West were no longer available. New solutions had to be sought.

The largest of the Latin American economies, the ones that had already established a small industrial base, turned to manufacturing certain consumer goods that they needed themselves. This selective encouragement, and later, protection, of the domestic manufacturing sector became the basis of an economic strategy called "Import Substitution Industrialization" (ISI), which was to last into the 1960s or even 1970s. To a certain extent ISI was successful. By the early 1950s industry had become the leading sector in the economies of Argentina, Brazil, Chile, and Mexico. By the end of the 1960s, as economic historian Victor Bulmer-Thomas notes, the countries that had adopted the ISI strategy saw the share of manufacturing in the Gross Domestic Product (GDP) rise to a level similar to that in the industrialized countries of the North.[1]

ISI has been called "the dream of national capitalism." It was the antithesis of economic liberalism, an approach that had its credibility destroyed during the Depression of the 1930s.* Those who shared this dream were nationalists who saw their countries emerging from the slump to follow in the footsteps of North America, Europe, and Japan—moving in the direction of greater industrialization (and thus fuller employment) and greater independence. These nationalists came from both the right and the left of the political spectrum—ISI was not, in the first decades of its existence, the exclusive property of either one side or the other.

ISI was by no means a form of socialism. As before the 1930s, capital remained in the driving seat. The states that adopted ISI policies continued to support private enterprise; indeed, they often actively welcomed it. In the case of Brazil, as Bulmer-Thomas shows, the private sector supported state enterprise both before and after a military takeover in 1964.[2] Still, the dictates of ISI did not equally favour all sectors of private enterprise. The traditional agro-exporters, such as the ranchers of Argentina, saw themselves as sorely victimized. But although this class suffered, the approach survived in continental Latin America. Only in Cuba was it destroyed.

One of the first steps of the ISI program took the form of the national-ization of industries and strategic resources such as oil. Here Argentina was a pioneer with the founding of Yacimientos Petrolíféros Fiscales in the 1920s. In Mexico the dangerous work of oil nationalization was carried for-ward under the government of Lázaro Cárdenas (president, 1934-40), causing a furore internationally. Although Mexican nationalization was seen as setting a bad example for other Latin American countries, the pol-icy continued to be widely imitated. In the 1940s the Brazilians formed Companhia Val do Rio Doce, a state-owned company that would extract iron ore. In the 1950s the Peruvians nationalized tin, and in the 1960s they nationalized the International Petroleum Company, a Canadian-registered subsidiary of Standard Oil, which became Petroperú. Even as late as the 1970s, the Venezuelans established state control over iron ore and bauxite production.

It was also during the 1930s, a time of crisis that saw a relaxation of the bonds of colonialism and dependency everywhere, that the Brazilian government (with U.S. assistance—the first time the Americans had invested in industrialization in the Third World) invested in steel and

---

* From the 1930s almost everyone, everywhere, was against liberalism: Nazis, communists, populists, nationalists, democrats. As an economic doctrine, liberalism was not to raise its head again until the 1970s. For an explanation of the fall of liberalism, see Hobsbawm, *Age of Extremes*, 1994, chapter 4.

worked towards a national oil policy. In 1939 the Chilean government set up a new state corporation, CORFO (Corporación de Fomento), to stimulate economic development. Just over a decade later, in 1951, Petrobrás was born in Brazil as a mixed private-public corporation monopolizing the exploration and exploitation of oil. Later in the same decade, under the presidency of Juscelino Kubitschek (1956-61), the pharaonic builder of Brazil's new inland capital of Brasilia, foreign investment was given every encouragement in Brazil for the purpose of expanding its industrial sector, especially the automobile industry. But the enthusiasm for a national economic policy in the succeeding decade proved costly, especially with the massive growth of the Brazilian national debt, partly amassed by Kubitschek in the building of Brasilia.

In Argentina government involvement and state investment in industrialization became particularly associated with Juan Perón, the most celebrated of all of Latin America's postwar political leaders. As president (1946-55, 1973-74), Perón's popularity rose to dizzying heights largely on the basis of his push to fulfil the national dream of economic modernity. The growth of industries meant an increase in the number of jobs, and between 1946 and 1954 the number of factories and the number of workers in Argentina grew by wide margins.

In the 1960s the industrialization of the larger economies of Latin America (Brazil, Argentina, Chile, and Mexico) seemed a virtual certainty, just a matter of time. From 1929 to 1947 Mexico's rate of industrialization had grown slowly but steadily from 14 per cent to 20 per cent, while Argentina's rate had climbed from 23 per cent to 31 per cent. Brazilian industrialization went from nearly 18 per cent in 1939 to just over 35 per cent in 1963. Between 1950 and 1974, manufactured goods jumped from 6 per cent to 18 per cent of Latin America's total exports. By the 1960s all of the larger countries were self-sufficient in the production of textiles and foodstuffs, the classic consumer goods. In comparative terms, this meant that the people of Mexico, Argentina, southern Brazil, Uruguay, and Venezuela were as well off as the people in the extremes of Western Europe: Ireland, Portugal, much of Spain, southern Italy, and Greece. In caloric intake and literacy rates, in numbers of doctors and television sets per capita, the people of these countries—that is, the majority of Latin Americans—were in roughly the same boat as the poorer Europeans. Although most of the larger Latin American republics remained a long way from the high economic standards of Western Europe and North America, they were even further removed from the more extreme poverty of most of the countries of Asia and Africa.

But even by the 1960s, serious economic problems had begun to surface. As in the 1930s, the balance of payments problem was central. Increasingly, the "policy-making elites," that is, the businessmen and their political and military allies, began to consider alternatives to ISI. They now viewed ISI as a mistake. Worse, they saw it as a sin, and those who clung to it had to be scourged. Turning their countries away from ISI would be no easy matter, because many people had become attached to its benefits. Violence as a matter of course thus became accepted, by businessmen and economists alike, as well as by their overseas backers. In Chile the private sector virtually went on strike against the interventionist regime of Salvador Allende (1970-73).

The alternatives to ISI included several possibilities, all of them focused on the promotion of exports. At the centre of the campaign was trade liberalization, that is, the banishing of inward-looking, in favour of outward-looking, growth. Such liberalization was to be financed by debt. But debt, like other narcotics, provides salvation only in the short term. After the Mexican government's default on debt in August 1982, which triggered a general "debt crisis," the banks halted their lending to Latin America. Thus began a new crisis, and new solutions. One of those solutions—and certainly not the least of them—was "regional integration," the first fruit of which was the North American Free Trade Agreement (NAFTA), which in turn also failed to provide the promised stairway to developmental heaven.

# Argentina: The False Promise of Perónism

Argentina is widely perceived as a national failure, one of the few countries that has moved from first-world to third-world status in only a few short decades. As recently as the 1920s, no one would have considered Argentina underdeveloped. With an apparently stable government, a highly literate populace, an unequalled prosperity relative to other Latin American nations, Argentina was perceived as one of the world's successful new democracies, equal in many ways to Australia, Canada, and the United States. Yet, despite this early promise, during the last fifty years Argentina has moved from crisis to crisis, sinking into deeper depths of economic turmoil, social disruption, political chaos, militarism, debt, and governmental irresponsibility. . . . What happened?[3]

Until the Depression of the 1930s Argentina had been ruled by an oligarchy with a rural economic base. Known as the *burguesía pampeana* (the *pampas* bourgeoisie), its main economic preoccupation was the production of wheat and beef for the export market. Its main social preoccupation was in guaranteeing its reproduction and hegemony in relation to other

Argentineans. This oligarchy was connected to the officer class of the military. To most senior officers of the Argentinean military, change meant chaos, and from the 1930s through World War II, many of them openly expressed an admiration for European fascism—that is, the political solutions of Mussolini, Franco, Salazar, and Hitler. The appeal of fascism was not surprising: at a time of social and economic disorder it offered the solution of order and the promise of racial patriotism. Yet, in general, Argentinean fascism had a different face and different manners than the fascism of Europe. Racial purity, for instance, was not a serious question. Because almost all of the indigenous inhabitants of country had been killed off, most Argentineans were of European origin. What Argentinean fascism did have in common with its European cousin was that it mobilized the working class behind the nation-state. Argentinean fascists, in the army and in the workshops, were ardent nationalists.

By the end of World War II, the world of Argentine politics had changed radically. The Depression, over which they had little control, had weakened the economic and therefore the political power of the *burguesía pampeana*. Then, during the war, overseas demands for processed and manufactured goods from Argentina had increased and the size of the industrial workforce had taken off: between the mid-1930s and the late 1940s the number of workers in industry increased from around half a million to about two million. A massive migration from the countryside to the cities, and to Buenos Aires in particular, had begun. Alongside the working class was a growing middle class, including small entrepreneurs. Sensing the decline of the bourgeoisie and a change in the established order of things, Argentina's officer class panicked and on June 4, 1943, carried out a coup that put its own generals in office.*

One general among the rest—Colonel Juan Domingo Perón (b. 1895)—held particular ideas about political management. In the new military government of 1943 Perón became undersecretary in the War Department and labour secretary, two offices that allowed him simultaneously to build up his own following in the army and to cultivate the growing and muscular working class. He succeeded in the latter by encouraging a series of reforms that included health benefits, job security, and pensions. By drawing the trade unions to himself, he detached them from their previous allegiances (particularly to socialism and anarcho-syndicalism). The workers were now given instructions not by

---

* Bourgeois decline was more an illusion than a reality. Many of the big landowners became big industrialists, concentrating shares in the same way that they had once concentrated land.

political leaders or trade unionists but by the managers of the Perónist state.

Perón's popularity soared. Amid the shouting "Perónism" was born, implying developmental nationalism, industrialization, increased employment, and higher standards of living for both the middle and the working classes. The army realized what was happening only too late. In another coup in October 1945, his superior officers forced Perón to resign. Organized by Perón's followers in the labour movement, crowds flooded the streets of Buenos Aires. The army vacillated and then backed down. When Perón ran for the presidency in 1946, he remained the most popular man in the country, and his victory was followed by buoyant economic times lasting until the end of the decade. This golden age was in large part financed by the $1.5 billion sterling and dollar balances that Argentina had accumulated by selling supplies to the Allies during World War II. The country could spend lavishly without having to borrow.

Perón made use of his popularity by securing his political base amongst the working class and the modern middle class, or petit bourgeoisie, while the rival cattle and wheat oligarchy continued to reinvent themselves as a modern bourgeoisie. But the price the working class paid was high; increasingly the trade union movement was subordinated by the state in a system known as "corporatism."* While the trade unions won great privileges for their members—everything from wage increases to holiday homes—their independence continued to slip away. The trade union leaders were appointed, and bribed, by Perón and his lieutenants, and the government could interfere in the affairs of the unions at will. Many trade union officials became Perónistas.

Adopted in 1946, Perón's Quinquennial Plan, a Soviet-style five-year plan appropriately Latinized, sought to simultaneously accelerate industrial development and guarantee national control. Consistent with the aims of ISI, this industrial development aimed at expanding the domestic market, at achieving mass consumption. Under the banners of populism (combined with a real, if unfocused, radicalism), economic nationalism became the battle cry. By 1948 Perón had nationalized the British-owned railway system together with the banking, financial, and communications sectors of the Argentinean economy. The state also took over the marketing of exports and the purchase of imports. The approach as a whole proved enormously popular.

---

* *Corporatism* implies the domination of the institutions of both the working class and the employers by the state. Its objects are industrial harmony and social peace, and its means are negotiations between the state, capital, and the working class.

Although Perón's populism had some elements in common with the rural populisms of the Canadian Prairies and the U.S. Midwest, his Argentina was politically a long way from the democracies of North America. Argentinean populism, like Italian fascism, was deeply tainted with repression. Perón's own party, the Partido Perónista, had its own thugs (called the *descamisados*, "the shirtless") employed to intimidate Perón's rivals and critics, not unlike the various blackshirts and brownshirts who terrified Europe in the 1930s. Their activities were complemented by the purging of the Supreme Court and its staffing with judicial ciphers sympathetic to Perón, in addition to the harassment of the labour movement. Still, Perónism was not essentially totalitarian. In Argentina there was neither terror nor a saturation of the civil society by totalitarian institutions, both of which were common among the fascist-tinted populisms of European countries from Germany to Rumania.

Perón's personal popularity was inseparable from that of his second wife, Eva Duarte de Perón (1919-52). "Evita," glamorous and dramatic, was a source of identification for the oppressed of Argentina, but her contributions were real. As Richard Bourne suggested: "As a Latin American personality possibly Eva's most revolutionary significance was that she was a woman. The fact that a woman was so obviously playing a leading role in one of the area's biggest countries opened up new horizons for women in every field."[4] More conventionally, she served as an evangelist for Perónism; her mission included the exaltation of her husband. More tangible was her success in her campaign for the enfranchisement of women in 1947. The Partido Perónista was complemented by the Partido Perónista Femenino. In the 1951 elections, when two million women cast their ballots for the first time, 6 women senators and 24 deputies, all Perónistas, were elected. Perón selected Evita to run as his vice-presidential candidate, a move the army vetoed.* When Evita died of cancer in 1952, Argentinean society submerged itself in grief.

By the time of Evita's death the Perónista state was running on empty. The country's exports had fallen back and its foreign reserves had largely dwindled away, spent on paying for the nationalization of transport, banks, and industry and then on subsidizing those sectors. With economic decline went a decay in income levels and living standards for Perón's supporters. The military's collective thoughts began to turn to mutiny.

Perón won the 1952 election fraudulently, although it is possible that

---

* In the early 1950s the election of a woman to a high state office would have been a notable event. The first elected woman head of state was Sirimavo Bandaranaike, who became prime minister of Ceylon (now Sri Lanka) in 1960.

he might have won it anyway. He had both organization and popular sympathy on his side, whereas the opposition was disunited and unknown. As protest against the policies of his regime mounted, Perón censored opposition newspapers and resorted increasingly to strong-arm tactics to silence his critics. Thus began what Juan E. Corradi calls "the reactionary phase of Peronism." Now turning against economic independence, Perón made it clear that he welcomed foreign, particularly U.S., capital into Argentina. According to Corradi, "U.S. and West European firms began taking over major sectors of Argentine industry. With tariff protection now working in their favour, U.S., German, and Italian firms developed . . . automobile plants and chemical complexes. The nationalist pretensions of the regime were simply thrown overboard."[5]

While beckoning to foreign capital, Perón imposed a freeze on wages and clawed back social benefits. Then, incredibly and mistakenly, he attacked the Catholic Church, which had hitherto tolerated his regime. He suspended the teaching of the Catholic religion in the schools and legalized divorce and prostitution. Although Argentina was not Spain or Ireland, the Catholic Church—already offended by the enfranchisement of women—commanded the allegiance of the vast majority of Argentineans, with piety still generally considered the most admirable of virtues. The Vatican struck back. Pope Pius XII excommunicated all government officials who had taken a part in the offensive against the church. This was a signal for further action, and in mid-1955 the middle class, now feeling the pinch of economic decline, engaged in mass demonstrations against the government. In September 1955 the first military revolts took place. The air force overflew Buenos Aires, and the navy threatened to bombard the city. On September 21, the army occupied the capital.

The officers did not act in a vacuum. Just as in a coup that was to come a decade later, the military officers made sure that owners of capital and the middle and lower-middle classes would support, or at least accept, their intervention. With these forces arrayed against him, Perón sailed upriver to Paraguay and then off into a more congenial exile in Spain. As soon as he departed, his government collapsed. Corradi provides a trenchant epitaph for this period:

> The Peronist government collapsed as soon as he departed. It was the end of what probably was the first instance of a political phenomenon that later became common throughout the Third World: nonaligned developmentalism in a mixed economy. In Argentina this phenomenon had taken the form of a pseudorevolution; a coalition of different classes and institutional bureaucracies within a capitalist framework, underwritten by the large funds accumulated by Argentina during exceptional years when the bonds of dependency

were relaxed. The alliance collapsed ten years later, when the funds had run out and import substitution could no longer sustain an independent industrialization process.[6]

The ISI program, the main strategy of the economic nationalists, had been mortally wounded in Argentina by the mid-1950s, and the following decades would see a slow and painful surrender by the economic nationalists to other forces.

## Post Perón

After a short interregnum, the military took power formally in June 1956, settling in for a rule that would last for almost 30 years, with only a short break in the mid-1970s. Its leaders, known in the contemporary Western political literature as "oligarchic praetorians," were determined to set the country on a fundamentally different course. From the end of 1955 to 1973 direct military rule alternated with elected civilian governments that were toppled when they failed to follow the conservative economic prescriptions of the military or proved to be too conciliatory to the Perónistas and the left. David Rock describes the quality of one of them, General Juan Carlos Onganía, who took power in 1966: "From the heights of [his] unexpected absolutism, he informed the country of the key ingredients of his preferences. . . . They were, in essence, those of a devout soldier, imprisoned by the narrowest of Catholic phobias in matters of sex, communism and art. An admirer of Franco's Spain, Onganía saw in it an example to be imitated in order to restore morals and order to a people he considered licentious and undisciplined."[7]

General Onganía and his officers were supported by most of the Argentinean bourgeoisie, much of the middle class, and by foreign interests. Even though there was a felt need among Argentina's new rulers that the economy would have to be denationalized, the urban working class demobilized, and the state restructured, attempts to do this enjoyed limited success. During the early years of military rule, while shifts at all levels were slowly taking place, a coherent program was lacking, and without coherent management the economy drifted out of control. Foreign debt increased, and inflation rose inexorably. Recession and mounting debt, rising in visibility from the early 1960s, began to bite hard on the population of what was Latin America's richest, best educated, and most urbanized nation—indeed, the continent's most Europeanized country. Political confrontation increased steadily, stimulated by a rise in food prices, a decline in public-sector expenditure, and a refusal to provide workers with wage increases. This confrontation was given a deeper Cold

War colouring from the early 1960s by the sensational successes of the Cuban Revolution. Guerrilla groups in the northwest of the country, in conscious emulation of the Cuban revolutionaries, regularly launched assaults on the forces of order.*

Through the crudest and most conspicuous forms of repression, the military dictatorship succeeded in keeping the lid on a smouldering society while overseeing the beginnings of a new economic program, this one based on *dependent industrialization*. The antithesis of ISI, this was industrialization by means of foreign investment and often in the form of foreign firms. It was, in other words, the denationalization of development. By 1971, out of ten principal industrial firms, eight were foreign-owned, and foreigners also owned more than half the private banks. Because foreign investment generally favoured using modern machinery in preference to creating more jobs or establishing higher wages, the members of the working class found their situations worsening. The prime beneficiaries of the new approach were the multinational corporations and especially the U.S. investment banks.

But by May 1969 the military's control had already begun to slip away. Major riots struck the cities of Rosario, Corrientes, and Córdoba, the most industrialized city in the country. These riots, known as the *cordobazo*, were led by university students and autoworkers. Uprisings followed in other cities. Strikes, guerrilla operations, kidnappings, assassinations, counterinsurgency operations by the military: Argentina displayed the symptoms of a country in the early stages of civil war. As the economy crashed downwards it broke through existing floors of inflation and unemployment. By 1973 the military, itself weakened by internal divisions, could no longer hold onto power.

## Neo-Perón

Even after its leader's overthrow, labour had largely remained loyal to the exiled Juan Perón while the Perónistas remained the most formidable and persistent bloc in Argentinean politics. Perón managed to pull certain strings from Spain, where he remained in comfortable exile. On May 25, 1973, the Perónistas elected one of their number, Héctor J. Cámpora, as president. Amid an almost universal elation, a government of national reconstruction was put into place. Reforms and plans for reforms rained down, leftists were installed in power, and leading officers associated with

---

\* There were five main guerrilla groups in Argentina, ranging from the Montoneros through two Perónista groups to two Marxist organizations. None were connected with either Beijing or Moscow.

the right were forced to retire. Perón himself was recalled from Spain to take charge of *his* movement. When he returned on June 20, 1973, as many as two million people were at the airport to meet him.

Almost immediately Perón proceeded to turn the clock back in the interests of his own tenure. To placate the right he replaced Cámpora and his leftist officials with functionaries of his own choosing, many of them conservatives. In new elections held on October 12, 1973, Perón himself became president. What had happened was no less than an internal coup: the Perónist right and its allies had crushed the Perónist left and its supporters. This heartened the conservatives—especially the army officers and businessmen—who were dismayed by the rebellion of workers and students and terrified at the thought of the collapse of order and authority.

The left responded to Perón's tilt to the right in a complicated physics of reaction. Urban guerrilla groups, the most important of which was the Montoneros, who represented the left-wing of the Perónista movement, now appeared. The guerrillas attacked the Perónista functionaries, the police, and the army. The army, in retaliation, murdered the guerrillas whenever possible, assisted by the Argentine Anti-Communist Alliance, a vigilante organization. In March 1974, with the complicity of Perón himself, the army went further; it overthrew the popular but left-leaning governor of Córdoba.

On July 1, 1974, Perón, the failed redeemer, died. His successor was Isabel Martínez de Perón, his third wife, who had run as his vice-president in the elections of the previous October. Although Isabel Perón could lay claim to being the first woman to serve as head of state in the Western Hemisphere, she was no more able than anyone else to keep the lid on the cauldron of Argentinean politics. In March 1976, in yet another coup, the military removed her from office.

## Bureaucratic Authoritarianism

The new military regime was headed first by General Jorge Rafael Videla, who ruled at the head of a military-led junta. Videla lasted until October 1980, when he was succeeded by retired Major General Roberto Viola. Together they formed what one political scientist has called the "bureaucratic authoritarian" (BA) mode of government. Viola was ousted in November 1981, replaced by the commander-in-chief of the army, General Leopoldo Galtieri, who would oversee the Malvinas fiasco. In July 1982 Galtieri was replaced by General Reynaldo Benito Antonio Bignone, who was in turn succeeded by Raúl Alfonsín after a landslide election victory.

The authoritarian bureaucrats may have been barbarous and incompetent, but they had a concrete economic and political crisis on their hands. The political dramas that had begun with Perón's 1955 ouster had weakened the country's authoritarian but populist political structure without replacing it with anything more substantial. Political partisanship now increasingly shaded off to sectarianism and terrorism. Since the coup of 1955 and especially since the Cuban Revolution (1959-60), large numbers of middle-class youth had become radicalized. Some of these youths became Montoneros, a centre-leftist political movement that adopted a complicated ideology of national self-sufficiency leavened with borrowings from Marxism and Catholicism. The Montoneros demanded independence from both capitalist and socialist countries, calling for, in other words, the creation of a space for international Third Worldism. In the early 1970s, with Perón still in exile, they saw themselves as a major force in national politics, but when Perón returned in mid-1973 he excluded them from any participation in politics and orchestrated their persecution by the police. From 1976, with the last of the Peróns removed, the military, with help from the vigilantes, sought to wipe them out completely, together with all others who opposed reactionary military dictatorship. The means adopted was a massive campaign of terror. One general boasted, "We are going to have to kill 50,000 people; 25,000 subversives, 20,000 sympathizers and we will make 5,000 mistakes." Another put a slightly different twist on the matter: "First we will kill all the subversives, then we will kill those who are timid, finally we will kill those who remain indifferent."[8]

The terror saw the disappearance of as many as 30,000 Argentineans. Some of them were guerrillas, but many more were trade unionists. Others were simply liberals and democrats seeking political change for the better. Many of them were tortured to death. Others were executed in prisons and in the streets, and an estimated 2,000 were thrown from airplanes into the Atlantic. Nor was escape from the juggernaut of military repression a simple matter: many political exiles were extradited from neighbouring countries based on secret agreements between those other military dictatorships and the Argentinean leaders.

Immediately after the military coup, the Confederación General de Trabajo (CGT), Argentina's trade union federation, had been interdicted. Its banning was just the first step in the assault on the working class. In reaction to the terror and assassination of the military regime, the trade union movement split and its numbers rapidly declined. A more conciliatory faction collaborated with the junta, while a more militant group continued to organize strikes.

The destruction of the trade unions facilitated a plunge of nearly 50 per cent in real wages in 1976. By 1977 the wage share of national income was at its lowest level since 1935. By removing the role of the state from key areas, and by withdrawing from economic management, the generals brought the barely adequate welfare system to a state of near collapse. Argentina, the land of wheat and beef, was now a country of malnutrition.

But the bureaucratic-authoritarian rulers of Argentina had no keys to paradise. Between 1975 and 1981, per capita GDP fell by 0.8 per cent per annum. By 1982 it was back to the 1970 levels. Capital fled the country, and industrial production was down by 50 per cent. "Argentina" writes William Smith, was "in the throes of the worst political, economic and . . . moral crisis in its history."[9] By early 1982, with economic decline continuing in a rapidly downward spiral, military rule had run out of credibility, except in the minds of the officers and the arms dealers. On March 30, 1982, the leaders of the CGT who had managed to survive the repression organized a mass rally. In doing this the trade unions were adding their protests to those of the Madres de plaza de mayo ("Mothers of the Square of May"), whose persistent and dignified demands concerning the whereabouts of the *desaparecidos* ("the disappeared ones") attracted the attention of the world media and were critical in discrediting the military. The "Mothers" succeeded, as one writer put it, in "turning their traditional private roles as mothers and wives to new public purpose."[10]

The misery and mayhem of Argentina under military dictatorship coincidentally came to a precipitous end immediately after the trade union demonstration. On April 2, 1982, in a state of deluded belligerence, General Leopoldo Galtieri effectively declared war on Great Britain. The prize of the war was ostensibly possession of the islands that the British called "the Falklands" and the Argentineans "the Malvinas." Some 9,000 Argentinean troops had occupied these islands after forcing the small British garrison there to surrender. The Malvinas comprised a largely deserted and windswept archipelago 8,000 miles from Britain and inhabited by 600,000 sheep and 1,800 humans. The Argentinean writer Jorge Luis Borges likened the conflict to two bald men fighting over a comb. Still, it seemed as though Galtieri had found a solution to the problem of the military's declining popularity and loss of initiative. Argentina's trade unions and political parties rallied behind them. *"Las Malvinas son Argentinas"* cried Argentineans from the left and the right.

Both Britain and Argentina assumed the support of the United States, but only one side received it. With a little help from her friend Ronald Reagan, the side of the British prime minister, Margaret Thatcher, won. Given the centuries of British experience in attacking poorly armed foreigners, and the Argentinean army's lack of experience (other than in attacking its own civilians), it was remarkable that the war hung in the balance for as long as it did.

The Argentinean dictators felt betrayed, and given their furious anti-communism and sycophantic pro-Americanism, perhaps they had every right to be. What they failed to grasp was that their status in Washington's global order was, when it came to the crunch, peripheral. Argentina was, strategically speaking, no Afghanistan. Indeed, as one former U.S. secretary of state unkindly pointed out, the states in the Southern Cone of Latin America (Argentina, Uruguay, and Chile) were a dagger pointing to the heart of Antarctica.

Argentinean patriotic opinion, excited by the military, rapidly drooped off into gloomy and frustrated detumescence. The captains began to bicker; some of them turned to drink. Their willingness to stay at their posts deserted them. It became evident, even to those most fervently pro-regime, that the Argentine military, despite all of its grand statements about defending the state and Christian civilization, was ineffective against foreign enemies. Worse, many of its captains had proven to be cowards when it came to fighting the British. Amid an intensifying campaign mounted by human rights groups, the junta began to dissolve.

On November 1, 1982, a mass grave of 300 unidentified persons was discovered; by the middle of the month the judges who had collaborated with the military murderers in the interests of their collective class began to be investigated from within the judiciary itself. In December the revived CGT organized the first general strike since 1975; at the same time a multiparty "March for Democracy" drew 100,000 demonstrators. Shaken as well by the sound of inflation crashing through the roof—it had risen to 200 per cent and was still climbing—the country's rulers made a promise of democratic elections.

In autumn 1983, as spring in the Southern Hemisphere began, Argentina was still trapped in a winter of discontent. Democratic elections were held on October 30, and for the first time in 40 years their results were not a foregone conclusion. With the Perónista movement divided, victory went to the head of the Unión Cívica Radical (Radical Party), Raúl Alfonsín (b. 1927), who projected an image of change and renewal.

## Democracy and Deterioration

Alfonsín had made a name for himself in the struggle for human rights under the military regime. When he attained power, the heads of the military were put on trial and many of them were convicted for what were in effect crimes against humanity, that is, mass murder as opposed to mere multiple homicide. On December 9, 1985, a civil court sentenced five of the military leaders who had ruled Argentina between March 1976 and

June 1982 to prison. Two of them, General Jorge Videla and Admiral
Eduardo Massera, got life sentences.

By this time much of the middle class was on its way to the poorhouse. Argentina, which had simultaneously one of the world's highest
rates of inflation (700 per cent in 1985) and one of the world's highest foreign debts ($50 million), was no longer even able to pay its U.S., Japanese,
and Canadian creditors. Soon after the elections Alfonsín presented
Congress with a draft law aimed at partially remedying Argentina's
spreading malnutrition. This was the Programa de Alimentario Nacional
(PAN), with the acronym spelling the Spanish word for "bread." In 1984
the state spent $120 million in food packages; this increased to $206 million by 1986.

Following an austerity plan that pushed inflation down to less than
100 per cent, and contesting two more elections—despite the rise from
the grave of the undead Perónistas—Alfonsín held on to power, becoming
by 1988 the longest-governing president in 25 years. But by 1989, another
election year, the country was again at the point of national crisis. Inflation
had returned, general strikes were widespread, military uprisings took
place in two of the provinces, and the poor had turned to looting the
supermarkets. Alfonsín lost the elections, leaving office five months earlier than planned. Shortly before he stepped down his government
declared a state of seige.

Alfonsín's successor, the Perónista Carlos Menem (b. 1935), took
office in July 1989. In his election campaign he had promised, "Follow me,
I will not fail you." His role models were the neoliberal champions of the
Western world: Margaret Thatcher, Ronald Reagan, and, somewhat surprisingly given what Argentineans had recently been through, Augusto
Pinochet. Almost immediately after coming to power he arrested the
entire leadership of the Partido Obrero (the Workers' Party).

Menem's march towards the right continued. Filling his cabinet with
conservatives, including the local representative of one of the country's
main foreign-owned transnational corporations, he launched into a program of privatization that shocked even his supporters. He had thousands
of state employees dismissed. Leading state-owned firms, such as Entel,
the state telephone company, and Aerolineas Argentinas, the national air-
line, were auctioned off for a fraction of their real value. *The Wall Street
Journal* commented that these two privatizations "more resemble corporate raids than stockholders' sales."[11] Both were sold for only a fraction of
their net worth. Most remarkable of all, Yacimientos Petrolíféros the profitable state-owned oil company, also disappeared into the private sector.
As Benjamin Keen notes, "Among Latin American oil producers,

Argentina was the only one to sell off its oil state monopoly, usually regarded as a 'strategic' asset, lock, stock, and barrel."

That Menem was able to prevail against those who opposed him was due to three main factors: most of the Perónista leaders of labour did not oppose him; he repressed the trade unions that did oppose him; and the Argentinean left was disorganized after years of repression. In March 1991 further cuts in state spending caused the loss of thousands more jobs as well as the loss of welfare, health-care, and education provision. Although this led to suffering for immense numbers of Argentineans, the IMF and the stock market reacted with satisfaction. Washington was no less pleased, offering to refinance Argentina's $21 billion foreign debt.

Inside the country, even by 1990, the crisis had deepened. With parts of the economy collapsing, an estimated 52 thousand people took part in looting in 15 of the country's 22 provinces. Congress admitted that the country was in a state of "social crisis." Reports indicated that the army and the police were carrying out joint exercises, and it was obvious that they were not planning to invade the Malvinas again. According to Georges Midré, "The authorities appear to have shared the opinion that the lack of food was, if not the sole reason, at least the central element among the causal factors leading to the uprising."[12]

Menem, faced with the possibility of an even more widespread social uprising, introduced another means of feeding the poor called "Solidarity Bonds." An estimated nine million families needed food subsidies, although only one million were being fed through the agencies of the state. By 1992, although both the PAN program and the Bonds had been terminated, the living conditions of Argentina's poor had continued to deteriorate.[13]

Menem, by now referred to as the Margaret Thatcher of the Pampas for his economic strategies, had turned himself into a major ally of the military, praising them for defeating subversion. In December 1990 he issued a general amnesty, releasing from prison General Jorge Videla and General Roberto Viola, the former presidents (1976-81). Later, in March 1995, when a retired naval commander confessed to being complicit in the murders of prisoners in the 1980s, Menem declared him a criminal and had him stripped of his rank.

In the May 1995 elections Menem managed to win 49 per cent of the vote. While neoliberals claimed this as a victory for the policies of the IMF, others pointed out that although Menem poured money into the campaign—he outspent his rivals by 50 to 1—only 38 per cent of voters cast ballots in his favour.[14] In response to a massive demonstration against his policies in July 1994, the Menem government openly discussed appropriating as much as $2.4 billion to create a new security force. As Keen points out, "Menem, who claimed to assume the mantle of Perón and to continue his work, had dealt a death blow to what remained of Perón's economic and political project. It remained to be seen whether Menem's neoliberal project, based on the sell-off of the national patrimony, the subordination of labor, and an alliance with domestic and foreign ruling classes, was more viable than the one he destroyed."[15]

# Brazil: From Kubitschek to Cardoso—and ISI to IMF

President Getúlio Vargas (1883-1954), who ruled Brazil twice (1930-45; 1951-54), was to Juan Perón as the Brazilian samba was to the Argentinean tango. Each danced slightly different steps to the music of the times, yet both wore the shiny shoes of national-populism tied on with the laces of corporatism.

It was in the first administration under Vargas that Brazil's industrialization, also carried out to the tunes of ISI, accelerated. Brazil's economy became more self-sustaining and less reliant on earnings from Brazil's major export, coffee, the crop that formed the main link between the country and the international economy. The two corollaries of industrial growth were, as Vargas realized, urbanization and social change. The cities, particularly São Paulo, expanded, and both the middle class and the working class grew in size and strength. Like Perón after him, Vargas used the workers against the bourgeoisie, buying their loyalty with higher wages and privileges such as a 48-hour workweek, paid annual vacations, pensions, health plans, and job security.

If these new classes were the winners in the process of capitalist industrialization, the losers were the traditional agricultural elite, the coffee bourgeoisie, and, to an even greater extent, the peasants. During his first 15 years in power Vargas, by overseeing industrial expansion, weakened the political power of the rural oligarchies. At the same time he paid them off by giving them the rights to the merciless exploitation of the peasantry.

Vargas had come to power during a time when the Depression was destroying the oligarchy that had ruled since the late 19th century. But like contemporary Argentinean politicians and property owners, he worried about order as well as development. This concern had drawn him to Italian Fascism and to the corporatist Estado Nôvo ("New State"), which had been erected in Portugal under the dictator Antonio Salazar. Brazil's version of the Estado Nôvo, established in 1937, gave the government the right to regulate certain aspects of foreign investment. The petroleum industry, for instance, was to be owned by Brazilians themselves. At the beginning of World War II, by means of a loan through the U.S. Import-Export Bank, the Brazilians founded a nationalized steel firm, the Companhia Siderurgica Nacional. Other industrial firms such as the Fábrica Nacional de Motores were founded during the war. "Between 1930 and 1945," writes Peter Evans, "the role of the state had changed dramatically."

> The construction of a centralized state bureaucracy had moved significantly forward, and the direct intervention of the state in economic affairs had accompanied it. Nowhere along the way is there evidence that the expansion of the state's role was undertaken as part of a "development project" of the local industrial bourgeoisie. They appear to have remained more as bystanders, pleased by the regime's ability to maintain control over the working class, sympathetic to the nationalist elements in the program, yet ideologically opposed to "statism."[16]

Vargas saw some form of corporatism as providing the order under which a measured progress could cautiously advance. This meant that the industrial working class would have to be cosseted, structured, and co-opted, just as it was later in Argentina. As for Vargas himself, he would stand like a Napoleon, without party and above all classes. And like Napoleon, his place would be guaranteed by the co-operation of the armed forces. In what we might call the conscience of the officer class there existed a nationalism that included the notion that the army had a sacred duty to guard the state. Precisely what kind of state the army had in mind would later become evident. The church, too, had a role, that of legitimation. The kind of state the church would willingly legitimate was not surprising; it, too, yearned for patriarchal authority and social order.

In 1945 Vargas was ousted by the same armed forces that had given him his political security. An army officer, General Eurico Dutra, held power for five years, leading a government that was pro-American and pro-economic liberalism at a time when economic nationalism and protectionism were still surging everywhere on the continent. Attempts by the government to have foreigners participate in the oil monopoly Petrobrás were fended off. *"O Petroleo e Nosso"* ("the Oil is Ours"), said its defenders.

The return of Vargas in 1951 was a repudiation of Dutras's liberal and internationalist policies. Nonetheless, Washington was still insisting that private investment was the only route to national development. Vargas retaliated, arguing that the Americans were trying to undermine Brazil's economic growth. A propaganda war broke out, but Vargas managed to maintain state control over the exploration and refining of petroleum. He also managed to oversee the establishing of a national development bank, which was used to finance Brazil's infrastructure and a state electricity company, Electrobrás.

The military—with a large faction of it congenitally anti-communist and suspicious of economic nationalism (which many of its leaders had supported in the 1930s)—began to increase pressure on Vargas. Many right-wing military arguments had been formulated in the supreme institution of military intellectualism, the National War College. Here, under the strong influence of U.S. military advisors, Cold War crusading pieties had been added to the older mysteries of Christianity and Civilization, which the officers had pledged themselves to protect. An explosive cocktail resulted, ignited by an awareness that at the Caracas conference of the Organization of American States (OAS), Washington had denounced communism as an international conspiracy that was in danger of infecting the otherwise healthy bodies of local political movements. Removal of local communists, therefore, was seen as a patriotic responsibility; one that would be repaid by U.S. military aid and co-operation.

The military had another grievance. The working class, or parts of it, was becoming privileged through better pay. Skilled workers were earning as much as junior officers, which was seen as a threat to the officers' social standing. The officers were therefore determined to rid Brazil of Vargas, blaming him for the breakdown of the status quo. By August 1954 the senior officers were demanding his resignation. Vargas refused to go, but then, quite unexpectedly, he chose a martyr's exit, shooting himself in the heart—a form of political exit that was to prove especially common among Latin American reformers. Their enemies to the right tended to favour shooting others.

Vargas was succeeded by Juscelino Kubitschek, an economic modernizer with an erector complex. He promised "50 Years' Progress in Five." His particular preoccupation was to develop the hinterland of the country and especially the vast and resource-rich Amazon Basin; so he expanded the infrastructure and founded a new capital in the northern interior, calling it "Brasilia." In the years of Kubitschek's presidency, Brazil entered one of its most dynamic periods of growth and prosperity, with both intermediate and capital goods industries expanding. And not being satisfied with merely Brazilian development, he proposed to Washington a program called "Operation Pan American," which was intended to eliminate poverty in the whole continent.

Official Washington, in the period before the Cuban Revolution, had only a limited interest in Brazil or anywhere else in Latin America. Even in the late 1950s, when he was presumably writing his famous book on economic development, W.W. Rostow thought that to forestall communism the United States should become involved in the modernization of Asia, the Middle East, and even Africa, but he was unworried by Latin America. Rostow thought that the continent, insulated by geography and the Monroe Doctrine from the world's power struggles, might develop "at a leisurely pace." As Van Gosse suggests, in this period Latin America had "dwindled to near invisibility."[17]

Although popular, Kubitschek's developmentalist solutions were costly and attracted many critics. By the time he was defeated in the 1960 election Brazil was suffering from high inflation and a huge national debt ($4 billion by 1961), which appears to have been the price for the improvements the president had overseen. Life expectancy had increased between 1940 and 1960 from 43 to 53 years, infant mortality had dropped, industrial production had increased, and industrial employment had come to double non-industrial (agricultural) employment.[18] In 1964 a report by the Economic Commission of Latin America summarized the extent of the nationalization that had been carried out within the Brazilian economy: "Brazil's public sector owns and directs the country's maritime inland waterway and rail transport facilities and its facilities for the production of petroleum and atomic fuel, controls most of the steel making capacity and is rapidly becoming the principal electrical energy producer. . . . It is also the principal iron ore producer and exporter."[19]

Economic nationalism had been joined by rural reformism as the main driving force in Brazilian politics. The focus for rural reformism was in the northeast part of the country. When *New York Times* reporter Tad Szulc visited the region in October 1960, he discovered to his horror that the region had been infected by anti-landlord and, worse, anti-U.S sentiments. He called the organizers "Fidelistas," that is, supporters of Fidel Castro.[20] Suddenly Washington had become interested in development and in Brazil.

Relations with Kubitschek's successor did not get off to a promising start. Janio Quadros showed himself preoccupied with the privileges that U.S. firms enjoyed in Brazil. In 1961 he introduced a bill into the Brazilian Congress to increase the tax on profits exported to the United States. Furthermore, he showed a lack of interest in the aid that the United States under President John F. Kennedy had decided to shower on Brazil as part of the "Alliance for Progress," the U.S. program introduced after the Cuban Revolution and designed to promote economic development as an antidote to revolution.* Even worse in U.S. eyes were the repeated

---

* The Alliance for Progress was announced in 1961, amid a fanfare of developmentalist

overtures that Quadros made to the left, both inside the country and internationally. It seemed as though an "independent" Brazilian foreign policy might be in the making. Indeed, while Quadros had no real intentions of joining the neutralist bloc, he did intend to form closer relations with African and Asian countries as well as with Brazil's neighbouring republics. This new interest did not exclude Cuba: he awarded "Che" Guevara Brazil's highest honour, the Southern Cross medal.

The flame of neutralism inevitably sent alarm bells ringing: by 1961 there were fears in the U.S. State Department that the Soviet Union had imperial designs on Latin America. Washington thought of isolating Cuba and carrying out a collective action against it, but few of the Latin American republics supported this course of action. "If we publicly declare that Cuba is a threat to our security," reported one Mexican diplomat, "forty million Mexicans will die laughing." In 1962 the CIA began its activities in Brazil, infiltrating peasant and labour organizations and recruiting local allies, especially within the army.

In Brazil, after a brief seven months in office, Quadros resigned, assuming that he would be returned with greater support. This was a miscalculation. Instead he was succeeded in 1961 by his vice-president, João "Jango" Goulart, once Vargas's minister of labour. According to Gerard Colby, Goulart saw himself as "Vargas' spiritual successor in the struggle to rid Brazil of foreign domination."[21] He was, like Vargas, a populist and a reformer but not by any stretch of normal imagination a communist. The State Department and *The New York Times* suggested otherwise; Goulart had, after all, been on a diplomatic mission to the People's Republic of China when Quadros resigned. And, as was the case with Quadros's neutralism, Goulart's gestures towards Third World solidarity were perceived as threatening U.S. interests—and so too was his program to restrict foreign business interests. (He supported a limitation on the export of profits by foreign companies and proposed the building of hydro-electric projects, which would diminish Brazil's dependence on foreign-owned companies.) Goulart also threatened the power of the large landholders by promising agrarian reforms.

---

rhetoric, by President Kennedy as a means of nullifying the effects of the Cuban Revolution (see chapter 3). The Alliance had two overlapping objects. The first was the modernization, or "commercialization," of agriculture by means of land reform. The need of the peasantry for land was subordinated to the requirement that the land be made into a source of profit. The second goal was the adoption of social and economic reform. To accomplish these ends the Inter-American Development Bank (IDB), established in 1959, would provide loans to all Latin American countries except Cuba. The Alliance barely survived the Cuban missile crisis of 1962 and was superseded by more violent programs that included the overthrow of governments, including that of Quadros's successor, Goulart.

In addition to foreign investors and the agrarian bourgeoisie (coffee planters and beef producers as well as mill owners committed to the export economy), other members of the elite were also worried by Goulart's policies. The Brazilian middle class became unnerved by the rising militancy of labour, especially in the northeast but also in the Alta Mogiana region northwest of São Paulo. The Brazilian army became alarmed by Goulart's appeal, above their heads, to the ordinary soldiers. Taken together, the bogeys of nationalist development (portrayed in the press as "Communistic"), reform, and independence in foreign policy were enough to convince his enemies that he was a threat. With more than a little help from their friends in Washington, not the least of which was the CIA, which had spent several millions in its campaign against the president, the army leaders marched against Goulart, forcing his resignation on April 1, 1964. The pro-American and right-wing General Humberto de Castelo Branco, a close friend of the CIA chieftain General Vernon Walters, replaced him.

## Darkness

The decade that followed the coup of 1964 has been called "the most dismal . . . in Brazil's life as a nation."[22] Even after that first decade the darkness continued; democracy was not to see the light of day in Brazil for 21 years. Politics beyond the local level became a charade; the only political parties were the ones controlled by the generals. The independent judiciary disappeared. Political repression and censorship became increasingly severe. Maria Helena Alves comments: "During the 1969-1974 period it was difficult to meet a Brazilian who had not come into direct contact with a tortured victim or been involved in a search and arrest operation."[23]

The payoff for all those who had opposed Goulart was attractive. The military government opened up Brazil's interior to foreign investment and suspended laws that had increased profit repatriation. It broke off relations with Cuba and sent Brazilian troops to join in the U.S. invasion of the Dominican Republic in April 1965. The army got to spend more on arms, usually purchased abroad, and on itself—guaranteeing its officers high salaries, security, and prestige together with a system of welfare otherwise available only in advanced social democracies. To justify their privileges, the officers wrapped themselves in the cloak of national security doctrine, asserting themselves as the defenders of the Christian nation against international communism.

During the Cold War this concept of "national security" became a key preoccupation of the governments of pro-Western regimes. The main threat to national security in countries such as Brazil and Argentina was seen to be internal and usually referred to as "subversion." Even if they worked for church organizations, subversives were seen as ultimately serving the ends of Moscow and were known as "dupes." In Brazil the font of wisdom regarding the matter of national security was the Escola Superior de Guerra (ESG), the National War College. The basic doctrine of the ESG specifically linked order and development and was called the "Doctrine of Political National Security and Development." But those who believed in the doctrine of "national security" appeared to be blind to a related issue: from the time of the 1964 coup Brazil's capitalism and even its lands were becoming increasingly taken over by foreigners—and not just Americans. By the late 1960s, for instance, Volkswagen of Germany owned 50 million acres in the country.

The doctrine allowed the enemies of the dictatorship to be stigmatized as subversives and victimized accordingly by being imprisoned, tortured, or murdered. This was particularly the case of the guerrillas of two movements, the National Liberation Alliance and the Popular Revolutionary Vanguard, who launched a campaign of "armed propaganda" featuring the assassination of soldiers, bank robberies, and other heroic and romantic adventures. In September 1969 the guerrillas even kidnapped the U.S. ambassador. While the guerrillas saw themselves as preparing the groundwork for urban and rural insurrections, their strategy backfired. The kidnapping of the ambassador was followed by a blitz in which as many as 10,000 suspected subversives were arrested and Congress was suspended. Within a few years most of the guerrilla leaders had been killed, and armed opposition to the military had virtually disappeared. Since the guerrillas lacked any real roots in Brazilian society or politics, any enduring legacy was limited. By 1973, the year of the coup in Chile, the destruction of the radical left was complete. In tandem with the policies of the junta in Chile, the military rulers of Brazil then led their country into a period of rigorous repression.

The military regime also replaced ISI with its opposite: economic liberalism. The doors of the Brazilian economy were opened wide for foreign investment and imports. Protectionism of any kind, where not abandoned, was disparaged. For a time under the military dictatorship, especially between 1968 and 1980, economic growth was dazzling. In some years the rate of growth reached double-digit figures: "the Brazilian miracle" was touted everywhere. Paul Cammack explains its policies and their results:

> Economic policy . . . sought to attract foreign and domestic capital into large-scale capital-intensive activity supplying consumer goods such as cars, televisions, hi-fi equipment and computers to the top end of the domestic

market, and goods ranging from processed or unprocessed primary commodities (soya beans and meal, orange juice, coffee, iron ore and pellets) to manufactures (such as steel, cars and commercial passenger aircraft) to the world market. The state played a key part in underpinning the "economic miracle" which peaked between 1967 and 1974 through massive investment in infrastructure and basic industrial production (notably in steel, hydroelectric and telecommunications), direct and indirect subsidies to private capital and the exclusion and repressive control of the majority of the population.[24]

Nigel Harris stresses the unrelenting role of the state even in the period of military rule: "Public spending, equal to 17 per cent of gross national product in 1947, was nearly a third of GNP in the early 1970s."[25] Internationally, Brazil was lauded for having established a favourable balance of trade.

## Children of the Miracle

In Brazil it was clear who the winners were. As early as 1971 *Business Week* was encouraging its readers to invest in Brazil, where, the magazine made plain, profit opportunities were just about the best in the world. "By the 1970s," writes José Luiz Fiori, "multinational corporations had taken the lead in almost all sectors featuring state-of-the-art technologies, coming to account for approximately 40 per cent of Brazil's industrial output."[26] And the losers? On July 21, 1974, *The Los Angeles Times* pointed out, "Despite Brazil's impressive growth rate, the gap between the rich and the poor is wider than ever." The richest 10 per cent did not merely get richer, they absorbed a full 75 per cent of the total gain in Brazilian income in 1964-75.[27]

A government study published in 1983 indicated that 70 per cent of the population had "a minimum daily calorie intake lower than necessary for human development."[28] Yet this was no surprise; more than 10 years earlier, in 1972, President General Emilío Garrastazú Médici had been forced to admit, "The economy is going well, the people not so well."[29]

The decline in wages and the increase in work time necessary for subsistence had another effect: the destruction of family life among the poor majority in Brazil. One study conducted by a parliamentary committee concluded that the number of abandoned and needy children was around 15 million, while the number of children living at the level of absolute poverty was around 25 million. In the North region, in the early 1970s, researchers found that 44.8 per cent of children—a total of 854,849—had been abandoned by their families.[30]

## Winners and Losers in the Brazilian Economic Miracle

| Economically Active Population | Income Concentration GNP Share Per Year (%) | | |
|---|---|---|---|
| | 1960 | 1970 | 1976 |
| Poorest 50% | 17.71 | 14.91 | 11.60 |
| Next-poorest 30% | 27.92 | 22.85 | 21.20 |
| Middle 15% | 26.60 | 27.38 | 28.00 |
| Richest 5% | 27.69 | 34.86 | 39.00 |

## Work Time Necessary to Purchase Minimum Food Ration

| Year | Necessary Work Time (per week) | Index |
|---|---|---|
| 1959 | 65 hrs, 5 min. | 100.00 |
| 1965 | 88 hrs, 16 min. | 135.62 |
| 1970 | 105 hrs, 13 min. | 161.66 |
| 1978 | 137 hrs, 37 min. | 211.45 |

Source: Maria Helena Moreira Alves, *State and Opposition in Military Brazil*, 1985, pp.111-12, 233.

## Democratic Solutions

The rise in oil prices after 1973, compounded by the debt rung up by the military dictators (which had increased from $12 billion to $50 billion between 1974 and 1977) began to erode the credibility of the Brazilian miracle. Anxious to regain its popularity, from 1974 the government started to relax its policies of repression. This led to increased protest on the part of both labour and church organizations and the growth, throughout the 1970s, of the official opposition party, the Brazilian Democratic Movement (MDB), which increased its number of deputies from 87 to 165 in the Congressional elections of 1974.

Still, the economic problems would not go away. By the early 1980s there was crisis at all levels, with a sharply declining GDP and a steeply rising rate of inflation (234 per cent in 1983). In 1982 the government began negotiations with the IMF aimed at finding solutions and also turned to the bankers of New York, who by this time were worried. They had loaned more money to Brazil than to any country in Latin America, indeed, to any country in the world. What if the Brazilians defaulted, worried the executives of Citibank who had loaned $436 million? By 1980 Brazil's foreign debt payments had represented 259 per cent of its total earnings, with 200 per cent considered the danger mark. Neither the Brazilian bourgeoisie nor their international allies found this situation acceptable.

By early 1984 collapse was in the air. Lacking credibility at home and abroad, the military surrendered the state to civilians. Yet even at that point the state maintained its powerful role in the economy of Brazil, owning as many as 19 of the 20 largest Brazilian companies, including Petrobrás, Electrobrás, and Telebrás.

When military rule ended in 1985, José Sarney (b. 1930), whose career in its earlier phase had been pro-military, became Brazil's first civilian president since 1964. But it was not until the end of 1989 that Brazilians got to vote again in presidential (as opposed to congressional and senate) elections. In the meantime, from the mid-1970s, participatory politics had continued to increase. By the end of a decade that also saw the emergence of movements demanding action on the cost of living, the liberation of political prisoners, and free speech in the universities, the trade unions, once severely repressed, had once again begun to express their discontent. A novel element in this expression was an attempt to form organizations of the working class. From the early 1980s the base of these organizations broadened to include not only industrial workers but also white-collar and agricultural workers. In 1982 the Partido dos Travalhadores (PT or Workers' Party) undertook its first electoral campaign, electing eight federal deputies and two mayors, which was at first seen as a bitter disappointment. The elections in 1985 and 1986 results were more encouraging, and in 1988 candidates from the Workers' Party won mayoralty elections in a number of Brazil's larger cities, including São Paulo.

Presidential elections were held in 1989 for the first time in 30 years. Brazil's nearly 84 million voters gave victory to Fernando Collor de Mello, a conservative populist representing big property, who narrowly defeated Luis Inácio da Silva, known as "Lula," the leader of the PT. Collor took office in March 1990, in the midst of deep crisis. Inflation had reached 2,000 per cent per year, and the toll of murders in Rio stood at 7,720 a year. A privatizer and modernizer who offered state-owned industries up for sale to the private sector, he promised a renewal of Brazilian capitalism by means of neoliberal reforms. He also promised to settle 500,000 families on agrarian-reform projects. Instead, he abolished the Ministry of Agrarian Reform altogether.

But Collor overreached himself; he was driven from office in the autumn of 1992, having been impeached for monumental corruption. As Paul Cammack predicted in late 1991: "Collor's perfection lay more in his ability to reflect the needs of the Brazilian bourgeoisie than to meet them; his record in office suggests that the crisis which produced him will also devour him."[31] He was succeeded by his vice-president, Itamar Franco.

Elections were held again in early October 1994, amid rumours of a

return of the military. Although leading in the polls in the early part of the
year, Luis Inácio da Silva of the PT was soundly defeated by Fernando
Henrique Cardoso of the Brazilian Social Democratic Party. Cardoso, a
leading dependency theorist and an exile in the period of military dictatorship, had returned to politics in 1977 as a member of the Brazilian Democratic Movement. Between 1985 and 1994 he had been a member of the
Brazilian Senate, but had no fixed ideological address. Supporting "Lula"
of the PT in his campaign against Collor, Cardoso subsequently served
Collor as an advisor. When Collor was deposed he was named by Itamar
Franco as his Minister of Foreign Affairs, shuttling back and forth to Washington where he cultivated important friendships and presumably won the
trust of the IMF as one of their proselytizers. His testimonials from Washington provided Cardoso with the neoliberal qualifications he needed to be
named by Franco as Brazil's Minister of Finance. It was here that he
gained immense popular support by restraining Brazil's galloping inflation
through a stabilization program called the Real Plan, named after the new
currency that he introduced. In the September prior to the national elections, inflation fell from 45 per cent to less than 2 per cent per month.
Unemployment, a consequence of the neoliberal reforms, continued to
increase.

In an analysis of the new Brazilian president's development models,
José Luiz Fiori argues that the "Spanish miracle" of Felipe González has
been adopted to serve as Cardoso's ideal. But, apart from the fact that this
model led to González's political defeat in the elections of April 1996, it
has been observed that the Spanish prime minister's economic liberalization and deregulation have led to his country's rapid deindustrialization.
Increasingly, in the 1980s and 1990s in Spain, industry's share of GDP fell
from 32.9 per cent to 24.2 per cent. Among the countries of the Organization for Economic Co-operation and Development (OECD), Spain, Fiori
notes, "sold the largest number of firms to foreigners between 1989 and
1993 because as the economy opened up, Spanish capital migrated to the
service sector. According to the World Economic Forum, Spain is now
among the least competitive nations of the OECD."[32] Spain's problems
include the highest unemployment rate in Europe in the mid-1990s as
well as high inflation. As one Spanish politician commented, "Spain has
begun to turn back without [first] going forward." Was this to be Brazil's
future?

In his farewell speech as he left the Brazilian Senate, Cardoso pointed
to a second model: Mexico. Brazil's 155 million people waited in hope: in a
December 1994 opinion poll, 78 per cent of those surveyed expressed
confidence that their lives would improve in 1995. Certainly, the lives of

many Brazilians must have benefited to some degree by the modest economic boom of the early 1990s. Yet even a 9 per cent growth rate in the last quarter of 1994 was not enough to persuade Cardoso to raise the minimum wage, the lowest in Latin America. After legislation to do this was passed by the Brazilian Congress in January 1995, Cardoso annulled the bill using his presidential veto.

By the mid-1990s Cardoso was presiding over one of the most socially polarized countries in the Third World, a South Africa on the western shores of the South Atlantic. Susanna Hecht describes this Brazil:

> With one of the higher levels of GNP per capita in the developing countries, Brazil has also the worst income distribution in the world. The minimum wage now fluctuates at less than fifty dollars a month with its purchasing power at almost the lowest level in the postwar period. In São Paulo, the rich centre of the richest state, more than a million people live in *favelas*— shanty towns—while another three million live in what are called *cortiços*. These are collective dwellings, basically old houses, which are divided up into small cubicles. Thirty families might thus share a bathroom, kitchen, and washing facilities. In this context, it is valuable to repeat yet another statistic: 54 per cent of Brazil's children live in families earning less than $35 a month. Of these, more than 25 million deprived children, some eight million, now live on the streets, occasionally returning home. Children have now replaced subversives as the main targets of death squads and policemen who routinely beat up, torture and kill children in order to hamper mugging and petty theft. Last summer [1993] child assassination by death squads hit international consciousness as eight kids were gunned down while they slept. [The Institute for Social and Economic Analysis, run by the Catholic Church] calculated from very sparse accounts that close to a hundred children a month are assassinated in Brazil's major cities. Indeed, in the 15-17 age group, 65 per cent of deaths are violent.[33]

By mid-1996 Brazil featured a growth rate of around 3 per cent, low inflation, increasing unemployment, a collapsing system of public health, and foreign reserves of $50 billion. Perhaps most revealing of all, in April 1996 television cameras caught a police massacre of at least 19 landless farmers—suggesting that the outcome of the battle for human rights in Brazil was far from over.[34]

# Chile: The Chicago Way

Chile's modern economy rose on the basis of two products of its soil: first nitrates, then copper. After World War II copper was responsible for up to 80 per cent of Chile's export earnings. Based on its sale Chile achieved a rate of industrialization and literacy that put it in the same league as the more advanced states of Latin America.

But the problem of slow economic growth continued to haunt Chile's impressive social and political postwar gains. By the early 1950s it was evident to some, at least, that the strategy of Import Substitution Industrialization had run its course. With widespread poverty still very much in evidence, the government increasingly relied upon deficit spending to keep per capita income high. By the 1960s the perception of economic exhaustion had spread, yet by the same decade the expectations of the working class had risen.

Chile's most impressive achievement was its political system. From the time its independence was first recognized, in 1823, Chile had suffered under military rule for only short periods. Its social system was less impressive: in common with Latin America as a whole, wealth was highly concentrated. A few firms, notably the U.S.-owned Anaconda and Kennecott copper companies, controlled most of the copper exports, while over half of the arable land was enclosed in large estates. Whereas the average large estate was around 23,000 hectares in size, half of Chile's farms averaged only 1.7 hectares. Between these peaks—the powerful foreign owners of mines and the local estate-owners on the one hand, and the poor workers and farmers on the other—stood a sizeable middle class, with many of its members surviving on the basis of state employment. In the mid-1950s the British economist Nicholas Kaldor pointed to what he regarded as a major problem in Chilean economic development: the low wages paid to labourers. Chilean wage-earners received only 20 per cent of the national income: this percentage could be compared to 59 per cent in the United States and 41 per cent in Britain. Kaldor saw Chile's "problem" as being "rooted in the excessive share in the national income of the propertied class."[35]

The United States was the main foreign investor in Chile. Chile's main economic value to the United States was as a source of copper, which was seen as a strategic resource. In the wisdom of the international security pundits, the important matter of access to this key element was best guaranteed by U.S. ownership.

Washington had begun to meddle in Chilean politics from the time of the presidential election of 1964, the year that Washington also became involved in the overthrow of João Goulart in Brazil. In that year, after six years in office, President Jorge Alessandri, a Conservative and a devotee of free enterprise, had stepped down. Alessandri's professed sympathy for U.S. copper interests had made his government unpopular at home during a time of rising economic nationalism. The two contenders for his succession were Eduardo Frei (1911-1982), the head of the Christian Democratic Party, and Salvador Allende (1908-73), the leader of a leftist coalition known as the Popular Unity Party, which included both socialists and communists. Frei was a reformer whose ideology stressed Christian and therefore evolutionary change. He repeatedly expressed his willingness to work within the framework of the Alliance for Progress being promoted by President Kennedy as an antidote to the "Cuban threat." Frei realized not only the dangers of antagonizing the United States but also the considerable advantages of co-operation. After all, the capital needed for his proposed reforms would have to come from the United States, and the CIA and U.S. corporations had already contributed as much as $20 million to his election fund. Frei became the first Chilean president in the 20th century to win an absolute majority of the popular vote.

Frei's economic program had two main components: the nationalization of most of Chile's copper industry, and agrarian reform. His government nationalized the holdings of the Anaconda Company and renegotiated agreements with Kennecott in 1970. According to the plan, the profits from the sale of nationally owned copper to foreign markets would help finance industrial development and agricultural improvement. Frei's government paid Kennecott double its book value as well as granting other compensation, such as the right to manage the nationalized mines and tax concessions. Because of Frei's repeated insistence that his government would by no means threaten U.S. interests in the country, the U.S. perception of his program and its reaction to his election were benign. Indeed, U.S. economic assistance to Chile under the administration of President Lyndon Johnson (1963-69) was, on a per capita basis, at one of the highest levels in the world. The form of this assistance was in long-term loans, which, even at a low rate of interest, considerably increased Chile's foreign debt.

After proclaiming the need to resettle 100,000 families on land of their own, Frei managed in his reforms to give land to somewhere between 11,000 and 37,000 (depending upon different criteria). In itself, this was a remarkable achievement. But in other areas the reforms fell short of the goals. Yet, despite limited results, by the time Frei left politics the role of the state in the economic, political, and social life of the country was deeply entrenched. According to Pilar Vergara, "Public spending as a per cent of the GDP increased from 35.7 per cent in 1965 to 46.9 per cent in 1970, public investment as a percentage of gross national investment rose from 61 per cent to 77 per cent, and the state expenditures in social programs went from 8.2 per cent to 9.4 per cent of the GDP—leading to an increase in public employment in these sectors from 119,000 to 153,000 people."[36]

While sympathetic to Chile's economic reform policies, Washington was not amused by Chile's foreign policy, which included criticism of the U.S. invasion of the Dominican Republic in 1965, a refusal to condone sanctions against Cuba, and support for Chinese admission to the UN. Instead of compromising with the U.S. foreign policy agenda, the Frei government increasingly moved away from it in the interests of both its own independence and greater regional sovereignty. This made Frei something of a role model among young nationalists of the late 1960s.

Frei was not eligible to run in the elections of 1970. The candidate of the far right was again Jorge Alessandri, but the right had split and its more moderate element ran their own candidate. On the left, at the head of the Popular Unity (PU) coalition, was Salvador Allende, Frei's old rival from the election of 1964.

## Allende

In the elections of early September 1970, Salvador Allende won by a narrow margin (with 36.3 per cent of the popular vote) and was confirmed in office by the Chilean Congress. He was the first Marxist ever to win a national election in the Western Hemisphere.

Aiming at the establishment of a socialist society without a revolution, Allende argued that he could effect a peaceful transition through democratic legislation. He appointed his supporters to a number of key positions within the Chilean state. He gave the secretary-general of the main labour organization the post of minister of the interior, for instance, thereby placing a leftist in charge of law and order. His government increasingly directed resources towards the poorer urban and rural dwellers.

Boldly venturing where Frei had only timidly trod, in July 1971 Allende nationalized U.S. and Chilean copper and nitrate firms as well as a number of other businesses and banks, while also raising the wages of workers and putting a ceiling on prices. He took the position that the superprofits earned in the previous years exempted Kennecott, Anaconda, and others from compensation. He expropriated more land, organizing it into state farms and co-operatives. By 1973 large estates of over 80 hectares had virtually ceased to exist. These measures were overwhelmingly popular, at least with those who benefited from them. When

Congress tried to block them, Allende invoked emergency powers. Altogether, according to Cole Blasier, the Allende government took over $680 million of the book value of U.S. private investment in Chile.[37]

Allende had made enemies in Washington, clearly, yet his most formidable problem was the world market. Copper prices were depressed from the moment he took office. After a year, partly because of the wage increases he had given to the working class, the Chilean economy was in serious recession. Direct financial assistance from Washington was completely cut off, loans from the World Bank, by this time under the management of former U.S. defense secretary Robert McNamara, were blocked, and the Inter-American Development Bank (where the U.S. had a veto) would grant only niggardly advances. As economic hardships became increasingly felt and the enemies of the Popular Unity coalition more loudly raised the alarm about the possibility of small property being nationalized, the large Chilean middle class (including small businessmen and white-collar workers who had voted for Allende) moved into the waiting arms of the upper class. The working class, public-sector employees, the poor, and a small part of the middle class continued to support the UP.

Adding to Allende's problems was the election of Richard Nixon as president of the United States in 1968. Nixon had made a career of anti-communism, and through the CIA his administration helped finance Alessandri's campaign, as they had Frei's. But Washington miscalculated; assuming that Alessandri would win easily, the U.S. government provided less money for his campaign than it had for Frei's. In mid-September 1970, immediately after Allende's election victory, the U.S. president of Pepsi-Cola introduced his Chilean friend Augustín Edwards to President Nixon in the White House. Edwards, a banker and the proprietor of Chile's main national newspaper, *El Mercurio*, warned Nixon that the new president was planning to socialize Chile's economy. Nixon, convinced that the Allende regime constituted a "national security threat," announced that "if there were one chance in ten of getting rid of Allende we should try it." If the CIA director, Richard Helms, needed $10 million, Nixon would approve it. The United States would cut its aid programs to Chile and "squeeze" Chile's economy until it "screamed."[38] Henry Kissinger, Nixon's national security advisor, confessed: "I don't see why we need to stand idly by and watch a country go communist due to the irresponsibility of its own people."[39] By the summer of 1973, Allende's opponents were well on their way to producing an economic plan that was to be brought into effect once the UP regime had been removed. By early September, Edwards was publishing copies of the plan in Chile.[40]

Following Kissinger's lead, the U.S. government did not stand idly by.

It spent tens of millions of dollars to destabilize Chile. Some of the funds went to sustain a nationwide truckers' strike that, together with other strikes, contributed to the immobilization of the economy in the second half of 1972. Even more went to opposition publications and political parties. At the same time Washington voted increased aid to the Chilean military, and talks between certain generals and the CIA became more earnest. It seems likely that the same generals authorized the October 1970 CIA assassination of General René Schneider, head of Chile's armed forces, who opposed the idea of military intervention against Allende's government.

In the Chilean congressional elections of March 1973, the right-wing parties attempted to win a two-thirds majority in order to impeach Allende. They failed miserably, and the UP actually increased its share of the vote to 43 per cent. In spite of the economic difficulties of the country, the working class remained behind the UP. The spectre of a permanent shift of political power to the left proved unbearable, not only to Washington and the middle and upper classes of Chile but also to a large part of the military.

## Pinochet

Mobilized behind General Augusto Pinochet Ugarte (b.1915), who up to that point had been a colourless figure of justifiable obscurity, the armed forces overthrew the Allende regime in a coup on September 11, 1973. Within hours of attacking the presidential palace, leaving it in flames with the president dead inside, the military rounded up and imprisoned leading members of the government. Then, as if to clearly establish their class purpose, the armed forces also attacked Santiago's working-class districts and slums using helicopters and tanks. "Thousands of suspected leftists were killed or detained," writes Peter Winn, with "many of them in outdoor stadiums or in concentration camps in the northern deserts or Antarctic islands."[41] Tens of thousands of Chileans were forced to flee the country. But to many others, the coup was a miracle: the president of the Supreme Court and a number of Catholic bishops expressed their thanks unctuously, while most of Chile's upper class and a large part of its middle class sighed with relief.

At first onlookers believed that the generals, recognizing that they were out of their political depth, would hand power back to the Christian Democrats. But by 1974 it had become apparent that they were determined to hold on to power themselves. It also became apparent that Chile was in the hands not of the military collectively, but of one general. Pinochet carried out a coup within the coup, promoting himself from being one of a trio of military leaders to the supreme command of both the military and the state. Several of his military rivals soon expired under mysterious circumstances. On June 17, 1974, the leaders of the junta signed Decree Law 527, giving Pinochet the position of Chile's chief executive. The regime was not to be the kind of joint dictatorship that had appeared in Brazil, Uruguay, and Argentina in the same decade; it was to become a one-man military government. In 1975 this fact finally dawned on the Christian Democrats, many of whose leading members had participated in the destabilizing of the government of Allende. In a token protest, they broke with the military regime.

As in Argentina after the military coup of March 1976, in Pinochet's Chile all vestiges of human rights were abolished. At least 3,500 Chileans were murdered, many by clandestine death squads that continued to work with insatiable sadism into the early 1990s. The junta smashed practically all of the organizations of the working class and even those of the middle class. Trade unions were completely atomized and their leaders assassinated. Public universities, which more than the private ones had provided support for Allende, were brought under the heel of the military. In one case, a general commanding a parachute regiment was appointed to head a university and dropped from an airplane into the university gardens. The effect was part of the theatre of terror that the military sought to perfect as a means of establishing an incontestable rule.

Jacobo Timerman, a victim of terror and tyranny in Argentina, wrote about the aftermath of the Chilean coup: "The entire country was occupied, and each general chose his own way of conquering the territory assigned to him. All the generals and admirals had dreamed of a war in which victory would allow them to take control of the cities of Bolivia, Peru, or Argentina, and so the occupation of Chile gave free reign to their fantasies, awakening such obsessions and desires as were thought to have been buried with Hitler in Berlin in 1945."[42]

Devastatingly, political parties were cut off from their social bases and their leaders forced to operate from exile. Without political organizations to support them, the living standards of workers and of the urban and rural poor began to decline catastrophically. Yet politics was not killed off; in the absence of political parties and trade unions, low-level organizations, under the protective umbrella of the Catholic Church, sprang up among the poor. The function of these was to offer security and succour, but they could not replace the broad-based political and trade union organizations that had been destroyed.

At first the main agent of terrorism had been the DINA (Dirección de Inteligencia Nacional), headed by Colonel Manuel Contreras, an officer who had made the pilgrimage to one of the Meccas of Western militarism, the U.S. Army Career Officers' School in Virginia. Contreras organized a car bombing of the exiled UP politician Orlando Letelier in the middle of Washington, D.C., in September 1976. But while U.S. authorities had no objections to political assassinations in principle—indeed, officials in the State Department, the CIA, and other branches of the U.S. government had helped organize assassinations all over the world—car bombs in the Free World's capital had to be deplored. The killing led to DINA's replacement by another intelligence organization, the Central National de Informaciónes (CNI). Although slightly less brutal, the CNI, like other paramilitary forces from the Andes to Afghanistan, quickly became tainted with corruption involving drug and arms dealing.

After an initial period of uncertainty, the Pinochet dictatorship announced itself converted to the new economic religion of neoliberalism: the neoliberal saviour was Milton Friedman, a disciple of Friedrich von Hayek at the University of Chicago. Friedman, who visited Santiago at the behest of his former students in March 1975, provided the revelation that if it were to be saved the Chilean economy needed shock treatment involving deep spending cuts. A month after his visit, one of his apostles was appointed minister of economic affairs. Meanwhile the nationalized U.S. corporations (Kennecott, Anaconda, and the telecommunications giant ITT) were given further compensation, the land reform program was partly reversed (28 per cent of expropriated land was returned to former owners), banks and firms were denationalized (auctioned off at between 67 per cent and 77 per cent of their net worth), and trade unions were banned. In 1976 Milton Friedman won the Nobel Prize for his contribution to monetary economics.

If Friedman was the saviour of the free market, his apostles were a group of young Chilean economists known as the "Chicago Boys." The previous "school" of structuralist economists who had promoted the strategy of ISI were now excluded from power. The "Chicago Boys" were both the designers and executors of the replacement economic policies identified with the Pinochet regime. According to Patricio Silva, these academics and policy-makers

> were more than simply the principle architects of economic policy; they were the intellectual brokers between their government and international capital, and symbols of the government's determination to rationalize its rule primarily in terms of economic objectives.... Cooperation with international business, a fuller integration into the world economy, and a strictly secular willingness to adopt the prevailing tenets of international economic orthodoxy, all formed ... a set of intellectual parameters within which the

technocrats could then "pragmatically" pursue the requirements of stabilization and expansion.[43]

In short, Chile became the first country in Latin America to adopt a neoliberal structural adjustment and stabilization program, including deregulation, world-market pricing, and privatization. As James Petras and F.I. Leiva point out: "Nowhere else in Latin America (or elsewhere) was the program adopted so completely and with so much doctrinal purity."[44]

The economic fate of Chile under the dictatorship, while guaranteed by the military, was therefore designed by intellectuals, particularly economists, possessing remarkable authority and posing as the disciples of a rational and value-free science. They claimed that because their interpretation of economics was the correct one, there was no alternative but to follow it. Anyone who did not, they pointed out, was not merely wrong, but wrong because he or she allowed ideology to subvert scientific thinking. The phrase "we have no choice," the war cry of neoliberals of all nations from the 1970s to the 1990s, now echoed in the Andes.

Through the late 1970s, as the grip of the "Chicago Boys" tightened, public spending declined and state enterprises were sold off. By 1975, real wages and per capita social spending had dropped to 63 per cent of 1970 levels. Unemployment between 1975 and 1981 averaged 18 per cent, three times higher than the average in the 1960s. By 1987 wages had fallen to 84.7 per cent of their 1970 level. The consequences were as appalling as they were predictable. By 1986 the World Health Organization was noting that Chile's caloric food consumption was so far below the minimum that the nation could be classified as a country "with nutritional deficiency."[45]

Conformity to the laws of the implacable and now exalted "world market" was not without certain rewards. Loans from the World Bank and the Inter-American Development Bank rushed forward to wash over the crumbling structures of Chile's increasingly derelict manufacturing economy. For those, particularly of the middle class and the bourgeoisie, who had hated the supply shortages of the Allende regime, the spending spree that followed the advent of the counter-revolution amply justified the dictatorship, which was the price to pay. Between 1975 and 1981 the number of cars in Chile doubled. By 1978 it looked as if the monetarist strategy had been vindicated: low inflation, a balance of payments surplus, and high growth rates led business circles to become euphoric. This was the case particularly of the few who had benefited by acquiring former state properties at bargain-basement prices. "Economic liberalization was supposed to produce economic diversity," writes Mary Helen Spooner, "yet the regime's policies, intentionally or not, led to a massive concentration of resources in the hands of a few business groups."[46]

As they sped ahead in their imported cars, humming the neoliberal tunes of the new regime, those in charge seemed to be paying little attention to fuel consumption. In fact the balance of payments indicator had moved across the line to the wrong side of "empty": the leaders were now running increasingly on borrowed fuel. Foreign debt soared from $4 billion in 1973 to $11.2 billion in 1980. Still, news from the outside world was reassuring; comparisons with the economic growth rates of South Korea and Taiwan continued to be celebrated, although sometimes with a sense of uneasiness. *Time* magazine (January 14, 1980), with a hint of misgivings, pronounced Chile "An Odd Free Market Success." But generally terms like *Wirtschaftswunder*, the word used to describe the West German "economic miracle" of the 1950s and 1960s, continued to be used freely— though without any reference to a key facet of the German miracle: a generalized improvement of living standards. Friedman himself proclaimed, "Chile is an economic miracle."

Friedman and the others, as it turned out, spoke too soon. In 1981 there were early warning signs of danger. Several major firms that had been regarded as symbols of the new regime became overextended and declared bankruptcy. In 1982-83 the global recession hit with full force. The high copper prices, which had provided around 95 per cent of Chile's export earnings, fell from $1.70 to $.52 per pound. More bankruptcies followed, the growth rate declined, debt mounted, and the monetarist miracle was denounced. By 1983 Chile's GNP was falling at an unprecedented rate, so much so that Chile's economy captured the record for the sharpest fall in GNP in Latin America. Chile's other record was its per capita debt, one of the highest in the world, a debt that consumed 80 per cent of the country's export earnings. Against a background of bankruptcies and general economic havoc, one Chilean observed, "The free-market policies of the Chicago Boys destroyed more private enterprises in the past year than the most radical sectors of Allende's coalition dreamed of nationalizing in three years; they have turned more middle-class people into proletarians or unemployed than any Marxist textbook ever described." Another economist said of the Chilean economy in 1984 that it was a "spectacular example of private greed masquerading as a model of economic development."

The economic crisis produced new opposition to the dictatorship at both the grassroots and the elite levels. The government, recognizing its own weakness, thrashed around, adopting one solution and then another. Ministers were shuffled, and in an attempt to save itself the state renationalized key firms. Gradually the economy was rescued from the brink of the abyss, although fatal injury may have been done to the manufacturing sector, where production fell by 22 per cent in 1982. By the mid-1980s recovery had begun, and neoliberalism was redeemed as the governing doctrine of the state.

By that time the economic basis of Chilean development had changed drastically, perhaps irrevocably, and Chile's place in the world market as a provider of non-industrial goods had been ensured. By the late 1980s, Chile's owners and planners had adopted the strategy of export-led growth based on agriculture, affirming the production of kiwis, grapes, wine, and apples, alongside the gains of a privatized (and increasingly foreign-owned) mining sector, as the engine for economic growth. As the decade wore on, the Camelot of more complete integration with the U.S. economy, a process called "globalization," became increasingly compelling.

By the late 1980s, the fate of the working class and the urban and rural poor had been sealed. The members of these classes were more poorly paid, less likely to work in factories than in the informal sector, and less secure, and they had fewer prospects than at any time since the coup. In 1987 the legal minimum wage had fallen to 65 per cent below, in real terms, what it had been in 1981. Apart from the very rich, and the very poorest 10 per cent of the country, whose standards had improved through state charity, the majority of Chileans had suffered from a palpable deterioration of social services and a decline in living standards. The dogged confidence of the neoliberals in Santiago and Washington remained, however, unshaken.

A verdict passed by Petras and Leiva may serve as an epitaph on the grave of the Pinochet years:

> Analysis of economic and social developments under the Pinochet regime supports this proposition: Poverty is the real product of capitalist development. Despite Pinochet's apparent preoccupation with extreme poverty and with government programs targeting indigent households, virtually all independent surveys have found that the military regime's economic policies dramatically increased the incidence and depth of poverty. By conservative estimates . . . the first phase of the military regime saw a 25 percent increase in the relative number of poor households and a 39 percent increase in the percentage of households whose members were desperately poor, unable to meet even their basic needs. [One study] based on the ability to meet "basic needs" in food, health and housing, showed that by 1985 over 45 percent of all Chileans remained poor and that 25 percent of these were indigent. And more recent data suggest that, if anything, the problem

worsened from 1985 to 1989, at the height of another boom. Clearly, the fruits of this boom were very unevenly distributed. By the end of the military regime, after five years of "renewed growth," 41 percent of families in Chile, representing 44.4 percent of the population and over half of the rural population, were at or were pushed below the poverty line by economic policy conditions well beyond their control.[47]

To be sure, the Pinochet regime did not invent poverty in Chile. It was widespread even before the coup. But have nearly two decades of military developmentalism helped or hindered it? Certainly, as Petras and Leiva point out, they have made it worse: "A revealing datum, an expression of growing impoverishment, was the reduction of 7 percent in the daily caloric intake of the poorest 40 percent of the population over the most recent period of recovery and growth. The daily caloric intake of the poorest 40 percent of the population was reduced from 2,019 in 1970 and 1,751 in 1980 to 1,629 in 1990."[48]

By the time the mid-1980s recovery had begun, even those who supported the Pinochet regime had begun to ask questions about the advantages of continued dictatorship. Many officers, particularly those in the air force, the navy, and the police, had been offended by Pinochet's concentration of power in his own hands, and many businessmen, now confident that the spectre of socialism had been banished, had grown to distrust the regime's competence in the field of economic planning. These groups, then, joined others whose thoughts had already turned northwards and who were considering the benefits of economic integration.

Protest had also re-emerged. A major strike, in May 1983, "broke the dyke of dictatorship." Up to this time the opposition had sheltered under the protection of organizations that had not been banned, including the church. Although many of the notables within the Catholic Church had welcomed the coup, the Catholic-organized Vicarate of Solidarity was the most effective human rights organization defending the victims of the regime. After the 1983 strike there was an increasing movement into the open, which was still not without its dangers.

The attitude of Washington also underwent a change. Until the election of President Jimmy Carter in November 1976, relations had generally been good. Then they declined, due in part to the assassination of Orlando Letelier. When Ronald Reagan was elected in 1980 they improved. From January 1982 the Reagan administration suspended the sanctions imposed by its predecessor, and Jeane Kirkpatrick, the Reaganite hatchet person who served as ambassador to the UN, flew to Santiago to give her blessings to the dictators. But from the time of President Reagan's second election (1984), U.S. foreign policy showed an increased hostility to the dictatorship that its own directors had helped to establish. An avowedly pro-regime ambassador was replaced by a representative who was more sympathetic to democracy, or at least to the idea of democracy within the limits of neoliberalism. And from around 1985, the U.S. economy, which had become visibly less competitive internationally, was looking for partnership with less competitive countries, particularly those in Latin America. These partnerships were to be guaranteed by such agreements as GATT and hemispheric free trade, which began to be discussed in Chile in the second half of the 1980s.

By 1986, the year in which Ferdinand Marcos in the Philippines and "Baby Doc" in Haiti were overthrown, Washington was offering financial aid to the dictator's political opposition. Human rights, its spokesmen had discovered, were not as secure in Chile as was desirable. In 1987 the Christian Democrats together with elements from within the Socialist party formed a coalition to struggle for free elections, which became the Coalition for the "No." Its aim was to fight the dictator in the promised plebiscite on his future.

## Democracy

Squeezed by a growing popular pressure for democratic politics from the bottom and a pressure from both the Chilean bourgeoisie and Washington from the top, General Pinochet had promised a plebiscite regarding the political road ahead. What chance was there, he thought, that *his* people would want to replace him with another group of indecisive and querulous politicians? What chance was there that these politicians could mount any kind of effective campaign? And anyway, hadn't Chile recovered from the recession of the early 1980s to see its economy growing steadily? There was every reason for confidence.

So the dictator allowed a plebiscite on October 5, 1988. Did the people want him to continue into the future as president? The answer: 55 per cent voted no, 43 per cent yes. Surprisingly, the regime accepted the verdict. To do otherwise would not only have flouted "international opinion" (in other words, the policies of Washington and the investment firms) but closed the door on any possibility of hemispheric free trade. The free presidential and congressional elections that followed, in December 1989, with over seven million people voting, were won by the anti-junta candidate, Patricio Aylwin, a Christian Democrat who was once the head of the Senate in opposition to Allende and now at the head of a broad front of centrist and leftist forces. In the Chilean Congress the Socialist Party was reborn, electing four senators and 17 deputies, compared to five senators and 29 deputies for their nearest rivals. For the first time women, who had previously been a mainstay of the conservative vote, turned away from the right.

On March 11, 1990, Aylwin was inducted as president. Although he had promised to make no changes to Pinochet's free-market policies, his administration increased spending on education, housing, and the poor. The number of officially defined poor Chileans began to decline, falling from five million to three million between 1990 and 1993. The administration also introduced bilateral trade agreements with Washington. (Secret talks on free trade with Mexico began in the same year.) The general, chagrined, retired to his palatial labyrinth, though not before he ensured constitutionally that he would remain head of the armed forces until his retirement in 1998 and that a significant share of the national budget would remain irrevocably allocated to the military. In 1993 Aylwin was succeeded by Eduardo Frei, son of the Christian Democrat president of the same name. Frei, Salvador Allende's Christian Democratic rival, also headed a centre-left coalition of parties and favoured increased social spending. The problems facing the government by the mid-1990s were formidable. According to Philip Oxhorn, "Advocates of the current development model admit that even with rapid economic growth, it will take 50 years to reduce extreme poverty to a minimum."[49]

Still, economic growth has occurred, together with low inflation, rising reserves, foreign investment, and declining unemployment. Inflation fell from 21 per cent in 1989 to 12 per cent by 1993 and then 8.2 per cent in 1995. Unemployment fell from 12 per cent in 1989 to 5 per cent in 1993. The annual average for economic growth from 1990 to 1993 was 6 per cent, with exports increasing in the same period by 9 per cent each year.[50] Chile had succeeded Mexico as the region's "star performer," though some doubters remained. "It cannot be expected," warned the authors of *Report of the Inter-American Dialogue*, "that democratic institutions will prosper under conditions of economic coercion, when millions of citizens are without a job, an adequate place to live, proper nutrition, basic education or hope in the future."[51] Even those impressed by Chile's economic record since the return to democracy confess to serious problems in both the health and educational sectors. "Teachers are poorly paid, often poorly trained, and have little motivation. . . . If reform of the educational system is difficult, then health sector reform is even more troublesome," comment Alan Angell and Carol Graham.[52]

The return of peaceful and consensual politics seems still somewhat uncertain. As late as March 1993 the Chilean police seized, raped, and tortured a woman they suspected of having information they needed. In July Amnesty International's human rights report on Chile found twice as many cases of torture in 1992 as in the previous year. At least until the sensational arrest and sentencing to six years in prison of General Manuel Contreras, the U.S.-trained head of DINA, in June 1995, no leading police-man had been charged in any case. As for Pinochet himself, among investors and conservative politicians alike, from Rome to Washington, he continues to be seen as "a man of historic vision and stature."[53]*

## Mexico: PRI, IMF, NAFTA, EZLN

Like Brazil and Argentina, the other large industrialized economies of Latin America, Mexico experienced rapid economic growth in the wartime and postwar years. And like them, this growth was connected to an ISI strategy. But the similarity ends there; unlike those other countries, politi-cal crisis did not spawn dictatorship. Mexico has been a singular case of political and social stability: "60 years of social peace," as Mexico's long-time ruling party, the Partido Revolucionario Institucional (PRI), liked to boast, at least until January 1, 1994.

With the end of World War II the tenure of President Avila Camacho, which had begun in 1940, came to a close. Camacho's regime had itself marked another closure—that of the revolutionary period in Mexican his-tory, which had begun in 1910. This revolution had seen its final phase during the presidency of General Lázaro Cárdenas del Rio, who had been elected in 1934 with the strong support of peasant and labour orga-nizations. Cárdenas implemented a far-reaching range of reforms, including the rapid transfer of nearly 50 million acres of *hacienda* (or large-estate) land to Mexico's peasants. By 1940 the *ejidos* (communally owned lands) contained 47 per cent of cultivated land, compared with 15 per cent in 1930. This was the first major agrarian reform in Latin American history. It was a huge political success, for it effectively destroyed Mexico's colonial and semifeudal landholding system, a sys-tem that continued to exist in other parts of Latin America into the 1960s. To complement this massive shift in proprietorship and to make the *ejidos* viable, Cárdenas's administration set up the Banco Nacional

---

* In the words of the Canadian mining magnate Peter Munk: Pinochet, "albeit you may not approve of the methodology, had the courage to single-handedly change the whole direc-tion of a whole continent. That man created a model that today, several years later, has generated more profit per capita in a Latin American forgotten country than in any other comparable period, in any other comparable country, with the exception of the last four years in North America." Munk's company, Barrack Gold Corporation, invested $500 mil-lion in Chilean gold mining concessions in 1995. That same year about half of foreign investment in Chile was in the mining sector. See *The Globe and Mail*, May 24, 1996, p.A10, June 9, 1996, p.A17.

de Credito Ejidal in 1935. The bank provided the loans necessary to support the *ejidos*.

Even more dramatic was the decision of the Cárdenas regime in early 1938 to expropriate the Mexican holdings of major foreign-owned oil companies, notably Royal Dutch Shell and Standard Oil of New Jersey. The nationalization of these firms was not based on any particular industrial strategy on the part of Cárdenas, but rather emerged out of the collision of the government's radical nationalist ideology and the oil firms' imperial pretensions. The corporations had challenged the sovereignty of the Mexican state by refusing to obey an injunction from the Supreme Court ordering them to increase the wages paid to their workers. Oil-fuelled nationalism was a phenomenon that would emerge again a decade later in Iran.

The international reaction to Cárdenas's bold move was immediate and predictable. Other Latin American countries praised it, and Britain and the United States imposed sanctions. But time was on the side of Cárdenas. The threat of war in Europe meant that the two great Allies, even if they had been otherwise disposed to do so, could not carry out effective action against either Mexico or the Cárdenas regime. President Roosevelt even went so far as conceding the Mexican right to expropriate, and by 1942 the oil companies had settled, at 4 per cent of their original claim. In the end, Cárdenas compensated British firms to the tune of $81 million while the U.S. companies received $24 million. Mexico thus became the possessor of a national petroleum company, Petróleos Mexicanos (PEMEX). In 1942 Mexico entered World War II on the Allies' side.

Under Camacho, in wartime Mexico, as elsewhere in Latin America, the basis for future industrialization was expanded. Some writers speak of an "industrial revolution" that included a huge increase in the production of pig iron, steel, and electrical capacity. This industrial growth was possible in large part because of a high wartime demand for Mexican minerals (including petroleum) and agricultural produce. It was facilitated by the policies of a government-owned industrial development bank, which took risks on long-term industrial projects that were well beyond the reach of local entrepreneurs. By most economic indicators, whether GDP, per capita product, or industrial output, Mexico made giant strides forward not only during the war but also in the following quarter-century.

Economic growth, though, does not mean equitable distribution. In Mexico, while per capita income increased from 325 pesos per year in 1940 to 838 pesos per year in 1946, the distribution of national wealth remained permanently skewed in favour of the wealthy. Within Latin America, the only country in which wealth was more skewed in favour of the rich was Brazil.

By the time of Camacho's successors, Miguel Aléman (1946-52), Adolfo Ruiz Cortines (1952-58), Adolfo López Mateos (1958-64), and Gustavo Diaz Ordaz (1965-70), both party and governing policies had changed radically. Tom Barry writes:

> Reform turned to counter-reform, and the corporatist structures given form during the Cárdenas *sexenio* [six year presidential term] became little more than bureaucratic channels of political control. The official rhetoric of the 1940-70 period included obligatory references to the populist and nationalist commitments of the state. But the government's policies and programs did not honor the social promises made by Cardenismo and instead shifted to accommodate dependent capitalism.[54]

Cárdenas's Partido de la Revolución Mexicana (PRM), founded in 1938, had changed its name to the Partido Revolucionario Institucional (PRI) in 1946. Acceptance of the idea that a revolution might be institutionalized signified that the creative confidence of the 1930s had become ossified. The PRI no longer represented the left-wing intellectuals, agrarian reformers, and champions of labour as it had in the 1930s. It was now increasingly a party of big businessmen and the technocrats who supported them. It was also a party umbilically connected to the body of the state.

The postwar Mexican state, that is, the PRI, now shifted the focus of its support from the peasants in the centre and the south to the private sector, and especially to the agricultural economy in the north and northwest, where large private holdings were prevalent (in the centre and the south more land was owned collectively). With increased support from the state, the large agricultural companies (which produced high-value crops for export, mainly to the United States) became more productive than the collective *ejidos*, which had less access to credit, water, and technological assistance.

While favouring the owners of estates and other big businesses, the state forced the working class onto the defensive. Prices went up, and wages were kept down. Cárdenas had once supported the oil workers against the international oil companies. Now when the workers struck for higher wages they were attacked by the army, an approach that the government justified as the price of industrial growth. The government kept wages low not only for industrial workers, but also for schoolteachers—so low that it was impossible to keep the schools staffed with competent instructors. School attendance in the rural areas was appalling; only 0.5 per cent of rural children finished the sixth grade.[55] As in Chile, reform proved next to impossible. In the early 1960s, when President López Mateos embarked upon a program of land distribution and nationalization of certain foreign-owned utilities, the private sector sent $250 million out of the country in a matter of days. López Mateos was forced to modify his position. Nora Hamilton and Timothy Harding conclude that from the decade of the 1960s private capital, not the state, was clearly in charge. Still, at that time at least it was mainly Mexican capital.[56]

In the decades between the early 1950s and the early 1970s, the Mexican economy boomed. Industrial output continued to grow with manufacturing increasing by an annual average of 7.6 per cent from 1950 to 1980. The GDP reached a rate (around 6 per cent) only matched by fast-growing economies such as West Germany, South Korea, and Japan. Real wages in manufacturing continued to rise. This was a growth led by the state sector, which included, notes Kim Moody, "over 1,100 enterprises including petroleum, steel, mining, railroads, airlines, and telecommunications.... American and other foreign capital was accorded a significant role in this industrialization process but within terms laid down by Mexican law and the Partido Revolucionario Institucional."[57]

By the early 1960s evidence of a disconcerting side-effect of economic development was becoming visible: the Malthusian spectre was beginning to haunt the daydreams of the modernizers. Since even before the war, the improvement in public health had led to a sharp rise in population. Now the mechanization of agriculture created other problems. Whereas in 1940 agriculture had occupied over 65 per cent of the economically active population, by 1970 it employed as little as 37 per cent. Between 1960 and 1979 the contribution of agriculture to the GDP had fallen from 16.2 to 9.0 per cent.

The fate of most of those forced to leave the land was low-wage employment, partial employment, or unemployment. The new generations, particularly if they were landless, left the rural areas to seek often non-existent jobs in the urban industrial sector. The towns and cities expanded phenomenally. Industry was able to employ about 10 per cent of a labour force that increased by 500,000 annually. From the mid-1930s to the mid-1950s, Mexico's population doubled from 16 to 32 million. By the mid-1990s it was 93.7 million. The population of the Federal District, which contains Mexico City, increased from 3 million in 1952 to 4.5 million only six years later. By the time of the 1990 census it was over 14 million. As well, the country's wealth was distributed only slightly less equitably than wealth in Brazil. "In 1963, half of the population received 15.5 per cent of the income—down from 19 per cent in 1950—while the top 10 per cent continued to receive approximately 50 per cent of the income. The income of the lowest fifth of the population did not increase in absolute terms between 1950 and 1963."[58]*

---

* Mexican statistics, or their interpreters, seem unusually unreliable on the point of income

In 1970, Luis Echeverría (b. 1922) was elected president. A populist in a hurry to change things, more than any of his predecessors Echeverría incarnated the spirit of Cárdenas. He revived *agrarismo*, the policy of agrarian reform that promoted the interests of the *ejidos*. In the arena of foreign affairs he sought to establish himself as a leading advocate of *tercermundismo* ("Third Worldism"), criticizing U.S. policies, offering recognition of China, and welcoming hundreds of the political refugees from Chile after the coup of 1973.

But at home time had run out for the last stage of ISI, which had been reincarnated as *desarrollo estabilizador* ("stabilizing development"). In August 1971, in the midst of a recession that had already slowed down economic growth, President Nixon imposed a 10 per cent tariff on Mexican imports, which abruptly ended the illusion that a special relationship existed between the two countries. By 1973 Mexican inflation was climbing and with it came a rise in prices. Echeverría responded by allowing wage increases and price controls on basic consumer goods. When businessmen complained and threatened the president with the spectre of capital flight, he lectured them on patriotism. In the place of *desarrollo estabilizador* he invented *desarrollo compartido*, "shared development," a recipe, not unlike the one proposed by Perón in his early years, intended to guarantee benefits to workers and peasants under the protective aegis of a caring but interfering state. Rural development was one of the main ingredients of this recipe. In the last moments of his *sexenio* Echeverría expropriated nearly 100,000 acres of privately owned land and handed it over to the *ejidos*.* The big landowners erupted in protest.

Echeverría's term in office was the last goodbye of the dirigisme—state-controlled planning—that was the political arm of the ISI approach; and it was the last epoch in which the Mexican state faced off against private capital, foreign and domestic. Yet these policies had unmistakeable effects. Peter Smith points out:

> The role of the state, already large, expanded sharply; real government revenue rose from around 8 percent of [GDP] in 1970 to roughly 12.5 percent in 1975. Public spending poured into housing, schooling and other development programmes. Agricultural credit increased. The nation doubled its

---

distribution; one survey showed that between 1984 and 1989 the share of the national income of the richest 10 per cent of the population had jumped from 32.8 per cent to 37.9 per cent, while the share of the poorest 40 per cent had shrunk from 14.3 per cent to 12.9 per cent. See Castaneda, *The Mexico Shock*, 1995, p.51.
* Barry refers to the distribution of a total of 20 million hectares and indicates that by 1988 the *ejidos* controlled 25 per cent of grazing land, nearly 10 per cent of farming land, and 8 per cent of forests. See Barry, *Zapata's Revenge*, 1995, pp.23, 14.

capacity to produce crude oil, electricity, and iron and steel. As a result, Echeverría proudly pointed out, the GDP grew at an annual average rate of 5.6 percent. Nonetheless, the expansion of state activity brought Echeverría into constant conflict with the domestic private sector.[59]

Echeverría was succeeded by José López Portillo (1976-82), whose policies stressed consensus-building rather than confrontation with Mexican big business. In his first address to the nation, Portillo explained that he sought to make a "treaty" with business. This softer, gentler, approach was made feasible economically by the 1976 discovery of immense new oil reserves. According to one estimate at the end of the decade, Mexico possessed almost 5 per cent of the world's proven oil reserves and around 3 per cent of its natural gas reserves. And the era of López Portillo was not one merely of oil discoveries, but one also of rapidly climbing energy prices. It was to be the bright sunset of Mexico's hopes for national development.

Mexico had now entered the ranks of those countries dependent upon oil revenues. From the mid-1970s, based on the optimism that oil engendered everywhere it was found, Mexico's ruling party borrowed heavily on world capital markets in order to modernize Mexico's economy and especially to increase the capacity for domestic food production. As in most other oil-reliant economies, apart from those in the sparsely populated countries of the Middle East, this approach proved to be disastrous. By 1981 world oil prices were dropping fast, and interest rates were on the rise. In debt to the tune of around $100 billion, and paying billions to foreign banks to service this debt, Mexico was now beset by rampant inflation, capital flight, and a chaotic situation on the financial and foreign exchange markets. The age of crisis had arrived. From then on, with brief remissions characterized by acceptable if not spectacular growth in 1984 and 1990, the Mexican economy would continue to perform badly. As a result most Mexicans would, year after year, suffer from declining standards of living.

## Mexico Redesigned

In August 1982 the Mexican government declared a moratorium on its debt, thereby launching the global "debt crisis" of the early 1980s. President Miguel de la Madrid (b. 1935, president 1982-88) faced the prospect of introducing reforms recommended by the wizards of international banking. Between 1980 and 1991 the World Bank handed Mexico a total of 13 loans, more than any other country had received. The reforms that the bankers demanded included the bitter medicine of the IMF's "structural reforms," a change from a focus on the domestic market to a focus on the export market, and the "opening up" of Mexico's economy. The role of the state in relation to the international market was to become even more severely limited. From the mid-1980s Mexico was "redesigned."[60]

The social costs of this redesign were high. Wages, which had been on the rise since the 1940s, were frozen, but prices increased. Unemployment grew, in large part due to the privatization or liquidation of 822 of Mexico's 1,115 state enterprises. Per capita real disposable income fell by 5 per cent a year between 1983 and 1988. From 1982 to 1991 the buying power of the minimum wage dropped by 67 per cent. At the same time the economists recommended a course of dieting. The Mexican Food System (SAM), which was established by López Portillo and proved to be the "last hurrah for the nationalists and populist reformers before the onslaught of neoliberalism," was closed down.[61] Government spending was cut in half, and as a result subsidies on some basic foods were eliminated. Additionally, in obedience to the IMF, de la Madrid undermined Mexico's commitment to food self-sufficiency and poured resources into the agro-export sector. This stimulated the large-scale capitalist producers in the north of the country, but starved those on the overcrowded farmlands in the centre (where some 90 per cent of Mexicans lived) and the south. By the end of the 1980s the cost of food imports, mainly from the United States, had risen to $5 billion. The reaction of the starving centre and south became most apparent, as we shall see, at the beginning of 1994, but even at the end of the 1980s some analysts were predicting that the IMF programs were not likely to ameliorate Mexico's economic crisis. Certainly, the years of President de la Madrid were a time of stagnant economic growth.

In the presidential elections of 1988 it seemed as if the PRI candidate, Carlos Salinas de Gortari (b. 1948), who like many of the richest Mexicans had studied in the United States, would be swept into office. His electoral theme was "modernization," and he spun the yarn of Mexico's imminent entry into the First World. The elite that formed Salinas's main backers was, according to Moody, "represented in the 37-member Mexican Businessmen's Council. These 37 leading business personalities control the country's top 71 private companies, which account for 22 per cent of the annual gross domestic product. These 37 were represented in the five largest privatizations, which amounted to 80 per cent of the value of all privatization up to 1991."[62]

But by 1988 the PRI had lost enough of its lustre that rivals felt they had a chance. Slightly to the left was Cuauhtémoc Cárdenas, son of the former president Lázaro Cárdenas and head of a coalition of left-wing elements known as the PRD (Partido de la Revolución Democrática), established in September 1988. Slightly to the right (that is, to the right of the now very right-tilting PRI) was Manuel Clothier, a millionaire corporate farmer who headed the Partido Acción Nacional (PAN), which had begun its days in the aftermath of World War II as a party of small property and piety. "Christianity and Capitalism" was its motto. By the 1980s PAN had two wings, the fundamentalists who still adhered to the old beliefs and a more powerful group representing the interests of big business. Its base of power was in the northern states of Mexico—Baja California, Guanajuato, and Chihuahua.[63]

Despite their apparent political differences, Cárdenas and Clothier agreed on one thing; that the monopoly of the PRI should be broken. But in the election held on July 6, 1988, the PRI, exercising its long-time penchant for violence and fraud, squeaked through. It, and the media it controlled, claimed that it had won a 50.3 per cent majority. Most Mexicans were sure that without chicanery Cárdenas would have won.

Once elected, Salinas put in place what amounted to a counter-revolution. Supported by a cadre of neoliberal technocrats, the Mexican version of the "Chicago Boys," his government moved rapidly rightwards. "Privatization" and "integration" became his battle cries. In June 1990 he announced that he had found the solution to the problem of Mexican development, that is, he had discovered the highway to high growth (5-6 per cent per year) that would lead the country into the First World. This was free trade with the United States, the same target that Chilean businessmen had set their sights on. Such an agreement was to be accompanied by continued denationalization and the dissolution of state controls over the economy. Geraldo Otero points out one facet of this approach: "As of 1982, all imports required previous government permits, with a top tariff of 100 percent and an average tariff of 27 percent. By 1990, no permits were required for most imports, and currently the highest tariff is 16 percent, with an average of 11 percent."[64] As state-owned firms were privatized, $70 billion in hot money poured into the country. The large U.S. brokerage firms and investment banks, such as Goldman Sachs (which coordinated the privatization), Salomon Brothers, and Citibank, had a field day.[65]

According to a Mexican journalist, "The booty of privatization has made multimillionaires of 13 families, while the rest of the population— about 80 million Mexicans—has been subject to the same gradual impoverishment as though they had suffered through a war."[66] Furthermore, according to research done by the Canada-Americas Policy Alternatives Group, the economic liberalization policies "created new opportunities for corrupt practices" on the part of the state. Critics have described the Salinas government's sell-off of state companies as "PRIvatization"—a "reference to the intimate connections" between business elites and the ruling party. Businessmen linked with Salinas gained key stakes in Mexicana Airlines, the National Bank of Mexico, and Banpais. In 1991 one of the biggest "prizes" of all, the publicly owned company TELEMEX, fell into the hands of one of Salinas's close friends and PRI finance committee members. Since then, according to the report, consumers have paid "among the highest rates in the world for a problem-plagued service which has scarcely changed its substandard quality."[67]

The negotiations for free trade began in mid-1991 and came to their successful conclusion at the end of 1993 when the U.S. House of Representatives passed the North American Free Trade Agreement (NAFTA). Citibank had led the U.S. corporate campaign to secure U.S. support. Wall Street rubbed its hands with delight: the Mexican economy was now wide open. Mexico, in the words of one writer, had been "forced to be free." As David Corn notes, NAFTA promoters, deploying statistical models, predicted that the U.S. trade surplus with Mexico, which was $1.7 billion in 1993, would balloon to $9 billion by the end of 1995.[68] During the "Summit of the Americas" in early December 1994, explained *The Economist*, "the Mexican miracle was lauded as a paradigm of successful economic reform and an example to the rest of the region."[69]

## "Mexican Miracle" to "Mexican Problem"

On January 1, 1994, the day NAFTA became effective and Mexico stood on the threshold of entering an economically integrated, neoliberal, and postmodern America, the wheels of the juggernaut of modernization started to come off. Two thousand Mexicans, variously labelled "peasants" and "Indians" (to distinguish them from their presumably more rational and less turbulent countrypersons), crashed into history. From the poor state of Chiapas in southern Mexico, men and women, most of them speaking Mayan dialects as their first language, emerged upon the scene in violent opposition to the progress whose victims they were certainly fated to be. Led by the Zapatista National Liberation Army (EZLN), they were, in most accounts, the victims of the modernization that had so preoccupied all Mexican governments in the previous half-century. Although Chiapas was rich in resources, particularly hydroelectric power, petroleum, and forest products, and was one of the top exporters of cattle, tobacco, soy beans, bananas, and cocoa, and the largest coffee producer in the country, many of the *campesinos* (small farmers) of the state had continued to live at the level of abject poverty. The governors sent by the PRI to rule over them had mainly worked to help themselves and the large-scale farmers and ranchers.* As Roger Burbach notes, the

> contrast between extreme wealth and poverty in Chiapas is, in large part, the result of the capitalist revolution that has ravaged the state. For the past twenty-five years, Chiapas has been convulsed by unprecedented economic transformations that have torn up the traditional agricultural economy and devastated the indigenous cultures. The Mexican state, responding to the interests of the country's emergent bourgeoisie and the demands of the international market place, has treated Chiapas as an internal colony, sucking out its wealth while leaving its people—particularly the overwhelming majority who live off the land—more impoverished than ever.[70]

The uprising in Chiapas provoked a political chain reaction that led to a meltdown both within the ruling PRI and on the national and international stock and bond markets. At first, between January and March 1994, the value of the peso declined by a mere 8 per cent—enough to bring most governments down—yet worse lay ahead. At the political level there was almost unbelievable mayhem, initially marked by the kidnapping of two corporate businessmen and a explosion in a bank in Monterrey. By March, Luis Donaldo Colosio, the PRI reformist candidate for the August presidential elections, had begun to offer more compromises to the rebels and their supporters, all of whom wanted more democracy and less manipulation. On March 16 he effectively repudiated many of his conventional big business backers when he signed an alliance with another rebel within the party, the mayor of Mexico City, Manuel Camacho, who had been seeking to form a centre of power partly within, and partly without, the party. On March 23 Colosio was assassinated. Soon speculation rose that the presidential candidate had been the victim of a conspiracy carried out by the dominant clan within the PRI. Colosio's successor then stepped forward in the form of Ernesto Zedillo Ponce de Léon (b. 1951), a party stalwart who had graduated from Yale University.

Zedillo won the presidential elections of August 21, 1994, with most Mexicans assuming the results had been massaged in the interests of the PRI. The losers were Cuauhtémoc Cárdenas and Diego Fernández de Cevallos of the PAN, although, because he virtually disappeared in midcampaign, there remained a suspicion that Cevallos threw the election. Francisco Ruiz Massieu, the secretary-general of the PRI, who was seen as

---

* In Mexico small farmers are those with 10 hectares or less and medium farmers those with 10 to 40 hectares. The existence of both of these groups is endangered, according to Barry, *Zapata's Revenge*, 1995.

a leading figure in attempts to democratize the party, was the biggest loser. On September 28, he, too, was assassinated. All indications suggested that, like the assassination of Luis Donaldo Colosio, this was an inside job. In any event the political rulers of Mexico, it now seemed, had lost the capacity to settle disputes among themselves peaceably. Was the stability that had characterized Mexican politics for half a century now at an end?

In December 1994 Zedillo moved into the *palacio nacional* just in time to see foreign reserves reach the bottom of the bucket. In nine months they had plummeted from $28 billion to $6 billion. Radical devaluation was the only choice. The weaker peso meant a huge increase in Mexico's dollar-denominated foreign debt. At $166 billion, it was now higher than it was in 1982 at the time of Mexico's "debt crisis."[71] To bail out the private banks the government was forced to spend more than the total acquisition moneys it had earned from the privatization of banks.[72] The U.S. trade surplus with Mexico, predicted to swell to $9 billion by the end of 1995, had turned into a Mexican trade deficit of $12.2 billion for the first nine months of the year.

"Only ten out of the twenty-four Mexican billionaires listed by *Forbes* in its 1994 ratings survived the peso collapse," noted John Ross in *The Nation* in late 1995. The poor, of course, fared even worse: "The Secretary of Social Development calculates that 2.5 million Mexicans have crossed the line from poverty to extreme poverty since January 1 [1995], adding to the 13 million to 18 million citizens who cannot, by United Nations standards, satisfy their daily nutritional needs. That is to say, nearly a fifth of the population is going to bed hungry every night."[73]

"The countryside was the part of Mexico most devastated by Salinista policy" confirms Jorge Castaneda. "The low prices of many products, competition from abroad, the high cost of credit, and the termination of subsidies and the whole panoply of state support all led to a genuine devastation of the Mexican countryside such [as] had not been seen within memory."[74]

As the peso declined, so too did the value of foreign investments in Mexico. With economic development smouldering on the runway, it was private capital that took off. Capital flight after the peso collapsed in 1994 amounted to $11 billion. The Clinton administration, not unconscious to the campaign contributions that Goldman Sachs had made to the cause of the Democratic Party, offered the Mexican government a $6 billion line of credit.

Even as late as December 1994 Mexico had been trumpeted as a "miracle economy." Now, quite suddenly, the pinup fluttered to the floor:

"The lure of Latin America's emerging markets has been shattered by an explosion in Mexico," confessed a shaken *Economist*. "Argentina's stock and bond markets were sent reeling. . . . Foreigners, who account for a large slice of investment in Brazilian shares, have been dumping these too."[75]

Meanwhile ex-President Salinas had thought better of remaining in the country. Rumours abounded; supposedly in exile in Canada, Cuba, or Ireland, apparently he did regularly return to his family home in Mexico. It was suggested that he had acquired a part of his ill-gotten gains ($120 million of which he had transferred out of the country) by offering protection to the lords of the Juarez drug cartel. Several members of his family had also been arrested for a wide range of crimes including the running of a money laundromat in Switzerland. His brother, Raúl Salinas, a middle-level manager, had not only been found with millions in several European bank accounts, but was also accused of the murder of his own brother-in-law, Jose Francisco Ruiz Massieu. Salinas's deputy attorney-general, Mario Ruiz Massieu, brother of the assassinated Francisco, also thought better of remaining in the country. He fled to the United States, where he was arrested for importing a large sum of undeclared money. In early 1996 Citibank, which had managed the movement of considerable amounts of money from Mexico to Switzerland, was co-operating with the U.S. Justice Department in its investigations.

Mexican annual GDP growth, having expanded to 3.7 per cent in the decade 1970-80, had declined to -0.7 per cent in the decade 1980-90 and then rose only to 1.4 per cent in 1996. By 1994, of Mexico's 92 million people, 24 per cent of rural dwellers and 8 per cent of urban dwellers were living in extreme poverty. Inflation in 1995, predicted at 19 per cent, reached 34.8 per cent. But the news was not all bad: nearly 60 per cent of the foreign multinational corporations in Mexico reported increased profits for 1995.[76]

# Summary

Starting in the years between the world wars and continuing until the 1970s or even early 1980s, populist governments in Latin America, unwaveringly sympathetic to the purposes of capitalism, sought to complement the political independence of their countries by achieving a greater degree of economic development. The road to more ensured economic growth invariably led through nationalization—not the same thing as socialism—and protectionism. Development equalled industrialization, as all leaders recognized, and industrialization required a securely protected domestic market. But almost from the first, industrialization had the double effect of creating new classes and threatening the hold of the old oligarchies. Many leaders, from Perón to Allende, recognized and encouraged this effect. But the oligarchies themselves, together with the newly emergent middle classes and foreign investors, feared disorder—and the spectre of disorder arose whenever programs of industrialization faltered. That they faltered was due in large measure to the inherent difficulties that less developed economies had in finding enough capital for investment and innovation and in affording the high rents demanded by the owners of that capital. Another problem was that when manufacturing did increase, it proved to be high-cost and inefficient.

Inevitably, then, when economic growth stagnated, crisis loomed. The workers and the middle class both quite rightly feared a decline in living standards. Competition for a shrinking pie led to raucous and often violent confrontations, at which point the oligarchies, now often supported by both a panicky middle class and the preponderant power in the hemisphere, would intervene. Under the supervision of the military, the ruling elites halted programs of national development and sold off selected national assets to the holders of capital. Development increasingly became dependent upon foreign investment. On a national level, on the whole, the richest got richer and the poorest got poorer. Increasing inequality became the hallmark of the period following the quarter-century of growth after 1945. By the later 1970s, with the rise of the debt crisis, the trumpet of economic development theory was playing the "last post" over the grave of ISI. Soon it would take up new tunes; all of these contained the word "export."

After the early 1970s the Pinochet regime in Chile had offered a new salvation: radical trade liberalization, usually called "neoliberalism." This approach, the opposite of ISI or "export substitution," was tried out globally—from Mexico to Vietnam. Yet the prosperity promised by the evangelists of liberalization and export promotion, after a brief and euphoric beginning, appeared illusive. National economic growth stimulated by foreign investment, even when impressive, was often unstable. While some people gained, and a few benefited incommensurably, most lost. During the recession of 1981-82, even Chile was struck by crisis.

Out of that crisis, from 1984, a new Chile emerged with an economy oriented away from the vain hope of industrialization and cured of economic nationalism. In this new Chile of agricultural and mineral exports and low wages, the guarantee of future prosperity was attachment to the U.S. economy via NAFTA. In this future there would be no place for Pinochet's Christian crusaders, who were returned to their barracks while

regimes dedicated to reducing inequality by increasing social spending
were elected to office. By 1995 Chile was making serious progress
towards acceptance as a serious partner in NAFTA. But, although it was a
leader of the Latin American pack of neoliberal reformers, Chile remained
too small to be much of an influence in the continent as a whole.

Brazil's authoritarian rulers of the 1970s and 1980s did not show any
particular vocation for market-oriented reforms. This was left to the liberals of the 1990s, first the discredited Collor and then the former *dependen-
tista*, Cardoso, who was from the outset apparently bent on emulating the
Spanish model of deep deindustrialization. The largest economy in the
region and one of the largest in the world experienced remarkable growth
in the late 1960s and early 1970s, but still no regime since the 1950s had
managed to halt economic and social deterioration. Growth, in the minus
range (-1.0 per cent) in 1992, was at 5.5 per cent in 1995 and 3.1 per cent
in 1996. The disparities in wealth between rich and poor, nevertheless,
had widened, and by the mid-1990s were as great as the disparities in the
living standards of Belgium and India. That Brazil has been given the
ironic nickname "Belindia" is a sour commentary on the stagnancy that
has only worsened in the past half-century. According to Castaneda, "In
1960 the poorest 50 percent of the Brazilian population received 17.7 percent of the national income; in 1970 its shared dropped to 15 percent; by
1980 that share had dwindled to 14.2 percent; and by 1990 it dropped to
10.4 percent."[77]

In Argentina, the home simultaneously of the most famous of the rad-
ical-populist leaders and the most infamous and incompetent military
regimes, malnutrition was by the 1990s in step with Latin America as a
whole: on the increase. By the mid-1990s, in common with Mexico,
Argentina was stuck in a trough of negative growth; rather than the 5 to 6
per cent high growth necessary to "take off," both Mexico and Argentina
continued to remain recalcitrantly earth-bound, outside the circle of the
successfully developing. Even the optimists who valiantly predicted a
growth rate of 2 to 3 per cent for the future were now admitting that the
level being achieved fell well short of what was needed to alleviate mass
poverty and, incidentally, guarantee a democratic political system.

What had happened throughout Latin America was indeed just the
opposite of those goals. The economic historian Victor Bulmer-Thomas
noted that various studies had confirmed the pre-World War II trend of
growing income disparity. The share of income received by the bottom
quintile (or 20 per cent) of the population in other regions of the world had
seen "a modest improvement" in the postwar years, but many Latin
American republics had continued to decline. According to Bulmer-

Thomas, by 1970 the average received by that bottom quintile for Latin America "was a mere 3.4 percent, compared with 4.9 percent for all developing countries and 6.2 percent for developed countries." He concluded that "the degree of income concentration was extremely high in Latin America," and "the concentration of income was becoming worse in precisely those countries (e.g., Brazil, Mexico) with the most dynamic performance."[78]

The political crisis that erupted in Mexico in the early days of 1994 suggested that the promise of prosperity accompanying a neoliberal and NAFTA future was no less a mirage than the other political and economic resurrections that were supposed to have taken place on the continent. As Castaneda predicted in a critical study of NAFTA:

> No country has ever attempted to develop an export manufacturing base by opening its borders so quickly and indiscriminately to more efficient and lower-cost producers. No nation today, not even the United States, has so willingly sacrificed an industrial policy or an equivalent form of managed trade. By unilaterally renouncing these advantages, Mexico will lose far more jobs in the next few years than it will create. Old industries and agricultural producers will die, be swallowed up, or join with foreign ventures, long before the new jobs arrive.[79]

By the mid-1990s the recent economic history of Latin America was such that Bulmer-Thomas was led to conclude, in a combination of optimism and apocalypticism, that there was a "ray of hope" for the 30 per cent of the population who were receiving 5 per cent of the national income. But for the 5 per cent who were receiving 30 per cent of the national income, he suggested, "a warning."[80]

To this Elizabeth Dore and John Weeks add a percipient note. "Today, we are on the cusp of a significant historical change," they say—a change that takes the form of "the relative decline of U.S. economic power." In 1966, they note, "The United States accounted for one-third of worldwide GDP. In the 1990s, this proportion has fallen to about one-fourth. The United States still dominates capital investment in Latin America. Yet Western European and East Asian . . . capital is increasingly important, marking what promises to be an increase in inter-capitalist rivalry in Latin America into the next century."[81]

Japan and other East Asian countries have emerged as "important players" in Latin America. The Japanese, for instance, largely financed the Brady Plan, aimed at restructuring the massive Latin American debt. Japan has replaced the United States as the largest donor to the World Bank and IMF and become the largest bilateral donor of foreign aid. In what is perhaps the most revealing example of the trend, the U.S. military base in Panama, Fort David, was closed down and converted into an industrial park backed by Taiwanese capital. Dore and Weeks conclude: "The historical parallel to these changes may well be the shift after the First World War from British to U.S. economic leadership in the capitalist world."[82]

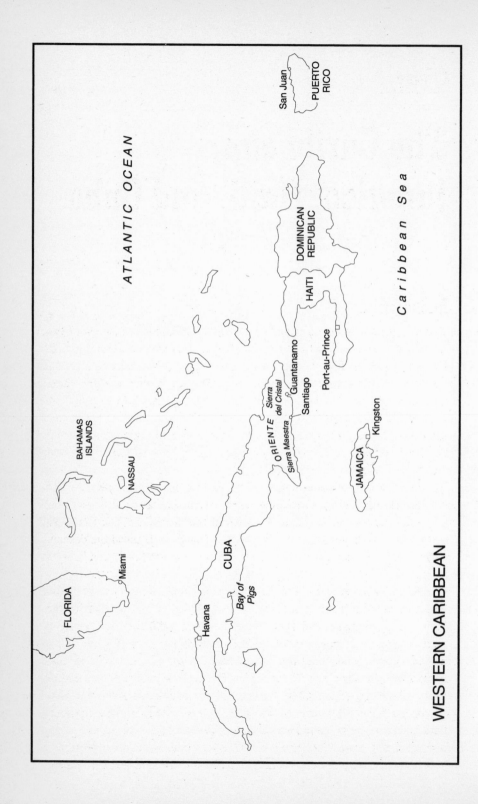

WESTERN CARIBBEAN

# Chapter 3

# The Caribbean: Jamaica, Haiti, and Cuba

## Background

Two overwhelming conditions have governed the history of the Caribbean archipelago, the chains of islands anchored in an arc running from just off-shore the coast of Florida in the west to the South American mainland in the east. First, and most shockingly, as a direct consequence of the European colonization that began in the last years of the 15th century, the indigenous population was almost completely exterminated. Second, in the place of those original inhabitants came the settlement of small numbers of Europeans, then larger numbers of Africans, and finally smaller numbers of Asians.

In most of the Caribbean islands the African population, often to some extent intermingled with the Europeans, became dominant. Only in Cuba, by far the largest island in the region, did the descendants of European settlers form a majority of the population—though in Trinidad the descendants of Indian indentured labourers came to equal the descendants of African slaves.

No three states in the same region have had histories as radically different as Jamaica, Haiti, and Cuba. In the heyday of mercantilism in the 18th century, Jamaica and Haiti were the most valuable possessions of their respective colonial rulers. The French colony of Haiti (then called Saint Domingue) occupied the western part of the island known as Hispaniola (sometimes called "Espanola"). The eastern part was occupied by Santo Domingo, which later became the Dominican Republic. In both Jamaica and Haiti not just the indigenous populations but also the local flora and fauna were annihilated to make way for imported slave populations and the crops they were compelled to cultivate. In consequence, both places became almost entirely occupied by people of African descent.

Beyond their populations of African origin and their brutal colonial pasts, from the early 19th century Jamaica and Haiti had little in common. In the last decade of the 18th century, the slaves of Saint Domingue tore the colony from the bosom of French colonialism with a violence that reflected the infernal oppression of the plantation system. Thereafter Haiti, as the independent republic of ex-slaves became known from 1804, sank into a morass of economic backwardness and despotism. Its government was a compact of mulatto merchants and politicians, supported by foreign bondholders and sustained by a hovering U.S. military presence, ruling over a majority of atomized and terrorized black smallholders.* While this continued, the land of Haiti became a perfect exemplar of "Oriental" avarice, violence, and impoverishment; a wretched African despotism existing at the very margins of political and economic existence yet living in the backyard of what, from the end of World War I, was becoming the world's most powerful economy.

The history of Jamaica, which was in the 18th century to the British what Saint Domingue was to the French—namely, the source of a notable wealth produced by slaves—can be told as a luminous example of humanity and enlightenment leading to emancipation and progress; that is, as a counterexample to the history of Haiti. In Jamaica in the first half of the 19th century, after a number of revolts that seriously threatened the continued dominance of the British, plantation slavery was abolished. In its place emerged a colonialism resembling the shape of things in certain African colonies—perhaps Sierra Leone or the Gold Coast. Under this colonialism a small class of literate Jamaicans was allowed to percolate upwards under the ever watchful eye of colonial administrators, missionaries, and a local white/mulatto oligarchy. Thanks in particular to a series of widespread labour revolts that shook the British West Indies in the late 1930s, the British rulers of Jamaica decided to implement a program of modest development and incremental self-government. They were motivated in this partly by the colony's declining profitability and partly by its growing economic ties with the United States. Perhaps rather than freeing Jamaica, the British were transferring it to new proprietors.

As early as 1900, the first Jamaican of African descent had been named to the non-elected Legislative Council. By 1910, 6 out of the 14

---

* Terms such as "mulatto" and "black" have important social if not biological meanings. Mulattos—the term originally applied to people of mixed European and African origin—are not necessarily lighter in skin colour than blacks, but they are almost invariably richer. This makes them, in some arguments, more Western. In Haiti mulattos were not a "race" or a "mixed race," but a social and political category. *Mulate pove cé nèg; nèg rich cé mulate*: "a poor mulatto is a black, a rich black is a mulatto."

members of the Legislative Council were partially or wholly of African
descent, and by the 1930s the Council was overwhelmingly "black." In
1936 the Jamaican Progressive League was formed to work for self-
government. Within a few years after World War II the move for self-
government had become a movement for outright independence. "Progressive" in the postwar period becomes a key word: until the mid-1980s
it is possible to imagine Jamaica "progressing," first under a *dirigisme*—
state-led planning and control—associated with both Alexander Bustamante and the Manleys and later under a neoliberalism identified with
Edward Seaga. But by the mid-1980s the seemingly forward movement of
history associated with the term "progress" had been halted.

Until the second quarter of the 19th century, Cuba, the largest island
in the Caribbean, had remained a backwater, sparsely settled by a population of mainly Spanish, not African, origin. In the second half of the 19th
century the Spanish, who had managed to hold on to Cuba while much of
the Latin American mainland became independent, began to import
African slaves in large numbers. While there were no slaves remaining in
the rest of the Caribbean, Cuba was in the midst of transforming itself into
an island of slave plantations that produced sugar using the most advanced
industrial equipment. This remarkable development was interrupted in
the last quarter of the century by the attempts of both free Cubans and
slaves to rid the island of Spanish rule. The movement for independence
reached a climax at the end of the century with an aborted war of independence, in the midst of which the Americans invaded to defeat the Spanish
and seize control of Cuba's future.

The Americans relinquished this future in the 1930s, but not before
ensuring that the country was handed to a *caudillo* (political boss) of their
own choosing. "Our man in Havana," from the point of view of Washington, remained in place until New Year's Day, 1959. The replacement of
what amounted to a dictatorship, by a regime of radical nationalists determined to seize control of Cuba's political and economic future, could not
be tolerated; indeed, until the present, it has continued to be anathematized with a passion that approaches religious conviction. That it has survived into the closing years of the century constitutes one of the most
remarkable chapters in the entire contemporary history of the Americas.

# Jamaica: "Betta Mus' Come"

During the Second World War the march towards self-government (that is,
"home rule," which excluded control over national development) accelerated in the whole of the British West Indies. In the previous decades,

several factors had united to induce the British Colonial Office to offer a small minority of Jamaicans increased political rights. One of these was the expansion of the middle class, particularly lawyers, teachers, and civil servants. Even though these professionals showed themselves immovably loyal to the British Crown, their demands were opposed by the white planters and merchants who, like white settlers elsewhere, made it plain that they thought that anything but white autocratic rule was unnatural. The hurricane of labour unrest that swept the whole of the West Indies in 1934-40 convinced London that the planters' position was untenable.

In 1941 Britain proposed constitutional reform, which was to include universal suffrage. In 1944 a "home rule" constitution was introduced, largely implementing reforms recommended by a committee of the Jamaican Legislative Council. At the end of the year a general election, with universal suffrage, was held for a House of Representatives—a first for the British West Indies. Two parties, the People's National Party (PNP) and the Jamaica Labour Party (JLP), competed. The PNP was Jamaica's first mass party and its head, after 1938, was the "Jamaican white" (or "mulatto") Fabian lawyer Norman Washington Manley (1893-1969). It was left of centre and thus reformist, with ties to the British Labour Party. The JLP, despite its name, was conservative and business-oriented, but backed by Jamaica's largest trade union, the Industrial Trade Union (ITU). The founder and leader of the JLP, Alexander Bustamante (1884-1977), was a favourite of the Colonial Office and, like Manley (the two were cousins), was a mulatto. He was also a populist with a program that was only superficially radical. According to Elizabeth Wallace, Bustamante "attacked members of the People's National Party as communists and atheists and the self-government they advocated as simply substitution of a brown man for a white on the backs of black men."[1] He won 23 seats in the 31-seat House. Because Jamaicans were on the whole strongly Christian, and because the message from the mainstream churches was persistently anti-communist, atheistic communists were seen as being a serious threat to the main values of Jamaican society.

In the 1944 vote only one other representative of the white oligarchy was elected. As a decisive collectivity in Jamaican politics, the whites had had their day—as Eric Williams of Trinidad later said in a famous speech, "The Massa Day Done." But the role of the whites as an *indirect* force in Jamaican politics was far from at an end. Having failed in 1944, most of the white oligarchy thereafter supported Bustamante.

For the half-century after the 1944 elections, this oligarchy—an armful of families—continued to dominate that part of the private sector of the economy not controlled by foreign capital. Four of the families—the

Ashenheims (owners of Jamaica's, and the anglophone Caribbean's, most important newspaper, the *Daily Gleaner*), the Henriques, the Issas, and the Matalons owned, or had major interests in, 107 companies. In his book *Class, State, and Democracy in Jamaica* Carl Stone refers to 15 "rich capitalist" families, most of which emerged as merchants in the late 19th and early 20th centuries and "the approximately 106 very wealthy members of the big capitalist class." Pre-eminent among this bourgeoisie are the Matalons, whose holding company, Industrial Commercial Developments, in 1983 accumulated around $19 million in pretax profits. As Stone explains, "The rich capitalist families in Jamaica have maintained a close relationship with foreign business interests."[2]

One historian of the West Indies, Gordon Lewis, was particularly scornful of these operations: "With few exceptions, the top class has been socially and politically reactionary; in economic terms, the junior partners of expatriate financial enterprise; and therefore mentally colonialist."[3] In later years, Michael Manley, Norman's son and political successor, reminded the great families that if they didn't like the Jamaica he was trying to create, there were five flights a day to Miami. Chillingly, at least for the Matalons and their friends, Manley may have picked up this attitude from Fidel Castro.

The families of the Jamaican oligarchy, besides owning important parts of the Jamaican economy, also profited as the local facilitators of foreign interests that controlled Jamaica's main assets: bananas, bauxite, and banking. Of the U.S. firms, United Brands was in bananas and Kaiser and Reynolds were in aluminum. The Canadian company Alcan was also in aluminum, with the Bank of Nova Scotia in banking. The British firms Tate and Lyle and Booker Brothers dominated the sugar industry, with Barclays in banking. The ties with international capital were often cemented by the presence of rich and influential Jamaicans on the boards of foreign firms.

When Bustamante and Norman Manley squared off in the election of 1949, Manley recognized that he would have to offset the ITU by organizing trade union support of his own. Indeed, many trade unions, particularly in the public sector, had grown impatient with Bustamante's conservatism, and with their support Manley won a larger share of the vote—though fewer seats—than the JLP. The main plank in the PNP platform was full and immediate responsible government, a position that the JLP insinuated was crypto-communist.

Still, the differences between the two parties were not great, and they became even less so after the PNP purged its left-wing element in early 1952. The purge was rewarded by the adherence of the Jamaican middle class (particularly the large civil service "salariat"), which shifted its support from the JLP to the PNP. According to Jamaican political scientist Carl Stone:

> From the 1940s to the 1960s the parties shared a belief that the state should provide aid and welfare to the poorer classes through social policies and public spending programmes; a view that the state should provide overall economic policy leadership for the private sector and assume a central role in promoting economic development through state funded projects; a perception of the need for some state regulation of the economy in the national interest; a broadly-held consensus that the state must provide social services for the citizens and economic services and infrastructure for those engaged in production through social reforms and legislation; and a common commitment to political patronage whereby scarce benefits that flow from government policies and expenditure (jobs, housing, contracts, etc.) are allocated to party supporters.[4]

In other words, both parties accepted a Keynesian and dirigiste role for the state. (For more on Keynesianism, see chapter 10.)

Where universal adult suffrage and Keynesianism combined most potently was in the fields of education and public health. Between 1950 and 1970, secondary school enrolment shot up from 15 per cent to 58 per cent. Infant mortality (per 1,000 live births) decreased from 118 in 1937 (in the Depression) to 81 in 1950 and then further to 36 in 1970. These changes were sustained by an unusual rate of GDP per capita growth between 1950 and 1960—at 6.5 per cent the highest in the Caribbean and Latin America.[5]

By 1953 Jamaica had internal self-government and Alexander Bustamante had become the Chief Minister. London retained control of Jamaica's foreign affairs and defence. By the mid-1950s, trade union power was on the decline and business interests had found a comfortable home in both parties. The paradigm for economic development in Jamaica was called the "Puerto Rican Model"—a rather simple construct based on the idea that cheap labour and geographical proximity to the United States should attract U.S. capital. The Jamaicans should provide the U.S. market with basic manufactured consumer goods; shirts, shoes, and the like. One obvious attraction of the Puerto Rican model was that it already functioned on another Caribbean island of approximately the same size. The first steps on the Puerto Rican path were taken in 1952.

Still, several factors might have indicated that what was good for Puerto Rico might not be good for Jamaica. For one thing, the Puerto Rican economy was almost entirely U.S.-owned. Some "80 per cent of the Puerto Rican economy is owned by U.S. multinationals," Michael Manley noted in 1982. "Foreign capital controls 90 per cent of the assets in manufacture, 70 per cent in banking and finance and 90 per cent in land, sea and air transport. This represents a drain of $2,216,200,000 in net profits and dividends annually. It is estimated that the total has been $40 billion since 1940."[6] As well, despite U.S. investment in Puerto Rico the island had seen a huge emigration to the mainland, largely a result of economic and social conditions. In the early 1980s, for example, 2 million out of 3.2 million Puerto Ricans were depending upon food stamps.

## Independence

From the mid-1950s both the JLP and the PNP sought to develop strong roots among all of the social groups of Jamaica. According to Stone, they "concentrated on mobilizing the bottom 40 per cent of the unemployed, the subproletariat, the poor and the lumpenproletariat who looked to them for patronage benefits and hand-outs."[7] The PNP won the elections of 1955 and remained in power until 1962, when Jamaica became independent. At the time, because the new country was in the midst of a spectacular economic boom, Jamaicans had every reason to be optimistic about its future. By the mid-1960s, when the boom was beginning to peter out, and threats to the postwar political order had started to show up. Rising unemployment had gradually dispelled the euphoria that had surrounded independence, and the poor, in particular, were getting only poorer.

According to Evelyne Stephens and John Stephens's assessment: "The development model of industrialization by invitation had produced growing unemployment and poverty next to growing affluence, which was aggravating the class and race conflicts in the society. These conflicts manifested themselves not only in labor militancy, political violence and the emergence of new radical groups, but even more threateningly in spontaneous riots and in increasing violent crime."[8] Earlier, in 1959-60, armed "Black Power" militants had engaged in a shoot-out with the army and the police. Two British soldiers were killed and over a hundred of the militants arrested. In 1963, in another confrontation, eight people were killed and three militants subsequently hanged. In August-September 1965 came attacks on the Chinese community—most of them the descendants of people introduced to the Caribbean as contract labourers in the 19th century and long the target of resentment by the poorest of Jamaicans. From early 1966 through the election of 1967, open wars took place not only between gangs and the security forces but also between the partisans of PNP and the JLP.

In April 1967, Hugh Shearer of the JLP won the national elections. A year later, on October 15-16, 1968, the "Rodney riots" broke out. Walter

Rodney, a 26-year-old Guyanese lecturer in history at the University of
the West Indies at Mona, near Kingston, had studied in London and taught
in Tanzania before returning to the West Indies. Rodney's ideology
included strong elements of black nationalism combined with dependency
theory and the unorthodox Marxism of the new left. The Jamaican minister of home affairs was later to try to convince the House of Representatives that "in my term of office and in reading of the records of problems
in this country, I have never come across a man who offers a greater
threat to the security of this land than does Walter Rodney."

The riots started after Rodney returned to Jamaica from a conference
of black writers in Montreal and was not allowed to leave his airplane—he
was banned from re-entering Jamaica. The government action provoked
demonstrations of students who were joined by gangs of urban youths,
together attacking the property of the wealthy, particularly of North American entrepreneurs. In Kingston they did a million pounds worth of damage, and more than ever lurid nightmares haunted the sleep of the
oligarchy.

## Manley and Seaga

In 1969 Norman Manley retired as leader of the PNP, succeeded by his
son, Michael, who went on to win the 1972 election campaigning on the
slogan "Betta Mus' Come." Michael Manley was a democratic socialist in
populist clothing. He was, that is, an adherent of the same general ideology that guided the British and Australian Labour Parties, the Canadian
New Democratic Party, and a number of European socialist parties, but
with a difference, which was that Manley was a Third World socialist. His
arguments were often wrapped in a populist rhetoric that might be called
"late Bandung." They stressed the existence of a Third World dominated
by a neocolonialist West and the need for Third World countries to adopt
policies of "collective self-reliance" that would put them on the road to
economic independence. These arguments echoed across the Caribbean
when demands for new strategies for development and new demands for
political independence were heard from such small islands as Grenada,
Dominica, St. Lucia, and St. Vincent between 1974 and 1979.

On the mainland, Manley's almost exact contemporary was the Mexican president Luis Echeverría (president 1970-76), who had a similar
nationalist-populist ideology. By the second half of the 1970s, with Chile's
Allende dead and Echeverría out of office, Manley had become the pre-
eminent hemispheric spokesperson for what remained of the still self-
conscious but non-communist Third World.

Given the Jamaican electorate's Christian religious background,

Manley saw the advantage of wrapping his program in a mantle not merely of populist but also of specifically biblical imagery. When asked to clarify what he meant by democratic socialism, Manley referred to it evasively, but not untruthfully, as "Christianity in Action." He stressed the social side of the Old Testament message even more by portraying himself as a biblical Joshua and his opponent as Pharaoh. Towards the black national-ists and Rastafarians of Jamaica he brandished a "Rod of Correction," which, he claimed, had been given to him by Haile Selassie, Emperor of Ethiopia and putative descendant of the biblical Queen of Sheba.*

Manley's program centred on two goals: to improve the lives of the majority of Jamaicans, and to make Jamaica's economy more independent of foreign capital. According to Anthony Payne: "Foreign capital was per-mitted to operate but, to an increasing extent, only on the state's terms, which included joint ownership. Local capital was equally encouraged but was required to distribute more of its profits to its workers in the form of higher wages and improved conditions. This populist model put the state in the driver's seat and temporarily won new welfare benefits for the poor and dispossessed."[9]

In the early 1970s the PNP introduced a reform policy designed to give smallholders more land. In education Manley promised free sec-ondary and university education as well as free uniforms and school meals in primary school. In housing the government managed to dramatically increase the stock of houses available to workers. Many of the programs were not successful, as Manley himself admitted. A major reason for fail-ure, as Stone points out, was the combination of "thin layers of leadership, thin technocratic skills and intellectual resources, lack of discipline among party cadres [and] rampant corruption and patronage excesses."[10]

During the election campaign of 1976, reggae star Bob Marley appeared at a bipartisan rally and sang his song "War."

---

* Black nationalism and Rastafarianism had their origins in Jamaica roughly between the two world wars. The pre-eminent black nationalist was Marcus Garvey (1887-1940), who pro-posed schemes for creating black pride and a black bourgeoisie. The Rastafarian move-ment rose in the 1930s, inspired by Haile Selassie's resistance to Italian imperialism. "Ras Tafari" was one of Haile Selassie's titles. By the 1950s the Rastas inspired the same dread in the minds of the British rulers in Jamaica as the Mau Mau rebels did in the minds of the British in Kenya. The Governor of Jamaica, Sir Hugh Foot, described the Rastafarians as "a sect of worthless hooligans and dangerous criminals." Both the Rastafarians and Mau Mau were seen as threats to Western civilization and progress; perhaps rightly, since the Rastas supported the autarky of self-sufficiency and considered Western civilization as Babylon. Even more shocking, rather than demonstrating communion with God by orderly kneeling and the token ingestion of wafers and wine, the disorderly Rastas inhaled mari-juana. Even the music associated with them, reggae, tended to show disrespect towards Western values.

That until the basic human rights
Are equally guaranteed to all
Everywhere is war.[11]

Whether Marley's sympathies for the PNP, played a strong role or not, Manley increased his seats in the 1976 general election from 37 to 47. Given the crisis of developmentalism across the Third World this was a surprising success. Manley had once suggested, in a reckless rhetorical flourish, that, with the victory of the PNP, capitalism in Jamaica had drawn its last breath. Quite understandably, this did little to comfort either the foreign investors or their local partners, neither of whom were inclined to tolerate the PNP under the best of circumstances. Worse, Manley had imposed a "Bauxite levy," which boosted Jamaica's earnings from its only exportable mineral from $23 million in 1974 to $195 million in 1979. Manley also nationalized the local offices of the British bank Barclays, merging it, in 1977, with a large Canadian bank, the Bank of Montreal, to create a large state-owned Jamaican bank, the National Commercial Bank.

The fear on the part of capitalist investors, such as the bauxite companies, that Manley was seriously bent on introducing what they called "tropical socialism" was enough to cause them to cut production and withhold investment. Local businessmen and administrators, particularly those of Chinese origin, migrated from Jamaica—mainly to Canada—in droves. Investment fell off.

For Jamaica's middle and working classes, the fear of communism, stimulated by the right-wing press, now became a serious matter. Then came a problem that no Jamaican regime—like other governments around the world—could possibly control: the rise of oil prices. In a single year, between 1973 and 1974, Jamaica's oil import bill doubled from J$65 million to J$177 million. Between 1972 and 1974 the country's public-sector debt—money borrowed to finance welfare and educational projects—rose by 56.7 per cent, from J$332.6 million to J$520.8 million.[12]

With oil prices rising, debt mounting, and the aluminum companies withholding investment, the Jamaican economy teetered towards collapse, pushed not a little by the IMF's draconian conditions, imposed as the terms for the loans in 1977 and 1979, and by a program of disinformation facilitated by the press both in Jamaica and in the United States. Manley himself suggested that Jamaica had been intentionally destabilized, much like Chile had been in the early 1970s, by an alliance of the U.S. government, the press, and capital. Anthony Payne finds this not improbable: "The weight of evidence makes it likely that the CIA was at work, in league with the JLP, the *Daily Gleaner*, and the opposition businessmen and trade unionists, to undermine the elected government in Jamaica."[13] The

*Gleaner,* for instance, moved from being merely partisan to being propagandistic from the mid-1970s under the editorship of Hector Wynter, who had been chairman of the JLP in the late 1960s. When Manley went to Cuba in July 1975, its provocations and distortions reached a new level.

Even though the government of Jamaica carried out all of the terms of a 1978 IMF agreement, the economy never recovered. Although the IMF has a record of reluctance in admitting to the failures of its prescriptions, in the Jamaican case it did indicate that it had erred in the medicine and dosage that it forced on the Jamaicans.

In 1980, after eight and a half years in power, Manley was driven from office in one of the heaviest electoral defeats ever suffered by a party in power. Right across the social spectrum, from the unemployed to the bourgeoisie, voters turned to the right in the form of the JLP under American-born and Harvard-educated Edward Seaga (b. 1930), in the hope of finding someone who could solve the problem of the national economy, that is, of their declining living standards.

Seaga's term in office coincided closely with the presidency of Ronald Reagan in the United States. Both promised deliverance of sorts. Seaga used the term to refer to the liberation of Jamaica from the strangulating restrictions of Manley's socialist policies. Reagan promised deliverance from defeating self-doubt for people at large, and deliverance from taxes for the rich. More than a little like the Canadian prime minister Brian Mulroney, elected a few years later in 1984, Seaga proved to be a supple U.S. client, a deal-maker, and a fixer. Seaga and Mulroney were both more opportunistic than dogmatic, and both promised to hitch their national wagons to the preponderant power in the hemisphere, the United States. According to Payne, within months of Seaga's election, "Jamaica had emerged as probably the most committed client state of the US government in the Caribbean area."[14] As one token gesture, Seaga had the Cuban embassy closed down. More importantly were the cuts: 30 per cent of government jobs were lost between 1980 and 1985; the cost of public administration as a percentage of GDP fell from 13.5 per cent in 1980 to a mere 8.5 per cent in 1988.[15]

Seaga's economic recipes for national development, like those of his Latin American neighbours, were thus taken out of the neoliberal cookbook that the IMF had so meticulously prepared in the 1970s. The renegotiation of IMF loans in tandem with the acceptance of IMF development guidance would, it was argued, buy Jamaica a more assured capitalist future. Because the IMF preferred a government like Seaga's to one like Manley's, its conditions were more generous. As it turned out, it loaned Seaga three times as much as it had allowed Manley. The World Bank was not far behind in its support. In 1981 Jamaica became the largest per capita recipient of World Bank loans.

Jamaica was also to be the beneficiary of a mini-Alliance for Progress aid scheme called the "Caribbean Basin Initiative" (CBI), wherein the investment of U.S. capital was promised to stimulate island development. The CBI, which came into effect in 1984, promised to give exports from the countries that subscribed to it a 12-year duty-free access to U.S. markets—a condition much like the one already operating vis-à-vis Puerto Rico. In the period of the Seaga government Jamaica also received remarkably high levels of other forms of assistance. But, as Anthony Payne and Paul Sutton note, the CBI was "crippled from the start."[16] As *Business Week* later admitted, it was "more a symbolic gesture" than an "ambitious program for economic stimulation."

The IMF schemes worked, at least in the *very* short term. After being starved of foreign capital, Jamaicans now saw investment flow into their country. In 1981-82, a consumer boom made it seem as though the repudiation of the PNP had paid off. As a result of the good times, Volvos and videos became accessible to more people. Still, Jamaica was still a long way from the promised land of a car in every garage or even a chicken in every pot.

The bauxite industry was at the centre of Seaga's blueprint for change: bauxite production was to more than double in three years. The production of alumina from bauxite ore was to be expanded from 2.4 million tons to 8.6 million tons as a consequence of foreign investment. But just as all this was beginning to happen, recession hit. The world demand for alumina dipped, and the U.S. aluminum giant Alcoa announced that it would *decrease* production in Jamaica. The other producers in Jamaica soon followed. By 1983 bauxite production, which had reached 12 million tons in 1980, fell to 7.3 million tons. In 1983-84 two major bauxite companies closed their doors. In turn government revenue and foreign exchange earnings plummeted, because bauxite was the source of as much as 70 per cent of Jamaica's foreign exchange.

The loss of revenue from diminished bauxite production was not offset by increases in other areas. Agricultural exports, particularly sugar and bananas, were also down. Finally, the dawning of a new tomorrow promised by the Caribbean Basin Initiative turned out to be largely an illusion. Neither foreign nor domestic capital rushed in where its owners had feared to tread under the Manley regime, and the Jamaican government found itself again with a balance of payments problem. By March 1983 the deficit had reached $150 million. The IMF demanded action in the form of a program of structural adjustment, and Seaga duly introduced austerity measures: new taxes, public spending cuts, import reductions. At the end of 1983 the Jamaican currency was devalued by an astonishing 43 per cent as a part of the IMF package. The commodities boom of 1981-82 suddenly seemed like a short-lived holiday that had taken place a very long time ago. From then on, as Payne notes, the management of the Jamaican economy by the Seaga government was largely a matter of "twists and turns."[17] Jamaica was a small country set adrift—and being buffeted helplessly by a strong wind blowing from the IMF headquarters in Washington.

By the end of 1983, with the JLP on the ropes, came a fortunate distraction. In Grenada, a tiny island just north of Trinidad, Maurice Bishop had led his New Jewel Party (NJP) to power in a bloodless coup in March 1979. The island seemed set, at least in the view of the Western media, to become the Cuba of the 1980s. Prime Minister Bishop annoyed Washington by spouting a developmentalist rhetoric that favoured the Cuban model, which, he said, "is now the best example in the world of what a small country under socialism can achieve." Even worse, he also talked about the building of a new Caribbean. President Reagan professed that socialist Grenada—with its total population of around 92,000—was a threat to hemispheric security. In October 1982 Bishop was assassinated by ultra-leftists in the island's opposition movement. President Reagan, perhaps reflecting on the tonic effect of the Malvinas campaign on the popularity of Margaret Thatcher, used the occasion to invade the island, with the Jamaicans, among other Caribbean nations, providing back-up. The whole affair served to discredit certain Jamaicans on the left, particularly the PNP, because Manley had supported Bishop's New Jewel movement as a "fraternal socialist party." But the invasion reflected positively on others, like the JLP, who detested Castro and Bishop and rejoiced in the idea of the United States as the policeman of the "Caribbean Basin." Soon afterwards Seaga called an election, which the PNP boycotted because a revision of the electoral lists agreed upon by both parties had not been completed. In the election, held in December 1983, the JLP won all the seats, providing the party with another five years it could use to adjust the island's economy in line with the requirements of the IMF. It was not the PNP's finest hour.

From 1984 to 1989 the JLP carried out further restructuring according to the dictates of the IMF and was rewarded with more loans and the rescheduling of more debt. But no loan fix could solve the country's chronic economic problems. Inflation remained high and unemployment reached over a quarter of the labour force. In January 1985 Kingston witnessed two days of protests and riots against IMF prescriptions. At the end of June the first general strike in Jamaica's post-independence history took place. Even the Industrial Trade Union, which had helped give birth to the JLP and had maintained an affiliation with the party, took part in the strike.

By now the economy was moving rapidly towards morbidity. At the beginning of the 1980s the country, at the edge of bankruptcy and subject to a CIA destabilization campaign, was convulsed by strikes, shootings by the army, and police and gang violence. The riots and protests frightened off tourists. Official forecasts predicted a decline of 6 per cent in GDP. The PNP was back at the top of the polls. Increasingly the Seaga government was being forced to reconsider its key promise about keeping the state out of the economy: it seemed that the state had to be reanimated if key national economic interests were to survive. Seaga, who had become almost completely disenchanted with his would-be benefactors, now made the same kind of maudlin appeals to the IMF that other Third World leaders, including Manley, had been obliged to make. Jamaica's people, he protested, could not take much more. But a joint team representing the IMF, the World Bank and the U.S. Agency for International Development (USAID) was immovable. It asserted that even more could be done by way of structural adjustments—that is, the Jamaican government could squeeze the people who had elected it even harder. Seaga, though, had reached the end of his rope; even he had to implement (in 1985) a Food Aid Program that gave food stamps to the starving. Here he was taking a page from the book of Argentina's Alfonsín, who, under similar circumstances, had introduced his Programa de Alimentario Nacional a year earlier. In a fairly conspicuous place within the Jamaican "free-market showcase" was a growing poorhouse.

## Jamaica's External Debt and Debt Service (1975-88)
## (in $ millions)

|                              | 1975 | 1980 | 1985  | 1988  |
| ---------------------------- | ---- | ---- | ----- | ----- |
| Total external long/ medium debt | 688  | 1867 | 3587  | 4002  |
| Debt service (accrued)       | 83   | 341  | 734   | 895   |
| Per capita debt              | -    | 875  | 1562  | 1699  |
| GNP                          | -    | 1166 | 759   | 1183  |
| Total debt service           | -    | 123  | 219   | 327   |
| Total net transfers (%)      |      |      |       |       |
| as % of GNP                  | -    | 2.8  | -7.7  | -14.5 |
| as % of imports              | -    | 6.8  | 13.4  | -33.1 |
| as % of exports              | -    | 4.8  | -9.9  | -22.9 |

Source: Panton, *Jamaica's Michael Manley,* 1993, p.82, Table 4.6.

In July 1986, by which year the country was running an external debt of around $3.7 billion, Jamaica held local elections. Because the PNP had boycotted the 1983 national elections, these represented the first chance for voters to register the popularity of the JLP. The verdict was unambiguous. The PNP won 126 of 187 seats, with the electorate clearly signalling that it wanted relief from the punishing demands of the IMF. With the reduction, at the end of 1986, of United States aid to Jamaica (which in the early Seaga years had been among the highest in the world on a per capita basis) and the slashing of Jamaica's import quota on sugar into the United States, the romance with the Reagan regime and its promises had hit bottom. Still, Seaga had to borrow money to keep the island's economy afloat. He got $132.8 million in January 1987, the fourth major loan since he had come to power. While the government avoided further devaluation, import, pay, and price controls became more stringent as the splits within the governing party began to show.

Despite an election budget in April 1988, full of goodies in the form of more public spending and particularly greater relief for the poor, and another IMF loan, this time for $114 million, the electorate was not seduced. Although 1987 had seen a slight improvement in the GDP (partly as a result of the drop in oil prices, partly because of greater exports of textiles and bauxite, and partly because of a greater inflow of tourists) the economy in 1988 showed signs of slowing down again. In the national elections of February 1989 the PNP under Michael Manley won 45 out of 60 seats.

In Payne's judgement, Seaga's gamble with a more abject form of dependency failed.[18] In his period in office Jamaica's rate of economic growth remained stunted, unemployment remained high, the infrastructure continued to unravel, and the external debt mounted—reaching $4.5 billion by the time he left office, a crushing burden for his successors. It would not be difficult to make the case that the economic sovereignty of Jamaica, so recently won from Britain, had been surrendered to the IMF, just as that of Puerto Rico had been long surrendered to the United States. It is unlikely, given the circumstances of the 1980s, that another government would have done any better. With all the heroic will in the world, Jamaica remained small, resource-poor, overcrowded, and easily dominated.

The few bright spots were the usual ones. A small group of already wealthy people had increased their wealth: "The share of labour income accruing to the top 20 per cent of the population jumped from 67 per cent in 1980 to 75 per cent one year later, a trend which continued throughout the 1980s. . . . In 1989, the World Bank estimated that the top 20 per cent of the population accounted for more than 60 per cent of income."[19]

After winning in 1989 Manley remained in power until health reasons led to his resignation in 1992. Almost from the moment of his return to power, his party made a screeching turn to the right. "Sensible politics," according to one leading U.S. daily, had returned. According to Trevor Monroe, "The new Manley government had no Left presence either in or around it, and declared a course of fundamental 'continuity' with Seaga's economic policy."[20]

Despite the PNP throwing overboard many of its left-wing commitments and trimming its sails to suit the inescapable winds blowing in from the IMF, the economy of Jamaica continued unalterably towards the shark-filled waters of dependency and deterioration. Debt-servicing consumed 46 cents of every dollar earned. The Governor of the Bank of Jamaica admitted that Jamaica could borrow no more. In September 1989, Jamaica failed the test set for it by the IMF. Deregulation and the sell-off, even giveaway, of state assets—hotels, land, telecommunications infrastructures—increased the sense of panic and despair. Manley's credibility, built up over a lifetime, began to evaporate, but he hadn't lost his sense of optimism. He predicted before leaving office that 1993 would see "the start of the greatest economic take-off in the history of Jamaica."

In March 1992 the competent and colourless Deputy Prime Minister Percival J. Patterson (b. 1935) replaced Manning as head of the PNP. According to the neoliberal analyst David Panton, "Under Patterson, Jamaica can either surge forward into the economically competitive world of the future or it can gradually withdraw into the politically-biased cocoon of the past."[21] In view of a worsening standard of living for the majority and rising inequalities, Panton may have neglected to consider a third possibility: neither forward nor backward motion, but, rather, the slow subsidence of a cruise ship stuck in the shallows, the mass of passengers trapped in the flooding lower decks, some of the affluent attempting to swim to the mainland with cash-stuffed pockets, officers still striking poses on the bridge, and the ship's owners, in the first-class cabins, still drinking their tea, albeit on a cracked and unmatching service.

# Haiti: Hope in Hell

Our Doc, who art in the National Palace for life, hallowed be Thy name....
Thy will be done in Port-au-Prince as in the provinces. Give us this day our
new Haiti and forgive not the trespasses of those anti-patriots who daily spit
upon our country.
    —Duvalierist version of the Lord's Prayer[22]

Throughout the 19th century, while the rest of the Caribbean remained under colonial rule, Haiti was free. Then, from 1914 to 1934, U.S. authorities occupied the country. They controlled the Haitian customs office until 1941, and they created the modern Haitian army as a force to police the peasantry. Racist as a matter of course, the occupiers preferred the mulattos to the blacks, and they put the mulattos in positions of authority. Within the stratum of people known as "mulattos"—about 5 per cent of the population—there existed an inner core of families numbering as few as five (the Mevs, the Brants, the Bigios, the Accras, and the Behrmanns). These were allied to, and became intermarried with, a small number of immigrant families, some of which had come from the Middle East.

The racism of the mulattos, which was essential to their self-image, was counterpoised by an ideology of *noirisme*, which was promoted among the minuscule black literati and celebrated the African origins of the majority. One of the earliest adherents of *noirisme* was François Duvalier, who, like the Senegalese ruler Léopold Senghor, the pioneer of *négritude* (from which *noirisme* was derived), was trained in medicine. But the difference between the two black "isms" was critical. In the simplest of terms, *négritude* was wrought as a means of cultural defence against colonialism, and *noirisme* as an ideological bludgeon against a domestic enemy, the mulattos.

At the end of World War II Haiti had almost nothing going for it except a century and a half of political independence. Even statistics were lacking—apart from those demonstrating that the territory that had once been the richest of France's overseas possessions was now the poorest in the hemisphere. As for the production of commodities, in the 19th century, as the rural population grew, the depletion and division of the land into smaller and smaller plots had inhibited the development of estates or plantations capable of producing a regular export crop. As a result one of the island's greatest exports was its own people. A steady stream of Haitians walked across into the Dominican Republic, where they were regularly victimized, brutalized, and virtually enslaved. If they were able to escape they set sail, often in inadequate boats, for the Bahamas and continental North America—with many of them drowning on the way. Still, the Haitian rulers stripped enough revenue from the remaining peasants to pay Haiti's debts, that is, the loans that the rulers took out to provide for their own needs.

When the Americans departed *physically* after World War II—politically they never quite left—black politicians rose to the top. The first of these was Dumarsais Estimé, who came to power in a coup in 1946, and the second was Colonel Paul E. Magloire, who overthrew Estimé in another military coup in May 1950. Magloire was in essence a puppet manipulated by the mulattos. The politics of having a black rule on behalf of mulatto interest was called *le politique de doublure*, "the politics of lining"—a black political shell served to conceal a mulatto lining. Magloire was himself forced out of office and into exile in 1956. In the period of Estimé and Magloire the economy of Haiti was in steady decline. There was no attempt to relieve the dependency on agriculture—coffee, sugar, and sisal, for the most part—an economic activity that was in steady decline.

## Papa Doc in Power

In September 1957, François "Papa Doc" Duvalier (b. 1907, "a simple country doctor," he called himself), previously associated with a U.S.-backed program to eradicate the infectious disease yaws, became president. He had not run for office in a vacuum; his rival, the populist Daniel Fignolé, had been forced to flee the island for his life. Immediately after Duvalier donned the sash of office, the army under General Antoine Kébreau and Duvalier's henchmen, the *cagoulards* ("hoods"), took up the cudgels that were considered necessary to cow the population into submission to his rule.

Duvalier promised the black majority self-esteem and development. His tenure in office, 1957-71, catapulted Haiti, hitherto one of the most obscure states in the Caribbean, into the limelight—as one of the world's most hellish places. His power took the form of an arch. One foot of the arch was secured by a secret police force, the Tontons Macoutes, the descendants of the *cagoulards*. The Macoutes were recruited from different elements within the black population: peasants, urban petty merchants, ex-soldiers, even the priests of voodoo, the *houngans*, who served as spies—"opportunists of every kind," notes James Ferguson, and unswervingly loyal to the dictator himself.[23] The opposite base of the arch was secured in the adherence of the Haitian merchant bourgeoisie. Ferguson describes the Duvalierists who straddled the Macoutes on the one hand and the mulatto merchants on the other:

> Duvalier and his supporters were primarily interested in plundering what they could from their fellow Haitians, irrespective of colour. The methods were many and various and were often ingenious. The state-controlled tobacco company . . . was effectively in Duvalier's hands and published no annual accounts. Gradually it extended its original monopoly to cover a range of commodities which included flour, sugar, motor cars, alcohol and electronic equipment. The profits from importing, distributing and selling all such goods could not be recorded or scrutinized.[24]

While the Haitian masses were particularly insecure and atomized, insecurity was ubiquitous; it afflicted even the mercantile elite. Whereas before the arrival of Papa Doc the blacks had been victimized, under his rule the mulattos came to be sporadically terrorized. This was not the randomness of some sort of master plan that understood the effective terror of unpredictability; this was the terror of a regime that was truly dysfunctional. In only the crudest ways did it work; those who did dissent openly and tried to raise rebellion met predictably horrible ends. As for Haiti's intellectuals, who were more mobile than the peasants, Montreal and New York became the centres of their resistance.

As for the shape of the promised development, Papa Doc certainly considered the "Puerto Rico" model. There were even wild hopes that the capital of Port-au-Prince might become the Hong Kong of the region. In the 1960s, certain U.S. industries moved to the island in their restless search for super-exploitable labour. They found that hungry Haitians were even more malleable than their brethren in Puerto Rico or Jamaica. But by the late 1970s it was apparent that the dream of a national economic upswing via large-scale implantation of foreign assembly plants was just that: a dream. By the end of the 1960s a slight rise in GDP had not been able to match the rate of population increase. A study published in 1977 disclosed that 86 per cent of the Haitian population relied on agriculture, with only 6 per cent occupied in industry.[25] A survey done the previous year disclosed that around half the population of Port-au-Prince qualified as "ultra-poor," that is, they spent over 75 per cent of their incomes trying to obtain 1,500 calories per day.[26]

## Baby Doc

The sickly and at times seemingly demented Duvalier had made himself "President for Life" in 1964, perhaps anticipating that for health reasons his tenure would be short. He also took care to ensure the succession of his unprepossessing son, the corpulent and dim Jean-Claude (b. 1951), known as "Baby Doc." But for most of his compatriots, the tenure of the father was not short enough. Papa Doc did not die until April 21, 1971. In a funeral oration, a judge in the Haitian Court of Appeal lost control of his grief. "This man was the Messiah!" he wailed. Somewhere between 30,000 and 60,000 people had been murdered by the Duvalierist state, and the country remained one of the poorest in the world.

Contrary to expectations, the transition from father to son was smooth. The new president, 19 years old, was installed on April 22, 1971, under the watchful eye of U.S. gunboats that were patrolling Haiti's waters to defend the status quo. Whereas Papa Doc was a devil with strong rural roots (as a country doctor and patron of the rural *houngans*) and a shrewd capacity to manipulate popular religion, Baby Doc was a monster of an altogether different gravity.

Even before 1980, when he married a daughter of one of the leading mulatto families, Michèle Bennett, the mulatto elite was again on the rise. Conspicuous among them was the shady Ernest Bennett, Michèle's father, a rich businessman who owned rural lands and Haiti Air and had the local BMW distributorship. His name had been linked with the drug trade between Latin America and the United States. These various sources of wealth gave him the means to spend several millions on his daughter's wedding to Duvalier, and it was this wedding, more than anything, that signalled the decline of the black elite and the renaissance of the mulattos. When Michèle Duvalier was confirmed as "First Lady of the Republic" in April 1982, Papa Doc's widow, Simone, the link between the creoles and the Duvalierist legacy, was forced out of the office, which carried with it a stipend of $100,000 a year.

For the mulattos, development was a more urgent question than it was for the blacks of the ancien régime. Baby Doc and his advisers were not entirely satisfied with living in a terrorized poorhouse. Like both dictators and democrats elsewhere, and even like Papa Doc, they yearned for economic modernity, which they believed could only come about through continued investment from one country, the United States. U.S. firms controlled much of Haiti's trade, and the United States was the main source of exports and imports. It was also the main guarantor of the regime's security. But by the administration of President Carter in the late 1970s, U.S. investment also carried with it a stipulation of "human rights" on the part of the receiving country. Port-au-Prince had to clean up its act, and a reforming dictatorship known as "Jean-Claudisme" was called into being. Jean-Claudisme was a blanket ideology, with both an economic and a political aspect. Central to the economic aspect was development, which was again to be based on the Puerto Rican model, and Haiti's pool of cheap, non-unionized labour once again proved to be a magnet for U.S. companies seeking to establish offshore assembly plants. Some of these plants were owned by members of the Haitian oligarchy themselves, such as the Mevs.

The Jean-Claudist strategy seemed to work. By the late 1970s 240 foreign firms had invested in Haiti. In the same years, tourism boomed, too. Club Med established a resort on a golden beach at a safe and well-patrolled distance from the mass of the Haitian poor, tens of thousands of whom starved in the famine of 1977.

Reforms, though, seemed unnatural to the hard-line Duvalierists, and so the government of Baby Doc vacillated between lukewarm change and feverish repression. The regime of unrelenting terror, which worked because rivals were liquidated before they had a chance to organize opposition, gave way to one of fitful terror, in which opposing tendencies, all of them supporting one or another form of dictatorship, emerged. One such tendency was embodied in the army.

Papa Doc had distrusted the army. In other republics in Latin America (for instance, in the adjacent Dominican Republic) the army had regularly acted as a loose cannon, quite capable of blowing away regimes that its generals felt were not acting in whatever interests they felt had to be defended. As a counterpoise to the army, Papa Doc had raised the Tontons Macoutes and bound them to himself. But Baby Doc, on the recommendation of Washington, had allowed the army to march back into state affairs. Better trained and equipped than the Macoutes, the army was back on the road to the power it had enjoyed in the days before Duvalier.

Although Baby Doc's regime had begun to appear more fragile by the early 1980s, it continued to receive the backing of the Reagan regime. The Haitian economy was severely unbalanced: for instance, while the country exported raw animal and vegetable products (not excluding human blood in the form of plasma), it relied on the importation of processed foodstuffs. The unbalance created a chronic trade deficit, largely in favour of the United States. In 1984 Baby Doc and his friends, in the name of the people of Haiti, were given $45.5 million from Washington in the form of aid. Little of it left the capital.

The economic situation worsened. The rural economy was undermined by a 1981 epidemic of swine fever that destroyed one of the peasants' main sources of cash income. The Americans recommended a porcine holocaust, the upshot of which was the destruction of the hardy and omnivorous Haitian peasant pig and its supersession by the drug- and cereal-dependent U.S. variety, which required an environment that could only be provided by the richer peasants. Indeed, the new pigs required lifestyles superior to most rural Haitians. At the same time the tourist economy had been smashed by the fear of AIDS, which had been imported into Haiti by North American tourists, spread through their interaction with Haitians in the sexual branch of the industry.

This economic collapse drove many Haitians to the edge. From 1972 they had taken to small boats and set sail for the United States as "boat people." By the early 1980s this influx of Haitians had become a problem for the United States. In 1981 some 6,000 per month were leaving the island. Tens of thousands more had emigrated to the Dominican Republic to join those who had been sold into forced labour by the Duvalier regime.

Even relatively privileged Haitians fled the country: by the 1980s there were more Haitian medical doctors in Montreal than in the whole of Haiti.

Then there was the question of religion. While the relationship between the Vatican and the various dictatorships of the Caribbean and Latin America was generally untroubled, one pope had excommunicated Papa Doc for persecuting missionaries. To no avail: the dictator had grown stronger by replacing foreign priests with his own clerical nominees. But in 1983 another pope announced that things simply had to change in Haiti and supported the efforts of priests and lay workers in their attempts to bring about social change. Just as rebels elsewhere sought to seize local radio stations, the church set up its own. "Radio Soleil" became Haiti's equivalent of Cuba's "Radio Rebelde" in the days before the overthrow of Batista.

Superficially, then, by the mid-1980s, the Duvalier regime had come to resemble the rule of Ferdinand Marcos of the Philippines, even down to Baby Doc's attractive consort, Michèle, a raptorial shopper who turned herself into a kind of junior Imelda. She was rumoured to have spent $1.7 million on a single spree in Paris. Ferguson points out:

> According to the World Bank . . . some 20,000 out of Haiti's 6 million population owned 40 per cent of the nation's wealth in 1983; another statistic revealed that 1 per cent of the population received 44 per cent of the national income. . . . The commercial and business sector of Port-au-Prince could thus boast an estimated 3,000 families who averaged an annual income of over $90,000. In contrast to this economic elite with its reputed 200 millionaires stood the average per capita income in 1980 of approximately $200 per year.[27]

Having entered the 1980s at the bottom of the hemispheric league under Baby Doc, Haiti as a whole only got poorer. According to the World Bank and the IMF, in 1985 public expenditure per annum on education amounted to $3.70 per capita, and on health, $3.44. For every secondary school, there were 35 prisons; for every secondary school teacher, there were 189 members in the army and police.[28]

Between November 1985 and Jean-Claude's departure in February 1986, resistance, repression, and reconciliation circled like vultures over the decomposing body of Duvalierism. At the beginning of January 1986, rebellion, known as the *dechoukaj* ("uprooting"), broke out in the impoverished town of Gonaives (the second largest in the country), where there was 80 per cent unemployment. By the end of the month the *dechoukaj* had spread to other parts of the country. Washington decided to end its life support. It announced first that it was withholding $26 million in agreed aid, and then it announced that Baby Doc had left the country—even though he was still there. The creation of this rumour of his exit had its effect, and Baby Doc got the message. Early in the morning of February 7, 1986, the First Couple boarded a U.S. C-141 cargo plane together with a number of their friends and relatives and a great deal of the country's portable wealth and were flown off to a luxurious exile in France. Already the home of another exiled sociopath, Jean-Bédel Bokassa of the Central African Republic, France was not unembarrassed by the arrival of the Duvaliers, while in Haiti Jean-Claude's people were delirious with joy at their deliverance.

## The Rise of Aristide

After the flight of the Duvaliers the *dechoukaj*—uprooting the supporters of the regime—continued. According to Amy Wilentz: "No one knows how many little Macoutes . . . were killed in the Dechoukaj in early 1986, perhaps more than a hundred. But the bigger fish, important mayors of towns . . . as well as chiefs of rural sections . . . and well-known Port-au-Prince swaggerers, were rescued from furious crowds and brought to prison under police protection. Some were later allowed to leave the country."[29]

The regime of Baby Doc Duvalier was succeeded by that of the Conseil National de Gouvernment (CNG), a junta dominated by the military and headed by Lieutenant-General Henri Namphy. Most of its members were Duvalierists, and more importantly they were supported by Washington. Washington had a number of concerns: it wanted stability in the interests of "regional security," an end to the tide of boat people, and some limitation to the flow of cocaine, which was being flown from the highlands of Colombia to the low places of the United States via Haiti. Again there was serious talk about modernizing Haiti's backward and derelict economy. The junta deregulated the Haitian state structure, which had been so profitable for the Duvalierists and U.S. firms. The effect of the closing down of state-owned factories and the removal of import controls was, predictably, disastrous. Small manufacturers and peasants both were undercut by a flow of cheap imported goods. In this chaos the army profited by controlling the inflow of imports and foreign aid.

The junta contained and then gradually limited and repressed the popular forces that had driven the dictator out of the country. Although it made a pretence of demobilizing the Macoutes, the junta did not, in fact, even disarm them. The regime went through the motions of setting a new constitution in place—it was approved by a referendum on March 29, 1987—but then blocked the transition to democracy altogether. On election Sunday, November 29, 1987, it oversaw a reign of terror unleashed by the Macoutes in order to prevent what would have been Haiti's first free elections.

The foreign policy-planners of the Reagan administration were now caught in a trap of their own making. They had not only backed right-wing candidates in the elections but had also trained and equipped the army and the paramilitary, which had prevented the same elections from taking place. The military coup didn't quite follow the U.S. blueprint for a return to democracy. Confronted with this double-headed monster, the U.S. government suspended a promised $62 million in aid, forcing the military to quickly stage a new election. Most politicians boycotted this next election, held on January 17, 1988—and all but 10 per cent of the population abstained from voting. It was won by Leslie Manigat, a 57-year-old political scientist who had spent 22 years in exile. When the new president appealed to the population to fall in behind him in the march towards national reconciliation, he found few followers. Nonetheless, despite a clear lack of support from Haitians in general, and the profusion of Duvalierists in both the army and the government, the U.S. government proclaimed his democratic qualifications. The Catholic Church fell in behind the new regime, now, as one report put it, "closing its eyes to the repressive apparatus of the dictatorship and the profound misery of the people."[30]

Manigat's rule lasted only 130 days, until June 19, 1988, when he was overthrown by General Namphy, who suspended the 1987 constitution and allowed the terror against the reformers to continue. But the cat was out of the bag; by late 1988, the eyes of the world were on Haiti and the Namphy regime was a pariah. Namphy himself was overthrown in a coup and trailed off into exile—to be succeeded by another general with connections to both Papa and Baby Doc, Prosper Avril. Although Avril could boast of neither popularity nor legitimacy, he could claim to have good relations with the U.S. government. Despite military rebellions against him by elite units within the army in early 1989, Avril, if he didn't actually prosper, survived. He was finally forced out of office on March 12, 1990, by which time even Washington's support had been dissipated. He handed over the interim presidency to Ertha Pascal-Trouillot, a woman of the bourgeoisie and a Supreme Court judge. Elections were once again scheduled. Pascal-Trouillot was, however, soon arrested on charges of complicity in an attempted coup. She fled to the United States in September.

On December 16, in the presence of hundreds of foreign observers, including former U.S. president Jimmy Carter, a relatively free election saw 60 per cent of the vote go to Father Jean-Bertrand Aristide, a brother of the Salesian order, parish priest of the church of Saint Jean-Bosco, liberation theologist, and unremitting opponent of the Duvalierist regime. Aristide had earlier been expelled from his religious order at the behest of Archbishop François-Wolff Ligonde, a cousin of Michèle Duvalier. Still, he had a huge popular following among the poor. He represented the popular church, the *ti-ligliz*, which had begun to organize the poor in Haiti in the 1970s but had been increasingly opposed by the church establishment as the Vatican swung around against liberation theology at the end of the decade. His party was called "Opération Lavalas"—*lavalas* being the Creole word for "flood."

> Aristide preached a brand of liberation theology that pleased no one except his extended congregation: the poor in the slums, the peasants . . . a scattering of young jobless lower-middle class youths with no future in the country, and a few liberals among the Haitian bourgeoisie and the exile community. He had all the right enemies. The Army hated him, because he mentioned colonels and sergeants and lieutenants by name in his sermons, and excoriated them for the abuses they committed against the people in their regions. . . . The American Embassy hated him, because he held the United States and its economic system responsible for much of Haiti's economic woes, and thus for the misery of her people, his congregation. The Church hierarchy feared him. . . . The very wealthy few in Haiti despised him also, because he accused them of betraying their countrymen and stated baldly that the system by which they enriched themselves was corrupt and criminal, and an offence against their fellow Haitians.[31]

But the Lavalas party had problems from the outset, including an attempted coup in January 1991 and violent rioting in the streets. The biggest official roadblock was its failure to obtain a majority in parliament. Parliament blocked 97 out of 100 of Aristide's proposed laws. In August 1991, thousands of Haitians appeared in front of parliament shouting "*Aba Makout Nan Lachanm*" ("Down with the Macoutes in parliament"). In September Aristide's government was overthrown by the army in a bloody coup, and Aristide was forced into exile in Venezuela. Many of his supporters, to the extent that they survived, also fled abroad. The Organization of American States imposed an embargo against Haiti.

The coup against Aristide was led by the mulatto General Raoul Cédras, whom Aristide himself had promoted to chief of staff. Haiti was now led by another drug-running dictatorship, sustained by money and propaganda from the CIA and using weapons from U.S. arsenals and instructors from U.S. agencies. The gangs these instructors trained were called *attachés*. Behind them stood the bloodstained paramilitary organization known as "the Front for the Advancement and Progress of Haiti (FRAPH)." Notable in the mix was a lack of toleration for the exiled Aristide on the part of both the Bush and Clinton administrations.

The U.S. government clearly saw Aristide as another of those dangerous radicals likely to disturb U.S. interests, however microscopic. Disinformation, disseminated by both private-interest groups and the U.S. state, worked to keep Cédras in, and Aristide out, of power. "Three months ago," Wilentz wrote in August 1994, "a U.S. Embassy cable claimed that human rights organizations were working with the Aristide government to exaggerate human rights abuses." It appeared that U.S. policy-makers were less concerned with restoring democracy than with regaining a more concrete stability. According to Wilentz, "participatory democracy" had become "too volatile, too dangerous, too unpredictable (all of these traits were attributed to Aristide in last year's CIA disinformation campaign)."[32]

Still, the pressure on U.S. immigration policy of the Haitian boat people, whose flight from Haiti's shores had stopped while Aristide was in office, was too great to bear. After negotiations between ex-president Carter (inventor, in his political heyday, of the political remedy known as "Somocismo without Somoza") and the Cédras regime, in mid-September 1994 U.S. forces invaded Haiti. In their wake, Aristide and his followers returned to power. In October Cédras, who had been on the CIA payroll since 1986, tamely left for exile in Panama, and Aristide moved into the presidential residence.

The Americans were now back in force, 60 years after they had last departed. Their military occupation lasted until February 1996, when they were replaced by Canadian forces. In the same month, in Haiti's first-ever peaceful transition of power, a new president, René Préval, a Belgian-educated businessman, was sworn in. The food, jobs, and justice that Aristide had promised had still not arrived.

# Cuba

Thomas Jefferson said in 1817, "If we seize Cuba, we will be masters of the Caribbean." Toward the end of that century, in 1898, the United States ostensibly took Cuba's side against Spain in the Spanish-American War and destroyed what remained of the Spanish Empire in the New World. For the next 40 years Washington and New York controlled the economy as well as the politics of a Cuba that was independent in name only.

In dominating the island, the Americans had every confidence that they were doing the right thing. Leonard Wood, the first U.S. military governor of Cuba, wrote to President William McKinley: "The people here . . . know they aren't ready for self-government. We are dealing with a race which has been steadily going down for a hundred years and into which we have got to infuse new life, new principles, and new methods of doing things." U.S. Senator Henry Cabot Lodge wrote to President Theodore Roosevelt in 1906 noting a "very general" disgust among Americans regarding the Cubans. There was a feeling abroad, he said, that the Cubans "ought to be taken by the scruff of the neck and shaken until they behave themselves." It was obvious to him that "some peoples were less capable of self-government than others."[33]

Roosevelt apparently agreed with those sentiments. The need for order led to U.S. support for dictators. The problem of dictators, that is, of *caudillismo*, had plagued the Latin American republics for a century and undoubtedly existed independently of the United States. Nonetheless, the solution to the question of order was not made easier by Washington's assumption that dictatorship was a necessity, both because self-government was inappropriate for Latins and because disorder was an evil. As a result, for the first third of the century Cuba was given order by a succession of U.S.-supported *caudillos*, including the notorious General Gerardo Machado, "the donkey with claws," who held power in 1925-33. Washington also refused to recognize the reformist regime of Ramón Grau San Martín (1933-34), who stepped into power when Machado fled. This was, in part at least, because Grau advocated the nationalization of utilities, agrarian reform, an eight-hour working day, and university reform.

Yet, although Washington's dominating presence remained, U.S. politicians did recognize the need for some reforms. After the fall of Grau, Washington annulled the Platt amendment, which had been passed in 1901 to allow the United States to intervene in Cuba in the interests of order, and passed a new law that granted Cuba a 28 per cent share of the U.S. sugar market. By this time nearly three-quarters of the sugar industry was in U.S. hands. In return for allowing the Americans to ship home the sugar that their firms produced in Cuba, the Cubans accepted a preferential tariff on 400 U.S. items. Here was a recipe that discouraged the import-substitution industries that other Latin American countries were beginning to build up, and that virtually guaranteed economic non-development.

## Fulgencio Batista and the Students

In the political crisis of the mid-1930s appeared an army sergeant named Fulgencio Batista (b. 1901). Batista, a labourer's son born in Oriente province, was to stay in power from 1934 to 1944. Only after Batista had retired to his luxurious estate in Florida in 1944—taking with him a fortune accumulated in power—did the Partido Revolucionario Cubano Auténtico (known as the Auténtico Party), Grau's party, finally attain power again.

Yet, in office the Auténtico Party was unable to resist the corruption that had infested the country. Grau himself was president in 1944-48 and succeeded by Carlos Prío Socarrás, who was both inept and corrupt. By the time Socarrás took over, the body politic was on its knees. In May 1947 the mayor of Havana, admitting that he could no longer control the corruption of his city, which had become a tourist Babylon ruled over by American gangsters, killed himself.

Out of the side of the Auténtico Party was formed in 1947 the Partido del Pueblo Cubano (PPC), also known as the Ortodoxo Party. The Ortodoxo Party was founded by Eddy Chibás, son of an owner of plantations and a railway, who had been a member of the radical student organization, the Directorio Estudiantil Universitario (DEU). The DEU had been founded in the 1930s at the University of Havana in response to Machado's dictatorship. Its ideology was homespun, utopian, and dyed with the colours of Cuban nationalism. Its program called for the severance of Cuba's dependency on the U.S. market and a building of economic ties with the wider world. It advocated nationalization of key natural resources, land reform, and labour legislation. Besides a political program, the DEU had a military branch, which made bombs. One of these bombs killed the president of the Machadoist Senate, and others eliminated his henchmen. Another almost got Machado himself. Run by a committee of 40 or 50 men, the DEU was the political grammar school through which every important political leader passed.

By the early 1950s, a familiar figure had recrossed Cuba's portals. Fulgencio Batista had returned to the island in 1948 when he was elected senator. When he seized power from the hapless Prío Socarrás administration in March 1952 public protest was feeble, with Batista maintaining that he had intervened to restore order and democracy. The instrument of his power had always been the army, which he had restructured after the coup of 1934, appointing loyal collaborators to key positions. His soldiers now saw him as simultaneously leading the nation to its destiny and pushing themselves up the promotional ladder.

The students saw him differently. Abandoning the DEU, in the late 1940s they formed rival "action groups," which attacked one another and the Batista government. As it had been in the 1930s, their ideology was utopian, populist, nationalist, and democratic. Certainly, few of the student activists had any interest in communism. The comrades of the Partido

Socialista Popular (PSP), the leading communist party in Latin America, had little interest in the students, either. Doggedly obedient to Moscow since its founding in 1925, its leaders had found it profitable to be accommodating to Batista, who allowed them legality.

The postwar economy of Cuba, which was almost entirely dependent on a single crop (sugar) and a single market (the United States), went from crisis to remission to renewed crisis. In common with other Latin American countries, from the early 1940s Cuba had benefited by wartime demand, which was followed by a postwar slump and, in response to world events, booms in the early and mid-1950s. The basis of the Cuban economy had remained unchanged since the mid-1920s; the rate of economic growth had exceeded population growth (thus increasing the GNP) only once since 1946. Throughout the 1950s the island produced around five million tons of sugar. Cuba would need to double this level of production to improve the lives of the population in general.

One consequence of the failure of sugar production to increase was a growing trade deficit with the United States. From 1902 to 1945, exports to the United States had constituted 80 per cent of Cuba's total exports. By 1959 they had declined to 69 per cent. Meanwhile, imports from the United States had risen from 66 per cent of total imports in 1911-40 to 75 per cent by 1956. Obviously, Cuba had become increasingly dependent on the U.S. market for practically everything (except sugar).

Not surprisingly, given the reciprocity treaties, the extensive U.S. ownership, and the profits that were so obviously and consistently leaving the country, anti-American feelings increased. To make matters worse for the Cubans, after the Second World War U.S. investment was diverted from Cuba to other Latin American countries, such as Brazil. While U.S. postwar investments in Latin America as a whole increased by 100 per cent, in Cuba they increased by only 24 per cent. And even though the Americans still controlled 42 per cent of total sugar production, the focus of their interest was shifting. So too was the interest of the minuscule Cuban bourgeoisie, which either exported its money or spent it at home on luxury consumption. The Cuban estate owners were left with an increased share of an asset of diminishing value, and the small farmers and landless labourers found themselves with increasing problems of survival. Yet sugar remained king. In the 1950s Cuba was the world's largest producer and exporter of sugar.

## Fidel

Fidel Castro (b. 1927) had been a student leader at the University of Havana in the late 1940s. His political ideas, as expressed in the 1950s and later, were naive, nationalist, and utopian. Like Chibás, a founding member of the party, he ran as an Ortodoxo candidate in the election campaign of 1952—which was cut short by Batista's coup on March 10. The British political philosopher John Dunn noted about Castro, the student leader on his way to becoming the most exceptional political figure in Latin America in the late 20th century:

> Castro's own political apprenticeship in the corridor gunfights of the University of Havana was not such as to lay emphasis on the finer subtleties of ideological commitment. He knew very clearly what he was against: the whole seedy Cuban political order with its intimate and degrading dependence upon United States power. He knew that it would be no easy feat to destroy it and he did not in consequence take the trouble to spend much time worrying about what exactly he would attempt to create in its place, if the opportunity came. Extravagantly brave and histrionically compelling, he was the perfect leader for a hopeless armed struggle.[34]

The coup concentrated the minds of the students; rather than trying to eliminate one another they now focused on removing the dictator. Members of the youth wing of the Ortodoxo Party planned commando attacks. Students belonging to the Movimiento Nationalista Revolucionario drew up plans to assault a military base outside Havana and to arrest Batista. They were betrayed and arrested.

What was to be done? In June 1953 the Auténtico Party met with other groups in Montreal to search for solutions, but failed to come up with anything concrete. Students again took matters into their own hands. On July 26, a group of them, including Castro, attacked the second largest military installation in the country, the Moncada barracks in Santiago de Cuba in Oriente province. The attack failed—of the 111 involved, 69 were killed, though only 8 in combat. Most were tortured and shot after being captured by irate members of the garrison. Castro was among the survivors, and in October 1953 he and others were brought to trial. He was sentenced to 15 years, his brother Raúl got 13 years, and others received shorter terms. But despite the crime and the verdict, Castro's five-hour self-defence during the trial was sensational—so much so that he reworked the speech in his jail cell and had it published as a pamphlet. The title of the pamphlet came from the last four words in his delivery. "Sentence me," he had said. "I don't mind. History will absolve me." Drawing on the liberal-humanist ideas of writers from St. Thomas Aquinas to Tom

Paine, Castro spoke of the sufferings of the Cuban people under Batista's dictatorship and the inequities of "underdevelopment." There is no serious evidence in his arguments of the ideas of Marx or Lenin.

The public, no less disgusted with the repression that followed the attack on the Moncada barracks than they were with the dictatorship and the corrupt military apparatus that sustained it, had found a hero. But the supporters did not include the Cuban Communist Party, the PSP. A letter in the Party paper, *Hoy*, characterized the Moncada assault as "a Putschist attempt, a desperate form of adventurism, typical of petty bourgeois circles lacking in principles and implicated in gangsterism."[35] As things transpired, these were bitter but nevertheless edible words.

Surprisingly, after the 1953 trial Batista's image seemed to improve. The new U.S. ambassador, Arthur Gardner, an appointee of President Dwight D. Eisenhower (inaugurated in January 1953), was an unashamed supporter of the dictator. So too was Eisenhower's vice-president, Richard Nixon, who likened Batista to Abraham Lincoln. At least as compared to the last years of the Auténtico Party government, the incidence of political gangsterism seemed to be on the decrease. On top of this, at a major conference of the sugar industry in London, Cuba was allocated a sizable slice of the world market. On this basis, Batista decided to call an election for November 1954. Elated with his overwhelming victory, in May 1955 the dictator gave amnesty to Castro and other prisoners who, once out, immediately began to organize using recruits from the Ortodoxo Party. While student revolutionaries continued a terrorist campaign against the Batista regime (which frequently caught them and left their bodies in the streets), Castro travelled to the United States to raise money for an armed insurrection. On November 25, aboard a 58-foot yacht, the Granma, 80 armed men set sail from Mexico. Aboard was Fidel, his brother Raúl, and an Argentinean doctor, Ernesto "Che" Guevara. Although their landing was a disaster and many of them were killed, enough survived to form guerrilla units in the Sierra Maestra of Oriente province. The Cuban revolution had begun.

The scale of the attacks was small because the guerrillas were few in number. Even after the handful of survivors had been joined by others, the total numbers in each of the main bands in Oriente province was just over a hundred. And because of the aura of romance that surrounded the youthful guerrillas in the mountains, it is easy to overlook the important urban networks that supported them and carried out an unrelenting propaganda war against the regime. Nor were the guerrillas alone in confronting the regime. In 1957, for instance, students attacked the presidential palace (an action ending in carnage), and there were public demonstrations by women and a general strike. Although the agricultural labourers in general played a small part in the uprisings against Batista, the support that the rebels received from the peasants in Oriente was also significant.

In February 1958, the clandestine radio station of the guerrillas, Radio Rebelde, went on the air. Increasingly disenchanted with the Batista regime, more and more Cubans tuned in and dreamed of deliverance at the hands of Castro and his guerrillas of the "26th of July Movement," as it was called. And as Cuban popular opinion shifted against the dictatorship, so too did opinion in Washington, which embargoed arms to the dictator. By mid-1958 there was a general acknowledgement of an acute political crisis gripping the country. Even the PSP and the Catholic Church began to oppose the Batista regime. Why not? In mid-May Castro stressed, "Never has the 26 July talked of socialism or of nationalizing industries." He spoke of the rights of free enterprise and of capital. Many onlookers were convinced by the rhetoric: by May 1958 a cell of M-26-7 had even been organized by the clerks in the Havana branch of the Royal Bank of Canada.

By the end of May Batista began his greatest and his last offensive against the rebels in the mountains. By this time rebellion had metasta-sized; the followers of Raúl Castro had moved from the mountains of the Sierra Maestra and established a base in the Sierra Cristal. The government offensive lasted until early August; by this time several of Batista's battalions had been destroyed and his high command was in disarray. At the end of June, Raúl Castro grabbed North American headlines when he captured ten U.S. and two Canadian citizens in a protest against support for the Batista regime.

From mid-October the rebels began their march westwards across the island. The State Department and the CIA began looking for replace-ments for Batista; they even sent an emissary to persuade him to capitu-late in favour of a caretaker government in order to keep the guerrillas out of power. But it was too late. From mid-December one large town after another fell to the insurgents. By the end of the year an estimated 90 per cent of the population supported the guerrillas, whose forces had increased to some 50,000. In the early hours of the first day of 1959 Batista, accompanied by a handful of his cronies and Meyer Lansky, a U.S. gangster resident in Havana, fled the country by yacht and private plane, taking with them around $300-400 million. Later the same morning two provincial capitals surrendered. The Argentinean doctor Che Guevara, whom Castro called "the most extraordinary of our revolutionary com-rades," entered Havana on the night of January 1-2 and Castro, now 33 years old, arrived on January 8. When the *caudillo* exited and the *Fidelistas* entered, the city exploded with joy.

## Guerrillas in Power

At first it seemed logical enough to compare Cuba with Venezuela, where another dictator, Colonel Marcos Perez Jimenez, had been toppled by democratic but non-communist insurgents. Castro was coy about his plans; certainly his professed political views were wildly eclectic. Sebastian Balfour argues that Castro and his closest followers had plans for a sweeping transformation of the island.[36] But along which lines? Certainly, there was little immediate evidence that the new regime was communist. For a honeymoon period lasting until Castro's trip to New York in April, U.S. reaction, while cautious, was not hostile. Vice-president Richard Nixon delivered the opinion that Castro was no worse than politically naive. Nixon had every reason to be cautious in his judgements. On a "goodwill" tour of Latin America's capitals in May 1958, he had been greeted almost everywhere with demonstrations against U.S. policies and in some places with riots. In Caracas, Venezuela, crowds stoned his car.

The honeymoon soon ended, as it was bound to. In the minds of the leaders of the revolution the options were limited, as Dominguez indicates: "Did Cuba's new government want a close relationship with the United States? Was this revolution committed to a Cuba open and profitable for multinational firms? Could its leaders make a genuine and radical revolution with the support of the United Fruit Company, Coca-Cola, the Chase Manhattan Bank or Standard Oil? Would Fidel Castro accept the economic austerity preached by the International Monetary Fund?"[37]

In June 1959, the new regime passed an agrarian reform law limiting the size of agricultural holdings and appropriating large landholdings. The law adversely affected both U.S. and Cuban property, though it promised compensation. Many foreign managers thought that the nationalization of U.S. property was inconceivable—or suicidal. After all, the U.S. secretary of state, John Foster Dulles, had announced, "The United States would not acquiesce in the rights of nationalization." The new policy put an end to the innocent and ambiguous phase of U.S.-Cuban relations. In July the State Department began drawing up plans to replace Castro.

Not all Cubans were keen on the reforms. The National Association of Cattlemen of Cuba, the Tobacco Growers' Association, the Bishop of Santiago, and the Auténtico Party all attacked the Castro government, five cabinet members resigned, and Provisional President Manuel Urrutia refused to sign revolutionary laws. Castro forced him out in July. Terrorism reappeared. From Florida, exiles in unmarked planes overflew Cuba dropping incendiaries. By 1960, 13 per cent of the cane fields had been set on fire.

Against a background of deteriorating relations at all levels, the

Americans began an economic blockade in October 1959. In December Castro was informed that the United States was considering a cut in Cuba's long-established—and key—sugar quota. In February, a Soviet delegation, including the First Deputy Premier Anastas Mikoyan, arrived in Havana and signed a trade agreement committing the USSR to buy sugar and provide trade credits. In the same month Cuba announced that it was moving towards national planning.

In early January 1960, the head of the CIA, Allen Dulles, presented President Eisenhower with the agency's plans for the sabotage of Cuba's sugar refineries. In March 1960 Eisenhower approved the training of exiles in Guatemala and a French ship loaded with arms and ammunition for the Castro government exploded in Havana harbour. In June and July, U.S.-owned refineries in Cuba refused to accept Soviet oil. They were nationalized, along with U.S. mines, hotels, and banks. In retaliation in July President Eisenhower cut off Cuba's sugar quota. In August Cuba nationalized all industrial and agrarian enterprises still in private hands, and by October any remaining U.S.-owned enterprises, including banks, had been nationalized. The U.S. response was a trade embargo. *"Patria o Muerte, Venceremos!"* Castro had cried at the end of a speech in March 1960: "Motherland or Death, We Shall Win!"

In November John F. Kennedy was elected president. In one of his last acts in office, on January 3, 1961, his predecessor Eisenhower had broken off diplomatic relations with Havana. By this time relations between Moscow and Havana were flourishing. Castro had even embraced the squat Soviet premier, Nikita Khrushchev, not just in public, but in public in New York. As early as July 1960, Khrushchev had spoken of Soviet missiles defending the Cuban revolution.

Kennedy's rival in the presidential elections, Nixon, had strongly identified himself with the anti-communist witch hunts of the early 1950s. To offset Nixon's claims, Kennedy had sought to establish himself as a reliable chief of the "Free World Colossus." He could thus afford to be no less hard-line on Cuba than Nixon. Advised by the same team of brilliant technocrats who were about to lead the United States into the tar pit of Vietnam, Kennedy opted to destroy the Cuban Revolution by supporting an invasion of the country by what two decades later would be called "contras." Specifically, these were the mainly white and affluent Cubans who had fled the island in the early period of the revolution and were now assembled around Miami. "Operation Mongoose," the largest operation the CIA had undertaken to date, was the means by which the serpent of communism was to be dispatched by its natural enemy, the Cuban middle class. The CIA head of the operation had in 1953 participated in the CIA-sponsored overthrow of the reform government of President Jacobo Arbenz of Guatemala.[38]

A central assumption of "Mongoose" was the belief that once armed liberators, obviously supported by Washington, had landed on Cuban soil, the Cuban people would rise up to throw off the shackles of communist oppression. This was a variant of the same theory that had led Castro and his comrades into the Sierra Maestra. As both Washington and, later, Che Guevara were to learn, the theory was faulty.

The invasion was launched on April 17, 1961. The invaders milled around in confusion on the Cuban beachhead, known as Playa Girón, the Bay of Pigs. The Americans refused to commit themselves to sending their own forces. The Cuban people did not rise up. The battle at the Bay of Pigs became, at once, a heroic victory for Castro and his supporters and a humiliating defeat for Washington. For although no U.S. personnel were directly involved in the landings, it was obviously a U.S. operation from start to finish. Where else had a U.S.-sponsored intervention fared so badly? The Bay of Pigs was not only a harbinger of the frustrating times that lay ahead for U.S. supremacy, but also, like the battle for Vietnam's Dien Bien Phu in 1954, a defining moment in the history of the Third World. Gabriel Kolko suggests that Washington feared Castro's neutralism as much as his Communism—that an anti-American neutralist "might galvanize far more successfully the latent nationalism of the region" and lead to a setback for U.S. leadership and influence and, worse, economic opportunity.[39]

Less than two months after the Bay of Pigs disaster, in an issue on "The Crisis in Our Hemisphere" (June 2, 1961), *Life* magazine sensationally predicted: "The climax of the struggle with Communism will come— soon." It quoted Castro: "The Andes will be converted into one vast Sierra Maestra of revolt." As if to demonstrate that politics imitates *Life*, on December 2, 1961, Castro declared himself a Marxist-Leninist. A new Cuban song echoed popular sentiment; its title: *"Cuba Sí, Yanquis No."*

There was nothing inevitable about Castro's conversion from nationalist to communist, according to Piero Gleijeses. Between the debacle at the Bay of Pigs and Castro's conversion, in July 1961, a senior Kennedy aid had met Che Guevara, by now Castro's left-hand man.

Cuba, Ché told [the aide], wanted "a modus vivendi" with the United States. "He said that they could discuss no formula that would mean giving up the type of society to which they were dedicated." But the Cubans were willing to accept limits on their foreign policy: "they could agree not to make any political alliance with the East—although this would not affect their natural sympathies." And Ché indicated very obliquely . . . that they could also discuss the activities of the Cuban revolution in other countries.

Kennedy categorically refused the olive branch. Instead he initiated
Operation Mongoose, the program of paramilitary operations, assassination
attempts and sabotage designed to wreck the Cuban economy and visit the
"terrors of the earth" on Fidel Castro. The lesson Kennedy drew from the
Bay of Pigs was not that he should talk to Castro, but that he should destroy
him.[40]

Then came another test for U.S. foreign policy: the missile crisis of October 1962. In August 1962 Washington became aware that the Soviets were
installing large-scale weapons systems in Cuban bases: first, anti-aircraft
missiles, and, second, short-range and medium-range missiles capable of
reaching the United States itself. In response, in a series of escalating
moves Washington mobilized troops and passed legislation that would vindicate U.S. intervention. The peak of the crisis came on October 22, 1962,
when President Kennedy announced that Cuba was about to be blockaded—in effect indicating that Soviet ships on their way to Cuba would be
stopped at sea.

For a few days the world seemed locked into a moment of gripping
international crisis; it appeared that if neither Washington nor Moscow
backed down there could be nuclear war. The U.S. Joint Chiefs of Staff
recommended an air strike on Cuba no later than October 30. But the
Soviets backed down; on October 28, they offered to cease construction of
missile bases in return for a U.S. pledge to honour Cuban integrity.
Remarkably, Washington willingly gave this pledge. The existence of Cuba
as a socialist state was thus guaranteed, or at least for as long as the USSR
existed. But what kind of socialist state was being created?

## Lider Maximo

Here is the paradox: freed from U.S. domination, Cuba became tied to the
Soviet Union; relieved of *caudillos*, Cuba came under the dictatorship of a
single leader, the *lider maximo*. And although from the 19th century
Cubans had fought for liberty, the most successful of these fighters, having
attained power, increasingly withheld it from his people. Yet, as Susan Eva
Eckstein takes pains to point out, in the three following decades Cuban
social, political, economic, and foreign policies, although continuously
dominated by a single regime (one headed by the former leaders of the
guerrilla army), were anything but constant. They shifted several times
from the early 1960s to the early 1990s as the regime moved forwards and
backwards in response to the pressures and protests of the Cuban people
and the exigencies of the external world.[41]

From the time of their defeat of the insurgents at the Bay of Pigs,

Cuba's rulers, while committed to the idea of "a rapid transition to communism," seemed inventive and pragmatic. Their detractors characterized this as "romanticism." Indeed, in October 1967, when Che Guevara was murdered in Bolivia where he had been attempting to establish a guerrilla base, W.W. Rostow rejoiced that he was the last of the romantic revolutionaries. But if some Americans regarded Che as a romantic, some Bolivians saw him as a saint. In the village of La Higuera in Peru, he is known as "San Ernesto de La Higuera," a protector of travellers and a guardian of women in childbirth.[42]

In a way Rostow may have been right. After Che's death, and especially after a huge failure of the sugar harvest in 1970, there was a decisive transformation in which the revolution, increasingly under the influence of Moscow, took a conservative and bureaucratic turn. This epoch was known as the "retreat to socialism." As in Mexico, revolution had become institutionalized; but worse, it had become totalitarian, at least in the sense that the *lider maximo* came to saturate the political scene, harassing and incarcerating all rivals to the right and left. As a result of dissidence being criminalized, most of Cuba's leading writers were forced to live in exile. Afro-Cubans who argued that there was still a racial problem in Cuba also became exiles.

In response to demands for more democracy in Cuba, and after organizing Cubans around a concept of *guerra popular* in the aftermath of Washington's invasion of Grenada in 1983, Castro argued, "We don't just have the vote, we have the weapons in the hands of the people. Can a people who have weapons in their hands be enslaved? . . . Can a policy be imposed upon a people who have weapons in their hands? And how can such a miracle be possible unless there's a total identification between the people and the nation, between the people and the Revolution?"[43]

Before this, in the 1960s, having nationalized most of Cuba's land, the revolutionary government decided that it would increase sugar exports as a means of financing industrial development. Throughout the 1960s sugar accounted for around 85 per cent of Cuba's exports, only slightly down from a level of 89.2 per cent in 1950. By the end of the decade, it was hoped that hitherto unattained levels of sugar might be harvested—10 million tons was the target. This effort failed, and by the mid-1970s it had become evident that the industrialization that sugar was supposed to have financed had also failed. In 1989, with sugar exports at 73.2 per cent, Cuba was still almost as dependent on sugar as it had been in 1950. The only difference now was that its markets were in the Soviet Union and Eastern Europe.

## Debt

Throughout most of the 1960s the Western commercial and diplomatic boycott of Cuba remained nearly complete. By the early 1970s, though, the boycott had relaxed and Cuba came out of quarantine. This change of heart was occasioned by the desperate search for borrowers on the part of the banks that had taken in petrodollar deposits after the increase of oil prices in late 1973. At the same time, the Cuban regime desperately needed to borrow to pay its bills. Castro and his comrades had every reason to believe that money borrowed could be repaid: in the mid-1970s sugar prices were high and the Cuban economy entered a period of unprecedented growth, estimated at 14 per cent annually between 1971 and 1975, the highest in Latin America.[44]

In the late 1970s sugar prices fell, and by the mid-1980s exports to Western countries had also slumped. Markets, like those of the European Economic Community (EEC), which produced beet sugar, had become more protective while others had turned increasingly to synthetic sweeteners. Nevertheless, the bankers who had loaned Havana money in the mid-1970s demanded interest payments. These payments (especially to Japan, Spain, France, and Canada) represented about 45 per cent of the value of exports to the West. By 1976, when Cuba's growth rate dropped to 4 per cent, a new Economic Management and Planning system had been introduced; by 1986 this system was deemed to have failed. Discouragement was widespread.

Perhaps nothing better indicated the increasing loss of faith in the capacity of the revolution to deliver material improvements than the emigration to Miami of more than 100,000 Cubans in 1980. Richard Bourne suggests that this exodus came as a huge shock to Fidel Castro, who assumed that most Cubans were, by and large, satisfied with the gains of the revolution.[45] Later in the decade there was further proof that the rot of decline had become widespread; several highly placed officials were arrested while others fled the country. Janette Habel writes of the late 1980s: "Waste and muddle in the management of the collectivized means of production had worsened, and social inequalities had grown. To this crisis of bureaucratic management were added the imbalances caused by the fall of raw material prices, as well as the effects of debt on an economy characterized by a structural trade deficit. The dependence of the Cuban economy on foreign trade is marked by a high level of imported goods, while Cuban products for export are limited."[46]

By 1992 Cuba was in the midst of the worst crisis since the revolution had taken place. According to Andrew Zimbalist, as recently as 1987-88, 84.2 per cent of Cuban imports had come from the Soviet Union and Eastern Europe.[47] Then came the collapse of the Communist regimes. Cuban imports from the Soviet Union alone fell by over 30 per cent in 1990 and dropped further in 1991. In 1989-91, Cuba lost $4 billion worth of imports from the Communist countries of Eastern Europe. Cuban sugar exports to the former Eastern bloc dropped from 469,000 to 55,000 tons. The dissolution of the Soviet Union at the end of 1991 ended the preferential pricing for Cuban sugar. By the early 1990s the price of raw sugar on the world market had dropped, and President Bush tightened the U.S. embargo on trade with the island. The policies of President Clinton did not diverge from those of his predecessor: at the U.S.-Russian summit in Vancouver in summer 1993, Clinton insisted on the Soviet cessation of oil deliveries to Cuba as a precondition to U.S. aid.[48] The leadership of a resurrected and non-Communist Russia showed no inclination to subsidize the continued existence of socialism in Cuba. "All told," writes Eckstein, "the Cubans assessed the cost of the collapse of Soviet-bloc relations at $5.7 billion in 1992. They lost 70 per cent of their purchasing power in three years."[49] Other European countries took a hard line on Cuban politics, as Eckstein points out:

> While opposed to Washington's interference in their own trade dealings . . . the aid ministry of the newly unified Germany announced that his country would send no aid to Cuba until Castro initiated political reforms. And the newly elected conservative government in Sweden cut off aid to Cuba. The Spanish socialist government even cut direct economic assistance from $2.5 million to $500,000; it denied Spanish exporter and investor requests for a credit line and credit guarantees. . . . In 1992, Cuba was the only Latin American country to receive no EEC aid.[50]

Cuba could only continue to cope by remaining flexible and stoic. While the citizens tightened their belts and got used to standing in long queues for food and other necessary goods, the government began encouraging foreign investment in nearly all sectors and undertook a wide range of marketlike reforms. Foreign ownership, which had stood at zero in the 1970s, crept up to over 50 per cent in some cases. The main new attraction for foreign investors was tourism, a sector with earnings that went from $200 million in 1989 to $700 million in 1993. Other hard currency-producing investment includes mineral and oil production and hard-currency clothing stores. The marketing of sex returned to Havana, although hardly at the 1950s level or even at that of most Western cities in the 1990s. At the same time, sugar production continued to plummet. While the dream of the 1960s was a 10-million-ton harvest, the reality of 1993 was 4.2 million tons. The main reason for this was the wretched price of sugar in relation to other commodities; in the early 1960s a ton of sugar had purchased 7.5 tons of oil; 30 years later it purchased 1.4 tons.[51]

## Cuba and the Third World

Cuba's commitment to the liberation and independence of the Third World came within three years of the fall of the Batista regime. In January 1962 the first Cuban arms shipment was sent to the guerrillas of the Front de Libération National (FLN) fighting against the French in Algeria. Some six months earlier the Cubans had recognized Algeria's exiled provisional government. Cuban military and medical missions continued as long as President Ben Bella was in power in Algeria. When he was overthrown, there was a brief lull and then good relations were continued.

Algeria was the avenue down which arms and military advisers passed to assist insurgencies in a number of African countries in the 1960s. These included Guinea-Bissau, under Portuguese rule until the mid-1970s, and Zaire, which was being torn apart by indigenous cliques each seeking to establish its own domination over the country's rich economy. Guerrillas trained in Algeria had infiltrated into Argentina in the spring of 1963 and began armed struggle early in 1964. Arms were also sent to guerrillas in Venezuela. A decade later, in 1973, when Jamaican Prime Minister Michael Manley was solidifying links with the Third World, Castro accompanied him to Algeria.

From 1966, when it founded the Asia-Africa-Latin America Peoples' Solidarity Organization (OSPAAL), until the 1990s, the Cuban leadership remained unwaveringly and conspicuously committed to what Fidel Castro has called "our Third World." In 1979 Cuba was chosen to host the Sixth Conference of the Non-Aligned Movement, and by the end of that decade as many as 35 countries were receiving Cuban military and economic aid. As late as 1987 in Moscow Castro stressed this commitment, making the point that if there were to be "peaceful co-existence" it must take place as part of "the struggle against the inequalities of development and the poverty which kills as many children in the Third World as a hundred nuclear bombs each year."[52] After that, although the question of murderous inequalities did not go away, the question of "peaceful co-existence" was narrowed to its essentials—relations with Washington.

Cuba's commitment took two main forms: involvement with other Third World states, especially in Africa, the Caribbean, and Latin America, and solidarity, in the form of political or diplomatic support, economic aid, and military reinforcement, with "anti-imperialist" struggles. This commitment was recognized even by those, like President Miguel de la Madrid of Mexico, whose record has not shown him to be entirely committed to greater independence from the West. "For Latin America, you represent the impassioned defence of our people's freedom and right to self-determination," de la Madrid said to Castro when he presented him with the Aztec Eagle Order in 1988.[53]

Throughout the 1960s Cuba's involvement with other Third World countries was limited because Cuba was ostracized by the members of the Organization of American States (OAS). After 1975—coincidentally the year that Prime Minister Manley visited Havana—global hostility towards the Cuban regime began to subside. Increasingly the Latin American states granted Cuba diplomatic recognition, and Cuba was allowed to join SELA, the Latin American trade organization. Even international bankers found good relations with the island an attractive proposition.

By the late 1970s, continuing the practice that had begun with medical aid to Algeria and in the mid-1970s had been extended to Jamaica, Havana was providing high levels of foreign aid in the form of doctors, technicians, and teachers to countries as far away as Vietnam and as close as Nicaragua. As many as 50,000 foreign students at a time were maintained in Cuba. Yet some instances of Cuba's military involvement called into question Cuba's "anti-imperialist" commitment. This was the case of Cuba's willingness to send troops to support the *derg*, the Ethiopian military dictatorship, whose murderous power rested on the possession of Soviet arms and whose main preoccupation, apart from domestic repression, was in defeating the genuine liberation groups within Ethiopia (the Eritreans and Tigrenians, in particular). Assisting the *derg* had nothing in common with the struggle against Western imperialism and everything to do with Soviet Cold War aims. And what words, other than "quixotic" and "opportunistic," can be used to describe Cuba's willingness to send troops in support of the incompetent but murderous dictators of Argentina, to fight the British over the Malvinas?

Much less equivocal was Cuba's willingness to send soldiers and airmen to fight the South Africans in Angola, a fight Cuba remained engaged in for a dozen years, until 1989, and which both forced Pretoria to withdraw from Namibia and helped to discredit the Botha regime (see chapter 5). The same willingness, in the face of consistent and serious threats from the United States, characterized Cuba's support for El Salvador's Farabundo Martí National Liberation Front (FMLN).

Piero Gleijeses, whose access to Cuban archives in Havana allowed him to trace the beginnings of Cuba's first venture into Africa in 1962, has convincingly argued that there is no evidence of Cuba being merely a Third World pawn of the Soviet superpower.[54] Cuba's "assistance to Algeria reflects a level of idealism that is unusual in the foreign affairs of great and small powers and that has continued to be part of Cuban policy towards Africa." Indeed, the Cubans did not follow the Soviet lead; for the most part they were in the vanguard.

## A Balance Sheet

The bottom line in assessing the success or failure of a Third World regime has to be not abstract "development" or statistical "growth," and certainly not its exportability as a "model" or its demonstrations of "solidarity" with other ostensibly revolutionary regimes. Why not consider the wealth of the poorest in tandem with industrial production? Janette Habel's comparative research shows substantial gains made in the lives of most Cubans:

> Between 1960 and 1980, the income of the poorest sections of the population of Brazil rose from $197 to $401 . . . while in Peru . . . it fell from $232 in 1961 to $197 in 1979. In Cuba on the other hand, the income of this same section of the population went up fivefold: from $182 in 1960 to $865 in 1982. . . . Finally, in spite of the crisis, industrial production . . . which represented 32 per cent of the material production in 1960, reached 46 per cent in 1981; in Latin America during the same period, it went from 32 per cent to 35 per cent, and in Brazil from 35 per cent to 36 per cent.[55]

The widely acknowledged improvements to the lives of most Cubans might, in themselves, explain the persistence of the Communist regime despite the boycott and blockade of the Western countries. Balfour argues for an additional reason:

> There is still no sign that the regime is under any serious internal threat. Its resilience cannot be explained away simply by fear, superstition or state repression, nor indeed by Castro's statesmanship. . . . The survival of the Castro regime thus far is due above all to the continued strength of nationalism in Cuba, which owes much of its force to the implacable hostility of the US government. It is a far richer vein than the oil reserves which foreign companies are exploring off the Cuban coast and on which the regime is pinning many of its hopes.[56]

# Summary

Jamaica, Haiti, and Cuba all had sugar, plantations, and slaves of African origin in common. In Jamaica and Haiti, after the abolition of slavery these slaves formed an overwhelming part of the population. In Cuba they formed a large minority.

In the period after 1945, the political histories of the three islands diverged radically. Jamaica became independent and relatively stable; unlike Haiti in the late 18th century or Cuba in the 19th and again in the late 20th century, it never had a revolution. Its overriding problems were simple—a relatively small size, a lack of capital and resources, and a dependency on foreign interests that controlled both the markets and the prices for its products. It also had no control over oil prices, so that when bauxite prices declined and oil prices rose the country fell into a debt trap. Indebtedness led to further poverty and dependency.

Two parties ruled independent Jamaica alternately, a right-centre JLP and a left-centre PNP; these followed different recipes for national independence and economic development. Neither managed either to shake the hold of the local oligarchy, which was committed to its own continued domination within a system of political and financial dependency upon the mainland, or to find new avenues to national prosperity. By the middle of the 1990s the Jamaican economy and society were continuing to flounder.

Compared to Haiti, however, Jamaica may seem like heaven with a few local problems. Contemporary Haitian history has been dominated by political monsters, most conspicuously Papa Doc and his son Baby Doc. Alongside them existed a whole apparatus of lesser devils, politicians of the utmost veniality, Tontons Macoutes, a security apparatus addicted to arbitrary terror, a religious hierarchy of unshakeable complacency, and an oligarchy of relentless greediness. All have ruled together in the interests of themselves and, usually, with the support of Washington. The change in this bleak situation came with the rise of the priest Father Jean-Bertrand Aristide at the head of a movement seeking reform. Both the oligarchy and Washington tried to keep Aristide and his followers out of power. Their main purpose in this was the maintenance of Haiti as a secure asylum in which the inmates would have little choice but to compete for work at wage rates among the lowest in the world. Only the frequent attempts at escape by the incarcerated forced a change that allowed Father Aristide to return from exile. Yet even this was hedged around restrictions allowing him to remain as president for only a single term.

Haiti, whose governments throughout the postwar period were viewed with an indulgent serenity by Washington and its Western allies, and whose oppositions were disparaged and undermined, surely provides a singular lesson. In the high places in the West where foreign-policy decisions are made, extreme levels of stagnation and starvation are tolerable over almost unthinkable periods of time. On the basis of the Haitian experience comes a chilling message: the rhetoric of human rights and Third World developmentalism notwithstanding, there is no bottom to the indifference of the rich countries towards even their most proximate neighbours, unless, of course, its citizens threaten to wash up on the shores of the mainland.

Until the mid-1950s Cuba was little more than an offshore Central American republic ruled through a local dictator with the blessings of the U.S. embassy on behalf of local investors and with the conspicuous support of the Communist Party. The Cuban Revolution, which ushered in the regime of Fidel Castro in the first hours of 1959, changed all this. Here was a seizure of power spearheaded by a handful of relatively elderly students possessed of both an eclectic arsenal and an eclectic nationalist ideology. The first limited nationalizations were aimed not so much towards the end of turning Cuba into a people's republic, but more towards the purpose of diminishing inequality, breaking the power of the old oligarchy, and, of course, guaranteeing national independence. After the briefest of honeymoons—less than 100 days—Washington decided that this direction could not be allowed to proceed. U.S. policy-makers then, through a series of calamitous miscalculations, pushed the Cuban regime into the arms of Moscow. For the following 30 years Cuba remained a socialist republic, economically tied to Moscow. Cuban citizens were able to enjoy both security and a relatively high standard of living and a sense of their own purposefulness within the Third World. The absence of any form of democracy was the price they paid for these gains. For those who remembered the Batista regime, a time when both democracy and security were lacking, and for those who knew of the conditions endured by the majority in other Caribbean and Latin American states, this was, perhaps, a sacrifice willingly made.

The Cuban revolution had its successes. In 1960, as measured in pupil/teacher ratios in primary education, Cuba stood thirteenth among Latin American countries. In 1988, it stood first. In population per physician, Cuba stood third in 1960 and second in 1984. In daily per capita caloric supply Cuba stood sixth in 1961-65 and third in 1988-89. In life expectancy Cuba stood third in 1950-55, and first in 1990. In infant mortality (deaths per 1,000 live births in the first year of life), Cuba had the best record in Latin America in 1945-49 and in 1990. Solutions to a difficult housing situation were less successful.[57] But with the evaporation of the Soviet bloc, Cuba's main trading partner and source of subsidies—and with crippling debt made more grave by the intensified U.S. blockade, even the benefits of the revolution began to unravel.

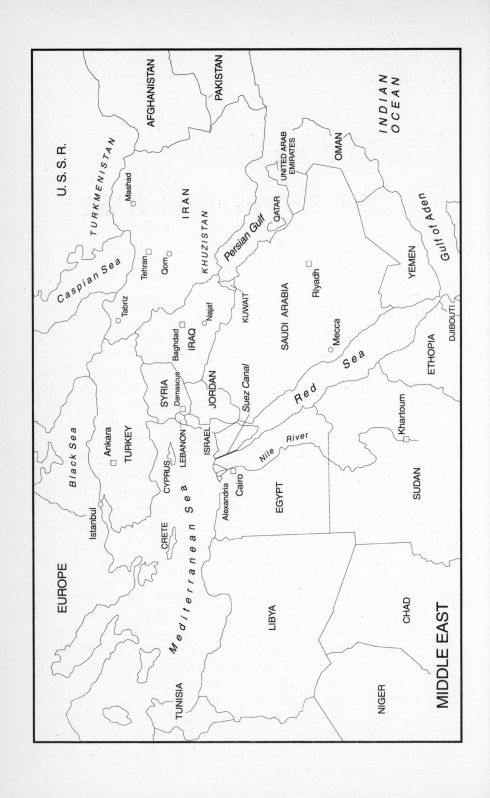

MIDDLE EAST

# Chapter 4

# The Middle East: Turkey, Egypt, and Iran

## Background

By 1945 the Middle East comprised mainly independent states, although the sovereignty of many of these countries was recent and incomplete. In the years after World War I, while Turkey and Iran had retained their autonomy and Egypt was released from a British grip, most of the Arab Middle East was divided into quasi-colonial territories known as "mandates." These mandates—Syria, Lebanon, Palestine, Transjordan, and most briefly of all, Iraq—were carved out of Arab lands that had been ruled for 400 years by the Ottomans, a Turkish dynasty. In 1920 the League of Nations gave over the territories in trust to the supervision of Britain and France—the idea of trust being like that of adoption. According to the public statements of the Western statesmen who dominated the League, Britain and France were rescuing the Arabs from their discredited Ottoman rulers. The idea was that London and Paris were entrusted to supervise the Arabs until they became politically experienced and mature enough to establish governments of their own.

Some of the mandates—Transjordan is perhaps the best example—had no reason to exist other than the convenience of Western statesmen, but despite this artificiality most of them became independent states between 1932 and 1948. The boundaries created by the League of Nations remained, for the most part, permanently fixed. When the British abandoned Palestine in 1948, Jewish settlers promptly turned the land into the state of Israel.

At the end of World War II, in spite of the disappearance of the mandates, the British managed to preserve their influence in the Middle East by means of local politicians who allowed them to hold onto their military bases, which, the British argued, were necessary to defend the region against communism. The Iraqis and Egyptians, for the most part finding this rationale unconvincing, forced the British to abandon these last footholds in their countries between 1949 and 1954. This brought to an end any substantial control of the Middle East by Europeans, although faded fragments of British power in the region fluttered on until 1971 when London finally ended its protective relationship with the Gulf states.

But the British withdrawal from the region overlapped with the installation of the Americans. The U.S. intrusion began in 1947 with the enunciation of the Truman Doctrine, which declared that the United States would "support free peoples who are resisting attempted subjugation by armed minorities or by outside pressures." Such countries would receive U.S. military and economic aid. The doctrine was used to establish a U.S. presence in Greece and Turkey (as well as justify sending troops to Korea). The intrusion continued with the founding of the settler colony of Israel as a U.S. ally-cum-client in 1948, and stretched even further with the enhancement of the U.S. military and economic role in the region, first in Saudi Arabia during World War II and later in Iran with the overthrow of the nationalist regime in 1953.

From the end of World War II the three largest states in the Middle East—Turkey, Egypt, and Iran—all followed different paths, but each of these paths, at least until 1979, led in the general direction of the West. Turkey was the most immovably pro-Western. Egypt was a problem, because the changes and growth its leaders sought led them to pursue a course of populist and often radical nationalism sustained by Soviet arms and policies of dirigisme and protectionism. Iran was the most mercurial of all: it shifted from populist nationalism in the early 1950s to pro-American developmentalism in the 1960s and 1970s, followed by a militant, cleric-dominated, anti-imperialism by the 1980s—and moving finally, by the mid-1990s, haltingly back into the waiting arms of U.S. capitalism.

# The Modernization of Turkey

Defeated in World War I—in which it sided with the Central Powers—in 1923 the Ottoman Empire was legislated out of existence. On its original Anatolian foundations the modern republic called "Turkey" was constructed.* Prominent among its political architects were senior army

---

* While the majority of the people of Turkey are Turks, that is, Turkish-speaking Sunni Muslims, Turkey is also the home of three million Kurds (about 20 per cent of the population) as well as other, smaller, minorities. The Turkish Kurds are part of a larger, contiguous, Kurdish population numbering at least 10 million whose other members live in Iraq and Iran. Long referred to as "a marriage of east and west," Turkey has a small part of its area, called Thrace, in Europe and a larger part, called Anatolia, in Asia.

officers trained according to Western military techniques. A half-century later theorists of political modernization were to draw on their experiment as one of the models for the modernization of the Third World.

The emergent Turkish state in the 1920s and 1930s was simultaneously modernist, secular, and authoritarian. In the sense that it overthrew the political, social, gender, and religious orders of the Ottomans, it was also revolutionary. Unlike the great revolutions of the 18th century in North America, France, and Saint Domingue, the Turkish revolution came not from below but, like the 19th-century revolutions of Latin America, from above. It has been argued that revolutions from above—those of Prussia, Japan, and Latin America, for instance—are predisposed to dictatorship, and Turkey was no exception.

From its inception the newly constructed Turkish state was dominated by a nationalist general, Mustafa Kemal (1881-1938), who became its first president. Assisting in his heroic, nation-building task was an intelligentsia trained in the final decades of Ottoman rule. Kemal and the elite that surrounded him organized the move of Turkey's new capital to Ankara in the centre of the country, abandoning the Ottoman imperial city of Istanbul (built on the continent of Europe). Ankara became a symbol of modernization for reformers throughout the whole of the Middle East.

Mustafa Kemal's one-man rule radiated through the country by means of a single party, the Republican People's Party (RPP). In a limited respect the RPP was like the PRI in Mexico: not really a party in the Western European or North American sense so much as a coalition of interests that formed a permanent ruling institution. But Turkey, unlike Mexico or even Egypt, had no powerful landed or commercial bourgeoisie: "The new population of republican Turkey, contained, in its overwhelming majority, a fairly homogeneous peasantry, provincial merchants, and a small urban petite bourgeoisie."[1]

From 1923 to 1950 the RPP monopolized political power. In those years Turkey was what has been called "a single-party state"—an oxymoron, because in normal usage political parties, like social classes, can only exist in relation to one another. The party's ideology, called "Kemalism," had six official planks: republicanism, nationalism, populism, statism, secularism, and reformism. Kemalism, in sum, was modernization speaking Turkish. A seventh unofficial plank was "developmentalism," which, at least in its Import Substitution Industrialization (ISI) form, came late. It did not emerge in Turkey until the 1960s.

Mustafa Kemal, who became celebrated in official propaganda by the name Ataturk ("father of the Turks"), died in November 1938, having accomplished in his lifetime the creation of the most Westernized, secular, and statist country in the Middle East, indeed in the whole "Orient." Like some of the leaders of Latin America, wooed by the fascism of Italy without ever becoming wholly fascist in all the trappings, Kemal and his followers sought to guarantee a stable future for Turkey through a marriage similar to the one Brazilians had commemorated on their flag—"Order and Progress." Yet two words were conspicuously absent from the proclamations of Turkey's political leaders: "democracy" and "class." In the absence of "democratic" the developmentalists of the 1950s and 1960s pressed other words into service to describe the Ataturk era: "progressive," "reformist," and "modernizing."[2] But Feroz Ahmad describes Ataturk's Turkey as a "police state," and as far as class is concerned, Atila Eralp writes: "The belief in an integrated, classless nation fused on the basis of national identity marks the ideological position of the bureaucratic elite since the inception of the republic."[3]

During World War II, recalling the disastrous consequences of being allied with the wrong side during World War I, Turkey remained neutral until February 1945, when it declared war on Germany and Japan. By early 1947 Ankara had totally abandoned its neutrality and leaped into the arms of Washington. The new U.S.-Turkey relationship was the central pillar of the Truman Doctrine, which was ostensibly proclaimed to keep the northeast Mediterranean and the "Northern Tier" of the Middle East free from communism. According to the terms of the agreement, in return for economic and military aid, the Turks would serve as sentinels patrolling the strategic frontier where the Middle East met the Soviet Union.

Turkey's conversion to the cause of the United States and its allies was unswerving during the following decades. Although nationalists themselves, the Turks became models of anti-nationalism and anti-communism. Their enthusiasm for the West was tireless and often a little exhibitionist. In 1950 Turkey's rulers supported the British in their attempts to maintain control of Iranian oilfields, and Turkish troops joined UN forces in the crusade against communism in Korea. In 1952 Turkey joined NATO as the only Third World country ever to become a member of this Western anticommunist military alliance: the price it paid was the recognition of Israel. To cap resolute fidelity to Western purposes, in November 1955 Ankara volunteered itself for membership in the U.S.-sponsored Baghdad Pact, a defensive alliance that in 1959 became the Central Treaty Organization (CENTO). This military and economic subservience to the West and its unwavering anti-communism won the hearts and minds of the developmentalists. They saw in Turkey, as they were also to see in Pakistan, the possibility of a staunchly Western East guided by modern leaders.

From the time of the Truman Doctrine, U.S. arms and loans flowed into Turkey in substantial quantities. Between 1947 and 1991, the U.S. government spent $9 billion on military aid to Turkey alone. But there were no free lunches. The cost of Turkey's pro-Western military modernization remained high, especially because any money paid for arms tended to be money lost for investment.

## Elections: 1950

The year 1950 saw Turkey's first multiparty elections and marked the beginning of the contemporary period of Turkish political history. In these elections the Kemalist Republican People's Party's adversary was the breakaway Democratic Party (DP), founded by a group of eminent members of the RPP who joined together to oppose the RPP's proposed land reform program. The election turned out to be a disaster for the RPP. After 1950 its members were to see the DP and its successors (the Justice Party, 1961-81, and the True Path Party and the Motherland Party in the 1980s and 1990s) remain in power for most of the remaining years of the century. According to Caglar Keyder: "By any measure the Democratic Party's accession to power in 1950 constituted a fundamental break in Turkish history."[4]

In economic terms the 1950 election represented, as Keyder puts it, "the transition from capitalism under bureaucratic tutelage to capitalism based much more solidly on market mechanisms."[5] In other words, political power shifted from the state bureaucracy towards the bourgeoisie. Still, compared to the advanced capitalist countries of the West, the Turkish bourgeoisie remained relatively weak and the bureaucracy, and especially the military, relatively powerful.

The DP, headed by Adnan Menderes (1899-1961), was a party of modernizing businessmen and property owners. Its leaders promised to turn their country into a "little America" within a decade. The means of achieving this goal were largely authoritarian: they continued the repressive policies of their predecessors, imposing press censorship, purging those in the universities and civil service who opposed them, and outlawing the rival RPP altogether in 1954. Political life for urban Turks in the mid-1950s would have seemed familiar to Argentineans, with at least one major difference, the role of religion. From the early 1950s the DP began to relax the official attitude towards Islam. Some of its leaders argued that religion was an individual right and no real threat to the secular state, and others maintained that religion was a glue necessary to social cohesion.

In the year of the DP victory, Turkey was still an agricultural country that had witnessed only moderate urbanization. Some four out of five Turks still worked in the fields. Istanbul, the grand capital of the Ottomans and still the commercial centre of the country, was smaller than it had been at the beginning of the century. Economic growth had been gradual, but hardly impressive.

These conditions changed rapidly. Carried along by a boom stimulated by the Korean War and European economic recovery, the Turkish economy of the early 1950s took giant steps forward. Cereal production, for instance, was 85 per cent higher in 1953 than in 1950, and the number of tractors, which farmers generally purchased on credit from the state, increased from 14,000 in 1950 to 44,000 in 1956. Villages in the interior of the country, hitherto cut off from the outside world, became connected to large towns and cities by a network of new roads. People and produce moved along those roads from the countryside into the towns. Between 1950 and 1960 the population of the four largest cities increased by 75 per cent, while between 1950 and 1980 Turkey's population increased from 20 million to 48 million. Agriculture became increasingly commercialized. Keyder stresses the tumultuous changes that characterized this period: "In Turkey, as in most peripheral countries, the scale of the change was devastating, especially since in terms of ideology, official and popular alike, stability and order had previously been considered the foundation stones of the society. Within a few years developmentalism and unbridled market freedom replaced such traditional values."[6] Not only was peasant life irreversibly transformed, but most of Turkey's leading capitalists also had their beginnings in the 1950s. By 1985 only 51 per cent of the Turkish labour force was employed in agriculture; this compared to 36 per cent in Egypt.[7]

As early as 1954, the boom stimulated by the Korean War began to slow down, and by the end of the decade the Turkish economy was in serious straits. Non-food imports had come to exceed exports by a wide margin. Menderes was forced to print more money and to turn to Turkey's richest benefactor, Washington. U.S. loans and military aid were not enough: foreign aid took the place of foreign investment. This aid was used to finance a program of Import Substitution Industrialization, which had been embarked upon in the early 1950s at the behest of Turkish entrepreneurs who wanted import restrictions in order to deal with the challenge of foreign imports. Through the process of protecting merchants against foreign rivals, Eralp notes, "Merchants were smoothly transformed into industrialists."[8]

## Coup: 1960

By the late 1950s, Menderes, once regarded as a folk hero, was being held to blame for the economic slowdown—even though, in the decade of his rule, the basis of the Turkish economy had changed substantially.

The Menderes regime was brought down by a military coup in May 27, 1960. At the forefront of this coup were junior officers, whose numbers had risen in the postwar period of military growth but whose salaries had stagnated. Highly nationalistic, they complained that democratic politics had led to corruption. The junior officers, banding together with their seniors to form a junta called the National Unity Committee (NUC), had few plans for the future although they spouted a populist and anti-capitalist rhetoric. Some of the senior officers had ties with right-wing sects. Their ideology, which stressed Turkish chauvinism, religious intolerance, and "traditional values," would also have been familiar to Latin Americans between the 1930s and the 1970s. While many of the junior officers wanted to hold on to power, the senior officers were determined to return to civilian rule, though not before cleansing the political system. To teach a lesson to all politicians and to reinforce the idea that the military was the guardian of the Kemalist state, they hanged Menderes and jailed a number of his leading supporters. They also interdicted the Democratic Party.

In reaction to the widespread discontent over Menderes's corrupt and heavy-handed rule, the NUC created a constitutional commission, which in turn recommended the establishment of democratic institutions and guarantees to form the basis of a new state. The conditions, remarkably liberal, included the expansion of civil rights, greater autonomy for the universities, and freedom to organize political and other associations. In spite of an increased role for the military, the reforms were widely applauded as a new beginning for Turkey's Second Republic.

The overthrow of Menderes had, however, created the precedent of military interventionism, and the first years of this Second Republic saw two more attempted military coups. Indeed, the 1961 Constitution institutionalized this by establishing a National Security Council (NSC), which included the heads of the armed forces and was given the right to advise the cabinet on matters concerning national security. The professional officer corps of the military was now a vested interest; its pay, amenities, and economic influence continued to grow throughout the decade. Its influence in the economy was guaranteed by OYAK, the Army Mutual Assistance Association, into which officers were obliged to contribute 10 per cent of their salaries. By the end of the 1960s, OYAK had become a major investment fund, with interests in automobiles (it owned 42 per cent of OYAK-Renault), tires, petrochemicals, and canning. In the 1970s and 1980s

OYAK moved into hotels and tourism. As Ahmad points out, the army's high command had now become committed to the system without being attached to any particular party.[9] The party leaders sought the support of the generals, rather than vice versa, and the generals were inherently hostile to groups such as the Workers' Party (WP), which wanted to modify the system of capitalist relations of which the military officers were now secure beneficiaries.

The 1960 coup established an economic regime that would last for the next two decades. This regime was dirigiste or "statist" in that it not only accepted the management of the economy by the state but also acknowledged that one of the state's main functions was the redistribution of wealth. The centrepiece of the new regime was an ISI program introduced through a 1963 five-year plan, which was opposed both by powerful rural landowners hostile to labour reforms and by private industrial capital, which did not want to see state industries reformed to make them more efficient. Despite this opposition, the plan went ahead.

In the second half of the 1960s the Turkish economy grew at a rate of close to 7 per cent. This growth was in part a consequence of Turkey's associate membership in the European Economic Community (EEC), which allowed Turkish workers to emigrate to Western Europe, where they were welcomed into the bottom level of the workforce. The remittances of these workers became important to the Turkish balance of trade. The integration of Turkish labour into the economy of Germany led to a change in dependency; Turkey now began to swing away from Washington towards Bonn.

From 1961 until 1965 the reconstituted and now legal RPP and the Justice Party, a centre-right formation in which the DP had been resurrected, governed in coalition. In October 1965 elections the JP won a majority under a new leader, Suleyman Demirel (b. 1924), an engineer who had worked in the United States as well as Turkey. The RPP, partly in reaction, moved to the left; its leaders became critical of Turkey's subservience to U.S. foreign policy interests and especially criticized the presence of U.S. and NATO bases and installations, which were scattered throughout the country. Further to the left, radical and political trade unionism crystallized in the form of the Workers' Party. The JP began to move closer to Islamic groups, establishing intimate, and lasting, connections with many of their leaders. Some among these were Saudi-financed. It also extended Islamic education throughout the secondary school system and set up higher Islamic schools in Istanbul and Konya.

The recruits to the Islamic organizations were often the casualties of the 1960s miracle of economic growth—that is, the victims of development. As the cases of Egypt and Iran show, these people were not the last to be recruited by the Islamists from the ranks of the dispossessed.

When Turkey had entered into an association with the EEC, its market had been swamped by Western goods, causing immense distress to small producers, artisans, and businessmen, all of whom had together formed the backbone of the JP. The policies of ISI led to similar consequences: the marginalization and disappearance of small owners and producers who became the victims of large-scale, and in some cases transnational, capital. These groups deserted Demirel, who, they believed, had sold them out. By the early 1970s they found their home in the right-wing and Islamist National Salvation Party (NSP), which attempted to offer protection against large foreign capital through state-financed projects and a weakening of relations with the EEC. The founder of the NSP, Necmettin Erbakan, regularly attacked Demirel for being pro-American and charged that Turkey's move to join the EEC was "'a product of a new crusader mentality,' because such a step would merely perpetuate Turkey's role as an economic underling of Western-Christian capitalism."[10] From the late 1960s, struggles between the militant and secular left and the increasingly powerful Islamist right produced spiralling urban violence. To make matters worse, the 1960s also witnessed the renaissance of Kurdish nationalism, which was to remain an undiminished problem for the rest of the century.

## Coup: 1971

On March 12, 1971, against a backdrop of political strife and Kurdish secessionism, and with Demirel ruling with only a paper-thin majority, the military moved in for the second time. Overthrowing the popular guarantees of the 1961 constitution, the military leaders banned, arrested, and incarcerated workers and intellectuals under the system of martial law. In July the Workers' Party was banned. In this, the second of what became known as "veto coups," state terror was used systematically. Again the similarities between Turkey and states of Latin America were apparent.

The politicians returned to take charge of the country in 1973, and a year later the RPP won the elections. The new prime minister, Bulent Ecevit (b. 1925), the leader of the radical faction of his party, expelled the landlords from the RPP and won peasant votes by supporting small producers against the large landowners, who were often linked to multinational corporations. Ecevit also took Turkey back into the Middle East by increasing co-operation with regional regimes, including Libya. Turkey recognized the Palestine Liberation Organization (PLO) and sided with the Arabs in the 1973 Arab-Israeli war. Ecevit enhanced his popularity as a patriot by ordering Turkish troops into northern Cyprus in 1974, ostensibly to protect the Turkish minority there from chauvinist elements within the Greek-Cypriot majority.

This invasion had several major consequences. First, it divided Cyprus into two parts, a Turkish north, which had been economically stagnant since the flight of its Greek population from their homes, and a prosperous Greek south. Second, the EEC boycotted Turkey. With the fall of the dictatorships in Spain and Portugal, the Europeans had become sensitive about democracy on their frontiers. Thirdly, partly as a result of this boycott, Turkey was driven to adopt a more Third Worldist line in foreign policy.

The most telling economic effect of the European boycott was that Turkey became unable to borrow money except from private institutions in the short term and at inflated interest levels. As well, further Turkish emigration to Western Europe was restricted, which blocked the flow of remissions and led to an increase of unemployment in Turkey. And during a period when the U.S. government was reducing aid to its foreign allies, borrowing became the only answer: between 1973 and 1980 the Turkish external debt increased from $3.25 billion to $16.25 billion.[11]

In late 1974 Ecevit resigned, and in the midst of crisis the government remained paralysed for nearly a year, until Demirel was able to put together a right-wing coalition government. From 1975 until the end of the decade, unstable political coalitions led by Demirel ruled a country not just polarized between left and right, and between Turk and Kurd, but also experiencing deepening economic difficulties. Violence was endemic, generally but not exclusively organized by the right-wing Islamist National Action Party, a partner in the coalition governments. The other source of violence was a guerrilla war launched by Kurdish separatists in the eastern provinces. By 1980 this uprising was costing 20 lives a day.

In September 1980, inspired by the revolution in Iran and the declaration there of an "Islamic Republic" in March, the National Salvation Party (NSP) held a massive rally. A return to Arabic script in religious texts and the veiling of women were already on its program, and its supporters were now demanding a return to Islamic law. Even more provocatively, the crowd at the rally refused to sing the national anthem. One of the fastest-growing parties on the right was thus openly repudiating secularism, a main plank of the Kemalist state. Anti-Westernism had become popular not only among the Muslim reformers but also among a wide range of parties from the left to the right.

## Coup: 1980

A third coup came on September 12, 1980. According to Ahmad, "The reason for the generals' intervention was their apprehension and their sense of urgency regarding Turkey's instability now that she had suddenly become strategically important to the West following the revolution in Iran."[12]

In the minds of Turkey's Western allies, perhaps the domestic crisis alone would have justified military intervention. In any case, the "loss" of Iran to the West, the declaration of an anti-Western Islamic Republic, the deterioration of stability in Lebanon, and the Soviet invasion of Afghanistan at the end of 1979 all provided the generals with an ironclad alibi for intervention. The generals' importance, not just to Turkey but to the entire Middle East political order, had been underlined by a Turkish-U.S. defence agreement signed on March 29, 1980. The Turkish invasion of Cyprus was now forgotten, and once again, as in the heyday of the Cold War, Ankara was linked to Washington; Turkey's contract as a policeman in the Middle East was renewed. U.S. funds now began to flow back into the country. Military aid increased from $125 million in 1978 to $500 million by the end of the decade.[13] The Saudis, too, proved to be generous to the new order. They saw Turkey as a bulwark of conservative Sunni Islam against Iran's explosive Shi'ism.

Initially the generals enjoyed a considerable amount of popular support. They had, after all, put a cap on the street battles between the different political factions. Slowly, over the three years in which they ruled the country, thanks also to the loans accompanying a Structural Adjustment Program designed by the IMF and World Bank, the economic situation improved. The price demanded by the economic stabilization plan was, as elsewhere, devaluation and restructuring; that is, the partial dismantling of the state and, ultimately, the neglect of the national market in favour of export promotion. Roger Owen suggests that by the 1980s the economy had more or less completed the ISI phase and was ready for its successor, export-based development.[14] In the early 1980s more of Turkey's products began to find markets in other Middle East states while economic ties with EEC countries decreased. Greater economic involvement with the region was accompanied by increased political involvement as well, and the ruling party began attempting to reconcile Islamist values with the Western practices that had long had a hold in the country. The government also addressed political matters. According to Ahmad: "The liberal constitution of 1961 was replaced by an authoritarian one based on the [French] constitution of 1958, the trade union movement was smashed, the universities were purged and centralized, the press was muzzled, the parties were dissolved and many former politicians banned from politics. The [army] High Command's aim was nothing short of eliminating politics from the system."[15]

With a certain change in the country's economic and political course thus guaranteed, political practice could be resurrected. In the elections of 1983 Turgut Ozal (1927-93) became prime minister at the head of the newly formed centre-right Motherland Party (Anavatan Partisi, or Anap), a second-generation descendant of the DP. Many of the leading lights of the Motherland Party had been recruited from the far-right National Action Party, some of whose militants had served in death squads that had murdered trade unionists, students, and leftists. Like Ozal himself, even though the ANAP was regarded by some as "the party of America," many of its members were associated with the Nakshibandi Sufi religious brotherhoods.[16] These organizations had been proscribed by law in the 1920s but nevertheless gained increasing numbers of recruits in the 1980s.

Ozal was the right man for the times. He had worked for the World Bank, and as president of Turkey's State Planning Commission he had introduced and then managed the program of economic restructuring designed by the Bank. During the period of military rule he had overseen the destruction of three of Turkey's four largest trade unions. He was also the first major Turkish politician to openly court the Islamic constituency: his pilgrimage to Mecca in July 1988 was but one element in this strategy.

The Motherland Party, strongly backed by Washington even when the Europeans complained of the suppression of human rights (and especially the Ozal regime's use of torture), dominated politics for the rest of the decade, winning elections again in 1987. Among the reasons for its appeal was the success of Turkey's exports on world markets and the inflow of foreign capital. The export success was closely tied to a lowering of wages by almost 50 per cent, which was a corollary of the suspension of collective bargaining rights, which had in turn come with the destruction of the trade unions and the rise of unemployment. Low-cost Turkish manufactured goods were now able to be sent off into the Middle East market, which had become all the more lucrative with the boom in oil prices and the expansion of markets following the Iranian Revolution (1979-80) and the outbreak of the Iran-Iraq war in 1980. Foreign capital flooded in for the same reasons that it entered Mexico under the presidency of Salinas— these included the selling off of public assets and the high interest rates paid for loans. The upshot of this combination of cheaper labour, increased exports (which grew from $2.3 billion in 1979 to $13.6 billion in 1991), and more loans (external debt increased from $25.5 billion in 1985 to $49

billion in 1990) was a growth rate of nearly 5 per cent. As long as the
growing debt was discounted, the country's economic gains seemed
remarkable. At least Turkey's rising U.S.-educated professionals, who
increasingly found themselves benefiting from key roles in the economy,
thought so.

Ozal's influence was based not just on his efforts to oversee Turkey's
remarkable growth rate, but also on his manipulation of almost limitless
patronage. Here again the case bore a strong resemblance to the workings
of Mexico's Salinas. Ozal played the religious card by incorporating
Islamist elements within his government. By doing so, he violated one of
the main canons of Kemalism, which prescribed that the state should
oversee secular education. The payoff for Ozal was that his party now controlled the religious vote.

Ozal's popularity was further enhanced by his demonstrable ability to
keep the military in government but out of politics. In July 1987 he exhib-
ited this talent by rejecting the high command's candidate for the office of
chief of staff. This was an indication not so much of the actual exclusion of
the military but its further integration into the economic structure
through establishing a military-economic complex.

Although Ozal's explicit motto had been "first the economy, then
democracy," the sacrifice of the latter did not ensure the success of the
former. By the end of the 1980s, political assassinations were still occur-
ring in the main cities, and the Kurdish insurrection had not gone away. In
1994 alone the military campaign against the Kurds cost $7 million.
Although an improved balance of payments situation lent credibility to
Ozal's economic policies, problems remained, especially high inflation and
unemployment. Income disparities became further exaggerated. As in
Latin America, the rich got richer but even a part of the middle class got
poorer. Ozal wisely decided that it was time to consolidate his gains, and
in October 1989, a few months after a wave of strikes had crashed against
his government, he had himself transformed into the President of Turkey,
an office normally reserved for a senior military man. His successor as
prime minister was a nobody, who quickly disappeared after the next
election.

The 1991 Gulf War gave Ozal a final opportunity to show his gratitude
to his Western allies. As well, because U.S. military assistance to Turkey
had dropped off in 1986, it was necessary to deliver some kind of reminder
that fidelity had its price. While the generals of the National Security
Council balked, Ozal demanded full support for the U.S.-led effort. The
Turks joined in the embargo of Baghdad with enthusiasm, while between 5
per cent and 10 per cent of the air strikes against Iraq were launched from

Turkish bases. But the war did not enhance the popularity of the Motherland Party. In the elections of October 20, 1991, the party fell to second
place behind a rival centre-right coalition, the True Path Party (TPP),
another descendant of the DP.* This coalition signalled the rise of Tansu
Ciller (b. 1946), the first female political leader in a Middle Eastern country (though not the first in a Muslim country). Her support came from the
liberal elements within the DP and JP. Sencer Ayata suggests: "They
hoped that the previous rural, provincial, and conservative image of the
[True Path] party would be replaced by an urban, liberal, and Western one
with the election of a modern, American-educated, female professor of
economics to the leadership of the party in power."[17]

By this time many Western onlookers, viewing with alarm the tri-
umphs of Islamic reformism (or "fundamentalism," as it became known in
the West) in both Iran and Algeria, had rehabilitated the domino theory
(which had worked so badly for them during the Cold War) and issued
earnest warnings that Turkey might retrogress into the dark night of anti-
Western religiosity. Their fears were not without cause: in March 1994
municipal elections the Refah, or Islamic Welfare Party (WP), got 19 per
cent of all votes nationwide. Ciller moved rapidly back to a more conventional centre-right position and began to strike alliances with religious
leaders.

The Welfare Party was a descendant of the National Salvation Party
(NSP), founded in 1972 and represented in parliament since 1973. Dissolved by the military after the 1980 coup, the NSP was reincarnated as
the WP in 1983. By the 1990s it had become the largest and best-
organized party in the country, with a strong grassroots movement and an
effective organization. In his analysis of politicized Islam in Turkey, Ayata
writes:

> The highly motivated, well-disciplined, and strongly committed activists
> believe in their political course as a mission ordained by God. They function
> at the community level, visiting every single quarter, street, and cluster of
> houses in the cities, gathering information about each voter and family sepa-
> rately, evaluating the data, and finding solutions for each problem. To pene-
> trate small communities, the young activists, including an army of women
> who can arrange home visits at any time of the day, have emerged as the
> party's major assets.[18]

---

* The Kemalite RPP had moved progressively leftwards since the 1970s, becoming, in 1985,
  the Social Democratic People's Party and then, once again, the Republican People's Party,
  in which form it won 49 seats in December 1995 elections.

Haldun Gulap provides a similar, if more generalized, analysis of the rise of the Welfare Party:

> *Refah*'s ascendance grows out of the crisis of mainstream politics in Turkey, a crisis manifest in an almost daily eruption of corruption scandals, in the protracted economic crisis, and not least in the ongoing military conflict between the Turkish government and the Kurdistan Workers Party (PKK). At a deeper level, *Refah*'s rise reflects a crisis of Turkey's ruling ideology [Kemalism]. . . . *Refah* challenges the basic pro-West orientation which this ideology directs and which currently represents the status-quo. *Refah* leaders have repeatedly, and apparently persuasively, made the point that "there are not several parties in Turkey; there are only two; *Refah* and all the others who unite in aping the West."[19]

Refah, Gulap points out, is not some mutant and atavistic strain of Islam returned from the past to haunt the future. It is the product of developmentalism, of the integration of Turkey into the world economy. Refah, like other Islamic reformist parties, "originates from the failure of the nationalist promises and social progress." By the 1980s, Gulap adds, "Turkey's development gap was still unclosed; its self-identity remained unsolved; and the dismantling of the protectionist welfare state by the Motherland Party had begun. The promises of statism, nationalism and developmentalism had failed."[20] The Islamist movement was able to build on the failure of that model.

In the elections of December 1995 Refah won the largest number of seats in parliament, 158 out of a total of 550. True Path won 135 and Motherland 115. Ciller, supported by coalition partners, remained as prime minister. On January 1, 1996, Turkey took another step westwards, entering the European Union's customs zone. The EU governments tactfully avoided the question of Turkey's appalling human rights record. According to Ertugrul Kurkcu: "During the centre-left coalition between 1991-1995, Turkey's human rights record hit bottom, with 2,000 extrajudicial executions and daily reports of torture during custody."[21] Membership in the union, the EU leaders told themselves, would ensure that Turkey would continue to move in a westward direction. Six months later, Necmettin Erbakan, a German-educated engineer at the head of the Welfare Party, became prime minister in a coalition government with the True Path Party. One of the planks of the True Path platform was the promotion of integration, not with the EU but with neighbouring Islamist states.*

---

* As Sami Zubaida points out, there is nothing surprising about Erbakan being an engineer: "Mainstream modern political Islam, whether promoted by the Muslim Brotherhood in the

# Egypt: Nasser's Developmental Nationalism, and After

Egypt emerged from World War II ruled by a king and occupied by a foreign power. By virtue of a treaty signed in 1936, the British had been conceded the right to maintain substantial garrisons in Cairo and Alexandria and to control a large amount of territory along the western bank of the Suez Canal. This military enclave, over which the Egyptians had no control, was known as the "Canal Zone." The existence of massive British forces in Egypt meant that the British ambassador in Cairo was on a par with the Egyptian king in political importance. The Egyptian bourgeoisie—landowners, merchants, and manufacturers—remained on the outside of this enclosure, watchful for opportunities to make their way inside.

During the war the Egyptian bourgeoisie had become consolidated and confident. The Depression of the 1930s had stimulated local manufacturing and guaranteed the emergence of an economy that was more complex and sophisticated than existed anywhere else in the Middle East. The Egyptian manufacturing bourgeoisie, like that in the larger states of Latin America, supported ISI.

The Egyptian king, Faruq, the largest landowner in the country, used the British as a counterweight against the major nationalist party, the Wafd. Although Faruq, by manipulating smaller political parties, kept the Wafd from power for years at a time, it was the only party with a well-oiled apparatus and strong grassroots organization. This political triptych—the king, the British, and the nationalist party—was destroyed by a military coup on July 23, 1952. The July coup, fomented by a group of young nationalists who called themselves the "Free Officers," was supported by what Caglar Keyder and Ayse Oncu call the "new middle class," a broad band of urbanized bureaucrats and technocrats, often only one generation removed from the countryside, who were themselves triply antagonistic: towards the bourgeoisie that had organized itself around the Wafd as well as towards the king and the British.[22]

After seizing power the Free Officers immediately deposed the king, catching the British completely caught off guard, though not the Americans. Officials in the U.S. embassy in Cairo were aware that a coup was in

---

Arab World, by Iranian revolutionaries, or by the main Islamist trends in Turkey, has explicitly accepted the science and technology of the West (while rejecting its cultural values) and implicitly adopted modern models of the state as centralized [and] bureaucratized. . . . Indeed, in Egypt and elsewhere, the ranks of the Islamists are dominated by engineers, technicians and medical professionals. This is also true for a good part of the Turkish Muslim intelligentsia." See Zubaida, "Turkish Islam and National Identity," 1996, p.14.

store. Several of the Free Officers had studied in the United States and held discussions with U.S. representatives (especially the CIA) in the months leading up to the coup. They did not feel the hostility towards the Americans as they did towards the British. Although the Free Officers may have been anti-colonial, they were not anti-American.

At first the newly installed military regime was headed by General Muhammad Neguib, an avuncular pro-Western figure. But Neguib served as a figurehead only until 1954, when he, in turn, was ushered out, replaced by the leader of the Free Officers, Colonel Gamal Abdul Nasser (1918-70). Major Anwar Sadat was one of Nasser's lieutenants in the new ruling junta, which called itself the "Revolutionary Command Council" (RCC).

The social origins of the new ruling group were distinctive; none of its members were from the old ruling class, known as the *pashas*. Their grandfathers had been peasants; they themselves were largely from the middle class or petit bourgeoisie. The military academy, open to them only in the 1930s, was the ladder to their social success. Nasser was among the first of his background to enter the academy. As young officers, Nasser and his comrades had been confronted by the fact of British military occupation (especially during World War II) and the powerlessness and corruption of their senior officers in the face of it. They blamed the loss of the 1948 war with Israel on this corruption. Although the members of the Revolutionary Command Council were Muslims, the RCC's ideas were secular, bourgeois, and technocratic—an updated variant of Mustafa Kemal's approach. The Nasserite junta was supported by a state-employed middle class together with the commercial petit bourgeoisie and the working class.

The coup and the birth of the RCC marked a decisive point in both Egyptian and Middle Eastern politics. On the first birthday of the coup, the new rulers banned the monarchy, and King Faruq, who had yachted off to exile to end his days corpulently in Capri, was to have no successor. Along with him went the political power of the *pashas*, the dominant class of landowners and lawyers who had controlled Egyptian politics since the birth of the Wafd Party at the end of World War I. The Wafd was also outlawed: together with the removal of the king, the party's banning seemed to mark the demise of the oligarchy.

The regime also banned the politico-religious organization known as the Muslim Brotherhood (Ikhwan al-Muslimin). The Ikhwan had emerged in the 1920s in the shadow of the British occupation and, despite regular persecution, had remained irrepressible, the main mass movement in the country. But the RCC was willing to go further than merely outlawing its opponents. Because one faction of the Ikhwan preached violence against the new regime, the RCC resolved to extirpate it; it hanged a number of its adherents, among them Sayyid Qutb, its leading intellectual light and the lodestar of Islamic revivalism in the contemporary Middle East. The regime was no more tolerant of threats from communists. One of its very first acts was to send several communist leaders to trial for sedition and to hang one of them. In the Nasserite prison camps, communists therefore rubbed shoulders with their opposites, the Islamic revivalists. The state also came down hard on independent feminist activities, annulling the Egyptian Feminist Union, which had been created in 1923, a year after Egypt had gained independence.

In August 1954, under pressure from both the new regime and the U.S. government, the British finally agreed to withdraw their 40,000 troops from the west bank of the Suez Canal, the Canal Zone, to which they had retreated when they were forced to evacuate Cairo and Alexandria after World War II. The consequences of this move were profound. First of all, the evacuation brought to a close the long chapter of European imperialism in the Middle East, which had opened in Napoleon's time. The French, Germans, Italians, and finally the British had all come and gone. Although the French were to remain in the Maghreb for a few more years, and the British were to retain a vestigial presence in the Gulf until the early 1970s, in essence the old empires of the Middle East were dead.*

A second consequence was that the United States became, briefly, the only major foreign power in the region. The U.S. government had become increasingly intolerant of the geriatric colonialism of its British allies and increasingly enthusiastic about its own prospects for dominating the oil resources of the Middle East. Already the leading Western power in Saudi Arabia by the end of the war, the United States had confirmed its position through building special relationships with Turkey in 1947, Israel in 1948, and Iran after the shah had been secured in power in a 1953 coup. A third consequence was that a wide range of Arab leaders, especially those espousing republican, secular, and developmental nationalism, turned to Cairo and Colonel Nasser for inspiration.

A final consequence was that the Israelis became even more deeply anxious about their neighbours. Israel had been at war with Egypt since 1948 and contending with Egyptian guerrillas since 1954. The removal of

---

* The Maghreb was the area to the west of Egypt including Libya, Tunisia, Algeria, and Morocco. In the 19th century the French had established protectorates over Tunisia and Morocco and had incorporated Algeria into France itself. Libya was colonized by the Italians from 1912 until the Italian defeat in World War II. The Algerian war of independence lasted from 1954 until 1962.

the British from the Canal Zone in 1954 ended the existence of a buffer between the two countries, and the Israelis, fearing attack by the Egyptians, became more concerned about providing themselves with advanced arms. Their purchase from France of supersonic aircraft in 1955 launched the contemporary arms race in the region.

At the head of Nasser's agenda was the restoration of Egypt to the role of the leading power, politically and culturally, in a reborn Middle East. In this brave new Arab world there would be room for no rival "isms"—not colonialism, Zionism, communism, the "fundamentalism" of the Muslim Brotherhood, the "feudalism" of Nasser's conservative enemies, or, even, feminism. Nasser was thus taking on all comers: the capitalist world, the communist world, and elements of the Arab world. The key to his success, such as it was, would be in his attempts to deal with these powers consecutively rather than simultaneously.

After Nasser came to power in 1953, the U.S. government promised him arms and development aid. Previously, by agreement with France and the United States, Britain had held a monopoly in supplying arms to the Egyptians and, as a result, the Egyptian armed forces were appallingly equipped. The Egyptian air force still flew the same kind of aircraft and the army still drove the same kind of tanks used in World War II. This was particularly galling to nationalist officers who saw the military infrastructure as a key part of national development. Yet, despite the promises, U.S. arms did not materialize: the West had, in effect, imposed an arms embargo on Egypt in order to protect the existence of the Israeli state.

Although he had misgivings about communism, Nasser saw that the only way to break out of the arms embargo was to negotiate with the Soviet Union, and in June 1955 he began talks with the Soviet foreign minister. This was Moscow's golden opportunity to breach the "Iron Curtain" that the West had built around the Soviet Union and its allies. The Soviet Union duly promised the Egyptians a deluge of arms of all types, including the most modern Soviet jet fighters. The West was aghast. In July 1956, in a blundering retaliation to this arms deal, the U.S. government unilaterally withdrew its financial support for the construction of a newer and larger Aswan Dam, which was to have been the grandest Western-backed development project in the whole of the postwar Third World. The dam was supposed to provide the water to irrigate tens of thousands of acres of land and provide electricity for industrialization. Without arms and a new dam, Egypt would remain insecure and dependent. Certainly there would be no hope of a renascent Cairo rising on the banks of the Nile to become the capital of a new, modern Middle East.

In what was the most audacious move in his career, Nasser struck back. The Suez Canal system (locks, docks, wharves, pilot boats, administrative offices) was owned and operated by the Suez Canal Company, a private firm with its head office in Paris. The canal had never been merely a waterway; from its 1869 opening in the heyday of empire it was regarded as a key strategic link with Asia. In the strategic jargon of the 1980s, it was a "choke point." It was also, like the companies that controlled oil production in Iran and Iraq, a symbol of Western dominance.

In the week after the withdrawal of the loan for the Aswan Dam, Egyptian troops occupied the local offices and facilities of the Suez Canal Company. On July 26 Nasser announced that the canal had become national property. Egyptians rejoiced in the action. Crowds chanted, "Long Live Nasser, Lord and Saviour of the Arabs." The British and French ground their teeth. Anthony Eden, the British prime minister, was particularly furious: Nasser and his fellow officers had helped destroy British credibility as a regional and world power. For the French, the Free Officers had not only seized the property of a French company but had also supported the Front de Libération National (FLN), the nationalist guerrillas in Algeria, by offering its leaders sanctuary and giving them air time on the Cairo radio program *Voice of the Arabs*, to which the Algerians listened attentively.

The Israelis, British, and French, assuming that the Soviet Union would not be willing to intervene and that the U.S. government would be acquiescent, invaded Egypt in the period October 29 to November 5, 1956. The Israelis attacked by land across the Sinai peninsula, moving towards the canal. The British and French flew bombers and paratroops from Cyprus (still a British colony) and dropped them onto the Canal Zone. The Egyptians were caught with their webbing down. Their forces offered only a token resistance, but they were able to effectively block the canal by scuttling ships in it—the measure that the British in particular feared most.

After hearing of the invasion, the U.S. government dropped a bomb of its own. The Eisenhower administration roundly and unequivocally condemned the invaders and insisted on a withdrawal. So too did the Soviets, somewhat relieved by the Western invasion because it took attention away from their own invasion of Hungary on November 4 and rendered any kind of joint NATO action there impossible. To make matters worse, the Saudis embargoed oil exports to France, and Arab saboteurs closed off Kuwait's oil export system. A run on the British pound started, with the value of sterling dropping and the cost of British exports shooting up as a consequence. The British suspected, quite reasonably, that this was the U.S. way of punishing them. Their armed forces were compelled to withdraw, and British Prime Minister Eden resigned. The French felt betrayed by both the Americans and the British. The Anglo-French-Israeli invasion was a miscalculation of heroic proportions. "Suez" would go down between "Dien Bien Phu" and "Bay of Pigs" on the granite memorials dedicated to Western neocolonial folly.

## Nasserism

Nasserism—with its high points lodged in the 1956 events—was an ideology that was secular, developmentalist, and socially and politically radical, in that it envisaged the redistribution of wealth downwards. It was also anti-communist and supported by the new middle class and the working class.

In spite of its anti-communism, Nasserism was a threat to U.S. regional interests. Washington's response to the Nasserism that it had helped bring into the world took the form of the Eisenhower Doctrine, launched just a few months after the defeat of the old West at Suez. The Eisenhower Doctrine offered economic and military aid to countries ostensibly threatened by communism; but because communism was hardly a serious threat in the Middle East and Maghreb—there were almost no Soviet fleets and bases in the region, while there was a U.S., British, and French military presence—the doctrine was intended as a defence against economic nationalism. That is, it was a defence against any attempt to remove any part of the Middle East from the hold of the increasingly U.S.-dominated "world market."

Among the Arab leaders two main alignments had emerged, one pro-Western (which had come to mean "pro-American") and the other nationalist. The young King Hussein of Jordan, Nuri al-Sa'id of Iraq, and the rulers of Lebanon were all pro-Western and welcomed the Eisenhower Doctrine. All of these, with justification, feared the growth of not only Egyptian influence but also nationalist radicalism. Still, many politically literate people in the Middle East saw the Eisenhower Doctrine for what it was: an attempt to perpetuate U.S. domination under the pretence of defending the area from the designs of Moscow.

Nowhere was this more the case than in Syria. In August 1957, the Ba'ath government in Damascus, which was, like that of Cairo, nationalist and secular, announced that it had discovered a U.S. plot. At the same time Turkish troops suspected of acting in the interests of Washington appeared to be massing on Syria's frontiers. The communists and their sympathizers in the Syrian government suggested that the best defence of Syria's sovereignty was merger with the much stronger Egypt. The ruling Ba'ath party was forced to follow this advice in order to preserve the governing coalition. The Ba'athis intended to play a leading role in the new Syrian-Egyptian coalition, a coalition that might become the basis of a reborn Arab Middle East.

The "United Arab Republic," the product of this exceptional merger, was born in February 1958. Within a few months, however, the Syrians began to suspect that they had made a horrible mistake. Nasser's pan-Arabism, it seemed, did not extend as far as considering the national susceptibilities of other Arabs. He gave the Ba'athis only a small number of seats in the new united party, the "National Union." New economic arrangements allowed for the free importation of Egyptian goods into Syria, but maintained Egyptian protectionism. Other Egyptian reforms that struck against Syrian businesses were no more palatable. Perhaps most horrifying was the descent upon Syria's capital, Damascus, of vast numbers of Egyptian bureaucrats.

In September 1961, the three-year-old United Arab Republic was liquidated. It had come as close to the dream of Arab unity as any two states were ever to come prior to the unification of the two Yemens in 1979. The fiction of unity was, nevertheless, kept alive by Egypt's preservation of the name "United Arab Republic" in reference to itself.

Nasser's policies in Egypt were more durable. His "Charter of National Action" of 1962 radically transformed the place of women in the country. By asserting that women were equal to men, the charter put women in a position to run for political office and fill jobs from which they had been previously excluded. Women now entered the universities in larger numbers and, there and in the workplace, increasingly cast off their veils in favour of Western dress. But there were limits to this gender engineering. Nasser kept clear of family law and avoided matters concerning polygamy and divorce. The administration thus created an opening for the few, but left the many still imprisoned.

Nasser had disparaged any system that did not guarantee social justice and an equitable distribution of wealth. So after nationalizing the Suez Canal Company, the regime sequestered a wide range of properties that had belonged to the British and the French in Egypt. These nationalizations, which led to a considerable expansion of Egypt's economic patrimony, strengthened the hand of the left within the government and led to the increased adoption of the term "socialism" to describe the Nasserite regime. The term gained increased currency with the expansion of Soviet economic aid from 1957 and the "Socialist Decrees" of 1961, by which the Egyptian state, according to Alan Richards and John Waterbury, "took over most large-scale industry, all banking, insurance, and foreign trade, all utilities, marine transport, and airlines and many hotels and department stores."[23] The centrepiece of this socialist developmentalism was the high dam at Aswan, part of a more wide-reaching five-year plan launched in 1957. As Richards and Waterbury point out: "The First Five-Year Plan embodied a straightforward ISI strategy, combining aspects of the easy (textiles, sugar, automobile assembly, pharmaceuticals) and hard (heavy engineering, steel, chemicals, and fertilizers) phases. It generated 1 million new jobs and growth rates of 6 percent per annum."[24]

Essential to the popularity of the Nasserite approach to economic development was a land reform program, which both increased the amount of land that could be cultivated through the building of the Aswan Dam and broke up the properties of Egypt's wealthy agrarian proprietors. In stages the government limited land ownership, cut peasant mortgages, and extended the period of payment for redistributed land, while at the same time encouraging co-operatives and promising irrigation and access to fertilizers and pesticides. Thus was the old class of *pashas* finally killed off, politically and socially if not corporeally. The effects of these reforms were palpable; average life expectancy rose as changes in income distribution and public health and education spread. The state sector expanded, with the bureaucracy growing from 350,000 employees in 1952 to 1.2 million in 1970. (Exporting bureaucrats to Damascus was thus a solution to a problem of oversupply in Cairo.) Within another decade the bureaucracy would almost double.

In 1962 Nasser made another stab at territorial unity. North Yemen, which could claim no particular strategic or economic importance, had escaped from both the clutches of the Saudis, who ruled the Hijaz area along the Red Sea to the north, and the British, who ruled Aden to the east. Possessing only the vaguest of frontiers, North Yemen was a backwater but, by the standards of the Arabian peninsula, one with a fairly large population. The North Yemen state itself was so minimal as to be almost transparent. In the 1930s the largest ministry had comprised six officials, two of them typists.

In the years after World War II, a small opposition had risen to address this somnolent status quo. One element was centred on the Free Yemeni Party, founded in Cairo during the war. The Free Yemenis had attempted a coup in 1948 but been crushed. The survivors fled to Cairo, and their cause was taken up by the Free Officers after 1952.

In 1962 pro-Nasserite officers in North Yemen revolted against the country's ruler, the unpopular imam Muhammad al-Badr. The Saudis, whose army had been trained by the United States, intervened on the side of the imam. What followed was a "proxy war" between the Egyptians and the Saudis fought on the territory of the Yemenis, with the Yemenis supporting their imam and the republican officers and townspeople relying on the Egyptians. At one point as many as 70,000 Egyptians had entered the country—almost as many as there had been British soldiers in Egypt a decade earlier. Despite this, Egypt was seen throughout the Middle East as representing the side of progress and the Saudis as incarnating Western dependency, feudalism, and reaction. The two main contenders finally agreed to a truce in August 1965, although neither side withdrew from Yemen until after the June 1967 Middle East or "Six-Day" War. The adventure cost the Egyptians several million pounds. "We never thought it could lead to what it did," Nasser confessed dolefully.[25]

On June 5, 1967, after provocations on both sides and especially Egyptian moves to secure military agreements with the Arab allies surrounding the Jewish state, Israeli planes attacked Egypt, destroying its air force on the ground. Strikes against Jordan, Iraq, and Syria followed. Without air cover, several thousand of the Egyptian troops sent to Sinai were killed. With no Egyptian army to bar its way, after less than a week the Israeli army had reached the Suez Canal. Within a few days the Israelis also occupied East Jerusalem and the West Bank of the Jordan River—both part of Jordanian territory after the British withdrawal from Palestine in 1948—as well as the Golan Heights of Syria. Israel had inflicted a humiliating defeat on its Arab neighbours, and in six days it had trebled the land area under its control. Although much later, after the peace treaty of 1979, Egypt was to reoccupy the territory it had lost in the Sinai, Israel remained in complete control of the formerly Jordanian West Bank territories.

A day after the war began, the Arabs took up another weapon, oil. On June 6, Saudi Arabia, Kuwait, Iraq, Libya, and Algeria banned oil shipments to the United States, Britain, and, to a limited extent, West Germany. By June 8 the flow of Arab oil had been reduced by 60 per cent. For Western consumers, the crisis deepened when in the same month civil war broke out in Nigeria, another major oil producer. Yet as a weapon the embargo failed. By July supplies were back to normal, and by September the embargo had been lifted. But the idea of a producers' strike to further political ends was not lost.

No Arab leader suffered greater humiliation than Nasser, who offered his resignation as president. Only widespread demonstrations convinced him to remain in office. Still, scapegoats were needed and the army furnished them, purging 50 leading officers. Nasser then tightened his connections with the Soviet Union, replenishing the military and devoting an even larger share of the national budget to arms.

The cost of military refurbishment was an expense the Egyptian economy did not need. Even before the war with Israel Egypt was having serious economic problems. Its second five-year plan (1962-67) had to be abandoned because of a lack of financing. The war led both to a loss of the oilfields in the Israeli-occupied Sinai and a falling off of tourism. Egypt entered a period of deep recession.

U.S.-brokered peace negotiations led to an official ceasefire with Israel, but just four months later, on September 28, 1970, partly as a result of exhaustion from those talks, Nasser died of a stroke. An epitaph written by the British journalist Robert Stephens, who knew Nasser through the 1950s and 1960s, reflects an unusually sympathetic Western view of the Egyptian leader:

> Nasser remains the most progressive ruler of modern times and the most important statesman thrown up by the Arab renaissance. His role as a leader of the anti-colonial revolution, one of the great world political movements of the twentieth century, is likely to be of enduring interest to historians. . . . His influence will continue to be felt in Egypt and the Arab countries for years to come in the movement of ideas and the course of political, social and economic development which he stimulated and helped to create.[26]

Although many of his grander pan-Arab visions came to nothing, Nasser's influence on Egypt's social and economic development was significant. In 1952 the Egyptian economy was primarily agricultural, relying mainly on the export of raw cotton for its export earnings. Industry was in its infancy. While agriculture produced 40 per cent of GDP, industry contributed only 15 per cent. By 1970 the contribution of industry had risen to 23 per cent, roughly the same as that of agriculture, which had declined. This had all been accomplished through the expansion of the public sector, while the private sector remained weak and dependent. When Nasser died, this dirigiste pattern of growth had already reached its limits. As John Waterbury points out, "The economy was stagnant, the bureaucracy expanding, and vested public sector interests [had] control over resources and the flow of communications."[27]

Another problem was Egypt's growth rate. At around 4 per cent in this period, in the period of Nasser the population had grown from 20 million to around 35 million—and would reach 50 million by 1986. Greater Cairo grew from 2.2 million in 1952 to 14 million in 1986.[28]

## Turning West

Nasser's immediate successor was Anwar Sadat (1918-81), one of his fellow Free Officers. Sadat's beginnings were inauspicious; indeed, they were quite bleak. Within months of Nasser's funeral his government became the butt of criticism and the target of demonstrations, especially by students. Seen increasingly as a midget standing in the shadow of a departed giant, Sadat was forced to cast about for some means of enhancing his stature, and he proposed an attack on the Israeli forces that had occupied the eastern bank of the Suez Canal. In the eyes of his Soviet military advisers, this was a desperate gamble.

The October 1973 War was launched simultaneously on October 6 by Egypt across the Suez Canal and Syria in the Golan Heights. Known as the "Yom Kippur War" because it took place on the holiest of Jewish holidays, the war unfolded in two stages. First came the attack by Egyptian jets, followed by an artillery bombardment across the canal. Then tanks and infantry made a successful crossing: to its own surprise, the Egyptian army smashed Israeli defensive lines and took up defensive positions. Throughout the Arab world came trumpetings of celebration. Disaster followed not long after. The Israelis regrouped and, rearmed by a U.S. airlift, not only pushed the Egyptians back across the canal but chased them into Africa. The road to Cairo lay ahead, defended only by a demoralized and shattered Egyptian army. At the same time the Israelis recaptured the Golan Heights. A shocked Sadat sued for peace. Washington and Moscow, the two main outside backers of the war, acted as referees and soon helped negotiate a ceasefire between Israel, Syria, and Egypt. The Egyptians had lost 7,700 men, killed in battle; the Syrians lost 3,500 and the Israelis 2,500.

The war had unexpected global economic consequences. In a gesture of solidarity with Egypt and Syria, the Arab members of the Organization of Petroleum Exporting Countries (OPEC) announced a second boycott: they would turn off their oil taps at the rate of 5 per cent per month until the Israelis withdrew from occupied Arab territories. Even the Saudis cut off oil shipments to the United States. Oil prices quadrupled, and the Americans decided that fighting the Cold War in the Middle East was a decidedly bad idea. By September 1975 the combatants had disengaged and the U.S. government had pledged huge sums of economic and military aid to both Israel and Egypt.

Although the Egyptians had clearly lost another war with Israel, Sadat emerged with enhanced credibility. Covering himself with the glory that followed from "the crossing," as the initial Egyptian assault against Israeli defences was styled, in April 1974 he proceeded to lay before his people a new blueprint for economic development. The central premise of his plan was formulated under the heading of *al-infitah* ("the opening up"), that is, liberalization, the antithesis of economic nationalism. It was what Ozal had initiated in Turkey before the coup there, and what was tried from the late 1970s elsewhere in the Third World, from Pinochet's Chile through Habib Bourguiba's Tunisia to Deng Xiaoping's China. In one scheme of thought it was the necessary response to the failure of ISI. Sadat also put an end to the program of "pan-Arabism" and dreams of Arab unity. In place of "the United Arab Republic," the country again became "Egypt." Perhaps exhausted after years of Nasser's rallies, exhortations, and vain schemes, not to mention military disasters, most Egyptians did not seem to mind.

A key to the *infitah* policy and its liberalization was privatization, which required the dismantling of the Nasserite system of economic development (called variously "Arab Socialism" and "bureaucratic capitalism"). Socialism in the Nasserite form had failed, it was now argued. The country had to be opened up to the stimulating effects of investment from both private domestic and foreign sources. Restrictions on foreign trade were to be removed. Yet still the public sector continued to grow throughout the 1970s and 1980s. In 1952, 2.2 per cent of the population worked for the state; by the end of the Nasserite era the number had risen to 3.8 per cent of the population (1.2 million); and by 1986 the figure had increased to nearly 10 per cent of the population (4.8 million) and 35 per cent of the labour force of 13 million.[29] In the early 1980s the public sector included nearly 400 companies and employed well over a million workers.

At the same time as repudiating the ISI program of Nasserism, Sadat took steps to change Egypt's political structure. The role of the army in both provincial government and the party overall was reduced to the point that soldiers no longer dominated the Arab Socialist Union, the mass party that Nasser had created in 1962.

One more objective of this economic policy was that the money from Arab oil production—which had reached grotesque heights as a consequence of the OPEC oil embargo—would make its way into Egypt. This money was to come both from other Arab states and from the million and a half Egyptians—technicians and teachers—who had gone overseas, particularly to the oil-producing economies, to seek their fortunes. To some extent this policy was successful. Investment increased and economic growth accelerated rapidly. In the decade of *infitah*, per capita GDP rates rose to 8-9 per cent per year.

But the promise of capitalist development remained stubbornly evasive. Generally speaking, the private sector was not able to create jobs, increase investment, or promote exports. According to William Cleveland, investors "tended to put their money into the purchase or construction of apartment buildings and office towers or into tourist-related ventures such as luxury hotels. They chose these low-risk, nonproductive investments over the uncertain performance of Egyptian industry."[30] Economic development was also restrained by the dead weight of Egypt's foreign debt, mainly due to arms purchases from the Soviet Union. *Infitah* was doomed to disappoint many of those who placed their hopes in it.

On the political side, Sadat offered greater freedom to the press and political parties. He allowed three parties, one on the right, one in the centre, and one on the left. The party of the centre, ultimately called the "National Democratic Party" and led by Sadat himself, became dominant, superseding the Arab Socialist Union. Surrounding Sadat was a circle of technocrats and securocrats and a group of plutocrats grown wealthy due to the new regime known as the *"infitah* bourgeoisie."

As part of his liberalization policy, Sadat reversed the agricultural tenancy laws that gave the peasants secure tenancy at fixed rates. The move caused insecurity and impoverishment. The poorest of the peasants fled into the cities. Greater Cairo, which by the 1970s had a population approaching 12 million, became choked with the homeless and the jobless. At the same time inflation rose rapidly. In January 1977, when the government succumbed to IMF pressure to reduce food subsidies, widespread riots swept the city and the army had to be launched against the Egyptian people.

The combination of internal socio-economic factors together with external factors, particularly the defeats by Israel in 1967 and 1973, worked to stimulate the rise of Islamic reformism, which had been dormant until the end of the 1960s. Prior to 1977, Sadat had enjoyed an understanding with the Muslim groups and made concessions to them by asserting Islamic law as the main source of Egyptian law. This was mainly a matter of short-term political convenience: he saw the Islamists as a weapon to use against the nationalists and the left, that is, against the Nasserites and the socialists. This rationale had come to an end, and now, as happened in Turkey and Iran around the same time, the Muslim reformers attacked both the West and Sadat's attachment to it. Muslim reformers had always been influential among the poor—they offered them rudimentary social services—and now they also became increasingly attractive to students, who were struck by the failures of secular nationalism and the growing poverty of the urban population. As would be the case of Algeria in the 1990s (and South Africa in the 1980s), impoverished youth, both students and the unemployed, became the shock troops of rebellion.

At the end of 1977 Sadat undertook another policy that he hoped would attract foreign investment and foreign aid. After 30 years of hostility he sought to negotiate peace with Israel, and in November, to the shock and horror of many in the Arab world, he made an official visit to Jerusalem and addressed the Israeli Knesset in search of *rapprochement*. The new relationship was consummated with Israeli Prime Minister Menachem Begin in a honeymoon environment at Camp David, the U.S. presidential retreat in Maryland, in September 1978, overseen by the beaming presence of President Carter. It was denounced, for different reasons, by almost all Arab countries and by the Palestine Liberation Organization (not surprisingly, because in the same year Israel had invaded southern Lebanon in an attempt to smash PLO bases there). Nonetheless, an Egyptian-Israeli peace treaty was signed in 1979. As an immediate consequence, Egypt was to regain the territory in Sinai that Israel had occupied since 1973. As a secondary result, Egypt was expelled from the Arab League, which had been founded in Cairo and dominated by Egypt since its inception. The league moved its headquarters to Tunis. No longer at the head of the Arab world, Egypt was now isolated.

Sadat's policies, however, had brought at least some benefits to many Egyptians. From the outset of the oil boom in 1974 until the mid-1980s, per capita income continued to climb steadily. The wealthy minority, in particular, was profoundly satisfied with Sadat. This was especially obvious in Cairo, where their ostentatious luxury conflicted so conspicuously with the grinding poverty of the poor. Unlike Nasser, who had a taste for austerity that won him the approval of his subjects, Sadat had grandiose material cravings. He moved into one of the palaces formerly owned by the deposed King Faruq, and the Egyptians came to refer to him as "Faruq II." Sadat's dependence on U.S. aid, to the tune of $2 billion a year, also came under heavy criticism, both from the neo-Nasserites, who had survived his repression and grown even stronger, and the Islamic militants, who had also managed to withstand the attacks by his police. In September 1981 Sadat ordered the arrest of 1,000 people suspected of plotting against him. Then, on October 6, at the annual Army Day parade, Sadat was assassinated by an army lieutenant who was a member of a Muslim reformist organization. "I have killed Pharaoh," the attacker gloated. Inside Egypt, only the wealthy mourned Sadat's demise. His neoliberal policies, magnified by his personal venality, had made him a pariah.

Sadat was succeeded by Muhammad Hosni Mubarak (b. 1928), who had been a senior officer in the air force until becoming Sadat's vice-president in 1975. Mubarak rebuilt the army, expanding its influence and replacing aging Soviet arms with arms from the United States, just as

Nasser had replaced outdated British stock with weapons from the Soviet Union. As in Turkey, the army became an estate within the state. Its officers lived in comfort, and even its non-commissioned officers enjoyed the perquisites of power. The army reached into the economic sector with the formation of the National Organization for Military Production and the Arab Organization for Industry, which were under its control. These organizations had a double interest: to provide the officers with secure (and inflated) incomes and to ensure the generals a supply of modern arms. In 1990, military industries, which had received massive investment from Saudi Arabia and some Gulf states under Sadat, produced about £1 billion Egyptian worth of military products as well as £600 million worth of civilian commodities. What President Eisenhower had alerted his country to was now emerging in Egypt—as it had already in Turkey—a "military industrial complex" of growing independence, rising inefficiency, and rampant patronage and profiteering.

But Mubarak had a problem that Sadat had managed to avoid: from the mid-1980s, per capita income began to decline precipitously. Discontent mounted. In February 1986 Egypt's main means of containing popular discontent, the Central Security Force, itself revolted. Three divisions of regular army troops were required to put the insurrection down.

The army now moved into the field of domestic security, which brought it face to face with Islamic reformists, who had become the chief force of opposition to the Mubarak regime. Because the reformists were regarded as a threat to the state, when they were arrested they were generally tried in military courts, which were both more severe and more arbitrary than civilian courts. Executions, some after military trials and some after no trial at all, increased in frequency. The antagonism between the state and the Muslim reformists reached a high point in 1987, subsided slightly around 1990, and rose again in the early part of the 1990s. Again, the situation was similar to the events that began to occur in Algeria in 1992. But whereas the Algerian reformists were united in a common front, the opposition in Egypt was not: the Egyptian movement was both more diverse and more complex.

Under the *infitah* regime the Egyptian bourgeoisie, which had suffered an eclipse under Nasser, made a spectacular comeback. By the end of the 1980s its members had moved on from merely acting as brokers for and minor partners with Arab and Western capitalists. According to S.E. Ibrahim:

> By 1990 the Egyptian bourgeoisie was pushing and pressuring for the 'privatization' of public-sector companies, floating the Egyptian pound, and for doing away with, or at least reducing, public subsidies on most basic goods

and services. In this respect, the Egyptian bourgeoisie has the International Monetary Fund . . . and other aid donors as formidable allies. The ruling elite of the Mubarak regime is divided and generally inept at responding to such demands. But on the whole it ends up by yielding piecemeal.[31]

Oil remained Egypt's leading export, but oil revenues dropped from $3 billion in 1982 to below $1.5 billion in 1986. At the same time, industrialization, the dream of Egyptians for over a century, stalled. Besides oil, the other main source of revenue was U.S. aid and foreign loans. Total aid and loans from all countries had reached nearly the $50 million mark in 1991, when, in payment for Egypt's denunciation of Saddam Hussein, the loans were partially forgiven.

In the aftermath of the 1991 Gulf War a massive infusion of aid, mainly from the United States, was directed towards Egypt. This aid together with fiscal reform reduced the foreign debt and the budget deficit to low levels while at the same time increasing foreign currency reserves and decreasing inflation. But in the years immediately after the Gulf War, economic growth slowed down to around 1 per cent (while the population growth rate exceeded 2 per cent). Income inequities persisted; per capita GDP fell from $680 in 1986 to less than $600 by 1993.

"The World Bank has caused more violent unrest in the third world than did the late Soviet Union," an Egyptian official observed.[32] Meanwhile, one anonymous but probably Western interpretation had the Egyptian state teetering on the abyss. "Cassandra," writing in the *Middle East Journal* about an "impending crisis" in Egypt, explained that against a background of increasing social misery, Egypt was in a state of inertia: "The Egyptian economy is suspended between a rigid monetarism, on the one hand, and an inefficient state capitalism on the other."[33] Political reform had been unsuccessful, and the National Democratic Party—which by the 1990s did not represent Nasserites, free marketeers, or Islamists— had lost its legitimacy, in large part due to the civil strife that qualified the era of Mubarak as the bloodiest period of Egyptian history in the century. The major actors in this civil strife were young Islamists and the security services. Both the security forces, whose members had staged a massive revolt in 1986, and the Islamists were busily recruiting members from the same impoverished youths. In spite of benefiting from a larger share of the national budget, the security forces were corrupt, divided, and exhausted.

As for the Islamists, they no longer comprised the same social groups against which Nasser had come down with a heavy hand, or with whom his successor, Sadat, had forged a compromise. By 1987 the Muslim Brotherhood had become the largest single opposition group in the national assembly. In the 1990s, according to "Cassandra," the Islamist movement became "further radicalized and intensified" as it came increasingly to reflect "the interests of the lower classes, rather than those of the middle and upper-middle classes." Now militants are more likely to be both younger and poorer—youths for the most part living on the margins of society in rural areas, suburban shantytowns, or city slums—and they tend to be less educated: "Whereas 80 percent of Islamist activists arrested in the 1970s were college students or graduates, by the 1990s they comprised only 20 percent." The Islamist insurgents, in other words, have for the most part become the "youths most negatively affected by Egypt's faltering economy."[34]

## Iran: Modernization and Reaction

Reza Khan (1878-1944) was a military strongman who had set himself up as shah (king) of Iran in 1925, just two years after Mustafa Kemal had installed himself at the head of the government of republican Turkey. He thus became Reza Shah, adopting the dynastic name "Pahlavi" soon after. Although Reza Shah lacked the revolutionary legitimacy and military heroism with which Mustafa Kemal was swathed and was thus never secure enough to lead Iran on the same path of "progress," his attempts to modernize and especially to secularize Iran were considerable. The Islamic clergy, at least, thought so. Iran's new king not only excluded them from political participation, but also banned their passion plays, denied them the right of self-flagellation, prohibited their funeral ceremonies, opened up politics to women, and outlawed the all-encompassing shawl (*chador*) that the religious leaders had insisted women should wear.

The effects of the shah's policies were to increasingly divide Iranian society between two poles: the "modern" and the "traditional." As Nikki Keddie explains, "The upper and new middle classes became increasingly westernized and scarcely understood the traditional or religious culture of their compatriots. On the other hand, the peasants and the urban bazaar classes continued to follow the ulama [Muslim clergy], however politically cowed most of the ulama were in the Reza Shah period. These classes associated 'the way things should be' more with Islam than with the West."[35]

When, in 1942, British and U.S. forces invaded Iran to secure the land route to their Soviet ally, Reza Shah, whose pro-German sympathies had made him unpopular, thought it best to step aside. He installed his 22-year-old son, Muhammad Reza Pahlavi (1919-80), in his place. The Allied occupation lasted until 1946. Thereafter Shah Muhammad Reza Pahlavi began to rebuild the power of the dynasty, which had been lost

during the occupation. To win the support of the *ulama*, he annulled much
of the legislation that his father had passed against them and their institutions. He also played up his piety.

Before World War II, Iran had been the principal oil producer in the
Middle East, with its oil pumped out of the ground, refined, and exported
by the British-owned Anglo-Iranian Oil Company (AIOC). The British government had been the major shareholder in Anglo-Iranian since 1914.
Anglo-Iranian and the British-Dutch firm Royal Dutch Shell together had a
controlling interest in the petroleum of neighbouring Iraq through a subsidiary of AIOC, the Iraq Petroleum Company. In the years immediately
after World War II, control of both Iranian and Iraqi oilfields gave the
British a position of dominance in Middle East oil production, leaving the
Iranians and the Iraqis as spectators on the sidelines, watching their oil
being pumped away. To them oil was not merely a commodity, then, it was
a symbol: its removal by foreigners for their own profit was a reminder of
their powerlessness.

By 1949, especially in the minds of the "modern" middle classes, students, and the working class, the nationalization of AIOC had become the
major issue in Iranian politics. The oil company itself had helped in this:
between 1945 and 1950 it had made a profit of £250 million and paid only
£90 million in royalties to Iran.

Immediately after the end of World War II, the rule of Shah Muhammad Reza Pahlavi was anything but secure. What he needed most was the
revenue to finance a modernization program and particularly to build up
his army. This was to come from the renegotiation of the oil agreement
with AIOC that he had signed in July 1949. The agreement was to be ratified by the Iranian *majles* (parliament), due to be reconvened in 1950. But
before the agreement could be ratified, the environment surrounding oil
agreements changed irreversibly.

In 1950 U.S. firms had agreed to give the Saudis a 50-50 split on oil
profits; Iran had been getting 20 per cent from AIOC. Iranian nationalists
were incensed by the obduracy of Anglo-Iranian, which refused to agree to
the same deal. Even the Americans regarded the AIOC as "self-righteous
and arrogant" and its policies as being characterized by "unusual and persistent stupidity." The ownership of oil proved to be a perfect issue around
which Iranian nationalism, dominated by liberals but appealing to many
sections of society, could mobilize. The leader of the nationalists was
Muhammad Mossadeq, whose political vehicle was the National Front, a
broad coalition of secular and religious interests. Mossadeq's political
influence and popularity were closely bound to his office as chairman of a
committee of the *majles* established to examine the ownership of Iranian

oil. In November 1950 this committee called for the nationalization of
AIOC.

To deal with the opposition of the nationalists, the shah appointed a
strongman, General Ali Razmara, as prime minister. The general was supposed to drive over the opposition like a tank and push through an agreement with the British oil company. Instead he was assassinated on March
7, 1951. Less than two weeks later the *majles* nationalized Iran's oil. Two
months later Mossadeq was elected prime minister. For his relatively brief
two years in power he was subject to a barrage of propaganda from the
West that depicted him, in common with many Third World leaders who
threatened the West's economic and military security, as being somewhere between eccentric and insane. Mossadeq was neither. He was not
only highly educated but also Western-educated, having studied in France
and Switzerland and holding a doctorate in law from the University of
Neuchâtel.

Mossadeq's first administration, notably cautious, attempted to
include, even court, favourites. He addressed the oil issue by first per-
suading the *majles* to elect four deputies from his own party to a parliamentary committee of five that was intended to implement the
nationalization law. In June 1951 he sent the committee to Khuzistan, the
main oil-producing area, to take over the oil installations. In July he broke
off negotiations with AIOC when it threatened him with countermeasures.
The moves caused great consternation in London, where throughout the
summer the British foreign secretary anguished over whether or not to
invade. Plans were made for the military occupation of Abadan, an island
at the head of the Gulf containing the headquarters of AIOC, along with the
largest refineries in the world. In the end the attack was called off. Certainly the British could have occupied the island of Abadan, but how would
they have been able to protect the pipeline that brought the oil to it? In
any case, the British were already heavily committed to the war in Korea
and sensitive to the growing crisis in the Canal Zone of Egypt, their main
base in the Middle East. On September 27 the Iranians moved in to
occupy Abadan, and Britain had evacuated the island by October 4. Nationalists everywhere in the Middle East saw the events as a major victory,
and the young officers in Egypt who were to lead the revolution the next
year were especially encouraged by it.

Mossadeq's success against AIOC was popular, and so too were his
reforms, which touched on agriculture, taxation, the judiciary, education,
and the electoral system. He confiscated some of the shah's widespread
lands, cut the palace budget, and gave the savings to the health ministry.
There is no evidence, however, that he wanted to replace monarchism

with republicanism. Nevertheless, by May 1953 much of the power that the shah had accumulated since the end of the war had been stripped from him. By mid-August Mossadeq was enjoying his finest hour, but he was already in trouble. As a reformer, he had offended the supporters of the shah, who included the heads of the military as well as religious leaders and businessmen. These groups were by no means comfortable with radical nationalism. Then there was the matter of destabilization: economic disorder was sown in the country by the boycott organized by the British and U.S. oil interests. Iranian oil exports plummeted from 666,000 barrels per day in 1950 to 20,000 in 1952.

The oil boycott had led to dwindling revenues. This loss in turn led to rising unemployment and escalating consumer prices that turned the middle classes, which had supported nationalization, against Mossadeq. His own National Party split, with the clerical leaders turning against him because of his nationalizations and enfranchisement of women. The U.S. government contributed further to Mossadeq's woes by cutting off all economic and military aid, which further encouraged the monarchist army officers to plot the prime minister's overthrow.

On July 25, 1953, President Eisenhower gave his approval to a plot to overthrow the prime minister of Iran. The CIA sent one of its leading conspirators, Kermit Roosevelt, to Tehran to help the British organize matters. Roosevelt took a suitcase full of dollars to buy the support of key generals and politicians. On August 16 the first coup attempt failed, and the shah scurried off, first to Baghdad, which was still ruled by a pro-British regime, and then to Rome. The Tudeh ("Masses"), the Iranian communist party, which supported Mossadeq's reforms, organized massive rallies to mark the shah's ouster. The U.S. ambassador made Mossadeq an offer he could not refuse. If he restored law and order, that is if he were to repress the Tudeh, U.S. aid would be forthcoming. Although the Tudeh had provided Mossadeq with the support he needed, Mossadeq was afraid of Soviet influence. As a result he took up Washington's offer and crushed the Tudeh using the army.

In doing so Mossadeq cut the ground from under himself. Elements of the army, whose leaders had been bribed with U.S. dollars, turned on him, and on August 19 his official residence was attacked by rebel tanks. Mossadeq was forced to surrender his power, the shah returned from exile, and both the National Party and the Tudeh were banned. Mass arrests, show trials, and executions, particularly of communists, followed. The persecution, lasting for more than a year, claimed 5,000 lives and drove another 50,000 people into exile. Mossadeq escaped the death penalty demanded by the state prosecutor, but was sentenced to internal exile. Power flowed back to the shah. According to Dilip Hiro, the coup "laid the foundation for royal dictatorship which lasted a quarter of a century. It destroyed any chance that Iran had of evolving as a Western-style democracy."[36] In view of Ayatollah Khomeini's later denunciation of the Americans for overthrowing Mossadeq's government, it should be remembered that when the coup took place many of Iraq's leading clerics, who despised the nationalists and feared the communists, actually welcomed it.

## Dictatorship and Development

The shah rewarded his U.S. backers by denationalizing Iran's oil production and dividing it among several oil companies. The five major oil companies each got an 8 per cent share, for a total of 40 per cent, and British Petroleum, the successor of Anglo-Iranian, got another 40 per cent. Royal Dutch Shell got 14 per cent and the French 6 per cent. "With the establishment of the Iranian consortium," writes Daniel Yergin, the historian of the U.S. oil companies in the region, "the United States was now *the* major player in the oil, and the volatile politics, of the Middle East."[37]

The shah rapidly consolidated his personal power after 1953; never again in the period of the monarchy would there be an independent prime minister. Equally, all other political institutions lost their independence and authority. Faithful generals, cosseted with high pay and perquisites, were promoted to key political positions while Iran was militarily bound to Washington through hundreds of millions of dollars received in military and economic aid. Security was reinforced with the setting up of SAVAK, the notorious secret police that the United States and Israel helped to organize from 1957. But the real secret to the shah's success was ballooning oil revenues: they climbed from $34 million in 1954-55 to $181 million just two years later. By the late 1950s, according to Hiro: "The Shah had laid the necessary political-economic infrastructure for rapid economic development under state-dominated capitalism: a process set to expand the size of the modern middle and upper classes—white collar professionals, and commercial and industrial bourgeoisie—and diminish the size of the traditional upper and middle classes: feudal lords, tribal chiefs, clerics, bazaar merchants and craftsmen."[38]

In 1958, to give his regime a veneer of democracy, the shah reintroduced electoral politics. Only two parties were allowed: the National Party, called the "Yes Party," and the People's Party, called the "Yes, Sir, Party."[39] These two royalist parties lasted until they were abolished in March 1975. Meanwhile, strikes remained disallowed. Yet while many among the modern intelligentsia were frustrated and parts of the working class and poor peasantry suffered, the modernizing landowners, upper civil servants, and sections of the commercial middle class closest to the ruler prospered.

Nonetheless, in 1960-63 Iran experienced one of its periodic economic crises. The government was spending too much on arms and the U.S. government wanted land reform and other liberal measures before it handed over any more loans. This was the period of the Alliance for Progress in Latin America, in which land reform was viewed as a remedy against revolution.

In 1963 Iran passed a Land Reform Act as the centrepiece of a reform package known as the "White Revolution." The objects of the act were twofold: to increase and legitimate the power of the shah and to break the power of the "feudal" elements in the countryside, where half of the land belonged to absentees. In itself, this move was laudable. From Mexico to Korea it had been shown that unreformed land ownership was an impediment to successful capitalist development. Of course, not everyone agreed. Land reform threatened not only the landed aristocrats but also the clerics who controlled lands through religious endowments.

To add insult to injury, in early 1963 the shah proposed enfranchising women and protecting families. From then on the honeymoon between the monarchy and the clerics was over. Among the most vehement of the clerical protestors against the agrarian reforms was a relatively obscure and junior cleric, Ayatollah Ruhollah Mousavi Khomeini (1902-89). Khomeini was, by comparison to most of his seniors, a radical. His position brooked no compromise with secular power.

Contrary to the proclamations of both Western academics and journalists, a unified Islam, or even a unified Shi'ism, has hardly ever existed. The political role of Iranian Shi'ism has been quite variable throughout history, and it is unusual in that its clerical leaders have often exerted a high degree of independence from the country's secular rulers. This has been so for several reasons: the decentralized nature of the country, the clerics' independent sources of revenue (from taxes and religious properties), their role as educators, and, finally, the traditions of Iranian Shi'ism itself, some of which (such as the independence of the *ulama* itself) were as recent as the late 19th century.

Iranians in the 20th century generally believed that individual believers could not interpret the Quran and the Traditions (*Hadith*) themselves, but that they should rely on scholarly experts, *mujtahids*. The leading and oldest of the *mujtahids* were known as *ayatollahs*. These tended not only to have immense religious authority but also considerable wealth and political influence, which was in part due to their close connection with the *bazaaris*, Iran's merchant class. The *bazaaris* were connected to the *ulama* in two ways: socially, because the sons of merchants often became religious leaders; and economically through the religious taxes and voluntary donations that the *bazaaris* paid to the *ulama*. During the economic boom of the 1960s, many new seminaries were financed by such donations. Later the support of the *bazaaris* would be essential to Khomeini while he was in exile.

Having railed against impiety, decadence, and corruption since the mid-1940s, by the early 1960s Ayatollah Khomeini was on his way to becoming one of Iran's most eminent religious leaders. His religious authority was buttressed by unusual personal qualities, including an undeniable charisma. Nikki Keddie stresses that at least some of his followers saw him in messianic terms.[40] His appeal for a return to true Islam, or at least his version of it, was coupled with a widespread nostalgia, on the part of those who listened to his sermons, for a simpler and more stable past combined with a growing revulsion towards the influences of the West. This revulsion was crystallized with the 1964 publication by the left-populist writer Al-e Ahmad of a book called *Gharbzadegi*, the title of which can be translated as "westoxification," which was to become a key word during the revolution of 1978-79.

The protest led by the Ayatollah against the reforms of the White Revolution was massive. In June 1963 thousands of Iranians took to the streets to denounce the autocracy. They were harangued by Khomeini, now on his way to becoming the doyen of the militant clerics. Many of his secular rivals and opponents believed that his leadership was temporary and that once his short-term goals were attained, he would move into the background. Khomeini was not only against the White Revolution, but also against the corruption of the shah's regime in general. He linked a critique of capitalist development with a moral critique. He was arrested, and more protest followed.

In the ensuing repression, in which the shah unleashed paratroopers and the SAVAK against the demonstrators and even went so far as attacking theological colleges like the famous Fayziyya Madrasa in Qom, several thousands were killed. For the time being, however, the combination of reforms and repression worked. The rebellion was crushed, and the White Revolution went ahead under continuing protest. By 1971, when the land reform program was officially ended, as many as 92 per cent of former sharecroppers got land. Richard W. Cottam suggests that this newly created class joined the securocrats and the newly made business elite to become the most fervent supporters of the shah.[41]

The lid was not kept on for long after the June 1963 uprisings. In October 1964, when the regime proposed diplomatic immunity for all U.S.

citizens in Iran, protest was renewed. Khomeini again spoke out, reminding his followers of the old "Capitulations" to European powers that had been granted, and opposed, in the 19th century.* He was deported to Turkey, from where, in 1965, he went to the Shi'a shrine city of Najaf in Iraq. He remained in exile in Najaf and later in Paris, a constant thorn in the side of the shah, until 1979. His criticisms stressed the squandering of national resources, the moral and political corruption of the shah and his sympathizers, and the machinations of the imperialist powers, especially the United States. They reached a wide public through the network of followers who remained faithful to him in Iran. He sent them sermons by cassette while he worked on the blueprint for the Islamic state that he was to establish in 1979.

Between 1963 and 1977 Iran boomed economically based on spiralling oil revenues. The average rate of growth in the 1960s was 11.3 per cent, which dropped slightly to 7.4 per cent in the 1970s. The shah's dreams of turning Iran into a major world power, industrially and militarily, seemed to be within reach. In January 1973 all petroleum production was once again nationalized—fortuitous timing, because from October to December of the same year, due to the Arab-Israeli war, prices rose from $2.55 to $11.65 a barrel. The cumulative oil revenue for 1974-77 was $38 billion. Between 1973 and 1974 alone oil revenue increased from $6.3 billion to $20 billion. Some of this growth was channelled into productive use—into agricultural and industrial development, improved transportation, and the development of human resources, for instance. This investment shifted the class structure of Iran, further eroding feudal relations while expanding the "modern." Yet agricultural production did not notably increase, and a massive exodus of rural labour, in part the product of increased birthrates and lowered death rates, was the consequence. In 1973-78 around 1.4 million people emigrated into the towns annually. Modernization in Iran, as everywhere, was highly disruptive.

Industrially and educationally the country's expansion was impressive. Between 1963 and 1977 the number of factories rose from 1,902 to 7,989, including steel mills, oil refineries, aluminum smelters, machine tool factories, and assembly plants for vehicles. The annual rate of industrial growth rose from 5 per cent to 20 per cent, and the education system expanded threefold. Students in secondary education increased from 14,240 to 277,500. The university population increased from 24,885 to

---

* The Capitulations were agreements made between Western powers and the Ottomans by which the Ottoman Sultan ceded his legal rights over Westerners. Under the agreements, suspected Western criminals in Egypt, for instance, would not be tried in front of local judges but before their own consular officials.

154,215, while Iranians in foreign, mainly Western, universities increased from 18,000 to 80,000. Large numbers of students went abroad to study because the level of scientific and technological education in Iran was low even by the standards of some other Third World countries.

The increasing impact of education was costly to the regime. According to Henry J. Munson, "Politically conscious Iranians had condemned [the shah] as an American puppet ever since the CIA returned him to his throne in 1953. And the expansion of education in the sixties and seventies greatly increased the number of such politically conscious people."[42] More and more of these people, like Khomeini, came to oppose the corruption of the autocracy. Much of the vast wealth generated by Iran's oil was pouring into the deep pockets of the shah. Not only were the Pahlavis the biggest landowners in Iran, but they were also the country's richest entrepreneurial family. A tax shelter known as the Pahlavi Foundation transferred even more money to the family. All told, perhaps $2 billion went into the shah's foreign bank accounts.

The most unabashed celebration of the shah's rapacity came with an orgy of legitimation that took place in October 1971 in the form of a grand celebration of 2,500 years of Iranian monarchy. The cost of this exhibitionism was between $100 and $200 million. The shah's handlers had 22,000 bottles of wine flown in for the celebration—this to a country lacking an adequate rural water supply and to a capital city with no serviceable sewer system. The combination of ceremony and alcohol was calculated to help people forget that the shah, despite his promotional claims ("King of Kings," "Light of the Aryans," "One Possessing Great Powers") was not really of royal stuff, but rather the son of a military strongman. The unforgiving and unforgetting Khomeini denounced anyone participating in the vainglorious bacchanalia as "a traitor to Islam and to the Iranian nation."

In spite of such denunciations, Iran continued to give the impression of unshakeable stability. Between 1963 and 1977 the shah's government maintained the status quo by massive expenditures on the military and police. By 1977 Iran had the fifth-largest military force in the world (its ranking had recently been improved by the sudden disappearance of the Saigon regime in Vietnam). Arms deliveries for 1978-80 alone cost $12 billion. Ervand Abrahamian noted, "Arms dealers began to jest that the *shah* read their manuals in much the same way as other men read *Playboy*."[43] Western defence contractors were ubiquitous and conspicuous. By 1977 60,000 of them were working in the country. Many Iranians resented their high salaries and ostentatious lifestyles.

In the 1960s and 1970s SAVAK had been expanded to spy on Iranians, with other agencies established to spy on SAVAK. According to Hiro,

"SAVAK had by now perfected its methods of intimidation: harassment; interference with mail and telephone; denial of job, promotion, passport or exit visa; pressures on the suspect's family and friends; arrest without charge; lengthy detention without trial; exile to outlandish places in the country; and finally the threat of murder."[44] To further bolster his autocracy, in March 1975 the shah abolished the two parties he had earlier invented and created a wholly new party called "the Resurgence," which was supposed to be a mass party organized to stretch from the grassroots to the peaks of society. The idea for the party seems to have been suggested to the king by Iranian students of political science on their return from the United States. As it turned out, this change may have taken Iran a step closer to revolution.

## Opposition

Despite oppression, the opposition, secular and religious, not only survived but also expanded, and because the closed political system allowed for no debate, violence became the most conspicuous means of oppositional expression.

By the late 1970s the secular opposition was of several different kinds. While the Tudeh had been virtually annihilated, Mossadeq's National Front had survived in a weakened form as an umbrella sheltering a range of groups opposing the regime. One of the main leaders of the National Front, Mehdi Bazargan (b. 1905), the son of a pious *bazaari*, had studied engineering in Paris in the 1930s and supported Mossadeq in the early 1950s. He was the representative of a reforming and modernizing tradition in the Middle East that went back to the 19th century and stressed the compatibility of Islam and the West, that is, of religion, democracy, and science. To Bazargan, it was not Western imperialism that was the cause of Iran's backwardness, but despotism and ignorance. He called for religious and secular reform and advocated an Islamic government run by secular experts committed to Shi'ism. His appeal was to the educated middle class. Bazargan was to play a leading role in 1978-79.

Dr Ali Shariati also belonged to the National Front. The son of a militant cleric, he was better known than Bazargan, perhaps because his views were more distinctly "Third Worldist," stressing as they did the possibility of developing indigenous means of resisting the juggernaut of Western values. Writers on contemporary Iranian history point out that his education in Paris in the early 1960s, at the time of the Algerian and Cuban revolutions, exposed him to the writings of Marx and Franz Fanon and led to sympathies with the aims of the Cuban Revolution. Abrahamian says that Shariati translated Guevara's *Guerrilla Warfare* and started to translate

Fanon's *Wretched of the Earth*, while Keddie reminds us that he had ties with Ahmed Ben Bella, the first Algerian president, who had particularly close links with Havana.[45]

"The core of his message," writes Cleveland, "was that Shi'ism was an activist faith that required its adherents to oppose injustice and to assert their cultural heritage in the face of Western models of development."[46] Like Bazargan, his appeal was strongest among the educated middle class, particularly students, for whom he provided "an ideology that fulfilled both their desire to remain loyal to their faith and their urge to undertake a revolution." Shariati, who criticized the conservative *ulama*, had considerable appeal for the liberal clergy. He died in mysterious circumstances in London in 1977, just as the final stage of protest against the Pahlavi dictatorship was taking off. Some Iranians claimed he had been murdered by SAVAK. Shariati was among the intellectuals who, according to Mehran Kamrava, initially spearheaded the revolution against the shah.[47]

Influenced by these intellectual leaders were the guerrilla organizations, the Marxist anticlerical Fedayan-i Khalq and the Islamic but leftist Mojahedin-i Khalq. The Fedayan, founded by university students, derived from the Tudeh. Its followers tended to come from secular backgrounds and believe strongly in class warfare and assassination. They carried out their first armed raid, against a police post, in February 1971; like the attack on the Moncada barracks by Cuban student rebels in July 1963, it was a bloody disaster. But, as in the Cuban case, it led to the emergence of a fully fledged guerrilla organization. Like the Cuban M-26-7, the ideology of the Fedayan was eclectic, drawing on the written works of Lenin, Mao Zedong, and Che Guevara. Unlike the M-26-7, in part due to the effectiveness of SAVAK, the Fedayan did not become a serious threat to the regime.

The Mojahedin came via the religious wing of the National Front. Its followers tended to be students of religious colleges, and its views were more like those of Shariati. In the early 1970s the Mojahedin received support from some of the pro-Khomeini clerics. Both groups believed that Iran was the victim of a U.S. imperialism that was cultural as well as economic. Both held that the regime of the shah had little popular support beyond the corrupt "comprador" bourgeoisie benefiting from connections to foreign capital, and that it could only rule by terror. By 1976, like the Fedayan, the Mojahedin had come under heavy attack from the secret police and the army. Between February 1971 and October 1977, 341 guerrillas were killed, with 177 of those deaths coming in gun battles and 91 by execution, and a further 50 murdered in jail cells. Most of those killed were under 35 years of age, and 39 of them were women.

There was among Iran's growing number of educated women, then, a tendency to be critical of the shah's role in the "Westoxification" of Iranian society. Leaders of these women joined the Muslim revivalists in denouncing the pernicious influence of the West. Together with their followers they expressed their resistance in material terms by devising a mode of dress that was less restricted than the traditional *chador*, but also less provocative than Western dress—a form they called *hajab-e islami*, or "Muslim dress."[48]

By 1977 several of the oppositional forces had united. The *bazaaris* in particular, resenting the price controls imposed by the ruling party in 1976 as a means of weakening their political and social influence, bankrolled the clerical enemies of the shah's regime. They contributed, according to Kamrava, some £20 million to Khomeini alone while he was in Paris, as well as funding strikes and hiring unemployed youths to demonstrate.[49] Among another segment of the middle class, the Westernized liberals, discontent manifested itself in the form of protests by groups like the Iranian Committee for the Defence of Human Rights and Freedoms. In common with other groups in Iran, the liberals were discontented over the unrelenting repression that continued to be a defining feature of the shah's dictatorship and with the regime's subservience to the United States.

Internationally, and especially in the United States, there was also a growing campaign against the regime. The election of President Carter, with his commitment to human rights, forced the shah to relax his repression, which in turn encouraged the opposition to come out into the daylight. In June 1977 three National Front leaders published an open letter to the shah denouncing his government for being "based on a system of despotism dressed up as lawful monarchy."

By November the opposition had moved onto the streets. Still, there seemed little cause for disquiet in the West. On a state visit to Iran at the end of 1977, Carter took a soothing approach: "Iran, because of the great leadership of the Shah, is an island of stability in one of the more troubled areas of the world." Only a few weeks later, in January 1978, protesting theology students from the religious centre of Qom clashed with the police, and 70 were killed. From exile Khomeini, whom the regime had attacked with scurrilous propaganda, praised the protestors and called for more demonstrations. Mourning ceremonies in February brought further protests in large towns. In Tabriz the demonstrations lasted two full days, and as many as 300 protestors were killed. Another commemoration was scheduled for March 29, and this time protests took place for two days in 55 towns. In Yazd, where the crowd shouted "Death to the Shah," participants were again gunned down: 100 died. On May 10 violent protests took place in 24 towns. The death toll mounted, forcing the regime to turn towards further reforms. In June onlookers were predicting that the crisis had ended.

By the first half of 1978, the remarkable rate of annual economic growth that had characterized the previous 15 years was plummeting, dropping to 2 per cent. During the summer of 1978 real wages started to fall, and unemployment started to rise, with a particular impact on the working class, which had hitherto been absent in large numbers from the demonstrations. The living standards of most Iranians, even those not involved in the modern sectors of the economy, were now falling quite rapidly.

The shah showed no sympathy. In June and July strikes increased, and 40 protesters were killed in Mashhad on July 22 in a demonstration including a large number of workers. Clashes occurred again at memorial services held seven days later in almost every large town. In Isfahan demonstrators took over the city for two days—and troops shot over 100 of them. At a memorial service in Abadan attended by 10,000 people the mourners shouted, "The shah must go." On August 28 the prime minister and his entire cabinet resigned.

On September 8, "Black Friday," the army confronted people mobilized for mass prayers to mark the holy days of *id el-fetr*, and at least 4,000 were killed. This was the turning point of the revolution, after which it could not be stopped. With strikes continuing through the rest of September, banks, refineries, and factories were all closed down. In October, in what amounted to a general strike, the closures were followed by demonstrations in bazaars, schools, newspapers, and government offices. In November, after 30 students had been shot down in the University of Tehran, protesters attacked the offices of foreign firms, luxury hotels, and banks. While Tehran burned, the shah (by now seriously ill with cancer) dithered. Strikes and demonstrations continued through November, with the religious leaders demanding his removal. The ten holy days of *Muharram*, beginning on December 2, were washed in blood. Some 700 people died in Tehran alone, and 135 were killed in Bazvin, some of them crushed under tanks. By the end of the celebrations half a million people were demonstrating in Tehran, and by the end of December the country's economy had ground to a halt, with local committees taking power in a number of places. The protesters made armed attacks against U.S. citizens and their property. The army was no longer willing to shoot at demonstrators.

The wealthy panicked. In September employees of the Central Bank of Iran had released a statement showing that 177 affluent Iranians had recently sent $2 billion abroad: 13 top military officers had alone exported $253 million. Knowledge of this transfer of wealth was bound to affect the morale of the army conscripts, who were paid $1 a day. By December French intelligence was reporting that the shah could not survive politically.

The counsels of the White House were divided. President Carter's human rights policy, which had contributed to the ouster of Somoza in Nicaragua, was having a disastrous effect on the American empire. The president's hawkish national security advisor, Zbigniew Brzezinski, wanted Carter to support the shah. Cyrus Vance, the secretary of state, wanted him to negotiate. Carter himself was indecisive, and by the end of 1978 Washington was apparently hoping the shah would be able to hand over power to a more acceptable but equally pro-American leader. Certainly the religious and secular radicals were to be kept at arm's length.

In early January 1979 the shah handed over effective government to Shapur Bakhtiar, one of the moderates of the National Front. Bakhtiar, now presiding over a regime that had collapsed in all but name, offered a number of reforms, including free elections, the cancellation of arms contracts, a halt on oil sales to Israel and South Africa, and the dismantling of SAVAK. Some opposition leaders indicated a willingness to support him. Khomeini called for more strikes and demonstrations, and the National Front insisted that there could be no peace until the shah departed. Strikes and skirmishes continued, not only against the shah but also against Bakhtiar. On January 13 an estimated two million people marched in 30 cities. The revolution of the urban masses—a revolution more like that of Paris in 1789 and Petrograd in 1917 than of China in the 1930s or Cuba in 1958—was under way.

On January 16 the shah fled to Cairo, the beginning of his long and pathetic flight away from the turmoil fostered by his modernization policies and repression. He delayed his departure for nearly a week in hopes of seizing the three royal crowns (the largest of which was studded with 3,380 jewels) and the Peacock Throne from the Central Bank. But the bank officials who knew the combinations of the locks had prudently disappeared. Crownless, throneless, and powerless, but hardly penniless, from Cairo the dying shah followed the setting sun into obloquy. What Eric Hobsbawm calls "one of the major social revolutions of the twentieth century" had taken place.[50]

## The Islamic Republic

On February 1, three million people turned out into the streets of Tehran to hail Khomeini's triumphant return from exile abroad. Khomeini refused to recognize Bakhtiar's authority and appointed Mehdi Bazargan. For over a week there were two governments. Then, unnerved, Bakhtiar fled, and Bazargan formed a government of secular moderates. Tension between his administration and the clerics quickly set in.

Khomeini, who was officially recognized as having supreme judicial authority, had little doubt about what had come to pass and what lay ahead. On March 30, 1979, following a national referendum, the monarchy was annulled and an Islamic Republic established. Although large sections of the population who wanted to be rid of the shah did not necessarily want a theocracy, experts went ahead to draft a new constitution, which Khomeini insisted would be "100 per cent Islamic." Clerics were guaranteed a dominant position within the state, and an "Islamic economy" was planned, aimed mainly at making Iran more self-sufficient and less dependent on oil. The country was through with any idea of liberal democracy and all its trappings. That model was seen, at least by the new clerical ruling establishment, as being Western and was therefore condemned.

On September 24, 1979, the Ayatollah told Muslims preparing to leave on a pilgrimage to Mecca: "My Muslim brothers and sisters! You are aware that the superpowers of East and West are plundering all our material and other resources, and have placed us in a situation of political, economic, cultural, and military dependence. Come to your senses; rediscover your Islamic identity! Endure oppression no longer, and vigilantly expose the criminal plans of the international bandits, headed by America!"[51]

Between the flight of the shah in January 1979 and an Iraqi attack on Iran in September 1980, the nation was in a state of rapid transformation. The Islamic leaders who dominated the Revolutionary Council forced Bazargan's resignation in November 1979. He was replaced in January 1980 by Abol-Hassan Bani-Sadr, who became the first president of the Islamic Republic: the *majles*, dominated by the Islamic Republican Party, elected Muhammad Ali Rajai, an inveterate enemy of Bani-Sadr, as prime minister. Bani-Sadr was himself to become a victim of the revolution, caught between Islamic radicalism and U.S. hostility to the kidnapping of American citizens. He was impeached in 1981.

By this time the Revolutionary Tribunals had started their work of trying and executing politicians and officers associated with the ancien régime. From mid-1981, largely in response to terrorist provocations, they turned on the left-wing Mojahedin-i Khalq. The Mojahedin, with an estimated 100,000 fighters, was only defeated by a reign of terror launched by the clerics. By 1982 the Islamic Revolution had crushed most of its internal enemies to the left and right and was able to devote its attention to building an Islamic society and to warding off an invasion planned by Iraq's Saddam Hussein.

With social justice high on the list of popular demands, land reform was back on the agenda. But thoroughgoing reform, while proposed by the government, was blocked by leaders of the religious establishment on the grounds that Islamic law justified private property. Not surprisingly, the religious leaders were backed in this regard by the wealthy merchants and industrialists. Other attempts to remove the economic and social privileges of the clerics also failed. Thus, by 1982, the revolutionary aspect of the Iranian Revolution had reached its peak. From that point it would become less radical, in social and economic terms, and more rightist.

In March 1980 the Islamic Republic began its educational reformation with the object of purging Western cultural values from the schools. In the summer of 1980 all colleges and universities were closed. When they opened again in the next year, the curricula had been cleansed of courses that were Western-inspired, especially the social sciences. Teachers were subjected to examinations based on their knowledge of Islam; those who failed were dismissed. Co-education was proscribed. Islam became the centre of the curriculum, and anyone with deficient religious credentials was excluded. The total number of university students, and especially the enrolment of women students, dropped sharply. The percentage of women students dropped from 40 per cent to 10 per cent. Although some resistance to religious influence showed itself throughout the 1980s, for the most part the clerics remained in positions of control.

Social behaviour was Islamized. Women were forced to wear the *chador*, music and dancing were banned, and Tehran's red-light district was burned to the ground. Correct behaviour was policed by the Islamic Guards, bodies of young zealots who harassed and, on occasion, executed accused miscreants. Khomeini also sought to turn the clock back in the matter of material expectations. Like Ghandi, he rejected the importation of Western consumer goods. Austerity was enjoined. In the time of the Prophet, he reminded his followers, people ate only one date a day.

On September 22, 1980, as the program of the Islamists was getting off the ground, Saddam Hussein's armies attacked Iran. There is little doubt that this invasion received Washington's assent. In November 1979, to the chagrin of President Bani-Sadr, the supporters of Khomeini had seized 57 U.S. foreign service personnel and would hold them hostage for 444 days. The "hostage crisis" provoked an astonishing hostility against the new regime in the United States. Other states in the Middle East—Saudi Arabia, Kuwait, and others—had every reason to fear an aggressive Islamic regime as well and supported Saddam Hussein with money and resources.

For his part, the Iraqi president had every reason to fear the likes of the Ayatollah, who had charged him with "attacking Islam and the Quran" and characterized his government as that of "the infidel Ba'ath Party." A large minority of Iraqis living in southern Iraq, along the frontier with Iran, were Shi'as; it was feared that these would turn against Saddam Hussein's regime. Furthermore, the Ayatollah abrogated the treaty that Baghdad had made with the shah, which guaranteed no support for the Kurds to the north.

The Iraqi invasion fostered patriotism and solidarity behind Iran's new rulers and allowed them to liquidate all of their internal rivals for power. It also carried a high economic cost. The first phase of the war lasted through 1982, by which time the Iranians had regained most of the territory seized by the Iraqis. A truce might have been sought at this point, but it wasn't. The war, after all, allowed the Ayatollah extraordinary leverage over his rivals.

By 1983 the conventional army had been so sorely depleted that a popular army, the *pasdaran*, had to be raised to supplement it. These two armies co-existed and managed to hold the Iraqi forces at bay until finally, after missiles had fallen on both capitals, Iraq announced a ceasefire on March 11, 1988, with Iran following suit on April 20. Meanwhile, more than a quarter of a million Iranians had been killed, and more than a million and a half lost their homes. Damages amounted to $650 billion, and the war in its final years had consumed 70 per cent of Iran's resources. "What a waste," commented one caricatural Western character in *Le Monde*, surveying a field of corpses. "Yes," sighs his companion, peering into a box of unsold missiles.[52] News later came out that during 1985 and 1986, while demanding an international arms embargo on Iran to isolate the "virus of fundamentalism," the U.S. government, through the offices of Israel, was secretly selling Tehran the anti-tank missiles that were being used to destroy the armies that Saddam Hussein was equipping from Western sources.

Well before the end of the 1980s the enthusiasm for the creation of an Islamic society had peaked and gone into decline. On June 3, 1989, Ayatollah Khomeini died. As was the case in Egypt with the death of Nasser in 1970, waves of grief swept the country. An Islamic politician, Ali-Akbar Hashemi-Rafsanjani (b. 1935), was elected fourth president. There had been two basic tendencies within the *majles* in the 1980s: the radicals, who abjured foreign investment and supported nationalization; and the conservatives, who favoured the private sector. Rafsanjani represented a third pragmatic tendency—the modern middle classes, including technocrats, civil servants, and businessmen—which rose between the other two.

After parliamentary elections in 1992, under the leadership of the newly elected Supreme Guide, Seyed Ali Khamenei, the conservatives, or rightists, prevailed. In terms of economic planning, both ISI and the Islamic economy were shelved. The government reversed the nationalizations, which had reached their high-water mark in 1982, and sold off state-owned industries in the industrial and service sectors. This approach was consistent with a development plan for 1990-94 that stressed "privatization and marketization of the economy, including the liberalization of foreign trade." The government adopted macroeconomic policies favoured by the IMF and encouraged by the World Bank. It welcomed foreign investment, and by mid-1992 it had rung up a foreign debt of $13.5 billion. The stock market in Tehran was reopened. In 1994 the U.S. oil companies Exxon, Texaco, and Mobil bought $3.5 million worth of Iranian crude, 24 per cent of Iran's crude oil exports. By early 1995 Coke and Pepsi, formerly denounced by the Iranian government, had returned, and the United States had reportedly become Iran's main trading partner.[53]

By the end of 1994, according to Ali Banuazizi, the legitimacy of the regime's leaders had worn out.

> With the clergy's direct involvement in the affairs of state, it was inevitable that they would come to be blamed for the ills of society and the failings of the government. But beyond such routine recriminations, the clerics' abuses of power, their mismanagement of the economy, their suffocating control over the cultural life of the country and, above all, involvement by some within their ranks in massive corruption schemes, have severely undermined their once considerable moral authority. The 'Islamic government' is fast losing the loyalty and trust of many who saw in it the promise of a new moral order.[54]

According to Fred Halliday, "By the early 1990s the story was circulating in Tehran that there was now only one authoritative Ayatollah left in the country: his name was "Ayatollah Dollar."[55]

# Summary

In Turkey the Kemalists dreamed of creating "an advanced and civilized nation in the midst of contemporary civilization."[56] Economically backward and lacking a mature and powerful bourgeoisie, they instead substituted the state, which they themselves ran. Although the Kemalist state was transformed after the election of 1950, its main object, modernization, and its main development policy, ISI, remained unchanged, and so too did the leading role of the army. To U.S. development theorists in the dawning years of their influence, which was also the coldest part of the Cold War period, the existence of a powerful and pro-American military in a country situated on the frontiers of both the Soviet Union and the Middle East could only be reassuring.

But as in the large economies of Latin America, the Turkish military could not keep its hands off the state. When the periodic crises that accompanied the attempts at economic and social development obtruded, the military stepped in—banning, jailing, executing, and generally terrorizing while representing themselves as the saviours of the nation. As in several Third World states, the military had an agenda of its own, which included a privileged role for its officer class. This role was no longer applauded by Western developmentalists. As Richards and Waterbury comment: "What is interesting to note is the total transformation in the way scholars interpret military rule. In thirty years we have moved from an image of them as revolutionary modernizers ushering in a new age to one of Mamlukes; heavy-handed, power-hungry bunglers, who act as impediments to economic growth and who rule by the use of threat or coercion."[57]

The integration of the military estate into the body of Turkish politics was one of the changes that occurred after the 1980 coup. The other was the abandonment of the long-standing strategy of ISI. By the 1980s, yet another political body had emerged, a renascent Muslim political community drawing on the dissatisfaction of those marginalized by the distortions created by modernization in its late 20th-century guise. Both Turks and Westerners characterized this politics as morally and politically reactionary, but it was reactionary in a different sense: in the sense of the law of aerodynamics, which states that for every action there is an opposite and direct reaction. If capitalist development was the action, Islamic revivalism was its reaction.

Nowhere in the Middle East up to the time of the Iranian Revolution was there a figure of such colossal influence as Gamal Abdul Nasser was in Egypt. Nasserism was the postwar form of Kemalism modified by the historical circumstances of Egypt. Mustafa Kemal had preserved the unity of Turkey from its enemies and promoted a secular modernism dominated by a military autocracy. Nasser sought to do the same. His attempts to unite the Arab world failed, but his attempts to destroy the old social and political system and build a new social and economic structure in Egypt were partly successful, as were his attempts to establish an independent, non-aligned foreign policy.

Nasser's legacy was only partly undone by his successor Anwar Sadat in the 1970s. Bowing to the force of winds from the West, which Nasser had resisted, Sadat seemed to have abandoned nationalism and Arabism in favour of globalism and Westernism. This cost him his life, and his successors were more prudent. By the 1990s the Nasserite state stood like the great colossi in the Egyptian desert, eroded and cracked, but otherwise apparently eternal. Swirling round its base were political currents driven by a revivalist religious ideology that rejected secular modernism and Western domination.

Iran was the crucible of development that exploded in the face of its Western Dr Frankensteins. Possessed of oil resources that the Anglo-Iranian Oil Company and the British government felt they must control, Iran became the arena of Cold War intrigue. The destruction of the nationalist but modernist prime minister, Muhammad Mossadeq, in 1953 and parties that supported him, the National Front and the Tudeh, and the apparatus of political repression built up over the next 25 years, conditioned the rise of an exceptional form of anti-Western nationalism.

In the place of Mossadeq came a royal autocrat whom British and U.S. oil interests and national security planners felt they could influence. Under the shah, Iranian capitalist development, fuelled by immense profits from oil, took place within a political cauldron with no pressure valve. By 1979 a social revolution of a magnitude exceptional in the postwar world destroyed the regime of the pro-Western shah and installed a theocracy that drew partly on classical Islamic models and vehemently denounced both Washington and Moscow.

The Iranian Revolution was a cause for rejoicing in much of the Third World and a source of bitterness and confusion in the West. Part of this confusion lay in the fact that it was both traditional and radical, revolutionary and counter-revolutionary. Where else, in the modern world, had a revolution been led by clerics allied with traditional merchants (*bazaaris*)? And when, since the great revolutions of the late 18th century, had an upheaval taken place "in which the dominant ideology, forms of organization, leading personnel and proclaimed goal were all religious in appearance and inspiration"?[58]

This Islamic Republic provoked fanatical response in the West, so

much so that when shortly after its inception it was attacked by its neighbour, Iraq, Western onlookers expressed widespread relief and even
approval. The large profits flowing to both Western and Soviet arms dealers made this approval all the more palpable. But by the early 1990s the
Iranian revolutionary regime, which managed to institute remarkable
social reforms, had, through venality and incompetence, lost most of its
popular appeal both at home and abroad.

As for the question of development in the Middle East as a whole: did
it take place? Richards and Waterbury conclude: "No country [in the
region] has built an industrial base that can withstand international competition, although Turkey and Israel have made important strides in that
direction. A great deal of industrialization has taken place, but it has been
highly protected, often allowed to become technologically obsolete."[59]

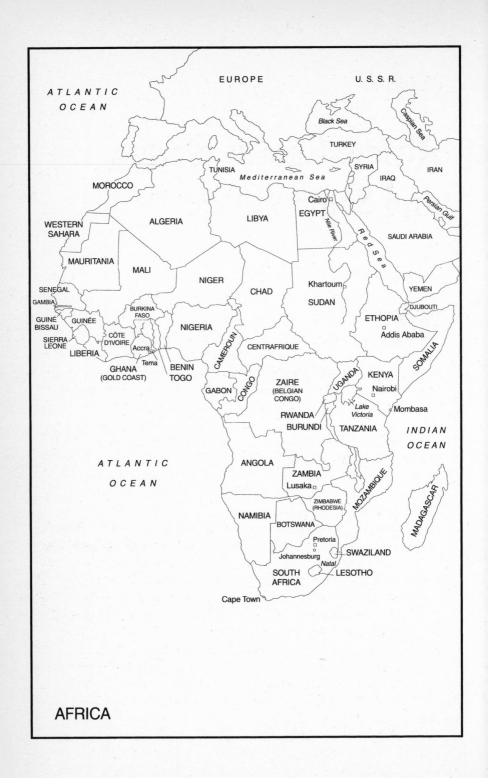

AFRICA

# Chapter 5

# Africa: Ghana, Kenya, and South Africa

## Background

Until the 19th century most of the African hinterland had remained beyond the reach of European control, but between 1875 and 1900, due to improved medical and military technologies, small European-led (but African-soldiered) armies conquered almost all of the continent south of the Sahara and north of South Africa. After deciding on the rules for the division of Africa at a conference held in Berlin in 1885, the major European powers—Britain, France, Portugal, Germany, Belgium, and Spain—sent off small bands of armed men to invade the continent and stake out its lands. This invasion—a kind of gold rush for territory—became known as "the scramble for Africa." Only Liberia, an unofficial U.S. protectorate, and Ethiopia remained independent.

In the partition of Africa, the British and French shared Western Africa, with the British getting the richest and most populous parts. The Belgians gained the enormous Congo, and the Portuguese got to keep the areas in which they had busily acquired slaves from the 16th to the 19th centuries, notably Angola, Mozambique, and Portuguese Guinea. The British also got the lion's share of Eastern Africa and shared the Sudan with the Egyptians. The Germans had to be content with the leftovers from the more powerful predators—scattered morsels of the continent in West, Southwest, and East Africa—though they lost these areas after World War I, when German Africa was redistributed among Germany's wartime enemies. Spain got a sandy territory south of Morocco and territorial scraps further down the coast.

On the basis of this partition and repartition, lasting from about 1885 to 1920, contemporary independent Africa was invented—in a way not dissimilar to how independent Latin America had been created in the early 19th century—that is, based on decisions taken elsewhere.

Even by the late 19th century, South Africa was an exception to many of the generalizations that could be made about the rest of the continent. In South Africa the process of European colonization began earlier and was more profound. It had gone on unremittingly, if unevenly, since the Netherlands East Indies Company disembarked Dutch settlers at the Cape of Good Hope in the middle of the 17th century. These settlers, who came to call themselves "Afrikaners," had "trekked" or migrated inland over the following centuries, encompassing and subordinating the African societies they met on the way, as well as transforming their own. Towards the end of the 19th century the Afrikaners were forced to confront the representatives of British mining capitalism who sought control of South Africa's gold fields. By the beginning of the 20th century, after fighting the Boer War (1899-1902), the British had defeated the Afrikaners and won control of the gold fields. A settlement in 1910 led to the emergence of the Union of South Africa, the first independent and modern country in Africa, but one in which the Africans themselves had almost no voice.

Colonial rule in most of Africa lasted from the time of partition until 1960-70, that is, for less than a century and in many parts of the continent for as little as 60 years. For most of Africa, the colonial era included several shorter periods: conquest, usually completed by the beginning of World War I (1870-1914); the war itself (1914-18); colonial consolidation overshadowed by the Depression (1918-39); a second war (1939-45); and finally nationalism and independence (1945-80).

In this overwhelmingly colonized continent, until the beginning of World War II there were no broadly based nationalist movements like the ones that had sprung up in Egypt and Asia in the aftermath of World War I. From the late 19th century a small number of men of African descent, generally of New World origins, did contemplate a united Africa, governed by Africans themselves, yet as late as the 1930s most educated Africans sought the reform, not the overthrow, of colonialism. They tended to remain loyal to the various crowns or republics whose headquarters were in London, Paris, Lisbon, or Brussels.

As the Depression deepened in the 1930s and Africans in many parts of the continent (in common with subject peoples from Pacific Asia to the Caribbean) became discontented with higher taxes, lower commodity prices, restricted opportunities, and shortages, discontent replaced contentment. The mutterings of protest replaced complacency. Starting roughly in 1935, strikes took place in many parts of the continent and small, usually Westernized, groups began to talk about self-rule. They were influenced by anti-colonial movements elsewhere in the world and by Africans who had taken up residence in Western countries. The inter-war stirrings were interrupted by World War II, which not only delayed attacks on the colonial system but also made those attacks inevitable in the long term.

As for the colonialists, in the 1930s their visions of Africa's future were not radically different from those in which they had found solace in the past. Certainly the word "independence" was on few lips. A British colonial secretary in 1938 declared with confidence that the spread of freedom, which the British themselves encouraged, was bound to be a slow process and would take generations or perhaps even centuries to achieve. The French wartime leader General Charles de Gaulle spoke in late 1944 of rebuilding the French empire as the basis for revitalizing the French nation.

Still, between the world wars some colonial strategists had the idea that changes would have to be made, and central to these changes was the word "development." A perception developed that the colonies could no longer be left to the laissez-faire policies of the previous decades, which, while often cruelly exploiting Africans, evinced little serious planning. Colonial development took a number of different approaches. The Portuguese, who had established the first colonies on the continent, were the pioneers of a highly integrationist strategy. From the late 1920s they sought to have their colonies—Angola, Mozambique, and Guinea—produce larger agricultural surpluses for the Portuguese home markets. This strategy was based on the exportation of cheap African cotton, often grown by forced labour, to subsidize the Portuguese textile industry. This cotton, transformed into textiles, would then be re-exported, in large part to colonial markets.

The Portuguese also devised a second means of making money in Africa. They sold the labour of the Africans in Mozambique to the mine owners of South Africa. In this exchange the Mozambicans got hardship and sometimes death, the white South Africans got extremely cheap labour, and the Portuguese colonial government got large amounts of gold. Portugal's colonial economic policies were focused not on the development of Africa but on the development of Portugal, the most economically backward country in Western Europe and, until 1974 at least, one of the most politically and, therefore, socially retrograde.

Britain, the most economically advanced of the West European colonial powers, promoted a different kind of relationship. British development policies, like British domestic politics, were relatively liberal. While they sought to enclose their African colonies within a bloc dominated by British commerce and finance, they also acknowledged a responsibility for African

well-being. Africans, thought colonial officials, businessmen, and missionaries alike, should be made less primitive and more modern.

In 1929 the British Parliament passed the Colonial Development Act,
which called for the provision of grants of up to a million pounds sterling
annually "for purposes of aiding and developing agriculture and industry"
in the colonies "and thereby promoting commerce with or industry in the
UK." By 1937 a leading colonial governor was parading the idea that "the
exploitation theory ... is dead and the development theory has taken its
place."[1] In February 1940, in the early stages of the war with Germany,
the Colonial Development and Welfare Bill was passed to provide investment in economic infrastructure. "Welfare" had become an issue because
of the political tumult that had rocked the colonial West Indies in the
1930s. The British had become increasingly aware that if some form of
colonial order were to survive, the conditions of their West Indian, African,
and Asian subjects would have to be improved. The French and Belgian
governments had similar ideas, although such considerations did not, on
the whole, occupy the Portuguese.

As for the Africans themselves, almost all of those who had heard of
"Progress" favoured it. Their view tended to be instrumentalist: progress
was a movement they had already been caught up in, a tide they had to follow. "We must emerge from the savage backwoods and come into the open
where nations are made," wrote a Gold Coast clergyman, Attoh Ahuma, in
a 1911 book.[2] A few years later another African commentator wrote in the
*Lagos Weekly Record*: "It is idle and fruitless to attempt to resist the
onward march and insidious influences of Civilization and Progress."[3]

The bias against the African past and against any non-Western forms
of development was absolute. The notion that progress meant Westernization was unassailable. It was *hegemonic* (that is, accepted as natural and
commonsense). The opposite of development—its failure—was primitiveness, with "primitive" equalling "traditional." Westerners rarely if ever
heard Africans admitting that they preferred primitiveness to progress,
although some Africans might have felt in their hearts that the old *political*
arrangements were the happiest, and others, notably the Westernized
literati, made romantic claims about the precolonial period. This is not to
say that some people did not have misgivings about the future. As one liberal colonial governor, Sir Bernard Bourdillon, explained:

> There are those who, with the real interests of colonial peoples at heart,
> look on the prospect of colonial industrialization with complete horror. They
> fear that it will completely disorganize native society and bring out all sorts
> of evils and vices and political troubles in its train. It is a fact that industrial-
> ization will mean considerable dislocation of native society, and that

dislocation will be attended by grave risks. Old sanctions and old standards of conduct will disappear, and new temptations will raise their heads.[4]

Bourdillon was expressing precisely the same fear that had made the blood of middle-class English people run cold in the 19th century: the fear of the social disorder that could accompany capitalist development.

### African populations
### (in hundreds of thousands)

|              | 1950   | 1985   |
| ------------ | ------ | ------ |
| Ghana        | 4,900  | 12,837 |
| Kenya        | 6,265  | 20,353 |
| South Africa | 13,683 | 31,593 |
| Nigeria      | 32,935 | 95,198 |
| Tanzania     | 7,886  | 22,751 |
| Ethiopia     | 19,573 | 42,271 |
| Mozambique   | 6,198  | 13,223 |
| Zaire        | 12,542 | 30,712 |

Source: Keyfitz and Flieger, *World Population Growth and Ageing*, 1990, pp.64-72.

The fates of two former British colonies, Ghana and Kenya, together with that of South Africa, are particularly revealing of certain trends in the history of African nations. Ghana, which was until the time of its independence called the "Gold Coast," had for most of the colonial period the highest per capita income of all African countries south of the Sahara, South Africa excepted, and was in the vanguard of the struggle for African independence. Like most other British and French colonies in West Africa, its economy was based on peasant agricultural production. Kenya, in East Africa, was, unlike the Gold Coast, a settler colony, in which production on farms owned by European settlers and British firms had a leading role. Nonetheless, unlike South Africa, the settlers did not determine government policy, which remained in British hands. Still, because of the influence of those settlers the process of Kenyan independence was more anguished. As an independent state it also followed a different developmental trajectory. Whereas in the 1980s it appeared that Ghana was not "progressing," Kenya (with Côte d'Ivoire, a former French colony) was touted as being one of Africa's model developing economies.

In the case of South Africa, the old colonial idea of separating and certifying people according to "race" became a systematic doctrine. This particular policy, called apartheid, was established to guarantee the privilege and dominance of the Afrikaner and Anglo white settler minority. It worked to keep Africans and Asians out of politics in the country for over 40 years after World War II. But perhaps as remarkable as the political system that was elaborated to serve apartheid was the country's economic development, the most dynamic in the whole of the continent.

## Colonial Gold Coast/Independent Ghana

At the end of the Second World War, one man in one colony with one agenda determined the direction of political change in British colonial Africa. The man was Kwame Nkrumah (1909-72), and the colony was the Gold Coast, in West Africa. The agenda was, essentially, the push for complete independence.

Among African colonies, the Gold Coast was peculiar in several ways. First of all, no European settlers lived there, which made it distinct from the white settler colonies of East and South Africa. Even the neighbouring Côte d'Ivoire had a few hundred French settlers who grew coffee and cocoa on plantations.

Second, although it had important gold mines, these mines were relatively less important in economic terms than agriculture. The Gold Coast was thus unlike the Belgian Congo (now Zaire), where there were no settlers either but mineral production was dominant. In the Gold Coast's agricultural economy the wealthiest sector, cocoa production, was in the hands of Africans, and these cocoa farmers had, on the whole, profited modestly from colonialism.* They had, in fact, become almost the richest of Africa's agrarian producers.

Trade with Western Europe, which had slowly increased between the 16th and the 19th centuries, created a thin crust of literate and Western-oriented merchants, lawyers, doctors, clerks, and catechists on the coastal areas of the Gold Coast. These Africans had begun experiments with local government even before the British forced colonial government on them in the late 19th century. Partly due to the unusual wealth of the Gold Coast's cocoa farms, education, mainly in the hands of Protestant missionaries, had thrust ahead from the 19th into the early 20th century, producing a diaspora of educated Gold Coast "natives" (as the colonists called

---

* Although Africans retained possession of the agricultural land in the Gold Coast, by 1945 many Africans were landless while others owned sizable farms. Thus even by late colonial times the term "cocoa farmers" usually referred to landowners who employed farm labourers. The term "peasant" here is therefore of little use because it does not distinguish between owners and workers. In her book *Development Economics on Trial: The Anthropological Case for a Prosecution* (1986), economic anthropologist Polly Hill disparaged the term "peasant" altogether, preferring to use the term "farmer" to apply to *all* agrarian producers.

them). Some of these people emigrated to other British colonies, like Nigeria, in search of work with private firms and colonial administrations, and sent their earnings home to build more churches and schools to educate more children. By the beginning of World War II, therefore, the educated, Westernized, African petit bourgeoisie in the southern part of the Gold Coast colony was unusually large and ambitious to get ahead. "Getting ahead" meant improving—and improvement implied change for the better.

By the end of the Second World War, the British, too, had accepted the necessity of improvement in the Gold Coast. Granting meaningful political power to Africans was a problem in colonies with white settlers, but this was not the case in the Gold Coast. Their political program was in advance of anything else in colonial Africa at the time. For the British one key was the continued nurturing of the educated elite of the Gold Coast, because cocoa and gold exports brought more foreign exchange into the "Sterling area" than the exports of any other colony excepting Malaysia.* Still, meaningful political power did not go as far as independence.

Two interdependent factors upset British gradualist timetables. One was a sense of growing frustration in the southern and most economically advanced part of the colony after the war had ended. African clerks, business people, demobilized soldiers, prosperous farmers, and youth were all thwarted by restrictions carried over from before the war to the postwar period. The restrictions limited imports and kept their prices high, but allowed British companies to fix the prices of African-produced exports and keep them low. On the whole, the Africans on the Gold Coast were less interested in such abstractions as independence than in the benefits that would come to them if they were able to ensure the removal of these restrictions.

Frustrated by the slow pace of change in the postwar period and antagonized by a perceived lack of gratitude for the Gold Coast people's contributions towards the war effort, a number of African leaders organized a boycott of British goods for February 24-28, 1948. The boycott was followed by a protest in Accra by African ex-servicemen dissatisfied with unfulfilled promises made to them during wartime. A panicky police detachment fired on these ex-servicemen, killing two of them. Rioting and looting followed in several towns, and foreign-owned shops and business premises were burned down. British authorities hastily

---

* The Sterling area comprised those countries and colonies from Hong Kong in the east to British Honduras in the west, all of which had currencies tied to the British pound and regulated by the Bank of England. The French equivalent was the franc bloc.

dispatched troops from the neighbouring colony of Nigeria and South Africa to restore order. In the end a total of 29 people were killed, with 200 injured. The episode by no means equalled events in Sétif, Algeria, where the French had killed thousands, and perhaps tens of thousands, of protesters in April 1945, or in Madagascar off the southeast coast of Africa, where following an insurrection in 1947 French colonial forces slaughtered more than 10,000 people. It was, nonetheless, a colonial crisis. More than that, the Gold Coast riots became the single most important political event in the whole period of British decolonization in Africa. Among other things, they proved to be the making of Kwame Nkrumah.

## Kwame Nkrumah, 1945-66

Kwame Nkrumah, born in 1909 in a village in the extreme southwest corner of the Gold Coast, had spent a dozen years outside the country, first studying in the United States and later living in London, England. He had been influenced to a limited extent by two West Indian social-ists, C.L.R. James (while Nkrumah was in the United States) and George Padmore (in England), and he had attended the Pan-African Conference in Manchester in 1945, a meeting organized by Padmore.* Initially, at least, James was not impressed by the young African student, who, he said, talked a lot about imperialism and Leninism but knew little about either of them.

At the 1945 Pan-African Congress Nkrumah staked his claim for "complete and absolute independence" for the Gold Coast. At the time, to most onlookers, the goal seemed outrageous: few people could imagine the Gold Coast or any other African colony becoming independent before the end of the century. Yet in the next couple of years Nkrumah fashioned himself into one of the best-known African nationalists in England, espe-cially after drafting "Towards Colonial Freedom," a manifesto demanding African independence in the next decade.

By that time some British colonial officials, such as Sir Bernard Bour-dillon, had already begun to think seriously about the social and economic betterment of colonial Africa, although their considerations for change remained almost invariably within an imperial framework. Britain's aim, Bourdillon insisted, should be "to produce healthy, prosperous, educated and contented peoples, capable of playing their full part towards ensuring

---

* Pan-African congresses had been organized by West Indians and African-Americans on an irregular basis since 1900. They became important forums for discussion of such questions as the political mobilization and emancipation of Africans and of Africans of the diaspora in North America, the West Indies, and Western Europe.

the welfare of the human race as a whole."[5] Colonial officials had begun to speculate about "self-government," which they saw as a form of limited autonomy within an all-encompassing imperial system—not the same as independence.

Not many Africans were as impatient as Nkrumah with this view. In early 1948 Nkrumah returned to the Gold Coast to take up the position of paid general secretary for a political body, but not really a political party, called the United Gold Coast Convention (UGCC), formed in 1947. This was a dignified and conservative association of chiefs, businessmen, and a hundred-odd African doctors and lawyers who shared the British political itinerary of self-government but wanted a slightly faster journey with fewer stops. It was somewhat like South Africa's African National Congress in its early phase. Nkrumah soon upset this group by proposing to turn the UGCC into a mass party with strong grassroots support.

The subsequent crisis of February 1948 came at a terrible time for the British Empire. In the previous year Britain had withdrawn from India, which had then gone through a bloody breakup of its parts. By late 1947 an impossible crisis had arisen in Palestine. At home the British economy was in a troubled state. In the British Colonial Office bewilderment mounted about what should be done. The newly arrived governor of the Gold Coast, Sir Gerald Creasy, was overwhelmed by the sudden turbulence in what was, after all, Britain's model colony in Africa. A conventional bureaucratic solution emerged: the government appointed a committee of enquiry, the Coussey Commission, which duly proclaimed what colonial figures like Bourdillon had already suggested. The British had a moral duty to "uplift" the Africans, and more colonial welfare was needed to improve literacy and turn peasants into citizens. The mother country had to accept greater African participation in policy-making. London, still in the midst of postwar reconstruction, and quite seriously short of funds, not surprisingly still wanted to keep its hands on the riches of the colony but was willing to share some of the wealth with the Africans. Thus the resources of the Gold Coast were to provide for both African development and British postwar recovery.

Nkrumah had other ideas. In 1949 he abandoned the listless UGCC to form his own party, the Convention People's Party (CPP). The CPP had the support of several grassroots constituencies—farmers, workers, and students—but its organizers were mainly colonialism's salariat, particularly clerks and school teachers. The most vital constituency was youth, and especially the poor youth whom the members

of the UGCC had derisively called "verandah boys" because they spent
their time loitering and even living in the shade of porches, unemployed.* Unemployment was one of the ghosts that always haunted the
developmentalists.

Nkrumah's political battle cry was radical: "Self-Government Now."
The "now" was, in the context of the times, highly significant. It was calculated to upstage the UGCC demand for "self-government in the shortest
time possible" and to discredit its leaders. Indeed, uttered by the same
man who had insisted on complete independence, it was deeply unsettling.
It was as though a black dance band was being asked to stop playing the
old favourite fox trots of the white and black middle-aged dancers and
move on to the beat of a more joyful and popular, African, musical program. Understandably, many on the dance floor performed awkwardly.

Nkrumah had no well-drawn map of the way ahead. His mentors,
such as Padmore, had equipped him with a few basic ideas—an anti-
communism and pro-Americanism cocooned in populism—and vague
ideas of pan-Africanism, but it was all quite innocent of any economic program that might fairly describe his political philosophy. A general strike he
tried to organize failed, and a state of emergency was declared. Nkrumah
was arrested and imprisoned. Afterwards the governor of the Gold Coast
tried to find moderates he could negotiate with, but none emerged. As a
result, Nkrumah remained at the head of the national movement, like the
Indian nationalists of a decade earlier, leading his followers from jail.

The elections for the Gold Coast's colonial parliament, known as the
Legislative Assembly—a body proposed by the Coussey Commission—
took place in early 1951. There were not to be elections in Africa of such
continental significance again until 1994 in South Africa. The CPP won 34
out of 38 seats and the UGCC 2. Nkrumah was released from prison to lead
the government, and for the next six years the country had a dual power
system. British colonial power, which was in descent, was gradually transferred to Nkrumah, whose independent power was ascending. In the last
election under British tutelage, in 1956, the CPP won 71 seats out of 104.
With this victory it became apparent that Kwame Nkrumah was going to
be the inheritor of the political kingdom.

The lessons that Nkrumah learned under his British mentors were

---

* Edward Kissi makes the point that the term "verandah boys" translated roughly into "the
  marginal" or "the hoi-polloi," that is, those who for one reason or another had neither
  homes nor full-time jobs and were thus forced to sleep on the verandahs of others. The
  "verandah boys" appropriated the term and turned it against the UGCC elite. I am grateful
  to him for this and other insights into the history of colonial Gold Coast and independent
  Ghana.

not the universal laws of politics, assuming such existed. They reflected, rather, the rules of the game as the British authorities saw them. There was to be no clean slate at independence, but rather a slate covered with the scribblings of Nkrumah's political mentors. What could these men advise? A basic principle was co-operation and constitutionalism as a means of maintaining "order"—a direction that demanded the exclusion of any radical alternative. The only palpable alternative was communism. Although only a few Africans in the Gold Coast had heard of communism, communists and even their literature were, nonetheless, banned.

Nkrumah quickly got the message. Soon after being released from prison, he had been invited to meet the governor. At an earlier meeting, wrote the Governor, there had been an atmosphere "redolent of mutual suspicion and mistrust." He noted, "We were like two dogs for the first time sniffing around each other with hackles half raised, trying to decide whether to bite or wag our tails. Soon afterwards, Nkrumah came to me alone and we were able to get to know each other. This time the hackles were down, and before the end the tails were wagging. . . . That was the beginning of a close, friendly, and, if I may say so, not unfruitful partnership."[6]

## Decolonization and Independence

In the years between 1951 and 1957 the British civil servants in the colonial government of the Gold Coast increasingly gave way to Western-educated Africans. The newcomers were paid at the same rates as the outgoers and had the same perquisites. In 1951-54 alone the number of Africans in the civil service trebled. They had all been taught the same rules by their colonial and missionary schoolmasters. As a result they were not only modern and "Westernized" but also tied, by kinship and social practices, to the societies they had been born into. They were thus in many respects pioneers in an uncharted social space that was between two worlds.

The rules that the members of this new class learned were, after all, the *only* rules for the peaceful transfer of political power, and stability was at the head of the list. Certainly none of these African civil servants, lawyers, and schoolmasters wanted any kind of revolutionary transfer of political power. With £200 million in reserves accumulated in British banks and the world price for cocoa generally moving upward, in the years leading to independence the economic prospects of the Gold Coast shone. In the period 1945-57, the value of Gold Coast exports rose from about £10 million to £100 million, while imports shot up from £15 million to £92 million. Cocoa prices climbed from £190 to £352 per tonne between 1948 and 1958. Gold exports more than doubled. Almost everyone could rejoice in at least some small material improvement to their lives. The political kingdom that Nkrumah was about to inherit seemed far from bankrupt.

On March 6, 1957, the colony of the Gold Coast ceased to exist. In its place rose an independent state within the Commonwealth, ostensibly a democracy, called "Ghana," with Nkrumah at its head. In what was his finest hour, his status and prestige in Africa were high. Only Nasser in Egypt could compare with him as a radical nationalist. And, like Nasser, Nkrumah placed the goal of development at the top of the political agenda.

Although Nkrumah took power just as the commodity boom of the early 1950s was slowing down, he began pushing to fulfil his hopes for spectacular national development. Under his increasingly dictatorial rule, an extensive harbour and industrial park were built at Tema, along the coast east of Accra, and the massive Akosombo Dam was raised on the Volta River to provide hydroelectric power. These endeavours remained the most ambitious feature of the years of Nkrumah's rule. Although the projects inevitably fell short of their goals and involved a great deal of wastefulness, Ghana's industrial production in general increased impressively, rising to much higher levels than in neighbouring francophone countries and being largely financed and managed by Ghanaians. Quite remarkably, Ghana was the first West African country to move into heavy industry, namely metallurgy, engineering, and chemical production. But, according to the Egyptian dependency theorist Samir Amin, the success of Ghanaian industrialization was limited, partly at least, because of a lack of co-operation from Ghana's French-speaking ex-colonial neighbours, whose economic policies were often designed by those who were more interested in co-operation with France than with other African countries: "The refusal of the other West African states to coordinate their own industrial plans with Ghana's was at least as much to blame for the difficulties and failures experienced in the country as were local corruption and mistakes."[7]

Whether or not we accept this indictment, one thing is clear: lacking either a substantial national or a large regional market, Ghanaian industrialization was doomed to failure. Even much larger countries that had been attempting to industrialize for a much longer time than Ghana—Brazil, Argentina, Chile, Turkey, Egypt, India—were learning how difficult it was to sustain industrial development in the cutthroat world of contemporary capitalism.

Nkrumah's attention, too, was very much given over to the question of continentalism. From 1958 he organized what was to become the first in a series of post-independence Pan-African conferences, which had as their aim the destruction of colonialism on the continent and the unity of the peoples of Africa. In 1958 representatives of the eight independent African states—Egypt, Ethiopia, Ghana, Liberia, Libya, Morocco, Sudan, and Tunisia—met in Accra. From this meeting emerged, first, the All-African People's Organization (AAPO) and, a few years later, in 1963, the Organization of African Unity (OAU). Also in 1958, when neighbouring Guinea declined to join the neocolonial French Union and was thereupon boycotted economically by France, Nkrumah lent the desperate government of the country £10 million. Here was a consistent theme; until the end of his days in power Nkrumah would offer sanctuary and support to nationalists everywhere in Africa. For this reason he was anathematized in the West.

But there was more to pan-Africanism than continental struggles against Western imperialism. Like the Third World unity evoked at Bandung in 1955, pan-African unity conveniently obscured the fact that although most Africans shared feelings of anti-colonialism, all of them were differentiated by access to material wealth and education. Throughout the continent there were rich and poor, well-paid African civil servants and unemployed youths, well-off farmers and poor farm workers. Nor did the wealthy generally sympathize with anyone who proclaimed the need to distribute the possessions of the rich among their poorer fellow Africans. Pan-Africanism was therefore much like nationalism: it plastered over the cracks dividing social groups and focused on foreign enemies. It encouraged myopia at the national level.

Both industrialization and pan-African unity were financed by reserves, that is, by £200 million in savings that had initially accumulated in Britain but at independence were returned to the control of Ghanaians. These reserves had been built up mainly through cocoa exports. But the "world price" of cocoa was determined by Western countries, which not only bought Ghana's cocoa but also encouraged Ghana's competitors to grow more of the crop. The resulting overproduction was responsible for a sharp decline in price in the early 1960s. To make matters worse, by 1961 Ghana's considerable foreign currency reserves had been almost entirely depleted. Still, the Nkrumah regime limped on until February 24, 1966, when it was overthrown in a military coup. Nkrumah was out of the country when this happened, and his supporters put up little resistance. Nkrumah never returned; the former president spent the rest of his life in exile in nearby Guinea, never again seeing the country to whose independence and development he had dedicated himself.

Politically, despite its grandiose projects, Nkrumah's regime had shown itself to be more than a little corrupt and seriously out of touch with its supporters. Despite the lamentations of his admirers, such as

C.L.R. James, when Nkrumah's ouster came it was welcomed not only abroad but also at home, by both the left and the right. Many of the leading CPP functionaries, like Alex Quaison-Sackey, one of Ghana's most notable international representatives, denounced him immediately after the coup: "The Army has taken power to liberate the people from oppression. The Ghanaian people will now have a free country and will not idolize a single man." The African farmers blamed Nkrumah for the low price of cocoa, the workers blamed him for low wages and high living costs, and disenchanted political supporters attacked him for cronyism and corruption. Many of these critics had been jailed by Nkrumah, and they were now released to make room for a new body of political prisoners. No one cheered Nkrumah's downfall more than the women in the market, Ghana's *bazaaris*, who had watched food prices increase over the previous years by several hundred per cent.

Yet in the light of the subsequent history of Ghana, and indeed of independent Africa, James's interpretation—that the fall of Nkrumah was a tragedy for Africa—seems understandable. Nor were Africans of the diaspora, like James, alone in viewing with sympathy the efforts of this African leader. Soon after the coup, Ousman Ba, the foreign minister of nearby Mali, denounced the putschists in no uncertain terms: "President Nkrumah's revolutionary work cannot be replaced and we do not accept that some musical comedy general, helped by policemen, should question the Ghanaian people's twenty years of struggle."[8] A quarter of a century later the English historian David Birmingham echoed the view that Nkrumah was indeed a remarkable leader who faced indivertible forces:

> Ghana was a prisoner of the West in every way at the time of the 1966 coup. Falling cocoa prices were not manipulated, as some liked to believe, to bankrupt Nkrumah's government, but the decline was a factor behind the coup. Efforts to find alternative markets in the Soviet bloc had proved disastrous, with cocoa sold to Russians turning up on the London commodity market to provide the Soviet Union with hard currency and to undercut the price of direct sales from Africa. Two days before the coup the price paid to cocoa farmers was again reduced in a profoundly unpopular budget move. This was in line with policy advocated by the International Monetary Fund, though the fund was concerned with orthodoxy, loyalty to the West and the reduction of government influence and not with radical innovation. The obverse of the falling commodity prices was the hard-sell strategy of industrial salesmen who continued to encourage Ghana to build up a debt beyond that which the economy could service. Terms of trade were running against all Third World countries, yet Britain guaranteed Ghana credits for a wholly ill-conceived project to build a shipyard at a time when ships could not be

sold even at giveaway prices. At the same time a West German firm advanced credits of no less than £60 million to make Ghana hostage to the German export drive.[9]

With the destruction of Nkrumah's regime, U.S. and Western European apprehensions concerning a radical future for Africa were stilled for a decade. In an article published a day after the coup, *The Times* of London suggested that if the generals "generate confidence, and want help, Ghana would be worth salvaging again."[10]

## After Nkrumah, 1966-95

The months after the coup were taken up politically by a prolonged wrangling over a new constitution and the selling off of state assets to private interests. Ghana was now run by a military junta led by Lieutenant-General Emmanuel Kwasi Kotoka and Colonel A.A. Afrifa. The junta, which called itself the "National Liberation Council," lasted for over three years until, after an election in August 1969, it handed over power to a civilian government with an inept schemer, Kofi Busia, as prime minister and another general, Edward Akuffo Addo, as president. Conventional and conservative, although democratically elected, Busia was regarded in the West with much more favour than Nkrumah had been. The World Bank lent him money interest-free, and Britain, France, and the United States agreed to a flexible schedule of debt repayments. Westerners profited from the continued sale of Ghana's national assets on the open market. Wealthy Ghanaians were able to transfer their money out of the country. But the economic situation did not brighten; indeed, Ghana's economy became more stagnant than ever. From exile Nkrumah commented on this situation in a book, *Dark Days in Ghana* (1968).

The increasingly authoritarian Busia fell from power in January 1972 when another military regime, this time under Colonel Ignatius Kutu Acheampong, intervened. Busia's unpopularity among the same people who had rejoiced in the ouster of Nkrumah was followed by a revival of sympathy for Nkrumah, and Acheampong tried to capitalize on this twist. After Nkrumah died in Bucharest on April 27, 1972, his body was returned first to Guinea, then, in July, to Ghana, where he was given a state funeral, a sign that the new regime was seeking legitimation through the rehabilitation of the former leader. At the same time, several of Nkrumah's former associates got jobs in the government, pan-Africanism was pumped up, and foreign investment came under renewed criticism. But these changes failed to halt the political carousel. In 1978 Acheampong was himself thrown off, to be succeeded by another general, Frederick Akuffo, who lasted only a year before he, in turn, lost his grip on power. By this time the economy of Ghana was in a "catastrophic" state. Between 1970 and 1983, according to Vali Jamal and John Weeks: "Almost every vital statistic one can think of had a negative sign. Agricultural output fell by 0.2 per cent per annum, industry by 4.2 per cent per annum, exports by 6.2 per cent and cocoa output by 6.1 per cent."[11]

The coup that destroyed Akuffo was of a different kind, at least for Ghana. It took place on June 4, 1979, and was led by junior officers and enlisted men with Flight-Lieutenant Jerry Rawlings (b. 1947) at its head. It had unusual popular support, but just over four months later, on September 24, Rawlings relinquished power and a new civilian president, Hilla Limann, took office. The economic crisis that brought Rawlings to the forefront continued. Ghana continued to be the only country in Africa undergoing a decline in measurable agricultural production. Although the Ghanaian GDP had grown comparatively slowly from 1960 to 1970, in the following decade it fell below zero. Ghanaians faced serious shortages of goods and a breakdown of state services. On December 31, 1981, at the head of a coalition of democratic forces including trade unionists and students, Rawlings returned, this time more permanently.

Rawlings's dictatorship, like Nkrumah's, was immensely popular at the outset. Claiming legitimacy on the basis of breaking with the corrupt old system (the system the British had handed to Kwame Nkrumah), Rawlings put himself at the head of the National Democratic Congress (NDC) and the "People's Revolution" that it directed. "This is not a coup," he explained. "I ask for nothing less than a revolution, something that will transform the social and economic order of this country. . . . We are asking for nothing more than proper democracy . . . to organize this country in such a way that nothing will be done . . . without the consent and authority of the people—the farmers, the police, the soldiers, the workers—you are the guardians."[12]

Few leaders in Africa in the last two decades have approached Rawlings's level of popularity. Behind him, a political rainbow comprising low-ranking soldiers together with worker and student organizations pushed hard for the reform of the political system. The regime forged links with foreign governments that saw themselves as socialist. Several hundred students and workers were sent to Cuba, for instance. Libya provided oil credits and subsidies without which the Ghanaian administration, faced with a depleted treasury, would have collapsed.

Facing Rawlings and his supporters were the representatives of the old order. Not surprisingly—given that the early 1980s was the heyday of Reaganism—it has been said that the U.S. embassy in Accra offered support to these forces. Several coups were mounted against the NDC, which led in turn to violent countermeasures. Ghana's unsolved economic problems continued to cast shadows of doubt on Rawlings's competence as an economic manager. Farmers protested and cut back on production for the market. By mid-1983, as in the last years of Nkrumah, food prices were out of control and the Volta Dam ran out of water in the midst of a great drought. Middle-class interest groups such as lawyers and Christian churchmen, groups that had supported the earlier Busia regime and were themselves supported from the U.S. embassy in Accra, denounced the NDC. As one U.S. writer notes, the Ghanaian state itself seemed to be withering away: "By the early 1980s it was apparent that Ghana had forfeited its elementary ability to maintain internal or external order and to hold sway over its population.... The Ghanaian state thus seemed to be on the brink of becoming less distinctive and relevant."[13]

Under intense pressure from both inside and outside the country, the NDC became increasingly divided between left and right. Rawlings's policies became more conservative and authoritarian. Leftists were arrested, sacked, or went into exile. After an unsuccessful coup attempt against him in November 1982, in 1983 Rawlings made his peace with the IMF and the World Bank and loans began again to flow into the country accompanied by prerequisite economic reforms. In Washington the U.S. president signalled his approval of the new developments in Ghana. Reagan had found another version of Jamaica's Edward Seaga, this time in Africa.

For a decade from 1983 Ghana became a model of redemption in the literature of the banks, lending institutions, and the journals promoting neoliberalism. Indeed, under the guidance of the World Bank's Structural Adjustment Programs, the country reached an annual growth rate of 5 per cent per year. Ghana defeated raging inflation, restored investor confidence, and paid off $600 million in debt. How had it done it?

The problem was, Ghana had made these strides, first of all, by borrowing more. In 1983, when structural adjustment was first imposed, Ghana owed $1.7 billion. By 1993 it owed $4.6 billion. In 1983 Ghana's external debt was 41 per cent of GNP; by 1993 it was 66 per cent. Ghana paid 13 per cent of its export earnings in debt servicing in 1980, and 23 per cent in 1993.[14] While exports increased, imports decreased. Yet even with increased exports, Ghana was on a treadmill, because as the cocoa farmers produced more, the price for cocoa plummeted (with a 48 per cent drop in 1986-89).

Not only were there fewer imports and more debt, despite increased production, but there was also more unemployment. Central to structural adjustment programs was "trade liberalization," which meant that any countries borrowing from the IMF and World Bank were obliged to remove tariff barriers. When the Ghanaians removed protection from their textile industry, the mills, faced with a flood of cheaper imports, were forced to close down, which in turn created unemployment. Alongside unemployed textile workers were unemployed civil servants, for the SAPs also insisted that state expenditures and institutions be cut back. Whereas Nkrumah had sought to industrialize Ghana, the World Bank was going in the other direction, presiding over a policy emphasizing the rural over the urban. The Bank was successfully forcing an abandonment of any attempt at industrialization. Between 1986 and 1991, although GDP grew by 4.8 per cent, employment dropped by more than 13 per cent.[15]

Two groups in Ghana benefited from this approach: the Western-educated, bureaucratic elite, and a sizable proportion of the country's cocoa farmers. As in other African countries, such as Kenya, the farmers were joined to the bureaucrats "umbilically," to use Bill Freund's term.[16] Although the rural poverty level remained the same at 37 per cent and the urban poverty level, at 59 per cent, was the highest in Africa outside of Ethiopia (which suffered from both drought and civil war), Ghana continued to be held up as a source of emulation by the IMF and the World Bank. This is less than surprising, given that under the aegis of the World Bank and the IMF Ghana's development became focused on the rural areas and the production of food and raw materials. Urban poverty declined by a much smaller degree, and, significantly, over 35 per cent of the Ghanaian population lived in urban areas by the mid-1990s.[17]

In late 1992 Rawlings and his NDC held elections for a transition to democracy, and in January 1993 they inaugurated the Ghanaian Fourth Republic. Rawlings was still personally popular, and the term "recovery" had become popular. At the head of the only effective political machine in the country and thanks to a great deal of strategic political spending, especially in the rural areas (on electrification and roads, for instance), he became president. The next year his administration laid off over 10,000 employees of the state-owned cocoa marketing board; their dismissal had originally been due in 1992, but this was not politically convenient given the elections of 1993. Still, Rawlings's government did not shun the role of the state: it pushed ahead on the project for increased rural electrification and protected other jobs in the public sector. By 1995 Rawlings's popularity had suffered a sharp decline following protests that erupted against his policies in 1993 and continued through the spring of 1995, when several people were killed in the midst of an Accra demonstration against the introduction of new taxes recommended by the World Bank.

By the middle of the decade the World Bank, having pronounced the

Ghanaian experiment in economic reform a success, was waiting to hand the torch of development to the private sector. Yet private capital was not forthcoming. Meanwhile, many of the problems of the pre-1983 economy seemed poised to return: growth had dropped to 3 per cent, the local currency, the cedi, continued to decline in value, interest rates remained exorbitant, unemployment soared, and capital and talent preferred to move, or to stay, overseas. The country found itself with one doctor for every 25,000 people, with 39.3 per cent of its people lacking "basic, or minimally essential human capabilities."[18]

The Bank was sticking by its 1992 promise of "accelerated growth," a promise that foresaw Ghana's economy moving upward to a position close behind the economies of the leading Asian countries. Certainly the basis of this takeoff would not be industrialization, for as Daniel Green pointed out, the basis of the country's economy—the export of the staples gold, timber, and cocoa—remained much as it had been in the colonial period.[19]

# Kenya: Emergency Evacuation

Colonial improvisation, marked by a confusion of purposes and stimulated by crisis, attained its most dramatic form in the East African colony of Kenya. After the beginning of the 20th century Kenya was settled by Europeans and South Africans whose interests were guarded by a sympathetic colonial government. The early promotional literature used to attract white settlers to Kenya referred to the colony as "a white man's country," suggesting a New Zealand with a slightly enlarged "native question." But the white settlers were soon to be disabused of any notions of power. As a British secretary of state told them, "No government in this country would ever agree to the claim on the part of the white settlers to govern on their own."[20] There were too few settlers and too many eyes on the colony to turn Kenya into another Southern Rhodesia.

Kenya's Africans, who could not be kept invisible because they outnumbered the whites by more than a thousand to one, were nonetheless supposed to be politically mute. They were to be seen working in the fields, but not heard in the assemblies. Africans were also discouraged from competing with the white settlers. Their access to land was restricted, and many of them were forced onto overcrowded reserves. They were forbidden to grow certain crops, and they received almost nothing in the way of economic assistance. Colonial provision for the health and education of the settlers was more than adequate; for Africans it was derisory.

In the 1940-45 period the white settlers in Kenya had a "good war."

Far from the battlefields, they enjoyed peace and profits. By 1945 they had every expectation that a white Kenya had a sunny future, and they intended to guide that future. During the war there had even been talk in official circles in London of some form of white self-government in Kenya—that is, of creating a duplicate South Africa on the Indian Ocean. Large-scale postwar immigration encouraged the white Kenyans in this belief. The settler population grew from 22,800 in 1939 to around 60,000 by the late 1950s. In the same period the African population increased from just under six million to just over eight million.

The Africans, for their part, had not had a particularly good war. Drafted into Britain's imperial armies, many had served as foot soldiers in the campaign against the Italians in Ethiopia, while some had even been transported as far away as Burma to fight the Japanese. Many of the African soldiers, including some future Mau Mau leaders, made contact with Indian nationalists who influenced their thinking about the British.* At home, others had continued to work as sharecroppers on white-owned farms. It was apparent to many of them that subsistence farming on the crowded reserves was heading for crisis. Large numbers of young people had flooded into Nairobi and Mombasa, where work and opportunity had been available during the war years. A few others had made money as farmers and small entrepreneurs.

In 1944 the governor of Kenya, Sir Philip Mitchell, had appointed the first African to the colony's Legislative Council. Mitchell, like Sir Bernard Bourdillon, was a paternalist. But towards Sir Philip, historians have seldom been kind. Mitchell appears to have been a dim if well-meaning colonial bureaucrat who believed in "multiracialism" (wherein a smattering of anglicized Africans might be allowed to hold responsible jobs in the colony) and to have feared that the European population might exploit the weaknesses of the African masses. He thought European emigration and investment were the best means of guaranteeing African development. Oxford-educated Eluid Mathu, whom he appointed, was a token African in an assembly of European settlers and officials together with a small number of Asian businessmen, most of whom had been recruited by the British for their commercial skills.

Other than Mathu and a second African, a Luo, appointed two years later, Africans lacked official representation in the Kenyan government. This was all the more objectional because the population of educated Africans was large and growing. By the late 1940s there were over 40,000 Africans in government service, notably at its lowest levels, as well as

---

* I owe this point and several others in this chapter to Bruce Berman, Queen's University.

many small businessmen and wealthy farmers. Thus there were almost as many propertied and literate Africans in Kenya as there were settlers.

## Mau Mau and Jomo Kenyatta, 1946-79

The Kikuyus were the largest ethnic group in Kenya, and it was mainly their lands, located in the pleasant and fertile "White Highlands," that the European settlers had appropriated.* In 1925 they had formed a political organization called the Kikuyu Central Association (KCA), which by the 1930s had been well on its way to acquiring a mass base among the Kikuyu peasantry and migrants. After being banned as subversive in 1940 the KCA continued to grow underground, alongside other smaller organizations. It was the main forum that its members had to air their grievances, which centred mainly around loss of land to the settlers.

In 1944 another organization, the Kenya African Union (KAU), was founded in the space created by the banned KCA. Its first head, Harry Thuku, had been involved in improving conditions for Africans since the 1920s. Thuku was succeeded by Johnstone "Jomo" Kenyatta (1890-1978), who returned to Kenya in 1946 after a decade and a half in Britain, where he had lobbied for the KCA and studied anthropology under the famous Anglo-Polish pioneer in that field, Bronislaw Malinowski. Kenyatta, like Nkrumah and other contemporary African leaders, bore the prestige (and carried the cultural baggage) associated with long sojourns in the West. By 1950 the KAU had built its membership up to around 150,000. Until it was banned in 1953, it remained moderate, elitist, and constitutionalist, with its main source of strength the modern and Westernized element among the African population.

While the KAU was not quite as constitutional and conservative as the Gold Coast's UGCC, the Africans on the crowded reserves and in the squalid townsites tended to see it as being ineffective. This was especially the case after the agricultural "disturbances" of 1947, which came as a consequence of the European settlers' attempt to force African squatters off their land in the White Highlands. The settlers proposed turning the Africans into an agricultural proletariat, available to white landowners as cheap labour. This had already become the fate of most Africans in the rural parts of South Africa. The government of Kenya supported this

---

* Some 40 major ethnic groups live in Kenya, divided into 120 subgroups. Four of these make up around 44 per cent of the population: the Kikuyu comprise around 20 per cent of the total, numbering (in 1993) some 5.3 million; the Abaluhya constitute 13 per cent and number 3.5 million; the Luo 12 per cent, around 3 million; and the Kamba about 2.8 million. Other groups include the Kalenjin (from which Kenyatta's successor, arap Moi, originated), the Meru, Maasai, Turkana, Somali, and Gusii.

project by allowing the Legislative Council to pass laws restricting both the land and livestock of Africans while increasing the number of days the landless Africans were expected to work for their white masters. This idea was at the same time both politically reactionary and economically radical. Politically, the attempt to subordinate Africans to Europeans was, by the middle of the 20th century, an anachronism. Economically, it was modern, because it sought to stimulate capitalist agriculture as the basis of economic development. That it was even considered underlines the depth of the British miscalculation, both in Kenya and in London, about the future of white rule in Africa. The approach was made easier to swallow by the continued exportation of colonial commodities, such as tea and coffee, to Britain, which saved the British government valuable dollars, because goods not produced within the sterling area had to be bought for dollars on the world market. The settlers and those who supported them in Britain made it clear that only whites could be trusted to produce these valuable export crops.

Gradually, mainly among the Kikuyu, a radical mobilization took place, including ex-servicemen, frustrated farmers, the landless, and youth who gravitated to organizations that were more militant than the KAU. These disaffected Africans were increasingly bound together in secret organizations by "oathing," that is, the pledging of solidarity with dire sanctions if the oaths were violated. Colonial repression, responding to a political situation that since 1947 seemed to be spiralling out of control with a series of strikes, demonstrations, and acts of violence, drove the African opposition underground. Invisible but alive in the racist fantasies of the white population, these organizations assumed monstrous forms.

By the early 1950s oathing had become a mass phenomena and more and more accompanied by physical attacks on those Africans, like the chiefs, who supported the colonial system and profited from it. The African parts of Nairobi were no longer under government control. Striking out often blindly, the colonial police made dozens of arrests of suspects. On October 20, 1952, just a few days after one of the colony's most faithful chiefs had been assassinated, a newly appointed governor of Kenya declared a state of emergency: all civil liberties and all legal protection of individuals were suspended. In essence the declaration acknowledged a state of civil war between the colonial regime and the majority of its African subjects. Amid near hysterical media coverage, orchestrated from London, troops were flown into Kenya from Britain and Egypt. The enemy was suspected of being everywhere; any African seen through the distorting binoculars of any white vigilante might be regarded as a "terrorist" and shot on sight.

The state of emergency lasted for seven years (1952-59) and marked the bloodiest and most repressive epoch in the postwar history of British colonial Africa. Africans were arrested, interrogated, terrorized, tortured, and murdered in astonishing numbers; according to some estimates, as many as 25,000 Africans (but just over a hundred Europeans) were killed. Of this number, the colonial government hanged over 1,000 Africans. The administration justified its actions on the grounds that it was preventing the destruction of Christian civilization in Africa by a savage and atavistic secret organization. The opposition was generally known as "Mau Mau," a phrase without meaning in any language, European or African. According to one British Colonial Secretary, "Mau Mau" was inspired by Satan. The bewildered head of the KAU, Jomo Kenyatta, whose experience among kindly colonial reformers in Britain, where he had lived for nearly two decades, had not prepared him for the racist hysteria that had become normal in Kenya, was framed in a show trial and sentenced in 1953 to eight years' hard labour. Policing the emergency cost the colonial government around £55 million. With the turmoil coming at the same time as the war in Korea, a troop build-up in Egypt, and another colonial emergency in Malaysia, the British government had to scrape money from the bottom of the defence barrel.

Despite the emergency, between 1954 and 1964 the GDP of Kenya increased from £112 to £212 million as substantial new economic interests emerged in the colony. The realization dawned on the Colonial Office that from the point of view of British capitalism, it was the benefits of Kenyan agriculture that contributed importantly to Britain's sterling reserves, not the prosperity of the settlers themselves. By the late 1950s the share of Kenyan assets owned by the settlers—with many of their farms being marginal—was no more than 15-20 per cent. According to Colin Leys:

> Once the Emergency had called into question the continuation of the whole
> colonial economy and the security of foreign investments generally, it was
> not surprising that the newer commercial and industrial interests, and even
> the ranches and plantation companies, found themselves willing if necessary
> to abandon the settlers, who had hitherto been allowed to speak for all for-
> eign interests, and to seek an alliance with the African leaders prepared to
> accept the private enterprise system and allow them to stay in business.[21]

These African leaders included the government-salaried chiefs, business-men, land and cattle owners, those with secondary education, and some ex-servicemen. The British began to negotiate with them. In 1959, the year when the state of emergency was lifted, and three years after Ghana's declaration of independence, London announced, to an amazed

African audience, that it was determined to effect a quick transition from internal self-government to outright independence. As a first step the British removed the legal restrictions that had defended the prized White Highlands against African settlement. This land was now transferred to both poor smallholders and to richer Africans through a series of settlement schemes financed by the World Bank and the U.S. Agency for International Development (USAID). Most of the Africans who got land in the Highlands were Kikuyus, although it had been the Maasai who had earlier in the century been forced to give it up to the British. Africans started to trickle back to lands to which no African had rights since the early 20th century.

At the same time a new constitution was accepted in which Africans had the majority of the elected seats in the Legislative Assembly. Kenya, once advertised as a "White Man's Country," was now repackaged as a "Developing Nation." As in the Gold Coast, economists, generally appointed by the British government, explained the rules for governing and expanding the economy of this country to the prospective African leaders. Large-scale state ownership (as in Ghana and South Africa) was not to be an issue, although the state took over certain regulatory agencies, including the Coffee Board, the Tea Development Authority, and the Tourist Development Authority. Foreign investment was to be encouraged. Steps were taken for the purchase of white farms and their redistribution to selected African farmers, many of them with close links to the newly emergent African political leadership.

The leading political parties were the Kenya African National Union (KANU), established in 1960 and the direct descendant of KAU, and the Kenya African Democratic Union (KADU). KANU represented the Kikuyu and Luo peoples, KADU the other peoples in the colony. In the general elections of 1961, which were intended to provide the government for an independent Kenya, KANU won and almost immediately secured the release of the elderly Jomo Kenyatta, incarcerated since 1953. The British, for their part, also made demands. They got the KANU leadership to agree that Kenya should remain in the Commonwealth, to welcome foreign investment, to guarantee the continued operations of foreign firms working in Kenya, to favour British trade, and to give preference to Western, over non-Western, trade and aid. There was little fear, therefore, that the newly born Kenya might be adopted out of the family of Western capitalist states.

## Independence

On December 12, 1963, Kenya became independent, beginning the "Kenyatta Era," which lasted until the death of Jomo Kenyatta on August 23, 1978. Despite a rhetorical commitment to the rule of law and to socioeconomic equality, by the end of the first decade the regime had become notable for the concentration of power in the hands of President Kenyatta himself. This power was at the centre of a web of patronage and favouritism that enriched a rising "homeboy" network, notably Kikuyu in origin. Many of its members were from Kenyatta's home district of Kiambu. Over the same decade, rival centres of political power were destroyed. KADU, the left-wing Kenya People's Union (KPU), and even dissident elements within KANU had all ceased to exist by the end of the 1960s. Opposition leaders, dissatisfied ethnic groups, and protesting students were variously harassed, threatened, repressed, and, if lucky, sometimes even bought out. Many of their leaders were fortunate to have survived at all, although this was not the case with Tom Mboya, Kenyatta's Luo heir-apparent. In July 1969 Mboya was assassinated, presumably on the orders of those within the ruling Kikuyu group who feared his influence. In March 1975 Josiah Mwangi Kariuki, a populist critic of the ruling clique, was kidnapped and murdered by senior police officers.

In the first decade of independence the Africanization of Kenya was rapid. By 1970 two-thirds of the area reserved for whites in the colonial period was returned to Africans. Of the 7.4 million acres in the White Highlands, 1.5 million went to small (African) farmers, 2.2 million acres to large (also African) farmers, and 3.7 million acres remained with (mainly foreign) plantations. A special allotment of 1.6 million acres was also set aside for wealthy African landowners. This purchase of lands from the white settlers was financed by loans from the British Treasury and the World Bank, loans that the new government of Kenya now had to repay.

For other Kenyans—those who did not have capital, could not get loans, or had no influence—the benefits were less substantial. As J.D. Hargreaves notes, "Landless squatters and labourers, former 'freedom fighters' emerging from the forests, and the growing numbers of urban poor were left to seek their personal Uhuru ['freedom'] in the open market."[22]

## After Kenyatta, 1979-95

By the time Jomo Kenyatta died in August 1978, Kenya had become the perfect model of what Western political scientists in the 1960s called the "African one-party state," that is, a single-party dictatorship. This dictatorship was legalized in 1982, and for the next decade no rival parties existed. Throughout the 1980s few Western governments seemed concerned about this political structure or, indeed, about the increased use of state terror to deal with dissidence, a practice followed by Daniel arap Moi (b. 1924), Kenyatta's successor. What did apparently matter was Kenya's stability and its steady growth. But that growth, though extolled, was not untroubled. First of all, Kenya had to contend with the energy crisis, a problem for all countries with no domestic supplies of oil or coal. It also had to face a currency crisis. After that came Kenya's diminishing ability to feed itself, and, finally, by the end of the 1970s it appeared that Kenya had the highest rate of population growth *in the world*. According to the 1969 census, the population of Kenya was 10,942,705; a decade later it had risen to 15,327,061, and by 1993 it was 26.4 million.[23]

Still, from the mid-1960s to 1980 the World Bank at least saw signs of progress: "Kenya's growth rates in manufacturing, agriculture, and the service sector were consistently higher than those of almost all other sub-Saharan African countries." So during the 1980s, Africa's supposed "lost decade," Kenya's decline was less dramatic than that of its neighbours. In its 1988 survey, the United Nations Industrial Development Organization (UNIDO) pointed out that Kenya's per capita GDP had grown at an annual net rate of 2 per cent during the period 1965-85.[24] Here, furthermore, was an African state that had simultaneously attracted foreign capital and fostered an African entrepreneurial class. Even critics of arap Moi's dictatorial regime seemed to be impressed by the process of "Kenyanization"—the replacement of foreign capitalists by Kenyans. The policy of the increasingly Kenyanized state was Import Substitution Industrialization, sustained by a manufacturing sector that had developed in the 1950s to produce goods for the internal market. Kenya exported very little of its manufactures. The state, always considerate of the market, it was proclaimed, had done what every developing African state needed to do; it had successfully incubated an indigenous bourgeoisie (known, perhaps more to their detractors than to the officials of the World Bank, as the "Wabenzi," or "the people of the Mercedes Benz"). Here, then, was the dream of African development finally come true.

But within Kenya problems surfaced at two levels. First, there was not only persistent but spreading poverty. According to the World Bank, in 1990 most Kenyans were not any better off than most Haitians. Nor was wealth in Kenya distributed with notable equity. In the 1990s, as in Haiti, the Westernized and wealthy elite—landowners, politicians, professionals, business people—remain at the top of the ladder. This elite, according to Norman Miller and Rodger Yeager, saw themselves "as a cohesive group" deserving of "prestige and economic well-being." While their incomes varied, they were clearly set apart from the poor and the lower middle class not only in income but also in style. The members adopted "British standards in clothing, housing, furniture, and entertainment. They lived in red brick tiled bungalows with well-tended gardens in Nairobi's residential sections. They played tennis, drank whisky, and owned high-priced cars. Indeed, the new African elite who had joined or replaced the white elite not only copied their life-style but often adopted their outlook." According to Miller and Yeager, critics, especially university students, accused this elite "of perpetuating the dualistic social system of colonial days and of favouring a system of mutual accommodation with the remaining whites."[25]

Below the elite other classes ranged from the less Westernized but still respectable middle class (or petite bourgeoisie) of clerks, teachers, nurses, skilled workers, small merchants, and middle-income farmers through the underpaid and underemployed to the urban and rural poor—the landless and jobless. The poor, as Miller and Yeager describe them, "include underemployed labourers, drivers, clerks, waiters, and scrubbers, who rarely earn more than . . . \$50 per month. Below them, the poorest of the poor consist of casual day workers and the outright unemployed, who may form more than 15 per cent of Kenya's urban adult population."[26] Among women in the country, 33.2 per cent were illiterate in 1993, compared to 15.3 per cent of the men.[27]

It has been suggested that Kenya's stability has depended upon the belief of the middle class that at least some of its male members, some day, would make it to the top. In reality, for most, this advancement was unlikely. For women, it was almost inconceivable. In the mid-1980s, 70 per cent of Kenya's female population was rural and functionally illiterate. According to the UN Development Programme, "Ironically, in rural Kenya women do most of the farming: studies have shown that women do 35 per cent more work than men."[28] In the towns—with an urban unemployment rate of 23.8 per cent in 1993—women constituted less than 20 per cent of urban job holders, and the jobs that they held were the lowest-paid.[29]

If Kenya's prime problem was poverty and an inequitable distribution of wealth, a second problem was the condition of the state itself. Bureaucratic incompetence and corruption had become endemic, and a national scandal. According to the auditor-general, by 1991 the financial position of the important Ministry of Commerce and Industry was impossible to ascertain: that is, no one knew where the funds that were supposed to be used to administer Kenya's economic development had gone. The cost of this corruption to the Kenyan people and to Kenya's Western aid donors, according to David Himbara, was about \$500 million.[30]

The corruption and incompetence of the state raised a serious question. The laissez-faire Kenya state had served, according to the developmentalists, as the nursery of the indigenous bourgeoisie. Now it appeared that the state had acted more as a piggy bank for the delinquent rich rather than an effective nursery. The real heroes of the saga of the capitalist development of Kenya were not the African wielders of state power at all. They were the small stratum of hitherto invisible Asian entrepreneurs, most of whom had emigrated from India in the colonial period. These, like Kenya's Africans, had been disparaged by the rulers of the settler state. They had also been ignored by the platoons of developmentalists who trooped to Kenya in search of the grail of development. By the 1980s it gradually became evident that it was Kenya's Asians, not the foreign capitalists or the African entrepreneurs, who through their successful establishment of a wide range of industries were responsible for much of Kenya's relatively impressive economic showing. If this were the case, and since Kenya was touted as a development success story—"Eastern Africa's economic powerhouse," as it was called—questions were bound to be asked. One of these was likely to be: did the Kenyan experiment in African capitalism really work? Another was: were the developmentalists deluded by their own wishful thinking?

## Development?

By 1990 the Kenyan state had come under severe pressure from its Western patrons for reasons other than the failure of its indigenous politician-entrepreneurs. In the 1970s and 1980s, Kenya had been a favoured recipient of Western aid and other kinds of support from such institutions as the World Bank and the UN. Much of this aid had been spent, perhaps even squandered, in supporting the state, that is, in sustaining a political apparatus that would otherwise have been depleted through the corrupt practices of its leaders.

But by 1991 both the EC countries and the United States, at the suggestion of the World Bank and the IMF, had begun to tie aid to reforms—both reforms in human rights and reforms in economic policies, including a curbing of corruption. In the 1988 national elections, for instance, charges of ballot-rigging and intimidation had been commonplace. In February 1990 Kenya's minister of foreign affairs, Robert Ouko, was murdered, like Tom Mboya and J.M. Kariuki before him, for political reasons. He was, it seems, seen as being a rival to arap Moi himself. The former minister of energy was arrested for complicity in Ouko's murder and for misappropriating foreign aid. In July 1990 there were riots in Nairobi and elsewhere, and in November a new opposition party was formed by one of the oldest of arap Moi's rivals, Oginga Odinga. In late December 1991, several cabinet ministers resigned to protest the president's failure to call elections. In January 1992, somewhere between 100,000 and 200,000 Kenyans participated in an anti-government demonstration in Nairobi. Food riots occurred later in the year.

Arap Moi was forced to trim his political sails. He allowed oppositional political parties to be revived and elections to be held. Benefiting from a divided and disorganized opposition, in December 1992, in the first multiparty elections since independence, the president and his party (KANU) won the election with only 35 per cent of the seats. But the victory provided arap Moi with only cold comfort, because both the richest and most populous parts of the country voted against him and several of his senior ministers were defeated. Nor did the rebuke of the electorate persuade the president to change his political ways fundamentally: three years later there were still regular reports of opposition politicians being assaulted by KANU goons.

# South Africa

With the unification of four former British colonies, the Union of South Africa was established as a self-governing (but not sovereign) state in 1910. The country thus became politically independent half a century before most African countries to the north.* In this independent country, with the short-lived exception of Cape Province, only people of European descent had the vote at any level of government. "Natives," as Africans were called, were represented by whites.

The rapid political changes that transformed Africa after the Second World War were blocked in the southern part of the continent. Indeed, in the four decades after the war South African history flowed in the reverse direction. While Africans in the colonial Africa to the north were gradually becoming more or less liberated, in South Africa they were, until the 1980s, becoming increasingly oppressed. This oppression was carried out under the name of apartheid ("separation"), which was both a political ideology (clothed in a biblical metaphysics that served to guarantee the security and prosperity of the European minority) and the key aspect of a program for economic development.

Yet apartheid did not become the *official* political doctrine of the

---

\* Complete political sovereignty came to South Africa with the Statute of Westminster in 1933. South Africa remained a dominion within the Commonwealth until 1961, when it became a republic.

South African state until the victory of the Nationalist Party in 1948, and it was not invented out of the postwar blue, nor were its roots even South African. The laws that upheld it in South Africa had their origins in the 19th century. Fundamental to these laws was the well-established yet simple 18th-century European credo that a hierarchy of races existed, that the "white race" was superior, and that other races, whether "yellow," "red," or "black," were inferior. Just as in the heyday of New World slavery, a belief was accepted, generally using evidence from the Bible, that the black race had been designated by God or Nature to serve the whites. In South Africa, as in large parts of the world until as late as the second half of the 20th century, only a minority of those who benefited from the belief found it abhorrent.

Within the country a number of organizations opposed the concept of a South Africa in which a minority of people of European descent dominated a majority of people of African descent. The most important was the African National Congress (ANC), established in 1923 on the foundation of the earlier, and more exclusive, South African Native National Congress (SANNC), formed in 1912. These organizations had come into being at precisely the time when the white rulers of South Africa were legislating furiously to limit political and economic opportunities for Africans and others—such as the "Coloureds" (people of mixed race) and the Asians (some of whose ancestors had arrived in South Africa in the 17th century). In 1911, for instance, the whites had passed the Native Labour Regulation Act, which relegated blacks to the status of a cheap labour force by reserving the better jobs for whites. In 1913 the Natives Land Acts separated whites and blacks in rural areas, giving the Africans ownership rights to a mere 7 per cent of South Africa's lands. In the next two decades other laws, such as the 1920 Native Affairs Act and the 1923 Urban Areas Act, restricted African mobility and opportunity in other ways.

At first attracting only Westernized and urban Africans who were mostly the products of missionary education, after World War I the SANNC and ANC broadened their appeal to include rural and uneducated Africans. Still, education remained the basis for African advancement both within the African political organizations and outside of then. Between the wars, when the protests organized by the ANC tended to be restrained and ineffective, the body was eclipsed by other, more militant organizations. But during World War II, when the cautious old guard was replaced by a new, more assertive generation, this tendency was reversed. Many of the members of this generation rose within the Congress Youth League (CYL), founded in 1943 and open to all Africans between the ages of 12 and 40. One of these younger activists was

Nelson Mandela (b. 1918). By the early 1950s the leaders of the CYL had a firm control of the ANC.

As part of apartheid's second plank, development, South African industrialization was kicked off in the late 1920s, based on an ISI program that sought to produce consumer goods, nurtured behind protective walls, mainly for the country's remarkably small white population, which never exceeded 20 per cent of the total. (Of this 20 per cent, just under 60 per cent were Afrikaners (Dutch or French descendants), and just under 40 per cent were "English." Nonetheless, it was the largest white population in all of Africa.) By the 1960s, the golden decade of apartheid, South Africa had become largely self-sufficient in producing such goods.

Another side to import substitution was not focused so much on the production of consumer goods as on national security. This led to the promotion of heavily subsidized state-owned industries, including ARMSCOR (armaments manufacture), UCOR (uranium refining), SASOL (oil refining and chemical production), and FOSKOR (fertilizers). By 1970 the public share of total fixed investment was 46 per cent. The state was by far the largest single proprietor within the South African economy. The South African version of state-controlled industrialization seemed thus to be successful in keeping the economy in local hands, provided that those hands were white.

Yet one major difference separated the ISI policies of South Africa from those of South America: the treatment of labour. South African industrialization, into the 1980s, was based on the superexploitation of Africans, who were meant to furnish cheap, largely unskilled labour while themselves remaining bereft of the benefits of industrial development. The entire legal apparatus of the state, reinforced by almost limitless violence against dissidents, was designed to ensure the continuance of these conditions.*

During World War II the economy of South Africa, like that of the Gold Coast and Kenya, had boomed. But unlike the colonial economies of Africa, the South African economy was based on an increasing industrialization. The mining industry, from which profits had been skimmed to provide investment capital for industry, had been largely nationalized. The South African state had gradually taken mining over in the years after World War I, so that whereas in 1917 some 85 per cent of dividends from the industry were paid to foreign owners, by 1963 the amount was down

---

* There are suggestive similarities between the development of capitalism in South Africa and the development of socialism in China. In both countries the majority of the population, legally domiciled in the countryside, was excluded from the benefits presumably created by their labour power.

to 27 per cent. The state-owned monopolies had also expanded in the same period. South Africa in 1945 had therefore become, at an economic level, a model for those who believed in capitalist development through state ownership. The country's economy had much in common with states on the other side of the South Atlantic.

Increasing industrialization in the interwar years had changed the complexion of the workforce, which had also grown impressively. Due to a massive influx of Africans from the impoverished rural areas into the cities, by the end of the war out of 361,000 industrial workers, 249,000 were black. These workers had become increasingly militant, and strikes had become increasingly frequent. In 1942 the biggest and most comprehensive strike in South African history took place. This militancy was tolerated because of the expanding markets and high profits guaranteed by wartime conditions, but with the end of the war it became viewed as a problem. As elsewhere in the Western world, measures to contain working-class militancy rose to a commanding importance on the government agenda.

If the militancy of the African working class was the main problem for South Africa's rulers, it was not the only problem. In February 1948, when the Accra riots took place in the Gold Coast, the first forcible blow was struck against British colonialism in Africa. But even earlier signals had gone out from other places, such as India, Palestine, Indochina, and Indonesia, that the designs for a postwar, reformed, neocolonial empire were no longer workable. Closer to South Africa, in 1945 in Algeria and 1947 in nearby Madagascar, insurrections against French colonial rule had broken out. In this twin context—of accelerated social change (and, particularly, increased African militancy) *and* the incipient breakdown of European control in the colonial world—the Reconstituted Nationalist Party (Herstigte Nasionale Party) won a surprise victory in South Africa on May 26, 1948.

## The Heyday of White Rule, 1948-76

The head of the victorious Nationalists (the "Nats"), Daniel Malan (1874-1959), was an active member of the Dutch Reformed Church. Indeed, so inseparably fused were this Protestant church and Afrikaner nationalism that the ideology both professed was called "Christian-nationalism." Upon hearing the news of his victory, Malan announced, "South Africa belongs to us once more.... May God grant that it will always remain so."[31]

Malan's government was more explicitly white supremacist than any of its predecessors. That many of his followers had sympathized with the

Nazis during World War II should not be surprising: sympathy for the Nazis, up to the point that they began to lose the war, was widespread in Europe and among European settlers everywhere. After all, the major preoccupations of Nazism were order, economic development, and race supremacy.

The Nationalists pledged to fashion a new South Africa by means of the apartheid system. Most of the essential elements of this system were already at least partly in place; it remained only to fuse them into one thoroughgoing regimen from which there would be no escape. The man who accomplished this was the implacable, Dutch-born, Dr Hendrik Verwoerd (1909-66), who served as minister of national affairs from 1948-58 and prime minister from 1958-66. Verwoerd brought to South African politics some of the same gifts that Ayatollah Khomeini brought to politics in Iran. He was a fundamentalist—in his case a Calvinist—and incapable in his own eyes of error. He was driven by a furious self-righteousness informed by religious visions that he claimed to have on a regular basis, which led to his belief that apartheid was divinely inspired. The clergy of the Calvinist Dutch Reformed Church only demurred from this line of interpretation under duress, such as in the aftermath of the 1960 Sharpeville massacre when a number of them proclaimed that apartheid had no scriptural (that is, biblical) foundation. Like most fundamentalists, Verwoerd explained his political philosophy in terms that schoolchildren could understand: "South Africa is a white man's country and . . . he must remain the master here. In the reserves we are prepared to allow the Native to be the masters: we are not the masters there. But within the European areas, we, the white people, are and shall remain the masters."

The apartheid system was installed by means of a series of particular laws meant to separate the races, break the political will of the majority Africans, and guarantee the accessibility and exploitation of their labour power. The Mixed Marriages Act of 1949 outlawed union between the races, while the Group Areas Act of 1950 gave the government sweeping powers to remove Africans from the towns and cities and to relocate them on the numerous reserves scattered throughout the country, with each reserve belonging to a "tribe."* These laws enforced the physical separation of the races and, at the same time, controlled African movement within the country. The reserves on which the "Bantus" were to reside were known as "homelands." The physical boundaries of the 10 specified

---

* Since most Africans in South Africa, like most North American Indians, had been urbanized, the meaning of the term "tribe" was ascriptive and political rather than social. Collectively Africans were called "Bantus" in white officialese, at least until April 1994, when they became full citizens.

homelands were defined in the "Promotion of Bantu Self-Government Act" of 1959. The areas were poorly endowed in land and other resources, lacked infrastructure, and, because they were widely separated, easy to control. Some of them, like Indian reserves in Canada, were made up of different sections separated from one another. Whether dispersed or not, each "tribe" got its own homeland. The various acts—such as the 1950 Group Areas Act, the Prevention of Illegal Squatting Act (1951), and the 1954 amendment to the 1936 Natives Trust and Land Act—led to millions of black people being forcibly ejected from "white lands." As Dan O'Meara points out, these people "were usually dumped unceremoniously to 'adapt or die' in remote and primitive 'resettlement areas.' The generally appalling conditions in these 'dumping grounds' regularly produced excruciating poverty, rampant disease and crippling infant mortality. The intense human suffering in places such as Dimbaza, Limehill, Soewater and hundreds of others provoked international outrage and led to charges of genocide against the government."[32]

With the establishment of the homelands, most Africans became "guest workers" in their own country, forced to carry passes that limited their residency in areas reserved for the whites. The Pass Laws were strictly enforced; Africans without passes or with expired passes would be jailed, fined, and sentenced to forced labour. Thus it was that Africans had fewer civil rights in South Africa than Yugoslav migrant workers had in Sweden or Turkish guest workers had in Germany. Having no rights to residence or naturalization in "white" South Africa, the Africans were doomed to perpetual migration—leaving the homelands to sell their labour, and returning to the homelands with goods bought in "white" South Africa, or to marry and have children, or when they were unemployed, or too badly injured, or too old to work.

Not all Africans suffered the same fate or had the same status. Many had the right to live in the all-African suburbs that ringed the white cities, places known as the "townships." In the homelands as well as in the townships, a fragile African bourgeoisie rose, comprising businessmen and lawyers, dependent on white South Africa for their legitimacy and security but able to acquire a modest wealth and education. As elsewhere in Africa, some members of this class came from the families of local chiefs. Nelson Mandela was one such, and so was his antagonist, Mangosuthu Buthelezi (b. 1928), appointed by the Nationalist government to rule the homeland known as KwaZulu.

## From Sharpeville (March 1960) to Soweto (June 1976)

It was against the apartheid system in general, and against the rigid appli-
cation of the Pass Laws that had been devised to control the movement of
Africans, in particular, that a protest in the town of Sharpeville in the
Southern Transvaal was organized on March 21, 1960. The protest was
one of a number organized hastily by the Pan-African Congress (PAC), a
black nationalist splinter that had broken away from the African National
Congress and stressed that the future of South Africa, which they called
"Azania," was to be black, not multiracial. The ANC had itself organized a
massive protest for ten days later. At Sharpeville as many as 10,000 people
turned up to demonstrate peacefully. Under the circumstances, in which
white security and prosperity depended upon African submission, there
could only be one official reaction: large-scale and visible repression. The
South African police attacked the protestors, killing 67 and injuring 186.

The effects of this repression were ultimately just the opposite of
what was intended, for in the gory ground of Sharpeville the seeds of a
new phase of resistance to apartheid were sown. But the process of
growth of this opposition was slow and painful, for it came at the beginning of the period of the most rapid economic expansion in South
Africa's history.

The year 1960 was memorable for more than Sharpeville. It was also
the vintage year of African independence, when Cameroon, Togo, Soma-
liland, the Belgian Congo, Nigeria, Mali, and Mauritania all became free
from colonial rule. By this year, too, other African and West Indian
colonies were poised for independence: Sierra Leone would become free
in the next year, and so would Tanganyika. Yet if the message of this global
tide of decolonization was not lost on South Africa's Africans, it seems to
have been inaudible to their rulers.

Hardly less propitiously, three months after Sharpeville another
nationalist movement was maturing in Mozambique, on South Africa's
northeast border. There, in June 1960, 300 protesting agricultural workers
were shot down in the town of Mueda by Portuguese security forces. This
massacre marked the beginning of a new stage of Mozambican anti-
colonialism, a stage given direction by the 1962 founding of the Front for
the Liberation of Mozambique. FRELIMO was to spearhead the colony's
struggle to independence, attained finally in 1975. A year after
Sharpeville, the other Portuguese colony in Southern Africa, Angola, was
also swept by rebellion. Thus the violent reaction of the police at
Sharpeville and the following repression were like a dyke raised to stop a
swelling continental tide.

Some outsiders were aware of this. The British had, after all, just lost most of their African empire. In South Africa they were particularly sensitive because of their huge investments. South Africa had soaked up more British capital than the whole of the rest of the continent. In February 1960, in a speech in Cape Town, British Prime Minister Harold Macmillan warned of the "strength of African national consciousness." But his white listeners were deaf to his hints.

In South Africa itself, after the Sharpeville massacre the cycle of rebellion and repression continued, with the forces of the state quite quickly gaining the upper hand. The PAC and ANC organized campaigns of resistance, although both organizations were outlawed and effectively smashed by 1963. They thus both remained largely ineffective until after the Soweto uprising in 1976. The high noon of white triumph came in a theatrical show trial in 1964, at the conclusion of which the ANC leader, lawyer Nelson Mandela, and seven others were jailed for life, charged with "sabotage and subversion." To the pique of many whites, Mandela narrowly avoided being hanged.

Into the void created by the suppression of the ANC and the PAC stepped the "Black Consciousness Movement," which became the main force of opposition to apartheid in the 1970s. The movement, formed in the late 1960s, had its political focus defined by an African student from Natal, Steve Biko (1946-77), who asked, "Who better to represent the oppressed than the oppressed themselves?" The question was especially directed at the white South African leftists who had such a powerful influence in the ANC. The slogan "Black Man, You Are On Your Own" encapsulated no less clearly the Black Consciousness ideology, although "black" did not refer exclusively to Africans. It was also, in this case, meant to include Indians and Coloureds.

Because of its doctrine of non-violence, Black Consciousness was not repressed by the authorities and in the early 1970s continued to grow, especially among high school and university students. But it never succeeded in winning mass support, and by 1973 its leaders, too, had been banned by the South African government—that is, effectively placed under house arrest. After the Soweto crisis of July 1976, the government came down even more heavily on the movement, arresting Biko and later murdering him in jail in September 1977. From that point on Black Consciousness declined, with other organizations taking its place, among them the United Democratic Front (UDF) and the Congress of South African Trade Unions (COSATU).

The state repression of the ANC, PAC, and the Black Consciousness Movement was affordable because of the remarkable boom of the South African economy. From 1948 to 1972, and especially from 1964 to 1972,

South Africa experienced one of the highest growth rates in the capitalist world; an average annual increase of 6-8 per cent. Foreign investment flooding into the country permitted South African defence expenditures to increase from $63 million to $1 billion between 1960 and 1975. The whites saw this spending as being quite acceptable; by 1970 they had replaced Californians as the world's most affluent people. For whites the promised land of Jerusalem-beside-the-Swimming-Pool had been reached. For Africans, the 1960s and 1970s were still Babylon-under-Cardboard, politically the bleakest period in contemporary South African history. Presiding over what O'Meara calls "a grubby . . . little police state" was the spirit of Hendrik Verwoerd. "I see the National Party today," he had proclaimed, "as a party which stands for the preservation of the White man, of the White government in South Africa."[33] The prophet could no longer proclaim his message in the flesh, however. He was assassinated by a deranged fellow white man in early September 1966.

Verwoerd's successor was a former minister of justice, Balthazar Johannes Vorster (1915-83), who had been interned during World War II for Nazi sympathies.* While he made it clear that he planned to follow in Verwoerd's footsteps, Vorster's options became quite different. Although in his early years as prime minister South Africa was still enjoying what Chris Alden calls "the halcyon days of the apartheid state," quite suddenly, in the early 1970s, South Africa's miraculous growth rate slowed down and inflation increased.[34] Foreign investment, once thrusting, shrivelled nervously. After 1972 came wave after wave, a swelling tide, of strikes and protests that crashed against the dykes of apartheid and brought an end to the tranquillity that had characterized the political scene since the 1960s. By the mid-1970s South Africa was experiencing both a recession and a huge balance of payments deficit. The rand was devalued twice in 1975 alone. Among the whites there was a whisper of worry. A leading businessman mused aloud about the necessity of some change, "if we are to keep all that we have."[35]

From outside the country came other shocks that amplified the distress of the South African state and brought the auditor knocking on the door: the increase in oil prices following the Arab-Israeli ("Yom Kippur")

---

* On the eve of World War II hundreds of Afrikaners became *Stormjaers* (Stormtroopers) in the pro-Nazi *Ossewabrandwag* ("Ox-wagon sentinel"). One of these was the Reverend Koot Vorster, brother of the future Prime Minister John Vorster. In an address to a student group on September 15, 1940, the reverend proclaimed: "Hitler's 'Mein Kampf' shows the way to greatness—the path of South Africa. Hitler gave the Germans a calling. He gave them a fanaticism which causes them to stand back for no one. We must follow this example because only by such holy fanaticism can the Afrikaner nation achieve its calling." Quoted in Bundy, *An Illustrated History of South Africa*, 1988, p.349.

war of late 1973; South Africa's main trading partner, Britain, joined the protectionist European Economic Community; and, most unnerving of all, a revolution in Portugal on April 25, 1974, followed a year later by the independence of Angola and Mozambique, both under Marxist governments. Some 500 years of Portuguese colonialism in Africa had come to an end. No longer was South Africa comfortably insulated from the rest of the continent by a sympathetic Portuguese colonialism.

Adding to the shock, on June 16, 1976, came "Soweto," the code word for a huge and bloody uprising lasting for three months and driven by schoolchildren, many of them influenced by the ideas of the Black Consciousness Movement. These children were in open revolt against the hopelessness of their lives and only tenuously linked to existing political organizations. The Soweto uprising was centred in one of the black townships near Johannesburg ("Soweto" deriving from "South-West Township"). Its most persistent images were of skinny schoolchildren throwing stones at armoured personnel carriers, of burning tires, and of policemen shooting at the schoolchildren—killing nearly 200 of them "officially" and as many as 600 to 700 unofficially.

The Soweto uprising was followed by revolts in other townships. According to O'Meara, "Like 'Munich' or 'Suez,' 'Soweto' was one of those rare historical catalysts which irreversibly transform the political landscape, whose very name becomes a metaphor for lessons learned by an entire society."[36] The event reversed what whites had hitherto thought was possible; some now began to wonder if the impossible was now inevitable. Less than a year after Soweto, in early 1977, the political commentator R.W. Johnson completed a book that raised the question many had been asking. Its title: *How Long Will South Africa Survive?*

Significantly, the Soweto events fell just a year after the fall of Saigon and just three years before the fall of the pro-Western regime of the shah of Iran and of the Somosa regime in Nicaragua. The period of the Soweto uprising represented the final great heave of the Third World against the last holdouts of postwar Western domination. Importantly, for this was the mid-1970s, everywhere that there was upheaval there was also television, so now people could watch and learn—about the possibility of urban insurgency, for instance. And, in many places, as in South Africa, people "making history" could even watch themselves. Furthermore, since the time of Sharpeville television had ended the possibility that massive public oppression could be engineered out of sight. So not only did South Africans watch their children being gunned down, but so, too, did the rest of the television-watching world. In sitting rooms from Delhi to Detroit people wondered if there wasn't something not quite right in the practice of white policemen killing black schoolchildren, randomly and publicly. By 1985 the kids in the streets had made many of the African townships ungovernable, thus raising another consideration, perhaps less humane, in the minds of foreign investors: what if the youngsters could not be brought under control?

As a result of the Soweto uprising, foreign investment, which had rushed into South Africa because of the attraction of high rates of profitability—and which in the early 1970s had already begun to decline—beat an even more hasty retreat. Over the next decade, the whooshing of imaginary dollars, pounds, and Deutschmarks as they fled across the ionosphere was accompanied by the moaning of a wounded South African economy and the lamentations of its white chiefs.

These white leaders responded to the Soweto crisis in several ways. They attempted, of course, to stem the tide of disinvestment. In 1977 the South African Defence Force (SADF) conceived of the "Total National Strategy" as the centrepiece of South Africa's self-redemption. The avowed objects of this strategy were to preserve "free enterprise" and rescue South Africa from "the Marxist threat." This "threat," it was alleged, came from two different directions: from the Marxist regimes to the north in Mozambique and Angola; and, at home, from the non-Marxist but nonetheless banned Black Consciousness Movement, and the banned ANC and organizations allied to it, one of which was the South African Communist Party (SACP). The SACP, outlawed in 1950, had come to life again after Soweto.*

The Total National Strategy combined terror (against the regime's enemies) with opportunities (for its collaborators, especially if they were African). For most of South Africa's black population it meant increased arrests, forced removals, declining living standards, and a hurricane of violence. In the decade of this policy's life, from 1978 to 1989, the mask of what one writer called "the democratic police state" was removed entirely.

To outsiders the claims of the Total National Strategy had limited plausibility. The Carter administration in Washington made it clear that the strategic value of the Cape of Good Hope was only slightly greater than that of Cape Horn—very limited, to say the least. (South Africa's

---

* The SACP had been formed in 1921. Although in the first decades of its existence its leadership was largely white, from the outset it was the only political party (that is, white political party, since non-white parties could not exist) open to all races and concerned with mobilizing the African majority. In the Cape, where, exceptionally, non-whites were allowed to run for municipal office, the SACP ran, and elected, a "Coloured" woman, Zainunissa Gool, in 1937. "Cissie" Gool was thus the first woman elected to any political office in Africa.

leaders had exaggerated fears concerning the political orientation of Jimmy Carter: "It will be exactly as if the Marxists had taken over," one of their spokesmen nervously suggested.) This projection failed the credibility test. Its failure to convince was reflected in the report of the Study Commission on U.S. Policy towards South Africa, published in 1981. The report came to the same conclusion as Johnson's book: time was running out for white South Africa.

## After Vorster

As the Americans predicted, the crisis would not go away and white South African political casualties began to mount. In early 1979, after a negative economic growth rate for two years, a new prime minister took over from B.J. Vorster. P.W. Botha (b. 1916), a hard-line former minister of defence, first sought to increase his own manoeuvrability by driving the right wing out of the Nationalist Party. He then concentrated power in the State Security (SS) Council, the chosen means for destroying the regime's main antagonists. Appointments to the SS Council were to be made exclusively by the prime minister himself. The Council, dominated by senior military officers, was mandated to deal with all matters of national security, from the price of bread to foreign policy. Parliament was sidestepped. The Chilean model of modernization guaranteed by repression had now arrived in South Africa; the epoch of the "national security state" had begun.

The idea of "national security" as a political doctrine had first emerged in the United States around 1950 as a program to combat communism at home and abroad. The idea of domestic and foreign policy being tied together to serve the single goal of preserving the status quo was exported to Third World countries as a means of combatting any political agendas that threatened the interests of the U.S. government and its allies. It was convenient to label these agendas "communist" and thus a threat to U.S. security, whether they were or not. P.W. Botha regularly spoke of the "Marxist threat." In the House of Assembly in July 1970 he explained, "The Western World—or the Free World, to put it more broadly—is being threatened by the global and total strategy under the leadership of aggressive communism."[37] When communism disappeared as a plausible threat, the practitioners of the "national security" strategy promoted the spectre of "international terrorism" to fill its place.

But as a means of turning back the clock to the happy days of white economic and political security, the Total Strategy and the SS Council could only be stop-gap measures. This became increasingly evident as the walls of apartheid began to fall inwards on its defenders, pushed by forces they could not control. A particularly hard blow was delivered when formerly white-ruled Rhodesia became independent under an African regime in 1980, now becoming "Zimbabwe." With Angola and Mozambique abandoned by the Portuguese five years earlier, the colonial *cordon sanitaire* was now entirely removed, and the white regime in South Africa was almost totally surrounded by unsympathetic African governments.

## Neighbours

For nearly a decade after its independence, Mozambique served as a sanctuary for guerrillas entering South Africa. Pretoria responded to this by training and financing its own version of *contras*, whose organization REN-AMO (Movement of National Resistance) succeeded by means of a calculated campaign of terror in devastating and depopulating large areas of rural Mozambique, thereby destroying the country's economy. From the South African point of view, the strategy worked. Under pressure from the *contras*, in March 1984, the government of Mozambique signed the Nkomati Accords, which closed off Mozambique to the guerrillas. But South Africa almost immediately flouted these accords and even went a step further by organizing the assassination in October 1986 of the President of Mozambique, Samora Machel. RENAMO meanwhile continued its devastating work, and by the end of the decade much of rural Mozambique was a wasteland terrorized by predatory guerrilla bands. The cost of this terror was hundreds of thousands of lives and as much as $15 billion, yet even the crucifixion of Mozambique could not guarantee redemption for white South Africa.

Whereas the South Africans were able to destabilize Mozambique at arm's length by using surrogates, in Angola the *contra* force, the pro-Western and tribalist UNITA (Union for the Total Independence of Angola), was less effective, especially since the Cubans had sent forces to help support the government. South African troops had invaded southern Angola in October 1975 to help UNITA overthrow the country's Marxist government, but the white warriors, outgunned by the Angolans and their Cuban allies, were forced to retire in March 1976. Inevitably the South Africans were drawn back into Angola, with even more disastrous results. In the battle of Cuito Canavale at the end of 1988, they were trapped by Cuban and Angolan government forces and, under threat of annihilation, forced to withdraw, not only from Angola but also from Namibia, which the South Africans had long controlled and used (against the protests of the UN) as a buffer state. In the eleventh hour of the Cold War, then, the Cubans had forced one of the West's most favoured allies to raise the white flag. On December 22, 1989, a set of agreements involving Angola, Cuba, and South Africa, underwritten by the superpowers, was signed at UN headquarters in New York. These led to Namibian independence on March 21, 1990—the last African colony to be freed from white colonialism.

## The End of Apartheid

The white minority's scramble towards a new, post-apartheid policy had unofficially begun as early as July 1985, when a number of white South African businessmen took the initiative to launch talks in Lusaka, Zambia, with the ANC. Their object was obvious: to prevent the deep wells of capitalism from being poisoned by the decomposing corpse of the ancien régime. The next month P.W. Botha promised sweeping reforms. But words were not enough; following the example of Chase Manhattan, foreign banks that had loaned funds to keep the ailing South African economy alive were demanding repayment. In one day, August 27, 1985, the value of the South African rand plummeted from 55 to 33 U.S. cents. Then, to the noisy protests of South Africa's allies abroad, including U.S. Vice-President George Bush and British Prime Minister Margaret Thatcher, sanctions were imposed, first by Washington and then by the European Community and other Western countries. The import into Europe of gold coins, steel, and iron was banned, as was the export to South Africa of arms. Corporate disinvestment accelerated.

Botha, who had proved unable to conserve the status quo, had been destroyed by forces over which he had little or no control. The country's security police had become increasingly unable to contain the revolutionary struggle on the streets, and the white government faced serious economic difficulties aggravated by sanctions and a loss of confidence on the part of international capital. The credibility of the government's claim that the apartheid regime was a necessary bulwark against international communism in Africa had collapsed.

In January 1989, after suffering a stroke, P.W. Botha announced his resignation, but he held on to the office of state president long enough to stage a historic meeting in August with Nelson Mandela, the ANC's jailed leader. The two got together in Botha's official residence in Cape Town. F.W. de Klerk succeeded Botha as head of the Nationalist Party, and like Botha announced his willingness to work for gradual political reform. An election in September 1989 left the Nationalist Party with a greatly reduced majority as both the Conservatives—who favoured stricter enforcement of apartheid laws—and the Democratic Party—calling for the immediate abolition of apartheid—gained ground.

South Africa's mammoth debt crisis continued to grow while apartheid's international allies, including Thatcher, urged retreat. The British prime minister became increasingly insistent on a negotiated settlement with the ANC, which would necessarily involve Mandela's liberation. Then, to the amazement of friend and foe alike, on February 2, 1990, the day parliament opened, de Klerk announced the lifting of the government ban on the ANC, the PAC, the South African Communist Party, and other proscribed organizations. On February 11, 1990, de Klerk released Mandela, who had by that point spent 27 years in jail. It was as if the thick steel bars that had secured the apartheid state had suddenly been cut through.

In the 1989 election campaign de Klerk had declared, "White domination, *so much as it exists*, must come to an end," though he promised to maintain white neighbourhoods and schools. In 1990 he still seemed to envisage a South Africa ruled by whites but supported by means of a strategy called "elite pacting," which involved calculating African collaborators such as the Zulu leader Mangosuthu Buthelezi, head of the communalist and reactionary Inkatha Freedom Party. Although he was supported by funds and weapons from Pretoria, and by right-wing patrons abroad, Buthelezi had few followers beyond the province of Natal, where the Zulus were in the majority. By the end of 1992, despite a campaign seeking to destabilize the ANC by means of the selective assassination of its organizers and supporters, the prospects of this alliance were effectively dead. By the end of 1993 it was evident that there would be no way of halting a national election that for the first time in South Africa's history would see the enfranchisement of *all* adults of *all* races.

South Africa's first democratic election, held on April 27-29, 1994, marked the final defeat of the apartheid system and resulted in the triumph of the ANC, the multiracial party that had most effectively fought against that system over the decades. The ANC, led by Mandela, won 62 per cent of the vote, with the National Party at just over 20 per cent. At 12:01 a.m. on April 25, 1994, the old South African flag signifying the ruling compact of Afrikaners and Anglos was lowered, replaced by a new flag symbolizing a reborn South Africa under African leadership. On May 2, F.W. de Klerk acknowledged that the National Party had lost power and on May 10, at noon, Mandela was sworn in as the new state president, overseeing a new "Government of National Unity." Nearly three and a half centuries of white advance and black defeat had come to an end.

In the December 1988-January 1989 issue of *Die Suid-Afrikaan*, Professor J.L. Boshoff wrote the obituary for the final stage of this epoch:

> What an appalling human tragedy apartheid has been. The Afrikaners' Frankenstein: their own creation has degenerated into a monster which now threatens to destroy them. . . . How reasonable and intelligent people could have voted for this laughable conception and endorsed it with ever

increasing majorities, is one of the great mysteries in the entire history of democracy. I am guilty myself. I voted for it.

It is obvious why apartheid failed. It could never have worked! ... Many people, knowledgable people, sympathetic people, warned us that it would not work. ... But we did not listen. All-knowing and arrogant, we pushed ahead. Do your damnedest! Lost opportunities, lost sympathy, lost insight into each other's aspirations, lost trust in each other's good faith. Forty lost years—years in which Afrikaners rarely confronted the implications of our situation of co-existence with others. Why should we have? The answer was so obvious—apartheid.[38]

The road from 1940, when Rev. Koot Vorster had advocated "holy fanaticism" as the salvation for the Afrikaner nation, had led nowhere, but the price of apartheid remained to be paid. To some extent the old South Africa lived on in the new. Now some black South Africans were getting richer, but massive poverty persisted. By 1996 the GDP per capita, at $3,370, was high by African standards but lower than other Third World countries such as Venezuela ($4,490), Chile ($4,480), Brazil ($5,230), and Argentina ($8,550). Unemployment was estimated at 50 per cent in 1994.

## South Meets South: South Africa and Brazil

Even with the end of apartheid, many white South Africans still preferred not to think of their country as "Third World" (or even "African"). But in the early 1990s South Africa had roughly the same income per head as Brazil, and if anything poverty in the African country was deeper and more widespread.

| 1992 | Brazil | South Africa |
|------|--------|--------------|
| GNP per capita | $2,680 | $2,530 |
| Life expectancy | 66 | 62 |
| Infant mortality (per 1,000 live births) | 65 | 70 |
| Maternal mortality (per 100,000 births | 150 | 550 |
| Adult illiteracy % | 19 | 35 |

Sources: UNDP, *Human Development Report 1994*; Macro-Economic Research Group, Cape Town, 1993; *New Internationalist*, March 1995, p.19.

As a beginning the new ANC government quickly introduced an ambitious Reconstruction and Development Program aimed at redressing social imbalances. It abolished all of the 10 homelands and took up the matter of establishing a new constitution. Certified on December 4, 1996, the constitutional document—to take full effect in 1999—would, it was said, "extinguish any legal legacy of apartheid." The document, "considered one of the most liberal constitutions in the world ... outlaws capital punishment, protects gay and lesbian rights and includes a Bill of Rights that guarantees equal rights for all."[39]

Another issue facing the new government was the settling of land claims. In the 1990s, with around 60,000 farmers owning 80 per cent of the farmland, a key issue was introducing a "just land dispensation." As one journalist put it, "Getting people settled on land they know how to farm is the only way to relieve joblessness and poverty."[40] And it seemed possible that, given the educational and social legacies of the history of apartheid, South Africa at the end of the 20th century would have difficulty developing a manufacturing sector outside the mining complex.

# Summary

Africa was liberated—that is, its political management was handed over to Africans—in two phases. The first phase began with the independence of Sudan in 1956 and Ghana in 1957, peaked in 1960, and was completed by the end of the 1960s. The second phase began in the mid-1970s when the Portuguese territories were set free. After them, Rhodesia became independent (a process involving the visit of Lord Soames, whose views we have seen in chapter 1) and, finally, in 1993, Eritrea. By the 1990s Sub-Saharan Africa contained some 44 independent countries with around 520 million people, just under half the population of India.[41]

English-speaking historians of colonialism have often used the phrase "transfer of power" to describe the process of African independence. The term, which the British used to describe the tumultuous process by which India had earlier become free of foreign rule, implies the genteel passing of majority shareholding from one member of the family firm to another: a painless, even amicable, process. The ceremonies that launched African independence sought to establish a certain finely drawn picture of this transfer: Africans were handed their independence by minor British royalty in fancy dress assisted by governors attired in feathers and swords; flags were lowered and raised, anthems old and new were sung, and soldiers saluted; limousines arrived and departed, doors slammed, champagne was drunk, and gravity was superseded by a barely controlled exuberance. All of this ceremony was designed for Africans to adore, adopt, or consume.

But the idea of a transfer of power in the sense of political and economic control turned out to be a misrepresentation of what took place. Africans, especially the nationalist elite, got limited political power but never the economic control on which all power must rest. The political power gave them, at best, the bureaucratic apparatus designed for colonial rule and the high salaries that usually came with that apparatus, as well as colonial boundaries, in some cases healthy bank deposits, the key to the cash drawer itself, access to loans, and a few obsolescent weapons. Many new nations were rather like the non-voting members on the boards of large firms: highly paid and well regarded, but ultimately powerless. Unlike India, African countries had neither an experienced and cohesive domestic bourgeoisie nor a mature and self-confident civil service.

In the years of independence, several leaders in the new nations attempted to break with Western domination—Kwame Nkrumah in Ghana, Sekou Touré in Guinea, Julius Nyerere in Tanzania, Amilcar Cabral in Guinea-Bissau, and Samora Machel in Mozambique, for instance. These attempts were in different ways frustrated, often by Western pressures and plots, not excluding assassination. Yet, even though the first generation of nationalists failed, the struggle continued.

The period of African independence was itself circumscribed by another epoch, that of phenomenal and worldwide capitalist growth (see chapter 10). The period from 1950, marked by the outbreak of the Korean War, to 1975, the final defeat of the U.S.-backed government in Saigon, saw the longest-sustained economic growth in world history. Africa both contributed to and benefited from this growth. According to D.K. Fieldhouse: "In those years the overall per capita growth rate for the whole continent averaged 2.4 per cent compared with 1.7 per cent for South Asia and 2.6 per cent for Latin America. . . . According to the World Bank, the rate of growth of GDP for the whole of sub-Saharan Africa slowed from 3.9 per cent in the 1960s to 2.9 per cent in the 1970s . . . while per capita income growth overall slowed from 1.3 to 0.8 per cent."[42]

Africans gained in two major ways from this growth, in health and education. In the two decades from 1960 to 1980 the number of Ghanaians who went to secondary school as a percentage of the relevant age group (known as the "school enrolment ratio") jumped from 5 to 36. In Kenya the number increased from 2 to 19, and in Côte d'Ivoire from 2 to 17. Thus if 2 out of every 100 secondary school-aged Ivorians went to secondary school in 1960, 17 went in 1980. In comparative terms, this suggests that with respect to secondary education these African countries were not very different from Britain a century earlier, when the school enrolment ratio was also around 17 per 100. John Sender and Sheila Smith underline this point: "The rate of progress, by any historical standards, has been striking: in the case of education, the number of children attending school in these countries grew very much faster between 1910 and 1960 than did the number of children attending schools in Europe in the boom years between the 1840s and 1880s." According to Sender and Smith, "The health gains, expressed in terms of life expectancy, also compare favourably with the rates of improvement in life expectancy achieved during the period of the Industrial Revolution in England." As well, they note that "the improvements in infant mortality rates in Africa, which are a reflection of improved food availability and distribution, of improved access to water supplies and of significant advances in female education" compare favourably with most West European countries.[43]

As for the important question of economic development, the results are more disappointing.

### African Exports

| | Total exports | Manufactured exports | | Other exports | |
|---|---|---|---|---|---|
| | (in U.S. millions) | | % | | % |
| Ghana | | | | | |
| 1960-69 | $286.40 | $2.86 | 1 | $283.54 | 99 |
| 1970-79 | 724.90 | 10.81 | 1 | 714.09 | 99 |
| Côte d'Ivoire | | | | | |
| 1960-70 | 302.45 | 10.49 | 3 | 291.97 | 97 |
| 1971-82 | 1,733.42 | 138.29 | 8 | 1595.12 | 92 |
| Kenya | | | | | |
| 1961-70 | 231.00 | 14.55 | 6 | 216.45 | 94 |
| 1971-80 | 799.20 | 94.63 | 12 | 704.57 | 88 |
| Tanzania | | | | | |
| 1962-70 | 227.78 | 28.05 | 12 | 199.72 | 88 |
| 1971-81 | 438.82 | 50.92 | 12 | 387.90 | 88 |

Source: Austin, *African Economic History*, 1987, p.247.

The example of manufactures as a share of total exports indicates that until 1980, no matter what kind of regime—whether the dirigisme of Nkrumah's Ghana, the "African socialism" of Nyerere's Tanzania, or the "open" economies of Côte d'Ivoire and Kenya—industrialization had contributed only a small part to the export earnings of most African countries. Like all other African economies, these particular ones could not escape the reality that most of their imports had to be financed from agricultural exports, and that the value of these exports not only proved unstable, but also declined over time in relation to most manufactured imports. Nor was there improvement after 1980: in the following years the GDPs of all of these countries dropped. Worse, having in the colonial period largely fed themselves, by the 1980s many African countries were dependent on food imports and handouts.

The value of African agricultural exports had fallen because, first of all, African exports had to be sold on international markets. In the postwar period, and especially from the 1960s, the selling price of agricultural commodities fell as new techniques and technologies were introduced that led to greatly increased crop yields. That is, as more intensive capitalist techniques of production and forms of labour organization were brought to bear on a commodity, the cost of production of that commodity diminished. Those who expanded their harvests by investing most in capitalist production could undercut the prices of those who continued to operate in the old ways. Increased production was rewarded with a larger share in the market. Conversely, for those whose production depended on supposedly "less efficient" and more traditional farming methods, the market slipped away. The way to safeguard against this was through increased investment, either by entrepreneurs or, where these were too poor or improvident, by governments. Yet few African countries had either the entrepreneurs or the governments that could do the job. The result was that small-scale African producers (chronically short of capital) were driven out of the market for cocoa, cotton, coffee, and vegetable oils.

Even in the early 1960s some writers had warned that Africa was off to an inauspicious start. Yet amid the tumults of independence and the sense of modest satisfaction based on the continent's economic performance in the 1960s, and in some cases into the 1970s, the warnings were largely ignored. Then, almost immediately following the crisis in oil prices in late 1973, the situation began to change rapidly. As the Nigerian historian J.F.A. Ajayi later wrote: "The optimism of development plans of the 1960s has given way to increasing frustration in the 1970s and disillusionment in the 1980s. The general lament is that this is not what was expected from independence."[44]

South Africa, ever the continental exception, had by the end of the Second World War become effectively independent of any outside power and rested in the hands of a domestic white ruling class committed to a policy of state-dominated industrialization financed largely by profits from mining. In 1948, just as the tide was turning against colonialism in the rest of Africa, white South Africans voted into office a government determined to guarantee through racist policies and a police state the dominance and high standards of living of the white minority within the country. For the next 40 years this government attempted not only to guarantee the country's industrial growth but also to retard the political participation of the majority of the population, based on high levels of violence and intimidation. One important corollary of this approach was an education policy that deprived the masses of Africans of anything but the most minimal education. After apartheid was finally defeated the new political configuration of the mid-1990s seemed set to survive, if not flourish, although a few years after the historic elections of 1994 the country's true economic development—that is, the push to create equal access to resources for all South Africans—remained to be seen.

The rest of the Sub-Saharan continent, unfortunately, was showing less promise. Steadily declining in economic terms from the late 1970s, by the 1990s most of Africa had become "the Third World of the Third World." By this time, a large question mark even hung over Kenya, which as recently as the 1980s had still been seen as a model for the rest of the continent. Third World analyst Walden Bello noted, "If current trends continue, the United Nations Development Program estimates that the continent's share of the world's poor, now 30 percent, will rise to 45 percent by the year 2000." And he added:

> Total debt for sub-Saharan Africa now amounts to 110 per cent of GNP, compared to 35 per cent for all developing countries. Cut off from significant capital flows except aid, battered by plunging commodity prices, racked by famine and civil war, and squeezed by structural development programs, Africa's per capita income declined by 2.2 per cent per annum in the 1980s. By the end of the decade it had plunged to its level at the time of independence in the early 1960s. Some 200 million of the region's 690 million people are now classified as poor, and even the least pessimistic projection of the World Bank sees the number of poor people rising by 50 per cent to reach 300 million by the year 2000.[45]

In one of the most stark of recent statistics, the World Health Organization has predicted that by 2000 life expectancy in Côte d'Ivoire, the Central African Republic, Congo, Uganda, and Zambia will drop to 42 years. The current life expectancy in the poorest countries is 43.[46] In Sub-Saharan Africa, with some of the poorest countries in the world, more than half the wealth is still in natural resources.[47] The task of making those resources work for the health and livelihoods—the full human capacities—of Africans in general remains one of the stickiest "development" questions for the future.

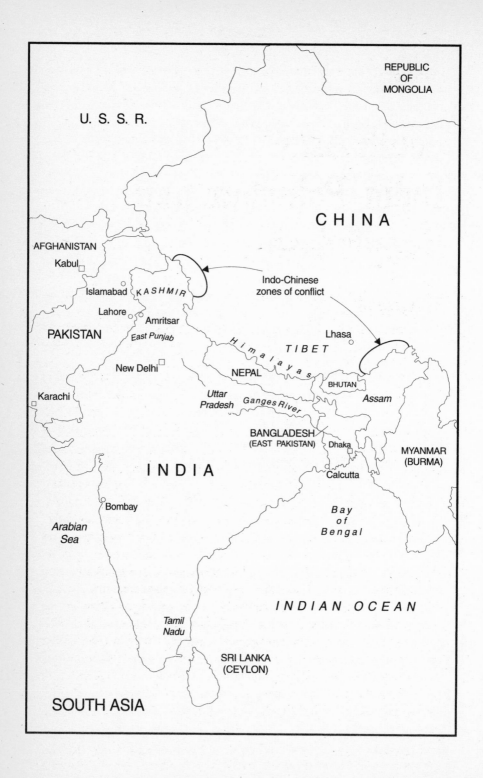

# Chapter 6

# South Asia:
# India, Pakistan, and Bangladesh

## Background

Mohandas Karamchand Gandhi (1869-1948) was the founding father of independent India and the Congress Party the vehicle of his success. The Congress Party—properly called the "Indian National Congress"—was formed in 1885, when British power in India was at its peak.* The early origins of the party meant that most other nationalist parties of the non-communist sort in the colonial and dependent world were either consciously modelled after it or, if not, resembled it strikingly. The Wafd in Egypt, *the* nationalist party of the Middle East in the first half of the 20th century, resembled the Congress Party to the extent that it too was virtually the sole party with a credible nationalist pedigree, a well-oiled apparatus of regional clientage, and a mass base. The Pan-African Congress, formed by Africans of the diaspora in 1900, and the South African Native National Congress, founded in South Africa in 1912, took their names from the pioneer Indian party.

Gandhi's brilliance rested in his gift of being able to combine in Indian nationalism the otherwise incompatible strains of Hindu traditionalism and European modernism. This combination of elements transformed Congress not only into a debating club dominated by lawyers and divided between "Extremists" and "Gradualists" (with the latter in control), but also into a mass movement, though one that remained under the control of the class that founded it. Hindu traditionalism, which called for a return to rural ideals combined with such distinctive religious practices as yoga, fasting, and sexual abstinence, was of great importance in the mobilization

---

* The British ruled India in part or in whole from the middle of the 18th century until independence in 1947. The term for British-ruled India was "the Raj" ("state" or "kingdom").

of the Indian masses. But its centrality should not obscure other factors, the most important of which was the tumultuous urbanization and economic transformation (and depression) that bore down inexorably on the Indian people in the first half of the 20th century.

At the beginning of the First World War Gandhi had returned to India from South Africa, where he had worked and prospered as a lawyer. More importantly, in South Africa he had established the practice that was to become the guiding philosophy of Congress until after independence: *satyragraha* ("non-violent political action"). Later he remarked, "South Africa gave me the start to my life's mission."[1]

By the time he returned to India, the Congress Party had adopted the idea of *swaraj* ("self-rule").* In 1920-21, in the midst of a massive turbulence sweeping the world from Ireland to China, Gandhi seized control of the party and created a new leadership. In the next two decades he transformed it into the greatest of the mass-based nationalist movements in the colonial world. His strategy was non-violent mass civil disobedience, and his most effective lieutenant was Jawaharlal Nehru (1889-1964), a lawyer's son who had been educated in a famous private school in England and at Cambridge. Nehru's views were not merely Westernized, they were Western. More surprisingly, given his background, they were also social-democratic. In 1929, as the youngest president of his party, he led Congress through the passing of the *Purna Swaraj* ("Complete Freedom") resolution, which proclaimed that the British government had "ruined India economically, politically, culturally and spiritually" and the time had come to "sever the British connection entirely."

Gradually, throughout the 1920s and 1930s and under the leadership of Gandhi and Nehru, Congress increased its pressure on the British occupiers, making it plain that the movement towards independence was irreversible. The question was when and on what terms? The advent of World War II both stifled the question and hastened the answer.

With the outbreak of war in Europe the leaders of Congress took the position that they, the Indians, and not their British rulers should have the freedom to decide whether they would become involved in the conflict. After all, the fight to maintain the territorial integrity of Poland was not necessarily of importance to India. Congress also wanted the Viceroy, the leading British colonial official in India, to guarantee that after the war India would be free to determine its own future. The Viceroy refused to

---

* *Swaraj* meant "self-rule" in the political sense of "independence" and the moral sense of "self-control." When Gandhi wrote, "The movement for Swaraj is a movement for self-purification," he meant that Indians must change not only their rulers but also their own attitudes.

give this guarantee, and so too did Winston Churchill, the British prime minister from 1940 to 1945. To combat the influence of the Hindu-dominated Congress, the British encouraged the All-India Muslim League, a political party of Indian Muslims founded in 1906, which had long demanded the creation of a separate Muslim state—"playing the Muslim card," this was called. But it would be wrong to think that the British did anything more than play a card that was already on the table. The Muslims, and particularly Muhammad Ali Jinnah, their leader, another London-trained lawyer, had designed and dealt the card. The idea of separate Muslim electorate representation within India had been discussed by Muslim leaders since the beginning of the century. In 1930 Muslim leader Muhammad Iqbal (1877-1938), a poet-philosopher, had called for the amalgamation of Punjab, Sind, and Baluchistan into a separate Indian state. By early 1940 the Muslim League had already drawn up the plans for what was, from August 15, 1947, to become "Pakistan"—the name, meaning "land of the pure," had been invented by Indian Muslim students in England in the early 1930s. Pakistan was to encompass two separate Muslim homelands, areas in which Muslims predominated. One of these was to be in the northwest, the state that Iqbal had imagined, and the other in the northeast, focused on Bengal. It was not evident in 1940 whether there were to be two different states or one state in two parts.

Jinnah's argument in favour of a separate Pakistan was nationalist and communalist.* Muslims, he said, could not live under the rule of a Hindu-dominated Congress. A powerful party of Hindus held the same position. The right-wing and communalist All-India Hindu Mahasabha (founded in 1915) argued that there was no room in an independent India for "minorities." By "minorities" the leaders of the Mahasabha meant Muslims in particular.

To many, the division of India along communalist lines was unthinkable. Modernist Indian thinking, like modern thinking everywhere, was deeply penetrated by the idea of universalism, the antithesis of religious or ethnic peculiarism. Hindus, Muslims, and others *should* be able to live together in harmony, it was thought. Furthermore, in both Britain and India, on the political left and across the broad centre, the unity that the Raj had brought to India was regarded as being of great positive benefit.

---

* "Communalism" used here refers to a politics based on the existence, real or imagined, of one or another religious community within a larger nation. In the context of Indian history, the main communalist politics were those of the Muslims, Hindus, and Sikhs. Communalism in Indian politics developed in the late 19th century, at the same time as the Congress Party. It should therefore be seen as an aspect of modern, not traditional, politics. I am grateful to Keith Meadowcroft for amplification of this point and for others in this chapter.

For Gandhi, Hindu-Muslim unity was one of the three pillars of *swaraj*. He pointed out that India's Muslims were descended from people who had once been Hindus. In discussions about the division of India, both Gandhi and Nehru used such terms as "vivisection" and "suicide." Others observed that in places like the hugely populated Bengal, Indian culture, excepting its religious aspect, remained undivided. Bengali Hindus (who according to the 1931 census comprised 44 per cent of the population of the state) and Muslims (who comprised 54 per cent) both spoke Bengali, dressed in the same way, and ate the same food. A debate was started that would continue over the succeeding years: were the Hindu and Muslim civilizations of India irreconcilably different? Or, as Ved Mehta was later to ask, did Indian Muslims not have more in common with Indian Hindus than with the Muslims in the rest of the world?[2] And would the differences between Hindus and Muslims not disappear in the melting pot of modernization?

In summer 1942 Gandhi attempted to launch a campaign of civil disobedience to persuade the British that they had no future in the country. "Quit India," the slogans of Congress demanded. "Leave India to God," Gandhi insisted. "If that is too much, then leave her to anarchy." This was a memorable demand, but not one calculated to move the British even in the most relaxed of times. They responded to the "Quit India" campaign without hesitation. Massive arrests followed, 60,000 all told. Gandhi was arrested but released later in the year. For the ninth time in his life, Jawaharlal Nehru was thrown in jail, where he remained until July 1945.

The British repression provoked demonstrations and even outright rebellion. Public buildings were burned, and the railway system was sabotaged. The British replied with escalating violence: troops firing on unarmed civilians, attacks from the air on Indian crowds, and public executions. From the point of view of the nationalists, two things failed to happen. The Indian army, made up of volunteers and numbering some two million by the middle of the Second World War, stood fast under its British commanders; and the Muslims also stood by the British, arguing that their communalism was above politics. Jinnah and the Muslim League deplored what they called the "open rebellion" organized by Congress. The British were relieved at this support and supported the Muslim League in return. By the end of 1942 the campaign for Indian independence had been smothered. There would be no more organized protest until the end of the war. Congress was desolated by the experience, and India was now irrevocably split between Congress and the Muslim League.

Yet even though the British had immobilized Congress, as Indian historian Sumit Sarkar writes, their "victory was ambiguous and with severe limits and had been possible only because war conditions had allowed really ruthless use of force. The British would never again risk such a confrontation."[3]

The Muslim League, which was not proscribed, would emerge in mid-1945 with renewed respectability and influence. League governments had sprouted in a number of key provinces in northern India (in some cases because local Congress leaders were behind bars), and the League leadership had learned to exercise tight control over them. Indeed, two would-be nations now existed within the bosom of the single colonial state. The British support for the Muslim League became more explicit: Jinnah would be allowed to veto any constitutional proposals laid before India's nationalist leaders.

The war, meanwhile, had wrought deep changes in the attitude of Indians. Mass suffering was acute, worsened by rampant inflation. In a famine in Bengal in 1943, between one and three million people perished. India as a whole experienced epidemics and food shortages caused by the requisitioning of rice for the army and for other parts of Southeast Asia. Another more or less invisible shift had also occurred: during the war the United States had replaced Britain as the most important source of India's imports. The United States, not Britain, would in the future come to represent "the West."

# The Birth of India and Pakistan

In elections held in India at the end of 1945, the Muslim League campaigned on a communalist platform, arguing that Muslims would be swamped by Hindus if the Congress Party prevailed in the elections. In large parts of India, Muslim voters were convinced by their appeals. The outcome of the elections was a triumph for the Muslims, at least in terms of seats won if not in terms of votes cast. The election confirmed that India had become irrevocably divided.

In late 1945 another factor also materialized. In 1939 Subhas Bose, a Congress Party radical from Bengal, had been re-elected to the presidency of the party and then forced to resign a few months later after opposition from Gandhi. After forming his own party, during the war Bose eventually crossed the lines and joined the Japanese, who were pressing hard on the eastern borders of India. He found his way to Berlin, from where he appealed, without success, to his fellow Indians to rebel against the British. In July 1943 he left Germany by submarine and arrived in Japanese-occupied Singapore, where he formed the Indian National Army (INA), made up of Indian troops captured while fighting alongside the

British. These soldiers were supposed to join the Japanese in liberating India. They failed miserably, and Bose himself died in a plane crash before the end of the war.

Towards the end of 1945 the British in India placed a number of INA officers on trial. The officers were defended by Jawaharlal Nehru, and the trial backfired for the British when the Indian public showed sympathy to Bose, whom they viewed not as a traitor but as a patriot.

A new Labour government in London, elected in 1945, dragged its feet at first on the question of India. Not only in India but elsewhere in the colonies its leaders still hoped that in some form or another the empire might be resurrected. For the time being they adopted the formula that "the governors must govern"—that Britain should rule the colonial empire, India included, not just resolutely but along conservative lines (because even for Britain's Labour government there was no independent socialist blueprint for imperial administration). For most people in Britain, of whatever political conviction, at the end of the war India was far down the list of concerns. (In the 1945 elections only 8 per cent of Labour candidates even mentioned India.) To send British troops off to die to hold onto India—as French troops were sent to die to hold Indochina and Algeria— would have been to commit political suicide.

With London proceeding with painstaking slowness, the official mind on the subject of India was undoubtedly stimulated by a series of mutinies beginning in early 1946, soon after the trials of the INA officers. The mutinies affected both British and Indian servicemen: the British because now that the war was over they wanted to be sent home and demobilized; the Indians because they no longer felt any virtue in serving the British. Sarkar calls the Indian naval mutiny at Bombay in February 1946 "one of the most truly heroic, if also largely forgotten, episodes in our freedom struggle." Taken together these revolts by Indian and British troops were "quite possibly the single most decisive reason behind the British decision to make a quick withdrawal."[4]

The British Labour government reacted decisively, at least as com- pared to its previous ponderous responses. It sent a delegation of cabinet- rank ministers to India with a mandate to plan for what they called "the transfer of power."

Negotiations between the British delegation, Congress, and the Mus- lim League took place in May and June 1946. No agreement was reached between Nehru, the Congress spokesman, and Jinnah, for the Muslim League, regarding the question of a united and independent India. The del- egation and the British Viceroy proposed a complex and unworkable scheme, but were pressed hard by the Muslim proposal for a separate state. In August the Muslim League declared a Direct Action Day to drive home its claims more forcibly. In Calcutta, the largest city in India and thus the largest city in predominately Muslim Bengal, the demonstrations resulted in violent confrontations between Muslims and Hindus. "The Terror" lasted for more than a year, from August 1946 to September 1947. By the end of 1946, clashes between Muslims and Hindus had spread to other parts of the country, and by 1947 riots had become chronic, causing thousands of deaths. The anarchy that Gandhi had preferred to British rule now loomed, and the unthinkable partition had become inevitable.

The collapse of the British Empire at that particular time was not limited to India. In February 1947 the British announced the withdrawal of their forces from Greece, where they were involved in a civil war on the side of the monarchy against local communists. That same month they withdrew from Palestine, their last mandate in the Middle East. And it was also in February 1947 that Churchill's successor as prime minister, Clement Attlee, rose in the House of Commons to announce the British withdrawal from India, set for no later than June 1948. Attlee appointed a new Viceroy: Sir Louis Mountbatten, who was not merely an earl, but also a handsome war hero—Mountbatten of Burma—the commander of the Allied forces in Southeast Asia. The dashing and regal Mountbatten negotiated the final British exodus from India, although along the way he had to scrap a plan, hatched in London, to Balkanize India by creating not only a separate Muslim state but also an independent Kashmir and perhaps other Indian Ruritanias as well.*

The British and the nationalists reached agreement, but not without great anguish. India would be partitioned, and two states established— India and Pakistan—with a boundary commission made up of both Hindus and Muslims determining the line of the incision. Pakistan would be made up of two widely separated halves: West Pakistan on the northwest side of India, and East Pakistan, with only 15 per cent of the territory—but 55 per cent of the population—at the mouth of the Ganges. Both India and Pakistan would remain members of the British Commonwealth. The official wealth of the Raj, everything from its railway cars to its paper clips, was to be divided according to a formula that gave the Indians 82.5 per cent and the Pakistanis 17.5 per cent. It was announced in Britain that the "transfer

---

* Kashmir, the largest state in India, was important because of its size and wealth as well as its strategic location. Its rulers both under the British and before them, the Mughals, were Hindus, the family of the Nehrus among them, but the majority of its four million people were Muslims. In the 1930s Kashmir had seen the growth of a political movement in which Muslims, Sikhs, and Hindus were all members. This movement demanded that the ruling maharajah share his power with other groups.

of power" creating an independent India and a sovereign Pakistan would take place at midnight on August 14, 1947.

This transfer was marked by two explosions. The more brilliant was the joy of Indians that their country was finally independent. The more devastating was the explosion of hatred of Muslims for Hindus, and vice versa, a hatred that had been exploited by all sides—British, Hindu, and Muslim—in the preceding years. It has been suggested that the British, who were after all still in control, could have done more to contain the violence, even by using forceful means against the rioters. Certainly, the spilling of "native" blood was never regarded with the same abhorrence as the spilling of European blood. In any event, the communal violence that accompanied the liberation of India and Pakistan cost as many as half a million lives. After it abated, in late August, an uprising in a corner of Kashmir provoked outright, but undeclared, war between India and Pakistan over control of the state. Fighting continued until a ceasefire was agreed to at the end of the year. Thereafter Kashmir remained partitioned. Millions of Kashmiri Hindus fled the state to become refugees in Delhi and Calcutta. The process of partitioning created over 10 million refugees.

Gandhi's attempt to stop the violence between Hindus and Muslims earned him the hatred of Hindu chauvinists, who attempted on several occasions to have him assassinated. On January 30, 1948, a member of a group that had split off from the Mahasabha succeeded in killing him. As Gandhi's successor, Nehru, lamented in a announcement broadcast throughout India: "The light has gone out of our lives and there is darkness everywhere."

Yet it was Gandhi, not the Hindu thugs, who, despite the violence associated with partition, had won the day. Gandhi had successfully mobilized the Hindu masses and steered them on a course that led away from communalism and ethnic hatred towards a modern nationalism, which was possibly the greatest achievement of any colonial leader in the first half of the 20th century.

# India: The Nehru Era, 1948-64

The period often referred to as the time of "Nehru's India" was the heroic age of the Third World. Between the independence of India and the death of Nehru in 1964 most of the colonial world fought for and won independence. For most of the newly independent states of Africa and Asia, it seemed, economic development was only a short distance off into the future. India in the Nehru Era was itself the most outstanding symbol of a

Third World state in the first flush of its freedom, a nation moving towards a certain, modern future.

Simultaneously the champion of his own country and of the Third World as a whole, Jawaharlal Nehru has been embraced by posterity as has no other non-Western leader before or since. Yet in his own lifetime Nehru was distrusted by many in the West. This was particularly true of the Americans, who, from the presidencies of Harry Truman through John F. Kennedy, generally distrusted Nehru and often despised him. Nor is it hard to see why. For Western movers and shakers, no more fearsome combination existed than nationalism, socialism, and bourgeois self-confidence.

In the opinion of Loy Henderson, the U.S. ambassador to New Delhi under Truman, the Indian prime minister was "vain and immature." In the characterization of the State Department's assistant secretary for Near Eastern, South Asian, and African Affairs, he was "a hypersensitive egotist." The *Detroit Free Press* hated his non-alignment in the early 1950s, fuming, "Nehru Likes Any Color Just So Long as It's Red," and referring to him as "the Prime Minister of an avowed red satellite, with Moscow's noose around his neck." In the middle of the decade President Eisenhower, after meeting the Indian head of state, wrote that Nehru suffered from an inferiority complex and schizophrenia. In November 1961, after meeting Nehru, Kennedy remarked that it was "the worst head-of-state visit I have ever had." His brother, Attorney-General Robert F. Kennedy, recorded that JFK "never liked Nehru" and found his arrogance and sense of superiority "rather offensive."[5]

This animus towards a man who so many, Europeans as well as Asians, found attractive was partly based in the threat Nehru posed to the U.S. view of the Third World. In any case, Western leaders could console themselves by remembering that compared to Mao Zedong, the other great Asian leader, Nehru was, in the main, quite amiable.

## Priorities: National Security

"First things must come first, and the first thing is the security and stability of India," Nehru told India's Constituent Assembly in November 1947.[6] The security and stability of India had got off to a traumatic start with the vivisection that had excised Pakistan from India the previous August. The dispute over the sovereignty of Kashmir came shortly after that, and sporadic fighting between Indian and Pakistani forces continued there until 1949, when Kashmir went through a second crisis. Obviously, the security of the new state was to be an abiding question.

Nehru's policies of national security united several objectives: the integrity and independence of India itself, anti-colonialism, international-ism, and neutralism. The major Western powers that India had to negoti-ate with in the Nehru years were on the whole committed to integrity and independence but hostile to Nehru's other policies. To them, India and its neighbours were seen as tokens in the greater game of world politics, in which there were only two main players. Indeed, since the 19th century the British had referred to the power politics being played out in Central and South Asia as "the Great Game." In the years after Indian indepen-dence similar metaphors of strategic gamesmanship were used: Western spokesmen talked of "playing the Chinese card," "falling dominoes," and "losing" China or Korea. The Indians, unwilling to be pawns, quickly learned the rules of the game themselves, which led them to play the United States off against the Soviet Union, getting arms from Moscow and food from Washington. Administrations in New Delhi also played other Western countries off against the United States and one another.

After the question of Kashmir had been neutralized (but not solved), other threats to national security arose, the lesser of which concerned the remaining European colonies in India. Two European states, France and Portugal, still had footholds on the subcontinent. The French voluntarily surrendered Pondicherry and adjacent enclaves in southeast India in the 1950s. Portugal, under the dictator Antonio Salazar in the 1950s and 1960s, would not release its Indian holdings for fear of the bad example this would set for its more valuable colonies in Africa. When Delhi sug-gested that Portugal abandon its colonies in Goa, Daman, and Diu on the west coast of the peninsula, nothing but bluster and bile flowed from Lis-bon, and from the mid-1950s a confrontation seemed almost inevitable. Even before independence the Indians had regarded the Salazar regime with unvarnished scorn, dismissing it as the "fascist and authoritarian administration of Portugal."

The Indian armies finally marched into Goa, and in just over 24 hours on December 17, 1961, the first European colony on the subcontinent, one that had existed since the early 16th century, ceased to be. Although the UN had condemned Portuguese colonialism, several Western countries— which would again support Portugal in Africa at the end of the decade— made disapproving sounds. The U.S. ambassador to the UN, Adlai Steven-son, intoned, "We cannot condone the use of force in this instance and thus pave the way for forceful solutions of other disputes."[7] But most of the Third World cheered, as did the states of Eastern Europe.

India's anti-colonialism was part of a continuum flowing from interna-tionalism to neutralism. The approach drew inspiration from the idea, pro-mulgated but hardly invented by the U.S. president Woodrow Wilson, that world politics should be open, settled by negotiation, and serve the interests of all people who should be free. Neutralism was the means by which independent countries would remain free of the games played by either the ex-colonial powers or the Great Powers, that is, the United States and the Soviet Union. Nehru put this succinctly in a 1946 speech:

> We propose, as far as possible, to keep away from the power politics of groups, aligned against one another, which have led in the past to world war and which may again lead to disasters on an even larger scale. We believe that peace and freedom are indivisible and the denial of freedom anywhere must endanger freedom elsewhere and lead to conflict and war. We are particularly interested in the emancipation of colonial and dependent countries and peoples, and in the recognition in theory and practice of equal opportunities for all races.[8]

India's approach carried more than just a sense of idealism. Nehru, among others, saw a real danger in adopting any position that would be unpopular in Washington, especially as the Cold War picked up momentum. Even before independence, in January 1947, a leading U.S. politician had asserted that the Congress Party was dangerously influenced by communists.

Two obvious threats to Indian independence existed. The first took the form of dissenting groups (politicians, army officers, religious leaders, minorities) within the country, groups that could be stimulated or at least supported in attempts to destabilize and even overthrow any Indian government whose policies seemed to threaten Western interests. The history of the Third World was to be replete with examples of this kind of internal destabilization; nationalist governments from Iran to Guatemala would be victims of it. But the enemy within was never a real possibility in India. A combination of the utter domination of the Indian political scene by the Congress Party and of Nehru's unrivalled position within Congress precluded it.

A second, more real, possibility involved Western use of regional rivals to threaten India. Given India's fortunate political geography, the only possibility in this regard was Pakistan. In 1950 Liaquat Ali Khan, the Pakistani prime minister, went to the United States to negotiate for arms, and he thereafter received them in substantial quantities. It appeared that India, whose forces the Pakistanis had confronted in Kashmir as recently as 1949, was the only likely target for these weapons. Tension between the two countries erupted again in 1950, with a massacre of Hindus in East Pakistan. By the mid-1950s Pakistan's hasty march towards Washington was commemorated by its membership in both the Central Treaty

Organization (CENTO) and the Southeast Asia Treaty Organization (SEATO), alliances motivated mainly by Washington's preoccupation with forming a bulwark against a southward-moving communism.

Nehru's hope was to create an independent bloc of Afro-Asiatic states that would not be a marionette in the hands of foreign string-pullers. His first steps in this direction came at an Asian Relations Conference organized in Delhi in 1947. A second conference met two years later. East Asian solidarity advanced a step further in October 1950, during the war in Korea, when Chinese premier Zhou Enlai sought to enlist Delhi as an intermediary to prevent UN forces from advancing any further towards the frontier with China.

Vilified for being a treacherous reactionary by the Soviet press and condemned as being a sickly neutralist by Washington, Nehru, who was both India's prime minister and its foreign minister, had to tread warily. Certainly, he appeared unafraid of considering what was in India's best interests, despite the protests of the Great Powers. There was even the possibility of playing off one of these giants against the other. Thus, faced with Washington's obduracy over the question of food aid, Delhi accepted Soviet food grains in early 1951 as part of a barter exchange. Here was the Great Game being played with new rules in which the Asian states were not merely pawns. While the Soviet Union played its food card against the United States' arms card, India played its Moscow card against Pakistan's Washington card. With Pakistan moving towards the Western camp, from 1953 Moscow cultivated India, even going so far as to take India's side over the issue of Kashmir. Nehru's biographer M.J. Akbar, an Indian journalist, explains India's rapprochement with the Soviet Union: "The most intelligent thing that the Soviets did was to build Indo-Soviet relations on the basis of Nehru's perceptions as much as on their own— unlike the Americans, who kept seeking to change Nehru into a champion of free enterprise. Nehru's socialism was as far from Soviet socialism as it was from U.S. capitalism, but the Soviets were not in the least bothered."[9]

## Third World Solidarity

Although mutual suspicion and the remembrance of past grievances destroyed the possibility of amicable relations with Pakistan, such a breach was not the case with India's other neighbours in South and Southeast Asia and further afield. From late 1954 Delhi was making plans to organize a summit of independent Asian and African nations to meet in Bandung, Indonesia, in April 1955. It was there, if anywhere, that a united Third World, as distinct from the collectivity of newly independent nations, was born.

In Nehru's view the essence of Bandung was an avoidance by the Asian and African states of military and economic entanglements such as SEATO, which bound smaller and poorer countries to the coattails of larger and richer nations by means of ultra-strong economic and military threads. Instead, he hoped that independence might be pursued through mutual reliance and economic development. At the economic level the Bandung Conference subscribed to the idea of Import Substitution Industrialization, but this was an ISI that was internationalist rather than narrowly nationalist. This approach advocated not only nationalism, self-sufficiency, and independence, but also self-help—economic and political as well as military—all within the Third World. Nehru, for instance, made it clear that he viewed the exploitation of Africa by Europe as one of the great crimes in history, and he argued that assistance for African development would be the special responsibility of India.

In international relations among the first fruits of the Bandung spirit was the support that Nehru gave to Nasser when Egypt nationalized the Suez Canal Company in July 1956. Nehru's unstinting condemnation of the Anglo-French-Israeli invasion of Suez in October-November 1956 was repaid by the remarkable popularity he gained in the whole of the Arab world. Despite its Muslim foundation, Pakistan's entanglement with the West precluded it from using religion as a means of solidifying support against India. Nasser repaid Nehru by supporting India over Goa.

Even before Nehru's support for Egypt over Suez, the scaffolding of solidarity that Nehru had attempted to build at Bandung in early 1954 was being pulled away. On October 7, 1950, a year after celebrating the birth of the People's Republic, China invaded Tibet. In the language of Chinese diplomacy the justification of the invasion was that Tibet was an integral part of China, which had, after all, invaded and defeated an independent Tibet in the 18th century. Therefore, claimed Beijing, there was no real invasion. And anyway, it argued, the theocratic regime of the Dalai Lama was reactionary and oppressive. Nehru did not doubt this, although of course the Tibetans didn't see it that way, nor did many other Indians. But Nehru, in the interest of rapprochement with China, swept the sovereign rights of the Tibetans under the carpet. Although this, in retrospect, might seem to have been an unprincipled and shortsighted position, Nehru had a limited range of choices available at the time. He was not able to contemplate chilling relations with a China that was already at war with the West in Korea—a war that was leading U.S.-commanded armies up the Korean peninsula towards Manchuria and seemed to be a prelude to further Western domination in Asia. Furthermore, for decades Nehru had hoped the day would come when India and China together would lead Asia out of the prison of colonialism. Tibet thus became the first sacrifice laid on the altar of Asian solidarity, and "appeasement" became one of the most painful foreign words to enter independent India's foreign policy lexicon. In April 1954, when India recognized Tibet as part of China, Chinese participation at Bandung was guaranteed, but the price that India would have to pay was not long in coming.

In winter 1955 a significant border incident occurred involving the crossing of Chinese troops into Indian territory. Nothing came of it. In the first part of 1959, there were more Indo-Chinese border incidents. After the Dalai Lama led a failed revolt in March 1959 against the Chinese in Lhasa, the Tibetan capital, the Chinese government began a massive repression of the Tibetans. Refugees flocked across the Himalayas into India, the Dalai Lama among them. In August and October several Indian border guards were killed. The Indian press sympathized with the Tibetans, amidst international accusations that the Chinese were, by a combination of murder and forced emigration, attempting to systematically exterminate the Buddhist religion in Tibet. The contemporary word for this—"genocide"—was barely more than a decade old.

In 1960 attempts to solve the border problem proved impossible, partly because the nearly 3,000 miles of mountainous frontier between the two countries had been so scantily surveyed. By 1961 the Indian government was charging that China was in "unlawful occupation of about 12,000 square miles of Indian territory." Nehru soon gave the Indian army orders to recover territories occupied by the Chinese (whether rightfully or wrongfully was a matter of opinion, given the cartographic uncertainties). On October 20, 1962, Chinese troops invaded India and war officially broke out. Over the next few days the Indians suffered a series of disastrous defeats as the Chinese advanced.

Perhaps the Indian military setback was predictable: Indians had fought bravely and even brilliantly in World War II, but that was under British command. No Indian officers had held major commands in wartime. Further, the Indian army was poorly equipped, and its officer corps had been corrupted through political meddling. The Chinese had been fighting inside and outside their country, under a wide variety of circumstances, for nearly half a century; as recently as the 1950s they had fought in northern Korea and Tibet. Neither paralysing cold nor mountains were unfamiliar to them. They had plenty of modern arms and competent and unified direction, and they were unflinchingly determined.

Buckling under Chinese attacks, the Indians on two separate fronts were overwhelmed in just ten days. (One front was to the north of Kashmir and the other east of Bhutan in northern Assam.) An Indian counterattack on November 14 was sent reeling in retreat. Some feared that the Red Army would enter Bengal. The only thing that stopped them from occupying Gauhati, the capital of Assam, was the policy of Beijing itself. Political crisis followed, and the Indian foreign minister since 1956, the ambitious and anti-American V.K. Krishna Menon, resigned. The nonaligned countries of the Third World, with the exception of Egypt, logically if disappointingly refused to align themselves with India. The war between India and China dealt a mortal blow to the idea of solidarity among nonaligned nations—the Indian prime minister had gone so far as to refer to the Chinese as "aggressors." Now, humiliated, Nehru turned to Washington for arms. On November 19 he requested *direct* U.S. military intervention. The next day, before Washington had time to respond, the Chinese declared a unilateral ceasefire. The Americans nonetheless offered India $60 million in emergency military aid, which complemented military assistance from the Commonwealth.

India's defeat at the hands of China, followed by Delhi's resort to military aid from Washington, destroyed the credibility of India and Nehru as the leading voice from the Third World. India's place was taken by China, which would hold that position for the next two decades. The idea of nonalignment was mortally wounded. In 1966, as India moved closer to the United States, China forged an alliance with Pakistan.

## Priorities: National Economic Development

After national security, the second preoccupation was national economic development—and here the objectives were obvious, because poverty in India was all-pervasive.

By 1950 an estimated 360 million people lived in India, the majority of them peasants, with about 70 per cent of the total engaged in agriculture. Everyone who had been alive at the time remembered the Bengal famine of 1943 and the millions of deaths from epidemics that followed. But in general and year after year, India's agriculture was in dire straits. Food production had only marginally increased since the beginning of the century and was not keeping up with population increases. Although there was no excess of land in India, the country's main problem was, in Western terms at least, inefficient and undercapitalized farming. Compared to other countries, India's rice and wheat yields per acre were low—indeed, India's average crop yields were among the lowest in the world. Food had to be imported and paid for by exports. Even with the imports, Indians suffered from malnutrition and the diseases, such as tuberculosis, associated with it. Life expectancy was half that of the industrialized countries.

The state of agriculture and the level of poverty suggested the need for drastic remedies, the foremost being a program of industrialization. At independence, even though powerful Indian industries existed, only about 6 per cent of GNP was produced industrially. This statistic revealed a problem in itself, because India was known to have vast mineral reserves. By one estimate in the 1960s India possessed at least one-quarter of the world's deposits of iron ore and one-third of the world's manganese, along with major quantities of other minerals, including petroleum.

Why had these natural assets not been used to greater effect? The conventional explanation was colonialism. Although industrialization had been stifled in many colonies, in India a process of actual "deindustrialization" had taken place from the late 18th into the late 19th centuries. Thanks to the economic policies of the Raj, as a proportion of its total production Indian industrial production was lower in 1950 than it had been two centuries earlier. Nonetheless, industrial production had grown slowly from the 1850s. The level of independent Indian capitalism had increased during World War I, and as in Latin America and many parts of the colonial world, business had been particularly stimulated by World War II. Even by 1939 British and Indian capitalists had put competition behind them and were hunting for profit as partners rather than rivals. Thus, from the viewpoint of British capitalism in India, independence was not an especially fearful prospect.

In the early years after independence foreign capital occupied a large place in the Indian economy, with most of this capital coming from the profits of previous investment. Foreign capital was dominant in several major industries (petroleum, rubber, private railways, matches, jute, tea, and coal) and played a large part in others. Banks, for instance, were 46 per cent foreign-owned, and electrical industries were at 43 per cent. Cotton had only 21 per cent foreign investment.

Indian-owned industry was highly concentrated. A few exceedingly large firms, in particular the Tata (the largest industrial and financial group), Birla, and Jain groups, had mammoth holdings. The Tata group, for instance, controlled more than 100 companies, and in the 1960s one of its industrial towns had a quarter of a million inhabitants. At the end of the war the Birla group managed nearly 100 companies as well as one of India's great banks and several newspapers.

## Plans for Growth

Superficially, India's plans for industrialization followed the blueprint of the Soviet Union, the pre-eminent model for rapid, large-scale, and socialist industrial modernization. The Soviet model was also to be the Chinese model, but the implementation of the first Chinese five-year plan was delayed by the Korean War (see chapter 8), making the Indian experiment with large-scale state-controlled industrialization the first in Asia. The difference between the strategies in communist countries and the Indian plan was that whereas the Soviets were forced to raise an industrial infrastructure on the bones of a hostile class of peasants, the Indians could pay for it, in part at least, through the debt the British had incurred in India during World War II—a debt that had risen to £350 million by 1945.

In April 1951 India launched its first Five-Year Plan. There are at least two ways of looking at this plan. According to the French Marxist Charles Bettleheim, the giant firms such as Tata and Birla helped design the plan in their own interests.[10] In the view of these firms, a strong state role in the economy was likely to enhance their security against foreign rivals and ensure healthy profits. The state would provide a trellis of economic regulations, a large public sector, and financial aid to private enterprise. State capitalism co-existing with private capitalism, as the Indian planners proposed, did not equal socialism.

A different view emphasizes that the main object of state capitalism was socialist, not capitalist: that is, public good, not private profit. This view underlines Nehru's credentials as a democratic-socialist; a position at odds with Gandhi's small-producer, peasant utopianism. As early as May 1929, Akbar indicates, a Congress resolution had emphasized that "in order to remove the poverty and misery of the Indian people and to ameliorate the condition of the masses, it is essential to make revolutionary changes in the present economic and social structure of society and to remove gross inequalities."[11]

In the same year Nehru had proclaimed his orientation: "I must frankly confess that I am a socialist and a republican and am no believer in kings and princes, or in the order which produces the modern kings of industry, who have greater power over the lives and fortunes of men than even the kings of old, and whose methods are as predatory as those of the old feudal aristocracy."[12]

Nehru and Congress were clearly of the view that the Indian state must occupy the commanding heights of the economy. It would do this by working the most important levers: finance, transportation, and industry. But the Indian economy was not to be a command economy of the Soviet and Chinese type. Most importantly, key sectors of heavy industry, agriculture, and the production of consumer goods and services were all to be left in private hands. So rather than following the Soviet model throughout, the Indian economy was to be somewhat like the mixed but essentially capitalist economies of postwar France and Britain. Nehru considered this socialism; Marxists like Bettleheim didn't. In 1954 the official goal of Congress was proclaimed to be "the establishment of a socialist pattern of society." But in the end the key sector of the economy, agriculture, remained less reformed than in either South Korea or Taiwan, which in hindsight suggests that Nehru's strategy was dirigiste rather than socialist, as Nehru claimed, and that India's economy was a highly regulated form of state capitalism.

The first Five-Year Plan (1951-56) was in large part an agricultural rescue operation, with a focus on increased food production. In its first year India had to import four million tons of wheat from the United States. Even though India continued to import food grains for the next two decades, food-grain production did increase by as much as 20 per cent, and the total national income grew by 18 per cent. As well, per capita income increased by 115 per cent and per capita consumption by 9 per cent.[13] The industrial side of the plan was also a success. If we take the value of industrial production in 1950 as standing at 100, by 1960 it had increased to 160, and by 1964, the year Nehru died, it had reached 280.[14]

A closely related second Five-Year Plan (1956-61), more costly and ambitious, moved beyond agriculture and the sense of crisis to stress ISI. Investment in agriculture fell to 17.5 per cent from 34.6 per cent in the first plan, and agricultural productivity, though continuing to rise, was matched by population increase. The investment in industrialization sought to establish a strong domestic manufacturing base, partly state-owned, aimed at providing India with both heavy industrial goods and power.

The second plan cost between two and three times as much as the first, and by 1956 the reserves accumulated during World War II were depleted. This meant that Indian public and private investment had to be supplemented by substantial foreign investment, which led in turn to debt problems, postponed only by other loans from foreign governments. The pattern was a familiar one in both Latin America and the Middle East.

A third five-year plan, accepted in 1961, pushed industrial development even more energetically, allowing India to claim the position of the world's seventh most industrially advanced nation. Like the second plan, the third was aided by foreign capital, particularly through a consortium of donors called the "Aid-to-India Club" made up of the United States, Britain, Canada, France, West Germany, and Japan. But while India was now able to export industrial goods ranging from locomotives to bicycles, the agricultural sector remained embedded in poverty, and in many places was stagnant. Education was seen as a partial solution to this stagnation. The third plan envisaged the education of 75 per cent of India's children in the age range of six to eleven years, which would produce an astonishing 50 million primary school pupils. While this goal proved unattainable, India's literacy rate rose to 23.7 per cent nationwide, from a level of about 10 per cent in the 1940s. The literacy level of women remained well below, at 12.8 per cent.

By 1964-65, Indian economic growth had run into problems, including drought and a war with Pakistan. Still, a modest growth of 3.5 per cent continued for two more decades. Ramesh Thakur points out:

> By the start of the 1980s, India had eased three of the tightest bottlenecks to economic development: shortage of savings for investment, dependence on imported food and lack of foreign exchange. High domestic savings meant that the resources for growth were found at home, so avoiding the double burden of a crippling government debt and an unmanageable foreign debt. Measures of social welfare improved: between 1951 and 1991 infant mortality was halved, life expectancy doubled and adult literacy trebled. The guru of the take-off theory of economic growth, W.W. Rostow, declared in . . . 1983 that India's economy had entered the post-take-off stage of the drive to technological maturity. By the end of the 1980s a much larger proportion of Indians had access to health and education benefits than before independence.[15]

On May 27, 1964, Nehru died in office. Like Mao Zedong, he had led his country in its age of heroic nationalism and gone on to enjoy the spring-time of its independence. And like Mao he died at home, of natural causes, and still in power—not through assassination, or in exile, or politically defeated, or even diminished. His successors would not be so fortunate.

## Indira's India, 1966-84

Lal Bahadur Shastri, who was selected by the Congress Party bosses because he was not likely to upset the status quo, succeeded Nehru as prime minister. When Shastri died suddenly in January 1966, he was succeeded by Nehru's daughter, Indira Gandhi (whose husband, Feroze Gandhi, was no relation of Mohandas Gandhi).

Like her father, in whose shadow and under whose influence she grew, Indira Gandhi (1918-84) had the kind of education reserved for the rich and sophisticated. She had gone to school in Switzerland and England and had impeccable nationalist credentials as a former leader of the Youth

Group of Congress and a major figure on the party's left wing. She was one of the few women imprisoned by the British during the Second World War. Nonetheless, at the time Jawaharlal Nehru died people knew of Indira Gandhi mainly as her father's companion. She had held no elected office. Party insiders soon repaired this by giving her a minor cabinet post as minister of information and broadcasting in Shastri's short-lived and turbulent government.

During the period of that government the second Indo-Pakistan war began, in September 1965, and was over within a month, by which time Indian troops were within a few miles of the Pakistani capital, Lahore. The Indian army was four times as large as Pakistan's and had been rearmed by the United States after the recent debacle with China in the Himalayas. After the ceasefire both Shastri and the unelected prime minister of Pakistan, General Muhammad Ayub Khan, took up the invitation of the Soviet Premier Alexei Kosygin and flew to Tashkent for talks to help settle the long-standing and mutual hostility between their two countries. The Tashkent summit, held January 4-10, 1966, advanced remarkably, in large part due to Shastri's capacity as a conciliator. A rosy future seemed to lie ahead for the two countries. Then, having played a statesman's role, Shastri died, and the question of succession returned.

The country's leadership seemed to present a David and Goliath competition, with David being not merely a woman but a woman with limited political experience and a left-wing following. Goliath took the form of Morarji Desai (1896-1995), a right-wing champion of India's big business interests. "Communists have always considered me their enemy no. 1," he boasted.[16] Desai was 69, and Indira Gandhi 48, but the party's elderly chieftains chose Gandhi largely because it seemed to them that as a weaker vessel she would be dependent on their support. Little did they know that they were electing the first Iron Lady of contemporary politics. Desai became deputy premier, but resigned two years later.

Indira Gandhi's election coincided almost exactly with a severe food shortage in Central India, which followed from the failure of the Asiatic monsoon rains to arrive in 1965, as well as Washington's growing preoccupation with Vietnam and communism in Southeast Asia. In October 1965 Washington assisted in the destruction of Nehru's former Bandung ally, Indonesia's Sukarno (see chapter 7), but was still seeking Asian friends. India's drastic need for food grains was convenient. In her Independence Day message on January 26, 1966, Gandhi announced that the United States had promised to supply enough grain to help India survive what had turned into a famine. Without U.S. food aid, certainly millions in the provinces of Central India would have starved. The rapprochement that had begun with the war with China had advanced another step; gone was the strategy of non-alignment and self-sufficiency. In March 1966 Gandhi flew to Washington to accept $435 million in financial aid to be used for India's fourth five-year plan.

Indira Gandhi's first term in office was a political trial by ordeal. Not only had it begun with an economic crisis produced by drought, but also the problem was averted only after an appeal to the United States. This was a humiliating turn of affairs for anyone who still aspired to non-alignment. The drought was followed by a demand for greater autonomy and territorial expansion of the state of East Punjab by the Sikh minority there. Gandhi's critics claimed, in addition, that the precipitous devaluation of the rupee, which fell from 4.76 to 7.50 to the dollar, was a mark of her obeisance to the United States. Devaluation meant that Indian goods would be cheaper, foreign goods would be more expensive, and foreign capital would be able to buy up large amounts of the Indian economy at bargain prices.

In the elections of 1967 the popularity of both Indira Gandhi and Congress fell calamitously. At the state level Congress no longer had a majority of total seats. Gandhi's leadership of the party remained weak. Desai still controlled the right wing of a party that was becoming increasingly divided. The final split came in 1969, with the death of the country's president, the constitutional head of the state. Gandhi wanted to secure her own candidate, V.V. Giri, a labour organizer and the country's vice-president, in his place. The right-wing, more elderly party leaders thought otherwise. After Giri won the election, in revenge the right-wing group expelled Gandhi from the party, charging her with indiscipline. The lower house of parliament continued to give her overwhelming support.

Now there were two Congress parties, Congress (O), the party of the geriatric guard (the "O" standing for "Organization"), and Congress (R), Indira Gandhi's party (the "R" for "Requisitionist"). Gandhi appealed over the heads of wealthy to the poor. She embarked on a program of nationalization, beginning with India's major banks, including the Central Bank. Gandhi's promise of land reform and the abolition of the allowances and privileges of India's hitherto independent princelings, the maharajahs, attracted even the communists, while the right-wing parties swung behind Congress (O).

In the national elections of March 1971 the struggle over the legacy of Nehru was finally settled. Gandhi, at the head of a left-wing coalition and riding on a wave of triumph that had come with the defeat of Pakistan in Bangladesh, won 350 out of 515 seats.

After her double triumph against the Pakistan army and her Congress rivals, Indira Gandhi moved quickly. In August 1971 her government signed a Treaty of Peace, Friendship, and Co-operation with the Soviet Union. Between 1972 and 1975 she carried out a series of nationalizations, at the same time moving to tighten her grip on the Indian political process. Congress became less democratic and more the vehicle for her authoritarian rule. In 1974 her government launched the fifth Five-Year Plan, which Thakur describes as "a frontal assault on poverty."[17] The means to achieve this end was to be an increase in food production, a goal that seemed to be within reach because of a huge breakthrough brought about by the "Green Revolution," which promised to continue a spectacular increase in the harvest of food grains. Gandhi proposed to enhance the gains made through crop production with other advances in land reform and birth control.

But by 1974 Indira Gandhi's government was in trouble. The claims that she had herself levelled against the corruption of the former Congress regime were now being levelled against her, her government, and even her family. The most visible target of these anti-corruption protests was her son Sanjay, a pampered playboy whom she had placed at the head of India's nationalized automobile production. After five years the nationalized firm had just managed to produce its first car.

The leaders of the coalition against Indira Gandhi's increasingly corrupt regime were J.P. Narayan (1902-79) and Morarji Desai, her rival in the race for the leadership of the party in 1966. Their party, the Janata Morcha—the "People's Front"—had among its allies many of those who had initially joined Gandhi against her Congress rivals: from left to right, Maoists, communists, socialists, communalists, conservatives, and cultists. Gandhi replied to the protest of her critics by crushing their strikes and jailing their leaders. The greatest blow against her credibility came in June 1975, when the Allahabad High Court found her guilty of electoral malpractice. The decision stimulated an avalanche of protest focusing on both the corruption and autocracy that had flourished under her government, and again Gandhi responded with violence. Towards the end of the month, imposing a state of emergency, Gandhi had her accusors arrested, and she suspended civil liberties. About 110,000 people were arrested and imprisoned without trial.[18] For Gandhi's enemies, it must have seemed as if the bad old days of British India had returned, and as in the days of the Raj, economic discontent underpinned the political protest. As Stanley Wolpert explains it: "With less than two thousand Indian citizens admitting to more than $1,300 a year of taxable income and more than four hundred million living on the knife edge of starvation . . . there was considerable reason to be discontented. And with at least one-third of the more than sixteen million annual college graduates of India unable to find jobs of any sort, it was hardly surprising to find educated youth in the vanguard of the opposition."[19]

With the help of her friends, the Russians on the one hand and the leading Indian capitalists on the other, along with the blessings of a bumper crop and high levels of investment, Indira Gandhi kept the lid on Indian affairs until 1977. Indeed, she screwed the lid down even more tightly after the emergency, co-opting or removing individual politicians and state governments alike—anyone who displeased her. When in January 1977 she somewhat abruptly let her opponents out of jail and announced elections for March, the opposition sprang back to life. The millions who for one reason or another had been offended by her government—in some cases by her jagged political style in general and in others by its particular excesses (forcible slum clearance without compensation, mass sterilization)—took their revenge. Her government was overwhelmed at the polls, and the Congress Party's political monopoly was brought to an end.

Both Indira Gandhi and her son Sanjay lost their seats in the backlash. Morarji Desai, who by then had the distinction of having been jailed by both the British and Indira Gandhi, became prime minister at the head of the Janata Party. "In voting Mrs Gandhi out in 1977," Thakur concludes, "Indians showed that while they can put up with much economic injustice, they would not tolerate tyranny. In accepting defeat gracefully, Mrs Gandhi confirmed that the norms of democratic transition of power had been internalized at the highest levels of India's political elite."[20]

The Janata Party's time in power was short and chaotic. Desai, at age 81, proved hopeless and inert, more interested in the high frontiers of yoga than in poverty and inflation. The party soon revealed itself as being hopelessly, even comically, incompetent. Splits occurred, with leading socialists, trade unionists, idealistic reformers, and young lions of all sorts flocking out of the party by mid-1979. Indira Gandhi's autocracy was now looked back upon as a kind of arcadian age. When Desai resigned at the end of July 1979 India's president called a new election for January 1980, which Gandhi won easily. Her party, with two-thirds of the seats in parliament, was now called Congress (I), for "Indira." Her favourite son, Sanjay, became her right-hand man—at least until June 1980, when he accidentally killed himself flying stunts in a private plane.

The last years of Indira Gandhi's Raj were anything but golden. In the northeast, among the people known as "tribals," rebellion and the threat of separatism appeared. In response the government enforced martial law. In the northwest came a different kind of havoc, as Soviet troops entered

Afghanistan in support of a pro-Soviet government. Opposing them were Muslim conservatives supported by Pakistan, which was, in turn, backed by Washington. In short order Afghanistan was to become Moscow's Vietnam.

More inflammatory because closer to home were affairs in Punjab, the most agriculturally prosperous and dynamic state in India. Some 10 million Punjabis were Sikhs, and 9 million were Hindus. A minority of Sikhs wanted greater autonomy in their own state, which they referred to as "Khalistan," which would be a sort of Sikh Pakistan.* While some Sikhs had agitated for a homeland from even before independence, between 1947 and 1980 only a minority were seriously concerned by the issue. After 1980, when Congress returned to power following its defeat of the Janata Party, militant reformists took over the independence movement. These reformists were led by a young Sikh monk called Jarnail Singh Bhindranwale (1947-84), who advocated the use of terror to get the Delhi government to make concessions.

The Sikh reformists murdered both moderate Sikhs and others. In the early part of 1984, with government troops in pursuit, Bhindranwale took refuge in the Sikh Golden Temple in Amritsar, near the infamous site of a 1919 massacre of protesting Indians by the British. On June 6, 1984, Indira Gandhi, by now no stranger to the use of force against political opponents, and with an eye to the advantages that strong action would bring to an election campaign due at the end of the year, launched her army against Bhindranwale and his followers in the Golden Temple. The temple was desecrated, part of it was destroyed, and Bhindranwale and his followers annihilated.

On October 31, 1984, Sikh militants had their revenge when Indira Gandhi was assassinated by two of her Sikh security guards. The escalation continued with attacks on Sikhs and their property in Delhi and elsewhere in north India. At least 3,000 Sikhs were murdered and 25,000 others left homeless. An official commission reporting on the slaughter could find no culprits. A report by the Indian civil liberties union pointed the finger at leading politicians in the Congress (I) Party.

---

* The Sikhs had emerged as a distinctive ethnic group in the early 16th century. "Unlike Christians or Muslims or any of the other minorities, Sikhs were at the centre of Indian politics, business, and national power," Ved Mehta states in *Rajiv Gandhi and Rama's Kingdom* (1994, p.49) After independence most Sikhs lived in the state of East Punjab, although Punjabi-speaking Hindus outnumbered the Sikhs there by more than two to one. In 1966 Indira Gandhi's government divided East Punjab into two states: Punjab, where Sikhs predominated, and Haryana, where Hindus predominated. Many Sikhs argued that a number of their towns had been included in Haryana and that they had therefore been swindled.

# Rajiv's Raj, 1984-91

Rajiv Gandhi, born in 1944, had led a quiet but privileged life until the time of his mother's death. Indolent and likeable and having neither academic aptitude nor political instincts, he had made a career as an Air India pilot. He became prime minister the day that his mother was assassinated, and within a few days called an election for December 24-27. The Congress Party (I) campaign had a simple slogan: "Remember Indira." The greatest electoral landslide in India's history ensued. "Our politics should be clean," Rajiv Gandhi stressed. "Mr. Clean," as he was called, promised a shining tomorrow.

Influenced by the neoliberal agendas promoted by Margaret Thatcher in Britain and Ronald Reagan in the United States, Rajiv Gandhi wanted to chart a new economic course for India, one that would free entrepreneurs from the restraints of government rules. But, as Mehta explains, this led to a dilemma: "He found himself trapped between giving entrepreneurs greater freedom to make money and keeping the loyalty of voters who were poor and whose situation was not going to improve, at least in the short term."[21] So although among those in both his immediate circle and business circles in general a consensus had grown that the planned, socialist economy would have to be at least partially dismantled, Rajiv Gandhi was a prisoner of politics. According to Mehta, "Rajiv's government could not dismantle the socialist structure, nor did he try to; it only opened up the country to more private enterprise than had existed before."[22] While a small class of wealthy, Western-oriented entrepreneurs profited considerably from Rajiv Gandhi's period in office, changes in the structure of the Indian economy were negligible. Certainly, the economy did nothing like "take off."

Many of the promises Rajiv Gandhi made in the first flush of his electoral victory came no closer to fulfilment. One of these concerned the Punjab, where, despite Gandhi's best efforts at conciliation, terror had continued to proliferate. The state became an occupied territory, governed under "President's Rule" (martial law), in which the terror of the Sikh militants was matched by a counterterror orchestrated by a Bengali governor and a Christian director-general of police. By 1992 sectarian violence had caused 4,768 civilian deaths.

In the northeast, where the "tribals" were in open revolt, the Rajiv Gandhi regime got off to a more promising start. Yet although Gandhi initially worked out accords acceptable to both sides, by 1988 the agreements had come unravelled. And by that time his former finance minister, V.P. Singh, had begun to make a nuisance of himself. Singh made a number of sobering disclosures concerning the corruption of the regime in the

matter of defence contracts, especially those involving the Swedish armaments firm Bofors. It seemed that persons close to Rajiv Gandhi were lining their pockets with public monies from kickbacks. In April 1987 Singh
was kicked out of the party, and thereafter he became as effective a leader
of the opposition as he had been a Congress cabinet minister.

Apparently confident that his majority in parliament would see him
through, Rajiv Gandhi announced a snap election for November 1989. The
major opposition parties, the Hindu-chauvinist Bharatiya Janata Party
(BJP), the descendant of the Hindu Mahasabha, and the Janata Dal agreed
not to field candidates against each other, and as a result Congress lost the
north and the centre of the country. By rights, since Congress still held
more seats than any other party, it could have formed a coalition government with one or another of the lesser parties and thus return to power.
But no other party was willing to join it. V.P. Singh, whose party had won
only 20 per cent of the seats, formed a new coalition government that
included the Janata Dal, the BJP, and the Bengali-based Communist Party
(Marxist). The coalition was unstable from birth, tottering on to a predictable collapse because of inevitable discord between partners whose
only real common interest had been to unseat Rajiv Gandhi.

In autumn 1990, with elections looming at the end of the year, the BJP
took up the communalist cause, leading a campaign for the restoration of a
Hindu temple on a site where a centuries-old mosque still stood. Violence
flared as the Hindus destroyed the mosque. The head of the BJP was
arrested, and in November V.P. Singh was forced to resign. The coalition
limped on until it collapsed in February 1991. New national elections were
slated for June 1991, but in the midst of the election campaign, on May 21,
1991 in the southern state of Tamil Nadu, Rajiv Gandhi was killed by a
bomb blast. His female assassin seems to have been a supporter of the
Tamil secessionists of Sri Lanka, who were aggrieved that the Indian army
had been used against them.

In June 1991, P.V. Narasimha Rao (b. 1921), a Tamil-language film star,
became prime minister at the head of a minority Congress government, a
position he held until defeated in 1996 elections. India remained trapped
in crisis. The Iraqi invasion of Kuwait and the Gulf War of early 1991 had
damaged the economy. In the 1980s it had seemed that the lethargic
"Hindu rate of growth" had been shaken off: industrial production had
increased by about 8 per cent per year, and India appeared to be the exception to the Third World rule of a growth of relative poverty in the decade.
Now, with the Iraqi invasion, oil prices rose again, and the Indian workers
whose home remittances had come to form an important source of foreign
exchange fled the Gulf in droves: 150,000 were suddenly back in India and

unemployed. Furthermore, Rajiv Gandhi's policy of trade liberalization had led to the country being swamped with imports that it could not pay for.

"When Rao became Prime Minister," Mehta states, "inflation was running at 14 percent; the budgetary process was out of kilter; foreign reserves were exhausted; India, with outstanding foreign debts of $71 billion, was the third-largest debtor nation in the developing world, after Brazil and Mexico; and, for the first time, it was in danger of defaulting on its debts."[23] The government had appealed to the IMF for a loan, eventually receiving over $2 billion. Rao's new government began its career by devaluing the rupee by nearly 20 per cent.

By the early 1990s voices began to be heard referring to "India's growing crisis of governability." London's liberal *Financial Times* excitedly declared, "The Raj is now nearing collapse" and concluded that Nehru's dynasty was at fault. Economic liberalism, it proclaimed, was the solution. The more conventionally conservative *Economist* made the same point: "The government must dismantle an unbelievably complicated system of restraints and rewards that, over the past four decades, has securely enclosed every area of life. . . . India must be opened up."[24]

Writing in 1993, Ramesh Thakur joined the chorus of laments over the failure of independent India's development program:

India's record has been a failure by the standards of its own ambitious targets. . . . The development perspective of the first five-year plan set the target of doubling national income per head by 1977; only half the target was achieved. The extent of poverty has barely been dented. In 1990, 410 million Indians (compared to 120 million Chinese) were still below the poverty line. . . .

India has fared badly in comparison both to the better and the badly off. In the 1950s India's share of world exports was 2 percent, of Third World exports 6 percent. By 1980 the figures had fallen to 0.4 percent and 1.4 percent respectively. In the mid-1950s India was the tenth biggest industrial power in the world; by the late 1970s it had declined to the twentieth. China as well as the four East Asian dragons [South Korea, Hong Kong, Taiwan, Singapore] have averaged growth rates more than double that of India over a sustained period of time. . . . In 1960 South Korea's GNP per capita was $87, India's was $73. In 1989 the figures were $4,400 and $340 respectively.[25]

In a book published two years later Thakur provided a more nuanced if no less censorious audit. Comparing India in the mid-1990s to India under the British Raj, he stated that India had "not fared too badly" in comparison with the 50 years of stagnation before independence. "It broke the pre-1947 economic stagnation, raised national income per head and strengthened the economic infrastructure," becoming "a vibrant and diversified industrial power in a remarkably short period of time."[26]

Thakur found that India's economy had grown three times faster in the two decades after independence than it had during the British Raj, "and faster than the rate of British growth during its comparable stage of development in the eighteenth and nineteenth centuries." Much of the credit for this growth, he said, must go to the public sector, although that growth might have reached a danger point: "It may also be the case that state-directed planning has enabled the private sector in India to grow strong enough to find the extensive public sector the main impediment to its further profitable expansion." Thakur pointed out the successes:

> High domestic savings meant that the resources for growth were found at home, so avoiding the double burden of a crippling government debt and an unrepayable foreign debt. In just forty years, infant mortality was halved, life expectancy nearly doubled and adult literacy almost trebled. . . . The considerable social improvements may not have reached the poorest Indians. Even so, today a much larger proportion of Indians has access to health and education benefits which before independence had been restricted to the privileged elite.

But those successes contrasted with stark failures: "More recent results, however, have been economic stagnation, structural rigidity and backwardness, desperate international infusion of capital to stave off defaults, and the persistence of poverty and inequality. India's record has been a failure by the standards of its own targets and the needs of its people. Its long-term growth rate pales into insignificance in a comparative context."

Although India had achieved capital accumulation and technical change based on state planning, these achievements did not bring improvements in productivity and welfare. Instead the country experienced rising unemployment, a growing dependence on imported capital goods and technology, and a generally ailing economy. As Thakur concluded, "In international economic exchanges, policy failures were reflected in a falling share of world exports, a depreciating currency and an inability to export sophisticated manufactures."

In a general election in May 1996 the Congress party, its powerful structure now a crumbling ruin, won the largest number of votes of any single party, but only 30 per cent of the total, lower than in any previous election. The BJP, which got fewer votes but won more seats, tried to form a government but failed to get the necessary vote of confidence in the lower house. During the election its candidates had promised to end the

"appeasement" of India's 110 million Muslims. India's president then
called on H.D. Deve Gowda, the leader of a bloc of 14 "social justice" parties known as the United Front, to form a government. The prospects of
this coalition were, from the outset, uncertain. Just possibly, the days
when a single party could run the country were over.

# Independent Pakistan, 1957-71

Muhammad Ali Jinnah (b. 1876), the London-educated barrister who
became Quaid-i-Azam ("Great Leader") of Pakistani nationalism, died on
September 1, 1948, seven months after Gandhi. It was Jinnah who had
complained in 1947 of the "mutilated, truncated, moth-eaten country created by the partition of British India." He had hoped that the Muslims
would rule over all of Bengal, including Calcutta, India's commercial capital, as well as the Punjab. Jinnah was succeeded by his right-hand man,
Pakistan's first prime minister, Liaquat Ali Khan (b. 1905), who was himself assassinated in October 1951. Although Jinnah was a visionary in his
own way, he was neither a Gandhi nor a Nehru. Thus his dubious legacy:
his party, the Muslim League, barely outlived him, and his state broke in
two in just over two decades after his death. Quixotically, while Jinnah was
a Muslim, and the justification of Pakistan was as a Zion for Muslims, he
was immovably opposed to establishing a theocratic state.

By the time of Liaquat's assassination Pakistan was already in trouble
from several directions. Muslims were offended by Liaquat's secularism,
and militarists were offended by his unwillingness to invade Kashmir. East
Pakistanis, who comprised over half the population of Pakistan and were
almost entirely Bengalis, felt oppressed and excluded from power by the
West Pakistanis, with whom they had nothing in common except their fear
of Hindu chauvinism and their religion; and even that was often a source
of friction. In schematic terms, the Sunni Muslims in West Pakistan had
much in common with the Muslims of the Middle East, while the Bengali
Muslims were more influenced by Hinduism. Muslim men in West Pakistan looked askance at the independence of women in the East.

The Pakistani bureaucratic-military elite was not made up of West
Pakistanis as a whole—that is of Sindhis, Baluchis, and people from the
North West Frontier Province—but mainly of Punjabis and *muhajirs* (emi-
grants) from the northern Indian province of Uttar Pradesh and from Bom-
bay. The *muhajirs* took control of the state from the time of Liaquat's
assassination until a 1958 military coup that put General Muhammad Ayub
Khan into power. Yet the problems they faced were insurmountable.
"From 1954 to 1958 Pakistan's political system degenerated into a farce,"

notes Omar Noman.[27] Ayesha Jalal is more sympathetic. While also stressing that the administrative bureaucracy hijacked the state, she underlines the real material and administrative poverty of Pakistan:

> With 23 per cent of the total land mass of the Indian subcontinent and nearly 18 per cent of the population—or more precisely 68.6 million out of 295.8 million in British India—the new state had less than 10 per cent of the industrial base in the two dominions and just a little over 7 per cent of the employment facilities. . . . In 1947 Pakistan's total industrial assets were worth only . . . approximately $112 million . . . of which the better part was owned by non-Muslims who had fled to India. Potentially self-sufficient only in foodgrains, Pakistan was the quintessential agrarian economy.[28]

Pakistan's grave administrative problems included a shortage of trained and experienced civilian and military bureaucrats. The Indian Muslims who emigrated to Pakistan were in every sense expatriates. Estranged from the India in which they had been born, they were unfamiliar with the Pakistan to which they had now moved. Preoccupied with the task of organizing an administrative and tax system, they failed to develop a workable political system balancing the interests of the diverse strands of Pakistani society—especially the regional elites, such as the great landowners, whose power over the local peasants was immense. Their attempts to raise taxes to sustain the civil and military administrations put them on a collision course with these regional politicians, who opposed the increasing centralization of wealth and fought for greater regional autonomy. The crises, both military and civil, that befell the bureaucracy of the new state immediately after its birth could only exacerbate their problems.

The first protest riots took place in East Pakistan in 1952 and were directed against the policy of imposing Urdu as the national language.* In provincial elections of 1954, the Muslim League was devastated by the United Front, a grouping of East Pakistan parties that wanted greater regional autonomy. Almost immediately after its election the United Front government was dismissed, and the administration of East Pakistan was placed under a governor from the west, an intervention that many in East Pakistan regarded as akin to colonialism.

---

* Urdu, related to Persian and written in Arabic script, had never been the vernacular language of any ethnic group, but was the court language of the Mughals and spoken by Muslims in the United Province of northern India under the Raj. Although it became the official language of Pakistan, Jinnah himself scarcely spoke it, nor did most Bengalis, Punjabis, Pathans, Sindhis, Baluchis, or other peoples who became Pakistanis, all of whom had their own languages. In some respects it was like Latin in medieval Europe or Hebrew in contemporary Israel.

The major, persistent, external nightmare was Pakistan's insecurity vis-à-vis India—a concern that drove its leaders into the arms of the United States and closed off any possibility that Pakistan might become enrolled in any bloc of either Middle Eastern or Third World countries. Its membership in CENTO and SEATO cast it as a pariah in the eyes of its neighbours.

For the Americans, Pakistan had, in geopolitical terms, a surfeit of attractive qualities: strategically facing the soft underbelly of the Soviet Union, nicely proximate to annoyingly neutralist India and able to provoke India over Kashmir almost at will, just east of the oil-rich Middle East but conveniently Muslim (and predominantly Sunni Muslim to boot), and with enough coastline on the Indian Ocean to claim to be a Southeast Asian state. Pakistan, like Turkey, thus possessed a kind of strategic glamour. Furthermore, the willingness of Pakistan's leaders to join both CENTO and SEATO gave its rulers credibility in the Pentagon and State Department, a credibility rewarded with lavish amounts of military equipment. This connection was gratifying to its soldierly elite, most of whom had come from "tribes" (like the Pathans) that the British had identified as "martial." U.S. Secretary of State John Foster Dulles, who toured the Middle East and South Asia in May 1953, had not been impressed by the political reliability of the Arab states, but Pakistan was a bright spot, he reported to the State Department—a country with the "moral courage to do its part in resisting communism."[29]

The leader of the 1958 coup, Ayub Khan (1907-74), was from one of the traditional ruling, landholding families of Punjab. Sent from Punjab to England to study in the military college at Sandhurst, he transformed himself into a Punjabi Colonel Blimp. A simple soldier, as he called himself, Ayub Khan was irrepressibly cheerful and co-operative. British and especially U.S. leaders and political analysts admired him volubly. After grabbing power Ayub Khan made himself chief of the general staff, prime minister, and president. In October 1959 his government cooked up a complex electoral system that limited the franchise to around 80,000 of Pakistan's hundred-odd million people. Those favoured with the franchise were called "basic democrats," and several months later this selected group was asked to say "yes" or "no" to a simple question: "Have you confidence in President Ayub Khan?" An incredible 95.6 per cent indicated "yes." This exercise, Noman commented in 1988, "made East European elections look glamorous."[30] Still, the stern military man almost glowed with the reflected approval of Washington. Samuel P. Huntington, the U.S. political analyst, gave the Pakistan leader full marks. "Ayub Khan," he wrote, "came close to filling the role of a Solon or Lycurgus or

'Great Legislator' on the Platonic or Rousseauian model." Men like him, Huntington affirmed, showed that military leaders could be effective builders of political institutions.[31]

Although as early as the late 1950s many in the Eisenhower administration had come to view the U.S.-Pakistani military alliance as an expensive blunder, in the early 1960s the World Bank and USAID, the leading official U.S. aid-giving institution, both approved of how military dictatorships executed policy. That these dictatorships destroyed the independence of the judiciary and press as well as academic freedom was seen as a small price to pay for economic development based on ISI policies and financed by foreign capital.

## Zulfikar Ali Bhutto

Ayub Khan's civilian front man was his protégé Zulfikar Ali Bhutto (1927-79), who had a background much like Nehru's. He was from a wealthy family, though landowning (like Ayub Khan's) rather than commercial, and had an extensive education abroad (at Oxford and the University of California at Berkeley). The difference was that Pakistan had no Westernized and democratic political culture like the one that had moulded the Congress Party in India, and it had no highly Westernized bourgeoisie. Bhutto was a landowner possessing over 100,000 acres and ruling over peasants whose relationship to him had a distinctly feudal flavour. His rise had begun in the mid-1950s, when a family friend, General Syed Iskander Ali Mizra, was appointed as governor-general. Mizra reappointed Ayub Khan as commander-in-chief of the army and Ayub Khan, impressed by Bhutto's cosmopolitanism and wit, soon appointed him as his advisor.

Ayub Khan and Bhutto were successful not only in attracting the support of Washington but also in cementing closer relations with China after the Sino-Indian war in the Himalayas in 1962. Apart from the brief respite after the three-week war of September 1965, Pakistani-Indian relations between the time of Nehru's death in 1964 and the final triumph of his daughter, Indira Gandhi, in 1970, were marked by chronic hostility, which reached its lowest point with the war in Kashmir, which variously smouldered and raged between April and August 1965, and which Pakistan quite palpably lost. In the words of Bhutto's biographer, Stanley Wolpert, the 1965 war became Bhutto's "political booster rocket."[32]

With a shrewd eye for the main chance, Bhutto abandoned Ayub Khan's dictatorship in early 1966, just after the Tashkent Summit that followed Pakistan's military defeat at the hands of India. Certainly the dictatorship seemed to be heading into rough weather. In March 1966 in East Pakistan, the Awami League under Sheikh Mujib ur Rahman (1922-75) had begun to campaign for independence from West Pakistan. The grievances of the Bengalis were simple; they were exploited and under-represented. They even used the term "colonial exploitation" to refer to their subjugation under the West Pakistanis—with the term partially justi-fied because most of Pakistan's foreign exchange came from the sale of jute from the East. Too much of the wealth of the East was used to benefit the wealthy in the West. The political system was skewed in such a way that although the Bengalis were the largest single ethnic group in Pakistan, and although most of the population lived in the East, only West Pakistanis at the head of West Pakistani parties were able to rule. In the decade 1956-66 an average of 4,946 riots a year occurred in East Pakistan. They had diverse causes, but in general were politically motivated.

Bhutto, the only Pakistani politician to emerge from the 1965 war with India with his popularity untarnished, launched the Pakistan People's Party (PPP) on December 1, 1967. Its motto was "Islam is our Faith, Democracy is our Polity, Socialism is our Economy, All Power to the People." Bhutto explained to his Pakistani brothers that the peoples of the Third World were "the most proletarian of the world" and "Therefore we have to cooperate, collaborate, get together, assist one another."[33] Some 22 families, the PPP claimed, had become the main beneficiaries of Pakistan's economic development, and Ayub Khan's family was among them. "They have sucked the blood of the people and have mercilessly looted them," Bhutto declared.[34] From the point of view of the moral economy of the rest of the country, and particularly East Pakistan, this situation was unpalatable, a source of deep grievance. Ayub Khan was considered a villain for having gambled and lost against the Indians in Kashmir.

Ayub Khan arrested both Sheikh Mujib and Ali Bhutto. Widespread protest followed, and the blood of students and workers began to flow onto the streets. Everywhere the chant "Long live Bhutto!" began to be raised. But by now Ayub Khan was seriously ill. In March 1969 he turned his government over to the commander-in-chief of the army, Yahya Khan (b. 1917), who even more than Ayub Khan consolidated military rule in Pakistan. Emboldened by the blessing of Washington and the World Bank, which promised him nearly half a billion dollars for the next year, he was determined to crush the independence movement in the East. Troops were flown into Dhaka, the capital of East Pakistan, and martial law was declared. The stick thus openly brandished, Yahya Khan then offered a slice of carrot to what he must have regarded as the donkey of popular sentiment. He promised general elections, the first since independence, for October 1970, but made clear that there would be no possibility of East separating from West.

On December 7, 1970, elections were held throughout Pakistan. In East Pakistan Sheikh Mujib ur Rahman's autonomist Awami ("People's") League won an astonishing 160 out of 162 seats. In West Pakistan Ali Bhutto's PPP won 81 seats. By rights the sheikh should have formed the new government of the whole of Pakistan. Although they could agree on little else, both Yahya Khan and Bhutto accepted that a government headed by the Bengalis was utterly unacceptable. (Indeed, Bhutto probably felt that government by anyone other than himself was undesirable.) The opening of the National Assembly, scheduled for March 1, 1971, was postponed. Bhutto and Yahya Khan flew to Dhaka for meetings with the Bengalis. When the talks broke down both leaders flew home, leaving behind them a large army of West Pakistan troops under one of their own, General Tikka Khan. Mujib ur Rahman responded, on March 26, by declaring East Pakistan dead and a new country, "Bangladesh," born.

The newly named Bangladeshis were ecstatic—flags were everywhere—but the West Pakistan rulers declared martial law and a civil war quickly ensued, with resulting victimization—of West Pakistanis settled in the East—and a subsequent repression by the largely West Pakistani army of Bengalis in the East. The (mainly Punjabi) troops of General Khan moved out of their barracks and slaughtered Bengalis wherever they found them. U.S.-made M-24 tanks manned by Punjabi and Baluchi crews shot down Bengali university students and their teachers without mercy. Women were mowed down in the markets. The sheikh was arrested and taken off to prison. By the end of April nearly a million refugees had fled into India, increasing to 10 million by the end of the year. India supported the East Pakistanis, and many of the Bangladesh refugees, armed by the Indians, returned to form guerrilla groups known as the Mukti Bahini, attacking the occupying army of West Pakistan. On November 23 the third Indo-Pakistani war broke out when Indira Gandhi ordered Indian troops to march into Bangladesh. The West Pakistanis, in turn, attacked India from the west, and so the Indian army once again marched into West Pakistan. On the eastern front, with the bulk of the population supporting the advancing Indians, the Pakistani army was quickly overwhelmed. On December 15, 1971, the Pakistani army in Bangladesh surrendered. Nearly 100,000 of its soldiers were now prisoners of the Indians.

Pakistan had now lost over half of its population. The Pakistan of the Muslim League had lasted only from August 15, 1947, to December 15, 1971, just short of a quarter-century. India had gained a grateful ally to the east, where before there had existed only an enemy. General Yahya Khan wisely resigned. Ali Bhutto, who had been made Yahya Khan's deputy just before the surrender of the Pakistani army at Dhaka, became prime minister. Sheikh Mujib ur Rahman survived incarceration to return to Bangladesh as prime minister, and the millions of refugees who had fled to India also returned. By early 1972 the government of India, under Indira Gandhi, had recovered much of the influence lost as a result of the country's defeat by China in the Himalayas.

## Pakistan Dismembered, 1972-90

What remained of Pakistan after the loss of Bangladesh was a country made up of one gigantic region, Punjab, which produced over half of the country's GNP, and three smaller ones, Baluchistan, North West Frontier, and Sind. The immigrants to Pakistan from India, the *muhajirs*, who numbered in the millions, were mainly concentrated in Karachi, the largest city and the commercial capital of the country. Pakistani politics was driven not only by the struggles between different social groups (landlords, peasants, Sunnis, Shi'as, Punjabis, Baluchis, *muhajirs*), but also by the dominance of the larger province and the bitterness of the smaller ones.

With the military discredited by the amputation of East Pakistan, Zulfikar Ali Bhutto's mandate as the first civilian ruler for 25 years seemed secure. His popularity was immense; no Pakistani leader had ever enjoyed such universal esteem. But Bhutto was unable to maintain the drive for change. Indeed, for much of his tenure in office the standard of living of the peasants and urban poor declined. The rhetoric of equality and development was sustained by the nationalization (in early 1972) of major industries (iron and steel, heavy industries, petrochemicals, cement, public utilities) and (in January 1974) of Pakistan's banks. But the cost was high: capital fled the country, and Pakistan's international credit ratings went into free fall. The indicators were now moving irreversibly towards the zero mark, and, worse, the tension between the communities in Pakistan increased. Riots began to erupt among the *muhajirs* and their Sindhi neighbours in Karachi and other cities.

In the face of mounting economic crisis, strikes, and political demonstrations, Bhutto came to rely increasingly on naked repression and manipulation. Blaming the West, in early 1972 he withdrew from the Commonwealth and SEATO and flew to Beijing, where he toasted Afro-Asian solidarity. In the same period he calumniated Pakistan's landowners and its elite civil servants. In 1973, capitalizing on the reaction in the Islamic world to the October war between Israel and its Arab neighbours, he launched an initiative that sought to ensure Pakistan a more permanent and central place in the minds of Muslims, and especially among those with bulging coffers, such as Libya and the Gulf states. By 1974, with his reputation as a Third World and Islamic statesman at its peak, and with his country's economy in deep disrepair, Prime Minister Bhutto's position had come to resemble that of other Third World reformers of the 1970s, from Allende to Manley to Ecevit to Indira Ghandi. All were waving for help, and all were sinking in the unforgiving waters of the world economy.

Besides substituting repression for reform, Bhutto, in common with other Third World leaders of the 1970s, sought credibility through a radical foreign policy, in particular trying to establish himself as a Third World leader by a closer identification of Pakistan with Islamic causes. In the name of independence, he also sought nuclear capability. But his "Third Worldism" earned him the hostility of the conservative pro-Western elites, and his nuclear policy earned him the enmity of the United States. In a way, then, he had become the Sukarno of his time: an Asian nationalist who had to be dumped.

By the end of 1976 many of the founders of the PPP had dropped out or been purged, with their places taken by zealous Muslims. As the Pakistani economy became even more battered, Bhutto tried to counter conditions by inspiring a cult of personality. Here China provided him with political inspiration. In unashamed imitation of the Maoist *Little Red Book* came his own red-covered *Bhutto Says: A Pocket Book of Thoughtful Quotations from Selected Speeches and Writings of Chairman Zulfikar Ali Bhutto*. But the cult of Bhutto never really did take off. He rigged and won a March 1977 election, but a combination of coercion and inflation cost him the support of those groups he had to rely on to face the combined opposition of the bureaucratic-military elite and the commercial-industrial bourgeoisie.

Against a rising crescendo of political protest, and fearing intervention by the army, he backed down and came to an agreement with the opposition for new elections, but the effort came too late. Like Sukarno, Bhutto was overthrown in an army coup. On July 5, 1977, the army, led by Commander-in-Chief Zia ul-Haq, whom Bhutto himself had promoted, returned to save the country from "chaos and disintegration." Behind the coup were two other forces: those who had at first supported Bhutto until his unwillingness to carry out either social or economic reforms became evident; and those whose material interests he had threatened.

A month later Bhutto was arrested, and he was eventually tried for dubious crimes. He was now regarded as a victim of the army, which led to a boost in his popularity, but this turn of affairs doomed him. Obviously, if he returned to power the army mutineers would find themselves in the dock. Furthermore, Bhutto had been instrumental in deposing another military ruler, Yahya Khan. On April 4, 1979, Zulfikar Ali Bhutto was hanged, to universal protest, in a Rawalpindi jail. The army, meanwhile, reassured the civilian population that it would relinquish power within 90 days.

## Zia ul-Haq

Bhutto's executioner, Muhammad Zia ul-Haq (1924-88), represented himself as another simple soldier and zealous Muslim. While he repeatedly assured the civilian politicians that he was committed to holding elections, he also took care to entrench his own political power. His regime oscillated from more repressive to less repressive, from militarism to restricted civilian participation, and from earnest to slack Islamism.

Between July 1977 and January 1986, Pakistan was ruled by martial law, and Zia was his own martial law administrator. The use of the terror of arbitrary arrest, torture, incarceration, and execution cowed his critics. Independent sources of authority, such as the judiciary, were once more neutralized. According to one account, "Zia banned political parties and introduced repressive laws like the Hudood and Zina Ordinance, under which a woman can only prove rape if she provides four Muslim male witnesses. Without such proof she faces imprisonment for adultery."[35]

Seeing the rise of Islamic reformism all around him, especially in neighbouring Iran, Zia sought, by elevating the role of the Sunni clergy, to enhance his own credibility among the princes who ruled the oil-rich states of the Gulf. His role as a guardian of Sunni Islam was made more credible by the Soviet invasion of Afghanistan in December 1979. With the Red Army on Pakistan's northern frontiers, wealthy Islamic regimes from Saudi Arabia to Libya opened their coffers, financing arms shipments to Islamabad. Washington, which had suspended both economic and military programs to Pakistan, also stepped in to help. In 1981 the United States provided Pakistan with $3.2 billion in military and economic assistance, and the CIA helped finance and organize the Afghani *mujahidun* against the Soviet invaders.* As Jalal points out, "After December 1979, the military not only ruled the roost in Pakistani society but acted as the defenders of a state deemed by the United States and the Western allies to be on the 'front line' between Soviet Russia and the 'free world.'"[36] With Russian troops poised to descend through the passes of Afghanistan to reach the Gulf and threaten the West's own vital supplies of oil, what did the West care about Zia's dictatorship, or Islamic fundamentalism, or the

---

* The term *mujahidun* (pl.) originally referred to soldiers of Islam, just as "crusaders" referred to soldiers of Christ. In modern times it is used to mean "guerrilla" or even "liberation fighter."

development of nuclear arms in Pakistan? Under these circumstances Zia was able to harvest a windfall of legitimacy from otherwise antagonistic ends of the ideological spectrum—all the way from the Shi'a fundamentalists in Iran and the Sunni reactionaries of Saudi Arabia on the one hand to Washington and its allies on the other.

Zia's regime also gained support from another direction. Noman argues that the remittances from Pakistani workers in the Gulf ($32 billion per annum at the peak) had improved the living conditions of tens of thousands of Punjabi households.[37] Punjabis, the most numerous of all of the Pakistani groups—they comprised 70 per cent of the 10 million Pakistanis who emigrated to the Gulf and other parts of the Middle East—lived in the not unrealistic hope that they might find jobs and therefore improved prospects as migrants. These hopes may have helped dilute opposition to the dictatorship.

Beneath the uneven surface of the Pakistani dictatorship, politics involving contending military and civilian factions continued to ferment. The prizes were compelling: Pakistan was not only the recipient of dazzling amounts of military aid but also the beneficiary of huge sums of humanitarian aid designated to sustain the three million Afghani refugees who had fled from the Soviet invasion. There was also a third source of profit for the military and civilian leaders: drugs. A large part of the guerrilla war against the Soviets and the regime they supported was financed by the export of substances, notably opium and heroin, derived from Afghani poppies.

In the struggle for control of this wealth, Zia ul-Haq was assassinated, together with key military advisors and the U.S. ambassador, on August 17, 1988, in a mid-air explosion aboard a Pakistani air force plane. Several possibilities came to the fore as suspects in the deaths: army rivals (two previous conspiracies to remove Zia had occurred within the army); a faction of the Pakistani intelligence service fighting for a larger share of the revenues from narcotics; one of the parties contending for the leadership of the Afghani *mujahidun*; and Shi'as who had been persecuted as a consequence of Zia's alignment with the Saudis. But after a two-year investigation the U.S. Federal Bureau of Investigation was not able to come up with a clear villain.

### The Rise of Benazir Bhutto, 1986-95

Zia's assassination opened the road for a return to party politics, and in November 1988 the army stood aside and allowed elections to take place. By that time another figure had arrived on the political scene, returning from exile: Benazir Bhutto (b. 1953), Zulfikar Ali Bhutto's intelligent, ambitious, and expensively educated daughter.

In the 1988 elections the PPP, the party of Zulfikar Ali Bhutto and Benazir Bhutto, won 92 out of 207 seats, while the Islamic Democratic Alliance (IDA), the party of Zia's partisans, won 54. In December 1988 Benazir Bhutto became prime minister, at age 35, the first woman to head a government in a contemporary Muslim state. Lacking an overall majority, her party was forced into alliance with the Muhajir Quami Movement (MQM), which commanded Karachi.

Her government lasted only until August 6, 1990. After the defection of her Karachi allies and bloody riots in that city, Pakistan's president, the ancient Ghulam Ishaq Khan, replaced her with an interim prime minister, Gulam Mustafa Jatoi, the commander of a ragtag coalition of PPP dissidents, army officers, regional chieftains, and religious leaders known as the Combined Opposition Parties (COP), formed in June 1987. Bhutto called this a "constitutional coup d'état," charging that military intelligence had been involved. In the elections to the national and provincial assemblies held in late October, the PPP was defeated conclusively. The Islamic Democratic Alliance (IDA) won 105 seats, and its leader, Muhammad Mian Nawaz Sharif, became prime minister. Sharif, a protégé of Zia, was strongly supported by the army.

By the early 1990s serious questions hung over the future of the Pakistani economy. Under Zia, through most of the 1980s the economic growth of Pakistan had been buoyant. Indeed, in 1980-86 the growth of the GDP had been in the 6 to 7 per cent range—higher than "rapidly industrializing" states such as Singapore, Malaysia, Thailand, and Indonesia.[38] Some of the sources of this growth were *conjunctural*—that is, dependent upon circumstances unrelated to the economic development of the country itself. Pakistan had, for instance, gained benefits from the remissions of Pakistani migrants working in the Middle East and from military and other aid invested in Pakistan as a result of the war in Afghanistan. But the Gulf War and peace in Afghanistan staunched the flow of both migrant workers and military aid. With the recession of the early 1990s, exports in 1991 declined by 30 per cent from the year before, with a current account deficit of $7 billion. In the early 1990s the state poured 88 per cent of its current expenditure into defence, administrative costs, and debt servicing, leaving little left for social or economic investment. The country's economy in the 1990s remained primarily based in agriculture—with 66 per cent of the population living in rural areas in 1993, and over 31 per cent of those living in poverty.[39] The main industrial activity was the processing and manufacturing of cotton goods. And at 3.1 per cent Pakistan had one of the highest population growth rates in the world. "There is a sense in which Pakistan's economy is living on borrowed time," Noman noted.[40]

Pakistan's disastrous economic situation was matched by crises on both the domestic and the external fronts. Despite an attempt by means of terror to control the province of Sind, the base of the PPP, by mid-1992 Sharif's grip on that area had become tenuous. And clashes with the Indian army in Kashmir had begun once again.

Sharif's declared solution to the country's economic problem was to liberalize and privatize the nation's infrastructure, while legitimating itself through the creation of an "Islamic welfare state." Parliament decreed that Islamic law would take precedence over civil legislation. The 1991-92 budget included an increase in military spending of 11.6 per cent and a decrease in social spending of 50 per cent. In May 1991 an "Aid to Pakistan" consortium made up of 14 countries and the World Bank approved over $2 billion in loans. The following year the World Bank engineered an additional loan of $54 million, and in April 1993 it added $100 million. Later in the year the IMF provided $1.6 billion and the World Bank a further $490 million.

On April 18, 1993, President Ghulam Ishaq Khan dismissed Sharif's government on the grounds of "maladministration, corruption and nepotism," and an interim government was established. On television the president accused the prime minister of having "unleashed a reign of terror" against his political opponents. Sharif promptly claimed that the president had acted unconstitutionally. In May the Supreme Court vindicated Sharif, and he returned to power, though not for long. With a PPP victory in elections held in October Benazir Bhutto again became prime minister. On November 14 Farooq Ahmad Leghari, one of Bhutto's most trusted lieutenants, was sworn in as president for five years. Leghari, a tribal chieftain and one of the largest landowners in the country, was, like Bhutto, an Oxford graduate. By early 1994 the PPP controlled not only the presidency and parliament but also three of Pakistan's four provinces. Only Baluchistan remained obdurately in opposition. But the PPP had little time to savour its victory.

By the middle of the decade political violence in Pakistan had reached levels unprecedented since the birth of the country. Much of the violence revolved around claims from the Muhajir Quami Movement that despite its control of Karachi, Pakistan's largest city, it had been deprived of political representation. The MQM asserted that the PPP had attempted to scapegoat the party as terrorists seeking to destabilize Pakistan. Benazir Bhutto certainly did nothing to conciliate its members when, in May 1995, she referred to them as "rats." By that time there was no doubt that the MQM had become the butt of Bhutto's repressive instincts. According to Amnesty International, in the first 15 months of the Bhutto administration not only had torture become widespread, but there had also been at least 35 extrajudicial executions.

Pakistan had also firmly entered the U.S. government's black book, marked down as a country considered to be financing "terrorist" activities, and according to Nicholas Macaulay the State Department saw the situation as unlikely to change in the near future: "To check torture, murder and mass arrests by the state institutions would rock the boat too violently." Although U.S. pressure led Bhutto to make efforts to curb the abuses of her own intelligence services, she herself was part of the problem, "part of the old social order and concerned to preserve her own power base." In the 1990s, Macaulay says, "The collapse of the Soviet Union has opened up the vast resources of gold, silver, uranium, oil and gas in the newly-independent republics of Central Asia to international exploitation in which Pakistan plans to play a leading role."[41]

# Bangladesh

Sheikh Mujib ur Rahman, elected as president of the Provisional Government of Bangladesh while still in a Pakistani jail, returned to his newly liberated country at the head of the Awami League, the party that had led the movement for Bangladeshi sovereignty. The Awami League consolidated its hold on the government of Bangladesh by winning the general elections of March 1973. The constitution of Bangladesh was not just modern, but enshrined secularism as one of its four cornerstones. The political program of the victorious Awami League was nationalist and dirigiste. Almost as soon as it took over state power it nationalized banks, businesses, and insurance companies, most of them owned by non-Bengalis, while handing out valuable import licences to its followers. It claimed to be socialist, too, but that rhetoric seems to have been due to the euphoria of independence.

In record time, and despite large aid remittances, especially from the United States—by the early 1970s quite obsessed with the politics of Southeast Asia—the government of Bangladesh became crisis-ridden. By mid-1974, for instance, the cost of living had risen as much as 500 per cent, and starvation was widespread. By 1975, according to one calculation, 61.8 per cent of the rural population could be classed as absolutely poor and 41 per cent as extremely poor.[42] The economy was out of control. Much of the blame, according to writer Talukdar Maniruzzaman, could be placed on the Bengali merchant class: "Unstable and impatient for material returns, they exploited nationalized industries, made easy money . . . smuggling jute, rice and relief goods to India, and simply frittered away their new wealth in non-productive expenditure, thus bringing about a sharp decline in the national economy and fuelling revolutionary political activity."[43]

That revolutionary political activity took the form of the Jatio Samaj-tantric Dal (National Socialist Party) and the Sarbohara (Proletarian) Party. Their protests were joined by those of the highly politicized Muslim leaders. The financing of these parties came by means of a hidden pipeline from Pakistan: after all, Bhutto had little love for the secessionist state, or for its leader. Mujib reacted to this challenge by turning to autocracy. He proclaimed a state of emergency (six months before Indira Gandhi was to do the same in India). He confessed that the problems of the nation were the crimes of his cronies: "corruption, profiteering, hoarding and smuggling." Parliamentary rule was a luxury, he argued, and democracy wasteful.

His move to take control of the situation was, as it turned out, a desperate and final act on his part. On August 15, 1975, Mujib and his family were assassinated by a gang of young officers working in cahoots with his own government, and the curtain came down on democracy in Bangladesh, where it would remain for the next 15 years. The government of Zulfikar Bhutto was the first to recognize the new regime.

By the time of Mujib's removal Bangladesh was moving more confidently into the world of Islamic reformism. The secularism enshrined in the constitution was abandoned. Islam was now to be the guiding principle of the state. The reasons for this shift were as much material as spiritual: Sunni reformist politics were being generously bankrolled by the Saudis while at the same time the oil fields of the Gulf offered attractive employment opportunities for Muslims everywhere. Economically, it made sense to be a Muslim reformer.

On November 3, 1975, a second coup was launched, only to be followed by five more coups in the same year. A situation loomed that threatened to resemble the coups and civil war in Nigeria just a decade earlier, but was forestalled by the rise of Zia ur Rahman (b. 1935), a general with a talent for reconciliation and political rehabilitation. Zia, however, was himself assassinated in a coup by dissident officers in May 1981. His successor, another general, Hussein Muhammad Ershad, purged the army of the faction that had assassinated Zia and rebuilt the officer corps on the basis of a collective enthusiasm for high salaries and perquisites, such as housing, superior medical treatment, and subsidized food—amenities often enjoyed by the officer corps in impoverished and indebted countries. This accumulation of privilege continued despite severe floods in May 1985, which left at least 10,000 Bangladeshis dead and 250,000 homeless.

By the time of October 1986 elections—marked by violence, fraud, and generalized intimidation and with only 2-3 per cent of the electorate voting—Ershad's legitimacy was in shreds. A year later the leading political parties united in demanding an end to the dictatorship. Undaunted, Ershad continued to hold power, and in November 1990, in the face of increasing demands for his resignation, he declared a state of emergency. He was deposed the next month amidst a mass upsurge of protest against his autocratic regime.

With Ershad's removal, democratic politics returned to Bangladesh. After a period of transitional government, elections in February 1991 saw Begum Khaleda Zia, the widow of Zia ur Rahman and leader of the centre-right Bangladesh Nationalist Party (BNP), installed as civilian prime minister—the third woman head of state in South Asia and the second in a predominantly Muslim country. By spring 1994 her opponents were charging her too with "official corruption and administrative inefficiency" and were attempting to provoke the same kind of mass intervention that had unseated Ershad in 1990.[44] The opposition parties boycotted parliament, and by the end of the year violent demonstrations against the governing party continued to rock the country. On December 23, 148 of 154 opposition MPs decisively resigned from parliament in an attempt to force the government to call new elections. Parliament was finally dissolved, and a general election called, on November 24, 1995.

# Summary

India had been the largest and richest land ever colonized by a Western power in the modern period. Partially transformed at all levels, and penetrated to its core by Western ideas, India remained for all that a land of peasants and precapitalist social structures. For India to be liberated from colonialism required a leader who could combine both "traditional," that is, non-modern, appeals with distinctly Western political practices. M.K. Gandhi was such a man. Leading the Indian National Congress from 1920 until his assassination in 1948, Gandhi mobilized and directed a mass of followers to form an irresistible force.

But the Hindu domination of the Congress Party threatened the large Muslim minority in India. Under Muhammad Ali Jinnah, the Muslims formed their own party, which, by playing off Congress against the British, gained recognition from India's colonial rulers. By the time of India's independence in August 1947, the country had been effectively trifurcated; two large parts of it, one to the northeast and the other to the northwest, became a separate country, Pakistan.

Gandhi's successor, Jawaharlal Nehru—articulate and urbane, and above all schooled in the political values of moderation and modernism in the England where he grew up—should have been regarded as an ideal leader from the viewpoint of the West. Instead he was seen as being dangerously unreliable. U.S. leaders preferred his antithesis, Ayub Khan, a general presiding over a backward dictatorship in Pakistan. Ayub Khan and his successors were more than willing recruits in the crusade to contain communism in Asia, for which they were rightly rewarded in arms and foreign aid favours.

Nehru's undoing was his idealism. Committed to the ideal of Third World non-alignment, his optimism and his spirit were crushed in October 1962, when Chinese armies burst through the passes in the Himalayas and forced him to abjectly accept U.S. military aid. His death in 1964 marked the end of the golden age of non-aligned "Third Worldism." He left behind a sprawling semi-democracy, partly industrialized, largely self-sufficient, but burdened with an apparently untransformable peasantry. While India's economy grew and industrialized on the basis of a succession of five-year plans, the mass of peasants, rapidly growing in number, remained for the most part stuck in a morass of poverty.

Nehru also left behind a lineage whose members were to provide the leaders for most of the remainder of the 20th century: his daughter Indira, prime minister from 1966 to 1977 and again from 1980 until her assassination in 1984; and Indira's son, Rajiv, prime minister from the day after his mother's death until his assassination in 1991. Rajiv Gandhi was the Anwar Sadat of India, the Shiva of destruction who tried to move India away from statism towards neoliberalism, initiating the process of selling off key segments of the public sector and opening India's doors to the supposedly therapeutic breezes of globalization. Even after Rajiv Gandhi's assassination, claims continued to be heard that if India were to find its way out of the political impasse it would have to undertake the destruction of the dirigiste state that his grandfather and mother had built up.

Meanwhile, after an unpromising start, Pakistan went nowhere. Ruled by a succession of generals from West Pakistan, Pakistan began showing morbid symptoms within the first decade of its existence. By 1970 East Pakistan was in open revolt and by 1971 it had, with more than a little help from India, transformed itself into independent Bangladesh. In what remained of Pakistan there was a short period of civilian rule under Zulfikar Ali Bhutto between 1972 and 1977. Until 1988, under the military dictatorship of Zia ul-Haq, Pakistan prospered, partly because of remittances from migrant workers in the Gulf and partly because of the profitable business of being on the West's front line against the Russians in Afghanistan. With the slump in the late 1980s, Benazir Bhutto came to power, but under her rule, by the mid-1990s, civil war had become a consistent Pakistani reality.

The beginnings of Bangladesh were hardly more propitious than those of Pakistan. Ruled by military dictators until 1991, it has remained overpopulated, underendowed, underindustrialized, and politically unstable.

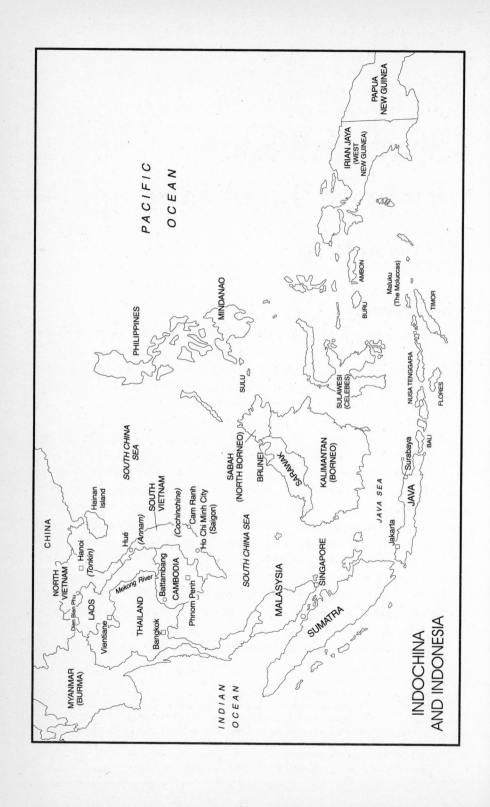

INDOCHINA
AND INDONESIA

# Chapter 7

# Southeast Asia: Vietnam, Cambodia, and Indonesia

## Background

By the beginning of the 20th century Southeast Asia, with the exception of Thailand, had been carpeted by colonialism from one end to another. The Dutch were amongst the earliest arrivals, creating a beachhead in the "Indies" at the beginning of the 17th century. The French came later, establishing themselves in a colonial federation known as "Indochina" in the second half of the 19th century. In so doing they extinguished the independent kingdom of Vietnam, which had existed longer than most European countries, and they absorbed the smaller kingdom of Cambodia. In the place of Vietnam, the French established three territories: one outright colony, Cochinchine, in the south, and two protectorates, Annam and Tonkin, to the north of Cochinchine. To these were joined two other protectorates, Cambodia, up the Mekong River from Cochinchine, and Laos, to the north of Cambodia. This federation comprising a single colony together with the four protectorates was known as the *cinq fleurs coloniales*, the "five colonial flowers."*

Significantly larger in extent and population than Indochina was the archipelago that became united first as the "Dutch East Indies" and later, in 1949, as "the United States of Indonesia." Indonesia encompassed 13,000 islands and spanned a distance equal to that between New York and

---

* Saigon, situated near the mouth of the Mekong River, was the commercial centre of the Indochinese federation as well as the capital of Cochinchine. Hué, the old capital of the kingdom of Vietnam, was the capital of Annam, and Hanoi the capital of Tonkin. Phnom Penh was the capital of Cambodia, and Vientiane the capital of Laos. The French governor-general of the Indochinese federation ruled from Hanoi, and the powerless Nguyen emperor, whose predecessors had ruled Vietnam, wiled away his hours in his palace in Hué when he was not spending his time and his allowance in the south of France.

Ireland. Its 1940 population was nearly 70 million, making it one of the most populous as well as most geographically extensive countries in the world.

The colonization of the Dutch East Indies began in 1619 and ended with the final conquests, of northern Sumatra and Bali, in 1909. As their control of the Indies grew, the Dutch became acutely conscious that their domination of this vast archipelago provided their own dwarf and resourceless country with a claim to major world importance. But even better was the wealth provided. The Indies were richer in agricultural produce and in minerals than any colony in the world, with the exception of India, and the richness sustained a considerable settler population of Europeans and Eurasians. The existence of these settlers suffocated any hopes the Indonesians themselves might have had of controlling the land.

Given the exploitable wealth of the colony, the status it provided for the Netherlands, and the employment it offered to the Dutch, it is no wonder that at the end of World War II, when the Dutch economy was a flooded ruin, the prospect of losing Indonesia was too daunting to be faced. A pamphlet published several decades earlier succinctly expressed Dutch fears: *Indies Gone, Prosperity Done*. But for many Indonesians—already bitter over Dutch exploitation and exclusion—the fatalistic capitulation of the Dutch army to the Japanese in 1940, followed by the rounding up of European colonists, meant that a return to colonial rule after the Japanese surrender was inconceivable.

# Vietnam Divided

In July 1941, a year after France itself had fallen to the Germans, the French colonial rulers of Indochina stoically signed a treaty with the Japanese that effectively placed the French colonial federation within the Japanese Co-Prosperity Sphere, the Japanese empire in Asia. According to this treaty, the Vietnamese and their neighbours would be ruled over by collaborationist colonial officials, contributing labour and resources to Japan's war effort. This arrangement lasted until March 1945, when in a sudden *coup de force* the Japanese took over Vietnam themselves, either flinging the French into prisons or driving them into the jungles. The Japanese then declared the whole of Indochina—Vietnam, Cambodia, and Laos—independent and placed tame local notables in charge. When Japanese power crumbled, a communist-dominated nationalist party, known as the Viet Nam Doc Lap Dong Minh, or "Viet Minh," rose to take over the newly created space.

In 1930 Vietnamese communists under the leadership of Nguyen Ai

Quoc, better known as "Ho Chi Minh," had been instrumental in forming the Indochinese Communist Party (ICP). The party launched its first wartime uprising in Cochinchine in November 1940, after Indochina had passed under the control of the French Vichy regime. It was here, for the first time, that the famous Vietnamese communist standard, the red flag with the yellow star, was flown. Within three months, the first guerrilla unit of the Viet Minh was formed in the northern protectorate of Tonkin. Viet Minh guerrillas continued to clash with the French until a Japanese coup in March 1945. With the French removed, but Japanese power in Asia clearly on the verge of extinction, the Viet Minh launched a co-ordinated effort to liberate Vietnam. Between the end of March and August one Vietnamese province after another fell to the guerrillas in a process of liberation that became known as "the August Revolution." Finally, in August 1945 the Viet Minh occupied Hanoi and there, on September 2, Ho Chi Minh read out the Vietnamese Declaration of Independence.

Other events cast a long and decisive shadow on Vietnamese independence. By September 1945 France had been liberated and Germany defeated. On August 15, Japan had surrendered. France's future, thought the leaders of the newly created Fourth Republic, depended on the redemption of its empire. This neo-empire was to be reconstituted not in its old and by then discredited form, but instead as a newly invented "French Union." Partnership and development were to replace domination and exploitation, it was solemnly affirmed. In September 1945, in the wake of an army of Indian troops under British command, the French began their return to Vietnam, and by early 1946 30,000 French troops occupied the country. The Viet Minh, poorly armed, outnumbered, and inexperienced in dealing with well-trained and experienced regular armies, was overwhelmed. In March its leaders were forced to negotiate a truce and accept the existence of the French-designed and dominated "Indochinese Federation" as the main Asian component of the newly constructed French Union. It appeared to the French that Vietnam was to be united with its siblings Cambodia and Laos, again to be nurtured at the breast of a caring France.

But both the French Union and the Indochinese Federation were doomed from the outset. In November 1946 the truce that the Viet Minh had been forced to accept was broken, and the First Vietnam War began. Over the next seven and a half years, the colonial armies of France, a motley collection of Frenchmen, Legionnaires, Moroccans, Algerians, and Africans, were never able to sustain the initiative, even with increasing quantities of U.S. arms—by the end of 1952 the U.S. government was paying 60 per cent of French war expenses in Vietnam; by 1954 this had increased to 80 per cent. The end for France came on May 7, 1954, after what was possibly the most decisive single battle in the whole of postwar history. On that day a heavily fortified French garrison in the Vietnamese-Laotian border town of Dien Bien Phu surrendered after being overwhelmed by the Viet Minh armies. For colonial peoples everywhere, "Dien Bien Phu" was as "Stalingrad" had been to the victims of the Third Reich: a source of inspiration and an icon for the struggles for independence. For the West, according to *The Times* of London (May 17, 1954), it represented "the most dangerous crisis since the end of the war."

During the time of the battle for Dien Bien Phu, a major international conference had been sitting in Geneva. Its main delegates were from the United States, France, Britain, the Soviet Union, and China, and its main task was to discuss Asia in the aftermath of the war in Korea. None of the leaders of these countries wanted further confrontation. The Soviets and the Chinese wanted co-existence with the West, and the Western powers, led by the Americans, wanted assurances that the spread of communism in Asia would be halted. With the sudden fall of Dien Bien Phu, discussions turned to the question of the French collapse in Indochina.

By July a solution had been worked out to satisfy all of the major powers. Vietnam was to be temporarily divided along the 17th parallel. Ostensibly this arrangement was intended to last only until national elections could be held. Until then the leaders of the victorious Viet Minh would rule the northern half of the country from Hanoi, and a provisional but non-communist government, sustained by U.S. military and economic assistance, would rule the south from Saigon. The north was to be known as the "Democratic Republic of Vietnam" (DRV) and the south as "the Republic of Vietnam" (RVN). Meanwhile the French packed their bags. They were supposed to oversee the administration of the country until internationally supervised elections could be held, but bitter at not only having lost their Asian empire but also having to hand it over to the Americans, they faded from the scene before this could take place. The dream of an Indochinese federation within the French union had turned to dust.

In reality the United States was now in charge; as the French had withdrawn from Vietnam, the Americans had taken their place. But, recognizing that elections involving the whole of Vietnam would result in a communist victory, the Americans worked to prevent them. Washington claimed, and its allies echoed the claim, that it was the communists who were obstructing the democratic process and preventing national elections. Most people believed them; communists, after all, had shown no commitment to electoral democracy anywhere else in the world.

Nevertheless, the Americans were forced to accept the existence of the DRV in the north as a short-term necessity; in the longer term Washington planned to roll back the Northern communists using the Republic of Vietnam as a base.

Following elections on October 23, 1955, the pro-American, anti-French, anti-communist, and Catholic Ngo Dinh Diem became president of the RVN. Around him was a clan of kinsmen and in-laws. The process of lionizing Diem began in the Western media and continued for the next several years. Diem, claimed *The Saturday Evening Post* in 1956, had saved his people from "the red tide of Communism in Asia." On May 11, 1961, on a visit to Saigon, where he announced Washington's support for the Diem regime, the U.S. vice-president, Lyndon B. Johnson, nominated the South Vietnamese president as "the [Winston] Churchill of the decade"—a great leader "in the vanguard of those leaders who stood for freedom." Privately, Johnson was more sceptical. "Shit, man, he's the only boy we got out there," he admitted.[1] Later, on April 9, 1961, with the help of the CIA, Diem was re-elected as president with 70 per cent of the vote. One CIA functionary in Saigon, William Colby, who would later head the agency during the overthrow of the Allende government in Chile, assured Washington that Diem's election "enhanced stability and encouraged hope for the future." Few were prepared to recognize, even in the early 1960s, that the Diem clan was "an indissoluble mixture of nightmare and farce," as Frances Fitzgerald was to comment in a remarkable book a decade later.[2]

Diem's main challenge, in his own eyes at least, was to prevent any change that he himself did not order. He turned the clock back on the limited land reform that had taken place before he had come to power, allowing the landlord class to repossess land and raise rents. But his greatest efforts went into extirpating all those who opposed him: communists, criminal gangs, religious sects, and even, ultimately, Buddhists. For a time, assisted in particular by the ubiquitous CIA, whose activities were financed by the export of opium, he seemed successful. By the late 1950s, using massive repression, he had ground the communists down to the point of annihilation. Out of 8,000 to 10,000 communists in South Vietnam in 1954, by the end of the decade only 2,000 to 2,500 had survived.

While the clock was being turned back in the RVN, a revolution was taking place in the northern DRV. From as early as August 1945 the relationship between peasants and landlords had been permanently reversed. The landlords had been put under increasing pressure, first to reduce rents and later, from mid-1949, to accept the redistribution of their lands among the landless. From early 1953 the tempo of this transformation accelerated, with the communists now seeking to destroy the landlord class entirely. Expressed in the language of the revolution, what they envisioned was "to liquidate the system of feudal land expropriation, establish the system of land ownership by working peasants, release land to the tillers and liberate the productive forces of the countryside."[3] The communists organized "struggle meetings," reminiscent of those in China in the late 1940s, and the landlords were denounced, divested of their property, and arrested. Until the end of 1955, wave after wave of reforms broke over the landlords and rich peasants, each wave liberating more villages, distributing more land, and stripping their proprietors of everything they possessed—livestock, tools, houses, clothes, furniture, even pots and pans. The campaign was referred to as a "Dien Bien Phu against feudalism in the North." The class of big landowners and rich peasants was destroyed. The numbers of victims of this repression are unknown. Estimates, inflated by the hot air of Cold War rhetoric, range from around 2,500 to 100,000, but Ken Post's 4,900 seems most credible.[4] In fact, the land reform program became so unpopular in some areas that in November 1955, in Nghe An in northern Annam, a peasant uprising occurred *against* Hanoi and had to be repressed by the People's Liberation Army. Despite this resistance, by the mid-1960s the DRV agrarian economy had been organized around nearly 30,000 agricultural co-operatives and 60 state farms. This policy affected nearly 90 per cent of peasant families.[5]

Besides land reform, the DRV government undertook a program of limited industrialization encompassed within the three-year plan of 1958-60.* Although the program aimed at laying the foundations for a new socialist system and raising the standard of living, unlike the great plans of the Soviet Union and China the DRV plan did not sacrifice agriculture in the name of heavy industry. It was nevertheless successful in increasing both heavy and light industrialization and expanding the size of the working class by nearly 50 per cent. A subsequent five-year plan (1960-65) confirmed the Soviet Union rather than China as the model for the socialist development of Vietnam. Nonetheless, on the occasion of the DRV's National Day in September 1962, Beijing declared that China and Vietnam were "as close to each other as the lips to the teeth."[6]

In the south, despite Diem's repression, in 1960 the communists

---

* Power in the DRV was monopolized by the Political Bureau (Politburo), which had 11 full, and 2 alternate, members. The best known of the full members in 1960 were Ho Chi Minh, Le Duan (who succeeded him as president in 1969), Pham Van Dong (prime minister), Vo Nguyen Giap (defence minister), and Le Duc Tho (who later negotiated with the Americans in Paris). Of the alternate members, General Van Tien Dung, the army chief of staff, was renown for organizing the final assault on Saigon in April 1975.

sprang back, forming the National Liberation Front (NLF), a guerrilla force composed mainly of southerners but supported by Hanoi and armed and supplied by China and the USSR. Non-communists also supported the NLF, driven into an alliance with the communists by Diem's relentless repression of practically all those who opposed him. By the early 1960s the situation in South Vietnam had shifted; now the Army of the Republic of Vietnam (ARVN) was in trouble. For the U.S. advisors the problems were confirmed at the landmark battle of Ap Bac in January 1963, when a small force of lightly armed NLF soldiers defeated a significantly larger contingent of ARVN troops complete with armoured personnel carriers, helicopters, and U.S. advisors.

In the deepening crisis, which had by this time infected even neighbouring Laos, the Americans made two decisions. The first was to support the removal of Diem, whose unpopularity could no longer be concealed; the president of the Republic of Vietnam and his brother were accordingly assassinated on November 1, 1963. Just what role the various agencies within the United States may have played in this affair has been debated, yet there is no doubt that ultimately Washington was responsible for his murder. Diem was replaced by the generals who had overseen his execution.

The second decision had even more dire consequences. Forgetting the lessons of Korea—which taught the hopelessness of using U.S. troops to fight land wars in the Third World—and prompted by the unshakeable optimism and moral righteousness of "can do" development experts like W.W. Rostow and Robert McNamara, the Americans increased their involvement in the civil war. Soon the word "quagmire" was to become a commonplace to describe what has since become known as the "Second Vietnam War." Between 1961 and the end of 1967, the number of U.S. soldiers in Vietnam increased from 3,000 to around half a million; beside them were 1.3 million South Vietnamese soldiers together with contingents from Thailand, Taiwan, Korea, Australia, New Zealand, and the Philippines. French President Charles de Gaulle had warned U.S. President John F. Kennedy about war in Indochina: "You will sink step by step into a bottomless military and political quagmire, however much you spend in money."

The turning point in the Second Vietnam War came with the NLF offensive at the time of the lunar New Year, known as Tet, which began on January 31, 1968. Without any doubt, the Tet offensive was a major disaster for the NLF. After scoring some notable early victories, its forces were subjected to staggering casualties. After Tet the southern NLF was increasingly replaced by units from the DRV. But, while the Tet offensive failed to achieve its objectives—of delivering a blow that would stagger or even topple the Saigon government—it did make a profound impression on U.S. and world public opinion. After the obviously well-planned attacks on some 30 South Vietnam cities, there could be no more doubt about the strength of the communist forces. Tet was an even greater disaster for the credibility of President Lyndon B. Johnson and his team of experts. Johnson felt it necessary to resign, and in the next presidential election his Democratic Party was defeated by the Republicans and Richard Nixon, who promised to remove the U.S. troops.

By 1970 troop withdrawals had begun. "Vietnamization" was the code word for the new strategy of letting the Vietnamese fight one another while the U.S. forces bombed the cities in the DRV. After March 23, 1973, the only Americans remaining in the south were advisors. And then, in late April 1975, came the collapse and rout of the Army of the Republic of Vietnam and the final flight of the Americans. By May 3, the communist regime, ruling from Hanoi, was in control of both halves of the country. The red flag with the yellow star now flew over the presidential palace in Saigon.

Vietnam was now united and independent, but the cost to the Vietnamese of the wars against the Western powers, first the French and then the Americans, was incalculably high. Vietnamese forests and fields remained poisoned by the herbicides used by the U.S. forces against their invisible enemies. A whole generation of Vietnamese had been devastated by the killing done by the Americans and their allies, and another remained crippled and deformed by the effects of poisonous chemicals. The U.S. Senate Subcommittee on Refugees estimated the *civilian* casualties resulting from the U.S. intervention at 400,000 dead and 900,000 wounded, with 6.4 million refugees.

Marilyn Young's figures have a different focus, but point in much the same direction. She calculates that in South Vietnam some 9,000 out of 15,000 hamlets were destroyed, along with 25 million acres of farmland and 12 million acres of forest; and 1.5 million farm animals were killed. The war had left "an estimated 200,000 prostitutes, 879,000 orphans, 181,000 disabled people, and 1 million widows; all six of the industrial cities in the North had been badly damaged, as were provincial and district towns, and 4,000 out of 5,800 agricultural communes." Young points to another lasting legacy: "North and south the land was cratered and planted with tons of unexploded ordinance, so that long after the war farmers and their families suffered serious injuries as they attempted to bring the fields back into cultivation. Nineteen million gallons of herbicide had been sprayed on the South during the war, and while the long-term effects were unknown in 1975 (and are not clear now), severe birth defects and multiple miscarriages were apparent early on."[7]

Calculating the U.S. losses requires a different arithmetic. No hamlets in Nebraska or villages in the Mississippi delta were among the settlements pulped by bombers or artillery. Of the 1.6 million Americans in combat, a disproportionate number were poor and black or Latino. The roll of those killed in action was not great, at least not compared to Vietnamese losses: 57,939 names are engraved on the Vietnam Veterans' Memorial in Washington. Most of those killed were between 17 and 21 years of age.

While the horsemen of the apocalypse stayed on the Asian side of the Pacific, for the duration of the longest war in U.S. history the United States did pay heavily in another way. In Joyce Kolko's summary:

> The worst world recession since the 1930s occurred in 1974-75. It was the culmination of a series of factors. Extremely important was the organic interplay of the effect of American aggression in Vietnam on the U.S. and the world economy. Had the war ended in 1968, the impact on the economy might have been similar to that of the Korean War. Lasting as long as it did, it had an organic effect on the whole world capitalist system. Many economists recognize that the Vietnam War helped undermine the dollar and the American economy—not just through increased expenditures overseas but also through the intense inflationary impact on the internal economy, increasing imports, overpriced exports, and especially the massive growth in the money supply to pay for the deficit.[8]

"And what did America have to show for all the treasure spent, all the lives lost, all the bodies crippled for life?" asks Stephen Ambrose. "Nothing, unless it was the lesson that Vietnam taught, whatever it may be. Few undertook to find out."[9]

# Vietnam United

Western pundits had warned of a bloodbath when Saigon fell. They conjured up images of the executions that had taken place in Hué at the hands of the NLF during the Tet offensive. But the bloodbath didn't take place. Instead some 100,000 people, most of them army officers and officials in the Saigon government, were taken away to "re-education camps," some for more than a decade. Many of them perished, partly due to the punitive austerity of the camps, some were executed, and 94,000 returned. By February 1988 only 159 former Saigon officials remained in detention.

From the outset unified Vietnam faced overwhelming problems.

From mid-1954 to April 1975 the predominantly agrarian economy of the Republic of Vietnam had been distorted, with the half-country reduced to dependence on a U.S. life-support system. One of the greatest effects of the war had been an emigration from the countryside to the towns, in part due to the recruitment policies of the Republic of Vietnam armed forces, which absorbed half a million men between 1964 and 1970. The loss of the labour power of so many peasants drove up rural wages and the price of domestically produced rice, but the price increase could not lead to a rise in output because of the labour shortage. As a result, although Vietnam had been a rice basket under the French and a rice exporter as late as 1964, by 1967 the south had become a net rice importer. To replace this lost production, the United States had imported rice into South Vietnam at subsidized prices, undercutting local prices. Those peasants still in the rural sector turned increasingly to market gardening for the U.S. forces.

After 1966, then, the Republic of Vietnam had a surplus of unfarmed land and a shortage of labour, and it was dependent on food imports. With landlords seeing agriculture as decreasingly profitable, capital made its way into the towns, where it found attractive investment opportunities in speculation and development. Where agricultural reform had taken place in the north, therefore, deformation was the experience in the south.

The U.S. evacuation suddenly cut off support for this distorted economy. The promise of reconstruction aid to Vietnam, made by President Nixon in a secret protocol that was part of the 1973 Paris peace agreement, was never fulfilled. The embargo continued under Nixon's successor, President Gerald Ford. After the inauguration of President Jimmy Carter at the beginning of 1977, permits were granted for $5 million in humanitarian aid to be sent to Vietnam, and Washington dropped its veto of Vietnam's admission to the UN. Delegations from the World Bank and the IMF arrived in Hanoi. On the question of mutual recognition, however, there was no agreement between the former enemies: the Vietnamese demanded that the Americans first accept the principle of providing reconstruction aid, and the Americans insisted on no preconditions to recognition.

The Vietnamese insistence on aid as a precondition in the Paris Peace talks led to a hardening of American attitudes. In May 1977, a motion was passed in Congress forbidding the State Department to negotiate "reparations, aid, or any other form of payment to Vietnam." In retaliation the Vietnamese released the text of Nixon's secret undertaking in which he agreed to provide aid without preconditions. In June 1977 an amendment to the foreign aid bill explicitly renounced Nixon's promise of aid, and all funding to any Indochinese state was prohibited. This meant that Vietnam was cut off from any international lending agencies that included a U.S. contribution. By December 1977 the Vietnamese were desperate and willing to accept a token amount of reparations, but the Americans were uncompromising. Further talks scheduled in Paris for early 1978 were never held, nor were diplomatic relations established. As far as the West was concerned, Vietnam may have won the war but it would be starved in the peace.

The view from Moscow and Beijing was, not surprisingly, different. In summer 1975, a little more than a year before the death of Mao Zedong, when the general secretary of the Vietnamese Communist Party, Le Duan, made a tour of Moscow and Beijing capitals, he was received with effusions of fraternal sympathy. A year later, when Van Tien Dung, organizer of the final assault on Saigon, visited Moscow, he was accorded the singular honour of being accommodated in what had once been Stalin's villa. The movement of Vietnam into the Soviet orbit was now under way. In July 1976 the reunified Vietnam changed its name from "the Democratic Republic of Vietnam" to "the Socialist Republic of Vietnam," and in December the Vietnamese communists changed the name of their party from the "Vietnam Workers' Party" (which it had been named in February 1951) to the "Communist Party of Vietnam." On June 28, 1978, the Socialist Republic of Vietnam joined COMECON, the Moscow-dominated economic bloc. By that time 60 per cent of Vietnamese trade was with the Soviet Union, and another 20 per cent with the countries of COMECON. Adhesion to COMECON led to a flow of Soviet aid that was essential to the development of hydroelectric projects and offshore oil exploration as well as to a counterflow of Vietnamese workers into Eastern Europe.

Just as there had been U.S. advisors in the Republic of Vietnam, there had been Soviet combatants on the side of Hanoi during the course of the Second Vietnam War. After the fall of Saigon, Soviet forces remained in Vietnam, with their numbers supplemented by even more Soviets who arrived to organize the air and naval base at Cam Ranh, which became the largest Soviet military base outside the countries of the Warsaw Pact. Jean-Claude Pomonti and Hugues Tertrais speculate that Soviet military aid was indispensable when Vietnam came to invade Cambodia in December 1978.[10]

Liberated Vietnam also quickly found itself facing disagreements with both China and Cambodia. The Chinese expected the Vietnamese to acknowledge the assistance Beijing had rendered over the decades by accepting a special and subordinate relationship that acknowledged China's dominant interest in Southeast Asia. They also wanted Hanoi to sever its relations with Moscow. Hanoi resisted this pressure. The

Vietnamese could hardly forget that their patriotism had been born a thousand years earlier in their resistance to China, and that Guomindang armies had occupied and pillaged their country as recently as 1946. The tensions were heightened by disagreements over the Spratly and Paracel islands in the South China Sea, places that both Vietnam and China claimed as their own. Such claims were taken all the more seriously because the Americans had discovered oil in the vicinity of these islands.

Cambodia's reluctance to accept Vietnamese patronage mirrored Vietnam's hesitations with regard to China. Just as the Vietnamese could never forget the Chinese invasions of Vietnam, the Khmers—the indigenous people of Cambodia—could not forget the Vietnamese encroachments on their territory from the 17th to the 19th centuries. Some members of the Khmer Rouge, as the party of the Cambodian communists was known, talked of *irredentism*, that is, of recovering lost territories. The Vietnamese leadership was hurt by such reminders and countered by stressing their role in the revolution in Cambodia. They were also alarmed by Chinese aid to Pol Pot after he had seized Phnom Penh. And not without reason: the Pol Pot faction had scores to settle with the pro-Hanoi faction of the Khmer Rouge.

The first victims of these Vietnamese-Chinese and Vietnamese-Cambodian tensions were the million and a half Vietnamese of Chinese extraction (called *Hoa*) who lived in Vietnam. The greatest concentration of these were in Cholon, Saigon's Chinese twin city. In 1951 about half a million *Hoa* lived in Saigon-Cholon. Few had become Vietnamese citizens, an option that had been offered to them. Under Diem, pressure had been applied to persuade the *Hoa* to become citizens, and from the 1970s the Hanoi regime was also concerned about their loyalty. After the unification of Vietnam this distrust was amplified. In January 1976, when the Vietnamese government ordered the *Hoa* to register their citizenship, most of them protested that they were Chinese. Afterwards they came under increasing pressure, with their rations cut and their newspapers suppressed. In January 1978 Beijing took up their cause, stressing that the *Hoa* were part of the Chinese nation. The *Hoa* who lived near the border areas with China were subject to increasing scrutiny and pressure, and by mid-1978 nearly 150,000 of them had crossed into China. This migration together with the nationalization of Chinese businesses encouraged other Chinese to seek exit visas. By May 1978 Beijing had charged its fellow communists in Vietnam with deliberately persecuting the Chinese in Vietnam. The claims were self-fulfilling: Hanoi then demanded not only that all Chinese leave the country, but also that they buy exit visas. Some 250,000 Chinese paid, setting off from Vietnam's shores in all manner of boats, with as many as 40,000 of them—"boat people," as they came to be called—dying at sea. The Chinese retaliated again in the way the Soviets had retaliated at the time of the Sino-Soviet split two decades earlier: they cancelled all aid and withdrew their technical and military advisers.

Simultaneously the crisis with Vietnam's other neighbour, Cambodia, deepened. The Pol Pot government in power in Phnom Penh launched a pogrom against all Vietnamese and Chinese settled in Cambodia as well as Cambodians suspected of being in sympathy with Hanoi. Thousands of refugees from Pol Pot—Vietnamese and Chinese, as well as Cambodian—fled to Vietnam.* Following this exodus the Phnom Penh regime launched a series of border provocations against the Vietnamese at the beginning of January 1977. Some accounts suggest that the Vietnamese lost as many as 30,000 troops in the ensuing two years of frontier wars.

The reaction of the Vietnamese was deliberate and effective. On December 25, 1978, during the dry season in Southeast Asia, Hanoi's armies crossed the border into Cambodia. Phnom Penh fell on January 7, 1979, and the occupation of the rest of the country followed in the next months. On the ruins of Democratic Kampuchea, the Hanoi-backed government of the People's Republic of Kampuchea (PRK) was installed. Something else lay in ruins: the communist solidarity of Cambodians and Vietnamese that had been envisaged by the founders of the Indochinese Communist Party. "The Red Brotherhood at War" was *The New York Times* epitaph for this split.

The Sino-Vietnamese conflict was a function of improved Sino-American relations, which was the work of President Jimmy Carter's hawkish National Security advisor, Zbigniew Brzezinski, who had as his object the welding of a close relationship with Beijing against Moscow. This relationship had the considerable attraction of being useable as a cudgel to punish Hanoi, which had, after all, caused Washington to lose a great deal of face. Brzezinski visited China in May 1978, and on December 15, 1978, the U.S. government announced the normalization of relations with China. A month later, in January 1979, Deng Xiaoping arrived in Washington to confirm the beginning of a new era in Sino-American relations. In February 1979, after Deng Xiaoping had denounced the Vietnamese as "hooligans" and "dogs," China invaded Vietnam.

The Chinese invasion was short and costly. It lasted only 16 days, during which time the Chinese occupied one major town for four days. The Chinese blew up this town, Lang Son, before evacuating in the face of

---

* Although critical of the Vietnamese handling of the *Hoa*, Beijing was silent regarding the fate of the thousands of Chinese murdered by the Pol Pot regime in Cambodia.

news that a Vietnamese regular division from Cambodia was on its way north. The Chinese suffered an estimated 30,000 casualties, all at the hands of the Vietnamese border guards. Deng, who had personally ordered the attack, lost face.

China also put pressure on Vietnam by supporting Pol Pot and his *banditti*. Indeed, Chinese assistance allowed the defeated remains of Pol Pot's force to continue fighting. Beijing's strategy was to bleed Vietnam in the killing fields of western Cambodia. Washington, too, supported Pol Pot; any enemy of Hanoi, thought Brzezinski, now at the peak of his influence, was a friend of America. The U.S. government would ensure that Vietnam remained an international outlaw while voting to provide the genocidal Pol Pot government with a seat at the UN. Under pressure, Japan and most Western European countries cut off their aid to Hanoi. The IMF, the World Bank, and the Asian Development Bank refused reconstruction loans. For a decade Vietnam remained isolated. In the same decade the evidence of Pol Pot's genocide surfaced.

But the Vietnamese did not blame all of their woes on the Americans and the Chinese. Since the death of Ho Chi Minh in 1969, the general secretary of the Communist Party had been Le Duan. After the fall of Saigon, Le Duan and those around him, in an understandably euphoric mood, planned to extend socialism to the southern half of their country. From 1978 they extended the collectivization of agriculture, accomplished in the north, to the south. They abolished capitalism, with accompanying upheavals. Following the same Soviet models already adopted in the north, they nationalized industry and centralized its management. They established production targets and prioritized heavy industry, marginalizing the production of consumer goods.

While the validity of comparing the same countries in wartime and peacetime is dubious, a case can be made for the claim that postwar Vietnamese socialism was beneficial to the majority of the population. Rice was now available at a low, subsidized price. Education and medical care were free. Yet the price for these basic needs was high: the Vietnamese economy was subsidized by the Soviet Union (until 1991) to the tune of $2 billion a year. This subsidization took several forms, one of which was the shipment, halfway around the world, of Soviet and East European steel for use in Vietnamese factories. Vietnamese farmers, particularly in the south, lost the incentive to produce because they were only able to sell 20 per cent of their production on the market. As a result Vietnam was reduced to importing rice from its neighbours.

When Le Duan died in July 1986, the Vietnamese economy was in a sad state, although already some change was in the air. Japanese investment, for instance, had begun to seep into the country, attracted by Vietnam's 64 million well-educated and industrious people and recognizable economic potential. Its effects, however, were slight. Neil Sheehan, who had reported from South Vietnam for *The New York Times* (winning a Pulitzer Prize for his efforts), revisited it in 1989. He was obviously both moved and depressed by what he saw: "Inflation was out of control at 600 to 700 per cent a year. The currency was becoming more worthless by the month, the official exchange rate 1,500 dong to the dollar, the black market rate 5,000. The stores were bare of consumer items. Vietnamese waited in long lines at the state rice shops for their monthly rations because the storage and transportation systems were breaking down too; rice was often simply not available."[11] By this time even the Vietnamese were admitting that their woes were not a consequence of the U.S. blockade.

Revitalization of the leadership of the Vietnamese Communist Party had actually begun several years before Le Duan's death. Within six months of his demise three other members of the Politburo "old guard" had resigned. The ostensible leader of the reformers was General Secretary Nguyen Van Linh, a southerner and a veteran of both the French and the U.S. wars. Rising to influence even before the Sixth Party Congress in December 1986, Linh initiated a series of economic reforms that anticipated those of Mikhail Gorbachev in the Soviet Union; Western journalists called him "Vietnam's Gorbachev." The reforms of 1987-88 condemned "bureaucratic centralism and subsidization" and began to renegotiate the relationship with the Soviet Union. They called for the abandonment of centralized planning and state subsidies and the adoption of free enterprise and foreign investment.

But, as in China in the 1980s, liberalization was at first carried out within limits; the "leading role" of the state was not abandoned. By 1989 Vietnam was leaving at least one crisis behind. Sheehan continued approvingly: "Rationing and subsidized prices for rice and all other commodities were abolished. People were told that they would have to buy what they needed in the open market. Capitalism was legalized and private enterprise encouraged. The currency was freed to find its true value; the artificial exchange rate was ended, and the dong was permitted to float at approximately the black market rate."

Hoping to cut down on inflation by shrinking the money supply, the government stopped printing money. It opened the borders to trade and passed what Sheehan called a "liberal foreign investment law" aimed at attracting capital from the West as well as from the Asian capitalist nations. It decollectivized agriculture, returning land to farmers under 15-year contracts "granted in exchange for amounts of rice fixed at the outset, the equivalent of a land tax in a Western country." The farmers could sell the rest of the harvest themselves.

"By the summer of 1989," Sheehan reported, "prices had stabilized, stores were filled with a spectrum of goods, inflation had fallen from 1988's 600 to 700 per cent to a projected 25 per cent for the year . . . rice production was up considerably, and the country was able to export rice in quantity for the first time since the 1930s."[12]

What Sheehan described represents an abandonment of the socialist model of development in favour of what some commentators call "the Taiwanese model" or "the Dragon model," though it is sometimes masked by the oxymoronic term "market socialism." The Taiwanese model was adopted not only by Taiwan but also by the other three "dragons" (or "Asian tigers," as they are also called)—South Korea, Hong Kong, and Singapore—as well as Thailand and even China. It was "export-led" and stressed profit on the basis of an expansion of the private sector and cheap labour recruited, in part, from those dismissed from state firms. The Chinese slogan "To get rich is glorious" was one of its mottos. The World Bank, more discreet, referred to "awakening the market."

The Taiwanese model was supported by the World Bank and the United Nations Development Programme (UNDP), and it carried considerable social costs. Even the World Bank had admitted that "one positive aspect of . . . socialist economies has been their preoccupation with the equitable delivery of essential social services—health, education and family planning. Evidence from Viet Nam . . . shows a remarkable pattern of social indicators, despite its low level of development."[13] Social services were now allowed to collapse.

There were further costs. With the market awakened, where once people had to line up, as Sheehan complained, now many starved. As Gerard Greenfield points out, "Record rice exports by state trading companies have coincided with 2.5 million people going hungry each year, and over 6 million people suffer from an inadequate calorie intake."[14] Gabriel Kolko records yet another facet of the capitalist development of Vietnam: "By the 1990s, the problem of corruption and fraud in the hands of Party members alone, not to mention the burgeoning criminality of yet others, had reached such epidemic proportions that it had eroded, to a degree only time would tell, the immense credibility that the Communists had won before 1975. Every senior Party leader publicly acknowledged this dilemma, but other than wholly insufficient expulsions, they could suggest no real alternatives."[15]

As the preoccupations of the Cold War receded, the possibility of an isolated Vietnam became even more remote. Gorbachev visited Deng Xiaoping in Beijing on May 15, 1989 (on the eve of the massacre in

Tiananmen Square). While no one was allowed to forget the past, better relations in the future seemed to be on the cards. The *Beijing Review* stressed, "China and the Soviet Union have the same social system." The *Washington Post* commented ruefully: "The Sino-Soviet split, while it lasted, was a great break for the West."[16]

In November 1991 Sino-Vietnamese relations were normalized, and just over a year later diplomatic relations between Vietnam and South Korea were established. In February 1993 François Mitterand visited Vietnam, and that summer the U.S. government authorized the international lending organizations to operate in Vietnam. The IMF, the World Bank, and the Asian Development Bank announced in December 1993 that they would make loans to Vietnam.

By 1993 Vietnamese oilfields were producing 110,000 barrels per day; by the end of the decade, it was anticipated, offshore oil would produce net export earnings of $1.5-$2 billion a year. In the National Assembly in December 1993 it was announced that the economy was expected to grow by more than 8 per cent a year. Yet in the previous year nearly half of Hanoi's residents believed that their lives had either not improved or worsened.[17] In February 1994 President Bill Clinton announced the lifting of the blockade of the country that was now being referred to as "the last great untapped business opportunity in Asia."

The socialist economic model had lasted in a united Vietnam for just under 20 years. The French journalist Jean-Claude Guillebaid provides a description of the forces that finally overcame it: "A resistance that neither B-52s nor Cobras could break is now defeated with chewing gum, Marlboros and Levis without a shot being fired. All over the country, kids strut around in Rambo caps. A pair of genuine Ray Bans is a coveted treasure. In Hanoi they sell fake 'Peugeot' stickers for Chinese bicycles. An American-made felt-tip pen turns you into a big shot. There is no defence against such riches."[18]

Still, an epitaph for all those killed by the British, the French, and the U.S. forces and their allies after 1945 may also be appropriate. By the mid-1990s Robert McNamara was confessing in his autobiography that it had been "wrong, terribly wrong" for his country to have got involved in Vietnam.

# Cambodia

When the Japanese snatched control of Cambodia from the Vichy French in March 1945, they allowed the shy and youthful Prince Norodom Sihanouk (b. 1922), whom the French had appointed king in 1941, to proclaim Cambodia's independence. Sihanouk abrogated all treaties with the French and set up a new government under the nationalist Son Ngoc Thanh, a Vietnamese Khmer who had spent part of the war in Japan. It was Thanh who, in July, proclaimed the need to awaken the historical grandeur of "Kampuchea," as he thought Cambodia should be rechristened.

The French, with no intention of decolonizing, returned after the surrender of the Japanese and reclaimed Cambodia, but now as an autonomous kingdom within the French Union. Elements of the former protectorate status remained: France was to retain control over Cambodia's defence and foreign affairs, while all the major departments of the government of Cambodia remained in the hands of the French officials of the Indochinese Federation.

With French help Sihanouk forced Thanh into exile, although Thanh's supporters remained, forming the first urban postwar nationalist party. They were opposed to both the French and Sihanouk, but by the early 1950s their lack of success had led their party to splinter. Some of them joined the rural guerrillas known as the Khmer Issarak ("Liberated Khmers"), which had emerged in the 1930s and had communist and non-communist branches. In a simple way these branches represented the two different paths that patriots might follow; in Vietnam both were combined in the Viet Minh, but in Cambodia they remained separate. Thanh's followers enrolled in the non-communist branch, which became increasingly hostile not only to its rival, but also to Sihanouk.

In November 1949, as the situation in Vietnam grew more desperate, France granted Cambodia and Laos an even larger measure of internal autonomy. French officials still held onto bureaucratic power, but the situation in Southeast Asia was moving too fast for the planners in Paris. In the previous month the People's Republic of China had been born. In February 1950 the Indochinese Communist Party (ICP), still dominated by the Vietnamese, declared that the masses in Cambodia and Laos should be mobilized for liberation. The next year the ICP dissolved itself; from then on there would be only national communist parties.

From its founding in September 1951, hundreds of Khmers joined the Khmer People's Revolutionary Party (KPRP), which became known as the "Khmer Rouge."* Within two years this faction would have some 5,000 men under arms and control large parts of rural Cambodia.

---

* Later the leaders of the KPRP changed its name to the Khmer Workers' Party (KWP); both the KPRP and the KWP are referred to as the Khmer Rouge.

After seizing power from the elected government in a coup in June 1952, King Sihanouk, up to that point a silent figure in Cambodian politics, announced that he would deliver independence to his country in three years. Some six months later, his political visibility further enhanced, Sihanouk had become an ardent and noisy nationalist. The French, who regarded him as little more than a dilettante, were unworried. Despite the war in Vietnam, they remained optimistic that Indochina would remain in their hands.

Putting himself at the head of a "Crusade for Independence," Sihanouk flew to Paris in early 1953 and bombarded the French government with demands that the government of Cambodia be transferred to himself. He got nowhere, and, worse, his considerable vanity was injured by Gallic indifference. He went on to Montreal, where he announced on Radio Canada that only if independence were granted to the countries of Indochina could communism in Southeast Asia be halted. He repeated the same message in visits to Washington and New York.

In the following months Sihanouk, who had become a national hero to Cambodians, succeeded in forging international support for Cambodian independence—which the French granted (in his absence) on November 9, 1953, on the eve of their total collapse in Indochina. In September 1955, in accordance with the Geneva agreements, elections were held in Cambodia. To run as head of state, King Sihanouk had abdicated the throne (to his father). There was still substantial opposition to his leadership from both the centrist Democratic Party and the leftist People's Party, but there was no doubt about his popularity. "To conservative Cambodians," write Grant Evans and Kelvin Rowley, "he was still the god-king. To radical Cambodians, he was the democrat who had won independence and given up the throne."[19] To give colouring to his ambitions, Prince Sihanouk formed a party known as the Sangkum Reastr Niyum ("People's Socialist Community") and conjured up an ideology that he called "Buddhist socialism." To ensure that his monopoly on power would be uncontested, he crushed the opposition, liberal and leftist, harassing and murdering its leaders and driving many of its survivors into the country, exile, or underground. "Brutality and intimidation were firmly established as instruments of state policy," comments Milton Osborne, Sihanouk's biographer.[20]

Prince Sihanouk, god-king and dictator, walked the tightrope of neutralism. Indeed, he was close to joining the greatest political high-wire artists of the contemporary period. During the 1950s, with Eisenhower as U.S. president and John Foster Dulles as U.S. secretary of state, neutralism was seen as constituting a dangerous and infectious doctrine.

Opposition to it, as Audrey Kahin and George Kahin explain, "constituted one of the defining features in the Eisenhower administration's approach to Southeast Asia."[21]

Sihanouk's first major sin, in Washington's eyes, was his refusal to join SEATO as it took control of the region from the French in autumn 1954. To demonstrate his independence of U.S. designs, Sihanouk participated in the 1955 Bandung Afro-Asian conference, where he struck up a friendship with Zhou Enlai, the foreign minister of the People's Republic. His second major sin flowed from this: he visited Beijing in February 1956. Zhou offered Sihanouk economic aid, and the two leaders signed a treaty of friendship. Osborne speculates that China offered to protect Cambodia against the DRV, "a state whose intentions the prince distrusted."[22]

But neutralism required that Sihanouk also find friends in the West. Only U.S. aid, after all, could ensure economic development and military competency. But the problems here were several, real and imagined. They included Sihanouk's dislike of one U.S. ambassador in Phnom Penh, a gauche cold warrior, and his failure to warm to another, whom Sihanouk found to be merely unsympathetic; a third, who arrived in Phnom Penh in 1964, Sihanouk sent packing back to Washington. In addition he found that the Americans, especially when he visited them in New York and Washington, did not treat him with the respect that he felt a god-king warranted. Finally he was concerned that he and the U.S. allies in the area—notably the Marcos regime in the Philippines and Diem in the Republic of Vietnam—were incompatible; he saw Diem as an outright U.S. puppet. From 1964, with the hawks in the White House on the ascent and pressing for an increased military commitment to Vietnam, U.S. relations with Cambodia went into an even steeper dive.

Yet despite rocky relations with Washington, until the second half of the 1960s Sihanouk's neutralism was largely successful. After all, it kept Cambodia in one piece and on the sidelines of the war in Vietnam. But other factors, inside and outside Cambodia, were shaking the wire on which Sihanouk balanced.

Social change within the country was one of those factors. In Cambodia, as everywhere else in the Third World, after decades of colonial neglect education had exploded after independence. By the end of the 1960s a million Cambodians were enrolled in primary schools and 100,000 in secondary schools. As elsewhere, too, few of the newly educated wanted to return to the fields after graduating from the classrooms. Most wanted to stay in the towns and seek their fortunes. Thus, some 10 per cent of the Cambodian population, mainly young males, found themselves in Phnom Penh, where from the beginning of the decade there was little for them to do because the urban economy was dominated by the Chinese and Sino-Khmers and the small civil service was already overstaffed. There was also the matter of a crisis in what we might identify as a moral economy, that is, the moral idea of the acceptable difference between the rich (merchants and bureaucrats, including many who had been trained by and served the French) and the urban poor (such as the students). Michael Vickery describes this situation: "Conspicuous consumption indulged in by the elite was no longer within the economy, but involved the acquisition of expensive foreign products, frequent trips abroad, hard currency bank accounts, and the construction of amenities modeled on those of Paris and New York.... Development, for such a consumption-oriented elite, meant luxury housing, western-style restaurants and bars, importation of automobiles."[23]

Phnom Penh, the magnet attracting the country's youth, reflected this divided world in which extraordinary and usually Western-designed wealth existed side by side with the most repulsive poverty. Originally a quaint backwoods capital, Phnom Penh had been transformed by Sihanouk into a magical cross between a southern French city, perhaps Nice or Cannes, and a Khmer Camelot. It was a place of broad boulevards, villas, a casino, a convent, a university, and a great cathedral situated alongside ancient temples and a monumental mock-traditional funeral pagoda built to contain the body of the prince's father, King Suramarit. Traversing the broad avenues were Western automobiles transporting the few, rickshaws carrying a minority, and a majority moving on foot. On the outskirts of the city were huge, and growing, slums. As in Cairo and Tehran, as the rural population increased and the rural economy stagnated, peasants poured into the capital.

Although vocally critical of this post-independence status quo, the critics of the regime remained terrorized and marginalized. Whenever they put up an electoral fight against Sihanouk, which they did on several occasions in the late 1950s and early 1960s, they were beaten down by a combination of chicanery and violence, made palatable by the prince's genuine popularity and the corruption that greased the wheels of state and society. After a crackdown following student riots in early 1963, the leaders of the left moved out of parliamentary politics altogether into clandestinity in the mountains of eastern Cambodia.

Leading these dissidents were Saloth Sar (1928-96) and Ieng Sary. Both of them were teachers who attracted young, urban Khmers repelled by Sihanouk's dictatorship and the corruption surrounding his regime and concerned about their own and Cambodia's future. Both had been students in Paris, where they had formed connections to the French Communist

Party. From France Saloth Sar had visited Yugoslavia after its break with the Soviet Union. He drew contrasts between Yugoslavia and the Soviet Union on the one hand and Cambodia and Vietnam on the other. Yugoslavia, he learned, was independent and communist; it was also successful in developmental terms. Saloth Sar had returned home in 1953 to join the Khmer Rouge guerrillas, whose headquarters were in the tribal areas in Cambodia's northeast. By the early 1960s he had become the Khmer Rouge secretary general. It is likely that he murdered his predecessor. Ieng Sary, his fellow student, became his deputy.

## War

A second factor that shook Sihanouk's balancing act was the intensification of the war in neighbouring Vietnam. From early 1964, as the fighting in Vietnam became more desperate, the military planners in Saigon and Washington became increasingly concerned about the military supplies known to be passing through Cambodia on their way to North Vietnam. The NLF was also using the highland bases in eastern Cambodia as "sanctuaries," that is, safe havens, particularly from air strikes. These refuges had expanded during 1966 and 1967. By this time, too, Cambodian-U.S. relations had reached the crisis point, and Sihanouk had slammed the door on U.S. aid.

By severing relations with Washington, Sihanouk cut himself off from the vital arms that the Americans had been supplying. Osborne notes that nearly one-third of Cambodia's arms came in the form of U.S. aid.[24] Without these arms, it soon appeared, it would become impossible to contain the insurgency on Cambodia's frontiers. By 1967 the increased activity of the Khmer Rouge, who were based in the same highlands as the Vietnamese communists, had begun to worry Sihanouk and right-wing elements in Cambodia, particularly the military establishment in Phnom Penh. The areas of the country over which the prince had control were shrinking, and it seemed the army could do little to arrest this trend.

Sihanouk's prudently nurtured neutralism was being eroded by internal and external forces: the Khmer Rouge rebels within Cambodia, and the Vietnam communists trespassing from the outside. His immediate solution was to pressure Hanoi to restrain the Khmer Rouge. He used the threat of closing down the supply route between the Cambodian port of Sihanoukville and the Vietnamese frontier. This route fed the Ho Chi Minh Trail, Hanoi's major supply artery passing from the DRV through Cambodia to the RVN. This tactic did not work. By 1969 Vietnam bases inside Cambodia had increased, and in the Cambodian border areas Hanoi, not Phnom Penh, called the shots.

Washington, now desperate to put pressure on the communists to the south, was determined to close down the refuges by other means. In mid-March 1969, within weeks of the inauguration of President Nixon, the United States launched "Operation Menu," Washington's code name for the secret bombing of the NLF and North Vietnam bases along the Ho Chi Minh Trail in eastern Cambodia. For his remaining year in power Sihanouk was aware of the bombing, but it remains unclear as to whether he invited it or merely accepted it as something he could not prevent. Much of this bombing was of heavily populated rural areas.

By that time both the Cambodian state and its prince were on the road to ruin. Recognizing this, the commander-in-chief of Cambodia's ill-armed armies, Lon Nol, took the chance to seize power in March 1970 while Sihanouk was in Moscow. Lon Nol, a rightist general, had been at Sihanouk's side since independence, with the prince entrusting him with the task of suppressing the communists since the early 1960s. Lon Nol had become prime minister in the October 1966 elections. In early 1967 he had squelched a peasant rebellion in Samlaut with great cruelty, by putting whole villages to the torch and killing hundreds, if not thousands, of peasants. Now, in the 1970 coup, some nationalists supported him, disenchanted not only with the prince's dictatorial rule but also with the excesses of his family, whose conspicuous consumption stood in stark contrast to the poverty of most of their countrymen. Others did not welcome his move, recognizing him for what he was, a dangerous reactionary.

To stimulate their support, Lon Nol renamed Cambodia the "Khmer Republic" and sent his troops to fight the Khmer Rouge guerrillas. He supported the U.S. bombing campaign, because among its victims were his communist enemies, both Cambodian and Vietnamese. But even with the aid of U.S. bombs, his forces had little taste for the job and were often wiped out by the better trained, better armed, and more competently led guerrillas.

By the conclusion of the U.S. bombing campaign at the end of 1973, some two million Cambodian soldiers and civilians had been killed and two to three million Cambodians had become refugees. It is generally accepted that in the crucible of chaos caused by this U.S. bombing, the elements were stirred together that gave Saloth Sar (now known as "Pol Pot") his victory. According to Ben Kiernan, the bombing "sowed a whirlwind" that the Pol Pot faction of the Khmer Rouge "was ready to reap." The bombing only solidified the Khmer Rouge's base and, just as importantly, it prevented the party from gaining power early on, during a time when, according to Kiernan, Pol Pot's "domestic and foreign policy extremism was far from generally accepted."[25]

David P. Chandler concurs: "Without the war, Pol Pot's coming to power, like Sihanouk's demise, is inconceivable."[26] By the time the Americans discontinued their bombing, the Khmer Rouge controlled around 60 per cent of Cambodian territory.

## Inferno

In May 1975, the same month that Saigon fell, the Lon Nol regime was toppled and Phnom Penh liberated by the Khmer Rouge. As one writer put it, for many who cheered the entry of the Khmer Rouge, it was the last happy moment of their lives.

The country that Lon Nol had renamed "the Khmer Republic" was now transformed into "Democratic Kampuchea," with its government headed by a trio comprising Pol Pot, Ieng Sary, and another former student from Paris, Khieu Samphan. The new government set out on a course to establish a national economy based on autarky, that is, almost total agricultural self-sufficiency, combined with ethnic and political cleansing. Pol Pot and his comrades may have been partly inspired by the Yugoslav and partly by the North Korean example. In any case, their common experience as students in Paris seems not to have disposed them to reproduce French civilization in the tropics.

First, Phnom Penh and Battambang, Cambodia's only real cities, were emptied of their inhabitants.* Urban Cambodians, whether or not they had any experience in the fields, were forced to become peasants working in agricultural co-operatives, particularly in the northwest, the country's centre of rice production, often under the most appalling circumstances. Phnom Penh's large Roman Catholic cathedral was totally demolished and the National Bank was blown up.

It has sometimes been argued that there was some justification for this severe approach, because the destruction of the country's economy and the influx of peasants had made feeding the overpopulated capital an impossibility. But this is scarcely an explanation for what happened. More credible is the argument that the leaders of the new regime had a millennial and anti-Western developmental vision deeply coloured by a racist nationalism that led them to destroy the previous economy and society and try to build a new one under their own control. This vision they pursued with a demonic single-mindedness. Chandler writes: "Money, markets, and private property were abolished. Schools, universities, and Buddhist monasteries were closed. No publishing was allowed; the postal

---

* The population of Phnom Penh was around half a million, with one-third being Cambodian, one-third Chinese, and one-third Vietnamese.

system was abolished; freedom of movement, exchanging information, personal adornment, and leisure activities were curtailed."[27]

Immediately after the fall of Phnom Penh, many of those associated with the former regime, including most of Sihanouk's family, were massacred. After them, it was the turn of the Vietnamese settled in Cambodia. Kiernan argues, "There is no question that Democratic Kampuchea waged a campaign of genocide against ethnic Vietnamese."[28] Then came those who resisted the edicts of the revolutionary leadership or were merely suspected of resisting. Many of these, perhaps 20,000—including practically all of the Khmer Rouge intellectuals outside of the Pol Pot clique—were tortured first at the regime's interrogation centre in Phnom Penh. Yet not even the members within the ruling clique were safe; many of them were also killed. Nor did the killing stop after the regime was apparently secure. An epidemic of purging took place from late 1976 through 1978 when Pol Pot (now known as "Comrade Number One") and his clique became aware of the growing resistance to their draconian and deluded development policies (known as "the Super Great Leap Forward"). The policies demanded the transformation of Cambodia into a "developed industrial country with great strength for national defence." Evans and Rowley describe one facet of these purges:

> The eastern region, one of Cambodia's most productive rice-bowls... became the scene of unrivalled brutality and destruction. Captured cadres of soldiers were killed on the spot; whole villages deemed unfaithful were massacred; and tens of thousands of people (perhaps hundreds of thousands) were forcibly deported to other regions, many only to be executed en masse when they reached their destinations. Most of the mass graves unearthed since the fall of the Pol Pot regime appear to date from this period.[29]

Many Cambodians voted against the Pol Pot regime with their feet: 100,000 fled into Vietnam.

Some critics suggested that despite the developmental rhetoric the revolutionary state of Kampuchea never did actually make it to its feet, and that terror operated to conceal the absence of effective administration. This view has now been overturned. According to Kiernan, "Despite its underdeveloped economy, the regime probably exerted more power over its citizens than any state in world history."[30]

Until it was invaded by Vietnam in December 1978, Cambodia was immured in a world of silence. Slowly the nightmare of "Pol Potism" was disclosed: forced labour, starvation, systematic torture, mass executions. How many died? It is still impossible to separate the deaths of those who perished from the starvation caused by the economic dislocation brought

on, directly or indirectly, by the U.S. bombing and those killed by the functionaries of the Pol Pot regime. Estimates of total deaths from both causes
range from over 700,000 to 1.5 million (out of a population of just over 7
million). Amnesty International, for instance, estimates one to two million
deaths from disease and 300,000 executions. Chandler suggests that more
than a million—or one in seven Cambodians—died from malnutrition,
overwork, and illness, with probably in excess of 100,000 executed.[31] Tens
of thousands more died in the conflict with Vietnam, which Chandler says
was almost certainly started by the Red Khmer. A more recent breakdown
suggests a total of 1,671,000 perished in the period 1975-79—that is, 21
per cent of the total Cambodian population.[32]

## Invasion

Although the Pol Pot government in Phnom Penh collapsed within a matter of weeks of the Vietnamese invasion, Democratic Kampuchea lived on
in two forms: in a guerrilla force, which numbered at most 20,000 in 1979
and was armed by China and Thailand, and as a presence at the UN, where
it was supported by the Chinese, the Americans, and the members of
ASEAN, the Washington-backed bulwark against communism that had succeeded SEATO in 1967 and included Brunei, Indonesia, Malaysia, Philippines, Singapore, and Thailand. Only by controlling the food donated by
international organizations was the Communist Party of Kampuchea (CPK)
able to survive—and mutate. From his forest hideaway, Ieng Sary
announced, "We are willing to forget the past and I hope that others, too,
will forget the past." Deng Xiaoping also came down on the side of amnesia when he said of Pol Pot, appropriately in the year 1984, "I do not
understand why some people want to remove Pol Pot. It is true that he
made some mistakes in the past, but now he is leading the fight against
the Vietnamese aggressors." At the beginning of 1981, Khieu Samphan,
who had succeeded Pol Pot as prime minister, announced, "No more
socialism."

U.S. and ASEAN support for Democratic Kampuchea and hostility
towards Vietnam lasted the whole of the 1980s. For over a decade, the
Khmer Rouge, although politically divided and largely ineffective, still
enjoyed the backing of Washington and the West. The Khmer Rouge guerrillas became a repainted version of the Khmer Serai ("Free Cambodia"),
which had been organized, probably with the help of the CIA, against the
government of Sihanouk in 1960. By 1986 Washington had given the
Khmer Rouge over $80 million worth of aid.

The Vietnamese, who had 200,000 troops in the country in 1980,
withdrew in 1988, but before pulling out they installed a client

government led by defectors from the Khmer Rouge. One of these was Hun Sen, who became prime minister. They also oversaw an agricultural decollectivization. For the first time in a decade, in 1988-89 the harvest was sufficient to feed Cambodia's eight million people.

Sihanouk, ousted by Lon Nol in 1970, had found refuge in Beijing. With the encouragement of Zhou Enlai, the Chinese prime minister, he had linked ideological arms with the Khmer Rouge and headed a "national front" government that lasted until after the fall of the Lon Nol government. Then, returning to Cambodia, he appeared at first as a figurehead in a government of national unity, although in reality he was a prisoner of the Khmer Rouge until the Vietnamese invasion. In the early days of January 1979, just ahead of the Vietnamese, he fled again to China. Oddly, at first he seemed to welcome this invasion by a communist state about which he had always shown grave apprehension: "The presence of the Vietnamese in my country today, humiliating and unpleasant as it is for us Khmers, is the only—and moreover imperfect—protection for the Khmer people against being massacred by the partisans, Pol Pot, Ieng Sary and other Khmer Rouge."[33]

But he soon changed his mind, or at least his position, and became the voice of the Khmer Rouge rump at the UN. Here he helped persuade the General Assembly, which the United States and China had also been lobbying, to vote in September 1979 to recognize Democratic Kampuchea. (The vote was 71 votes to 35, with 34 abstentions. No Western country voted against, although several, including France and the Scandinavian countries, abstained.) Sihanouk also formed his own party and launched his own guerrillas, who operated in Cambodia alongside the forces of the former Khmer Rouge against the Vietnamese-backed People's Republic of Kampuchea (PRK) government. Throughout the 1980s and into the early 1990s, he moved between Beijing, Jakarta, and New York, negotiating his own return and a settlement that would guarantee elections in Cambodia.

Meanwhile, several changes had taken place beyond Cambodia itself; as Vietnamese communism transformed itself out of existence, a rapprochement developed between Beijing and Hanoi. And Washington had preoccupations elsewhere. Cambodia had become a "broken-backed state."

## Resurrection?

By the end of 1991 a Supreme National Council for Cambodia had been negotiated into existence. This was one of the dividends of the rapprochement between Beijing and Hanoi, on the one hand, and a peace plan brokered by the Security Council of the United Nations, on the other. The

Supreme National Council represented the Khmer Rouge, the supporters of Sihanouk, and the PRK. In July 1991 Sihanouk, still in Beijing, was elected its president. A peace agreement was signed in Paris in October, and Sihanouk returned to Phnom Penh in November, now recognized as the head of the Cambodian state. Hun Sen, who had been the foreign minister and then prime minister of the PRK government, became prime minister. Khieu Samphan arrived with him. A Pol Pot mouthpiece to the last hour, he narrowly missed being lynched by the crowd.

The war wound down in 1992. National elections, supervised by the United Nations Transitional Authority in Cambodia (UNTAC), were held in May 1993 and won by the party of none other than Prince Norodom Sihanouk, now leader of the United Front for an Independent, Neutral, Peaceful and Co-Operative Cambodia (UFINPCC). Hun Sen, at the head of the People's Party, was the loser. Despite attempts at reconciliation, the Khmer Rouge boycotted the elections and afterwards threatened the secession of the seven provinces it dominated. These tensions led to a renegotiation of power and the subsequent emergence of a coalition government, with Sihanouk now becoming king and head of state. The first prime minister, taking power in mid-1994, was Sihanouk's son, Prince Ranariddh, leader of the UFINPCC; the co-prime minister was Hun Sen, who, despite losing the election of May 1993, refused to step down.

Meanwhile, UNTAC had hurriedly left, leaving behind a corrupt and inefficient government ruling over a country that had become not only a world centre for drug trafficking ("Medellin on the Mekong") but also the world amputations capital. According to a report by the special representative of the UN secretary general for human rights in Cambodia: "Members of the armed forces in Cambodia continue to enjoy wide and effectively uncontrolled powers of arrest, detention and even execution." His report underlined "the involvement of high regional and provincial military officers and their units in criminal activities."[34] These military officers remained loyal to Hun Sen, who continued to control every level of administration down to village level.[35]

By 1994, still controlled by Pol Pot, the Khmer Rouge was little more than a warlord's rabble financed by a lucrative trade in timber and gems with businessmen in Thailand. In August 1996 Ieng Sang defected with his troops from what remained of the Khmer Rouge forces under Pol Pot. After he claimed that Pol Pot alone had been responsible for the Khmer Rouge holocaust, Ieng Sang was granted an amnesty. As William Shawcross commented, "A leader of what has long been acknowledged as one of the most odious regimes in modern times has been pardoned for reasons of political expedience."[36]

# Indonesia: Independence and the New Order

In 1936 the governor-general of the Dutch East Indies, B.C. de Jonge, estimated that in another three hundred years the Indonesians would be "ready for some kind of autonomy." This would have been a source of reassurance to both the 270,000 Dutch and Dutch Eurasians in the Indies and those at home in the Netherlands. For the Dutch and Eurasians in Southeast Asia it meant that they could enjoy the privileges for which they were qualified largely by accident of birth, privileges that included a near-monopoly on government jobs. For the Dutch, thousands of miles away in the Netherlands, who had never seen the Indies, it meant a guarantee of the 13.7 per cent that the Indies contributed to their national economy.

The Indonesian nationalists saw the situation differently. They were offended by a system that kept jobs and wealth out of their hands and pumped profits and their tax money across the seas. Yet when they protested they were likely to fall victim to the heavy repression that most often ended in confinement in internment camps in the most remote parts of the colony. Most of the leading nationalists had spent time in these camps.

A scant six years after de Jonge's optimistic estimate, Dutch control over the greater part of the archipelago had melted away. After surrendering more or less without a fight to the advancing Japanese armies in early 1942, members of the colonial administration had their turn to be marched off to internment camps, where they stayed until the Japanese surrender on August 15, 1945. Meanwhile the Japanese, short of trained administrators, appointed Indonesians to run the occupied country. By 1943, when the tide of war was turning sharply against Tokyo, the occupying Japanese went a step further. They began to offer the Indonesian nationalists the means to conduct propaganda against the West. They also trained militia that they hoped to use against the returning Western forces.

Two days after the Japanese surrender Indonesian nationalists declared the birth of their country. Achmed Sukarno (1901-70) was proclaimed president and Muhammad Hatta vice-president. In November of the same year, in Surabaya, the army of the infant republic, of which the militiamen trained by the Japanese were a key component, fought its first major battle against the Dutch. For four years the nationalists struggled against and negotiated with the returning colonists, whose increased desperation was matched by the decreasing popularity of their cause even among their U.S. benefactors. U.S. Marshall Plan dollars had, after all, been siphoned off by The Hague to fight the war in the Indies. Despite the Netherland's use of U.S. equipment and conscription of 100,000 soldiers, by March 1949 the Indonesian guerrilla forces had the colonists on the run.

## Independent Indonesia: The Sukarno Era, 1949-66

The Republic of the United States of Indonesia was born in 1949, bound artificially to the Netherlands by undertakings that attempted to establish a Netherlands-Indonesian Union. This was supposed to be the local equivalent of the French Union (which barely worked) and the British Commonwealth (which lasted, at least for a while). But the relationship between The Hague and Jakarta deteriorated rapidly. In 1954 the Indonesians withdrew from the Union, and in 1957 they nationalized Dutch firms. Still the Dutch tried to save face by holding onto the western part of New Guinea, which the Indonesians called "West Irian." In 1960 there was renewed military confrontation, and in August Indonesia finally broke off relations with the Netherlands. Two years later West Irian was brought under a temporary UN trusteeship, only to pass over to full Indonesian control in May 1963.

Between 1945 and 1966, Achmed Sukarno presided over what was the world's fifth-largest independent state and the world's most populous Muslim country.* Sukarno, a Western-educated engineer, half Javanese and half Balinese, was a Muslim and a social-democrat. He had founded the Partai Nasional Indonesia (PNI) in 1927—with its slogan "Indonesia Merdeka" ("Free Indonesia")—and by 1930 the party had more than 100,000 members. The Dutch, arresting him as an agitator, forced him to spend nine years in detention and exile.

The ideology of the PNI, which was more implicit than explicit, reflected Sukarno's genius. A little like Gandhi's, it was a rich and eclectic combination of Western elements, such as liberalism and Marxism, and native ideas, such as those derived from Hinduism, Buddhism, and mysticism. Only once did Sukarno spell it out: in June 1945, in an informal speech to other nationalist leaders, he made reference to his "Five Principles"—nationalism, internationalism (also called humanitarianism), representative government, social justice, and belief in God in a context of religious freedom. The Kahins make the point that the independent Indonesian government was one "in which most leaders were unsympathetic to an increase of foreign capital and dedicated to the idea of its eventual displacement by a predominantly socialist economic order."[37]

---

* "Muslims" in Indonesia were not a single, homogeneous group. Some Muslims were Muslims above all; others had various dominant identities in addition to being Muslims. Thus the concept of Indonesia as a "Muslim country" can be misleading.

The eclectic nationalism of the new government seemed to be just the right thing for a largely peasant population, which, although predominantly Muslim, also comprised large regional minorities with different religious and ethnic backgrounds. There were dissenters, of course. The most persistent were Muslims who launched what was, for a decade after 1948, a stubborn guerrilla war in the mountains of central Java. For Sukarno the Muslim parties, and especially their far-right members, posed a much greater threat than did the adherents of the country's other major secular party, the Indonesian Communist Party (PKI). Indeed, out of fear of the most militant of the Muslim elements, the PNI embraced the PKI.

Between 1949 and 1957, with no elections being held, Parliament was made up of appointees from the major parties. Increasingly, this method of rule was found to be inefficient and unsatisfactory. In 1959 Sukarno announced the abandonment of this system of government and the creation of a dictatorship with himself ruling over an appointed assembly. He glorified this new system with the name "Guided Democracy." Marginalized, his vice-president, Muhammad Hatta, resigned. But Hatta was not alone in his opposition to Sukarno's usurpation of power. Many of the leading officers in the army also opposed Sukarno, although they did not so much lament the absence of democracy as the centralization of power in Jakarta and the diminution of their own influence, which was strong in the regions.

The three pillars of "Guided Democracy" were known as NAKASOM (an acronym standing for "Nationalism, Religion, Communism"). Under its sheltering roof in the assembly, and under Sukarno's domination, all political groups were simultaneously represented. NAKASOM thus ensured representation of the PKI. In 1965 Sukarno went so far as to appoint a few members of the party to the most marginal posts in his immense cabinet. The most important of these became minister of sport.

Since the PKI had at least three million members (and was thus not merely the oldest Communist Party in Asia but the largest legal Communist Party outside the Soviet bloc), Sukarno could hardly exclude it. Although the communists had launched an insurrection against the PNI in 1948 (known as the "Madiun rebellion"), in the years after its defeat it restored its credibility by distancing itself from both Moscow and Beijing and embracing a resolutely nationalist policy.

Sukarno's commitment to non-alignment led him to cultivate relations with the People's Republic and to accept Soviet aid alongside that from the West. Like other nationalist leaders, he played one side off against the other. When Washington refused to supply him with arms, like Nasser in Egypt he turned to the Soviet Union. These two aspects of his policy—tolerance of the PKI and openness with regard to the Soviet Union and China—bound together by Indonesia's hosting of the Bandung conference, suggested to some that Sukarno was the kind of lurching nationalist who, like Nehru, might in the end veer closer to Beijing or Moscow. This is precisely what many in Washington felt, and it is what led senior figures in the Eisenhower administration to try to topple him in 1958 by covertly supporting a military mutiny. This action was, according to the Kahins, "the largest, and to this day the least known of the Eisenhower Administration's covert militarized interventions."[38] For nearly a year the Americans trained and armed the rebels in Sumatra and the Celebes, even providing them with aircraft that bombed Sukarno's forces. In the end the rebellion was quelled, partly because of the effectiveness of the Indonesian army, partly because of splits among the rebels.

For the Indonesians, the political cost of the insurgency was high. Both the army and the presidency gained the kind of strength that would allow them to maintain their control over the country's political and economic life for decades, and parliamentary government was effectively destroyed in the long term. "At the same time," according to the Kahins, "the civil war struck a devastating blow against any future prospects for a devolution of power from the central government in Jakarta to the regions or any significant measure of decentralization and local autonomy. Indonesia became an authoritarian centralized polity, both in the closing years of Sukarno's rule and under the Suharto regime which succeeded it."[39]

Furthermore, in 1959, under pressure from army leaders, Sukarno did away with the 1950 liberal constitution and restored an authoritarian version set out in the final days of the Japanese occupation. He banned the party of modernist Islam and replaced the elected parliament with a presidentially appointed body, although he also tried to safeguard the surviving large parties, including the Communist Party, as a counterweight to a possible military takeover.[40] So, as the Kahins emphasize, it was the U.S.-supported rebellion that nudged Sukarno even further along the road towards authoritarianism.

Other problems followed the end of the insurrection. In one of the last attempts to secure their influence in Southeast Asia, the British proposed the creation of a federation of territories that would run from Malaya through Singapore to the petty colonial outposts on Borneo (Sarawak, Brunei, North Borneo). London announced the birth of "Malaysia" on September 16, 1963. The British were unwilling to wait for the outcome of a UN mission organized to enquire whether or not the people of Sarawak and North Borneo were actually willing to be confederated. There is every reason to think that they were not.

Sukarno was irritated by the idea of a neocolonial client confederation in a region that he hoped to dominate, especially because Borneo was one of Indonesia's central islands. This led him to a blustering adventurism that consisted of sending ill-trained armed parties to invade Malaysia in 1964. The parallel between Sukarno and Nasser, who had dispatched his armies to Yemen two years earlier, is striking: both saw themselves as regional gatekeepers, not just nationalists but supernationalists. The difference is that Sukarno had considerably less control over his army than Nasser did over his. Most of the Indonesian generals would have no part in Sukarno's invasion schemes.

Indonesia's military leaders in the 1950s were ambitious and fissiparous. Many opposed Sukarno's appointment of General Abdul Haris Nasution as the chief of staff in November 1955. Often regionally based, and supported by local merchants and politicians, the officers were capable of resisting orders from Jakarta and even of rebelling against the government. They were also not above a kind of warlordism in which they took control of local sources of wealth, part of which they distributed to loyal soldiers. When Dutch-owned assets were nationalized at the end of 1957, the generals took a large share. Their massive mismanagement of the nationalized industries and plantations put them on a collision course with the powerful left-wing and communist unions. Such collision seemed guaranteed by 1963, as the economy was falling apart and inflation shooting up.

By the mid-1960s one of the leading generals was General Raden Suharto (b. 1921), who had risen up the promotional ladder throughout the 1950s. By 1965 he had reached a rung on the seniority ladder just below Nasution's deputy, General Ahmad Yani. Suharto had been accused of embezzlement before going into the army, and while in the army he was removed from his command because of corruption. He went into the smuggling/import/export business with Liem Sioe Long, a Chinese entrepreneur. The Liem-Suharto connection proved to be an enriching experience for both; by 1989 Liem was reckoned to be one of the world's fifty billionaires. According to Michael Vatikiotis, Liem owned companies that accounted for 5 per cent of Indonesia's GNP.[41]

On October 1, 1965, following a coup attempt in Jakarta, much of the leadership of the army was captured and executed, including General Yani. It is impossible to be certain about the sequence of events that followed, because a shroud of censorship was soon thrown over the affair. What is clear is that the coup was suppressed by units under General Suharto, whom Sukarno was forced to designate as responsible for "the restoration of security and order." The army was now in charge: a bloodbath followed in which most of the victims were members of the PKI. In one interpretation, armed parties of assassins were guided by lists of leading communists maintained by the U.S. embassy in Jakarta.[42] Certainly, as the Kahins comment, "American input went beyond mere approbation and encouragement." When the putschists turned to Washington for weapons "to arm Moslems and nationalist youth in Central Java for use against the PKI," they admitted this was part of an army policy "to eliminate the PKI." Washington responded swiftly and sympathetically.[43]

The PKI was annihilated; its banners would never flutter again. Estimates of the number of murders orchestrated by the army and other anti-communists (including some Muslim student organizations in a leading role) range upwards from 450,000 to a million. Kiernan argues that what took place in parts of Indonesia in 1965-66 should be compared to what happened in parts of Cambodia a decade later.[44] On the island of Bali alone, 40,000 to 100,000 out of a population of 1.8 million were killed. The repression as a whole lasted for more than a decade. In the later 1970s, as many as 100,000 people were shut up in government dungeons, including thousands of artists, intellectuals (especially teachers), and civil servants accused of varying degrees of closeness to the PKI. A CIA report stated: "In terms of the numbers killed, the anti-PKI massacres in Indonesia rank as one of the worst mass murders of the 20th century, along with the Soviet purges of the 1930s, the Nazi mass murders during the Second World War, and the Maoist bloodbath of the early 1950s."[45]

As far as the army was concerned, it no longer had to contend with rivals for power.

## The Suharto New Order, 1966-95

The pogrom was welcomed by the United States and Britain in particular, and by the West in general. In March 1966 Sukarno, who had not been among the victims of the first coup, was finally ousted in a second coup and a new regime under General Suharto was installed. Arguments for neutralism and criticism of British arrangements in Malaysia were now stilled. Relations between Jakarta and Beijing and Moscow were severed. In its political connections, at least, Indonesia left behind the non-aligned world of Bandung and fastened itself to the West. One sign of this was Suharto's leading role in the 1967 formation of ASEAN, the collection of U.S. military allies in Asia. Suharto's regime—called, like Mussolini's in the 1930s, the "New Order"—made Sukarno's eclectic authoritarianism look almost innocent. Besides presiding over a police state that suffocated political life, the military dictator halted land reform and proscribed what remained, after the bloodbath, of trade union and peasant organizations.

Military dictatorship served the double function of destroying any residue of the Bandung movement and attracting foreign capital, particularly U.S. and Japanese, which was happy to invest in an orderly and resource-rich Indonesia. Tax incentives offered even more encouragement; they were a central part of a foreign investment law passed in 1967. By 1977 the Americans and the Japanese had invested $8 billion in Indonesia. By the end of the decade a state-owned, dirigiste, economy was rising fast.

For all their commitment to foreign investment, the generals of the New Order, no less than Suharto himself, were economic nationalists, and for good reason. By 1974 the heights of the Indonesian economy, private and public, were dominated by an interlocking directorate comprising themselves and Chinese businessmen. Absent from the leadership of civil government departments as late as 1957, by 1982 the generals had succeeded in heading 47 per cent of them.[46] *L'état, c'est nous* ("We are the state"), they might have boasted, for the generals rewarded themselves handsomely—so much so that by 1977 the U.S. Securities and Exchange Commission complained about the kickbacks they were demanding. Until the mid-1980s at least, independent capitalists were scarce.

The generals were more than merely looters, although the term "economic philosophy" might overstate their interest in ideas. According to Richard Robison, the Indonesian military rulers "envisaged a program of state-led capitalist development to form an integrated national industrial economy which included capital, intermediate and consumer goods industries."[47] Thus "national development" based on ISI had become a central dogma. As committed to this dogma as the generals were the new class of civilian state managers (many of them economists) who served under them. At the highest level these men had staggering power. None seemed concerned with such soft issues as "human rights." All of them were obsessed with "growth."

If the generals commanded and the economists planned, the infantry of the state was its civil service. This grew parasitically, from 608,000 in 1963 to over 3 million by 1986—a rate of growth, as John Bresnan points out, that exceeded that of the population in general and matched the GNP.[48]

The security of the regime, the centrality of the economists, and the expansion of the civil service were all spokes in a wheel lubricated by one commodity, oil, which was the country's principal, indeed dominating, export. As a result of the rise in oil prices in the last part of 1973, Indonesia had enjoyed a sudden boom that propelled the national economy out of the bottom group of Southeast Asia's larger nations. By the early 1980s, with oil prices still buoyant, energy sales as a proportion of total export earnings had reached 70 per cent and were rising.

Overseeing oil production was Pertamina, the huge, tentacled state enterprise that ran not only the oil and gas industries but also petrochemicals and steel. Pertamina, operated more as a fief than a firm, was controlled by General Ibnu Sutowo, one of the leading pro-Americans in the late 1950s. Sutowo, accountable only to the army leadership, enjoyed close relations with Japanese businessmen who had an unquenchable need for oil to feed their supertankers.

By the time he had been forced to step down as manager of Pertamina in 1976, General Sutowo, through imprudent borrowings, spendings, and pilferings, had plunged the company into $10 billion in debts. Since he was a close crony of Suharto, however, Sutowo was never brought to trial. Indeed, given that his policies had bled Pertamina dry, it was appropriate, perhaps, that he became head of the Indonesian Red Cross. He also got to keep the Jakarta Hilton, just one of his more profitable investments. General Sutowo would probably be among the first to agree with the verdict of Michael Vatikiotis, a Jakarta correspondent for the *Far Eastern Economic Review*, who commented that "not all regimes born out of the barrel of a gun are bad."[49]

But we should not be distracted by the mammoth gains accumulated by the few. The many also benefited from the oil boom. In the decade 1970-80 per capita income almost doubled. At the same time Indonesia expanded its infrastructure of basic health and education facilities, giving the country one of the highest levels of primary school enrolment rates in the world (93 per cent). By the mid-1980s Indonesia, once a major rice importer, was close to self-sufficient in this major staple. Key to this was the government's subsidization of fertilizers and pesticides, using profits from oil.

## Disorders

By 1977, a year of parliamentary elections, students, who had earlier protested against the Japanese domination of the Indonesian economy, had become actively engaged in criticizing the military dictatorship and its policies, one of which was the regime's consistent violation of human rights. In part, at least, they were thinking about Timor.

On December 7, 1975, a day after Secretary of State Henry Kissinger and President Ford visited Jakarta, Indonesia's armies invaded the eastern end of the island of Timor, to the east of Java. Eastern Timor had been part of the Portuguese, not the Dutch, empire, and when the Portuguese revolution took place in 1974 a small group of nationalists had declared Timor independent. Washington, anxious, no doubt, about the fate of the region after the fall of Saigon, and aware that Marxist regimes were about to sweep into power in the ex-Portuguese colonies in Africa (Guinea-Bissau,

Angola, Mozambique), declared the Timor nationalists to be communists. Their destruction by Jakarta's army was felt to be a necessity. In the invasion and the repression that followed, as many as 200,000 Timorese were killed, out of a population of only 720,000. In 1976 Timor was incorporated into Indonesia as a province, although Jakarta had not succeeded in extinguishing the guerrilla movement that had established itself there. The UN declared the occupation illegal, but did nothing about it. Not surprisingly, for the Americans, the Japanese, and even the Canadians, the sweet smell of money concealed the stench of the dead. A former British defence minister confessed, "I don't really fill my mind much with what one set of foreigners is doing to another." He had sold the Indonesian generals ground-attack aircraft worth more than £500 million (some $700-800 million).[50]

By the early 1980s the Suharto regime was beginning to face other problems. One was the decline in income from oil, due to a recession in the oil market. Oil prices remained depressed from 1982 to 1986. A second was that the kind of state capitalism (oil-financed heavy industrialization) fostered by the New Order was felt to have outlived its purpose. "Deregulation" and "diversification," applied elsewhere in the Third World, now became the watchwords that foreign advisers insisted upon for Indonesia. But deregulation was problematic, because a large slice (40 per cent in 1986) of state enterprises was controlled by the same group that ran the state: Suharto, his family, and generals. These people were reluctant to commit economic suicide. Import Substitution Industrialization had been good to them; they didn't want to accept that the party was over. The problem was not merely one of wealth, it was also one of staying in power. The subsidies lavished on food production, and which had benefited ordinary Indonesians, conflicted with the interests of GATT, which had as one of its central purposes the replacement of self-sufficiency with reliance on open markets.

Under pressure from the IMF and World Bank, Indonesia adopted selective deregulation and moved ahead with diversification. The state began to withdraw from the economy, while export-led growth came to replace the older ISI policies. Immediately after one of his ceremonial re-elections in 1983—elections in Indonesia take the form of unanimous support for Suharto by the Consultative Assembly, which he, himself, appoints—Suharto announced the abandonment of a wide range of oil-financed heavy industrial projects: a petrochemical complex, an electrical-generating program, and an alumina plant. The immediate consequence of the fall of oil prices was a slump in the economic growth rate, to 4.4 per cent in the middle of the 1980s.

In the longer term, the new policies were successful. Growth rebounded to around 7 per cent by the end of the decade, and many of the corrupt tentacles of the public service were lopped off. In 1985, for instance, in a radical move the notoriously corrupt customs service was disbanded and handed over to a private Swiss firm. According to Vatikiotis: "The share of non-oil exports as a percentage of total exports increased from 31 per cent to 50 per cent in the period 1978-87. By 1990, there was no longer talk about Indonesia's reliance on hydrocarbon exports."[51] Even as export-driven growth slowed down among the rest of Asia's "miracle" economies, Indonesia maintained a relatively high rate (6.5 per cent, equal to South Korea's growth rate). Manufactured exports grew from $501 million in 1980 to $16.1 billion in 1982.[52] Most exports were of the labour-intensive type: textiles, garments, footwear, electronics, furniture, toys, and sporting goods. Although the big beneficiaries of the country's growth were inevitably the Suharto family and friends, there were millions of other beneficiaries as well.

Still, the economic shifts of the 1980s inevitably provoked more dissent. Building opposition had never been easy, because the state repression was generally swift and brutal; there was even a special term for the work of the government death squads, *"penembakan misterius,"* or "mysterious shootings." After the student protests in the 1970s, for instance, student life was "normalized" by violent means. As recently as 1989, one student had been jailed for eight years for selling copies of a proscribed book. In the same year the army killed between 41 (the official figure) and 200 people in a protest over land tenure. "Mental ideological screening" became mandatory for applicants seeking jobs in the military, the civil service, the press, and legal aid societies—or even as shadow puppeteers. Dissent was further regulated by the Suharto family's ownership of all three television stations plus a major publishing group.

Spaces for protest did still exist, particularly in the religious domain. In September 1984 Muslim preachers, focusing on the tyranny and corruption of the regime and the poverty of a part of the urban population, were able to foment an uprising, which again came up against a wall of repression: as many as 63 were killed. Other manifestations of popular discontent were registered later in the year and throughout 1985. In the absence of an effective politics of opposition, a populist Islam, such as the movement growing in the Middle East, was becoming the vehicle for protest by the disinherited. The New Order remained vigilant against any upsurge of militant Islam, and a number of Muslims were charged with attempted subversion of the state.

In early 1986 Ferdinand Marcos had fled from the Philippines.

Gradually the fact that he and his cronies had plundered the state for billions of dollars became public knowledge. Awareness of General Suharto's gouging practices dawned more slowly, mainly because of censorship, and reaction came even more slowly for the less obvious reason that under the New Order the standard of living for the majority of Indonesians had improved significantly.

In the following months and years, while Marcos suffered the gilded purgatory of exile and obloquy, the Indonesian elite became understandably nervous, but hardly morose. The family members of Suharto Inc. continued to acquire control over the most profitable areas of the economy.[53] In November 1994, in a feature on the Suhartos, the *Observer* estimated the fortune of Suharto père at £10 billion in 1989.[54] The paper reported that his oldest daughter, Tutut, vice-president of the ruling party, was combining "money-making and jet-setting with a love of politics. Her principal company, Citra Lomtoro Gung, manages a system of deeply unpopular toll roads. Her other interests range through wood pulping, educational TV, radio, publishing and pharmaceuticals." One of the companies owned by Titik, Suharto's second daughter, had "joined British investors in a £400 million project to build a mammoth cement works in Sumatra." Suharto's sons, Sigit and Tommy, were partners in the manufacturing and trading Humpuss Group. Bambang, another son, had become the most successful of all family members in business: "His firm Nusantara owns hotels, coal mines, property, paper mills. He made a fortune out of a monopoly on the import of plastics; he got a monopoly of the trade in oranges in Kalimantan but lost money when his excessive greed caused farmers to revolt." The *Observer* was perhaps too gallant to mention Suharto's wife, Tien, a queenly figure with a taste for diamonds, referred to by some as "Tien Per Cent." From the cocoon of the state, thus, rose the butterflies of independent capitalism. Apart from the messy business of human rights, often excluded entirely from the literature on the subject, Indonesia was becoming a developmental dream.

Nonetheless, by the mid-1990s the word did seem to be getting around about the Suhartos and the policies of the Indonesian state. In early 1994 Toronto's *Globe and Mail* featured a story headlined "Economic Miracle Bears Fruit—for the Few." Filling its moral sails with a breeze that had been blowing intermittently but apparently unnoticed since the student protests against corruption in the mid-1970s, the newspaper noted, "Rampant nepotism, cronyism and lavish displays of luxury are fuelling bitterness in Indonesia about President Suharto and his family." A few months later a writer in *The Guardian* commented, "Indulgent Western attitudes may change now that Suharto can no longer guarantee 'stability.' "[55] Since reforms would be difficult, a sacrifice was required. One of the leading Chinese businessmen in Indonesia, Eddy Tansil, was given a 17-year prison sentence over a fraudulent $430 million letter of credit he had obtained from a state bank. Arief Budiman has suggested that Tansil's trial signifies a power shift within Indonesia and the rise of a mainly Indonesian big business group.[56]

In any case, though enthusiastic about the business opportunities, the West remains unimpressed by Indonesian business practices. The "Corruption Index," produced by the Berlin-based Transparency International, elected Indonesia as the world's most corrupt country, but not before John Pilger had written in the London-based *New Statesman and Society* that General Suharto had seen Indonesia's "continued international respectability vanish; and now its domestic tranquility may be dissipating. This is not to say that a coup is likely; the military's repressive force pervades Indonesian society: yet seldom a week passes when the limits of its control is not tested by an increasingly confident popular resistance."[57] Pilger says that the trend suggests "a reawakening of the mass movements" that existed before 1965.

By the standards of the IMF and other Western policy-makers, Indonesia was reckoned to have "good prospects" in the 1990s. Its rate of GDP growth by the middle of the decade was over 7 per cent and expected to stay there. Politically, as Pilger argues—and especially with an aging Suharto and the problems of succession—for the first time in many years the dictatorship in Indonesia may be operating on increasingly shaky grounds. Still, according to Indonesia specialists attending a 1992 conference the recent events by no means indicate that the "tide of history" in the country is finally moving in a democratic direction.[58]

# Summary

Independent Indonesia was born on August 17, 1945; independent Vietnam was reborn on September 2, 1945. Although both were to be shortly after invaded by imperial forces, Indonesia survived to become independent in 1949. The independence of a united Vietnam was impounded until April 1975, by which time it had suffered two wars and seen several millions of its people killed, maimed, and dislocated.

Vietnam's revolution represents the last great communist upheaval of the 20th century. After defeating the world's greatest military power after two decades of war, Vietnam, now united, emerged with a socialist economy under a communist government allied simultaneously with Moscow and Beijing while being totally boycotted by the West. Only with the breakdown of communism and the market reforms of the late 1980s did Vietnam, following the example of China, embark on the road of capitalist development. Transformation proceeded at record speed. By the mid-1990s, only a few slogans remained as reminders of the communist past.

Cambodia went from protectorate status under the French, to independence, to membership in the French Union, and to independence again, all within eight years. Between the break-up of Indochina following the defeat of the French at Dien Bien Phu in May 1954 and the fall of Phnom Penh to the Khmer Rouge in May 1975, Cambodia was dominated by one of the most persistent and opportunistic political leaders in the whole of the Third World, the sometimes god-king Prince Nordorom Sihanouk. Then, as a result of U.S. bombing and the ascendancy of the Khmer Rouge, Cambodia disappeared altogether into a silence broken only when the full horror of the atrocities committed by the Pol Pot regime became apparent. Collapsing under the swift offensive of the communist armies of Vietnam in January 1979, the Pol Pot government-in-hiding was given a new lease on life through recognition and support by Washington and its allies, and including the People's Republic of China. By the 1990s, even after the Pol Pot regime had been formally disowned by its Chinese and Western sponsors, the legacy of the U.S. intervention in Indochina lived on in the mayhem underwritten by the superpower.

The Indonesia that was born in 1945 and became securely independent four years later was headed by Achmed Sukarno, one of Asia's loudest and most successful nationalists in the postwar period. Sukarno fits into no easy mould; he was no military modernizer like Kemal in Turkey or Pahlavi in Iran; no communist like Ho Chi Minh or Mao Zedong. Nor was he an opportunistic nationalist-come-lately like Cambodia's Sihanouk. In some respects, such as his socialism and his enthusiasm for Third World unity, he shared common ground with Nehru.

Like Mossadeq in Iran, Sukarno tolerated the communists of the PKI because they supported him and because he feared the political and Islamic rightists more. Unlike Mossadeq he did not turn on them: but like Mossadeq, Sukarno was overthrown in a U.S.-encouraged coup against which he was able to offer little or no resistance. The massacre of as many as half a million Indonesians that followed his ouster has been compared to the massacres conducted by Stalin, earlier, or under the Khmer Rouge a decade later.

Sukarno's successor was one of the many anti-communist military modernizers that Washington and the West welcomed for their capacity to secure Western interests in the Third World. Unlike others of this ilk, however, General Suharto was immoveable. After coming to power in 1965 he remained the ruler of Indonesia for the next three decades, presiding over a state that showed itself to be a model of orderly development. Indonesia was thus the best vindication of the political development strategies of the 1950s and 1960s, which claimed that rule by military elites could provide the stability necessary for successful economic growth. Because the economic success of Indonesia, like that of South Korea, has been of the command type, by the 1990s the Suharto dictatorship, also in common with that of South Korea, had come under increasing pressure to open the economy to foreign investment and ownership. One lever used against the regime, that of human rights, can be seen as a prime instance of Western opportunism, because Washington in particular, and the West in general, cheered when half a million were massacred in the coup of 1965 and remained generally silent during the subsequent repression of the Timorese.

But the similarities between South Korea and Indonesia should not blind us to their differences; neither the standard of living nor the sophisticated industrialization of South Korea has been reproduced in Indonesia. And while South Korea's military rulers of the 1970s and 1980s were, from the mid-1990s, regularly seen as penitents in chains, stoically awaiting long prison sentences, the ruling families of Indonesia, still ruling with an iron fist, thus far remain exempt from prosecution.

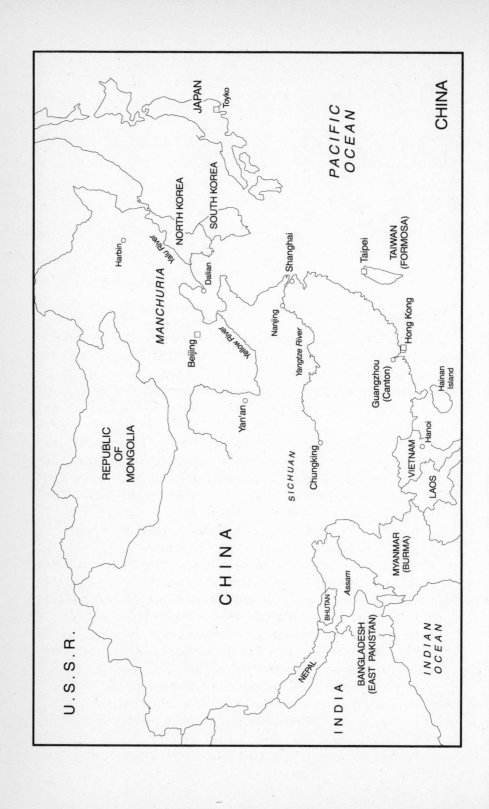

# Chapter 8

# China

## Background

In 1912 the last Manchu emperor of China handed over power to the first republican president, Sun Yat-sen (1866-1925). The founding father of republican China was a nationalist, modernizer, and democrat. His party, the Guomindang (GMD), or Nationalist Party, represented the interests of China's westernizing bourgeoisie, which, having grown up mainly on the South China coast, aspired to create a country that was united, modern, and capitalist. Most westerners wanted the same for China, although many sought to perpetuate their own influence in the country. The Americans, for instance, wanted a China tinctured with Protestantism, devoted to progress, and tied via the Pacific to U.S. commercial interests. The Japanese had only slightly different ambitions.

From the 1860s China's leaders had sought to defend China against foreign demands by means of a state-directed military modernization. The "Self-Strengthening Movement" of the latter part of the 19th century was a modernizing reform movement organized by officials of the state and aimed at establishing arsenals and shipyards that would produce the guns and ships that would defend China against outsiders. Originally guided by imperial officials, the movement was taken over in the republican period by China's nascent bourgeoisie, which was bent on its own version of economic modernization. The GMD was their party. The golden age of this bourgeoisie, that is, their greatest period of economic expansion and political power, was in the second and third decades of the 20th century. After that, as China once again became divided, it became painfully evident that the "nationalist revolution," the revolution in which industrialists and merchants sought to lead China through both an economic revolution and a political revolution, had failed.

"A whole generation of politicians and intellectuals—and not only within the Guomindang—was influenced by Japan's decision to modernize half a century earlier and was convinced that China's future also depended on its ability to 'modernize,' to model itself on the West, which meant adopting free capitalist enterprise, parliamentary democracy, and intellectual liberalism. From 1921 to 1929, this 'Western path' proved to be impracticable," concluded three French historians writing in the late 1970s. Over a decade later Jonathan Spence echoed the same conclusion when he wrote that after seizing power the Chinese Communists adopted the Soviet model for economic development "after the failure of Guomindang attempts at reform along Western lines."[1]

After a turbulent and largely unsuccessful period of trying to unify a China divided by warlordism, Sun died in 1925. His successor, Chiang Kai-shek (1888-1975), was also a nationalist, an anti-imperialist, and a modernizer, but rather than being a democrat he was a military dictator. Superficially, at least, one might see his resemblance to Reza Shah of Iran. Both were modernizing militarists, but neither could compare to Mustafa Kemal in either legitimacy or effectiveness. Chiang had studied in military schools in China and Japan, and had also been sent to the Soviet Union to study military techniques. He believed, in his own words, "that to be in the army is the highest experience of human existence as well as the highest form of revolutionary activity." Chiang had other experiences as well; in Shanghai he had been connected to the underworld and worked on the stock exchange, although accounts differ as to whether he was a broker or merely a clerk. More importantly, he was married to the daughter of a Bible salesman, Charlie Song, whose other daughters had married Sun Yat-sen and a major financier.

Facing the Nationalists was the Chinese Communist Party (CCP), born in 1920 in the wake of the great protest movement of 1919 known as the "May Fourth Movement." Inspired by the Bolshevik Revolution, the Chinese Communists also sought a modern and secure future for China, but one that was socialist rather than capitalist. Chiang had allied with the Communists in a common front against regional warlords in the early 1920s, but, fearing the militancy of China's young working class and the demands of a dissatisfied peasantry to whom Communist appeals were directed, he turned on them in 1927, massacring them in Shanghai and in other cities and towns where their numbers had grown formidably. For the next 22 years a civil war was fought across China, sometimes raging with great ferocity, other times burning more slowly. The Communists, outmanned and outgunned, were forced to retreat from the cities into the countryside, establishing their main base after 1935 in the caves of isolated and impoverished Yan'an in north China. There, in the second half of the 1930s, Mao Zedong (1893-1976) rose to pre-eminence. Whereas other communist leaders, following the Soviet example, had placed their faith in urban workers, Mao had discovered the revolutionary potential of the peasants. He compared them to "a tornado or tempest, a force so extraordinarily swift and violent that no power, however great, will be able to suppress it."

Although they were enemies, the leaders of the GMD and CCP had a common aim: the unity and rejuvenation of China and its liberation from both Western and Japanese imperialism. The interests of the two imperialisms were similar but not identical. Leaders in Western countries such as Britain, France, Germany, and the United States, interested in "free trade imperialism," saw China as a potential market and a cheap source of labour. To this end, they had established enclaves on the Chinese coast and forced Peking (now Beijing) to give them rights to conduct trade and establish their missionaries in the interior. Japanese interests were more conventionally colonial. The imperial party in Tokyo wanted direct, even if partial, control over China. After the Sino-Japanese war at the beginning of the 20th century Japan had taken possession of Formosa (later called "Taiwan"). Some Japanese leaders envisioned a united Asia under Japanese domination forming a bulwark against the West.

## Republican China at War, 1931-45

In September 1931 Japanese forces invaded the Chinese region of Manchuria, moving across the Yalu River from Korea, which they had occupied since 1910. A year later actual annexation took place, with Tokyo turning Manchuria into a puppet state called "Manchukuo." The seizure of this territory was the precursor of World War II in East Asia, a war that was to last until August 1945. It was the first step towards the fulfilment of a Japanese "mission," nurtured by intellectuals and politicians since the end of the 19th century, to spread "Japanese civilization and ways to every corner of the world." From these dreams emerged the idea of the Greater East Asian Co-Prosperity Sphere, "in which China and Japan, under Japan's vigorous and martial leadership, would claim their rightful place in the world, even if it took war to persuade China of the correctness of this course."[2]

Not satisfied with the massive acquisition of Manchuria, over the years 1933-35 the Japanese launched a two-pronged attack against Shanghai and into the adjacent provinces. The armies of Chiang's Nationalists and those of the warlords allied to them offered only limited opposition. Chiang's tactic was called "trading space for time." He hoped to preserve enough of his armies to survive the Japanese invasion and later smash the Communists as he had done once before.

As the Japanese advanced southwards, Chiang's government abandoned its capital at Nanjing and retreated to Chongqing, a remote and backward city on the Yangtze River in the south-central interior, in Sichuan. By 1938 almost all of China's major economic assets were in Japanese hands: the great ports, the industrial and commercial centres, and the richest and most populous parts of the country. Chiang's dream of re-establishing a powerful and united nation went up with the smoke that rose from China's devastated cities as the Japanese assault continued.

At the beginning of the war with Japan, Communist forces numbered a mere 30,000 men. These soon increased, reaching half a million by 1940 and over 900,000 by early 1945. The population of the Yan'an region under Communist rule numbered between 25 and 44 million, expanding and contracting depending on the Communists' capacity to resist Japanese pressure. There were Communist bases elsewhere in China as well, particularly in the south of the country, some beyond Japanese lines and others behind them.

From the late 1930s, then, China was divided into three parts, with the Japanese holding Manchuria and the eastern coastlands, the Communists holed up in Yan'an, and the Nationalists in Sichuan in the interior. Chiang and his generals waited in the hope that the Western allies would defeat the Japanese. As military leaders they were unimpressive. In the assessment of the U.S. Joint Chiefs of Staff: "We feel that, at most, not more than one-fifth of the Chinese Army is capable of sustained defensive operations."[3] The Chinese troops, conscripts who were often at the point of starvation, were generally enervated and frequently sought to save themselves by mass desertion. But Chiang was right about one thing: once the United States had entered the war, Japan would ultimately be defeated. This defeat, Chiang and his cronies hoped, would leave him free to pursue his war to extinction against the Communists.

From late 1937, a month after the Sino-Japanese war had begun, the CCP had agreed to postpone its struggle against the Nationalists in the interests of establishing a united front against the Japanese enemy. An uneasy alliance was thus forged between the governments of Chongqing and Yan'an. In theory this alliance remained in force throughout the war, although in reality it began to come unstuck in 1939 and broke down entirely in January 1942, when Chiang's forces attacked and inflicted heavy casualties on the poorly armed Communist New Fourth Army in central China. From 1942 on, Communist activities were completely banned in Nationalist areas, and Communists were arrested and often killed when discovered. Chiang maintained between 150,000 and 500,000 men to blockade the Communists in their stronghold in the northwest, men who might otherwise have been deployed in fighting the Japanese.

The tenacity with which Chiang held on, and thus occupied around 40 per cent of all Japanese military forces, was rewarded by his Western allies. At the Cairo conference in November 1943, where he met with Churchill and Roosevelt, "Generalissimo" Chiang Kai-shek, despite Churchill's scepticism, was elevated to membership in the "Big Four"—the prospective leaders of the postwar world. It was agreed at Cairo that the "unequal treaties" of the 19th century, the treaties that allowed foreigners special rights in China, would be annulled, and that Taiwan and the Pengpu islands should revert to Chinese sovereignty. Neither Hong Kong nor Macao were to be surrendered, however, nor was there any suggestion that Western capitalism in cities like Shanghai or Canton would have anything but a secure future.

In September 1944 Republican China took its seat at the conference at Dumbarton Oaks at which the outline for the founding of the United Nations was sketched; China was to be given a permanent seat on the Security Council, alongside its three "Big Four" partners, the United States, the Soviet Union, and Britain. It is apparent that Washington (if not London) placed a good deal of faith in a renascent China, one that would include Manchuria and be resolutely anti-communist. None of the Great Powers, not even the Soviet Union, anticipated that within five years of the surrender of Japan the reborn China would become the world's most populous communist state.

By 1944 political discontent was rife everywhere behind Nationalist lines. After a famine in the winter of 1942-43 in which two to three million people had died, rural resentment mounted. Militarily, the incompetence and corruption of both the Chongqing government and its officers in the field were exposed. Winston Churchill thought that the inclusion of China as one of the "Big Four" was "an absolute farce." China was not invited to the Yalta Conference in February 1945—even though it was the Yalta meeting that would decide that the Soviet Union should enter the war in Asia within three months of Germany's surrender. In return for attacking Japan, the Soviet Union would be allowed to re-annex the southern part of the Sakhalin Peninsula and the Kurile Islands, which it had lost in the Russo-Japanese war; lease the naval base at Lushun; return to the internationalized city of Dalian (Darien), and have "pre-eminent interest" in the railways of Manchuria. Not only were the Chinese unaware of this agreement but, apart from Roosevelt himself and Harriman, the U.S.

ambassador to the Soviet Union, most other members of the U.S. government were in the dark about it.[4]

By late 1944 strong oppositional currents were at work within China and even within the GMD. By the time of the GMD Sixth Party Congress in May 1945, elements in the party denounced the pervasive corruption, opportunism, inefficiency, disregard for public welfare, and decline of morale in party, government, and army. There was talk of removing Chiang.

The Seventh Congress of the CCP was held from April 23 to June 11, at the same time as the Sixth Congress of the GMD, which it intended to eclipse. Most significantly, it was held at the very dawning of the postwar world—in the narrow crack of time between the defeat of the Third Reich and the surrender of Japan; and the Congress anointed Mao Zedong as undisputed leader of the CCP and elevated "Mao Zedong Thought" to the status of the guiding ideology of Chinese communism.* Political power was increasingly centralized in his person, and references to the Soviet Union and, indeed, the international revolutionary movement were dropped. The Congress pledged to continue the work of establishing popularly elected coalition governments throughout the liberated territory. In a report called "On Coalition Government" presented to the Congress, Mao proposed the creation of a common-front government based on an alliance of workers, peasants, and the national bourgeoisie. The "comprador" bourgeoisie, that is, Chinese capitalists working for foreigners, was condemned; it would have no place in the new China. Private national capitalism was therefore to be protected and encouraged, at least into the undefined future when, following the logic of the Marxist scheme of historical development, it would be replaced by socialism.†

Since it had been invaded by Germany in June 1940 the Soviet Union understandably had shown only a limited interest in events on the other side of the continent. Then, on August 8, 1945, less than a week before Tokyo capitulated and in accordance with its undertakings at Yalta, the Soviets declared war on Japan. With breathtaking speed, Soviet forces overran all of Manchuria and North Korea. By August 19 the soldiers of the two Red armies, Soviet and Chinese, had linked up.

---

\* David Goodman describes "Mao Zedong Thought," also known as "Marxism-Leninism-Mao Zedong Thought," the official ideology of the CCP, as "the codification by Mao of Marxism-Leninism as applied to Chinese conditions." Goodman makes the point that in its heart Mao Zedong Thought was highly nationalistic. See Goodman, *Deng Xiaoping and the Chinese Revolution*, 1994, p.55.

† The Chinese Communists recognized four classes as being on their side: the national and petty bourgeoisies (which included the liberal professionals), workers, and peasants. All of these classes are represented as small stars on the Chinese flag, beneath a larger star that represents the Communist Party.

## The Chinese Civil War, 1945-49

Even with the defeat of the Japanese, the Chinese Communists had a difficult road ahead of them. However corrupt his government and incompetent his generals, in August 1945 Chiang could claim authority over all the
country's major cities, its entire industrial base, and most of its population.
His armies numbered over 2.5 million men, more than double those of the
Communist forces. They were materially superior in every respect. It is
no wonder that at the end of the war both Washington and Moscow placed
their bets on the Nationalists; every precedent told them that modern
weapons plus large armies were unbeatable, especially when confronted
by poorly armed peasants. China, a poll at Princeton University in 1944
disclosed, was regarded as second only to Canada as a trustworthy peacetime ally. And why not? U.S. advisors were everywhere in Nationalist
China, in the army, in the government, and even at Chiang's elbow.

Joseph Stalin continued to acknowledge the Nationalists as the sole
responsible government of China and maintained that the Communists'
divisions should be dissolved into those of the Nationalists. The Communists themselves quite reasonably regarded this as a recipe for suicide.

On August 28, 1945, Mao Zedong and Zhou Enlai, his right-hand man
in the area of foreign affairs, together with a representative of President
Roosevelt, flew from the Communist capital, Yan'an, to Chongqing to discuss the future of China with Chiang Kai-shek. The Communists made it
clear that they expected the GMD to abandon one-party rule and establish
a National Assembly. The Nationalists basically agreed. In the meantime,
Chiang insisted, the Communists should hand over the administration of
the areas they ruled. Mao and Zhou stalled.

The Americans had given Chiang the task of accepting the Japanese
surrender not only on mainland China but also on the island of Taiwan and
in the northern half of Vietnam. Chiang ordered the Japanese army commander in China to defend Japanese positions against the Communists
until his Nationalist troops arrived—even ordering him to attempt to
retake positions lost to the Communists earlier—which led to clashes
between the Japanese and the Communists after the official Japanese surrender. Despite their undertaking of non-intervention, the Americans also
did their best to help Chiang. They airlifted over 100,000 Nationalist soldiers to the cities of the north and northeast and sent over 50,000 U.S.
Marines for occupation duties until Chiang's forces could arrive. The U.S.
motives were transparent: "The long-term objective of the United States
was to encourage the development of a relatively strong and friendly
China capable of serving as a counterweight to the Soviet Union and open
to the penetration of American capital."[5] So U.S. policy was clear: peace

and support for a reformed government led by Chiang, and, if this proved unworkable, war and support for a reformed government led by Chiang.

In mid-November 1945 Chiang began to fight his way into Communist-controlled Manchuria with his U.S.-equipped units. From early January 1946, negotiations were begun in the ostensible hope that the conflict could be brought to an end. Wide-ranging agreements, including a cease-fire that was to last until June 30, were reached. Unfortunately, despite the widespread longing for peace among the Chinese people, there was no means to enforce the agreements; peace never had a chance. By March both sides were fighting again. The government offensive of July 1946 marks the official beginning of the civil war, which the Communists called the "Third Revolutionary Civil War."

U.S. supplies continued to flow to China. By late 1945 the Americans had delivered enough equipment to supply 39 of Chiang's divisions as well as build up his air force. In August 1946 the U.S. government handed over $900 million worth of aid, most of it military. The Americans took control of Chiang's finances and expanded his army, navy, and police. The United States secured trade agreements that made it China's major trading partner. But U.S. attempts to underwrite Chiang's government were undermined by two factors: the corrupt and inept leadership of the Generalissimo's governing clique; and the United States' own wavering between enforcing a power-sharing agreement between Chiang and the Communists and loading the GMD with enough arms to crush Mao's armies.

Throughout most of 1947, despite the frenetic and spiralling appeals of the U.S. China lobby (which mainly represented the interests of businessmen and the Protestant churches), the policy-makers in Washington became increasingly depressed and inert. Desperately, in 1948, when the Nationalist cause was all but lost, the U.S. government provided Chiang with a further $275 million in economic aid and $125 million in military aid. Truman's representative in China, General George Marshall, had hoped unrealistically that China's liberals would save the day: but they lacked the power to exercise a "controlling influence."[6] By 1948 both the national bourgeoisie and the liberal professionals in China had become opposed to Chiang's government and joined the workers and students who supported the CCP. Where communist ideology failed, spiralling inflation, due in large part to the incompetence and venality of the Chiang regime, had convinced them of the hopelessness of the Nationalist cause.

After Chiang had smashed Communist organizations in the towns—beginning with his massacre of workers in Shanghai in 1927—the Communists' power had shifted to the countryside, where much of the peasants faith in the Communists was based on the CCP's rural social and economic policies. At the centre of these policies was land reform, which to a large extent had been suspended during the war in the interests of a common front of all of the people, landlords as well as peasants, against the Japanese. But in early 1946 the program of land reform recommenced with a vengeance, taking the form of a broad frontal attack on a wide range of issues: rural landlord tyranny, poor wages, high taxes, corruption, and banditry, thieving, and lax morals. The objects of reform were material and political: more equitable distribution of land being the most important. The compact between the CCP and the peasants, particularly the poor peasants, would prove indestructible, at least until the disaster of the Great Leap Forward in 1957-59.

The attacks were not carried out by the Communist Party members so much as by the peasants themselves. In this way the peasants were educated in the question of landlord and rich peasant exploitation and became enrolled, or mobilized, in the struggle against those who oppressed them. Of course, the mobilization of the masses was liable to lead to excesses, but this was justified as a necessary side effect of a rural revolution that was without doubt highly popular among the peasants. An additional benefit was that the victorious struggle for land had led the peasants to join the armies of the CCP. These had been reorganized from July 1946 by Lin Biao as the "People's Liberation Army" (PLA). The Communists now possessed a conventional army rather than a guerrilla force.

In the first year of the civil war, from July 1946 to June 1947, the superior government forces seemed to carry all before them. With the exception of the industrial city of Harbin, they seized all the cities and towns in the northeast. The Communists remained on the defensive, melting before Chiang's troops and leaving the GMD armies the apparent victors. Like Chiang before them, they were trading space for time.

In autumn 1946 Mao Zedong and the commander of the Red Armies, Zhu De, outlined the strategies their forces would follow: concentration and annihilation. The enemy would be engaged with as strong a force and as much speed and mobility as possible where he was weakest, and then liquidated; his arms and even his soldiers would be absorbed by the PLA. The control of territory was not the goal. This strategy was remarkably successful. By the end of 1947 the Communists had secured control of most of China north of the Yellow River as well as important pockets in central China.

Until October 1947 Stalin played a waiting game. Soviet aid to the Chinese Communists had been minimal. Then Stalin decided to throw in his lot with Mao. According to a study based on recently opened Russian archives: "Soviet armies had captured a huge arsenal from the Japanese . . . in Manchuria, and up to this time the Soviet commanders had refused Chinese Communist overtures to acquire it. The material involved, including tanks and heavy artillery, was sufficient to equip 600,000 men. On instructions from Moscow, the Soviets transferred the arsenal to Mao's men."[7]

The People's Liberation Army was also equipped with excellent U.S. arms abandoned by the surrendering or fleeing forces of Chiang's generals. Indeed, whole armies and cities switched sides with amazing facility. By 1948, half the arms supplied by the Americans to Chiang were in Communist hands, giving Mao's forces the means of reoccupying the cities they had been driven out of two decades earlier. By this time Washington had all but given up hope for Chiang: Japan, it had been decided in late 1947, was to be the main U.S. counterweight to the Soviet Union in East Asia.

The last phase of the war was marked by three decisive campaigns fought between the early autumn of 1948 and the end of January 1949. On January 31, 1949, Peking fell. In the victory parade General Motors trucks pulled U.S. artillery through the streets. U.S. tanks followed U.S. armoured cars, and many of the luckiest Red Army soldiers rode in Jeeps and wore U.S. uniforms—all captured from Chiang's forces. On April 21 the Yangtze was forded on a 300-mile front, and all of south China lay in front of the Communists. In the same month Chiang abandoned his capital at Nanjing and was accompanied in his flight to Canton by a single foreign ambassador, that of the Soviet Union. Shanghai, at the mouth of the Yangtze and the greatest city in China, capitulated to the Communists on May 27, 1949. In October Canton fell, and by December Chiang had completely abandoned the mainland. Dean Acheson, Truman's secretary of state, provided a trenchant obituary for the armies of the Guomindang state: "The Nationalist armies did not have to be defeated; they disintegrated. History has proved again and again that a regime without faith in itself and an army without morale cannot survive the test of battle. . . . The Communist leaders have foresworn their Chinese heritage and have publicly announced their subservience to a foreign power, Russia."[8]

One of the leading figures in the broad-fronted and decisive campaigns of 1949 was Deng Xiaoping (b. 1904). Deng had been among the small group of students who lived in France in the 1920s and, like Zhou Enlai and Ho Chi Minh, joined the French Communist Party. A veteran of the struggles of the 1930s and a major figure in the war against Japan, in the coming years he was to become Mao's successor. After the fall of Peking, Deng remained in the southwest region of China, where he served as a kind of proconsul for the new state.

Since the spring of 1949, Chiang had been shipping government gold reserves, guarded by elite regiments of his army, out of Shanghai to Taiwan, the offshore island ruled and developed by the Japanese for half a century between 1895 and 1945. The GMD invasion of Taiwan was accompanied by the arrest and execution of thousands of Taiwanese who protested against the new occupation. By December 1949, with U.S. protection, Chiang's government had established itself securely; thus was born what the Western press, using its Portuguese name, called "Formosa"—a U.S.-supported outpost facing "Red China," under the control of the remnants of a government that the Americans themselves admitted had lost all credibility.

# The People's Republic, 1949-76

With most of Chiang's armies either smashed or decamped, on October 1, 1949, the birth of the People's Republic of China was declared. The announcement fell not quite at the mid-point in the cycle of communist victories in the 20th century: 32 years after the fall of St. Petersberg and 26 years before the fall of Saigon. Whatever else was to follow, one of the main objects of all of the three great Chinese leaders had been accomplished: the instability and insecurity of China had come to an end; and order, stability, and the promise of economic justice had arrived.

In the United States the "loss of China" was traumatic: "To have Free China become Communist seemed a national disaster," wrote John King Fairbanks.[9] President Truman was blamed for the crime of strategic negligence. Republican Senator Joseph McCarthy blamed the loss on communists and communist sympathizers in the State Department, which was duly purged of many of its most experienced officials. But even before the impact of "McCarthyism," the State Department itself, together with the same media that joined in the crucifixion of its officials, was propagating the idea of a global "Communist Empire" controlled from the Kremlin.

That there was some substance to the idea that Truman's loss was Stalin's gain was underlined by Mao's visit to the Soviet capital in December 1949, when the new Chinese state was barely two months old. Onlookers had not yet realized that considerable distrust existed between the Chinese and the Russian Communists. Moscow had, after all, supported the GMD and urged reconciliation upon the Chinese Communists, right up to 1947. Only the advance of the Cold War, and in particular the enunciation of the Truman Doctrine in the spring of 1947, persuaded Stalin that he should shift his support from Chiang to Mao.[10] Now Stalin saw Moscow as the capital of a communist world that included China.

Mao Zedong proclaimed himself Chairman of the new Chinese state under the banners of a "democratic coalition" that ostensibly included a range of political parties other than the CPP. But it was obvious where the power lay; all of the leading ministries were headed by Communists. In the government of the People's Republic, Zhou Enlai (1899-1976) became the foreign minister, Zhu De (1886-1976) the commander-in-chief of the armies, and Liu Shaoqi (1898-1969) vice-chairman. In 1954 Deng Xiaoping became successively secretary-general to the CCP Central Committee and, two years later, general secretary of the CCP.

The first priority of China's new government was rural reform. The Agrarian Reform Law of 1950 turned landless peasants into private land-holders. Military victory had ensured land redistribution throughout the country along the lines established in the previously liberated areas—at the expense of wealthy landowners, immense numbers of whom were arrested, tried, and executed. Collectivization was not undertaken for several years (until 1955-56) on the grounds that Chinese peasants might resist it. What the People's Republic did want was an agricultural surplus that could be used to fund industrialization. What it did not want was the kind of mass repression carried out against reluctant middle peasants (kulaks) that had marked Soviet history in the 1930s.

Although the government nationalized the commanding heights of the economy (banking, trade, railways, and heavy industry), it initially left many firms in private hands, praising their owners as members of the national bourgeoisie. Landless and powerless politically, they were no longer a threat. The "comprador" bourgeoisie was not tolerated. "Comprador," like "kulak," was a pejorative; in fact, it was often a death sentence.

With the model of rapid Soviet industrialization in mind, the Chinese Communists moved rapidly to reconstruct and strengthen the country's ravaged and backward economy. Their focus was the kind of heavy industry that would encourage both higher agricultural productivity and secondary industry—that is, the steel, coal, chemicals, and machinery that would produce the tractors and fertilizers that would make agriculture more productive. But the Communist regime had inherited an agriculture that produced only limited surpluses for the market and an industrial base that was almost defunct. Where could the surplus be found to invest in the heavy industry that would produce the industrial goods that would stimulate agricultural productivity? One answer was the Soviet Union: Soviet aid in the form of plant and technicians would allow the Chinese economy to take off.

## The First Five-Year Plan and Revolutionary Transformation, 1953-57

The damage done to China's economy by the civil war and the Korean War (1950-53) delayed long-term economic planning. When it did arrive, it was modelled on the five-year plans of the Soviet Union and seen as the means to a "transition to socialism." This approach entailed not only economic changes, particularly in the form of an emphasis on heavy, even giant, industry, but also social changes, including the rapid expansion of a proletariat and an elite class of state technocrats. The administrators who presided over this transformation included Liu Shaoqi and Deng Xiaoping.

On March 5, 1953, before the first plan was implemented, Joseph Stalin died. The formal and fraternal ties that existed between Peking and Moscow were emphasized in the state-controlled Hsinhua News Agency release of March 10, 1953: "Joseph Vissarionovich Stalin, the greatest genius of the present age, the great teacher of the world Communist movement . . . has departed from the world. . . . Comrade Stalin's contribution to our era through his theoretical and practical work is beyond our estimation. Comrade Stalin is representative of the whole of this new era of ours." It was a case, clearly, of formulaic lamentations and ostensible solidarity: at Stalin's funeral Zhou Enlai occupied a privileged spot in the midst of Stalin's Soviet successors (and not with other foreign mourners). Solidarity was repaid with material generosity; the five-year plan was carried out with the help of thousands of Soviet experts and Soviet materials. Mixed Soviet-Chinese companies were formed for mining and aviation. What doubt could there be in the outside world that the solid Red ice sheet that was already grinding down on the peoples from the Baltic to the South China Sea was on the move?

In general terms, measured by the increase of steel, coal, electricity, oil, cotton, grain, and even school graduates, the five-year plan was a success. The autarky of the backward regions was dissolved, and a national market expanded on the basis of both increased trade and the building of roads and railways. Agriculture, though, stagnated although agricultural surpluses were appropriated at artificially low prices as a means of financing industrial reconstruction. By the end of 1956, almost all peasants had been organized into co-operative units that pooled land, cattle, and tools. Unlike the process of collectivization in the Soviet Union in the 1930s, which was unpopular and saw millions killed by merciless Stalinist officials, the Chinese peasants collectivized quietly. Within three years the co-operatives had grown in size and were employing full-time administrators whose purpose was to ensure the procurement of cheap agricultural products to feed the urban population.

Under the first plan, then, rural areas were sacrificed on the altar of urban industrial growth. Also sacrificed was rural public health and welfare, which received little investment. Nevertheless, the adoption of simple measures of public hygiene combined with the cessation of wars led to rapid population growth. The 1953 census, the first taken using modern methods, revealed a population of 582.6 million. By 1957 the number reached 646.5 million. In a mere four years, China's population had *increased* by around 64 million. The increase alone was more than the population of the largest country in the Middle East or Africa or Latin America. Given both this rise in population and the catastrophes of the previous century, in 1957 there seemed little doubt that communism had benefited China's 646.5 million people.

Throughout the 1950s China's international prestige grew, especially in the Third World. China's relations with its neighbours—India, North Korea, and the Mongolian People's Republic—were good and getting better. Internationally, Zhou Enlai increased China's visibility by attending the Geneva conference in April 1954—a meeting convened to discuss détente in Asia and which continued on to fix the future of Indochina. The Chinese made an even greater splash with their participation at the 1955 Bandung conference. The presence of Zhou in Indonesia, a populous and rich Asian country with a large and well-organized Communist Party, did not pass unnoticed in the West. Yet international communist solidarity was already declining. In the Soviet Union, especially after the denunciation of Stalin by his successor Nikita Khrushchev in 1956, the idea of the continuing revolutionary transformation of society appeared to be passé; in China it did not.

The differences between the two countries became apparent in spring 1957. In the months before, Mao himself had encouraged China's intellectuals to speak out against political abuses. "Let a hundred flowers bloom, let a hundred schools of thought contend," Mao had said, and criticism of the party followed.[11] Would there be a softening of communism, as in the Soviet Union, or a liberalization as attempted in Hungary? No. Suddenly and viciously the party leaders, including Liu Shaoqi, Mao's heir apparent, and Secretary-General Deng Xiaoping, turned on the intellectuals, accusing them of being anti-revolutionaries. Abandoned by the party leadership, including Mao, the intellectuals found themselves exposed and defenceless, and a political massacre unprecedented in the postwar years followed. Jonathan Spence notes:

> By the end of the year, 300,000 intellectuals had been branded 'rightists', a label that effectively ruined their careers in China. Many were sent to labor camps or to jail, others to the countryside not just to experience life on the land for a year, but into what was essentially a punitive exile that might last

for life. . . . A whole generation of bright young party activists were similarly penalized, among them some of China's finest social scientists, scientists and economists.[12]

Although Spence mentions a figure of 300,000 victims, other sources suggest 400,000 to 700,000. Their punishments presaged those that would be inflicted later on the intellectuals in the Cultural Revolution.

Were they set up by Mao on the assumption that once they had identified themselves they could be destroyed? Jung Chang, in a popular anti-Mao memoir, says they were. Writers like Spence and Jean Chesneaux say not.[13] In any case, not surprisingly, the population in general seems to have gone along with their victimization.

## The Great Leap Forward, 1957-59

After the purges of the intellectuals came another revolutionary spasm. The Great Leap Forward was inspired by a dream of development: its proponents argued that China should seek to catch up with 150 years of Western progress in only 15. This dream was prompted by several specific considerations. Agricultural production was not keeping up with population increases, and militarily China appeared frighteningly vulnerable to the U.S. missiles positioned on Taiwan—weapons that could carry nuclear warheads. There was also a growing disenchantment with the Soviet Union, both its leadership and its models. Under Khrushchev the Soviet Union seemed to be moving away from socialism in dangerously revisionist directions. Finally, Mao was dismayed by what he regarded as the decline in revolutionary spirit among the Chinese people and the decline of party unity. So, in late 1957 a series of new projects, many of them involving immense amounts of human labour, were organized to mobilize the peasants. A new slogan was promoted: "More, faster, better, cheaper." The government introduced communes to replace co-operatives and abolished private property. The 50,000 communes, ranging in size from a few thousand to as many as 70,000 households, became the backbone of Chinese agriculture.

At first the results of this revolution in rural production seemed promising: in the summer of 1958 the government reported an unusually large harvest. An excited Mao Zedong gave a speech attributing this result to "the all-round, continuous leap forward in China's agricultural production and the ever-rising political consciousness of the 500 million peasants." Few in China's governing circle dared to try to awaken him from his utopian dream. One exception was the defence minister, Marshal Peng Dehuai. At a special Party conference held in June 1959, Peng Dehuai wrote Mao a personal letter criticizing the Great Leap. Although Peng was one of Mao's oldest and closest comrades, he was accused of forming a "rightist opportunist clique" and dismissed from his post, banished to obscurity. Peng's fate served as yet another powerful deterrent to those who might otherwise consider dissidence.

Stark reality ended the dream of a Great Leap Forward. The record harvest of 1958 was exposed as a bureaucratic fraud: the reported 375 million tons of grain had not been harvested; rather, perhaps as little as 215 million. China fell back to the earth, dazed. Worse than that, the enforced introduction of communes led to a devastating famine that swept China from 1959 to the early 1960s. Millions of peasants, many forced by state procurements to turn over the grain they needed for themselves and their families, died of starvation; estimates go as high as nearly 50 million, although a figure of just under 30 million seems more likely. (By comparison, according to a UN estimate, 9 million Chinese were killed in the Sino-Japanese war between 1937 and 1945, a figure that increases to 11-15 million if loss of life due to famine and other causes is included.)[14] At the height of the Great Leap Forward famine, state grain procurements reached 45.4 per cent of the total marketed grain crop; some 20 years later this figure was only 21.8 per cent.[15] According to one historian, the famine surpassed any other famine or natural disaster in China in the 20th century.[16] Another, Jasper Becker, argues that the famine "was entirely man-made"—a famine made by Mao. Agricultural production was not the only sector that plummeted: both heavy and light industry declined, heavy industry by a catastrophic 47 per cent in 1961 over 1960.[17]

Yet because the famine arose from political, not natural, causes, recovery, for those who survived it, was rapid. By 1964 output levels were back to pre-Great Leap levels. Nonetheless, as one argument puts it, the Great Famine turned China's peasants against collectivization and sowed the seeds of reform.[18]

By the early 1960s, the disenchantment of the Chinese leadership with the Soviet Union had become complete; the Sino-Soviet relationship, overtly fraternal, occasionally warm, although generally cautious, was now at an end. In 1960 the Soviet aid experts in China were called home, and the next year Peking attacked Khrushchev for "revisionism," which meant that he was inclined towards capitalism. From that point began a new epoch in Chinese history, one in which the Soviet Union played a generally antagonistic part.

## The Cultural Revolution, 1962-65

In the period 1962-65 the underlying tensions between the two poles within the CCP broke the surface. The right had encouraged what amounted to petty capitalism, that is, a greater role for the market and individualism, seeing an increased role for the technocrats (especially economists and planners) in running the country. The left wanted to extirpate capitalism and individualism, and thus "revisionism," and demanded that power be held in the hands of the people (or rather in the hands of the increasingly elderly party functionaries, who regarded themselves as the representatives of the people). The struggle was complicated by personal ambition and metaphysical nuance.

Although recent writing on China may have exaggerated personal rivalries, it is as well to consider them in broad terms. On the one hand was the ambition of an aging Mao Zedong himself. After the disaster of the Great Leap, Mao had retired to the political sidelines. He claimed that the Chinese revolution was being corrupted by policy conservatism and bureaucratic inertia, with certain elements within the party "taking the capitalist road." These elements were being tolerated, if not supported, by his old comrades-in-arms—Liu Shaoqi, the vice-chairman, and Deng Xiaoping, general secretary, in particular. Deng Xiaoping had said: "As long as we increase production, we can even revert to individual enterprise; it hardly matters whether a good cat is black or white—as long as it catches mice, it is a good cat." This homely metaphor, coined as a pragmatist's attempt to put economic planning ahead of political rectitude in the shadow of the Great Leap disaster, was to be associated with Deng for the next three decades.

At a party congress in September 1962, Mao issued his battle cry, "Never forget class struggle!" but the battle was not joined until three years later. On Mao's side was the ambitious Lin Biao (1907-71), who had become the defence minister in 1959 when Peng Dehuai was purged for criticizing the Great Leap Forward. Through the promotion of the cult of Mao's personality within the People's Liberation Army, Lin Biao had placed himself as a faithful servant on Mao's right hand. A second Mao ally was his third wife, Jiang Qing, who had hitherto kept out of the political limelight. An actress who had become disturbed by the conservatism of Chinese theatre, her agenda was centred on cultural cleansing. She was soon to become a leading figure of the Cultural Revolution Authority, which became the revolutionary inquisitional bureaucracy. Unmatched in hysterical incantations, Jiang Qing's group claimed that China was still "under the dictatorship of a sinister anti-Party and anti-Socialist line which is diametrically opposed to Chairman Mao's thought. This sinister line is a combination of bourgeois ideas on literature and art [and] modern revisionist ideas on literature and art."[19]

The struggle between left and right grew more intense through 1964 and 1965. Both sides accepted that there had been backsliding. The return of capitalist commercial relations was reported, with an example being the selling of poultry and produce on the open market. The peasants, it seemed, had grown disillusioned with socialist values. But there was disagreement as to what was to be done: whether to permit a slight expansion of capitalism or exorcise it by revolutionary renewal. The old solidarities of the generation of the Long March and Yan'an unravelled further as former comrades took one side or another. Two poles gradually emerged, both being interpretations of the essential nature of revolution and socialism. At the highest level these were represented by Mao on the one hand and Liu on the other, with Deng Xiaoping leaning towards Liu and Lin Biao towards Mao.

Mao opposed Liu's insistence on using the party to discipline those who did not conform to authority. He thought that existing authority tended to favour bureaucratism and the status quo. The ordinary people, the "masses," Mao said, should be openly involved, as they had been in the attacks on the landlords in the Yan'an period. In the People's Liberation Army, support for Mao's view was disseminated through the use of the *Little Red Book* (officially known as *Quotations of Chairman Mao*), the catechism with a red plastic cover that Lin Biao had used to propagate Mao's basic ideas. This book of catchy revolutionary invocations became the ultimate authority for the struggle that followed. Lin Biao, on his way to becoming one of the greatest political salesmen of the century, claimed that Mao was "our great teacher, great leader, great supreme commander and great helmsman." Soon these affirmations were on a hundred million lips.

After several years of sparring, the "Great Proletarian Cultural Revolution" was launched. It began, the official histories say, on November 10, 1965, and convulsed China for the rest of the decade. The Chinese themselves referred to it as "China's Second Revolution." Within the next three years almost all of the country's political structures and practices had been affected by the struggle between two interpretations of Chinese communism. The main vigilantes of the Cultural Revolution were the self-elected "Red Guards," young workers and students who, throughout the country, verbally and physically attacked all those whom they deemed to be political conservatives ("advocates of the bourgeois line"). As many as 10 million Red Guards were encouraged by Mao himself in a series of eight immense meetings held in Tiananmen Square from mid-August

1966. As a result of their attacks, which did not spare those in the ruling apparatus, for a period of two years public order in China was on a knife's edge. Not only did the left fight with the right, but leftists quarrelled with ultra-leftists with increasing violence. Party cadres, teachers, students: all became grist for the mill of this Chinese reformation. No one was spared, not Liu Shaoqi, not Deng Xiaoping, not their families. In some confrontations hundreds were killed. According to the journalist K.S. Karol, who a few years earlier had watched, admiringly, the rise to power of communism in Cuba, in April and May 1967 there were 133 armed battles with as many as 63,000 victims.[20] Attacks on the "Four Olds"—Old Customs, Old Habits, Old Culture, and Old Thinking—even led to assaults on property: old buildings, old temples, old art objects, and even old towns and villages were destroyed.

The Cultural Revolution peaked in January-February 1967, but as late as September of that year the fever was still so high that Mao, Lin Biao, and Zhou Enlai feared that increasing episodes of factional fighting might degenerate into a Hobbesian "war of all against all." It took until the second half of 1968, by which time the PLA itself had intervened against the Red Guards (under the banner of "Support the Left and Not the Factions") for the situation to stabilize. By spring 1969 the temperature of the "second revolution" was dropping. By that time Liu Shaoqi had become one of its victims, removed from the presidency of the People's Republic and expelled from the Communist Party. He died miserably in 1969, the year the faithful evangelist Lin Biao was anointed as Mao's successor. Deng Xiaoping was forced to leave Beijing in October 1969 and spent three years in exile under house arrest. His oldest son, Deng Pufang, was permanently paralysed after being defenestrated by the Red Guards.*

Within a couple of years the tide of counter-revolution had exhausted itself and annihilated the main force of the revolution itself: hundreds of thousands of Red Guards were exiled to the countryside.

How is this unprecedented convulsion in the most populous country in the world to be understood? The French Marxist historian Jean Chesneaux, not surprisingly, was in sympathy with its goals. Writing in the late 1970s he called it "an expression of the tensions and conflicts surrounding *the fundamental choice of a type of society*."[21] In this interpretation, the justifiable object of the Red Guards and their mentors, including Mao Zedong, was to block tendencies that would have led to the corruption of socialism, as had happened in the Soviet Union under Khrushchev. The journalist

---

* By the time of the Tiananmen massacre, Deng Pufang, known as the "crown prince," was said to have made a fortune as a profiteer. See Brook, *Quelling the People*, 1992, p.66.

Karol, who visited China in 1965 and again in 1971, and whose contributions to the left-wing French weekly *Nouvel Observateur* and the equally left-wing English *New Statesman* recounted the events of "the second Chinese revolution" with sympathy: "To my mind, it is a certainty that this movement did not take the name of revolution in vain. The tens of millions of Chinese who battled during those years were really putting their individual and collective fate at stake. Moreover, if the form taken by this ordeal was unexpected and baffling, the same cannot be said of the beliefs that impelled the leaders to unleash the storm."[22]

Other later writers have shown markedly less sympathy. From the vantage point of the early 1980s the Cultural Revolution was increasingly seen as an unmitigated disaster. In Immanuel C.Y Hsu's stern judgement: "Though in appearance an endeavour of noble idealism, the Cultural Revolution ushered in a decade of destruction and disorder. The party was decimated. Industry, agriculture, and science suffered severe losses. Disruption in education left a generation untrained."[23]

Later, swimming with the tide of denunciation of everything communist, the U.S. Pulitzer Prize-winning journalist Harrison Salisbury stressed the personal aspects of the Cultural Revolution, especially Mao's desperate attempt, as his vision became corrupted by age, to hold onto power.[24] Salisbury and others describe Mao's machinations against the background of the torments inflicted upon its victims: the humiliations, tortures, and executions; the shattering of China's education system; and the exhaustion imposed on the party and the army as millions of people were purged, interrogated, banished, "re-educated," and tormented.

Certainly the list of victims, even eminent victims, was long. It included Liu Shaoqi, author of *How to Be a Good Communist* and once considered to be Mao's successor to the leadership of the party. Liu was reviled, abused, and ultimately denied the medical attention he required. After a short interval, even the winners became losers: in less than two years after Liu's death Mao turned his back on his disciple Lin Biao. In an epilogue to the Cultural Revolution—in an event as sensational and bizarre as it was obscure—Lin and his family fled China in a jet that crashed in Mongolia on September 13, 1971, killing all. Lin Biao, who had anathematized Liu Shaoqi as "a traitor and a scab" in 1969, was himself denounced as a "renegade and traitor" by Premier Zhou Enlai in 1972. These personal fates seem to give credence to Spence's verdict that "the Great Proletarian Cultural Revolution showed that neither Mao nor the CCP seemed to know how or where the nation should be heading."[25]

In February 1972, and despite the torrents of rhetoric against capitalism that had flowed in the years of the Cultural Revolution, Mao received

President Richard Nixon in Beijing. It was an extraordinary meeting in which two doomed leaders, a president who had made his career as an anti-communist and a chairman who had just emerged from an ultra-communist reformation, signed protocols underwriting the status quo.

The effect of the Nixon visit was to underline Spence's suggestion that the Chinese leadership had lost its way. Even after the death of Liu Shaoqi, China's leaders continued taking shots at one another, often in a highly ritualized form. An attack on China's foreign minister, Zhou Enlai, who had been a major backer of the opening to the West, for instance, was implied in a criticism of western classical music, especially Beethoven and Schubert. The attack was led by a clique of four people, known as the "Gang of Four," who operated around the aging and increasingly with-drawn Mao. The leader of this gang was Jiang Qing, Mao's wife and the pillar of the disastrous Cultural Revolution, who with her cronies had won important leadership positions at the Tenth Party Congress in 1973. Deng was an immediate victim of this attack; he more or less disappeared from political life in the autumn of 1975.

Within a decade after the Cultural Revolution, the old order was coming to an end, due to natural causes. Mao Zedong's last public appearance was in 1973, at the Tenth Party Congress. He died in September 1976, aged 82, just nine months after Zhou Enlai (and a year after Chiang Kai-shek). With the demise of Mao, Zhou, and Chiang, and before them, Liu and Lin, a generation that had risen in the wake of the great political uprising of 1919, and that had steered Chinese history for over half a century, had passed.

In 1975, a year before he died, Mao expressed his thoughts in a poem to Zhou Enlai, whom he knew was also dying:

> Loyal parents who sacrificed so much for the nation never feared the
> ultimate fate.
> Now that the country has become Red, who will be its guardians?
> Our mission unfinished, may take a thousand years.
> The struggle tires us, and our hair is grey.
> You and I, old friend, can we just watch our efforts being washed
> away?[26]

## Judgements

The assessments that followed immediately after Mao's death were generally sympathetic, in part because the late 1970s, in the West, was not yet a time for the settling of scores with communism. Thus Edward Friedman: "Mao Tse-tung actually was one of the greatest political innovators in human history."[27] Maurice Meisner, writing a full decade after Mao's death, provided an even more considered eulogy, but one hardly less sympathetic:

> The legacy that Mao Tse-tung bequeathed to his successors was thus a most ambiguous and contradictory one, for it was marked by a deep incongruity between its progressive socioeconomic accomplishments and its retrogressive political characteristics. On the one hand, Mao "created a nation" . . . fulfilling in the early years of the new regime many of the unfinished tasks of China's abortive bourgeois revolution. The Maoist era also established many of the preconditions for socialism: the beginning of China's modern industrial revolution; the abolition of private ownership of the means of production, a necessary if not sufficient condition for socialism; and the retention . . . of a vital socialist vision of the future. On the other hand, Maoism retained essentially Stalinist methods of bureaucratic political rule; generated its own cults, orthodoxies, and dogmas; and consistently suppressed all forms of intellectual and political dissent. Mao, to be sure, regarded the bureaucracy he created as a great evil, but the only remedy he could devise to restrain his own creation was to rely on his personal prestige and the force of his own personality. Neither in theory nor in practice does the Maoist legacy include institutional safeguards against bureaucratic dominance.
>
> Thus at the end of the Mao era China resided in that misty historical realm of socioeconomic orders that are neither capitalist nor socialist. . . . Maoist China was not capitalist because it had abolished the essential condition of capitalism—private property and private ownership of the means of production. It was not genuinely socialist because the masses of producers were denied the means to control the products of their labor, nor did they have the means to control the state, which increasingly stood above them as both the economic and the political manager of society. If the Maoist regime was by and large successful in carrying out the "bourgeois" phase of the revolution, it proved incapable of achieving the proclaimed "transition to socialism."[28]

Finally, the verdict of Eric Hobsbawm:

> However much we may be shocked by the record of the twenty Maoist years, a record combining mass inhumanity and obscurantism with the surrealist absurdities of the claims made on behalf of the divine leader's thoughts, we should not allow ourselves to forget that, by the standards of the poverty-stricken Third World, the Chinese people were doing well. At the end of the Mao period the average Chinese food consumption (in calories) ranked just above the median of all countries, above fourteen countries

in the Americas, thirty-eight in Africa, and just about in the middle of the Asian ones. . . . The average expectation of life at birth rose from thirty-five years in 1949 to sixty-eight in 1982, mainly owing to a dramatic and—except for the famine years—continuous fall in the mortality rate.[29]

There was, then, tangible improvement in the lives of the Chinese people after the revolution. The question remains: was this because of the policies of Mao Zedong or in spite of them?

# Reform and Modernization in the Epoch of Deng Xiaoping, 1976-95

Mao's successor as guardian of the nation and chairman of the Chinese Communist Party, Hua Kuo-feng, was a sixth-ranking vice-premier who owed his rise to power largely to the Cultural Revolution. Handpicked by Mao, primarily to block Deng, Hua was a party hack—grey, opportunistic, and inept, the creature of more powerful interests, and elected to hold the ring long enough to allow for a realignment of power. These interests were those behind the Gang of Four on the one hand, and the senior political cadres and military leaders who detested, and while Mao was alive at least, feared the Gang of Four, on the other.

At first Hua went to great lengths to establish his credentials as a Maoist. Then gradually he replaced the more rigid policies of Mao's later years with a more liberal cultural policy, which included arresting the Gang of Four by means of a pre-emptive strike. This broke the back of the ultra-left opposition and ended their monopoly of power in the cultural sphere. In December 1976, members of the Gang were arrested and indicted for forming an "anti-party clique." Their crimes included treason. Their downfall marked the end of Maoism.

Up to this point, Hua was still wading in the political shallows. After cultural policy came the slightly deeper water of educational policy; the universities and research institutes that had been the victims of Mao's cultural revolution were revived in the form in which they had existed in the 1950s. But then Hua went still deeper. Above all he sought to leave his mark as an economic modernizer. In February 1978 he introduced his "Four Modernizations," which laid the plans for massive investment in heavy industry, energy production, and infrastructure. But this ambitious project was his undoing; China did not have the means to invest the huge sums needed to finance Hua's projects, and Hua's credibility dribbled away as the projects were gradually abandoned.

As Hua's power ebbed, the prospects of Deng Xiaoping rose. Deng was the last of the original generation of communists, and like others of that generation, he bore the scars of half a century of political battles. In particular, and in contrast to Hua, he was marked by the purges of the Cultural Revolution. Many of his supporters—other victimized party cadres and intellectuals (known as the "rehabilitated cadres faction") as well as the tens of thousands of former Red Guards once deported to the countryside—identified him as the man to right the wrongs and remove the obloquy from which they had suffered. Other supporters were economic liberals, that is, reformers who advocated economic and especially rural reform. Maoist development strategy, they thought, had worked for the ten great years, 1949-59, but had since broken down with catastrophic results. The Great Leap Forward (1958-60), in their eyes, was not only the grave digger of tens of millions of peasants but also of China's socialist agrarian policies. Some two decades after the Great Leap, China's leaders were forced to acknowledge that 100 million peasants still did not have enough grain to eat.[30]

Hua failed in efforts to keep Deng out of power by implicating him in nefarious political activities, and a rehabilitated Deng soon made his way to the top, along the way displacing Hua's supporters, the Maoist rump, in favour of his own allies. By the end of the Third Plenum of the Party's Eleventh Central Committee, which met December 18-22, 1978, Deng had achieved dominance and Hua was supreme in name only. Hua's policies were eclipsed by those of Deng, who launched a program of "socialist modernization" that placed a ban on struggles of the "mass" variety. Thus there would be no more struggles within the revolution.

That same Third Plenum gave the political sanction to reconcile China's socialist planning with the market. According to conventional political wisdom, these meetings first kindled the beacon that illuminated China's economic liberalization. Another interpretation offers that economic liberalization had already begun, illicitly to be sure, in the countryside as early as the end of the 1950s, and that by 1978 it was well under way.[31] For the next decade it would lurch forward, out of the control of China's rulers.

The month after the rehabilitation of the market had been announced, in January 1979, diplomatic relations with the United States were established. Deng, whose political dominance in China continued to be secured as more and more of his rivals were dropped from leadership positions, capitalized on this new connection in a triumphant tour of the United States. Coincidental with this rapprochement with the United States was China's invasion of northern Vietnam on February 17, 1979. Although the military campaign was a disaster, it helped secure the relationship between Beijing and Washington. In 1979 Deng became *Time* magazine's "Man of the Year."

In June 1981 Hua resigned as chairman of the CCP, and within a year he had almost vanished politically. Deng's Maoist rivals had also been dispersed. Deng was now on top. To signal his triumph, a program of revision of the reputation of Mao was begun under the abstract heading of a critique of "ultra-leftism" and in the concrete form of the show trial of the "Gang of Four," which began in November 1980. Although most systems of criminal justice exhibit signs of theatricality, the trial of the "Gang of Four" was more than theatre, it was a judicial Peking Opera. It raised but could not explicitly answer the question: how responsible was Mao Zedong himself for the disasters of the past? Deng and his comrades decided that they must not go all the way: Mao had made "mistakes," true enough, but his status as a revolutionary and a modernizer could not be seriously undermined without threatening the legitimacy of the entire system. Mao was thus spared the fate of Stalin.

After the Fifth Plenum of the Eleventh Central Committee (February 23-29, 1980), the official reversal of the economic policies associated with Maoism was in full flood. Premier Zhao Ziyang announced:

> In economic work, we must abandon once and for all the idea of self-sufficiency, which is characteristic of the national economy. All ideas and actions based on keeping our door closed to the outside world and sticking to conventions are wrong. . . . By linking our country with the world market, expanding foreign trade, importing advanced technology, utilizing foreign capital, and entering into different forms of international economic and technological cooperation, we can use our strong points to make up for our weak points.[32]

In essence, the strategy of export-led development called the "Taiwan model," which had previously been adopted by Japan and the rapidly growing capitalist economies of Pacific Asia, was now being embraced by the People's Republic. Many in Taipei, the capital of Taiwan, must have gloated.

One of the first changes was the increased toleration for ownership of private plots of land. Although peasants were already pushing this ahead illegally, from an official point of view this and other changes were carried out uncertainly, for the reformers were still some way from acknowledging the incorporation of capitalist models for China and therefore had to conceal change under a cloak of Marxist economic jargon. Then, with increasing confidence borne by an inexorable tide of peasant demand for change, the "free marketeers" began to jostle socialist planners to the edge of the stage. They were encouraged by the upward creep of living standards, as peasants gradually inundated the markets with their own produce, and pedlars and vendors became ubiquitous. By 1983 the commune system, the backbone of China's socialized economy, had broken down. In its place, although most land was still legally owned by the state, production and distribution of agricultural surpluses were left to the peasants themselves, generally working on family farms. Land could now be rented and labour hired. Even before this, state enterprises right across the board were given increased autonomy. Orville Schell states, "By the end of 1982, there were 2.63 million private industrial and commercial enterprises licensed in China, involving nearly 3.25 million people. . . . By the beginning of 1984 this figure had doubled, to 5.86 million private industrial and commercial enterprises, which were employing over 7.5 million Chinese."[33] By 1994, according to David Goodman: "The state sector of the economy only produced a little over half of the output value of industrial production, compared to close on 80 per cent in 1978."[34] Kate Xiao Zhou argues that the state sector had faded to an even greater degree, even earlier: "Central planning, the symbol of the socialist state, controlled only a little over 10 per cent of all industrial production by 1992."[35]

An "open door" policy cleared the way for an influx of foreign capital, while special economic zones and "open" cities attempted, with a good deal of success, to emulate the conditions existing in the advanced capitalist parts of East Asia, particularly Hong Kong. By the mid-1980s, three of China's four special economic zones, described by Richard Baum as "hyperactive enclaves of commercial laissez-faire" and plagued by "smuggling, profiteering, and currency manipulation," were in Guandong province, birthplace of Sun Yat-sen and ancestral homeland of China's attempted but unsuccessful bourgeois revolution.[36]

By the mid-1980s several developments that reflected this liberalization were evident. The gross value of agricultural output had increased at an annual rate of about 9 per cent since 1978. The grain harvest of 1984 was the largest in Chinese history. Living standards saw a continued improvement, and rural per capita income doubled in a five-year period. The rural gains came partly because the peasants' response to the incentive of the markets had led to a rise in output, but it was also partly due to a vast urban migration of peasants, which led to a building boom in both rural and urban areas, which in turn led to improved housing. Building was now in the hands of private firms, and peasants became construction workers. In the making was a rural bourgeoisie alongside rural agricultural workers and peasants, plus an urban bourgeoisie, involved in construction manufacturing, distribution, and transport, among other things, as well as an urban proletariat.

Inevitably, even "socialist modernization" (also known as "the semi-market economy") has a down side. While there was an increase in the value of the production of most agricultural commodities from oilseed to cotton, grain production, the centre of the agricultural economy, slumped, in large part at least because of government price controls. If these controls were removed, it was thought, and grain were to be sold at prices set by the market, the result would be spiralling inflation. A number of foreign observers issued warnings. To William Hinton, an agriculturalist who had been watching China since his first visit in 1937 and had written sympathetically on the Cultural Revolution, the consequences of liberalization for agriculture on the vast grasslands would be disastrous. Hinton predicted that overgrazing would lead to desiccation.[37] Other Western visitors noted extensive deforestation in some areas and the neglect of key public works, such as the irrigation system, much of which had been constructed in campaigns of mass mobilization in the 1950s. Similarly, others noted the breakdown of the public health system, one of the most undisputed successes of the revolution (which had led to average life expectancy increasing from 35 to 68 years): the proportion of the population with access to health care was reduced from 80-90 per cent in 1979 to 40-45 per cent in the mid-1980s. Maurice Meisner saw an even bleaker aspect of liberalization:

> The most disturbing long-term consequence of market reform has been the rapid growth of socioeconomic inequality in the countryside, raising the prospect of new class divisions and social conflict. As might have been anticipated, those better endowed and politically better placed have had far greater success in heeding the government's injunction to "get rich" . . . in a market-oriented rural economy. . . . Thus a new social class structure, albeit still in embryonic form, has emerged in the Chinese countryside: an elite group of successful entrepreneurs who own machinery or operate commercial and service enterprises, hire wage laborers, and accumulate capital in a diverse variety of private business endeavors; the great mass of peasants increasingly differentiated by income and function, and ranging from the relatively prosperous to the relatively impoverished; and a rural *lumpenproletariat* made up of wage laborers and semi-employed or unemployed youth, some of whom roam the countryside in criminal gangs.[38]

In 1984, 35 years after the founding of the People's Republic, the balance of payments, which had hitherto been healthy, began to fall into serious deficit. In the first six months of 1985 China's foreign exchange reserves dropped by more than one-third, the price of the purchase of 89,000 Toyotas, 16,000 vans, 2.9 million television sets, 252,000 videocassette recorders, and 122,000 motorcycles.[39] Inflation started to rise rapidly and continued to do so throughout the decade, and prices started to ascend steeply.

By 1985 criticism had begun to be voiced concerning the consequences of "socialist modernization." It came from several quarters. Two of the older cadres, Chen Yun and Peng Zhen, for instance, were critical of the substitution of liberalism for the planned economy. They were particularly concerned that the abolition of the policy of state procurement had led many peasants to abandon grain production. In reply to their uneasiness, Deng was adamant: reform must go ahead, there could be no turning back.

Other criticism came from the students as well as the political elite who had access to the press. One such member of the elite was Hu Yaobang (b. 1916), general secretary of the Communist Party from 1980 to January 1987, who was thought to be Deng's appointed successor. The problem that Hu and the reformers on his side raised was crime and corruption, which had become pandemic and had led to illegal currency dealings and the development of an immense black market. Perhaps as many as 100,000 motor vehicles a year were being smuggled into China, as well as tens of thousands of motor cycles, televisions, vcrs, and other expensive luxury commodities. Much of this was funnelled through the Special Economic Zone on Hainan, an island off the southern coast of Guandong. Senior government officials were deeply implicated; indeed, through illegal economic activities they and their progeny, who invariably remained immune from persecution, were constituting themselves as a new class. Many intellectuals, particularly economists, however, remained enchanted by Western economic theories, which they wanted to discuss more openly.

The most compelling question in the minds of the students was the question of human rights. Fang Lizhi, an astrophysicist and vice-president of the Chinese University of Science and Technology at Hefei, was in the vanguard in raising this question. He suggested to his students that the right to enjoy democracy was an inalienable one and that governments did not have the prerogative to bestow liberties on citizens; rather, citizens gave governments rights. "China cannot have economic development without democracy," he argued, which made him a hero in the eyes of students and a villain in the eyes of the conservative Party leaders.

Deng reacted promptly and bitterly, claiming that "bourgeois liberalization," of which he was, of course, the godfather, was a threat to stability. He claimed that it was an attempt to turn China towards capitalism. The right way for China, affirmed Deng, was the socialist way. Deng's answers did not satisfy the students, who by the end of 1986 were agitating for democracy on a regular basis. Reacting, Deng demanded the sacking of those on the Central Committee who were in favour of "bourgeois liberalism." He also increased his repression of the dissident students and forced the resignation of General Secretary Hu Yaobang. In her discussion of Hu, Merle Goldman describes him as being at the centre of China's "democratic elite."[40] Hu, blamed for not being firm enough, was sacked and disappeared temporarily from public view. He was replaced by Zhao Ziyang, who had also been a protégé of Mao Zedong.

By 1988 the party leadership was more distracted by inflation and a sagging economy than liberalization. Deng's solution, at first opposed by Zhao but supported by Li Peng (b. 1929), the premier-designate, was towards even greater liberalization.* The consequence was alarming. Economists began to talk of hyperinflation. Premier Li Peng felt obliged to admit that inflation was retarding the improvement of the living standard and in some places even lowering the standard of living. The Party was forced to step in and tighten fiscal and monetary policy; further liberalization was put on hold. Zhao, unfairly made the scapegoat for Deng, was removed from all control of economic policy. The students now renewed their campaign for human rights. Just as their campaign was warming up, Hu Yaobang died suddenly on April 15, 1989.

## A Dream of Democracy

The death of Hu Yaobang provided an opportunity for open dissent. Within hours of his death the "Beijing Spring" had begun; a day later, on April 16, 4,000 university students marched to Tiananmen Square in the centre of Beijing to place memorials proclaiming Hu the "Soul of China." Other banners carried the slogans "Long Live Democracy," "Long Live Freedom," "Down with Corruption," and "Down with Bureaucratism." On successive days ever larger numbers of students assembled in the square. By April 22, the day of Hu Yaobang's funeral, their numbers had increased to 100,000, and China's "Democracy Movement" was fully evident.

Deng's reaction to this increasing protest initially took the form of threats in the press. One notice complained of "an extremely small number of people with ulterior motives" who were opposed to "the leadership by the Communist Party and the socialist system."[41] This approach backfired: by the end of the month the crowds in the streets had continued to

---

* Li Peng, the son of a "revolutionary martyr," was adopted by Zhou Enlai and his wife, Deng Yingchao, in 1931.

increase. In mid-May, when another Communist modernizer, Mikhail Gorbachev, came to visit Beijing, the students exploited the opportunity to demonstrate their grievances. Large parts of the welcoming ceremony had to be called off because students had taken over Tiananmen Square. On May 17 a million people marched through Beijing in support of the students and their demands. Led by Li Peng, the party leaders, at first divided on how to handle the situation, finally opted for repression. They imposed martial law on May 20. On May 23 a million people marched to demand Li's resignation and the revocation of martial law. On June 2 unarmed troops were confronted as they tried to take up positions around Tiananmen Square, and the next day more troops were moved into Beijing. By this time the number of soldiers on the scene had reached at least 150,000. That evening armed troops backed up by armoured personnel carriers and tanks unleashed an attack on the demonstrators. By the following day, June 4, units of the People's Liberation Army had killed 2,000 to 3,000 unarmed people. "Down with Deng Xiaoping!" they had cried as they fled. In his testament to their persistence and valour, Tim Brook writes: "The night was over. So too was the Democracy Movement and everything the students and their supporters hoped to achieve. By taking the Square, the Army had crushed opposition to the Party. It had also shattered the minds of an entire city and an entire generation. The students trudged . . . to their campuses like people in a nightmare, some hysterical, most in tears, all dazed and exhausted. The dream was over. From now on, it would be the old story: intimidation, settling of scores, silence."[42]

Of those killed in early June, most were workers and clerks, fewer were students. Estimates range from 2,600 to 3,000 dead, 20,000 wounded, and up to 7,000 arrested in Beijing alone.[43] Goldman states: "Although the student and intellectual leaders were interrogated, subjected to arrest, deprived of their jobs, and put under surveillance, they were not executed as were scores of workers who had participated in the demonstration. . . . Most of those killed in the June 4 crackdown were workers or bystanders." Brook makes a similar point: "It was the workers who were the fodder for PLA guns, not the students."[44]

The clean-up in Tiananmen Square was followed by a witch hunt for those implicated in the protest movement, with many hundreds jailed. Of these, many workers, but no students, were eventually executed. According to Goldman: "If the June 4 crackdown revealed how little China's political system and leadership had changed over the decade, the demonstration itself revealed how much Chinese society had changed in the same period."[45]

The people of Beijing regarded Premier Li Peng as morally bankrupt, and he never became party secretary. The new secretary was Jiang Zemin, the dull and cautious mayor of Shanghai who was thereby put in the position of heir apparent to Deng. Zhao became yet another of Deng's victims, accused of trying to "split the party." After Deng instructed him to make a formal confession of error, Zhao defiantly refused. After that he was forced into the shadows. Deng referred to the Tiananmen protest as "the anti-party and anti-socialist turmoil." He congratulated the army for restoring "stability and order."

But the Communist Party was chastened by the protest; Deng himself even admitted that a major outbreak was almost an inevitable consequence of a growing disenchantment with corruption and inflation, especially on the part of youth. In the months after Tiananmen, the Chinese press shifted its focus from the arrest of dissident workers and students to the arrest of corrupt officials. The special shops for leading cadres were closed. There was a move against nepotism. There were even executions for economic crimes. At the Fourteenth Party Congress in October 1992, Jiang Zemin praised Deng as "the general architect of reform and opening up and of the modernization drive in relation to socialism in China." He said that it was the task of the Congress "to use comrade Deng Xiaoping's theory of building socialism with Chinese characteristics as a guide," to "quicken the pace of reform, opening up and modernization." Earlier Zhao Ziyang had spoken of a "socialist planned commodity economy." Now Jiang spoke of an attempt to build "a socialist market economic system."

After the Tiananmen massacre, economic reform languished briefly before being revived in late 1990. In December 1990 the Shanghai stock exchange opened, and by the end of the next year the Shanghai market listed 100,000 individual investors. In 1991 a securities exchange was opened in the Shenzhen Special Economic Zone. In February 1992 Deng went on a tour of the special economic zones in the south of China to assure the people there that making money was as glorious as ever. A month later, the *People's Daily* announced that "active and prosperous financial markets will bring the country innumerable benefits" and "a joint-stock economy can serve our socialist construction."

But, as Orville Schell and Todd Lappin comment, the rush to liberalize was not without hazards. Referring to the riots in Shenzhen in August 1992, which were stimulated by something close to a millennarian belief that possession of shares in newly listed companies on the stock market would provide access to quick riches, Schell and Lappin note that the "riots gave a hint of how ill-equipped China is to deal with the consequences of the reckless pace of economic reform that Deng has unleashed." Rather than being the hoped-for "providential cash cows that can be milked endlessly by investors and factory managers alike," China's new stock exchanges turned out to be "delicately balanced markets capable of sending devastating shock waves throughout the Chinese economy if not managed correctly." China's political system was still not equipped to deal reliably with periods of financial crisis. Indeed, according to Schell and Lappin, "The Chinese government is a faction-ridden snake pit of warring party leaders who range from neo-Maoist hardliners to Westernized liberals. In the absence of a stable political system, and a legal system that cannot be overridden by political considerations, resolution of conflict depends almost entirely on a 'big leader,' in this case Deng Xiaoping, now 88."[46]

In the future, Schell and Lappin predict, the chaos that surrounds China's "strangely eclectic economy" might provoke insecurity and upheaval and work to destabilize the political power of the centralized state. If that does not happen, then something else might: that is, inequality. While the growth rate in some of China's southern regions approaches 20 per cent, other parts of the country, as many as one in three Chinese counties, are becoming increasingly impoverished.

More recently, as Perry Link points out, in the poorest parts of the country as many as 50 million people cannot afford tea daily and are chronically short of drinking water. Yet these people, rural and disorganized, are not likely to be the problem. Unrest is more likely to come from those better off: the less poor peasants in the countryside and workers, teachers, and office workers in the cities and towns, people who have begun to suffer from wage cuts, rising inflation, and lack of security, especially with state enterprises being sold off to the private sector. "During 1993," according to Link, "peasant uprisings occurred in 20 of China's 29 provinces; in the same year industrial workers . . . staged more than 6000 illegal strikes and joined more than 200 riots."[47] While Western governments, transnational corporations, and business weeklies celebrate the "fastest growing market in the world" and applaud the government's "search for a stable economic policy," tight monetary control, and reform of state enterprises, more alarmist voices point to China's increasing trade deficit, inflation, and the likelihood of a "hard landing" for the economy in the very near future. And yet others, like Vaclav Smil, allude to the catastrophe that lies even further ahead when constant demographic growth intersects with the depletion of resources (land, water, and fuel)—all under the looming cloud of a degraded environment.[48]

# A Dead Religion

Whatever may come to pass, rumours of the demise of the influence of Mao Zedong do not seem to have been greatly exaggerated. Writing on December 26, 1993, Mao's one-hundredth birthday, Richard Baum concluded:

> Today, less than eighteen years after the Chairman's death, few traces of his quintessential zeitgeist remain. Maoism—the spartan, puritanical ethos fashioned by a tight-knit group of Chinese revolutionaries in the 1930s and 1940s—is moribund. Though "Marxism-Leninism-Mao Zedong Thought" remains the official state religion, it is a religion largely devoid of faith—and of faithful; its true believers, once a fearsome phalanx, have dwindled to a mere handful of senescent old men. In place of Mao's austere, colorless collectivism there has emerged a new, upscale, entrepreneurial ethos, euphemistically labelled "socialism with Chinese characteristics" by China's reform-minded senior patriarch, Deng Xiaoping. In Deng's China, to get rich is glorious, not treasonable.[49]

Earlier, Daniel Kelliher noted that the Communist Youth League, the main conduit that led peasant youth into party membership, "sank into miserable straits in the countryside. The head of ideology for the Youth League's official journal admitted in 1983 that 'in most rural areas the League has ceased to function.' "[50]

By 1995, while Deng Xiaoping had virtually vanished from public view, his successor had not emerged. But for whoever succeeds Deng—Jiang, president since 1993, or his main rival, Premier Li Peng, or perhaps some more shadowy figure—the way ahead seems fraught more with hazard than opportunity. Jonathan Mirsky, East Asia editor of *The Times* (London), states:

> Any leader faces serious problems. China's National Academy of Sciences recently predicted that it will take at least a century for the country to reach the economic levels of the developed world. The population is swelling despite the one-child-per-couple policy. . . . Grain production is rapidly dropping as farmers leave the land. More than 100 million ex-peasants roam the country looking for urban work, committing crimes and having uncounted babies. State employees in the cities are restive because of low wages. Crime and corruption soar, and an inflation rate on consumer goods of 25-40 percent impoverishes workers. Foreign investors are becoming disenchanted with the never-quite-appearing China miracle.[51]

In 1975 Mao Zedong had asked: "Now that the country has become Red, who will be its guardians?" In 1992 his sometime protégé, Deng Xiaoping, asked the same question: "As long as we, the older generation are still around . . . the hostile forces know that change cannot happen. But who can guarantee this once we old people pass away?"[52]

# Summary

China's history in the 20th century began and ended with the problem of modernization and order: communism was but one solution to this problem. From the Republic born in 1912 under the sign of capitalist development to the regime of the CCP buried in the 1990s to the laments of the Old Guard, the fault lines of contemporary Chinese history have been between autarky and nationalism on the one hand and liberalism and globalism on the other. Both Westernization and anti-Westernization have thus far each failed once, yet the problem remains.

For nearly half a century Mao Zedong presided over the triumph and ultimate decline of the regime of "Sinified Marxism." Under Mao the CCP first offered an alternative to the corrupt and incompetent regime of Chiang's Nationalist Party and then, with the defeat of Chiang, reorganized the state and economy to guarantee China's territorial integrity and security. The price of Mao's dictatorship was high. The consequences of the purges and revolutions after 1949 were dire: certainly millions, and perhaps tens of millions were killed either violently or silently. The mayhem of the Cultural Revolution, generally seen in its time as a necessary renewal of communism, guaranteed its antithesis, the rebirth of the very forces it had intended to extirpate: namely, Western-inspired democracy and its corollary, economic liberalism. Writing in mid-1994, and quoting Margaret Thatcher with favour, historian Immanuel Hsu pointed the way to the liberal and democratic future that lay ahead:

> Continued economic prosperity will give rise to a growing middle class in an emerging civil society, in which the new rich and powerful—the entrepreneurs, the bankers, the investors, the stockholders and the professionals—will demand greater political participation and the rule of law, popular elections, and a voice in legislation and budgetary decisions. Step-by-step the government will find it necessary to accommodate them, and eventually—perhaps early in the 21st century—a Chinese-style "restrained" democracy may emerge.[53]

Hsu's Whiggish prophecy, with "democracy" replacing Protestantism, bears a remarkable resemblance to the U.S. blueprint for the redemption of China as sketched out at the beginning of the 20th century—except that capitalists, not Christians, now seem to have received the mandate to lead

China into the future. Many writers, like Mirsky, Smil, Link, Schell, and Lappin, seem to interpret its chances of success as being no greater than they were over 80 years ago, while the IMF predicts that China's economic growth rate will continue at a rate sufficient for the country to maintain itself as the world's third largest economy. Yet, Brook states, "China's predicament [is] as a poor country in an international environment dominated by the developed capitalist world. In the end, the issue is not Communism. It is imperialism: the economic subordination of the underdeveloped world by the developed capitalist world."[54]

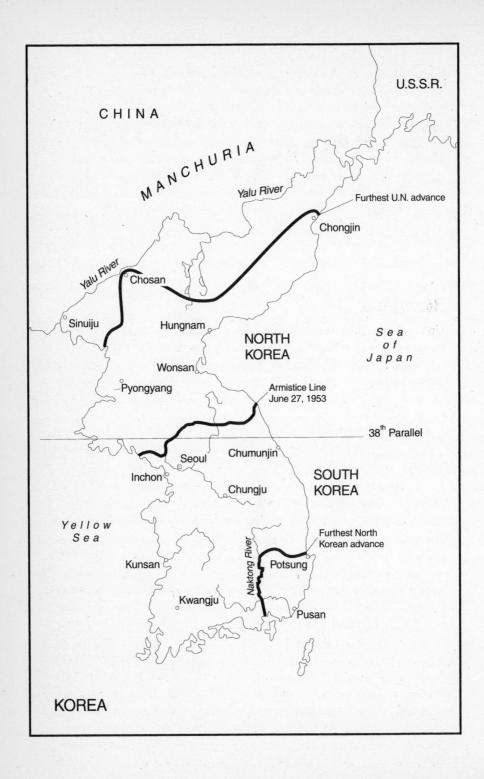

# Chapter 9

# Two Koreas

## Background

Until the Kanghwa Treaty of 1876, when it was coerced by Japan to open its doors, Korea remained sheltered from the tumults of the expanding world trade of the 19th century. With justification, Western writers caricatured Korea as "the Hermit Kingdom." The economy on the peninsula lying between China and Japan was completely preindustrial, depending almost entirely, for instance, on human and animal transport. Korea even lacked a generalized money economy: it was not until the arrival of the Japanese that the yen replaced rice and barley as the medium of exchange.

In the years that followed the Kanghwa Treaty, during the final spasm of the Yi dynasty (which had ruled Korea since 1392), capitalism began to take hold, stimulated largely by Japanese trade. By the end of the century and into the first decade of the next the Japanese were vying with China and then Russia for control of the country. In 1910, five years after defeating the Russians in the Russo-Japanese war, the Japanese invaded outright. Korea, which had existed as a unified state since the seventh century AD, became a colony.

Under Japanese rule, capitalist growth came even faster, which was all the more remarkable because no Western European colonialism ever encouraged industrialization in its colonies. As historian Carter J. Eckert points out: "What is striking about the colonial period [1910-1945] to the student of Korean socioeconomic history is, first of all, the extent of industrial growth that did take place in spite of Korea's colonial status. Second . . . is that colonialism did not preclude considerable numbers of Koreans from taking an active part in such industrial growth."[1] Perhaps the term "considerable number" is too sanguine: Alice H. Amsden refers to the same class as "a wafer-thin stratum of Korean capitalists" that "was deliberately cultivated to further collaboration."[2]

The attractions for Japanese investments, besides nearness and political control, were considerable. As well as a strong centralized government, Korea had abundant cheap labour. Perhaps even more importantly, it served as a convenient corridor for Japanese expansion into Manchuria and had plentiful resources for hydroelectric development. Heavy industries such as chemicals, fertilizers, steel, and production of war *matériel* thus gained a footing in the north, with light industry such as textiles, printing, machine tools, and manufactured food in the south. In addition the south, a flat terrain with richer soil, was more suitable for an irrigation-supported agricultural development. In the early years of colonial rule, manufacturing represented less than 7 per cent of Korea's total output. By the end of the 1930s, by which time Korea had been transformed into a logistical base for the invasion of Manchuria, manufacturing had reached nearly 30 per cent.[3] As well, a major shift in agriculture included a deepening commercialization. In 1910-12, when the Japanese took over, the market value of all crops stood at 318 million yen. By 1939-41, it had reached 1,875 million yen. Rice production increased from 67.4 million yen in 1910-12 to 142.8 million yen in 1939-41.[4] The transformation as a whole, from about 1935, marked the beginnings of Korea's industrial revolution.

While the Japanese had stimulated higher levels of agrarian production and laid the foundations for the modern development of manufacturing, transportation, and commerce, these advances were directed more at annexing the Korean economy to Japan's than at fostering independent growth. Like modernization everywhere else in the world, ruthless expropriation and exploitation of peasants were the price. Eui-Gak Hwang explains:

> According to statistics compiled in 1930 about 75 per cent of Korean farming families fell into serious debt. More than 70 per cent of those debts were payable to Japanese financial institutions, at interest rates of 15-35 per cent a year. The only way to avoid starvation was to abandon the farm; indeed, many went to Manchuria or Japan, only to find it no easier to settle there.... It is evident that [the] combination of land taxes, high rents, and the extension of Japanese ownership, in addition to curtailing domestic consumption, was the means employed to provide rice for export to Japan.[5]

Apart from migration and starvation, many Koreans who lost their lands became tenants, while others were absorbed by industry, mines, and railway work. In 1910 Korea had practically no working class; by 1941 it had nearly 1.3 million industrial workers. During World War II, hundreds of thousands of these workers were shipped to Japan to work, especially in the mines, where around a quarter of a million laboured (and died) under the most primitive conditions.

## Resistance and Collaboration

Koreans had resisted foreign domination from the time that the Japanese had forced them to open their doors to foreign trade. Students were at the centre of this resistance, which also included peasants and Western-influenced intellectuals. At the time of the Versailles conference in 1919, two million Koreans had shown themselves hostile to Japanese colonialism and in support of the movement for Korean independence. The first nationalist parties appeared in the next decade, along with the beginnings of long-standing divisions in Korean politics between communists on the left and liberals and others on the right. Korean communists, united behind the Korean Communist Party, formed in 1925, were supported by Chinese communists and the Soviet Union. Liberal nationalists were largely inspired by the Christian churches, and in the postwar years most political leaders had affiliations to these churches. Many Korean patriots were both Christian nationalists and communists and, like the capitalists, co-operated with and benefited from the Japanese occupation. According to Amsden, "Though the foreign aggressor was universally hated, the privileged elites collaborated with it to avoid social change, and the impoverished rural masses tolerated it in the absence of better alternatives. Nevertheless, in Korea, nationalism found an ideal climate in which to grow."[6]

During the Second World War, as was the case everywhere else within Japan's Co-Prosperity Sphere, the screws were tightened on the Koreans both as producers and as sources of labour. Higher taxes and price inflation were used as fuel for the Japanese war economy. By 1942 the tax rate was three times higher than in 1936, and the Japanese were conscripting hundreds of thousands of Korean men and women for military and industrial purposes. In an attempt to stifle the inevitable rising tide of nationalism, the Japanese interdicted the use of the Korean language, even compelling the Koreans to change their family names into Japanese. These repressive measures, as often happens, backfired, fanning rather than quenching the nationalist flames.

# The Birth of Two Koreas

After Japan's collapse in August 1945 the political situation in Korea was volatile. Everywhere fear and loathing were accompanied by a clamour for change. New political parties, people's committees, trade unions, and organizations of peasants, youths, and women demanded a new course. The immediate demands were for independence without foreign interference and the exclusion of collaborators from the body politic.

During this period the dream of a "People's Republic" of Korea emerged, pushed mainly by left-leaning nationalists of the Committee for the Preparation of Korean Independence (CPKI), many of them communists. But these communists were Koreans first and communists second, as Bruce Cumings suggests:

> Communism in Korea in 1945 did not signify a deeply held world view, or adherence to an authority residing in the Kremlin, or commitment to Marxist internationalism. . . . Its adherents could scarcely be distinguished from nationalists and conservatives in their belief in the uniqueness of the Korean race and its traditions and the necessity to preserve both, or in their understanding that a unique Korea required unique solutions. What did distinguish Left from Right was (1) a commitment to a thoroughgoing extirpation of Japanese influences in Korea, with all that this implied for Korean society and for Koreans who had profited from colonial rule; (2) a commitment to mass politics and mass organization and to the social equality that this implied; (3) a commitment to the reform of Korea's "feudal" legacy, feudalism being a code for gross inequalities in the allocation of resources, particularly land.[7]

On September 6, 1945, several hundred members of the CKPI gathered in Seoul to announce the formation of the Korean People's Republic (KPR). The government of this incipient republic comprised mainly nationalists who were untainted by collaboration with the Japanese. The cabinet, including members of both the political left and right, was headed by an absent Protestant pastor, Princeton graduate, and nationalist, Syngman Rhee (1875-1965), who had not yet returned to Korea from the United States, where he had been in exile since 1912. The leaders of the resurrected country formed the government in some haste so that it should be in place when the Americans arrived. They saw the possibility of tutelage under the Americans as a distinct hazard.

The antithesis of the CKPI was the Korean Democratic Party (KDP), formed a few weeks later. This was the main party of the right, containing, at the visible level, patriots, notables, and intellectuals, and, less visible, large landowners and wealthy capitalists, many of whom had profited from co-operation with the Japanese. Its founder was Kim Song-ju (or Kim Il-Sung, as he was later known), whose family in the period of the Japanese occupation had established the largest Korean-owned textile mill. Its goals, beyond opposition to the KPR, were vague—it could hardly admit to favouring landlordism, private ownership of industry, and the rehabilitation of opportunists and traitors. It stood reality on its head by claiming that the CKPI and the new KPR were collaborationist and reactionary. The party was soon to weld its fortunes to the interests of the Americans, who would be willing to support it rather than accept the radical nationalism of the CKPI.

On the other side of the Pacific Ocean, different plans were being formulated. Some six months after the Atlantic Charter had been signed in August 1941, President Roosevelt had implied that Korea was one of the countries from which the yoke of tyranny would be removed. Again, at the Cairo Conference in 1943, the Koreans were referred to as being a people "enslaved," and promises were made that they should become "free and independent." But just before the end of the war, Washington changed its official mind. President Roosevelt said that he thought Korea might be ruled as a Big Four trusteeship for anywhere from 5 to 25 years. In May 1945 one of his envoys, Harry Hopkins, was sent to Moscow to persuade Stalin of this scheme.

With the Soviet declaration of war on Tokyo on August 8, 1945, and the imminent collapse of Japan itself by early August, this plan was hastily revised. The fear in the West was that the Red Army, which had quickly moved into the peninsula, might occupy the whole of Korea and turn it into a kind of Asian Roumania. In a hastily improvised attempt at damage control, Washington quickly decided, on August 10-11, that Korea should be divided between the United States and the Soviet Union into two trusteeships, with the dividing line along the 38th parallel. Presented with the idea, Stalin acquiesced.

## The Making of South Korea, 1945-50

U.S. troops were rushed to the newly demarcated South Korea from Okinawa, arriving on September 8, 1945. Wartime ideas about liberation, freedom, and independence were forgotten. The head of the U.S. army of liberation, General John Hodge, instructed his officers that Korea was an enemy of the United States and therefore subject to the terms of the Japanese surrender. The U.S. administration imposed on South Korea was known as the "United States Army Military Government in Korea." It involved 72,000 men and had been designed for occupation duties in Japan. Although some of its officials spoke Japanese, almost none spoke Korean. It refused to recognize the KPR.

By mid-October 1945 Syngman Rhee was on his way to becoming head of the new South Korean government. Returning to Seoul after an absence of 33 years, Rhee had become the prima donna among nationalist exiles. Although disowned by the rival Korean Provisional Government, the mainstream party of political exiles, he had acquired several well-placed patrons. The most steadfast of these was the New York publisher and sometime deputy-director of the Office of Strategic Services (the parent of the CIA), Preston Goodfellow. With Goodfellow's help, Rhee had won the sympathies of General Hodge. In U.S. eyes Rhee's most sterling qualities, other than his resolute patriotism, were his fanatical anti-communism and his dogged pro-Americanism. Although Rhee was able to disguise himself upon his arrival in Seoul as an impartial senior statesman mediating between left and right, soon the mask dropped and he began to work overtly with the rightist KDP.

South Korea's political direction was ensured by the Americans within the first few months of their occupation. By mid-November 1945 the U.S. forces of occupation under Hodge, supported by General Douglas MacArthur, the Supreme Commander of Allied Forces in Japan, had effectively declared war on the Korean left. Trade unions were assaulted and strikes were prohibited. Land reform, in a country in which high rates of tenancy had become even more entrenched under the Japanese, was brought to a halt. As one U.S. colonel commented: "Our mission in Korea is to keep the absentee landlords from being chucked out.... Korean masses want farm land divided up among those who work it. Our job is to force those labourers to pay rent." The colonel said the Russians had committed the "atrocity" of "having expropriated and divided up the large estates of the absentee landlords and given them to small fry."[8]

By ensuring that rightists gained control of the bureaucracy and the main instruments of repression—the police, army, and judiciary—the Americans also made sure that a pro-American, anti-communist dictatorship would emerge from the elections planned for 1948. Two of the key elements in this dictatorship were the Korean National Police (KNP) and the National Defence Force (KNF). The KNP, formed around the nucleus of the Japanese colonial police, was headed by two KDP organizers. The KNF became the Republic of Korea Army (ROKA) in December 1948. Its officers were largely ex-members of the Japanese and Guomindang armies. The first chief of staff of the ROKA, Won Yong-dok, had been a lieutenant-colonel in the Japanese Kwantung Army. None of the officers had fought in the anti-Japanese resistance.

One of the first tasks of the newly formed national military force was the repression of the 1946 "Autumn Harvest" uprisings, which were launched against the policies of the military government. This suppression marked the end of both peasant activism and of the "People's Committees" that had helped lead them. The repression continued through the following years with the closing of opposition newspapers and banning of opposition parties. But rural revolts continued, as did military mutinies.

By mid-1947 22,000 people were locked up in Korean jails, and among them were 7,000 leftist political prisoners. It was in these circumstances, and against the protests of all parties except the KDP, that elections were held in May 1948. To the delight of Washington, which had UN observers supervise the elections, the KDP won. The UN observers, who declared that the elections were "a valid expression of the free will of the electorate," had managed to visit only 2 per cent of the polling stations. The Republic of Korea (ROK) was born on July 19, 1948, and by June 1949 the United States had withdrawn its occupation forces. By September 1949 the number of political prisoners in ROK jails had risen to 36,000. Between the liberation and June 1950, various forms of political violence led to an estimated 100,000 casualties.

## The Birth of North Korea, 1945-50

The Soviet occupation of North Korea was atypical, compared to the occupation of Eastern Europe. The Soviets had advanced into North Korea on August 8, the day they declared war on Japan and exactly a month before the Americans landed in the south. Upon receiving the Japanese surrender they withdrew into the background, handing over power, their own arms, and an arsenal acquired from the Japanese to local communists under Kim Il-Sung, a guerrilla leader who had been trained by, and served, the Soviet armies against the Japanese. Kim (1912-94) was not the only major Korean communist leader. Several others managed to remain on the scene into the 1950s.

As early as August 25, 1945, the Soviet command in Pyongyang had authorized what was still known as the "United Korean Communist Party" to take over the government. By mid-September the Soviet occupation authorities were working through local People's Committees. Almost immediately, with the active support of the Soviet army, the colonial coalition of Japanese occupiers and local collaborators—officials, landlords, and industrialists—was swept away. Although there were fewer landlords and fewer bureaucrats in the north to take into account, still the Soviet occupation, with its active support of leftist-led groups, achieved a stunning transformation. In Cumings's summation: "Within nine months of the liberation, landlordism had disappeared, the land had been redistributed, major industries had been nationalized, radical reforms had eliminated the worst abuses of the factory system and had established formal equality for women. Within a year of the liberation, a powerful mass party enroling hundreds of thousands of Koreans and a rudimentary army provided the organization and coherence that Korean politics had so long lacked."⁹ A North Korean government had emerged that was popular, well-organized, and dictatorial. Kim not only destroyed his "bourgeois" enemies, but also liquidated many of his rivals within the Communist Party, many of whom were his seniors, and more experienced.

Following the destruction of the landlords, which was largely completed on the initiative of poor peasants and agricultural labourers themselves in early 1946, the government organized some 11,500 rural co-operatives. Land was not immediately collectivized; this was to come a few years later, in 1950. Cumings suggests that this land reform provided the Pyongyang regime with a "vast reservoir of popular goodwill."¹⁰

Equally popular was labour legislation promulgated in June and July 1946, which provided for an eight-hour day, social security, and equality for women. At the same time major industries and enterprises were nationalized. By the end of summer 1946 the dictatorship of Kim Il-Sung was firmly in place and the Korean Workers' Party (KWP) had emerged as the single political representative of the revolution. Non-leftist political parties ceased to exist, and press freedom was stamped out. Surveillance and repression were normalized. Behind Kim's power was the *poandae* or "People's Guards." As in Eastern Europe, police power was exercised in the name, if not necessarily in the interests of, the people. In 1948, the year the Democratic People's Republic of Korea was formed, the North Koreans also created the Korean People's Army (KPA). By 1949, with the end of the civil war in China, as many as 100,000 Korean soldiers who had fought on the side of the Chinese People's Liberation Army joined the KPA.

## The Korean War, 1950-53

By 1950, corruption and mismanagement had so seriously undermined the effective functioning of the economy of South Korea that Washington threatened to remove its backing for the regime. This was no inconsiderable threat: the Americans were contributing around $120 million per year to keep Seoul afloat. Then came a reprieve: deepening East-West antagonism following the establishment of the Chinese People's Republic in October 1949 led the U.S. Senate to reverse its decision to withdraw support. A new aid package encompassing both South Korea and Taiwan was announced.

Despite renewed U.S. support, in the elections at the end of May

1950 Rhee's party won only 67 out of 210 seats. Rhee reacted by arresting a number of the opposition assembly members. Then, after months of cross-border provocations, on June 25 troops from communist North Korea crossed the 38th parallel. The U.S.-trained Republic of Korea Army crumbled, Rhee fled, and on June 28 Seoul fell.

In the four decades since 1950 arguments have proliferated as to the origins of this invasion: who really started it, and why? To what extent were Moscow and Beijing involved? A recent attempt to provide answers to these questions, based on newly opened archives in Russia, suggests that Kim convinced an uncertain Stalin that the destruction of the Rhee regime would be simple and swift and that the United States would not intervene. Stalin approved of Pyongyang's preparations and supported the re-equipping of its armies, but Mao was not consulted.[11] According to the authors of *Uncertain Partners*, "Keeping Mao out of the picture was Kim's intention," partly because North Korea was considered to be in the Soviet, not the Chinese, sphere.[12] Even at this early point in the Cold War there was thus no unified communist bloc, directed centrally from Moscow, as Western analysts liked to imagine. Instead, there was a fissured communist world with two dominant parties, alongside a number of smaller ones from Belgrade to Pyongyang that were attempting to maintain some degree of autonomy by playing the larger regimes against one another.

In Beijing the outbreak of war in Korea came as a shock. China had every reason not to want a major confrontation on its frontiers. Having only just themselves emerged from nearly two decades of foreign occupation and civil war, the Chinese leaders scarcely wanted to squander scarce resources warring against a coalition of foreign armies led and bankrolled by the world's number-one superpower. Aggravating the problem was Korea's strategic location as a corridor leading to the industrial heartland of China.

In the first stage of the war, from June to late August, the ROK armies and their U.S. ancillaries were sent reeling southwards: around 38,000 KPA soldiers almost drove five ROK divisions of around 50,000 troops into the sea. While this retreat was taking place the Americans and their Western allies were preparing for the decade's greatest anti-communist crusade. On June 25 President Harry Truman ordered the evacuation of American civilians from South Korea, the delivery of ammunition and other supplies to the ROKA, and the dispatch of the U.S. Seventh Fleet from the Philippines to the waters separating Korea from Japan. On June 27 Truman announced that "the Communists have gone from the stage of subversion to that of armed world conquest." The Security Council of the United Nations quickly approved a resolution introduced by the U.S.

government recommending "that members of the United Nations furnish such assistance to the Republic of Korea as may be necessary to repel armed attack and to restore international peace and security in the area." The majority of the members of the Council favoured this motion; Egypt and India abstained. Denis Stairs makes an important point:

> The decision to repel the North Korean invasion by force was an American decision, just as the decision to refer the crisis to the Security Council was at American behest and in the American interest. The United Nations did not itself decide collectively to condemn the aggression and then to obligate its members, including the United States, to take action to stop it; rather, the United States decided to oppose the aggression and then to ask the members of the United Nations for moral and material support.[13]

By the end of June, Canada, Britain, Australia, New Zealand, and the Netherlands had pledged assistance to the U.S. government in this cause. On July 8 Britain and France jointly introduced to the Security Council a resolution creating a UN force under a unified command. The resolution requested that the United States "designate the commander of such forces." Thus it was that the UN forces were placed under General MacArthur in Japan. MacArthur was responsible to the U.S. president, not the UN. He and his commanders deployed the UN forces as they, and not the other national governments, saw fit. Units of the Canadian army and air force, for instance, were regularly used in ways that contradicted the instructions of the Canadian Department of National Defence.

By the end of August the ROKA and the reinforced U.S. units that fought beside it had been pushed back to a tightly circumscribed area around Pusan on the southeast coast of the Korean peninsula. By early September this compacted force had grown to become almost twice the size of the KPA, whose soldiers were not only significantly less well armed but had no air or naval support.

The counterattack began shortly after September 11, when the U.S. National Security Council authorized total war. The cities, towns, and road system of North Korea were to be bombed without regard for civilian casualties. On September 15 U.S. forces made a massive landing at Inchon, Seoul's port on the west coast. At the time this was regarded as a brilliant stroke by General MacArthur, enhancing his prestige and his self-image even further. The KPA, stretched out from the 38th parallel to the south of the peninsula, was thus outflanked. Advancing rapidly with few casualties, UN forces captured Seoul 11 days later. Meanwhile, the besieged and by now U.S.-led army had burst out of the Pusan perimeter and was advancing rapidly northwards, pushing the North Korean army back in disarray. A scant two weeks after the Inchon landings, the first ROK forces were crossing the frontier into North Korea. By the end of the first week of October U.S. troops had also crossed the frontier and were advancing northwards.

With South Korea liberated, the first phase of the Korean War had come to an end. According to Jon Halliday and Bruce Cumings, "The war for the South left 111,000 South Koreans killed, 106,000 wounded and 57,000 missing; 314,000 homes had been destroyed, 244,000 damaged. American casualties totalled nearly 5,000 dead, 13,659 wounded and 3,877 missing in action. North Korean casualty figures are not known."[14]

After crossing the 38th parallel the ROK army and its U.S. allies pushed north almost unopposed, without ever seriously considering the possibility that China might be stirred into action as the allied army moved towards the Chinese frontier. But there should have been no doubt about which side Beijing would take. On June 27 the *People's Daily*, the official organ of the government of the People's Republic, published an editorial attacking both the Rhee regime and U.S. policy. On August 1 the Beijing government criticized American imperialism and called the North Korean struggle "completely just." It referred to North Korea as "our good neighbour." As of July "volunteer" units of the People's Liberation Army (PLA) began being transferred to the northeast. Nevertheless, throughout most of the early autumn, U.S. intelligence agencies predicted that China would not enter the war, despite Beijing's message, relayed through the U.S. consul-general in Hong Kong at the beginning of September, that China would send forces to North Korea if UN troops crossed the 38th parallel. The Chinese made this threat even more pointedly at the end of the month. It was ignored, even as the North Korean buffer collapsed and UN armies moved closer to the industrial heartland of China.

The allied ranks took on an air of great complacency as they advanced northwards, assuming that the North Korean armies had been physically liquidated. Instead, the North Koreans had evaporated only to crystallize again south of the Yalu River, on the Chinese border, towards which the Americans and their allies were being remorselessly drawn. As late as October 22, U.S. advisers were concluding that the KPA was no longer capable of an organized defence of the shrinking territory that it still held. On October 25 the ROK and U.S. armies came in contact with the first Chinese soldiers, who had crossed the Yalu from the middle of the month in immense numbers, undetected despite U.S. air superiority. By November 27, when the UN forces reached the banks of the Yalu, over 300,000 Chinese troops occupied what little remained of communist-ruled North Korea.

Of modern and industrialized North Korea little was left either, for where towns and factories had once stood there was now only rubble. The large town of Sinuiju near the Chinese border, for instance, had been removed from the face of the earth. By November 25, according to an official dispatch, a large part of the area between the Yalu River and the enemy lines to the south was "more or less burning." Soon the area would be a blackened and barren wilderness.[15]

When reports finally began to reach the Western allies of a force of half a million regular Chinese soldiers straddling the Yalu, they began to have misgivings about a further advance towards the river. Canada, Britain, France, and a number of other powers wanted to withdraw further south to the narrower waist of North Korea and create a buffer zone between themselves and the Chinese. General MacArthur wanted to push ahead and "finish the job."

For a short period from November 7 to 26 there was a stalemate along the Yalu. At this juncture, 22 MPs from the ruling Labour Party in Britain filed a motion in the House of Commons proposing that peace talks be opened. Although there was little criticism of the conduct of the war in the United States, the British socialist weekly *The New Statesman* forcefully expressed the opinion that MacArthur "seems intent on turning the Korean War into a world war." On November 23 the British foreign secretary sent a conciliatory message to Beijing in the hope of promoting a peaceful settlement. The Chinese responded by releasing a hundred U.S. and South Korean prisoners, together with a message that China did not want war.[16] But the British initiative did not go down well with MacArthur. In mid-November he charged them with "appeasement," an epithet recycled from the Munich crisis in which Britain had sold out Czechoslovakia to the Germans a dozen years earlier. But compromise was in the air. Even the U.S. Joint Chiefs of Staff had begun to discuss removing the UN forces to a position well south of the Yalu.

Unfortunately, the hour of disengagement had passed. On November 27, 1950, North Korean and Chinese troops, with limited Soviet air support, struck back against the UN forces, which by this time had become precariously dispersed.* The North Koreans, thought to be destroyed, threw 150,000 troops against the UN forces. The Chinese force was even larger, at around 200,000 soldiers. Washington was panic-stricken. The attack was to be what Secretary of State Dean Acheson referred to as

---

* Initially Stalin had refused to allow his forces to become involved in the war. On October 14 he changed his mind, and by late November Soviet pilots were flying their first combat missions. As many as 200 Soviet pilots were killed in the war.

"one of the most terrific disasters that has occurred to American foreign policy, and certainly ... the greatest disaster which occurred to the Truman administration."[17] Truman himself confessed moodily: "It looks like World War III is here."[18] MacArthur wanted the option of using atomic weapons; he seems also to have requested chemical weapons.

MacArthur's forces, shattered and divided, retreated southwards in disorder. The ROK troops threw away their arms and fled on foot, their officers preceding them in whatever transport was available. Although they had fewer troops than the Chinese and North Koreans combined, in all other respects the forces under MacArthur's command were superior. On January 4, 1951, Seoul fell for the third time. The Chinese advance was broken off on January 7 but launched again at the end of the month. After this the communist forces, their supply lines stretched to the limit, were gradually pushed north of the 38th parallel. Seoul was recaptured by the UN forces (for the second time) on March 14.

As in early November, peace again threatened to break out. On the first day of spring, MacArthur was informed that Washington had decided to limit military operations to the south of the 38th parallel, partly in response to the demands of the U.S. allies, partly because of a disinclination to continue fighting with China. While Washington was preparing ceasefire initiatives, MacArthur waded in with further provocations that undermined them. To this challenge to Truman's authority, the general soon added another; in a right-wing journal he published a criticism of Washington for not arming more South Korean troops. The allies of the United States were now deeply disturbed, not to say horrified. For Truman, MacArthur had outlived his usefulness. On April 10 the president sacked the general. "There were no tears shed in the Canadian capital" and probably few elsewhere among Washington's nervous allies.[19]

Now the war was, once again, at a stalemate. Communist offences in April and May stalled. Only Rhee still talked seriously of reunification, which the Americans knew could only be attained through war with China. In mid-May a resolution was tabled in the U.S. Senate "urging that a Korean armistice be arranged along the 38th parallel by 25 June." Others took up the theme in the UN. After informal meetings with George Kennan of the State Department, on June 23 Jacob Malik, the Soviet ambassador to the UN, called for a ceasefire and the withdrawal of troops to either side of the 38th parallel. Two days later Beijing informally signalled support for the Soviet peace proposal. On July 10, peace negotiations began between the North and South Korean and Chinese and U.S. representatives. In October these negotiations were being carried out at Panmunjom. Initially, the talks were expected to last for just a few weeks, but they went on until well-past mid-1953. Meanwhile the Americans hammered the Chinese and Koreans from sea and air, wreaking further destruction on a country already devastated.

Until the bitter end Rhee tried to impede the peace negotiations. On 18 June he organized a mass escape of over 27,000 Korean POWs, which infuriated Eisenhower and Churchill, who each began to contemplate a means of getting rid of the Korean leader. But Rhee's good luck saved him: in response to his threat to block the peace negotiations, the communists launched a massive assault against the UN forces on June 24-25, inflicting heavy casualties. The spectre of more fighting haunted both the Western leaders and the UN troops themselves, most of whom had grown tired of the war. On July 13 the forces in the north launched yet another attack, with a huge number of resulting casualties. At this point, with some two million troops facing off against one another, the Americans decided that there would be an armistice whether Rhee supported it or not. As a result the armistice was signed on July 27, 1953, by the North Koreans, the Chinese, and the Americans, but not by the South Koreans. Afterwards the U.S. government signed a mutual defence treaty with Rhee and undertook direct control over the ROK army and the stationing of massive contingents of U.S. troops in the country. To the bitterness of a divided nation was added the sour taste of a foreign dominance that had continued for most of the 20th century.

By the time the armistice was finally signed, several important changes had occurred at the international level. In January 1953 Dwight D. Eisenhower replaced Truman as president of the United States. The war, it is generally conceded, had lost Truman the presidency. More importantly, on March 5, 1953, Stalin died. The first phase of the global Cold War had come to an end.

## Losers and Winners

Between late June 1950 and late July 1953 some 3 to 4 million Koreans died, out of a population of around 30 million when the war started. Between 500,000 and 1,000,000 Chinese soldiers were killed as well, with the Americans losing 54,246 men, 33,639 of them killed in battle. Other forces—Turks, Greeks, French, Canadians, and British—saw 3,194 killed in battle. One of MacArthur's successors, General Mark Clark, commented dolefully: "I gained the unenviable distinction of being the first United States Army commander in history to sign an armistice without victory."[20] The cost of the war also fatally undermined, and split, the British Labour government, which had binged on rearmament partly as a consequence of the war and fell from power in October 1951. Finally, it drained Chinese resources that were badly needed to reconstruct the country after its own long civil war.[21]

The war did save, at least temporarily, Rhee's political career, and the deep pockets of his clan were filled with money diverted from U.S. foreign aid projects. Others benefiting included Chiang Kai-shek—the future of his fortress in Formosa was guaranteed—and Japan. As Tom Kemp explains in his discussion of Japanese industrialization, "It was fortunate for some industries, and for the economy as a whole, that the Korean War and an intensification of the Cold War took place" in the early 1950s when the Japanese needed a new industrial push. "American military spending and stock-piling meant orders for machinery, steel, chemical products and armaments. Japan became a forward military base and arsenal for operations in Korea."[22]

One other important direct consequence, even inadvertent benefit, came from the war. In the three months in which the KPA occupied the south in 1950, the communists largely destroyed the long-established system of land tenancy. After the war the Americans, mainly to pre-empt the communists, discouraged its resurrection. The effects of the forced land reform were far-reaching, as Amsden points out: "Reform redirected idle capital away from land speculation to manufacturing and uprooted a class that had not proved itself progressive. It relieved the bottleneck in food supply, which in turn dampened inflationary pressures. It created a far more equitable income distribution." As well, by breaking the power of the large landholders, the land reform made the way clear for a "strong centralized state power."[23]

# The Development of the Republic of Korea, 1953-95

After the armistice, South Korea's continued rule under Syngman Rhee was, like the regime in North Korea, dictatorial and sustained by a foreign power. Between 1953 and 1958 U.S. aid (excluding military assistance) averaged $270 million a year, nearly 15 per cent of the annual GNP. Then came the reckoning: by 1959, with aid reduced and various projects of postwar reconstruction completed, the economy fell into a state of deep depression. Policy experts in the West predicted that South Korea was not going to make it, and officials in Washington decided that Rhee was no longer the man for the job. This judgement was assisted by the advent of a mass social revolt in 1960, which brought an end to the First Republic (1948-60).

The 1960 revolt was ostensibly against venality: too few had grown too rich, too fast, due to the reconstruction boom of the late 1950s, and too many had been left behind. The precipitating cause of the revolt had come in April 1960 with the murder of a student who had been protesting against fraudulent electoral practices. Students throughout the country had risen up in anger, and when Rhee called in the army to crush them, the army refused to budge.

University and high school students were joined by junior civil servants and even middle-ranking army officers. The generalized and growing opposition—with a hint of possible revolution—led to Rhee's resignation on April 27. Elections in the summer gave power to the Democratic Party, but the period of democratic government was short-lived. In May 1961 a military coup led by General Park Chung Hee (1917-79) and supported by younger officers, most of them trained after 1945 and thus more consciously pro-American than anti-Japanese, gained control of the country.

As for the circle around the deposed Rhee, its end was swift. The dictator's chosen successor, Vice-President Lee Ki Pong, was murdered by Rhee's adopted son. The Rhee clan, which had infested the Korean state high and low, lost its controlled access to the goods of the land. Rhee retired to Hawaii, where he died in 1965.

## "Soft Authoritarianism" in South Korea, 1961-79

The South Korean military remained in power for 25 years following the coup of 1961. Behind them stood Washington and the West, unanimous in the view that South Korea was an outpost of the "Free World." U.S. generals both financed and commanded the military arm of this outpost, the ROKA. Beside them stood tens of thousands of U.S. troops, a situation that demands comparison with that found in the Republic of Vietnam in the early 1960s.

General Park's main excuse for overthrowing the government had been the Cold War recipe: communists were on the verge of taking over the country, and only the patriotic armed forces could save it. Yet however real the fear of communism, Korea's rulers had a certain justification for sleeplessness: they were, unlike the generals in Argentina or Chile, on the front lines of the global struggle between communism and capitalism. Park's coup was generally welcomed by modernization theorists who argued that soldiers prevented chaos and ensured economic growth. In the period of Park's rule (1961-79), a time described as being one of "soft authoritarianism," military and economic aid flowed generously into the country.

Park presided over the Golden Age of South Korea's economic growth. Yet, despite its gloss of modernity, the Park era ended with a

Gothic flourish. The general was assassinated by the head of the Korean CIA in October 1979.

In the two decades of the Park dictatorship—a time in which South Korea became the world's developmental state *par excellence*—the South Korean economy completed the transformation from an economy based on agriculture to one of comparatively high levels of industrialization. The country's GNP increased from $1.2 billion at the end of the Korean war to $1.8 billion at the beginning of the Park era to $61.8 billion in 1979. The growth continued after Park's death, reaching $164 billion in 1988. The average annual growth rate increased from 4.3 per cent in the postwar 1950s to 10 per cent by the end of the 1980s. The average annual per capita growth rate of 7.1 per cent made South Korea one of the fastest-growing economies in the world. Park himself likened this transformation to the great periods of modernization in other Third World countries: the Meiji reforms in Japan, Sun's modernization in China, Mustafa Kemal's revolution in Turkey, and Nasser's revolution in Egypt.

Still, this Golden Age was not without its peculiarities. The South Korean industrial revolution was not born, like the English industrialization that W.W. Rostow had studied, into an agriculturally based society without the aid of outside forces. Korean development, its foundation already laid during the period of the Japanese occupancy, was stimulated by a deluge of military and economic inputs from the United States. The growth also involved extensive government intervention: dirigisme ruled. South Korea's industrial expansion was not a celebration of free-market principles, but the opposite. Shortly after seizing power Park nationalized the banking system to give the state control over domestic interest rates and foreign loans. The government also implemented severe price controls over 110 commodities, and it strictly controlled capital flight. According to Amsden, "Legislation passed in the 1960s . . . stipulated that any illegal overseas transfer of $1 million or more was punishable with a *minimum* sentence of ten years' imprisonment and a maximum sentence of death."[24] The shadow of the noose thus hung over the free movement of money, although the threat did not apply equally to those at the top of the political pyramid. And protectionism was everywhere; it became so exalted that in the 1960s the smoking of foreign cigarettes was regarded as being unpatriotic.

The Korean government also encouraged legal monopolies organized by large industrial conglomerates (the *chaebol*), by limiting the number of companies it allowed to enter any field. Nora Hamilton and Eun Mee Kim state: "The state-*chaebol* alliance was critical for the rapid growth of the *chaebol* to become some of the world's leading industrialists, as the state provided low interest rate loans and other protective measures to support their growth. . . . This alliance was based on the exclusion and repression of labour. Repressive labour policies kept workers' wages much lower than those of their counterparts in the other nations, and prohibited labour unions."[25] By 1984, according to one estimate, sales by the top ten *chaebol* accounted for 67 per cent of the Korean GNP.[26]

## After Authoritarianism, 1979-90s

The period between the assassination of Park in 1979 and the elections of late 1992 was dominated by two oppositional figures, Kim Dae Jung and Kim Young Sam. Supporting them were many of the generation of young Koreans who had grown up in the 1950s, people who were increasingly unwilling to accept the legitimacy of Park's continued dictatorship.

Their pro-democracy demonstrations began as early as spring 1980 with a major political manifestation in the provincial capital of Kwangju. "The Kwangju Rebellion," which saw as many as 200,000 people taking to the streets, was the greatest political crisis in Korea since the end of the Korean War; it was the Tiananmen Square of Korean politics. It was put down by troops, many under U.S. command, with a brutality that shocked the world. Estimates of deaths range from the official 200 to an unofficial 2,000. Some 15,000 participants in the revolt were arrested and taken to special "re-education camps." Kim Dae Jung was tried and convicted of sedition, but managed to escape with his life, mainly due to U.S. pressure. The incident and its aftermath—the protest, massacre, mass arrests, re-education—suggest that South Korea, despite the "miracle" of its development, was, even at the beginning of the 1980s, as repressive a dictatorship as existed in the communist world or Latin America.

The Kwangju Rebellion forced Park to accept constitutional reforms, but it did not bring to an end popular hostility to the dictatorship. Further protest came in June 1987, with nationwide demonstrations against the government. The slogan of the democratic movement of that year was "Autonomy" (that is, independence from foreign interference), "Democracy," and "Unification."

In December 1987 democratic elections were held for the first time since the Park coup of 1961. The democratic opposition, led by the "two Kims," Kim Dae Jung and his ally, Kim Young Sam, could not unite, and so Roh Tae Woo, a former general and Park's chosen successor, won the election. By the time of the presidential elections of December 1992, Kim Young Sam had pulled a double-cross. Abandoning the opposition and joining forces with Roh Tae Woo and Kim Jong Pil, a plotter in the coup of 1961 and the founder of the Korean CIA, he now came to represent a pro-big-business coalition known as the Democratic Liberal Party (DLP). To the dismay of his former allies, he won.

By the early 1990s, GNP growth had fallen to 4.9 per cent, still impressive by Western standards but a long way from the growth rate of over 12 per cent in the peak years of developmental dictatorship. Given the trade liberalization being pushed on all countries under the aegis of the General Agreement of Trade and Tariffs (GATT), it seemed that the Korean trade surplus with the United States would continue to fall, which gave rise to speculation in the West that the Asian model had exhausted its potential. Whether or not this was the case, the serious decline of Kim Young Sam's popularity in local elections in July 1995 suggested that he had exhausted his own potential. Nor was his predecessor, former president Roh Tae Woo, safely out of the woods of popular wrath. Double-crossed by his former ally Kim Young Sam, in November Roh was imprisoned in connection with a slush fund that had operated in his favour when he was in power: Roh was accused of having illegally obtained at least $653 million. In December ex-president Chun Doo Hwan, who had seized power in 1980, was also imprisoned for political crimes, in particular the assassination of Park in 1979 and the Kwangju massacre of May 1980. A secondary offence was in connection with a sum of $1.2 billion that he had illegally amassed. President Kim Young Sam called the arrests the beginning of a "great revolution," adding that Koreans must be ready to "get rid of the military culture and the specters of the coup d'etat in order to protect democracy."[27]

Whether the Korean politico-economic tiger can be regarded as an example for other Third World states in their quest for democracy and development is, then, highly debatable. *The Economist*, a magazine that has never shown itself bashful in preaching the lessons of neoliberal development around the world, had by 1995 tempered its praise for this particular model:

> South Korea's expansion, like that of other Asian tigers, resembled the rapid development of communist states. In the 1950s some Eastern European economies achieved spectacular growth by squeezing more and more savings and labour out of their people. But this kind of authoritarian advance is neither pleasant nor sustainable.
>
> South Korea's labour policies were especially unpleasant. The country was built by men who worked appalling hours, led by obsessive bosses.... Kim Woo Choong, who founded the Daewoo industrial group in 1967, never took a day off until his son was killed in a car crash in 1990. His employees were expected to work 6 days a week, 12 hours a day, until the mid-1980s. Anyone who protested got fired, or jailed. Under Park Chung Hee as well as

under South Korea's next soldier president, Chun Doo Hwan, labour disputes were generally resolved by troops, tear gas and truncheons.[28]

Political life under South Korea's generals, the same weekly admits, was
not always much better than life in North Korea.

Indeed, the adopted economic strategy—one guaranteeing intensive
labour exploitation and consumer deprivation alongside high levels of military expenditures—suggests that South Korea does have a great deal in
common with the economically advanced communist states of Eastern
Europe, such as Hungary. South Korea, the largest (in area) and most populous of the "Four Dragons," stands as a good example of what might be
loosely called "developmental fascism" (the twin of the "developmental
communism" of Eastern Europe). It could even be that the combination of
political democracy and neoliberalism that the United States in particular
is anxiously trying to tie to South Korea's future is likely to undo the
developmental miracle, achieving much the same results as the same
forces have done in Eastern Europe.

# The Development of the Democratic People's Republic, 1953-90s

The war had brought devastation to North Korea. The U.S. blanket bombing had destroyed almost all the industrial plant and much of the irrigation
network. In Pyongyang only two multistorey buildings survived. In the
rural areas the revolution that had overturned the landlords was succeeded by a counter-revolution in which landlords, carried northwards
with the UN armies, now victimized those who had victimized them.

## Socialism Triumphant

The move to socialize ownership by collectivizing farms as co-operatives
began immediately after the armistice of July 1953 and came out of both
necessity and ideology. Between August 1953 and November 1954 the
number of co-operatives increased from 174 to 74,000. By 1958 all private
land had been absorbed into collectives, and by the following year almost
no vestige of private ownership remained in the rural areas—not land, animals, machinery, or even tools.

The rural co-operatives accounted for almost all food production.
State collective farms, the other form of agricultural organization,
accounted for about 10 per cent of the total. The government allowed private ownership for plots of under 100 square metres only. Ipyong J. Kim
provides a sketch of a model state collective farm covering 2,300 hectares

and supporting a population of 3,400.[29] The farm was worked by 1,200 farmers organized into 20 work teams. The main crop was rice, but the farmers also raised cows, oxen, rabbits, and chickens. The farm supported 11 nursery schools and 14 day-care centres and had its own technical high school. A team of ten physicians ministered to its inhabitants. Each household in the collective had a sewing machine and a television set.[30]

The average co-operative was much smaller, including only about 80 families that together cultivated just over 300 acres. Individual peasants were left with small vegetable gardens and fruit trees as well as pets and bees. Over time co-operatives diminished in number and expanded in size: while 16,000 of them had existed in 1957, only 4,000 remained in 1958. Socialized agriculture produced impressive rates of agricultural growth, with production almost trebling between the armistice and 1970, and doubling again by the mid-1980s.[31] That collectivization produced such results was in large part due to the technological revolution accompanying the social revolution. Irrigation, electrification, and mechanization were all prioritized, as was the increasing use of chemical fertilizers. A CIA report published in 1978 admitted that "grain production had grown more rapidly in North Korea than in South, that living standards in rural areas 'have probably improved faster than in the South' and that 'North Korean agriculture is quite highly mechanized, fertilizer application is probably among the highest in the world, and irrigation projects are extensive.'"[32] The United Nations Food and Agriculture Organization accepted that North Korea was first in the world in terms of rice production per hectare. The country attained food self-sufficiency by the early 1980s, giving credence to Kim Il-Sung's promise in 1970 that the food problem had been solved.

Industrial development appeared to be far behind agricultural development, but was nonetheless respectable. Following the blueprint of Stalinist industrialization, the state favoured heavy industry over light, consistent with the principle of *juche*, which involved working to develop the capacity to produce almost everything that the country required. In important respects, even given the damages inflicted by U.S. bombing during the war, North Korea had considerable industrial advantages over South Korea. Even before the end of the Second World War, 75 per cent of heavy industry had been concentrated in the North (and 75 per cent of light industry in the South). Most chemical fertilizers, upon which agriculture depended, were produced in the North, along with most hydroelectric and mining power. By 1988, according to Cumings, the per capita figures for North Korea were suggesting that the industrial economy was by no means "a basket-case." Cumings's assessment was that the North was not doing badly in delivering the goods of the "second industrial revolution"—"steel, chemicals, hydroelectric power, internal combustion engines, locomotives, motorcycles and various sorts of machine-building items." It was, though, lagging "far behind" in the communications technologies of the "third industrial revolution"—"electronics, computers, semiconductor chips."[33] North Korea also did well in arms production. During the Iraq-Iran War it provided as much as 40 per cent of Iraq's arms imports.[34]

Central to the organization and success of the North Korean economy was the ruthless organization of labour. Like the three-year and five-year plans, labour organization imitated the Stakhanovite movement in the Soviet Union and the Great Leap Forward in China. Workers were organized in teams and urged to create new production records. Incentives were moral, not material; rewards took the form of titles and medals.

In common with other communist states, therefore, the economy of North Korea was of the "command" and "closed" type: it was planned by the state and isolated from the capitalist world economy, at least until the mid-1980s. From 1947 North Korea's economic development was organized in a series of agricultural and industrial plans. The first of these plans covered only single years, but by the 1970s they included periods of six and seven years. The last seven-year plan covered the period 1987-93. Pyongyang has always boasted that these plans exceeded their quotas in almost all respects, and the claims seem to have been justified. In the 1950s and 1960s North Korea enjoyed truly impressive rates of growth. In 1954-56, during a three-year plan, the average growth rate of the economy was 41.7 per cent. In 1957-61, during a five-year plan, it was 36.6 per cent. In the late 1950s North Korean growth was three times greater than growth in South Korea.[35] A good deal of this growth was financed by aid from other socialist countries: according to one source, the total Soviet, Chinese, and East European aid to North Korea in the formative period of 1946-60 was over $1.8 billion.[36]

## Kimilsungism

Alongside the agricultural and industrial revolution came cultural and ideological revolutions. The basis of the cultural revolution was improved education, with mass literacy the target. The ideological revolution had more unusual aims. Its target was to guarantee a peculiar kind of state and society, and its subsidiary effect was to ensure the dictatorship of a single man at the head of a small ruling group. From the armistice in 1953, Kim Il-Sung, known variously as "the Great Leader," the "Respected and Beloved Leader," and the "Iron-Willed and Ever Victorious Commander," consolidated his power in North Korea on the basis of a control over society that many Western writers have argued was nightmarish in its thoroughness. Gavin McCormack, for instance, notes how authority became increasingly centralized, with the country increasingly run by an iron discipline: "The population was classified into categories of reliability and subjected to intense campaigns of ideological moulding and mobilization; a fine mesh of surveillance was woven over all, and severe sanctions reserved for the deviant."[37]

This totalitarian ideology, labelled by Western writers, at least, as "Kimilsungism," had several goals. It was an attempt first of all to fashion a Korean form of Marxism; in this regard it acknowledged derivation from Mao Zedong's attempt to create an original Chinese Marxism. It was also an attempt to modernize without sacrificing ideology. The debate over how much communism should be sacrificed to guarantee progress was an old one and often described in terms of the opposition between "Red," that is the aim of socializing the system, on the one hand, and "Expert," that is, the aim of modernizing it, on the other. How much redness could be sacrificed to the aims of expert technique?*

A further goal in the new ideology of the DPR was *sadae*, or "serving the big." According to this approach, as Young W. Kihl notes, "Those in leadership positions perceive their role as one of active command; those on the receiving end accept their role as one of blind submission."[38] Thus, as in Confucianism, the leader was the father of his subjects. Kim Il-Sung was such a father. The state directed all of the apparatus of modern communications and propaganda towards reinforcing Kim's paternal role. It rewrote history where necessary and invented history where it couldn't be rewritten. Kim was glorified as "the greatest philosopher-politician in the annals of human history" and "the greatest military strategist the world has ever known." "Kimilsungism" developed magical and incantatory aspects. According to the annals of the movement, the entire crew of the fishing boat *Minchungo*, caught in a tempest in March 1963, was saved after chanting passages from Kim's biography.

The result of all this was a surrealist cultism at a level astonishing in the contemporary period. Tai Sung An described the scene in the early 1980s: "The entrance to every public building has a large painting, mural, or mosaic of the leader as do the subway stations. All citizens wear Kim buttons on the left breast. Every room visited by Kim on one of his continual on-the-spot guidance tours is marked by a red plaque with gold

---

* Recalling Deng Xiaoping's claim that it didn't matter whether the cat was black or white as long as it caught mice, "Kimilsungism" maintained that it was possible to breed red cats who perfectly combined the qualities of mouse-killing *and* communism.

letters giving the date of his visit. Glorification of Kim is the main theme of dances, songs, operas, and films. Everyone is expected to devote some amount of time daily to the study of Kim's works."[39]

But however much he was deified, Kim Il-Sung was not immortal, and beginning in the early 1970s he gradually relinquished power to his son, Kim Jong-Il (b. 1941), who had been another object of the same cult of leadership. Kim Jong-Il's position was confirmed in August 1984, by which time he, too, was generally known as "Dear and Beloved Leader." Western commentators noted from the start that this communist Baby Doc did not seem to be made of the same stuff as his father.

Until the end of the 1980s, Kim Il-Sung tried to walk a tightrope between the Soviet Union and the Chinese People's Republic. In December 1979, for instance, Kim joined Beijing in denouncing the Soviet invasion of Afghanistan. Less than six months later Kim sent a telegram expressing Pyongyang's solidarity with the same regime in Kabul that Moscow had intervened to protect. The regime also retained its commitment to Third World liberation and its hostility to the United States. No opportunity was ever too slight for Kim to attack the reputation of Washington and its allies. Of Japan he wrote in the early 1970s: "The Japanese militarists most zealously follow the U.S. imperialists in their 'two Koreas' plot. While stepping up their renewed invasion of South Korea, the Japanese militarists, hand in glove with the U.S. imperialists, are actively pushing ahead with the plot to create 'two Koreas.' "[40]

As for the United States, in a pamphlet breathlessly titled "Answers to the Questions Raised by the Chairman of the Costa Rica-Korea Association of Friendship and Culture," Kim wrote, "The U.S. imperialists and their stooges are now more undisguised in the manoeuvres to provoke a war in Korea and are resorting to every sinister trick to rig up 'two Koreas.' "[41] The stooges included the rulers of South Korea. Kim Young Sam was awarded the title of "abominable flunkeyist traitor" and "dyed-in-the-wool pro-American stooge."

This feverish opprobrium was not entirely without justification. In the early 1980s, 4,000 U.S. servicemen were added to the 40,000 already stationed in South Korea, and military exercises involving more than 200,000 U.S. and Korean troops were carried out at the beginning of every year. Even in the early 1990s thousands of U.S. troops were still stationed in South Korea. These troops and those of the ROKA remained under U.S. command. This situation in which the U.S. military commands the armies of another sovereign nation is, as Cumings points out, unique in the contemporary world.[42]

## Socialism in Crisis

Despite the denunciation of Tokyo, Pyongyang had begun to open its doors to Japanese imports in the late 1970s. Kim's motives were obvious enough: South Korean industrial growth had begun to outstrip development in the North. The North's GNP was $3.6 billion in 1965 and $4.4 billion in 1970, and the South's was $2.5 billion in 1965 and $8.6 billion in 1970. By 1988 the chasm had widened even more spectacularly: $27.6 billion for the North and $164 billion for the South.[43] The combination of the sudden rise in oil imports (after 1973) and the decline in the prices of its own exports, notably minerals and metals, drove the North to seek outside help, which took the form of imports of machinery and even plants from Japan and Western Europe. A decade after Kim's speech to the chairman of the Costa Rica-Korea friendship society, North Korea passed a law that permitted joint ventures with foreign capitalism. By 1987 the country was involved in 50 joint ventures, 44 of them including Koreans resident in Japan. The consequences were predictable: between 1970 and 1974 North Korean debt had reached only $1.7 billion; by 1989 North Korea owed around $4.1 billion, with $2.23 billion of this owed to non-communist countries.[44] In addition to the accumulation of debt, by the beginning of the 1990s the country was suffering widespread food shortages that had reached almost famine proportions.

Despite the universally proclaimed success of North Korean economic growth, the country's 1990 per capita GDP was about one-sixth of South Korea's per capita GDP. By the early 1990s North Korea's growth rate was in the minus range, indicating, in terms of economic development, that North Korea was regressing. Soviet aid—invisible to many of those impressed by the great leaps made in North Korean agriculture—undoubtedly played a part in this discrepancy.[45] Favoured as a socialist ally, North Korea had been sustained economically by the Soviet Union, which provided technical assistance and "friendship" prices for oil at lower than prevailing free market prices. The collapse of the Soviet Union removed the props holding up the economy of North Korea. Oil imports from the Soviet Union had been at 2.18 million tonnes in 1987, but had been cut in half by 1992, when the Soviet contribution dried up entirely. According to McCormack, "In the summer of 1992, it was reported that not a ship moved in Wonsan harbour, that smoke was rising from less than half the chimney stacks around Pyongyang, that large scale army manoeuvres had ceased altogether, while air force pilots were reduced to four hours practice per year."[46] In 1993 the North Korean GDP was $20.5 billion, while South Korea's was at $328.7 billion. By 1994 income per head in North Korea was one-eighth of the income in South Korea, and by early 1996 the

North was suffering from a devastating famine, in part brought on by floods that had destroyed the cereal harvest.

Talks on arms control and the reunification of Korea had begun in 1990 but moved at glacial speed. On July 9, 1994, on the verge of the first summit between the leaders of North and South Korea, Kim Il-Sung, "the Great Leader," the world's longest-surviving political head of state and most senior Stalinist, died after a record 49 years in power. His succession by his son Kim Jong-Il, "the Dear Leader," was completed without any notable disturbances. Attempts by Washington to persuade Pyongyang to abandon its nuclear weapons program in return for the normalization of diplomatic and trade relations, apparently successful in August 1994, were abandoned in spring 1995. By the end of 1996, reported *The Far Eastern Economic Review*, North Korea's national economy had virtually ceased to exist.[47] With malnutrition reported throughout the country, a mass exodus of North Koreans across the Chinese and South Korean frontiers had begun.

## Summary

Korea existed as a unified country for a millennium before it was opened up to foreign trade at the end of the 19th century. In 1910 it was invaded and colonized by the Japanese in the first phase of their project of creating an East Asian empire. Unlike their West European and U.S. rivals, the Japanese encouraged industrialization, although the Korean role in this should not be exaggerated. This industrialization was scant consolation to most Koreans, who suffered doubly from economic exploitation and the political and cultural repression of a harsh regime of colonialism. Under this colonialism the two main forms of Korean nationalism were established: in simplified terms, a liberal, Christian, and pro-Western form on the one hand, and a pro-communist form on the other. Even the Korean communists were nationalists and not, as Cold War propaganda frequently proclaimed, the puppets of the Kremlin. Arguably they were therefore red-tinted patriots more than deep-dyed Marxists.

Japanese rule over Korea continued until August 1945, leaving an economically and socially distorted Korea to its inheritors. In August 1945 troops from the Soviet Union invaded from the north and in early September of that year armed forces from the United States advanced from the south. Korea was sawn in half. Indifferent to the interests of the Koreans themselves, both Washington and Moscow installed their own candidates in power, with Syngman Rhee becoming Washington's dictator of choice in the Republic of Korea and Kim Il-Sung Moscow's choice in the

Democratic Republic. Over the next 50 years South Korea was to become one of the West's most immoveable "bulwarks against communism."

The invasion of the South by North Korea in June 1950 was an attempt to solve a problem that has troubled all Koreans since the Great Powers sentenced their country to political vivisection at the end of World War II. The problem was division; its solution, unity. Kim Il-Sung proposed to unite the country under his own rule, but the short-term effects of his attempt were catastrophic. The long-term effects are more ambiguous. Surely, it was argued, had Korea not been a cockpit of Cold War enmities, the capitalist development of the South would not have been as advanced as it is today. There can be little doubt that most contemporary South Koreans see such development as desirable. Whether most North Koreans actually rejoice in the status quo is more open to question. Meanwhile the issue of unification, which entered a new stage after the unification of Germany in 1990, remains urgent. With unification under Pyongyang inconceivable, unification under Seoul seems the only possibility. Byoung-Lo Philo Kim, pessimistic concerning the prospects for unification in the 1990s, addresses the benefits that would be derived from a reborn Korea: "As a unified nation, Korea would be the world's twelfth most abundant country in labour force and the world's twentieth wealthiest country in the size of its economy; both will be the best markets for each other; the wasteful military defense burdens which combined are the world's fifth largest in military personnel and the thirteenth in military spending, will be diverted to the construction of a powerful economy."[48]

Before unification takes place, Kim suggests, the standard of living of the North will continue to decline as will, inevitably, military expenditures. South Korea, which in the mid-1990s still served as the base for 36,000 U.S. troops, will have to end its military subordination to Washington:

> The American military presence in South Korea profoundly affects political alignments in both the South and the North. It lightens the military burden of South Korea. It also impedes democratization in the South, and in the North it strengthens xenophobic hard-liners centered in the military who are engaged in a growing struggle with more moderate, outward-looking elements within the ruling Workers' Party. The U.S. military withdrawal from South Korea is an important factor for the future development of both South and North Korea.[49]

Yet, as Perry Anderson warns, Korean unification seems almost imponderably difficult for several reasons, not the least of which is that the regimes of both North and South have sustained themselves through exaggerating the threat posed by their Korean neighbours.[50] But perhaps more important is the matter of the economic gulf. Average productivity and per capita income in the North are somewhere between a fifth and a tenth of those in the South. The financial costs of the smaller South absorbing the larger North would be incalculable, not to say insufferable. Anderson's conclusion is therefore that the burdens of unification would be mammoth. Moreover, if carried out with anything but delicacy—a quality decidedly lacking among the political bosses on both sides of the frontier—unification could lead to a "nightmarish chaos."

# Chapter 10

# What Was Development?

## Introduction

"Development" was the promise of universal economic growth along the routes pioneered by the leading countries of the West. "Growth" implied steady economic expansion and sophistication in the form of industrialization. The inevitable corollary of such growth was to be a basic improvement in the conditions of life. People would eat more, grow taller, become more literate, live longer, and enjoy fuller lives. Women would enjoy a greater measure of emancipation. Some of these gains could be quantifiable; the normal measure of economic increase, called "growth," was codified as "Gross Domestic Product" (GDP).* A GDP of over 2 per cent per annum for several years running was a sign of steady growth; a GDP of 8-10 per cent was regarded as a wonder; and over 10 per cent as a miracle. The average growth rate of OECD economies, the most fully developed of all, was steady but declining in recent decades: 4.3 per cent per year in the 1970s, 3.3 per cent per year in the 1980s, and 2 per cent in the mid-1990s.

For the Third World, though, even rapid industrialization, as we've seen, did not guarantee upward mobility within the capitalist world economy. For instance, Thailand, Malaysia, and Indonesia—all "wonder-economies"—had average annual rates of growth between 1980 and 1988

---

* Gross Domestic Product (GDP) refers to the total output of goods and services produced within any country in any year. Gross National Product (GNP) refers to GDP plus overseas earnings.

   In some cases the value of using GDP as an indicator of a nation's economic health is misleading: what are we to make of the fact that although Costa Ricans had a life expectancy equal to that of Americans, the per capita GDP of Costa Ricans was only one-twelfth that of Americans? Even "rapid growth" can be misleading: in 1995 Vietnam's growth rate was a spectacular 9.5 per cent, but in the same year the country's per capita income was a dismal $220.

that were among the highest in the world, at 6.8 per cent, 7.3 per cent, and 13.1 per cent respectively. Yet in their per capita incomes all three countries lost ground compared to the OECD countries and to Japan and the Four Dragons (South Korea, Taiwan, Hong Kong, and Singapore).[1]

Besides the prospects of economic growth, "development," as it turned out, was also "Americanization," which implied a certain cultural and political change as well. This was the promise of "McWorld," a gustatory metaphor for globalization. Just as curries, sushis, and couscouses would surrender to hamburgers, so other cultural commodities would either be replaced by American equivalents or imitate them. This surrender would take place gradually from the top of society downwards; that is, as incomes rose, Western cultural practices and Western commodities— suits, supermarkets, hairdos, food, marriage practices, language—would trickle down through elites to the masses below. A fine spray of shopping sprees at Macy's, apartments in Miami, and villas in Switzerland would bathe the Third World elite, while a waterfall of Coca-Cola and Ray-Bans would rain down on the many.

The ruling classes of countries as far from U.S. shores as Morocco and Indonesia would therefore all be carried by the developmental tide towards cultural, and bourgeois, America, simultaneously the terminus and pinnacle of the Western world. Even if they had been, earlier in their colonial histories, introduced to French or British or other European cultures or politics, the pressures now would be to follow the American path in the pursuit of progress.

From the end of World War II through the "development decade" of the 1960s, the probability that many non-Western economies would "take off" was a universal article of faith. Initially the leading candidates for rapid development were in East and South Asia: Japan, South Korea, Hong Kong, Singapore, and, after the bloodbath of 1965, Indonesia. These East Asian "NICs" (Newly Industrialized Countries) were not going to be alone for long; at different moments it was predicted that they would be joined by Brazil, Chile, Mexico, Argentina, Turkey, Iran, Thailand, Philippines, Vietnam, South Africa, and even Nigeria. But by the mid-1990s the happy face of developmental optimism was masked by gloom; the list of states that were "developing" had grown shorter by the year. Even the "miracle economies" seemed to be in danger. South Korea, toasted as a model developer since the 1970s, seemed two decades later to be wobbling, to the point that in 1996 it was said by the *Financial Times* to be suffering the "worst economic performance in three years." China, the land of almost unbelievable economic advances in the 1980s and early 1990s, had become a source of anxiety: "Signs of unease grow in Beijing over the economy," read the headlines of the same financial daily.[2] And even if economic pessimism could be banished, as it was in many of the more buoyant economic reviews, there was another problem: "Asia is booming, and its boom is an ecological catastrophe."[3] If East Asia looked economically insecure, who, in the last years of the century, could predict blue skies for the economic and political futures of even the most promising countries of Latin America, let alone the poor nations of Africa?

By the second half of the 1990s the normal usage of the term "development" had mutated: "development" had now come to mean a modest increase in "industrialization," that is, an improved capacity to produce textiles, sports shoes, furniture, or even a solid GDP based on the export of resources, agricultural products, or low-tech industries. Indonesia was an "emerging giant" that had developed wonderfully by the late 1990s; yet one recent development enthusiast had to admit, "For all its success, Indonesia is still a very poor country."[4]

"Development," the record shows—and the histories in this book illustrate—has had mixed success, but, more predominantly, it has had notable, even extreme failures in the postwar period. In general, as Tom Athanasiou puts it, "Globally, the economy is doing well, but the same cannot be said of the people."[5] Part of the problem has been not just the political and economic crises of the countries themselves but the role of the leading institutions and "regimes," which, despite avowals that they were meant to facilitate development, seemed to inhibit and distort it, or even prevent it. These institutions, far from having any claims to belonging to the "world," as titles such as the "World Bank" or "World Trade Organization" would seem to indicate, or even of being "international," are mainly U.S.-dominated, for the perfectly simple reason that in the period 1945-95, U.S. power was globally predominant.

By the late 1990s the shelf date of the idea of universal development seemed to have expired. By the time of the publication of the World Bank's 1996 *World Development Report* no mention was made of "development" or "developing countries" in the table of contents. "Developing countries" had now often become "emerging markets." Even countries seem to be going out of fashion. From the mid-1980s, library shelves began to be filled with books explaining how the modern state had outlived its usefulness: quite reasonably, too, as many modern states appeared to have reached the ends of their national warranties—the former Soviet Union, the former Yugoslavia, Czechoslovakia, Liberia, Zaire, Somalia, Sudan, Iraq, Pakistan, perhaps even Canada—they might all, it was suggested, soon expire, at least in their current forms. For the metaphysical abstraction known as "the market," it was argued, states were becoming unwanted baggage; after all, they impeded "free trade," which had become the grail, with so many bankers and economists in hot pursuit of it. But in whose interests did the markets speak? And by what democratic process were the bankers and investment brokers elected to rule the universe?

## The Road to the West: Ideas and Elites

From the beginning of the 19th century, ideas such as "progress" and "modernization" penetrated the non-Western world through local elites who came to be seen, and see themselves, as "modern." Although these elites had based their programs for political advancement, economic development, and social change on Western models, the content of these programs generally adhered to the contours of local history. The reaction of the elites in Turkey, for instance, was conditioned by both the peculiarities of Ottoman history and the specificity of several centuries of Ottoman-Western contact. The elites in Japan, where the West was hardly visible until the mid-19th century, had been conditioned by their isolation, so that they formulated considerably different programs. Thus the terms "modern," "Western," and, latterly, "development" resonated differently in Turkish and Japanese ears.

Neither in Turkey nor in Japan, nor anywhere in between, did advocates of modernization suggest a complete uprooting of the indigenous and its replacement with a Western substitute. Even if this was desirable, it was not possible. Thus for most modernizers, the ideal was a grafting of Western technique onto an indigenous stem: as the Chinese official Feng Kuei-fen (1809-74) put it at the dawn of the Self-Strengthening Movement: "Learn the superior techniques of the barbarians in order to control the barbarians." The barbarians, of course, were the Westerners who were attempting to beat down China's doors in order to evangelize about trade and God.* The purpose of "self-strengthening" was to acquire Western arms and military techniques to defend China—not just the country itself, but the imperial status quo—from the winds of change that blew from the West. One of the leaders of the movement, Tseng Kuo-fan, built an arsenal with machines purchased from the United States. On his staff was one Yung Wing, the first Chinese graduate from Yale.[6]

Not just in China but elsewhere too a variant of the Western model

---

* Trade and God were not, in the minds of some Westerners, entirely separate considerations. Sir John Bowering, Queen Victoria's representative in Siam, was one of these. "Free Trade is Jesus Christ and Jesus Christ is Free Trade," he confessed. Quoted in Anderson, "Murder and Progress in Modern Siam," 1990, pp.34-5.

was held up for emulation. This was the Soviet model: *"Vive les Soviets"* cried the Muslims who marched through the streets of colonial Algiers in the mid-1930s.[7] And in the period after World War II Red modernizers were to be found everywhere from the China Sea to the Caribbean. After the Chinese revolution, they were no longer mainly from Moscow; civil and military experts from Beijing would go where both Western and Soviet experts had gone before them; and from Algeria to Zaire and from Managua to Angola there would also be Cubans.

The Japanese have always been the most successful among Asians in the adoption of Western techniques. Like the Chinese "Self-Strengtheners," the Japanese in the 19th century did not Westernize to become Western; their goal was to make actually existing, non-Western, Japan more viable. This was, indeed, a common strategy in Asia. By the beginning of the 20th century most Asian political leaders and thinkers wanted a future in which the most ineffective and corrupt local practices would be replaced by the best and most efficient imports from the United States or Western Europe. Westernization was therefore used as an anti-dote both against the West itself and as a bulwark against changes that were unacceptable to the social and political status quo. In China this approach seems to have returned in the last decade of the 20th century. According to the *Far Eastern Economic Review*, the "spiritual civilization" campaign of President Jiang Zemin is a reaction to the zealous free marke-teering associated with Deng Xiaoping. Those who support Jiang agree that something is rotten in the country: "Provinces ignore Beijing. Cor-ruption and crime are rampant. The rich grow richer, the poor poorer. A spiritual malaise grips the Middle Kingdom." For these problems "Dengism" and the United States were held to blame. "Burn Down Hol-lywood," advised a chapter in a popular anti-foreign tract, while another study showed "that the overwhelming majority of young Chinese consider the U.S. their arch enemy."[8]

The Middle East has also recently been pilloried as another "civiliza-tion" inveterately hostile to the West. John Esposito notes parallels between the Muslim world and 19th-century China: "The modernization through Western models initiated by Muslim rulers was primarily moti-vated by a desire to strengthen and centralize their power, not to share it. . . . The rulers' primary interest was in military, bureaucratic, and tech-nological reform, [but] not in substantive political change."[9]

Of the reforming Middle Eastern states, Egypt is usually held up as a classic example. Under Muhammad Ali, the Ottoman-appointed governor who ruled in the first half of the 19th century, modernization rushed in. New elites, called "the French knowers," helped to establish Western higher education and transfer Western techniques in armaments manufacture, military organization, medicine, and printing. Leaders were given traditional Islamic education but then sent off to Paris to further their schooling in "the ways of the world." Of particular importance was the attempt at state-sponsored industrialization: the building of factories in which a newly born Egyptian working class, using Egyptian cotton, produced textiles for export. Together with the factories and the workers came a certain amount of Western culture, some elements of which, like the Cairo Opera House, built in the 1860s, were restricted to the landowning class, the *pashas*. Yet, paradoxically, Westernization, even when it divided Egyptians along class lines, helped to make concrete the idea of Egyptian-ness; that is, it helped educated Egyptians of all classes to imagine themselves as being members of the same community. This was particularly the effect of the introduction of printing presses and the production of Arabic-language newspapers, the first of which became available as early as 1828.

For a time the Egyptian elite's admiration for the West was not tempered by the threat of domination. Eventually, though, it became apparent that Westernization was more often than not accompanied by a profound racism on the part of Western officials and merchants; this racism had a functional value in that it allowed the levers of power, and the jobs behind those levers, to fall into, and remain in, the hands of Westerners. It also made the Westerners feel good: "The British middle class gloried in . . . their status as a *Herrenvolk* ["master race"] in the east," writes Indian historian C.A. Bayly.[10] But the Egyptians and other peoples in the East did not glory in their status as *Untermenschen* ("inferior people"). When resistance to creeping British control took the form of a full-scale uprising, it was met with an equally full-scale British invasion in 1882.

Nearly a century later it was the degrading and corrupting influence of Western culture that repelled the most important Muslim thinker of the 1950s, Sayyid Qutb. Qutb, a leading figure in Egypt's Muslim Brotherhood, had travelled to the United States in 1949 to study and was scandalized and repelled by what he saw. He was particularly abhorred by the moral permissiveness he saw in the form of the free mixing of the sexes in public places and by the free use of alcohol. In his writings he inverted Western "Orientalism" to produce an equally topsy-turvy "Occidentalism," describing Americans "as being violent by nature and as having little respect for human life. . . . American churches were not places of worship as much as entertainment centers and playgrounds for the sexes."[11]

What Qutb and his ilk had to offer in the place of the morally bankrupt West, and its evil twin, communism, was the "third way": a religion,

Islam, that would attempt to reform politics and halt the process of what the Iranians were later to call "Westoxification." But beyond repudiating capitalism and demonizing Marxism, the revivalists' blueprint for the economic future was vague and contradictory. Still, to others, especially the dispossessed for whom economic blueprints were hardly part of the struggles of daily life, revivalist Islam offered a compelling view of a political and social world in which Muslims could enjoy dignified and secure lives as members of a coherent and caring community and find freedom from the stigma of being outsiders.

Significantly, the Egyptians who trickled towards the Muslim reform movements in the 1970s were different from their ancestors in the 19th century. By the late 20th century Egypt had become industrialized and urbanized: half its population no longer drew their incomes from the land. Nor was it a country of *pashas* and peasants, separated by a thin stratum of educated clerks and small merchants.

Egypt's social transformation is apparent in the membership of the reformist organizations. Many of the reformists were recent emigrants from the villages and small towns; while they looked forward to the future, they also looked backward to a romanticized rural past. In the process of pulling themselves up from peasant status into the middle and lower middle class they had often become highly educated, even by Western standards. "The majority," writes Esposito, "had university degrees in modern scientific and technical professions like engineering, medicine, science, and law rather than in religion or the humanities." These products of a Westernized education system turned against the West for two reasons: jobs and alienation. If they had jobs, they were generally poorly paid; otherwise they were underemployed or unemployed. And they abhorred the corruption of the world and the loss of what they imagined to be "traditional" values. As Esposito points out, "The wealth and ostentatious lifestyles of the rich contrasted starkly with the poverty and massive unemployment of overcrowded ghettos, and the clash between Western and traditional Islamic values in dress and social (especially sexual) mores on the street and in the media was a further source of scandal and outrage. While the freedom and delights of city life proved seductive for some, for many Islamically minded young Egyptians modern Egyptian life produced a sense of isolation and alienation."[12]

How far to go Westwards, then? Not very far, suggested Abd al-Hamid ben Badis (1889-1940). A great Algerian reformer (whose father had served the French colonial government and whose brother was a French-trained lawyer), ben Badis made his position clear: "Islam is my religion; Arabic is my language; Algeria is my fatherland." Yet if those

Algerians who followed ben Badis were drawn to Islam and Arabic, and others were equally attracted by the West, still others were attracted to both. David Gordon, who wrote about Algeria in the 1960s, just a few years after it had successfully won its independence from France, noted:

> Moslem Algerians, after the war [1954-62], found themselves between two worlds; the modern Western world and the world of their historical Moslem Arabo-Berber past. Alienated from both, Algerians were now to take the initiative in coming to terms with both. The Revolution was to be a struggle both for entry into the modern world and for a revitalization of Islamic values. It was to be a rejection of both the deadening hand of a corrupted past and of France. All colonial revolutions are characterized by this duality, of course, but in the case of Algeria the duality . . . was especially marked.[13]

Those who sought to dam and divert Western influence were invariably opposed by those who wanted more, not less, of what the West had to offer. Students of the different regions of the Third World have tended to ignore this group, the "Westernizers," and their political, economic, and cultural programs. In the case of the Middle East, this omission has led to the drawing of an oversimplified schema in which the much-studied reformist, revivalist, or revolutionary Muslims are seen as pitting themselves not against their own pro-Western elites, but against a hallucinated West and its demonized representatives. Yet, up to the present, except in a minority of Middle East states such as Libya, Iran, and Afghanistan, the Westerners, counting the Saudis among them (despite their revivalist façade), have remained dominant. Even leaders like the Egyptian President Anwar Sadat, who wore the mantle of "the Believer President" and under whose aegis the Islamic reformist organization enjoyed a renaissance, were immovably pro-West in everything from their Washington-oriented foreign policies to their Western-cut suits.

Despite their invisibility in the works of academic writers of the Third World, the pro-Western elites have been an essential part of the history of developing countries ever since their inception. It is easy to caricature their venality, as André Gunder Frank did when he accused them of being "an integral and supportive part of the metropolis-satellite system," people "dependent on the continual exploitation of the poor," and "mere links" in a chain of oppression that connected "the great financial and industrial centres of the world" to the beaten-down peasantry. These elites, he predicted, "would therefore resist any change."[14]

This representation of the pro-Western elites as being as essentially unattractive as their "fundamentalist" kinsmen has a substantial history. Keith Buchanan culled the following sketch of the culture of the ruling

family of Côte d'Ivoire, the Houphouet-Boignys, from *Time* magazine
(June 8, 1962): "The Ivory Coast's First Lady is coiffed by one of the most
exclusive Paris hairdressers ... and dressed by Dior whose salon is
strategically located across the street from the Houphouet-Boigny's
apartment.... The affluent Houphouet-Boigny's also have a villa in the
stylish Swiss resort of Gstaad (her six-year-old adopted daughter Hélène
is attending school in Switzerland)."[15]

Like them or not, certainly the cost of the sumptuary habits of the
Houphouet-Boignys and their fellow Third World bourgeois—the great
ruling political clans of Kenya (the Kenyattas), Mexico (the Salinases),
Haiti (the Duvaliers), Iran (the Pahlavis), Pakistan (the Bhuttos), and
Indonesia (the Suhartos), as well as their conjoiners, is immense. It can be
measured, in part, in terms of *capital flight*, the removal of capital from one
country to a safe haven and luxury bolt-hole in Florida, Switzerland,
Southern France, and even, in the recent (1996) case of the Bhuttos, a
multimillion-dollar estate in Southern England. At one point in the 1980s,
for instance, Latin American and Caribbean citizens owned assets in the
United States estimated at over $200 billion—only slightly less than the
$208 billion in loans that U.S. banks had made to Latin American nations.
The IMF reported that Africa had lost about $30 billion to capital flight
between 1974 and 1985. In another estimate, the figure for the years
1972-82 alone was well over $100 billion. As Volkmar Kohler, a former
West German secretary for development, once confessed: "We have to
work with elites who have no interest in seeing the poorer classes in their
societies advance."[16]

Yet it would be an oversimplification to suggest that the road along
which Third World countries have moved since 1945 has been dominated
by only "Westerners" and "anti-Westerners." Another group has consistently marked its presence with demands for an independent, non-aligned,
"third way." This group has sought neither a revival of the past nor a
future saturated with Western models. Its leaders have been nationalists
and Third Worldists and they have sought to assure the welfare of the
majority rather than of the minority. Those who were interested in seeing
the poorer classes advance have been thwarted and disparaged (as "utopi-
ans," "mystics," "communists," "Hitlers"), whether they take the form of
aristocrats like Mossadeq, upper-class socialists like Nehru, middle-class
reformers like Manley and Castro, intellectuals like Guinea-Bissau's liberation fighter Amilcar Cabral, religious leaders like Haiti's Aristide, lower-
class officers like Eygpt's Gamal Abdul Nasser, or the thousands of anonymous peasant and trade union leaders who have risen, and disappeared, in
the Third World in the last half-century.

# Reactions: Masses and Movements

Despite remarkable urbanization throughout the 20th century, even in the 1990s most of the people of the Third World remain as peasants, their livelihood earned in the countryside—in or associated with agriculture—rather than in urban areas. In his book *Age of Extremes*, Hobsbawm argues that only three regions of the globe have remained dominated by peasant populations: Sub-Saharan Africa, South and Southeast Asia, and China.[17] But if we add to these the heavily populated regions of the Middle East, where countries such as Turkey and Egypt have over half of the labour force employed in agriculture, and a country like Mexico, where around 40 per cent of the population is still employed in the agriculture sector, we soon get a predominately agrarian/rural Third World. In Ghana and Kenya, two countries considered earlier in this book, peasants form 59 per cent and 81 per cent respectively of the labour force. Even in Latin America as late as 1955, 51.5 per cent of the workforce was engaged in agriculture.[18]

In many places, peasants—sometimes with the help of urban elites, and sometimes without—had resisted Western domination of all sorts. Although they had often been overwhelmed, their resistance to the economic and political systems imposed by colonial governments or by the descendants of colonial governments, in common with the resurgent Islamic movements, was often reborn after periods of dormancy.

For instance, writing about the settlement of Huasicancha in the Peruvian highlands, Gavin Smith speaks of a culture of opposition that has been developing throughout history: opposition by the indigenous Huanca-speaking peoples to the Quechua-speaking Inca rulers; opposition to the Spanish colonists and their regimes of forced labour; and, finally, opposition to *hacienda* owners who attempted to monopolize their land.[19] The opposition to *haciendas* continued for over a century, until the 1970s. When this opposition finally reached a climax, in the 25 years between 1947 and 1972, it took the form of what was "unquestionably one of the largest peasant movements in Latin American history" and was connected with an unpopular development policy implemented by a new government. "This widespread rural initiative" Smith argues, "was neither the result of well-synchronized guerrilla groups manned by cadres brought up in the middle-class suburbs, possessing degrees in sociology or political theory and trained in Moscow or Havana, nor of peasant leagues well-organized for the coordination of political activity." Rather, the mobilization was based on "a series of local initiatives lacking a centralized leadership or organizational infrastructure."[20]

Here, then, is the opposite to the elite-driven Islamic movements, a genuinely popular political mobilization, centred on the question of land,

and guided by local people with its roots deeply buried in local history; a movement unburdened by intellectuals or "isms."

How exceptional are such locally led peasant movements? The answer depends on how we define leaders, as the case of Mexico illustrates. Until the Cuban revolution, Mexico had been the only Latin American state that had seen the colonial structure of land ownership broken. As late as 1910, colonial landholding patterns had prevailed. While some *haciendas* controlled millions of acres, 95 per cent of the rural population owned no land at all. Of the numerous Indian communities, for instance, fewer than 10 per cent owned land. In early 1913 Mexican peasant leaders, responding to the cry of "Land and Liberty," rose up against the government. These leaders were members of a new class that identified itself as neither Indian nor creole (of European descent but born in the New World); they were *mestizo* (of mixed European and Indian ancestry). According to Burns, they were "impoverished, sons of peasants, virtually illiterate in their childhood, looking more to their Indian than to their Spanish past, unknown and unheralded," and they re-created Mexico in their own image, destroying the colonial landholding system and creating a new system that recognized communal ownership of land.[21] But the Mexican peasants were not alone in their rebellion; they had powerful allies among the urbanized, Western-educated elite, and the revolutionary ideas of this elite owed everything to Western Europe and the United States. The Mexican Revolution was therefore simultaneously peasant-led and elite-led, Western and anti-European. Significantly, while the peasants may have made the revolution, the ministers of the first government of Mexico after the revolution were chosen from among the elites, not from among the peasant leaders.

The inauguration in 1920 of President Alvaro Obregón marked the beginning of postrevolutionary Mexico. Under Obregón a land reform program was launched that redistributed three million acres. At the same time the government initiated an educational program that, for the first time, built schools and brought teachers to peasant communities. José Bascencelos, the education minister responsible for the expansion of the school system, preached a doctrine repudiating spiritual and cultural Eurocentricism and invented, in its place, "Mexicanism," at the centre of which was a new race, the *mestizo*. According to Burns, "Mexico's intellectuals rallied to the cry. A new sense of nationality and pride—brilliantly evident in art, architecture, music, dance, and literature—engulfed Mexico." Whereas in the Middle East Islam became the foundation stone of resistance to Westernization, in Mexico organized religion, in the form of Catholicism, soon became the centre of the opposition to the revolution. As a result, in the 1930s, church and state were essentially at war.

Although the 1960s have been characterized as the great decade of revolutionary movements in Latin America, the 1970s did not see their end. It was, however, the end of the "high visibility" social movements in the region. During the next decade, the 1980s—characterized as being the worst period in the contemporary history of Latin America—Arturo Escobar and Sonia E. Alvarez note that there has been, in practically every country in the region, "an impassioned experience of resistance and collective struggle on many fronts, even if less visible than in former decades."[22] The fronts in question include rural struggles, struggles for the emancipation of women, attempts to defend the environment, and civic and cultural movements. These struggles have been distinctive enough that they have been referred to as "the new social movements." The *rondas campesinas* in northern Peru, for example, have been described as "one of the largest and most sustained rural movements in late 20th century Latin America."[23] Developing in the early 1980s after the *haciendas* had been legislated out of existence, and exploding in the early 1990s, the *rondas campesinas* focused on two interrelated questions: the corruption of government officials and an unsupportable government agrarian policy. Although the earliest leaders of the campaign included teachers, lawyers, and priests, the *rondas campesinas* had everything in common with the broad front of movements in Mexico in the 1990s: movements involving peasants, workers, teachers—indeed, citizens of all sorts—struggling for a rainbow of goals.

# Rules of the Game: Institutions, Regimes, and Practices in a Golden Age

By the end of the century—despite the varied national manifestations of "development" in the Third World, and the complicated responses of both elites and majority populations—certain large global structures have had the effect of overriding the national and universalizing the general. These institutions were created to guarantee the capitalist development of the West, and of the United States in particular, and in the process came to dominate the dependent capitalist development of the Third World. But by the early 1990s the cost of such domination was perceived as having led to the United States' loss of economic, although clearly not its military, preponderance.* The effect of this perception was that the United States was

---

* My concern is not with whether or not the United States did actually lose its economic

transformed from a nation besieging the world with its message of economic and cultural superiority to one besieged and wondering who to blame. Just as significantly, the apparent U.S. economic deterioration has been accompanied by vertiginous Third World decline—and not necessarily a decline in national product as symbolized by GNPs and GDPs, but a decline in the living standards of most people.

## Morning in America

At the conclusion of World War II, the United States was, in one succinct phrase, "the Free World colossus." Never in history had a country been so economically powerful and its citizens so individually prosperous. In 1945 U.S. industrial production was double the average of the five prewar years; the United States produced half of the world's coal, two-thirds of its petroleum, and more than half its electricity. The U.S. GNP had swollen from $90,500 million in 1939 to $211,900 million in 1945—or from $691 to $1,515 per person. In 1938 U.S. shipyards had constructed the equivalent in tonnage of one-sixth of the British merchant marine (the world's largest). In one wartime year alone, 1943-44, the yards produced a tonnage equal to one and a half times the same merchant marine. In 1945 the United States held 80 per cent of the world's gold and three-quarters of its invested capital. The U.S. military capacity had grown by leaps and bounds. According to Melvyn P. Leffler: "Its strategic air force was unrivalled. Its navy dominated the seas. It held a monopoly over humanity's most intimidating weapon, the atomic bomb. The United States had preponderant power."[24]

With the country's capitalist rivals either raising their hands in gestures of surrender or holding them out in gestures of supplication, Uncle Sam had reason to walk tall. Both Germany and Japan, the most formidable rivals for preponderance, had gone from being strutting imperial powers to cowering and conquered territories administered by former enemies.

Not only the enemies but also the allies had been badly wounded in the war. Charles de Gaulle was later to write: "As the tide [of war] retreated it suddenly exposed, from one end to another, the mutilated body of France." The Netherlands and Belgium, the other colonial powers

---

preponderance; it is that in the early 1990s several important writers claimed that this was the case. By the mid-1990s, taking into consideration U.S. economic recovery, which began in 1991, and the serious political and economic problems of rival economies (Germany and Japan, in particular), the "declinist" argument seems less persuasive than it had been earlier. Still, writers such as Tom Englehardt, in *The End of Victory Culture*, 1995, do indicate that something in the nature of power has been lost along the way.

of northwest Europe, were, if anything, in worse shape: flooded, plundered, disordered, and destitute. Britain was unique among the major capitalist democracies in not having been occupied, yet with the country having lost more than a quarter of its economic assets as a result of the war, its rulers recognized that, in general terms, it had ceased to be a power of the first rank in the game of postwar politics. As for the Soviet Union, in January 1946 a U.S. Naval Intelligence report commented, "Economically, the Soviet Union is exhausted." Still, the Soviet Union was, in military terms, a power to be reckoned with; indeed, it was *the* other world power.

Given this state of affairs—and with widespread fears of global chaos and revolution—order had to be restored, and this restoration would be primarily a U.S. responsibility. Indeed, the exercise of this responsibility by means of two major programs, one political and the other economic, forms the main narrative thread of postwar history.

The political program was based on an argument voiced by both U.S. and other Western leaders that the greatest threat to a peaceful, prosperous postwar world was communism and communist-inspired nationalism. This argument was particularly convenient for the European colonial powers, because it allowed them to apply for U.S. financial credits, arms, and general sympathy to help reimpose a modified and more efficient colonialism. They argued that if communist-inspired nationalism prevailed, wide-ranging parts of the "underdeveloped" world would be lost to the West. This West was now christened "the Free World," and "Freeworldism" became the ideology of the Cold War political world order.

The antidote to the threat of communism—which came, first, from the direction of Moscow and, later, from Beijing as well—was applied in two stages: "containment" followed by "rollback." The U.S.-led war in Korea was the first major war of containment in the Third World, and the war in Vietnam was the second, but many smaller wars and skirmishes also took place, as well as even more interventions in the form of coups. In many places and in many situations, as we've seen in earlier chapters, nationalism and communism were successfully rolled back.

## Bretton Woods

Postwar economic programs for a new world order were based on the assumption that if global economic stability were to be ensured, U.S. supervision and U.S. capital were essential. The rules for the new world order were hammered out at the United Nations Monetary and Financial Conference held in July 1944 in the rambling Mount Washington Hotel in Bretton Woods, a holiday resort in New Hampshire. "Bretton Woods" was to become the shorthand for globe-girding economic agreements in the way that "Versailles" became the shorthand for political agreements after World War I.

In Bretton Woods the representatives of nearly 50 states had come together, though not, of course, as equals. Besides the United States and Canada, most were from Western Europe and Latin America. India, China, and the Philippines were also there, as was Ethiopia. South Africa was there, represented by its white government officials.

It is no coincidence that Bretton Woods was in the United States; almost all of the dominant international institutions that provided the superstructure for the postwar world were established and guided from the United States: the United Nations, the World Bank, the International Monetary Fund (IMF), and the great scheme for Western European economic rehabilitation, the Marshall Plan. The U.S. treasury secretary had explained to his president his intention to move the financial centre of the world from London, where it had been since the 19th century, to Washington. U.S. conservatives and isolationists, who might have otherwise been hostile to supranationalist institutions, accepted the ones invented at Bretton Woods, confident in the knowledge that the bodies would be U.S.-controlled.

At the outset the discussions about trade in the postwar world were dominated by the United States and Britain, the two leading capitalist countries at the end of World War II. The famous British economist John Maynard (Lord) Keynes led the British side. Keynes had been the hero of a revolution in economic thinking that began to gain ground in the 1930s. Keynes and his followers believed that unregulated capitalism had been the source of the Depression, and the Depression had been the cause of World War II. Keynes advocated more state intervention in the economy to ensure full employment, which would underpin general security and prosperity. Insecurity, it was widely assumed, had led to the desperation and dictatorship that had put the world on the road to World War II. Keynes was also a great iconoclast: "Practical men, who believe themselves to be quite exempt from any intellectual influences, are usually the slaves of some defunct economist," he wrote.

The two leading teams of negotiators did have somewhat different visions of what lay ahead for both their national economies and the world economy in general. Basically, the British wanted U.S. credit to rebuild the economies of Western Europe (including their own) and to stimulate the economies of the colonies. The colonial economies would complement those of the metropolitan countries. Keynes saw London remaining as the financial centre of the empire and of some (if not all) non-imperial countries as well. The Americans, by contrast, wanted the dismantling of the protective tariff walls that Britain and other imperial powers had built around their empires. The United States' future depended on unimpeded access to the world's markets and raw materials. In sum, the United States wanted free trade. In 1944, as 50 years later, free trade was seen as being necessary for the fullest development of capitalism. It was therefore bound to be the ideology of the preponderant capitalist power.

## The International Monetary Fund (IMF)

The IMF was the more important of the two major institutions conceived at Bretton Woods; its actual birth and that of the World Bank took place at Savannah, Georgia, in February 1946. In the months after the 1944 meetings at Bretton Woods, Washington's attitude towards the reconstruction of global capitalism had shifted. Less tolerant of rival centres of economic influence (such as the British Empire/Commonwealth or the French or Netherlands unions) and more concerned with their own country's primacy, the U.S. negotiators at Savannah flexed their muscles more frequently. This disillusioned those, like Keynes, who held a more internationalist perspective. He died a few weeks after the Savannah meetings, doubtless in a disappointed frame of mind.

The IMF's overriding aims were regulation and stabilization—to regulate the marketplace of the "free world" in the interest of stability and free trade. The term "world" is key: the IMF has always claimed to be acting in the interests of global economic well-being; national or regional questions could never be allowed to impede universal requirements. The directors of the IMF, not local leaders, would get to interpret what was good for "mankind." Just as the directors of General Motors had claimed that what was good for GM was good for America, the directors of the IMF were able to say with equal confidence that what was good for America was good for the world.

The IMF had five original concerns: convertibility, exchange, currency, credit, and adjustment. Convertibility required that all national currencies could be exchanged with all others, which was the opposite of currency control, which restricted convertibility from one currency to another and had been common before World War II. Most advanced countries postponed convertibility until the end of the 1950s, but since then even most Third World countries have accepted it. The Soviet bloc countries held out until the bloc disintegrated. Convertibility meant that national governments had diminished control over the relative value of their currencies.

The second concern, exchange, required that convertibility be handled at fixed rates. The object was to prevent countries from manipulating their currencies to their own advantage, a practice common in the 1930s. The Bretton Woods negotiators agreed that the value of the U.S. dollar should be tied to the price of gold and the exchange rates of all other countries should be tied to the dollar. Countries with U.S. dollars could exchange them for gold.

Currency required an internationally acceptable and available monetary unit, and this concern also led back to the U.S. dollar, the most acceptable currency in the postwar capitalist world. The United States guaranteed that the dollar would not be devalued, so that other countries would be confident about keeping it in their reserves. Devaluing in relation to the dollar, as the British did in 1968, was regarded as a sign of economic weakness and an admission of political mismanagement.

A system of credit was needed because international trade inevitably led to balance of payments problems. By 1978 the total amount of money available for loans had reached $39 billion, of which the United States contributed 21 per cent. By 1995 the Fund's 179 members had contributed a total of $226.2 billion, of which $52.4 billion had been loaned out. This money was loaned on a short-term basis to countries in need "on the understanding," according to E.A. Brett, "that they adopt policies to deal with the problem which the IMF considered appropriate."[25] Unless the IMF's solutions to a country's economic problems were accepted, there would be no loans, a factor that came to be known as "conditionality." The IMF had no leverage on economic strategies in non-borrowing countries.

In all of this the United States was influential from the beginning, at least partly because voting strength within the IMF was proportional to contributions, and the U.S. quota has always been the largest. This power led to initial disagreements with Washington's European partners, but in the late 1940s their economic weakness was decisive. Washington had little difficulty in imposing its will.

Some four decades after the Bretton Woods agreements, criticism of the IMF had become a major intellectual pastime among developmentalists. The 1980 Brandt Commission report, *Global Challenge*, which confronted the problem of global economic disparity, criticized the IMF for putting the burdens of economic reform primarily on the poor countries and largely ignoring any responsibility on the part of the rich. But the IMF was unmoved, as it was 15 years later on its 50th birthday. Its executives had an ecclesiastical confidence that not only what was good for the IMF was good for the world, but also what was wrong with the world could be made right by the IMF.

## The World Bank

The second product of the Bretton Woods conference was the International Bank for Reconstruction and Development (IBRD), later known as the "World Bank." The original purpose of the Bank was to provide, in the words of its own charter, for "the development of productive facilities and resources in less developed countries" and for the promotion of a "balanced growth of international trade." But because of the reluctance of its Western founders to contribute, it had no money of its own. For its investments it turned to the bond market, by which means it had raised about a billion dollars a year by the end of the 1960s.

The governing body of the World Bank, like that of the IMF, reflected the economic status of its members. Thus it was ruled by representatives of the richest countries. Unlike the IMF, its president has always been an American. Most of its senior officials were Americans, British, French, Canadians, and Germans. Its researchers were often Indians, Egyptians, and Spanish-speakers. The largest contingent of clerical workers was Filipino.

### The World Bank: Main Shareholders and Voting Power, 1981

| Country | % | Country | % |
|---|---|---|---|
| United States | 20.84 | India | 3.28 |
| United Kingdom | 7.44 | Canada | 3.22 |
| Germany (West) | 5.06 | Italy | 2.94 |
| France | 5.05 | Netherlands | 2.25 |
| Japan | 5.04 | Belgium | 2.13 |
| China | 3.47 | Australia | 1.90 |

In 1960 the International Development Association (IDA) was established as an offshoot of the World Bank to make loans to countries too poor to afford the terms of the Bank itself, a concept that the United Nations had been pushing. Most of the IDA loans were "soft," often requiring no repayment for at least 10 years, but they were hardly interest-free. Thus, from the 1960s onward, the term "World Bank" refers to the IBRD plus the IDA. With the introduction of the IDA, the World Bank was moving rapidly from postwar reconstruction to economic development, and by the end of the decade the shift was complete. Presiding over this new phase in the history of the World Bank was Robert McNamara, a heavyweight figure in the Kennedy and Johnson administrations who became president of the World Bank in early 1968 after serving as U.S. defense secretary from 1961 to early 1968—that is, through the period of the build-up of the war in Vietnam. Among the U.S. policy elite McNamara had a stature even greater than that of the developmentalist Rostow. In their study of the World Bank, Susan George and Fabrizio Sabelli remind us that McNamara's close identification with the Vietnam War earned him the sobriquet "Butcher of Vietnam."[26] Like Rostow, an obsessive anti-communist, McNamara had pioneered such concepts as the "body count" and fostered such murderous weapons as cluster bombs and chemical defoliants. He praised the Dow Chemical Company for its "service to the Free World." Dow manufactured the napalm that the U.S. air force dropped on Vietnam.[27]

There would seem to be a somewhat macabre ideological overlap between the manufacture and systematic counting of bodies and the fastidious counting of dollars. It takes the form of a belief that, based on exclusively quantifiable information, rational calculations and decision-making can be ensured. The old-fashioned term for this was "positivism." The 19th-century positivists believed that the secrets of the universe would be disclosed by the prudent accumulation of facts. McNamara was a modern positivist, a believer in the magical reliability of numbers; one leading U.S. politician referred to him as "an IBM machine with legs," although it appears as though he often made up the data as he went along.[28]

In the first months of his World Bank presidency, true to form, McNamara concentrated his attention on augmenting the numbers: he raised more money than had been collected in any previous calendar year. In the 19 years to 1968, the Bank had financed 708 projects at a total cost of $10.7 billion. In McNamara's first term, from 1968 to 1973, 760 new projects were undertaken at a cost of $13.4 billion, and the staff of the Bank increased by 120 per cent. According to McNamara's vision, the more money that was borrowed, the more likely Third World economies were to develop. Because loans by the Bank were apparently viewed as Guarantees of Good Housekeeping, other banks and donors opened their purses, too. There seemed to be no downside; developmentalist dogma predicted that the loans would yield growth, and growth would guarantee the paying off of loans. Certainly, no one in the Bank predicted anything like the debt crisis that followed in the 1980s, by which time the phenomenon of loan pushing had become known as "reckless credit expansion."[29]

In 1973, when McNamara discovered "rural development," he explained it to the annual meeting of the World Bank: "The question is what can the developing countries do to increase the productivity of the small farmer. How can they duplicate the conditions which have led to very rapid agricultural growth ... and combat rural poverty on a broad scale." A couple of years later the Bank reported: "Traditional peasants need to be modernized; they need to be given access to capital, technology, and adequate assistance. Only in this way can production and productivity be increased."[30] The Bank would help make life better for the rural poor of the Third World by helping them become more economically rational. The question of the teeming urban poor, whose numbers continued to increase, was postponed. In subsequent decades the Bank's attention turned to issues of women's welfare and later to the environment and even the survival of workers within the global system that it had designed.

But by the end of 1981 unanticipated problems rose. Most states in the Third World had borrowed heavily, on relatively easy terms, in the 1970s and early 1980s, to finance the development for which they yearned and that Western experts recommended. While the World Bank had encouraged specific development strategies and offered to organize their financing, the Bank could not either guarantee their success or pick up the tab if they failed. By the early 1980s a mammoth problem had emerged: it had become clear that development had not taken place, or at least not to the extent required. Third World borrowers found themselves in the position of needing to borrow even more money, but now against a background of falling primary product prices, to pay off their development loans. Loans were made to pay off loans, and the Third World borrowers were becoming net exporters of capital. Because all development requires the investment of capital, its export constituted disinvestment and therefore anti-development.

By early 1982 McNamara had been replaced by a former Bank of America president, A.W. Clausen, and the interest rates on bank loans were at nearly 10 per cent. Some debtors owed more than they could earn from exports: "The external debt service as a percentage of exports was 179 percent for Argentina, 129 percent for Mexico, 122 percent for Brazil, 95 percent for Venezuela, and 91 percent for the Philippines." As for the poorer African countries, according to Joyce Kolko, "By 1985 sub-Sahara Africa's forty-two countries owed $135 billion, or 35-40 percent of exports, compared to 9 percent in the mid-1970s. Governments began to increase their production of commodities to meet their foreign-exchange demands for debt service and essential imports, and the overproduction drove prices down further. Over the same period their average per capita national income fell between 10 and 25 percent. . . . By 1985 one-fifth of all IMF loans were in Africa."[31]

Small and copper-dependent Zambia was one of the most stricken by this situation. Zambia's GNP was 27 per cent lower in 1984 than in 1974, and its per capita income had fallen by two-thirds since 1981. The social consequences of increased poverty were notable: despair, drunkenness, and disease all increased markedly. According to President Nyerere of neighbouring Tanzania: "Africa's debt burden is now intolerable. We cannot pay."[32]

The debtors were also in deep trouble in Latin America, too, and in 1982 Mexico became the first to announce that repayment was impossible. Still, no attempts were meant to forge a common front against the lenders. Debtor nations negotiated one by one and broke ranks when general agreements were attempted, and, one by one, they attempted to stem the flow out of their countries towards the lending countries. In 1985 Peru declared that it would pay only a fixed proportion of its export earnings. In 1987 Brazil refused to pay interest until better terms were negotiated. Soon Bolivia also refused to pay. When the banks eventually negotiated a highly profitable "buy-back" scheme that netted them huge tax breaks, the Bolivian government redeemed its debt at 11 cents on a dollar. In 1987 Zambia, a small-time player in the field of international finance, withdrew from the IMF altogether. Yet despite this general debt disaster, both the IMF and the World Bank continued to urge many Third World states— China and India among them—to increase their development debt.

### The "Borrowers' League Tables," 1993

| All-time Champion Borrowers | Most IBRD Outstanding Loans | Highest Outstanding Debt (1992) |
|---|---|---|
| India | Mexico | Mexico |
| Mexico | Indonesia | Brazil |
| Brazil | India | Indonesia |
| Indonesia | Brazil | India |
| Turkey | Turkey | China |
| China | Philippines | Argentina |
| Argentina | Argentina | Korea |
| Korea | Colombia | Turkey |
| Nigeria | Nigeria | Egypt |
| Morocco | | Nigeria |
| | | Algeria |
| | | Philippines |
| | | Pakistan |

Source: George and Sabelli, *Faith and Credit*, 1994, p.44.

Partly in response to the unnerving debt crisis, the World Bank and the IMF, as well as state-controlled aid agencies such as the U.S. Agency for International Development (USAID), jumped onto a new 1980s bandwagon called "structural adjustment." The claim of Structural Adjustment Programs (SAPs) was that they would consciously shift the direction of development by accelerating it. The great agencies would offer financial assistance to help with balance of payments difficulties on the proviso that a Third World country would accept a package of policies ensuring its return to financial balance. The contents of the program were more or less the same throughout the Third World: the liberalization of foreign exchange and import controls, the devaluation of the currency, and the deflation of domestic demand. After enduring this Draconian economic medicine, Third World economies were expected to return to health and join the ranks of the developing.

As part of this solution to the economic problems of the Third World, from the early 1980s the World Bank pushed for privatization of national economies. Privatization was part of a series of measures associated with the economic doctrine known as "neoliberalism" that was designed to shrink the state or, in other words, to reduce expenditures on such state-run areas as health and education. With Keynesianism now dead, the new economic doctrine called for the reduction of state interventionism. The downsizing of the state, said the economic theorists of the Chicago School and their followers everywhere, was necessary for the continued viability of capitalism.

Since the end of World War II, publicly owned firms such as oil companies and banks had become normal and ubiquitous in both the developed and the less developed worlds. The postwar rehabilitation of capitalism had been closely connected with the growth of the public sector. In India, the most populous of the non-communist Third World countries, for instance, in the 1970s "of the 101 largest companies (by value of assets), thirty were state-owned (including the nine largest, covering 60 percent of the total assets)."[33] Now the World Bank and the IMF set out along the path of stripping the public sectors of Third World countries of many of their most valuable possessions and turning them over to an elite of locals and foreign buyers: state oil companies, television networks, banks, airlines were all auctioned off in the decade from the mid-1980s to the mid-1990s.

Writers who accept the premises of neoliberal economics cite the examples of Chile, Ghana, Turkey, and Indonesia as countries that accepted SAPs and thereby achieved relative economic success. Other critics argue that structural adjustment exacerbated rather than solved the debt problem. Often, as in developed countries, privatization provided easy pickings for the rich, because nationalized firms were sold off, to either foreign investors or local elites, at prices far below their real value. Local buyers generally had to borrow capital internationally, which led to great benefits for some but often debt and distress for national institutions. Local populations were not insensitive to the declining living standards and pain that often followed. Throughout the 1980s and early 1990s, powerful demonstrations against the World Bank and IMF became common enough that they had their own name: "IMF riots."

Through all this, the World Bank and the IMF were represented by their advocates as being, like the market itself, above the normal commercial melee and unconnected with the material interests of those who governed them. Not all were taken in by this, however. Julius Nyerere of Tanzania appeared among the dissenters. In 1985 he stated, "The IMF has become largely an instrument for economic and ideological control of poor countries by the rich ones ... in enforcing the unilateral will of the powerful."[34]

## The General Agreement on Tariffs and Trade (GATT)

Yet another institution, the General Agreement on Tariffs and Trade (GATT), was the unexpected outcome of U.S. initiatives and three conferences held between October 1946 and March 1948 to oversee the formation of a global marketplace. U.S. dominance of this market was taken for granted, and by the mid-1960s GATT was often perceived as a "rich man's club."[35]

The GATT charter, signed by 23 countries (11 of them in the Third World), came into effect in January 1948. With a secretariat in Geneva and a set of rules governing negotiations over tariffs, by the early 1990s GATT had 109 members, including all of the OECD as well as the majority of developing countries and even Hungary, Czechoslovakia, Poland, and Rumania.

Since its emergence GATT has organized eight sets of negotiations or "rounds," the most important of which was the "Tokyo Round," which took place between 1973 and 1979. The "Uruguay Round" began in 1986 and concluded at the end of 1993. In all of these rounds the prime purpose was to encourage non-discrimination between countries and the progressive reduction of tariffs, which was to be done by exercising the principle of reciprocity: any country that broke the rules of the GATT would be liable to retaliation from its main trading partners. The 1995 GATT agreement authorized the establishment of the World Trade Organization (WTO), which replaced GATT. (Among other differences, whereas GATT was essentially a set of rules and was conceived of as a provisional measure, the WTO is an institution and forms a permanent commitment for its member states.)

Although each member of GATT had but one vote, the organization was anything but democratic. Most decisions were made as a result of

negotiations between the great economic blocs within the capitalist oligarchy known as the Group of Seven (G7)—the United States, Canada and
members of the European Union, and Japan. These accounted respectively
for 36 per cent, 34 per cent, and 19 per cent of the total output of the then
25 OECD members, that is, a whopping 89 per cent of the total output of
the industrialized world. Nor surprisingly, then, as Kevin Watkins points
out, "Whatever the skills of negotiators from the South, for the most part
they are like extras on the GATT stage; the show can't go on without them,
but nobody is remotely interested in what they have to say."[36] At the
Brussels GATT summit in December 1990, the U.S. chief negotiator, Carla
Hills, had a staff of 400 advisers—more than the staffs of all of the African
and Latin American delegations put together. Even then, Hills and her
team did not represent U.S. interests in the abstract: the lobbying of the
multinational corporations saw to that. Rather, the U.S. team argued for
the corporations—in the form of IBM, Citibank, and American Express.
Among other things, "We want to abolish the right of nations to impose
health and safety standards more stringent than a minimal uniform world
standard."[37] On the European side, Hills's opposite numbers also argued
on behalf of great multinationals—Unilever, Hoechst, Bayer, and British
American Tobacco. It is difficult not to conclude that GATT and its successor, the WTO, represent a parliament of titans watched by noisy but generally ineffective paupers sitting on the back benches.

The most pressing and divisive issue in the GATT Uruguay Round
was agricultural trade reform. According to Watkins, writing before the
concluding agreements of December 1993:

> The U.S., espousing an aggressive free market ideology, has attempted to
> use the GATT as the multilateral extension of domestic farm policies adopted
> in the mid-1980s. These have been aimed at consolidating its market domi-
> nation through the use of a variety of direct and indirect subsidies to dump
> farm surpluses on to world markets. Under the GATT regime advocated by
> the U.S., farm protection would be phased out globally, thus removing barri-
> ers to U.S. export dumping.[38]

## The Food Regime

Infinitely more obscure than the international financial and trade institutions was the postwar "food regime," which had neither a home nor an
acronym but existed as a set of political and economic priorities and con-
ventions nonetheless. It was also like the menu at McDonald's—highly
advertised, persuasively packaged, accessible, and, even to the poor, compelling.

The food regime, also established after the end of World War II, had as its purpose the setting down of agreed-upon regulations to govern production and consumption, not just of human food but also of animal feeds, such as soy and maize. The export of food, including stimulants (tea, coffee, cocoa, marijuana, opium), was, after all, the basis of many Third World economies.

The first period of the food regime was roughly that of the "golden age" of postwar capitalism, from 1947 to 1973.[39] In this period of uncontested U.S. dominance, Washington passed a succession of laws that were not only intended to protect U.S. food producers but would also enable the United States to use food as a means of achieving strategic and other objectives: food could be used to make friends and to twist arms. As a result of U.S. food aid policies, recipient countries were forced to modify both their own food policies and the eating habits of their peoples. Thus, as in other areas, the U.S. government captured its partners in a net of relationships designed to meet the requirements of U.S. domestic producers (farmers producing wheat, for example) and U.S. agricultural corporations (agribusinesses), as well as U.S. foreign policy goals.

The establishment of this regime had several visible consequences. One was the increase in meat-centred diets everywhere in the West. The effects of this increase were particularly profound in Latin America, where much of the beef and animal food was produced. Another was the shaping of Third World production to conform to Western appetites. From the 1950s the United States cultivated Third World import markets to absorb existing U.S. wheat surpluses. At the same time, U.S. agriculture undermined the markets for Third World agricultural products. For instance, sweeteners using corn competed with sugar, and U.S.-produced soya oil undermined Third World vegetable oils, peanut oil and palm oil particularly. Arturo Escobar summarizes the consequences of this shift:

> Countries that were self-sufficient in food crops at the end of World War II— many of them even exported food to industrialized nations—became net food importers through the development era. Hunger similarly grew as the capacity of countries to produce the food necessary to feed themselves contracted under the pressure to produce cash crops, accept cheap food from the West, and conform to agricultural markets dominated by the multinational merchants of grain. Although agricultural output per capita grew in most countries, this increase was not translated into increased food availability for most people. Inhabitants of Third World cities in particular became increasingly dependent on food their countries did not produce.[40]

By 1973-74 a new crisis ushered in the second period, from late 1973 to the 1990s. With their own tropical crops in decline because of a shrinking export market, many Third World countries had become desperately dependent upon U.S. food grains. At the same time vegetable oil prices had also increased. These changes meant that the Third World countries had to borrow money to enable themselves to buy the oil to cook the food that they may or may not have received as charity. The loans incurred put them in the power of the lords of financial discipline—the World Bank in particular. The main form of discipline was to be structural adjustment.

This second period saw the addition of a new market, that of the Soviet Union. In the 1980s the Soviet Union became a major importer of U.S. food grains. By now a kind of reciprocal dependency had developed: the new Third World (including part of the former Eastern bloc) became dependent on imports of U.S. food grains, but the United States became dependent on Third World markets, especially as U.S. industry became increasingly less able to compete with the production of Pacific Asia and Western Europe. Japan, meanwhile, sought to develop diversified sources of food grains to reduce reliance upon the United States. By stimulating new centres of food production in the Third World, Japan was destabilizing the system carefully nurtured by Washington since 1947. Also in the 1970s Washington found a new source of distress, this time in the form of the "New Agricultural Countries," or NACs. One of these was Brazil, whose production of oilseeds and meal cut deeply into U.S. markets.

A major preoccupation of the leading GATT negotiators had become, therefore, to shore up the crumbling foundations of this postwar food order, which now included not only the G7 states (particularly France) but also the NACs.

## The Aid Regime

In the postwar era the acceptance of the idea that aid is a necessary and irreplaceable part of the structure of the contemporary world economy has led to the formation of yet another regime. The granting of foreign aid is, therefore, not usefully seen as the outcome of humanitarian concern driven by a superior Western conscience that empowers the airplanes of this or that country to fly off to Biafra or Rwanda with a few tons of food (amid great media hurrahs). The aid regime is better understood as a facet of the trade practices of the dominant economies that have guaranteed the subordination of many of the economies of the Third World.

Contemporary aid has three visible forms; money and technology or technique aimed ostensibly at encouraging or supporting development; money for arms and training; and money and goods for health and emergency relief. All three forms come from the same sources and often the same institutions, and these are almost invariably Western. The modern genealogy of aid takes us to the expansion of imperialism in the 19th century—Christians preaching the missionary position on modernization theory: the "do's" and "don't's" of nudity, sexuality, morality, punctuality, frugality, diligence, and accumulation. Missionary aid was a source of power for Christians, indigenous and foreign, whose views about the necessity of Western trusteeship seldom diverged from those of the colonial powers who were their hosts. From the 1930s its beginnings in the days of the colonial powers, development aid had as its first priority the strengthening of the metropolitan (that is, British or French), not the colonial, economies and was to be used as a form of social engineering.

But these instances of postwar aid to the non-Western world pale by comparison to the aid given by the United States to Europe under the auspices of the European Recovery Program, better known as the Marshall Plan. This plan dispensed over $13 billion between 1948 and 1952 to Western European countries. Its motives were not purely philanthropic, because it sought to provide the Western European economy with the means to buy U.S. goods. While this may not have been charity in its purest form, it was certainly an intelligent expression of self-interest. All Western Europeans welcomed it, and several communist states sought (but didn't get) it. The Marshall Plan was intended to be part of the re-creation of a new global order. By tying the European economies to that of the United States, the aid forcefully limited the recipients' options. "The Marshall Plan, as well as subsequent aid programs, was as much directed against 'national capitalism' as against socialism or communism," states Robert E. Wood.[41] That is, like the programs of the IMF and the World Bank, aid inhibited forms of development that did not suit the donor.

In the Third World, within this new postwar global order, aid was to have two major objects: to ensure that the economies of the Third World functioned efficiently, because the prosperity of the West was closely connected to the purchasing power and raw materials of the non-West; and, just as in Europe, to discourage the development of national capitalism or communism in any form. Postwar U.S. aid to European states with colonies was used to influence or even destroy independence movements. The British in Malaysia, like the French in Indochina, got invaluable military aid from Washington in their attempts to destroy communist nationalism. Regimes that defied the interests of the Americans, like Mossadeq's Iran or Goulart's Brazil, were destabilized by being cut off from loans and aid; and once Washington saw that government was back in the hands of compliant regimes, loans and aid flowed in once again. So aid was used as a hammerlock to hold Third World countries in place as dependent associates in a U.S.-dominated system—even though this hammerlock was passed off, wherever possible, as an embrace of solicitation.

While the forms of aid have varied historically they have always conferred a major "feel good" component on their benefactors; young (mainly white) Americans in the Peace Corps in the 1960s, whose numbers reached nearly 16,000 in 1966, could feel that they were following the dictum of their president, who said, "Ask not what your country can do for you—ask what you can do for your country." The young (mainly white) volunteers from other Western countries, from CUSO in Canada or VSO in Britain, for instance, together with *coopérants* from France, knew that what they were doing in Peru or Uganda was not for themselves, it was for the people of the Third World. This form of aid was at its peak from the early 1960s to the early 1970s. The various volunteers also functioned as missionaries in reverse; they carried the gospel of "Third Worldism" back to the industrialized countries they came from, stimulating the credo that Westerners would be "partners" in the development of the non-West. The idea of partnership seemed to be less paternalistic than previous relationships. By the mid-1990s the sense of righteousness on the part of the givers had not completely disappeared. "The First World confers much largesse on the Third World," begins John Stackhouse, a development-issues writer for Toronto's *Globe and Mail*, continuing on to explain how the World Bank "has long built foundations on which individuals [in the Third World] could build better lives."[42]

Aid was therefore never what it seemed to be; it was more concerned with the discipline that is a frequent corollary of charity than it was with simple humanitarianism. If aid were simply humanitarian, it might be logical that either the most needy or the most promising got the most aid. But neither did; most U.S. aid, for instance, has gone to the most reliable and the most respectable from the point of domestic political and "national security" considerations. The greatest aid recipient, by any standards, has been Israel; another major beneficiary is Egypt. One-quarter to one-half of all U.S. foreign aid has fallen into the "military security" category. In the mid-1980s, at the height of the U.S. counterinsurgency program in Central America, El Salvador got 5 times as much aid as Bangladesh, even though Bangladesh had 24 times as many people and was 5 times poorer than El Salvador.[43] Awkwardly, despite this aid, infant mortality rates in El Salvador climbed in the 1980s when the "free market" regime oversaw the decline of public services, such as adequate and clean water.

There are clear cases in which aid simply mitigates the harmful effects of other development policies: the aid to health systems administered by the U.S. Agency for International Development is an example. As

Merideth Turshen points out, the policies of the U.S.-dominated IMF and World Bank have caused a decline in national health care systems all over Africa.[44] At the same time USAID provides funds for U.S. organizations that provide Africa with forms of health and medical aid. A more macabre instance of this is to be found in Rwanda. The French sold arms to the rulers of Rwanda in autumn 1993, trained soldiers in the use of those arms, and sent military and medical aid in the form of soldiers and doctors to protect those being killed as a result of the ensuing genocide in spring 1994.[45]

Most public health aid is, in any case, not dispersed overseas, but spent in the donor countries. Food aid expenditures are no more philanthropic: U.S. food aid, which constituted 31 per cent of U.S. aid to developing countries between 1953 and 1970 and 24 per cent between 1971 and 1981, has, according to Wood, "probably cost the United States nothing at all because the cost of price support and storage in the absence of the food aid program would have amounted to about as much as 'giving' it away."[46]

This is not to deny that aid, of both the development and military varieties, has been essential to development in at least a few countries. For instance, South Korea, a bastion of anti-communism, received nearly $6 billion in economic aid, and more in military aid, between 1946 and 1978. For most of the 1950s and 1960s, while the South Korean economy was becoming industrialized, this aid represented about half of the income of the Korean government. Taiwan received nearly $6 billion in economic aid in the same period, accounting for about 34 per cent of the country's total gross investment. The whole of Africa, by comparison, received $5.6 billion over the same period, indicating the close connection of most major aid beneficiaries to U.S. strategic interests.[47]

Still, a number of countries with little or no "national security" value have become habituated to aid payments. This was particularly the case of those states in Africa where, by the end of the 1980s, aid represented more than 5 per cent of GDP. Indeed, it was in that decade that Julius Nyerere made the novel plea that it was the humanitarian duty of the West to provide aid to the poorer and less developed nations, including his own country, Tanzania. In the banking capitals of the West, this idea was regarded as being risible; indeed, its opposite, that charity should be given to only those who could provide some kind of security or profit dividend, was the central tenet of aid policy towards the Third World.

International aid (excluding that from the World Bank) to the Third World generally peaked in the decade between the mid-1960s and mid-1970s and then declined. While aid did not invariably diminish in absolute terms, it did so in terms relative to the needs of the Third World. This was particularly the case in the 1980s, the decade of crisis. A second major decline began in 1993 and continued through the middle of the decade. In almost no countries—with Norway and Denmark the exceptions—did it reach the 1 per cent of GDP that was held out as being the United Nations' goal.

### Aid from selected countries as per cent of GNP

|        | 1960 | 1965 | 1970 | 1975 | 1980 | 1985 | 1994 |
|--------|------|------|------|------|------|------|------|
| Canada | 0.19 | 0.19 | 0.44 | 0.58 | 0.41 | 0.46 | 0.43 |
| France | 1.35 | 0.76 | 0.62 | 0.66 | 0.64 | 0.71 | 0.64 |
| U.K.   | 0.56 | 0.48 | 0.40 | 0.42 | 0.39 | 0.31 | 0.31 |
| U.S.A. | 0.53 | 0.57 | 0.31 | 0.26 | 0.26 | 0.27 | 0.15 |

Source: United Nations, *World Development Report*, 1985, p.208; Randel and German, eds., *The Reality of Aid*, 1996, p.15.

### Recipients of aid from Development Aid Committee of OECD (1994)

| (Figures for Canadian aid in square brackets) | | |
|---|---|---|
| Sub-Saharan Africa | 32.3% | [41.3%] |
| Latin America and Caribbean | 10.1% | [12.6%] |
| South and Central Asia | 11.6% | [18.9%] |
| Central and East Europe (including former USSR) | 14.6% | [ 5.2%] |
| Middle East and Maghreb | 12.4% | [ 5.5%] |
| Other Asia and Oceania | 19.1% | [16.5%] |

Source: Randel and German, eds., *The Reality of Aid*, 1996, pp.13, 102.

By the 1990s aid was increasingly being used to service debts. In 1993-94, of every three dollars of development loans, two went straight back to the World Bank to repay debts, and part of the remaining dollar was used to repay credits to the IMF. It becomes evident that many countries can only service their external debts when the donors provide the resources for them to do so. Those countries, which are mainly in Africa, are known as the "Severely Indebted Low Income Countries" (SILICS) and pay more to their creditors than they receive. In 1987-93 Britain, for instance, received over $1.5 billion from the SILICS. About half of SILIC debt repayment, however, is of the "multilateral" kind, that is, payable to the World Bank and IMF.[48]

# Ordering Arms

A third "development" regime concerns the sale of arms. At the end of 1945 only two Western nations, the United States and Britain, had viable and substantial arms industries. Other countries, such as India, Sweden, Canada, and Spain, produced only small arms (light artillery, rifles, machine guns) in small quantities. Although parts of the world from East Asia to Western Europe were saturated in arms of all kinds, immense areas, including Africa and most of the Middle East, either had no arms or sported relatively few modern "heavy" arms.

The Americans and the British attempted with some success to divide the world into exclusive arms markets. The British got most of Africa, the Middle East, and South Asia, the French got the rest of Africa, and the Americans supplied (and trained) a colourful range of customers: the Guomindang regime in Taiwan, the French in Indochina, the Filipino oligarchy, the Greek monarchists, the Turks, and Papa Doc in Haiti.

By the early 1950s the marketplace was becoming more clamorous, but most of the stall-holders still had only small arms on display. The Americans and the British still controlled the large arms market, comprising jet fighters, tanks, and warships. This was both profitable and politically valuable; their aircraft and tank producers could finance the development of new models by selling off the old. And because there was little or no competition and the demand was greater than the supply, it was a seller's market.

In the Middle East, particularly after the Tripartite Agreement of 1950 (which sought to prevent military escalation in the region) most of the tanks and fighter aircraft were, by agreement with the Americans and the French, British-made. The situation changed dramatically in 1955, when the French sold the Israelis supersonic jets that were far superior to anything possessed by the Arab air forces. The Franco-Israeli agreement drove the Egyptians, who had only been able to acquire a trickle of second-rate British jets, into the arms of Moscow, which supplied them not only with a fleet of MiGs but also an armada of modern tanks. "The Egyptian-Soviet arms deal of September 1955 was probably the turning point in the postwar arms trade," write John Sutton and Geoffrey Kemp.[49] By the time of the "Suez Crisis" of October-November 1956, the Middle East arms race was already off to a flying start. By the late 1960s the ranks of the major Western arms suppliers had broadened considerably with the appearance of West Germany, Sweden, Canada, Switzerland, and Belgium. By the 1980s the Middle East was to account for 40 per cent of all global arms purchases.

The primary stimulus to arms production was war, and in the postwar period war—by any other name, and sometimes with no name at all—was always fought in the Third World (counting Greece during the civil war of 1946-49 as part of the Third World). From the Greek and Chinese civil wars in 1946 through to the Gulf War in 1991, tens of wars in the Third World consumed record consignments of U.S., Soviet, and other arms. In the war between Iran and Iraq in 1980-88, the two oil-rich Middle Eastern states together spent $64 billion. That war proved a bonanza for the arms trade. France had sold Iraq $11.5 billion of military equipment by the end of 1986, and hundreds of millions of dollars worth of arms to Iran.[50]

After the 1988 truce French arms salesmen swept down on Baghdad to replenish Saddam's arsenal. In 1990 Hussein signed a contract with the French firm Aerospatial to produce ground-to-air missiles and purchase 100 Mirage and Alphajet fighters. Although Iraq was France's main market for arms in the Middle East, the French were not alone. The Salon Militaire held in Baghdad from April 28 to May 2, 1989 featured 200 exhibitors. In January 1990 Italy sold Iraq 11 warships for $4 billion. A French writer spoke of *"ce commerce fabuleux."* By 1990 Iraq had a foreign debt of $75-80 billion, much of it incurred to buy arms.

Nor was Africa exempt from this gun craze. According to Richard Sandbrook, "Between 1973 and 1978, the value of weapons sold or donated to the continent of Africa increased ten-fold, from $300 million to over $3 billion annually. The Soviet Union was the most bountiful arms supplier, accounting for about one-half the total, followed by France (25 per cent) and the U.S. (13 per cent)."[51]

Third World countries have always produced some weapons. Although largely dependent on U.S. supplies during World War II, even the Chinese nationalists produced a limited range of small arms. But the real leap in Third World production came after 1970, and especially after the oil prices increases of 1973. By 1980 Brazil, North and South Korea, Israel, India, Pakistan, Turkey, and China were among the most active exporters, although their sales were insignificant compared with the USSR (30.1 per cent of the market in 1982), the United States (26.2 per cent), France, the United Kingdom, West Germany, and Italy, which accounted for 84 per cent of all sales to the Third World. In the 1980s the People's Republic of China (PRC) was the largest of the Third World exporters of military equipment, with its closest competitor, Brazil, lagging far behind.[52]

The granting of foreign aid has long been connected to the supplying of arms. In many cases countries got aid only after they had bought arms. In other cases they got aid to offset the purchase of arms. In early 1994 a scandal exploded in Britain surrounding an alleged connection between a

## Leading Third World Recipients of Major Conventional Weapons, 1991-95

(at constant 1990 prices)

|                    | $ millions |
|--------------------|-----------:|
| 1. Turkey          | 8,096      |
| 2. Egypt           | 7,138      |
| 3. Saudi Arabia    | 7,092      |
| 6. India           | 5,158      |
| 7. China           | 4,747      |
| 9. Taiwan          | 4,228      |
| 11. South Korea    | 3,778      |
| 12. Kuwait         | 3,363      |
| 13. Thailand       | 3,318      |
| 14. Pakistan       | 3,212      |
| 16. Iran           | 2,790      |
| 18. Indonesia      | 2,120      |

Source: Stockholm International Peace Research Institute (SIPRI), *Yearbook*, 1996, pp.413,465-7

## Leading Suppliers of Major Conventional Weapons, 1991-95

(at constant 1990 prices)

|                        | $ millions |
|------------------------|-----------:|
| 1. U.S.A.              | 61,879     |
| 2. USSR/Russia         | 15,879     |
| 3. Germany (Fed. Rep.) | 10,156     |
| 4. U.K.                | 6,611      |
| 5. France              | 5,582      |
| 6. China               | 5,159      |
| 12. Canada             | 876        |
| 14. North Korea        | 743        |
| 23. Brazil             | 228        |
| 24. South Korea        | 184        |
| 26. South Africa       | 139        |
| 28. Pakistan           | 130        |

Source: Stockholm International Peace Research Institute (SIPRI), *Yearbook*, 1996, pp.413,465-7

## Market Share of Leading Suppliers

|  | % share of total arms sales 1993 | 1994 | Arms sales ($ billions) 1994 |
|---|---|---|---|
| U.S.A. | 61.5 | 60.2 | 89.3 |
| France | 12.0 | 11.3 | 16.7 |
| Germany | 5.3 | 5.0 | 7.4 |
| Japan | 4.5 | 5.1 | 7.5 |
| Italy | 1.7 | 1.8 | 2.7 |
| Israel | 1.7 | 1.7 | 2.5 |
| India | 0.6 | 0.6 | 0.9 |
| South Africa | 0.4 | 0.4 | 0.6 |

Source: Stockholm International Peace Research Institute (SIPRI), *Yearbook*, 1996, pp.413,465-7

£1.3 billion defence contract with Malaysia and a £234 million aid contract to build a hydroelectric dam. Britain had apparently brokered another deal with Indonesia, which bought £500 million worth of military equipment from Britain while being offered an aid sweetener of £65 million to build a power station. According to the World Development Group, Britain had made similar arrangements with Thailand, Nigeria, Ecuador, Jordan, and Oman.

After the Gulf War of 1991, inquests and reports documented the spider's web connecting the Western arms suppliers to their Iraqi customers. Although both the United States and Britain had supposedly embargoed the sale of arms to Saddam Hussein during the Iraq-Iran war, both countries still supplied him with arms and intelligence. Intermediaries in this trade included the CIA and a whole range of more conventional manufacturers, suppliers, and bankers. In the end, Americans, Britons and others ended up fighting armies and disarming paramilitaries that their own merchants of death had recently armed.

In some cases disarmament proved problematic. In the 1980s, Washington supplied the Afghani "freedom fighters" with shoulder-launched ground-to-air missiles to use against the invading helicopters of the Soviet Union. When the Soviet forces withdrew, the Afghanis were left with valuable assets for which they had no use, so they began to sell them on the international market, making them available to anyone with the money and the right connections. Here, then, is the Western nightmare predicted by Tom Athanasiou and sensationalized by any number of writers of thrillers: "Since weapons proliferation is at all levels unimpeded by any serious efforts at control, we must assume that the poor of the future will be armed to the teeth."[53]

## GDP and Sales: Nations and TNCS

Ranked by annual GDP and sales in dollars, 1988

| | | | |
|---|---|---|---|
| 1. | U.S.A. | GNP | 4.8 trillion |
| 2. | Japan | GNP | 2.8 trillion |
| 3. | Germany | GNP | 1.2 trillion |
| 4. | France | GNP | 950 billion |
| 5. | Italy | GNP | 830 b. |
| 6. | U.K. | GNP | 700 b. |
| 7. | Canada | GNP | 440 b. |
| 8. | China | GNP | 372 b. |
| 12. | India | GNP | 238 b. |
| 15. | Mexico | GNP | 178 b. |
| 16. | Korea | GNP | 171 b. |
| 20. | GM | sales | 121 b. |
| 21. | Ford | sales | 93 b. |
| 26. | Exxon | sales | 80 b. |
| 27. | Argentina | GNP | 80 b. |
| 28. | South Africa | GNP | 79 b. |
| 29. | Royal Dutch Shell | sales | 78 b. |
| 30. | Saudi Arabia | GNP | 73 b. |
| 31. | Turkey | GNP | 64 b. |
| 34. | IBM | sales | 60 b. |
| 37. | Toyota | sales | 51 b. |
| 38. | G.E. | sales | 49 b. |
| 40. | BP | sales | 46 b. |
| 42. | Israel | GNP | 45 b. |
| 53. | Egypt | GNP | 34 b. |

Source: Lairson and Skidmore, *International Political Economy*, 1993, pp.252-3.

## Transnational Corporations (TNCS)

Among the major institutions of the postwar world are the several hundred transnational corporations that have had a powerful, if uneven, effect on the economies of the Third World. In their contemporary form—GM, Ford, Exxon, Royal Dutch Shell, IBM, Nestlé, Samsung, Toyota—the transnational corporations first appeared in the 1960s, although their antecedents go back to the beginning of the century. By the 1970s they had become a global force; there was even a certain apprehension that they were going to take over the world.

Yet the transnational firms should not be seen in isolation but rather as a part of the emerging transnational economy—as part of a network of economic activities that had escaped the bounds of the national states that had originally nurtured them. According to Eric Hobsbawm, the three most obvious aspects of this new transnationalization were the transnational firms themselves, the new international division of labour, and offshore finance.[54]

The earliest form of contemporary economic transnationalism, and, by the 1990s, the most persistent, was not that of the TNCs themselves but of finance. Richard J. Barnet and John Cavanagh refer to this phenomenon as the "Global Financial Network," defining it as "a constantly changing maze of currency transactions, global securities, MasterCards, euroyen, swaps, ruffs, and an ever more innovative array of speculative devices for repackaging and reselling money."[55]

One aspect of the Global Financial Network was "offshore finance," with the term "offshore" being used because Western firms registered themselves in tiny countries, like Liechtenstein and the Turks and Caicos islands, where taxes and restrictions were minimal. Corporations that have subsidiaries the world over frequently organize their transactions to minimize the taxes they pay. They do this through a device known as transfer pricing. If the corporate parent "sells" goods or services to a subsidiary based in another country, the corporation can choose to declare the profit from that transaction in whichever country taxes are lowest, or perhaps even a third country in which another subsidiary (which may or may not consist of a brass plaque, a registration number, and a fax machine) exists solely for that purpose. Business advocates frequently argue that the free play of market forces must be allowed to set the rules of the economic gain. But in real life many transactions take place within corporations—without any reference to the market.

The currency of offshore finance was the "Eurodollar" (often known as "Eurocurrency," which was the same thing). The Eurodollar was the U.S. dollar held in foreign banks over which the banking laws of the United States had no control. Eurodollars originated in the early 1950s as dollars kept by the Beijing government in a Soviet bank in Paris—out of the reach of Washington. In the following decades U.S. dollars overseas accumulated enormously, thanks to U.S. spending, especially on the military. By the 1970s, the lending and borrowing of Eurodollars had become big business. Hobsbawm states:

> The net Eurocurrency market rose from perhaps fourteen billion dollars in 1964 to perhaps 160 billions in 1973 and almost five hundred billions five years later, when this market became the main mechanism for recycling the Klondike of oil-profits which the OPEC countries suddenly found themselves wondering how to spend and invest. The USA was the first country to find itself at the mercy of these vast, multiplying floods of unattached capital that

washed round the globe from currency to currency, looking for quick profits. Eventually all governments were to be its victims, since they lost control over exchange rates and the world money supply. By the early 1990s even joint action by leading central banks proved impotent.[56]

Throughout the 20th century, huge corporations had become transnational as they moved from the industrialized centres of capitalism, particularly the United States, stalking sources of cheaper labour and new markets, driven by the need for increased profit. At home profitability had reached an impasse. Abroad, cheap labour and resources, lower taxes, and few environmental and health controls were attractive. By the mid-1980s the TNCs numbered in the hundreds and controlled between a quarter and a third of all production and a larger percentage of its trade. According to Watkins: "In 1985, the combined size of the world's largest 200 TNCs exceeded $3 trillion, equivalent to nearly one third of global GDP."[57] Yet, despite the development of transnational trade, 90 per cent of global production was aimed at domestic markets: that is, most of what was produced in the United States and in the European Union was consumed in those same markets, not exported. "The national bases of production and trade remain for the domestic market," insists Michael Mann, who also argues, "It is doubtful whether, in many respects, capitalism is more transnational than it was before 1914."[58]

Most TNCs have been U.S.-owned; otherwise they are European (especially British) or Japanese. Few were from the Third World. Such TNCs accounted for the lion's share of U.S. exports—as high as 97 per cent, according to Brett.[59] Furthermore, although many TNCs moved into the Third World, most of their investment was in the developed countries. In 1975, for instance, only 26 per cent was in the Third World, and this amount was on the decline. Yet they had a huge influence in the Third World. In agriculture, for instance, "six TNCs control the distribution of 60 percent of the world's coffee, three TNCs sell 75 percent of the bananas, fifteen control more than half of the world's sugar trade, two TNCs control half the wheat trade, and two companies produce more than half of the farm machinery."[60] One firm, Cargill, has come close to monopolizing the coffee market. To talk thus about "the coffee market" is to talk, to a large extent, about what the family that owns Cargill decides. But Cargill's principal interest is not even coffee, it is grain, in which it is also the world's largest trader. Cargill controls 60 per cent of the world's grain trade, and it and five other grain companies control 96 per cent of U.S. wheat exports and 95 per cent of U.S. corn exports. "The same companies handled 90 percent of wheat and corn trade in the Common Market, 90 percent of Canada's barley exports, and 80 percent of Argentina's wheat exports,"

Barnet and Cavanagh found.[61] When the United States negotiates on matters concerning grains, Cargill does the homework and presents the papers to the government. It was once said by the fatalistic that Man proposes and God disposes; in cereals Cargill both proposes and disposes.

What does this transnationalization lead to? A U.S business executive working for the National Cash Register company expressed the view from the cash register with a pleasant straightforwardness: "I was asked the other day about United States competitiveness and I replied that I don't think about it at all. We at NCR think of ourselves as a globally competitive company that happens to be headquartered in the United States." In Eric Hobsbawm's view, "The most convenient world for multinational giants is one populated by dwarf states or no states at all."[62]

# Crisis: The 1960s to 1990s

The "Golden Age" of contemporary Western capitalism is said to have begun around 1950 and continued, after a slowdown between 1958 and 1964, into the early 1970s. The historian of the United States' half-century of dominance, Thomas J. McCormick, suggests that the American "high tide" came in the late 1950s and early 1960s and that, after a short period in the mid-1960s, the ebb-tide began to move with increasing certainty in the period 1968-76. "The United States," he notes, "came to bear a striking resemblance to Great Britain a century earlier."[63] This was Britain on a downhill slide.

In the best years of this period, the advanced Western economies had unprecedented growth rates of more than 4 per cent, rising to as high as 5.2 per cent, while even some low-income countries achieved rates as high as 4.4 per cent. A small number of rapidly developing countries gloried in truly astonishing rates: South Korea's "economic miracle" produced rates above 10 per cent overall for two decades and in manufacturing alone above 20 per cent for ten years.

But even in the early 1960s there were intimations, noticed by almost no one, that postwar prosperity might be as mortal as that of earlier epochs. One indicator was the "dollar overhang," a term referring to the excess of U.S. overseas liabilities over domestic foreign exchange reserves, including gold. By 1965 U.S. reserves were only $15.45 billion while its liabilities were $25.18 billion.[64] The next year President de Gaulle of France, perhaps partly resisting U.S. or any other strategic or economic hegemony, demanded that the United States convert a substantial amount of his country's dollar holdings into gold. If the Americans had allowed the conversion it would have weakened the dollar, but the U.S. allies stepped in and it didn't happen. The Americans were not alone in their woes. By 1967, after a long battle with their balance of payments, the British were forced to devalue, and in 1968 the French followed suit.

Between 1967 and 1971—the years of the most furious fighting in Vietnam—the U.S. deficit expanded from $2.9 billion to $19.8 billion. To deal with this problem, an essential element of the Bretton Woods system was simply liquidated. On August 15, 1971, President Nixon announced that the United States was unilaterally abrogating the Bretton Woods agreement by ending dollar-gold convertibility. In that same year growth in the advanced economies had halted. Nixon's intervention, which led to a devaluation of the dollar, together with wage and price controls, hitherto unheard of, got the U.S. economy going again, but the damage inflicted on world monetary order was severe. For capitalism the two decades of certainty appeared to be over, with a new era of instability, sharp currency fluctuations, and long-term recession setting in—although it could be debated whether this shift represented a disaster for the capitalist system or, rather, simply the exchange of one capitalistic epoch for another version, reorganized and with a new order of dominance.[65]

U.S. defence expenditures played a major part in this global shift. From the Korean War onwards, U.S. military outlays were significantly higher than those of its Western rivals. Much of this expenditure was overseas and benefited countries, such as Japan, that were becoming industrial competitors. While rivals invested in modernizing their social and economic infrastructures, the United States spent its efforts in an arms industry that was, in general economic terms, unproductive. The main U.S. beneficiary of this expenditure was what President Eisenhower, in the last year of his mandate in 1959, had called "the industrial-military complex"—the firms, such Lockheed, GM, or Litton, that made the arms and equipment and had intimate and not particularity discreet relations with the generals who disposed of them. According to Joyce Kolko, the long duration of the Vietnam War "had an organic effect on the whole world capitalist system." Along with other factors, the war had an inflationary impact on the whole economy through "increasing imports, over-priced exports, and especially the massive growth in the money supply to pay the deficit."[66]

## Fin de Good Times

For a short time after Nixon's readjustments to the international monetary system, the postwar boom staggered forward. In 1972-73, there was rapid economic growth and a leap upwards in the levels of world trade, connected with an investment boom. Countries in the Third World were jubilant as raw materials prices reached record highs.

Conventionally the end of the long boom (and the beginning of the recession of the late 1980s and early 1990s) is associated with the increase in oil prices at the end of the Arab-Israeli war of 1973. In three months, between October and December 1973, the posted, that is, official, price of oil almost quadrupled, going from $2.55 to $11.65 a barrel. By 1974, after further price increases, the price of oil had quintupled. All OPEC countries benefited from price increases, but the leader in the battle to push up oil prices was the shah of Iran, who needed money to finance his modernization projects. President Nixon complained strongly. The shah was unrelenting. Of the people of industrial nations, he said, "They will have to realize that the era of their terrific progress and even more terrific income and wealth based on cheap oil is finished."[67]

Less than two years after the oil shock, in November 1975, the heads of the six most advanced economies—the United States, Japan, Germany, France, Britain, and Italy—came together in a "summit." Representatives of these countries, known as the G6, and then, when Canada joined, the G7, had met before but never so earnestly. Their principal preoccupations were two linked issues: the slowdown in economic growth in the West, and especially in the United States, and price inflation, which had been stimulated by the rise in oil prices. Economists were only just beginning to see that the U.S. economy, which had been growing at an annual rate of 3.4 per cent after inflation over the century from 1870 to 1972, was now growing at a rate of only 2.3 per cent. This worrying slowdown, which was to continue into the 1990s, was mainly the fault of a decrease in productivity—that is, in the output of goods and services per hour of work.

The governmental brain trusts were not at all certain as to what could be done about the decline in output—perhaps it would recover on its own. But they saw inflation as a problem they could do something about; and they saw it as a much greater problem than unemployment, which was also rising. One way to curb inflation, they argued, was to cut social spending. From the second half of the 1970s throughout the 1980s and into the 1990s, politicians campaigned and governors of banks were elected and re-elected on the basis of the persuasiveness of their arguments in favour of cutting social spending, and, as we've seen, the same cutting solutions were to be applied to the Third World. Arguments for raising taxes to maintain levels of social spending, or for removing tax benefits for the wealthy, went unheeded, if they were heard at all. Indeed, in the United States in 1981-82, and in Britain and Canada thereafter, governments actually cut the amount of taxes paid by the most affluent sectors of the populations.

Now, when the representatives of the G7 countries contemplated the causes of the crisis of the mid-1970s, they observed that since the end of the Vietnam War there had been major shifts in what is called the "international division of labour," that is, the distribution among nations of the different tasks of world production and trade. This distribution, which many argued was "natural," gave some countries the blessings of advanced industry and others the less attractive benefits of providing labour, minerals, or agrarian commodities. What indeed had happened was that industrialization had crept out of the previously industrialized world into the so-called Newly Industrialized Countries (NICs). In his wide-ranging critique of Western development theories, Ozay Mehmet states: "Taiwan, South Korea, Hong Kong and Singapore emerged as the pioneering set of countries graduating out of the class of developing countries and into the coveted group of Newly Industrialized Countries (NICs). Graduation of the Dragons came right on the heels of the Japanese Miracle and it caught Western development theorists by surprise. These theorists were still preaching ISI strategy for the Third World when the Dragons had discovered export-led growth!"[68]

In the 1970s the growth of these NICs was accelerated by two factors: firms moved out of countries in which labour was dear and towards countries in which it was cheap; and they moved in the direction of "markets." Modern factories and refineries, built by Western firms, sprung up where few or none had existed before: in Mexico, Poland, Saudi Arabia, and Thailand. The economic growth was also aided by a political factor: the element of state capitalism. There was no "hidden hand" at play; on the contrary, dirigisme ruled supreme. Governments, mainly very conservative and often openly repressive, supported industry and directed economic growth. Regarding South Korea, for instance, Nigel Harris notes: "In the sixties and seventies, the state dominated the entire process of rapid economic growth. . . . The heart of Korean development was as state capitalist as any East European economy and as Keynesian as any West European state democracy."[69] Indeed, some countries in Asia had done so well, in large part because of the key role the state had played in directing and supporting economic expansion, that they avoided the downturn in the 1970s and their growth was accelerated. In Asia as a whole, growth figures for 1975-77 were higher than in 1967-72. The Asian golden age, it appeared, was about to succeed that of the West.

By contrast, the 1970s were the end of the Western golden age. By the mid-1970s the most advanced economies were being hurt by overcapacity in world markets. There were now too many producers of steel, ships, and shirts, and many of them could produce more cheaply than

Western countries. Most were bent on exporting manufactured products. Between 1973 and 1982 the NICs doubled their productive capacity. By 1982, they were producing 17 per cent of the world's crude steel, for instance, while steel production in the United States especially, but in the OECD countries as well, had gone into a sharp decline. After the mid-1970s, six Third World countries—Brazil, Argentina, Mexico, Taiwan, South Korea, and Venezuela—had become steel exporters. By 1979 Mexico had modern "direct reduction" mills and planned to sell its technology overseas. Even China, generally regarded as a great market for Japanese steel, paid the French and Swiss to provide the means to expand its production.

A major market for steel had been the U.S. auto industry. According to Joyce Kolko, "The United States's share of the total world auto output dropped from 50.4 percent in 1960 to 24.5 percent in 1980. Japan's rose over the same years from 4.9 percent to 28.8 percent, and the Japanese steel industry benefited from this expansion."[70] Korea also produced steel and cars to compete with the United States. Between 1973 and 1984 Korean steel production climbed from 1 to 12 million tons annually. In 1974 South Korea produced 9,100 cars and, in 1979, 114,000. Hyundai planned to produce between 5 and 6 million cars by 1991, of which around 3 million would be exported. In 1984 a U.S. undersecretary, forgetting the pledges of Bretton Woods, appealed to the world steelmakers not to sell technology to the Koreans because their exports of 5.7 million tons were perceived as threatening the U.S. output of 75 million tons.[71]

An already grave economic situation worsened. In late 1978 and early 1979, with the revolution in Iran bringing about the downfall of the shah and the second oil price shock, panic words like "free-for-all" and "anarchy" began to be heard in the West. In June 1979 line-ups at the gas pumps of the United States were seen as harbingers of apocalypse. President Jimmy Carter, who seemed unable to straighten things out, or at least unable to give the impression that he could, was replaced by 1980 by Ronald Reagan, who seemed made for the role. After defeating Carter Reagan said, "America is back." Optimism as a growth restorative had been reinvented but, better than that, new policies had been conceived.

The decade of the 1980s was one of increased turbulence. Against the 1970s background of perceived economic decline, U.S. policies of "military Keynesianism" gained ground and military spending rose rapidly. President Reagan promised his fellow countrypersons a "600-ship Navy," stimulating the part of the economy that survived from military procurements—the defence industries—and that consumed masses of both steel and manpower. In the mid-1980s the U.S. economy rallied on the basis of

military expenditures and massive borrowing (especially by means of bond
sales to Japan). When Reagan entered the White House in 1981 the federal budget deficit was $74 billion, and when he left in 1991 it was more
than $300 billion. In 1973 interest payments had been 7 per cent of the
total budget in 1973, and in 1992 they stood at 15 per cent.[72]

The high levels of defence expenditure in the 1980s were connected
to a perception that parts of the Third World were spinning out of Washington's control—a perception that had come to the fore with the fall of
Saigon. After its losing battle with "one of the poorest people on earth,"
according to Giovanni Arrighi, the great power of the United States had
"temporarily lost most, if not all of its credibility as the policeman of the
free world." Now local forces jumped into the vacuum, springing up all
over the map—not just in South Asia and Indochina but in Portugal's
African colonies and in Zimbabwe, Central America, and the Middle
East—in the attempt to take control over their people's destinies.[73] In late
1978 and 1979 Washington's watchman on the Gulf, the Pahlavi regime in
Iran, self-destructed, and at the end of the same year the Soviet Union
invaded Afghanistan. Maps in popular political weeklies showed readers
how Afghanistan was on the doorstep of the Gulf—and the West's main
supply of oil. Just south of the Rio Grande, in Nicaragua, the Sandinistas
had wrested power from Anastasio Somoza, the Batista of Central America. In the Eastern Caribbean a new revolutionary Grenada was located at
what was alleged to be one of the great strategic crossroads ("choke-
points") in the region. In Europe socialist governments came to power in
France and Spain.

A second, more severe recession began in the United States in 1980
and spread abroad, lasting until 1983. In the OECD countries unemployment rose faster than at any time since the Depression. As productive
capacity declined, onlookers witnessed frequent discussions of the "rust
belt" and "sunset industries" in the northern United States and saw sor-
rowful photos of British industrial plants being sold to the highest foreign
bidder. Governmental response came in the form of a more restrictive
monetary policy, with high interest rates a common prescription aimed at
remedying economic illnesses. The tight U.S. monetary policies hurt
Third World trade by reducing the demand for products from the South.
With declining exports came soaring payments to service debt. According
to Arrighi, "Latin American service payments . . . increased from less than
a third of its exports in 1977 to almost two-thirds in 1982. The ensuing
generalized state of *de facto* bankruptcy completed the reversal of the fortunes of Third world states in world financial markets."[74]

By 1984, fuelled by the record U.S. expenditure on arms, the climb out of the recession was under way, although high interest rates guaranteed greater debt in the future. An overvalued dollar had disastrous effects on the U.S. export trade. According to Joyce Kolko, "The United States lost 23 percent of its export share between 1980 and 1984 and saw a 20 percent increase in its imports relative to its GDP."[75] Recovery was fuelled not by production but by the growth of the retail service industry, with the expansion of that sector stimulated by imports.

In 1982, for the first time since 1945, U.S. direct investment abroad also declined (by 2 per cent). Foreign investment in the United States increased by 13 per cent. By 1984 the United States had become a net importer of capital for the first time since before World War I. By 1985, 30 years after its triumphant emergence from World War II, it was a net debtor. According to Joyce Kolko, "After sixty-five years as the world's creditor, the United States in 1985 became its largest debtor." Most of this indebtedness was connected to the cost of military expenditures. The United States, in the words of Paul Volcker, chairman of the Federal Reserve Board, had become "hostage" to foreign capital.[76] Others said that U.S. government policies had fallen hostage to the Federal Reserve—a clear recognition, seldom made with reference to the Third World, to the relationship between indebtedness and sovereignty.

Not surprisingly, the bankers in New York and the decision-makers in Washington did not sit idly by as the U.S. economy became decreasingly competitive. Just as, a century earlier, capitalists had sought vulnerable resources and markets in Africa and Asia to assuage another crisis, in the mid-1980s the Americans turned to the developing economies of their own Third World backyard. Free trade imperialism, caged for decades, was again released from captivity: beginning around 1985 Washington began to bang on the doors of the national economies of Mexico, Brazil, and Argentina demanding greater access to their markets in the name of a doctrine called "liberalization," which called for restructuring of national debts and agreement with World Bank plans for structural adjustment. Secret NAFTA negotiations with Mexico were held in January 1990; bank privatization took place in May 1990. U.S. imports flooded Mexico, where they were consumed mainly by the middle class. By late 1994 Mexico's foreign debt was overflowing and reserves had reached rock bottom. By that time the rich had begun to transfer their millions out of the country to safe havens in the United States, Switzerland, and the Cayman Islands—with Citibank suspected of offering them a helping hand.[77]

# Japan

Japan had been devastated during World War II, suffering from the destruction of nearly half of its industries. But with the Korean War, Washington turned its energies to supporting a program of Japanese economic recovery. At the time there was no fear that Japan would become a major competitor, but in the 1950s and 1960s the country's leaders showed themselves to have other ideas. They were determined to return to the front ranks of the industrial powers, and they did this by means of promoting a program of capital-intensive and high-technology industry.

In this program "the plan" took precedence over "the market." In the case of the Japanese economy, "the plan" was drawn up by two key ministries, the Ministry of International Trade and Industry and the Ministry of Finance. The term "laissez faire" was not heard; little was left to unseen forces. In the three decades from 1960 to 1990 Japan's GDP growth exceeded that of both the United States and Germany. In the decade 1961-70 it exceeded 10 per cent. "Miraculous recovery" was a term frequently used.

By the middle of the 1980s, despite reassurances from conservative political leaders that "America was back," disturbing (or at least confusing) economic graphs showing that the United States was in economic trouble continued to provoke concern. By early 1985 it had become apparent that Japan was the world's biggest creditor and that in the 1984 fiscal year it had a trade surplus of $45.5 billion. The Japanese had managed the remarkable feat of having a trade surplus with almost all Western countries except Switzerland.

"Korea came along and saved us," admitted a U.S. secretary of state, and "the *us* included Japan." U.S. military spending during the Korean War and later during the Vietnam War provided a great stimulus to the Japanese economy. By the late 1950s, just over a decade after it had been utterly desolated by war, Japan had begun to establish itself securely in overseas markets. Still, other than in the area of textiles, Japan was still scarcely seen as a competitor to the advanced economies of the West. In 1955 Japanese industry barely produced 69,000 cars. Then came the full force of the heat of the rising sun. By 1968 Japan was producing over four million cars, and its exports of cars and other expensive consumer goods were on the increase. By the mid-1980s Japan had become the largest car exporter in the world.

Its success was linked to several tightly linked factors. They included an exalted, and often exaggerated, role for the state in the export sector, especially through the Ministry of International Trade and Industry, and official encouragement of uniquely Japanese trading companies, which came to control over half of the country's import-export trade. These companies, with no parallels in the West, acted simultaneously as bankers, insurers, warehousers, and distributors. Still, a much smaller part of the Japanese economy was nationalized than in the leading Western countries.

The Japanese were highly protectionist; their markets were not wide open in accordance with free market doctrine. Even foreign investment was kept at arm's length. As late as 1994, due to the obstacles placed in the way of foreign investment by the Japanese state, industries, and banks, Japan had the lowest rate of foreign investment of any G7 country. The state in Japan, not the free market, had the decisive role. The developing economies in Pacific Asia, such as the Four Dragons, took Japan as their model. As Arthur MacEwan stresses, "In no case . . . has successful export-led growth been directed through the sort of deregulation that might be called 'free trade,' the sort of deregulation that is called for in the neo-liberal project."[78]

In early 1995 *The Economist*, writing on the phenomenon of Japan's new nationalism, admitted, "Where Japan walks, western fears are seldom far behind."[79] The new phobia was that the Japanese would forge an alliance with their Asian neighbours, in whose economies they had been investing since the 1970s. This alliance would be against the West. Already, at the November 1994 summit of the Asia-Pacific Economic forum (APEC), Japan had refused to support the U.S. demand for freer trade, arguing that the emerging market economies of Asia needed protection. Worse, the Keidanren, the association of Japanese big business, suggested that Japan should back the East Asian Economic Caucus (EAEC). This was a trade organization that had been invented to exclude the United States.

But by 1994 it seemed that the Japanese economy too had stalled. For the fiscal year ending March 31, 1994, Japan registered an economic growth of a miserable 0.2 per cent. The average share on the Japanese stock market was down around 40 per cent of its 1989 high. There was talk of financial collapse. *Time* magazine crowed, "Japan no longer has the wind at its back." In July *Le Monde diplomatique* carried the headline *"Le Japon en panne"* and made references in the article to Japan breaking down, the "end of the Golden Age" and "the end of the myth of excellence"—and that "something is rotten in the state of Japan." A World Bank report for 1994 predicted that 25 years in the future the three leading economies would be China, the United States, and, in third place, Japan.[80]

# The Economic Development of the Third World

At the end of World War II, most of colonial Asia, Africa, and the West Indies had been integrated into the world economy as a source of primary products. The extent of this integration varied. Laos, Cambodia, upper Burma, Afghanistan, and non-Soviet Central Asia, parts of Africa, Amazonia, Paraguay, New Guinea, and the Atlantic coast of Central America had been bitten off but barely chewed. Other parts of the world—such as Bolivia and Peru, the *pampas*, northeast Brazil, the South African Rand, the Zambian Copperbelt, the Maghrebian plain, India, Cochinchine, and Java—had been thoroughly chewed over and their wealth absorbed into the bloodstream of the capitalist world system.

Many colonies were part of the semi-autarkic imperial commercial and monetary blocs formulated in the 1930s as a response to the failures of international trade. The destruction of these blocs was one of the prerequisites for the liberalization of trade in the postwar period and thus a U.S. preoccupation. The means of this destruction was decolonization. Inevitably, as colonies became states, their ties with their former colonial masters weakened.

But the ex-colonial world was not satisfied with simply escaping the political bonds of colonialism. All independent countries wanted to grow economically, and this "development" required income from trade to finance industrialization. In the first paragraph of the first chapter of his *Industrialization in the Western World*, Tom Kemp states:

> There is scarcely a country in the modern world where an improvement in the material level of living is not regarded as a desirable goal by rulers and ruled alike, and where industrialization is not seen as the necessary means to achieve it. History is clearly on the side of this view. The nations which are rich and powerful possess a technologically advanced industrial base, capable of turning out a large volume of manufactured goods. Nations which are poor and dependent have little or no industry and are primarily agricultural.[81]

By 1995, although some claimed that the service sector was the industry of the future, world trade was still principally in manufactures.

For the newly independent countries, then, the big question of development was a simple one: how to industrialize or, in exceptional cases such as India and China, how to expand from an industrial base that already existed. This question had been addressed in China from the late 19th century and in Latin America from the late 1920s. One solution was to industrialize by first building a platform of agricultural exports. In the 1950s and 1960s this strategy seemed realistic, because the prices for agricultural commodities was generally high, which was in turn partly because of the wars in Korea, Vietnam, and elsewhere. But this state of affairs barely lasted into the 1970s, by which time food prices had begun to fall. At the same time oil prices rose sharply. The prospects for industrialization in many countries declined concomitantly. But in Pacific Asia this was not the case; the transition to industrial capitalism had taken place.

## Third World Developers

In 1992 and 1993 China had an average GDP growth rate of 13 per cent, the fastest growth of any country in the world. In the first quarter of 1994 China's GDP dropped only slightly, to 12.7 per cent. Since around 28 per cent of the world's population lived in China, this was particularly impressive. The forecast rate of growth for Singapore was only slightly less, at 11.6 per cent. Thailand's rate was 8.2 per cent, Malaysia's 8.1 per cent, Indonesia's 7 per cent, Taiwan's 6.1 per cent, and Hong Kong's 5.6 per cent.[82]

Beloved by economists and institutions like the World Bank, GDP and GNP growth rates in the abstract can be misleading. China and Singapore may have been in the same growth rate leagues, but it seemed unlikely that countries with large populations like China would ever reach Singapore's level of development or standard of living. No matter what its growth rate, China would always remain among low-income countries; and, equally, despite an amazing GDP, Indonesia still had a per capita income of only $650. Some 27 million people in Indonesia still live in absolute poverty.[83]

The "Four Dragons" or "Asian Tigers"—South Korea, Hong Kong, Taiwan, and Singapore—had been developing continuously since the 1960s, and by 1995 had most of the qualities of the poorer to middling states of the European Union nations: they were industrialized (agriculture contributing no more than 10 per cent to their GNPs; industry around 40 per cent); their industry was capital-intensive and based on high technology; they were consuming four times as much energy as their Asian neighbours; their 75 million inhabitants were exporting 5 times as much as the over one billion Chinese of China, and 17 times as much as the 850 million Indians. Their collective GNP was almost the equivalent of China's. In ranking measured by GNP, South Korea was 16th, Taiwan 20th, and Russia 15th.

How the Four Dragons came to be developed while countries in Latin America had failed, and how they had escaped the debt trap, form one of the greatest debates in contemporary development studies. But, for one thing, all of the Dragons developed to a great extent thanks to U.S. aid and

Japanese investment. The development strategy they used was also just the opposite of ISI, which the Latin Americans favoured. The strategy was known as "export-based development" and favoured production, generally of light-industrial and consumer goods, rather than heavy-industrial goods, aimed at the external rather than the internal market. None of the Dragons developed on the basis of the strategies recommended by the IMF and the World Bank—that is, on the principles of the "free market." Rather, all of them developed within the embrace of "the plan"—that is, the dirigiste and protectionist state. Finally, they were all small: two of them, Hong Kong and Singapore, are essentially islands. It is doubtful just how far their lessons can be applied to larger, more complex countries.[84]

## The Non-Developers

Given that agricultural exports, or commodities, were seen as being a necessary base for economic development, the prices that producers got for those exports in the postwar period became a key factor. For instance, tea, the staple agrarian export of Sri Lanka, earned 2.61 rupees a pound in 1954. In 1969 it earned 1.53 rupees a pound. This price collapse came as a result of increased worldwide production for the market—particularly from Kenya, Uganda, and Malawi in East Africa. Given a shortfall of income, every year between 1966 and 1975 the Sri Lankan government borrowed on the average $60 million. According to Paul Harrison, by 1975 Sri Lanka owed $1 billion, and the cost of paying back capital and interest devoured 20 per cent of its export earnings each year.[85] As the income of Sri Lankans fell, they were able to buy fewer manufactured goods, and the country's nascent manufacturing sector lost much of its domestic market.

Tanzania's main export earner was sisal, a raw material used in making rope. In the early 1970s, when sisal prices were high, the country prospered. The first spot of trouble came in late 1973, after oil prices started their sharp incline and the government had to dig deeply into its pockets to pay its fuel bill. Things grew worse: by 1976 sisal prices had tumbled down to around 50 per cent of the 1954 prices, in large part because natural rope was being replaced by synthetic products. Further catastrophe followed with the recession of the early 1980s, which saw commodity prices collapse once more.

For a period in the 1950s and 1960s Ghana was the world's major producer and exporter of cocoa. The selling price for cocoa rose from 21 cents a pound in 1949 to 58 cents in 1954. Just as Ghana was about to be born the price dropped to 27 cents, although, as if vindicating independence, it bounced up again in 1958 to 44 cents before dropping to 17 cents in 1965, the year before Nkrumah was overthrown. By July 1977 the price was up to 23 cents. Yet by the early 1990s Indonesian cocoa production, having undercut Ghana's cocoa in price, was poised to overtake Ghana in production.

Countries producing other commodities—sugar, bauxite, bananas, copper—followed much the same pattern. The combination of steadily falling world prices, as in the case of Sri Lanka, or rapidly fluctuating prices, as in the case of Ghana, led Harrison to conclude:

> Primary products, with very few exceptions, are a bad business to be in if you want a steady livelihood, but most of the developing countries depend on just one, two or at most three commodities. Hence their balance of payments, and the foreign exchange they need to buy machinery for their fledgling industries, are completely at the mercy of the fickle commodity trade winds. In the mid-seventies, many countries still had all their eggs in a single basket. Two thirds of Chad's exports were cotton, two thirds of Chile's were copper. Wood made up 65 per cent of the Congo's exports, sugar four fifths of Cuba's, cocoa two thirds of Ghana's. Three quarters of Liberia's produce was iron ore, sugar nine tenths of Mauritius's, cotton and yarn three fifths of Egypt's. Tea accounted for three fifths of Sri Lanka's exports, copper for three fifths of Zaire's and nine tenths of Zambia's. Coffee was a major earner for many countries, amounting to 37 per cent of Haiti's exports, 43 per cent of Rwanda's, 48 per cent of Ethiopia's, 50 per cent of Colombia's, 61 per cent of Uganda's and 84 per cent of Burundi's.[86]

When we talk about Ghanaian cocoa or Sri Lankan tea, we should visualize the producers of this country bearing their products to some marketplace, where the price is determined by some complicated and generally imperceptible power. This marketplace is the physical manifestation of an economic abstraction known as "the market" or "the free market." Much of world trade, though, is determined not by the "free market" but by the TNCs. The world's banana trade, for instance, is dominated by three food transnationals, United Brands, Standard Fruit, and Del Monte, which control almost the entire process of production and distribution. A UN study showed that for each retail dollar spent on bananas, less than 12 cents stayed in the exporting country, while 38 cents went to the multinationals involved.[87]

## Back to GATT

By the early 1990s it had become clear to more than one observer that the industrialized countries had imposed their own agenda on the latest round of GATT negotiations, rather than allowing the talks to raise and address the economic problems of the Third World. According to Watkins, "Many issues of vital concern to developing countries—such as the linkages between their debt and trade problems, depressed and volatile commodity prices, technology transfer and the restrictive business practices of western companies—have been excluded from the negotiations. Others, including the removal of trade barriers erected by the North over the past decade, have been consigned to the status of negotiating side-shows." Led by the U.S. government, the richer countries worked "to restructure the rules of world trade around the interests of powerful transnational corporations."[88]

The leading countries had conceived of a two-tier system centred, for the time being at least, on a competitive alliance between the three major blocs: the U.S.-dominated NAFTA, the German-centred EU, and the Japanese-led East Asian bloc. The benefits of commerce based on the 1993 agreement would go largely to those blocs, while according to OECD estimates less than a third of income gains would go to the South, and those gains would go overwhelmingly to China and a few upper-income Southeast Asian countries. Because of a loss of preferences in the European market, Sub-Saharan Africa would actually lose income.[89]

The agreement permitted capital to move without restraint to places with the lowest wages, where pollution controls were absent and human rights protection minimal. Consumers in the North might be able to buy their goods more cheaply, but the price would be paid (or not paid) in the Third World. More world trade would be concentrated in the hands of a few giant companies.

The countries of the Third World, which had little choice but to accept the agreement, would experience social dislocation and political instability on an unprecedented scale. About two billion people, around 40 per cent of the world's population, are dependent on small-scale agriculture for their sole source of income. Perhaps 40 per cent of them could be driven from the land over the next 10 to 20 years by the GATT deregulation of the world trade in grain. Their farms may be "inefficient" compared with the vast mechanized cultivation of the United States, but those farms happen to be what keeps them alive.

# Audit

After World War II and especially since the 1950s, the Third World seemed to be slowly developing—its economies had become even more integrated into global trade patterns and more industrialized, and the living standards of its people had begun to slowly rise. In 1965 manufactured goods accounted for only 16 per cent of the exports from the Third World, but by the early 1990s they had reached around 66 per cent. By the 1990s Third World markets absorbed 25 per cent of the industrial world's exports and a staggering 40 per cent of the exports of the United States. Most spectacularly, the Four Dragons moved into the suburbs of the developed world. Indonesia lifted itself out of the morass of the 1950s to see local living standards improve remarkably: from the end of the 1960s to 1992 annual per capita incomes went from $50 to $650.

Yet by the 1990s there was massive disappointment. Even Latin America, the richest continent in the Third World, had failed to meet development expectations. As Victor Bulmer-Thomas points out, "The economic development of Latin America since independence is a story of unfulfilled promise . . . not one republic has achieved the status of a developed country."[90] According to World Bank calculations, nearly a third of the region's people lived in poverty in 1989, up from 27 per cent a decade earlier; and for the adjacent states of the Caribbean, "The outlook for the 1990s does not look promising," the World Bank admitted.[91]

In the last decade of the 20th century, not only did relatively more people live in poverty in large parts of the Third World, but despite increasing its share of the world's trade the Third World also remained peripheral. Asia's share of world trade in 1993, for instance, was a mere 15 per cent. India's share of world exports in 1950 was 19 per cent and in 1994 was 0.5 per cent. Globally (as well as locally) there was still a great divide between the rich and poor. According to Watkins, "Some three-quarters of international trade and investment flows still take place between the industrialized countries, which account for just 15 percent of the world's population. There is a further concentration of economic power within these countries."[92] This economic power is also translated into power on the political or policy-making fronts, whether it is the U.S. government's tight monetary policies, the GATT agreements, or the World Bank and IMF strictures. Few Third World nations have had significant influence over the major trading or financial institutions that shaped the postwar world. Simultaneously, decline in the larger Third World economies—not Sri Lanka and Ghana, but Egypt and Argentina—went back to the failure of the ISI policies favoured by nationalist regimes in the first decades after World War II, followed by the failure of the later anti-protectionist policies of the 1970s and 1980s.

Until the 1980s, Western-dominated institutions had almost invariably argued that development—as they, themselves, defined it—would take place, providing their prescriptions for local improvements were followed. Those prescriptions changed on a regular basis, and most often ignored powerful local considerations, especially the specifics of local history. "Take-off" was to happen on runways that had paved over local historical development. Furthermore, the prescriptions skirted certain questions altogether: the need for Western profits from loans, for instance, or the role of Western consumption. Although by the 1990s the industrialized countries had 26 per cent of the population, they accounted for 81 per cent of energy consumption, 70 per cent of chemical fertilizers, and 87 per cent of world armaments. According to Escobar, one U.S. citizen was spending "as much energy as 7 Mexicans, 55 Indians, 168 Tanzanians, and 900 Nepalis."[93]

Almost invariably, development was meant to satisfy needs as defined in the West, with the focus shifting according to the latest trends.[94] In both the 1980s and 1990s, development circles stressed the search for and encouragement of "civic culture." Third World countries lacked grass-roots political institutions independent of governments, thought the developmentalists of the World Bank, and thus "governance" was invented and books on governance began to fill library shelves. As a report by the Canada-Americas Policy Alternatives (CAPA) notes, "good governance" in the definition of the World Bank and the IMF included "an efficient public service, a [high quality] judicial system . . . the accountable administration of public funds . . . respect for the law and human rights at all levels of the government, a pluralistic institutional structure, and a free press." In theory, the "good governance" model promoted values of "transparency, accountability . . . predictability, trust, responsiveness, professionalism, [and] anti-corruption."[95]

In the literature of politics and development the word was now everywhere: scholars had to address the question of Third World "governance" if they were to command serious attention and win research grants. It became a proposition universally acknowledged that the Third World needed more and better "governance" if it were to advance. Only occasionally was it acknowledged that the strategies imposed by World Bank and the IMF demolished schools, health programs, and infrastructures, thus creating the disorder that made effective "governance" unlikely.

But, as the CAPA report acknowledges: "Since the introduction of the notion of good governance, privileged neo-liberal business elites and technocrats have controlled the policy-making process in Latin America. Thus, good governance has been associated with, and subordinated to, the promotion of economic liberalization as a means of economic and democratic development. After more than a decade of SAPs and their severe social impacts, CAPA sees little in the way of sustainable democratization and development." The report concludes:

In most countries, economic liberalization and adjustment have compromised initiatives for social and political democratization. Social indicators reveal grim realities of poverty, illiteracy, and malnutrition. Income disparities have increased, creating larger groups of poor people, illiteracy, and malnutrition. Income disparities have increased, creating larger groups of poor people, without access to minimum quality health care or basic education. Simultaneously on the political front, a disorganization of the public participatory spaces has taken place, as manifested in the decay of political parties and the dramatic decline of trade union organizations.

Prior to the discovery that Third World states were lacking in "good governance," it was widely held in the West that their peoples were lacking in other qualities that entitled them to the claim of modernity. Where development didn't take place, therefore, the conventional Western assumption had been that women had the wrong attitudes to child care, or men had the wrong attitudes towards women, peasants had the wrong attitudes towards forests, or, from the 1970s in particular, retrograde customs or the state baffled the free working of the market. More development plans were thus drawn up (in Western centres) and more NGOs, more Western volunteers, more consultants, more conferences, and more journals were required.

Few attempts were made to generalize about the disastrous effects of developmentalism; industrial deaths at Bhopal in India, military deaths in Guatemala, ecological death everywhere. Most of the time these collateral costs, like the civilians caught in cross fire, were sublimated, rationalized, or just dismissed. Of course, this was not invariably the case. Sometimes those in authority admitted that the difficulties were great. In 1988 the chief economist for the World Bank admitted, "We did not think that the human cost of these programs could be so great, and economic gains so slow in coming."[96]

From the 1980s, two changes became evident. One, argues Escobar, rose from the grassroots and sought to transform development, that is, to provide an alternative, locally defined, development.[97] The most publicized example of this, if not necessarily the most important or effective, appeared in the 1994 rebellion in Chiapas in Mexico. Yet where these grassroots initiatives might lead in broader terms is yet to be seen; certainly the great food multinationals, the arms interests, the great names— General Motors, Citibank, Rockefeller, Nestlé—have shown no evidence of having changed their collective mind about the future. Still, many of the successful rebellions against modernization and development have been successful despite the hostility of governments and elites.

The second change of the 1980s was more bold but hardly more

innovative; it took the form of the outright rejection of "Westernization."
Outside the Tehran Hilton in the early 1990s hung a banner in Farsi:
"Modernization not Westernization." Following the May 1996 election in
India in which the Hindu-chauvinist BJP emerged with the largest number
of seats, its national secretary announced: "We are against Westernization.
India's culture is 1,000 years old." The defeated prime minister, P.V.
Narasimha Rao, had "failed to convince the nation that five years of eco-
nomic liberalization and stable central government had bettered people's
lives."[98] The message of the Islamic reformist Refah (Welfare) party in
Turkey, the popularity and prospects of which continued to rise into 1996,
and the "fundamentalist" Islamic Front for Salvation (FIS) in Algeria, overlap: both, in common with the Islamic Republic a decade earlier, challenge
Westernization but not modernization.

The alternative to Westernization seems bleak. Indians from left to
right regard Hindu chauvinism, however modified for the purposes of
political expediency, as horrifying. In Iran the heyday of the ayatollahs was
marked by incompetence and corruption, in Cambodia Pol Potism was
beyond nightmares, and in Algeria the struggle between a ferocious Westernized state apparatus and the terrorism of Islamic reformism has left the
majority despairing on the sidelines. In the words of the banned Algerian
popular singer, "Cheb" Khaled:

> Le baraka a foutu le camp
> L'égoism a effacé le solidarité
> Où sont les hommes d'antan?
> . . . Reste la fuit . . .
> Mais où?

> Fortune has forsaken us
> Egoism has erased solidarity
> Where are the men of yesterday?
> . . . Only escape remains . . .
> But where?[99]

# Notes

## 1 The Third World: From Western Perspectives

1 Keddie, *Iran and the Muslim World*, 213.
2 Williams, *Keywords*, 58.
3 Eastman, *Family, Fields and Ancestors*, 159, 167.
4 Williams, *Keywords*, 103.
5 Kataoka, *Price of a Constitution*, 85.
6 Dulles, "Policy for Security and Peace."
7 Quoted in Hane, *Eastern Phoenix*, 94.
8 Laffey, *Civilization and Its Discontented*, 4.
9 Quoted in Laffey, *Civilization and Its Discontented*, 11.
10 Quoted in Hall, "Negotiating Caribbean Identities," 10.
11 Quoted in Spurr, *Rhetoric of Empire*, 31.
12 Quoted in Said, *Culture and Imperialism*, p.xvii.
13 LaFeber, *Inevitable Revolutions*, 37-8.
14 Quoted in Berman and Lonsdale, *Control and Crisis in Colonial Kenya*, 144.
15 Louis, *British Empire in the Middle East*, 226.
16 Quoted in Kataoka, *Price of a Constitution*, 31.
17 Wolf, *Europe and the People without History*, 5.
18 For a fuller discussion of the history of the idea of "Western civilization," see Novick, *That Noble Dream*, 311-14.
19 Flower, *Serving Secretly*, 256.
20 Quoted in Kesselman, "Order or Movement?" 139.
21 Wolf, *Europe and the People without History*, 4-5.
22 Bernal, *Chinese Socialism to 1907*, 5.
23 Kennedy, *Rise and Fall of the Great Powers*, 539.
24 Kennedy, *Preparing for the Twenty-First Century*, 310.
25 Much of what appears in the following paragraphs draws on information in Cowen and Shenton, *Doctrines of Development* (1996). I am grateful to Bob Shenton for letting me see a manuscript version of his book in advance of publication.
26 *Far Eastern Economic Review*, April 28, 1994, 66.
27 Moughrabi, "Media and the Polls," 38-40.
28 Quoted in O'Brien, "Modernization, Order, and the Erosion of a Democratic Ideal," 356.
29 Quoted in Escobar, *Encountering Development*, 3.
30 Lerner, *Passing of Traditional Society*, p.vii.
31 Escobar, *Encountering Development*, 215.
32 Mason, "Stages of Economic Growth Revisited," 117.
33 McCormick, *America's Half-Century*, 120.

34 Huntington, *Political Order in Changing Societies*, 47.
35 Ibid., 157.
36 Richards and Waterbury, *Political Economy of the Middle East*, 359.
37 Chomsky, *Necessary Illusions*, 284.
38 Lehmann, *Democracy and Development in Latin America*, 26.
39 Baran and Hobsbawm, "Stages of Economic Growth."
40 Bagchi, *Political Economy of Underdevelopment*, 39.
41 Lehmann, *Democracy and Development in Latin America*, 28.
42 Leys, "Underdevelopment and Dependency."
43 Hutton, *State We're In*, 67.
44 Kay, *Latin American Theories of Development and Underdevelopment*, 202.
45 *The Guardian Weekly* (London), April 21, 1996, 16.
46 World Commission on Environment and Development, *Our Common Future*, 43.
47 Escobar, *Encountering Development*, 193-4.
48 Gosse, *Where the Boys Are*, 1994.
49 Buchanan, " Third World," 5-16.
50 Staniland, *American Intellectuals and African Nationalists*, 22-8.
51 Quoted in Bello, *Dark Victory*, 7.
52 Escobar, *Encountering Development*, 217.
53 Davies, "Who Killed Los Angeles?" 40.
54 Huntington, "Clash of Civilizations?" 22-49.
55 Kaplan, *The Atlantic Monthly*, February 1994, 44-76; David, "Why the Third World Still Matters," *International Security* 17, 3 (Winter 1992/93), 138.
56 *Le Monde*, Oct. 23, 1992; *Le Monde Diplomatique*, April 1993; *London Review of Books*, March 11, 1993; *La Presse*, May 28, 1993.
57 Bello, *Dark Victory*, 95-7.
58 Ibid.
59 *The Globe and Mail* (Toronto), April 6, 1995.
60 Escobar, *Encountering Development*, ch.6.
61 Barber, *Jihad vs. McWorld*, 199.

# 2 Latin America: Argentina, Brazil, Chile, and Mexico

1 Bulmer-Thomas, *Economic History of Latin America*, 283.
2 Ibid., 356.
3 Shumway, *Invention of Argentina*, p.x.
4 Bourne, *Political Leaders of Latin America*, 267.
5 Corradi, *Fitful Republic*, 69.
6 Ibid., 70-1.
7 Rock, "Argentina, 1930-46," 129-30.
8 Quoted in O'Brien and Cammack, *Generals in Retreat*, 49, 82, fn28.
9 Smith, "Reflections on the Political Economy of Authoritarian Rule and Capitalist Reorganization in Contemporary Argentina," 37.
10 Winn, *Americas*, 308, 344.
11 The information in this and the two following paragraphs are based on Keen, *History of Latin America*, vol. 2, 324-5.
12 Midré, "Bread or Solidarity?" 358.
13 Ibid., 362.
14 Burkett and Richards, "Argentine Election Results," 4.
15 Keen, *History of Latin America*, vol. 2, 326.
16 Evans, *Dependent Development*, 89-90.
17 Gosse, *Where the Boys Are*, 25.
18 Schneider, *"Order and Progress,"* 193.
19 Quoted in Evans, *Dependent Development*, 93.
20 Cited in Leacock, *Requiem for a Revolution*, 14-15.

21  Colby, with Bennett, *Thy Will Be Done*, 423.
22  Schneider, *"Order and Progress,"* 195.
23  Alves, *State and Opposition in Military Brazil*, 125.
24  Cammack, "Brazil," 22.
25  Harris, *End of the Third World*, 84.
26  Fiori, "Cardoso among the Technopols," 18.
27  Burns, *Latin America*, 254.
28  Alves, *State and Opposition in Military Brazil*, 233.
29  Sader and Silverstein, *Without Fear of Being Happy*, 20.
30  Alves, *State and Opposition in Military Brazil*, 113.
31  Cammack, "Brazil," 54.
32  Fiori, "Cardoso among the Technopols," 21.
33  Hecht, "Love and Death in Brazil," 130.
34  *Financial Times* (London and New York), June 6, 1996, 1.
35  Petras and Leiva, *Democracy and Poverty in Chile*, 37.
36  Vergara, "Changes in the Economic Functions of the Chilean State under the Military Regime," 86.
37  Blasier, *Hovering Giant*, 262.
38  Landau, *Dangerous Doctrine*, 106.
39  Quoted in Constable and Valenzuela, *Nation of Enemies*, 23.
40  Petras and Leiva, *Democracy and Poverty in Chile*, 41-2, fn10.
41  Winn, *Americas*, 323.
42  Timerman, *Chile*, 4.
43  Silva, "Technocrats and Politics in Chile," 394.
44  Petras and Leiva, *Democracy and Poverty in Chile*, 21.
45  Oxhorn, "Popular Sector: Response to an Authoritarian Regime," 68-9.
46  Spooner, *Soldiers in a Narrow Land*, 166.
47  Petras and Leiva, *Democracy and Poverty in Chile*, 35.
48  Ibid.
49  Oxhorn, "Popular Sector: Response to an Authoritarian Regime," 71.
50  Angell and Graham, "Can Social Sector Reform Make Adjustment Sustainable and Equitable?" 208.
51  Quoted in Nun, "Democracy and Modernization: Thirty Years Later," 16.
52  Angell and Graham, "Can Social Sector Reform Make Adjustment Sustainable and Equitable?" 210.
53  *London Review of Books*, Sept. 22, 1994, 26.
54  Barry, *Zapata's Revenge*, 25.
55  Meyer and Sherman, 1991, 645.
56  Hamilton and Harding, *Modern Mexico*, 96.
57  Moody, "NAFTA and the Corporate Redesign of North America," 100.
58  Quoted in Hamilton and Harding, *Modern Mexico*, 1986, 97.
59  Smith, "Mexico Since 1946," 371.
60  Moody, "NAFTA and the Corporate Redesign of North America," 99ff. Much of the data that follows, though not necessarily the interpretation, draws from Moody's article.
61  Barry, *Zapata's Revenge*, 41.
62  Moody, "NAFTA and the Corporate Redesign of North America," 101.
63  See La Botz, *Democracy in Mexico*, 62, 123.
64  Otero, "Mexico's Political Future(s) in a Globalizing World Economy," 321.
65  *The Nation*, March 6, 1995, 307.
66  Quoted in Petras and Vieux, "Twentieth-Century Neoliberals," 76.
67  Canada-Americas Policy Alternatives, *Focus on Corruption*, 3-4.
68  *The Nation*, Jan. 1, 1996, 19.
69  "Survey," *The Economist*, Jan. 9-15, 1995, 1.
70  Burbach, "Roots of the Postmodern Rebellion in Chiapas," 115.
71  *The Nation*, March 6, 1995, 308.
72  *Mexico Times*, Dec. 22, 1995.
73  *The Nation*, Dec. 18, 1995, 782.

74 Castaneda, *Mexico Shock*, 144.
75 *The Economist*, Jan. 7-13, 1995, 59.
76 Barry, *Zapata's Revenge*, 49-50; *Mexico Times*, Dec. 18, 1995, 36, 38.
77 Casteneda, *Mexico Shock*, 215.
78 Bulmer-Thomas, *Economic History of Latin America*, 313.
79 Castaneda, *Mexico Shock*, 48.
80 Bulmer-Thomas, *Economic History of Latin America*, p.v.
81 Dore and Weeks, "Changing Faces of Imperialism," 13.
82 Ibid.

# 3 The Caribbean: Jamaica, Haiti, and Cuba

1 Wallace, *British Caribbean*, 58.
2 Stone, *Class, State, and Democracy in Jamaica*, 38-9, 45.
3 Lewis, *Growth of the Modern West Indies*, 187.
4 Stone, "Power, Policy and Politics in Independent Jamaica," 21-2.
5 Ibid., 22, 24.
6 Manley, *Struggle on the Periphery*, 30-1.
7 Stone, "Power, Policy and Politics in Independent Jamaica," 34.
8 Stephens and Stephens, *Democratic Socialism in Jamaica*, 56.
9 Payne, "Liberal Economics Versus Electoral Politics in Jamaica," 29.
10 Stone, quoted in Panton, *Jamaica's Michael Manley*, 45.
11 Bob Marley, "War," 1976; my thanks to Alex Home-Douglas for this reference.
12 Panton, *Jamaica's Michael Manley*, 37,42.
13 Payne, *Politics in Jamaica*, 59.
14 Payne, "Liberal Economics Versus Electoral Politics in Jamaica," 33.
15 Panton, *Jamaica's Michael Manley*, 80.
16 Payne and Sutton, *Modern Caribbean Politics*, 21.
17 Payne, "The 'New' Manley and the New Political Economy of Jamaica."
18 Payne, "Liberal Economics Versus Electoral Politics in Jamaica," 52-3.
19 Panton, *Jamaica's Michael Manley*, 91.
20 Monroe, *Cold War and the Jamaican Left*, 3.
21 Panton, *Jamaica's Michael Manley*, 187.
22 The Duvalierist version of the Lord's Prayer was invented to commemorate Papa Doc's election as president for life in 1964. Quoted in Ferguson, *Papa Doc, Baby Doc*, 49.
23 Ferguson, *Papa Doc, Baby Doc*, 40-1.
24 Ibid., 53-4.
25 Labelle, *Ideologie de couleur et classes sociales en Haiti*, 76, and n5.
26 Lundahl, "Underdevelopment in Haiti," 42.
27 Ferguson, *Papa Doc, Baby Doc*, 70.
28 Ibid., 90.
29 Wilentz, *Rainy Season*, 53.
30 *La Presse* (Montreal), Dec. 8, 1988; author's translation.
31 Wilentz, *Rainy Season*, 112.
32 *The Nation*, Aug. 22-29, 1994, 184.
33 Quoted in Balfour, *Castro*, 13.
34 Dunn, *Modern Revolutions*, 219.
35 Karol, *Guerillas in Power*, 139.
36 Balfour, *Castro*, 65.
37 Dominguez, "Cuba Since 1959," 460.
38 Much of the narrative in this section is derived from Gleijeses, "Ships in the Night."
39 Kolko, *Confronting the Third World*, 142.
40 Gleijeses, "Ships in the Night," 42.
41 Eckstein, *Back from the Future*.
42 *Libération*, Oct. 7, 1992.
43 Quoted in Benglesdorf, *Problem of Democracy in Cuba*, 143.

44 Eckstein, *Back from the Future*, 51.
45 Bourne, *Castro*, 295.
46 Habel, *Cuba*, 5.
47 Zimbalist, "Teetering on the Brink," 407-13.
48 Eckstein, *Back from the Future*, 95.
49 Ibid., 93.
50 Ibid., 95.
51 Ibid., 107.
52 Habel, *Cuba*, 29.
53 Quoted in Stubbs, *Hearts and Minds in Guerilla Warfare*, 91.
54 Gleijeses, "Cuba's First Venture into Africa," 191-2.
55 Habel, *Cuba*, 212.
56 Balfour, *Castro*, pp.viii-ix.
57 Eckstein, *Back from the Future*, Tables 4.1, 5.1, 5.2, 224-6; and Dominguez, "Cuba Since 1959," 121.

# 4 The Middle East: Turkey, Egypt, and Iran

1 Keyder and Oncu, "Introduction," 6.
2 For developmentalists on Turkey, see, for instance, Huntington, *Political Order in Changing Societies*, 221, 347-52; and Lerner, *Passing of Traditional Society*, 136-66.
3 Ahmad, *Making of Modern Turkey*, 104; Eralp, "Turkey in the Changing Postwar Political Order," 209.
4 Keyder, *State and Class in Turkey*, 124.
5 Ibid., 124.
6 Ibid., 137-9.
7 Oncu, "Street Politics," 275.
8 Eralp, "Turkey in the Changing Postwar Political Order," 211.
9 Ahmad, *Making of Modern Turkey*, 130-1.
10 Hiro, *Between Marx and Muhammad*, 57.
11 Eralp, "Turkey in the Changing Postwar Political Order," 214.
12 Ahmad, *Making of Modern Turkey*, 174.
13 Eralp, "Turkey in the Changing Postwar Political Order," 219.
14 Owen, *State, Power and Politics in the Making of the Modern Middle East*, 157.
15 Ahmad, *Making of Modern Turkey*, 13.
16 Kurkcu, "Crisis of the Turkish State," 5-6.
17 Ayata, "Patronage, Party and the State," 46.
18 Ibid., 52.
19 Gulalp, "Islamist Party Poised for National Power in Turkey," 54-6.
20 Ibid.
21 Kurkcu, "Crisis of the Turkish State," 7.
22 Keyder and Oncu, "Introduction," 7.
23 Richards and Waterbury, *Political Economy of the Middle East*, 196-7.
24 Ibid.
25 Quoted in Yapp, *Near East since the First World War*, 221.
26 Stephens, *Nasser*, 580.
27 Waterbury, *Egypt of Nasser and Sadat*, 260.
28 Yapp, *Near East since the First World War*, 218-19.
29 Aly, "International System and State Policies," 194-5.
30 Cleveland, *History of the Modern Middle East*, 339.
31 Ibrahim, "Egypt's Landed Bourgeoisie," 37.
32 *New York Review of Books*, April 6, 1995, 34.
33 *Middle East Journal*, 49,1 (1995), 9-27.
34 "Cassandra," *Middle East Journal*, 49,1 (1995), 20.
35 Keddie, *Roots of Revolution*, 111.

36 Hiro, *Iran under the Ayatollahs*, 36.
37 Yergin, *The Prize*, 477.
38 Hiro, *Iran under the Ayatollahs*, 41.
39 Abrahamian, *Iran between Two Revolutions*, 420.
40 Keddie, *Iran and the Muslim World*, 169.
41 Cottam, "Iranian Revolution," 79.
42 Munson, *Islam and Revolution in the Middle East*, p.ix.
43 Abrahamian, *Iran between Two Revolutions*, 436.
44 Hiro, *Iran under the Ayatollahs*, 54.
45 Abrahamian, *Iran between Two Revolutions*, 465; Keddie, *Iran and the Muslim World*, 170.
46 Cleveland, *History of the Modern Middle East*, 400-1.
47 Kamrava, *Revolution in Iran*, 114.
48 Tohidi, "Modernity, Islamization and Women in Iran," 122.
49 Kamrava, *Revolution in Iran*, 121-2.
50 Hobsbawm, *Age of Extremes*, 454-5.
51 Quoted in Munson, *Islam and Revolution in the Middle East*, 3.
52 Le Monde, *L'Histoire au Jour Le Jour*, 966.
53 *The Economist*, March 25, 1995.
54 Banuazizi, "Iran's Revolutionary Impasse," 5.
55 Halliday, *Islam and the Myth of Confrontation*, 75.
56 Ahmad, *Making of Modern Turkey*, 53.
57 Richards and Waterbury, *Political Economy of the Middle East*, 359-60.
58 Halliday, *Islam and the Myth of Confrontation*, 48.
59 Richards and Waterbury, *Political Economy of the Middle East*, 431.

# 5 Africa: Ghana, Kenya, and South Africa

1 Cowen and Shenton, *Doctrines of Development*, 295.
2 Quoted in Davidson, *Black Man's Burden*, 39.
3 *Lagos Weekly Record*, March 6, 1915.
4 Bourdillon, *Future of the Colonial Empire*, 53-4.
5 Ibid., 22-3.
6 Quoted in Fitch and Oppenheimer, *Ghana*, 36.
7 Amin, *Neo-Colonialism in West Africa*, 244-5.
8 Quoted in Fitch and Oppenheimer, *Ghana*, 8.
9 Birmingham, *Kwame Nkrumah*, 92.
10 Quoted in Fitch and Oppenheimer, *Ghana*, 7.
11 Jamal and Weeks, *Africa Misunderstood*, 103.
12 Quoted in Brittain, "Ghana's Precarious Revolution," 50.
13 Young, *Colonial State in Comparative Perspective*, 5.
14 United Nations Development Programme (UNDP), *Human Development Report 1996*, 173.
15 Ibid., 57.
16 Freund, *Making of Contemporary Africa*, 241.
17 UNDP, *Human Development Report 1996*, 171.
18 Ibid., 27.
19 Green, "Ghana's 'Adjusted' Democracy," 58.
20 Quoted in Berman, *Control and Crisis in Colonial Kenya*, 184.
21 Leys, "Underdevelopment and Dependency," 42.
22 Hargreaves, *Decolonization in Africa*, 195.
23 UNDP, *Human Development Report 1996*, 179.
24 Himbara, in Berman and Leys, *African Capitalists in African Development*, 70.
25 Miller and Yeager, *Kenya*, 78-7.
26 Ibid., 78.
27 HNDP, *Human Development Report 1996*, 139.
28 Ibid., 52.
29 Miller and Yeager, *Kenya*, 83.

30 Himbara, in Berman and Leys, *African Capitalists in African Development*, 73.
31 Quoted in Bundy, *Illustrated History of South Africa*, 370.
32 O'Meara, *Forty Lost Years*, 69.
33 Ibid., 109, 117.
34 Alden, *Apartheid's Last Stand*, 19.
35 Quoted in O'Meara, *Forty Lost Years*, 197.
36 O'Meara, *Forty Lost Years*, 180.
37 Alden, *Apartheid's Last Stand*, 1996, 30.
38 Quoted in O'Meara, *Forty Lost Years*, 1.
39 AP release, in *The Globe and Mail*, Dec. 5, 1996, A20.
40 Jenny Morgan, *The Guardian Weekly*, Sept. 15, 1996, 22; David Ransom, *New Internationalist*, March 1995, 10; *The Globe and Mail Report on Business*, January 1996, 106.
41 UNDP, *Human Development Report 1996*, 179, 228.
42 Fieldhouse, *Black Africa*, 71.
43 Sender and Smith, *Development of Capitalism in Africa*, 62-3.
44 Quoted in Young, *Colonial State in Comparative Perspective*, 213-14.
45 Bello, *Dark Victory*, 54.
46 *The Guardian Weekly*, Sept. 22, 1996, 21.
47 UNDP, *Human Development Report 1996*, 64.

# 6 South Asia: India, Pakistan, and Bangladesh

1 Quoted in Dalton, *Mahatma Gandhi*, 16.
2 Mehta, *Rajiv Gandhi and Rama's Kingdom*, 186.
3 Sarkar, *Modern India*, 404.
4 Ibid., 423, 411.
5 McMahon, *Cold War on the Periphery*, 62, 89, 218, 224, 281.
6 Quoted in Akbar, *Making of India*, 509.
7 Quoted in McMahon, *Cold War on the Periphery*, 282.
8 Quoted in Akbar, *Making of India*, 484.
9 Akbar, *Making of India*, 495.
10 Bettleheim, *India Independent*, 145.
11 Akbar, *Making of India*, 466.
12 Ibid., 466.
13 Ibid., 472.
14 Rothermund, *Economic History of India*, 133.
15 Thakur, "Restoring India's Economic Health," 138-9.
16 Frankel, *India's Political Economy*, 227.
17 Thakur, *Government and Politics of India*, 314.
18 Ibid., 338.
19 Wolpert, *New History of India*, 398.
20 Thakur, *Government and Politics of India*, 341.
21 Mehta, *Rajiv Gandhi and Rama's Kingdom*, 77.
22 Ibid., 79.
23 Ibid., 164.
24 Quoted in Mehta, *Rajiv Gandhi and Rama's Kingdom*, 157-60.
25 Thakur, "Restoring India's Economic Health," 139-42.
26 This and the following quotations are from Thakur, *Government and Politics of India*, 314.
27 Noman, *Political Economy of Pakistan*, 12.
28 Jalal, *State of Martial Rule*, 64.
29 McMahon, *Cold War on the Periphery*, 160.
30 Noman, *Political Economy of Pakistan*, 27.
31 Huntington, *Political Order in Changing Societies*, 251, 261.
32 Wolpert, *Zulfi Bhutto of Pakistan*, 92.
33 Ibid., 112.

34 Ibid., 144.
35 *New Internationalist*, September 1995, 36.
36 Jalal, *State of Martial Rule*, 326.
37 Noman, "Pakistan and General Zia," 44-5.
38 Noman, "Pakistan and General Zia," 47.
39 UNDP, *Human Development Report 1996*, 171, 177.
40 Noman, "Pakistan and General Zia," 50.
41 Macaulay, "Karachi Slays Me," 12.
42 Bagchi, *Political Economy of Underdevelopment*, 241-2.
43 Maniruzzaman, "Bangladesh," 218-19.
44 *Far Eastern Economic Review*, April 21, 1994, 19.

# 7 Southeast Asia: Vietnam, Cambodia, and Indonesia

1 McCormick, *America's Half-Century*, 150.
2 Fitzgerald, *Fire in the Lake*, 135.
3 Post, *Socialism and Nationalism in Viet Nam*, vol. 1, 187.
4 Ibid., fn90.
5 Post, *Socialism and Nationalism in Viet Nam*, vol. 3, 179, 184.
6 Ibid., 147.
7 Young, *Vietnam Wars*, 301-3.
8 Kolko, *Restructuring the World Economy*, 20-1.
9 Ambrose, *Rise to Globalism*, 257.
10 Pomonti and Tertrais, *Viêtnam*, 24.
11 Sheehan, *After the War Was Over*, 17.
12 Ibid., 18-19.
13 World Bank, *Awakening the Market*, 28.
14 Greenfield, "Development of Capitalism in Vietnam," 205.
15 Kolko, *Anatomy of War*, 569.
16 Evans and Rowley, *Red Brotherhood at War*, 24-2.
17 Kolko, *Anatomy of War*, 591.
18 Guillebaid, *Return to Vietnam*, 73.
19 Evans and Rowley, *Red Brotherhood at War*, 20.
20 Osborne, *Sihanouk*, 86.
21 Kahin and Kahin, *Subversion as Foreign Policy*, 9.
22 Osborne, *Sihanouk*, 102-3.
23 Vickery, *Kampuchea*, 22-3.
24 Osborne, *Sihanouk*, 166.
25 Kiernan in Kiernan and Boua, *Peasants and Politics in Kampuchea*, 284.
26 Chandler, *History of Cambodia*, 282.
27 Chandler, *Brother Number One*, 1.
28 Kiernan, *Pol Pot Regime*, 460.
29 Evans and Rowley, *Red Brotherhood at War*, 99.
30 Kiernan, *Pol Pot Regime*, 464.
31 Chandler, *Brother Number One*, 4.
32 Kiernan, *Pol Pot Regime*, 458.
33 Cited in Kiernan, "William Shawcross: Declining Cambodia," 56.
34 *Far Eastern Economic Review*, April 27, 1995, 32.
35 Shawcross, "Tragedy in Cambodia," 43.
36 Ibid., 45.
37 Kahin and Kahin, *Subversion as Foreign Policy*, 17, 37.
38 Ibid., 10.
39 Ibid., 217.
40 Benedict Anderson, *London Review of Books*, Aug. 24, 1995, 19.
41 Vatikiotis, *Indonesia under Suharto*, 178.
42 This suggestion appeared in "US agents drew up Indonesian hit list," *The Guardian*

(London), May 22, 1990. But as Benedict Anderson argues, the destruction of the PKI and its failure to re-emerge cannot be blamed on any imperialist power. See Anderson, "Rewinding 'Back to the Future,'" 137.

43 Kahin and Kahin, *Subversion as Foreign Policy*, 230.
44 Kiernan in Chandler and Kiernan, *Revolution and Its Aftermath in Kampuchea*, 142.
45 Quoted in Kahin and Kahin, *Subversion as Foreign Policy*, 228.
46 Bresnan, *Managing Indonesia*, 109.
47 Robison, *Rise of Capitalism in Indonesia*, 147.
48 Bresnan, *Managing Indonesia*, 105.
49 Vatikiotis, *Indonesia under Suharto*, 34.
50 Pilger, "On Her Majesty's Bloody Service," 18. For the massacre of people from Timor, as well as in northern Sumatra, where 2,000 civilians were killed between 1989 and 1993, and West Irian, where hundreds have been killed, see Amnesty International, *Power and Impunity*, 50-8.
51 Vatikiotis, *Indonesia under Suharto*, 40.
52 Aswicahyono, Bird, and Hill, "What Happens to Industrial Structure When Countries Liberalise?" 345.
53 Vatikiotis, *Indonesia under Suharto*, 5, 50-5.
54 *The Observer* (London), Nov. 13, 1994.
55 *The Globe and Mail*, Feb. 1, 1994; *The Guardian*, June 28, 1994.
56 *Far Eastern Economic Review*, Dec. 22, 1994, 21.
57 *The Guardian Weekly*, Aug. 20, 1995, 3; *New Statesman and Society*, June 16, 1995, 14-15.
58 Bourchier and Legge, *Democracy in Indonesia*, 316.

# 8 China

1 Chesneaux, Le Barbier, Bergere, *China from the 1911 Revolution to Liberation*, 346; Spence, *In Search of Modern China*, 541.
2 Spence, *In Search of Modern China*, 389-90.
3 Hsu, *Rise of Modern China*, 637.
4 Leffler, *Preponderance of Power*, 81.
5 Hsu, *Rise of Modern China*, 636.
6 Ibid., 629.
7 Goncharov, Lewis, and Xue Litai, *Uncertain Partners*, 14.
8 In Schurmann and Schell, *Republican China*, 368, 370.
9 Fairbank, *United States and China*, 350.
10 Goncharov, Lewis, and Xue Litai, *Uncertain Partners*, 57.
11 Chesneaux, *China*, 73.
12 Spence, *In Search of Modern China*, 572.
13 Chang, *Wild Swans*, 281; Spence, *In Search of Modern China*; Chesneaux, *China*.
14 Hane, *Eastern Phoenix*, 9.
15 Kelliher, *Peasant Power in China*, 122.
16 See Lardy, "Economic Recovery and the First Five-Year Plan," 371.
17 Becker is quoted in Link, "Plant Less, Produce More, Harvest Less," 3; for the industrial decline see Goodman, *Deng Xiaoping and the Chinese Revolution*, 65.
18 Zhou, *How the Farmers Changed China*, 13.
19 Quoted in Spence, *In Search of Modern China*, 603.
20 Cited in Chesneaux, *China*, 157.
21 Chesneaux, *China*, 153-4.
22 Karol, *Second Chinese Revolution*, 4.
23 Hsu, *China without Mao*, p.vi.
24 Salisbury, *New Emperors*.
25 Spence, *In Search of Modern China*, 617.
26 Quoted in Meisner, *Mao's China and After*, 428.
27 Friedman, "The Innovator," 300.

28  Meisner, *Mao's China and After*, 444-5.
29  Hobsbawm, *Age of Extremes*, 470.
30  Kelliher, *Peasant Power in China*, 89.
31  Kelliher, *Peasant Power in China*; Zhou, *How the Farmers Changed China*, esp. ch.3.
32  Quoted in Schell, *To Get Rich Is Glorious*, 115.
33  Ibid., 21.
34  Goodman, *Deng Xiaoping and the Chinese Revolution*, 90.
35  Zhou, *How the Farmers Changed China*, 231.
36  Baum, *Burying Mao*, 175.
37  Schell, *To Get Rich Is Glorious*, 68-83.
38  Meisner, *Mao's China and After*, 476.
39  Baum, *Burying Mao*, 175.
40  Goldman, *Sowing the Seeds of Democracy in China*, 25-61.
41  Brook, *Quelling the People*, 29.
42  Ibid., 150.
43  Simmie and Nixon, *Tiananmen Square*, 198-9.
44  Goldman, *Sowing the Seeds of Democracy in China*, 336-7; Brook, *Quelling the People*, 168. Brook's analysis of the period of the protest and the massacre remains at once the most considered and compassionate; Brook (p.169) gives the figure of about 2,600 killed.
45  Goldman, *Sowing the Seeds of Democracy in China*, 338.
46  Schell and Lappin, "China Plays the Market," 743.
47  Link, in *New York Review of Books*, June 9, 1994.
48  Smil, *China's Environmental Crisis*.
49  Baum, *Burying Mao*, p.xi.
50  Kelliher, *Peasant Power in China*, 220-1.
51  Mirsky, *The Nation*, June 19, 1994, 888-9.
52  Quoted in Goodman, *Deng Xiaoping and the Chinese Revolution*, 102.
53  Hsu, *Rise of Modern China*, p.viii.
54  Brook, *Quelling the People*, 209.

# 9  Two Koreas

 1  Eckert, *Offspring of Empire*, 5.
 2  Amsden, *Asia's Next Giant*, 33.
 3  Hwang, *Korean Economies*, 16-17.
 4  Ibid., 15.
 5  Ibid., 15.
 6  Amsden, *Asia's Next Giant*, 28,
 7  Cumings, *Origins of the Korean War*, 86.
 8  Quoted in Cumings, *Origins of the Korean War*, 209.
 9  Cumings, *Origins of the Korean War*, 382.
10  Ibid., 417.
11  Goncharov, Lewis, and Xue Litai, *Uncertain Partners*, ch.5.
12  Ibid., 153.
13  Stairs, *Diplomacy of Constraint*, 50-1.
14  Halliday and Cumings, *Korea*, 95.
15  Ibid., 115.
16  Stone, *Hidden History of the Korean War*, 196-7.
17  Quoted in Stueck, "March to the Yalu," 233.
18  Quoted in Halliday and Cumings, *Korea*, 126.
19  Stairs, *Diplomacy of Constraint*, 320.
20  Quoted in Karol, *Second Chinese Revolution*, 51.
21  Halliday and Cumings, *Korea*, 200-6.
22  Kemp, *Industrialization in the Non-Western World*, 43.
23  Amsden, *Asia's Next Giant*, 37.
24  Ibid., 17.

25 Hamilton and Kim, "Economic and Political Liberalisation in South Korea and Mexico," 116.
26 Amsden, "Third World Industrialization," 17.
27 Quoted in Mesler, "Ghosts of Kwangyu," 56.
28 "A Survey of South Korea," *The Economist*, June 3-9, 1995.
29 Kim, *Communist Politics in North Korea*, 52.
30 Ibid.
31 Barkin, "Food Self-Sufficiency in the Democratic People's Republic of Korea," 31.
32 Quoted in Cumings, *Two Koreas*, 70.
33 Cumings, *Two Koreas*, 65.
34 Ibid., 71-2.
35 Kim, *Two Koreas in Development*, 121; Amsden, *Asia's Next Giant*, 40.
36 Kim, *Two Koreas in Development*, 120.
37 McCormack, "Kim Country," 27-8.
38 Kihl, *Politics and Policies in a Divided Korea*, 16.
39 An, *North Korea in Transition*, 132-5.
40 The quotations in this paragraph, as well as other materials included, I owe to Neil Peden.
41 Kim Il-Sung, "Answers to the Questions Raised by the Chairman of the Costa Rica-Korea Association of Friendship and Culture," Pyongyang, 1975, 4-5.
42 Cumings, *Two Koreas*, 81.
43 Kim, *Two Koreas in Development*, 67.
44 Ibid., 122, 83.
45 See, for instance, Barkin, "Food Self-Sufficiency in the Democratic People's Republic of Korea."
46 McCormack, "Kim Country," 36-7.
47 *Far Eastern Economic Review*, Oct. 10, 1996, 26-7.
48 Kim, *Two Koreas in Development*, 206.
49 Ibid., 207.
50 Anderson, *London Review of Books*, October 17, 1996, 29.

# 10 What Was Development?

1 Arrighi, *Long Twentieth Century*, 336.
2 *Financial Times*, Sept. 4, 1996, 11, Sept. 6, 1996, 4.
3 Athanasiou, *Divided Planet*, 125.
4 Hill, *Indonesian Economy since 1966*, 240.
5 Athanasiou, *Divided Planet*, 14.
6 Hsu, *Rise of Modern China*, 279.
7 Ruedy, *Modern Algeria*, 140.
8 *Far Eastern Economic Review*, Oct. 3, 1996, 22-8. I thank Dr Robin Porter of Keele University for pointing this article out to me.
9 Esposito, *Islamic Threat*, 53-4.
10 Bayly, *Indian Society and the Making of the British Empire*, 201.
11 Esposito, *Islamic Threat*, 127-8.
12 Ibid., 137-8.
13 Gordon, *Passing of French Algeria*, 50. I thank Michael Brett of the School of Oriental and African Studies, London, for drawing my attention to this passage.
14 Quoted in Lehmann, *Democracy and Development in Latin America*, 28.
15 Buchanan, "The Third World," 10-11.
16 Quoted in Lairson and Skidmore, *International Political Economy*, 246; see also Jamie Swift, "The Debt Crisis," in Swift and Tomlinson, *Conflicts of Interest*, 87; Barnet and Cavanagh, *Global Dreams*, 370.
17 Hobsbawm, *Age of Extremes*, 291.
18 See Burns, *Latin America*, 230. For a comparison of Turkey and Egypt, see Oncu, "Street Politics," 275. According to Oncu, although Egyptian statistics reveal a somewhat smaller agricultural population, these figures do not take women into account, which Turkish

statistics do. For Mexico, see Smith, "Mexico Since 1946," 1991, 330. For Ghana and Kenya, see Jamal and Weeks, *Africa Misunderstood*, 1993, 7.

19 Smith, *Livelihood and Resistance*, 1, 59.

20 Ibid., 11-12.

21 Burns, *Latin America*, 198-9.

22 Escobar and Alvarez, "Introduction," 1-2.

23 Starn, "'I Dreamed of Foxes and Hawks,'" 90.

24 Leffler, *Preponderance of Power*, 2-3.

25 Brett, *World Economy since the War*, 69.

26 George and Sabelli, *Faith and Credit*, ch.2.

27 Much of the following section draws on George and Sabelli, *Faith and Credit*.

28 Halberstram, *Vanity Fair*, September 1996, 244.

29 Mehmet, *Westernizing the Third World*, 108.

30 Escobar, *Encountering Development*, 162.

31 Kolko, *Restructuring the World Economy*, 203, 207.

32 Quoted in Kolko, *Restructuring the World Economy*, 207.

33 Harris, *End of the Third World*, 145.

34 Quoted in Riddell, "Things Fall Apart Again," 68.

35 Mehmet, *Westernizing the Third World*, 107.

36 Watkins, *Fixing the Rules*, 36-7.

37 Quoted in Athanasiou, *Divided Planet*, 177.

38 Watkins, "Agriculture and Food Security in the GATT Uruguay Round," 38.

39 Harriet Friedmann, who has written most persuasively about the food regime, outlines its main epochs in "The Political Economy of Food," 29-57.

40 Escobar, *Encountering Development*, 104.

41 Wood, *From Marshall Plan to Debt Crisis*, 25, 40-4.

42 *The Globe and Mail*, Feb. 4, 1995.

43 Wood, *From Marshall Plan to Debt Crisis*, 11.

44 Turshen, "US Aid and AIDS in Africa," 95-101.

45 *Le Monde*, June 24, 1994.

46 Wood, *From Marshall Plan to Debt Crisis*, 14.

47 Nolan, "Assessing Economic Growth in the Asian NICs," 47; Kiely, "Development Theory and Industrialization," 154.

48 Van Hees, Bokkerink, Pettermann, and Pepijn, "Another Reality of Debt," 28-30.

49 Sutton and Kemp, "Arms to Developing Countries," 5.

50 Klare, "Deadly Convergence," 141; Kolko, *Restructuring the World Economy*, 154.

51 Sandbrook, *Politics of Africa's Economic Stagnation*, 105.

52 Bitzinger, "Arms to Go," 84.

53 Athanasiou, *Divided Planet*, 301.

54 Hobsbawm, *Age of Extremes*, 277.

55 Barnet and Cavanagh, *Global Dreams*, 17.

56 Hobsbawm, *Age of Extremes*, 278.

57 Watkins, *Fixing the Rules*, 9.

58 Mann, "As the Twentieth Century Ages," 117.

59 Brett, *World Economy since the War*, 87.

60 Kolko, *Restructuring the World Economy*, 175.

61 Barnet and Cavanagh, *Global Dreams*, 229-30.

62 Hobsbawm, *Age of Extremes*, 281; for the NCR quote, see 403.

63 McCormick, *America's Half-Century*, 125, 155.

64 Brett, *World Economy since the War*, 119.

65 Keegan, *Spectre of Capitalism*, 47; Arrighi, *Long Twentieth Century*, 313.

66 Kolko, *Restructuring the World Economy*, 20-1.

67 Quoted in Yergin, *The Prize*, 626.

68 Mehmet, *Westernizing the Third World*, 110.

69 Harris, *End of the Third World*, 41-2.

70 Kolko, *Restructuring the World Economy*, 126.

71 Harris, *End of the Third World*, 30, 40-1.

72 Arrighi, *Long Twentieth Century*, 316-7.
73 Ibid., 321-2.
74 Ibid., 323.
75 Kolko, *Restructuring the World Economy*, 48.
76 Ibid., 49, 197.
77 *The Globe and Mail*, June 6, 1996, B10.
78 MacEwan, "Globalization and Stagnation," 133.
79 *The Economist*, Jan. 14-20, 1995, 13.
80 *The Guardian Weekly*, Dec. 31, 1995, 12; *Time*, March 13, 1995, 64.
81 Kemp, *Industrialization in the Non-Western World*, 1.
82 *The Economist*, May 14, 1994, 116, 118; World Bank, *Indonesia*, 2.
83 World Bank, *Indonesia*, p.xiii.
84 See Kiely, "Development Theory and Industrialization," 141.
85 Harrison, *Inside the Third World*, 335.
86 Ibid., 338.
87 Ibid., 348-9.
88 Watkins, *Fixing the Rules*, 2-3.
89 Watkins, "Letters to the Editor," *The Guardian*, Dec. 17, 1993.
90 Bulmer-Thomas, *Economic History of Latin America*, 410.
91 *The Economist*, Dec. 11-17, 1995; World Bank, *Caribbean Region: Current Economic Situation*, p.x.
92 Watkins, *Fixing the Rules*, 6-7; see also *Far Eastern Economic Review*, April 28, 1994.
93 Escobar, *Encountering Development*, 212-13.
94 Mehmet, *Westernizing the Third World*, chs.3-5, provides a good survey of the theoretical shifts in the postwar years.
95 Canada-Americas Policy Alternatives (CAPA), *Focus on Corruption*, 5-6.
96 Quoted in Bienefeld, "Capitalism and the Nation State," 96.
97 Escobar, *Encountering Development*, 215-6.
98 *The Globe and Mail*, May 10, 1996, A14. My colleague Dr Homa Hoodfar observed the banner outside the Tehran Hilton.
99 Reporters Sans Frontières, *Le drame algérien*, 52; author's translation.

# Bibliography

## Books and Articles

Abbasher, Jamal. "Funding Fundamentalism: The Political Economy of an Islamic State." *Middle East Report*, 172,21,5 (September/October 1991): 14-17, 38.

Abbott, Elizabeth. *Haiti: The Duvaliers and Their Legacy*. New York: McGraw-Hill, 1988.

Abrahamian, Ervand. *Iran between Two Revolutions*. Princeton, N.J.: Princeton University Press, 1982.

———. *Khomeinism: Essays on the Islamic Republic*. Berkeley: University of California Press, 1993.

Adleman, Jeremy. "Post-Populist Argentina." *New Left Review*, 203 (January/February 1994): 65-91.

Agernon, Charles-Robert. *La Décolonisation Française*. Paris: Colin, 1991.

Ahmad, Feroz. *The Making of Modern Turkey*. London: Routledge, 1993.

Akbar, M.K. *Nehru: The Making of India*. London: Penguin, 1989.

Alavi, Hamza and Teodor Shanin, eds. *Introduction to the Sociology of "Developing Societies."* New York: Monthly Review Press, 1982.

Alden, Chris. *Apartheid's Last Stand: The Rise and Fall of the South African Security State*. Houndmills, England: Macmillan, 1996.

Alves, Maria Helena Moreira. *State and Opposition in Military Brazil*. Austin: University of Texas Press, 1985.

Aly, Abdel Monem Said. "The International System and State Policies: The Case of Egypt," in *Developmentalism and Beyond*, ed. Oncu, Keyder, and Ibrahim: 177-203.

Ambursley, Fitzroy and Robin Cohen, eds. *Crisis in the Caribbean*. New York: Monthly Review Press, 1983.

Ambrose, Stephen. *Rise to Globalism: American Foreign Policy since 1938*. New York: Viking Penguin, 1988.

Amin, Samir. *Neo-Colonialism in West Africa*. Harmondsworth, England: Penguin Books, 1973.

Amsden, Alice. *Asia's Next Giant: South Korea and Late Industrialization*. New York: Oxford University Press, 1989.

_____. "Third World Industrialization: 'Global Fordism' or a New Model?" *New Left Review*, 182 (July/August 1990): 5-31.

An, Tai Sung. *North Korea in Transition*. Westport, Conn.: Greenwood Press, 1983.

Anderson, Benedict R. O'G. *Java in a Time of Revolution: Occupation and Resistance, 1944-1946*. Ithaca, N.Y.: Cornell University Press, 1972.

_____. "Murder and Progress in Modern Siam." *New Left Review*, 181 (May-June 1990): 33-48.

_____. "Radicalism after Communism in Thailand and Indonesia." *New Left Review*, 202 (November-December 1993): 3-14.

_____. "Rewinding 'Back to the Future': The Left and Constitutional Democracy," in *Democracy and Indonesia*, ed. Bourchier and Legge: 128-42.

Angell, Alan and Carol Graham. "Can Social Sector Reform Make Adjustment Sustainable and Equitable? Lessons from Chile and Argentina." *Journal of Latin American Studies*, 27,1 (February 1995): 189-219.

Appiah, Kwame A. *In My Father's House: Africa in the Philosophy of Culture*. New York: Oxford University Press, 1992.

Armstrong, P., A. Glyn, and J. Harrison. *Capitalism since World War II: The Making and Breaking of the Great Boom*. London: Fontana, 1984.

Arellano-López, Sonia and James F. Petras. "Non-Government Organizations and Poverty Alleviation in Bolivia." *Development and Change*, 25 (1994): 555-68.

Arrighi, Giovanni. *The Long Twentieth Century: Money, Power, and the Origins of Our Times*. London: Verso, 1994.

Association of Concerned African Scholars. "The CIA, Department of Defence and African Scholars." *Review of African Political Economy*, 55 (1992): 107-8.

Aswicahyono, H.H., K. Bird, and H. Hill. "What Happens to Industrial Structure When Countries Liberalise? Indonesia since the Mid-1980s." *Journal of Development Studies*, 32,3 (February 1996): 340-63.

Athanasiou, Tom. *Divided Planet: The Ecology of Rich and Poor*. Boston: Little, Brown, 1996.

Austin, Ralph. *African Economic History*. London: James Currey, 1987.

Ayata, Sencer. "Patronage, Party and the State: The Politicization of Islam in Turkey." *The Middle East Journal*, 50,1 (Winter 1996): 40-56.

Badran, Margot. *Feminists, Islam, and Nation: Gender and the Making of Modern Egypt*. Princeton, N.J.: Princeton University Press, 1995.

Bagchi, Amiya Kumar. *The Political Economy of Underdevelopment*. Cambridge: Cambridge University Press, 1982.

Bakhash, Shaul. *The Reign of the Ayatollahs: Iran and the Islamic Revolution*. London: Unwin, 1986.

Balfour, Sebastian. *Castro*. Harlow, England: Longman, 1995.

Banuazizi, Ali. "Iran's Revolutionary Impasse: Political Factionalism and Societal Resistance." *Middle East Report*, 24,6,191 (November-December 1994): 2-8.

Baran, Paul and E.J. Hobsbawm. "The Stages of Economic Growth." *Kyklos: International Review for Social Sciences*, 14 (1961): 234-42.

Barber, Benjamin R. *Jihad vs. McWorld*. New York: Random House, 1995.

Barkin, David. "Food Self-Sufficiency in the Democratic People's Republic of Korea." *Bulletin of Concerned Asian Scholars*, 18,4 (1986): 20-40.

Barkin, David. *Distorted Development: Mexico in the World Economy*. Boulder, Col.: Westview Press, 1990.

Barlow, Robin and Firket Senses. "The Turkish Export Boom: Just Reward or Just Lucky?" *Journal of Development Economics*, 48 (1995): 111-33.

Barnet, Richard J. and John Cavanagh. *Global Dreams: Imperial Corporations and the New World Order*. New York: Simon and Schuster, 1994.

Barry, Tom. *Zapata's Revenge: Free Trade and the Farm Crisis in Mexico*. Boston: South End Press, 1995.

Baum, Richard. *Burying Mao: Chinese Politics in the Age of Deng Xiaoping*. Princeton, N.J.: Princeton University Press, 1994.

Bayart, Jean-François. "The Historicity of African Societies." *Journal of International Affairs*, 46,1 (Summer 1992): 55-79.

Bayly, C.A. *Indian Society and the Making of the British Empire*. Cambridge: Cambridge University Press, 1988.

Bello, Walden. *Dark Victory: The United States, Structural Adjustment and Global Poverty*. London: Pluto Press, 1994.

Bengelsdorf, Carolee. *The Problem of Democracy in Cuba: Between Vision and Reality*. New York: Oxford University Press, 1994.

Beresford, Melanie. "Vietnam: Socialist Agriculture in Transition." *Journal of Contemporary Asia*, 20,4 (1990): 466-86.

Bergère, Marie-Claire et al., eds. *La Chine au XXe Siècle: D'Une Revolution à L'Autre, 1895-1949*. Paris: Fayard, 1989.

Berman, Bruce J. *Control and Crisis in Colonial Kenya: The Dialectic of Domination*. London: James Currey, 1990.

_____ and Colin Leys, eds. *African Capitalists in African Development*. Boulder, Col.: Lynne Rienner, 1994.

_____ and John Lonsdale. *Unhappy Valley: Conflict in Kenya and Africa*. London: James Currey, 1992.

Bernal, Martin. *Black Athena: The Afroasiatic Roots of Classical Civilization*. 2 vols. London: Free Association Press, 1987, 1991.

_____. *Chinese Socialism to 1907*. Ithaca, N.Y.: Cornell University Press, 1976.

Bettleheim, Charles. *India Independent*. New York: Monthly Review Press, 1971.

Bianco, Lucien. *Origins of the Chinese Revolution, 1915-1949*. Stanford, Cal.: Stanford University Press, 1971.

Bienefeld, Manfred. "Capitalism and the Nation State in the Dog Days of the Twentieth Century," in *Socialist Register 1994*, ed. Ralph Miliband and Leo Panitch. London: Merlin Press, 1994: 94-129.

Bill, James A. and Wm. Roger Louis, eds. *Musaddiq: Iranian Nationalism and Oil*. London: Tauris, 1988.

Birmingham, David. *Kwame Nkrumah*. London: Macdonald, 1990.

Bitzinger, Richard A. "Arms to Go: Chinese Arms Sales to the Third World." *International Security*, 17,2 (Fall 1992): 84-111.

Blachman, Morris J., William M. Leogrande, and Kenneth Sharpe. *Confronting Revolution: Security through Diplomacy in Central America*. New York: Pantheon Books, 1986.

Blasier, Cole. *The Hovering Giant: U.S. Responses to Revolutionary Change in Latin America, 1910-1985*. Pittsburg, Penn.: University of Pittsburg Press, 1985.

Bourchier, David and John Legge, eds. *Democracy in Indonesia: 1950s and 1990s*.

Monash Papers on Southeast Asia, no. 31. Clayton, Victoria: Centre of Southeast Asian Studies, Monash University, 1994.

Bourdillon, Bernard. *The Future of the Colonial Empire*. London: S.C.M. Press, 1945.

Bourne, Richard. *Political Leaders of Latin America*. Harmondsworth, England: Penguin Books, 1969.

_____. *Castro. A Biography of Fidel Castro*. London: Macmillan, 1986.

Brass, Paul. *The Politics of India since Independence*. Cambridge: Cambridge University Press, 1990.

Bray, Marjorie W. "Latin America's Debt and the World Economic Crisis." *Latin American Perspectives*, 16,1,60 (Winter 1989): 3-10.

Brenner, Philip. "Cuba and the Missile Crisis." *Journal of Latin American Studies*, 22 (1990): 115-42.

Bresnan, John. *Managing Indonesia: The Modern Political Economy*. New York: Columbia University Press, 1993.

Brett, E.A. *The World Economy since the War: The Politics of Uneven Development*. London: Macmillan, 1985.

_____. "Voluntary Agencies as Development Organizations: Theorizing the Problem of Efficiency and Accountability." *Development and Change*, 24 (1993): 269-303.

Brittain, Victoria. "Ghana's Precarious Revolution." *New Left Review*, 140 (July 1983): 50-61.

Brook, Timothy. *Quelling the People: Military Suppression of the Beijing Democracy Movement*. New York: Oxford University Press, 1992.

Brown, Michael Barrett. *After Imperialism*. London: Heinemann, 1970.

Buchanan, Keith. "The Third World." *New Left Review*, January-February 1963: 5-16.

Bull, H. and A. Watson, eds. *The Expansion of International Society*. Oxford: Oxford University Press, 1984.

Bulmer-Thomas, Victor. *An Economic History of Latin America since Independence*. Cambridge: Cambridge University Press, 1994.

Bundy, Colin. *An Illustrated History of South Africa*. Montreal: Reader's Digest, 1988.

Burbach, Roger. "Ruptured Frontiers: The Transformation of the US-Latin American System," in *Socialist Register 1992*, ed. Miliband and Panitch: 239-53.

_____. "Roots of the Postmodern Rebellion in Chiapas." *New Left Review*, 205 (May/June 1994): 113-24.

Burns, E. Bradford. *Latin America: A Concise Interpretive History*. Englewood Cliffs, N.J.: Prentice-Hall, 1986.

Burkett, Paul and Donald G. Richards. "Argentine Election Results." NACLA *Report on the Americas*, 29,3 (November/December 1995): 4, 46.

Calloni, Stella. "The Horror Archives of Operation Condor." *Covert Action Quarterly*, 50 (Fall 1994): 7-13, 57-8.

Cammack, Paul. "Brazil: The Long March to the New Republic." *New Left Review*, 190 (November-December 1991): 21-58.

Campbell, Bonnie K., ed. *Political Dimensions to the International Debt Crisis*. New York: St. Martin's Press, 1989.

Cardoso, Fernando Henrique. "Dependency and Development in Latin America." *New Left Review*, July-August 1972: 83-95.

_____ and Enzo Faletto. *Dependency and Development in Latin America*. Berkeley: University of California Press, 1979.

Carothers, Tom H. *In the Name of Democracy: U.S. Policy toward Latin America in the Reagan Years*. Berkeley: University of California Press, 1991.

Carrère d'Encausse, Helène and Stuart Schram. *Marxism in Asia*. London: Penguin Books, 1969.

Cassandra. "The Impending Crisis in Egypt." *The Middle East Journal*, 49,1 (Winter 1995): 9-27.

Castaneda, Jorge G. *The Mexico Shock: Its Meaning for the U.S.* New York: New Press, 1995.

Catley-Carlson, Margaret. "Aid: A Canadian Vocation." *Daedalus*, 117 (1988): 319-33.

Chaliand, Gerard. *Revolution in the Third World: Myths and Prospects*. New York: Viking, 1977.

Chandler, David P. *Brother Number One: A Political Biography of Pol Pot*. Boulder, Col.: Westview Press, 1992.

_____. *A History of Cambodia*. Boulder, Col.: Westview Press, 1992.

_____. *The Tragedy of Cambodian History: Politics, War and Revolution since 1945*. New Haven, Conn.: Yale University Press, 1992.

_____ and Ben Kiernan. *Revolution and Its Aftermath in Kampuchea: Eight Essays*. Monograph Series No.25. New Haven, Conn.: Yale University Southeast Asia Studies, 1983.

Chandra, Bipan. *India's Struggle for Independence*. Calcutta: Penguin Books, 1989.

Chang, Jung. *Wild Swans: Three Daughters of China*. London: Harper Collins, 1993.

Chapuis, Robert. *Les Quatre Mondes du Tiers Monde*. Paris: Masson, 1993.

Chatterjee, Partha. *Nationalist Thought and the Colonial World: A Derivative Discourse*. London: Zed Books, 1986.

Chen, Jerome, ed. *Mao*. Englewood Cliffs, N.J.: Prentice-Hall, 1969.

Chesneaux, Jean. *China: The People's Republic, 1949-1976*. New York: Random House, 1979.

_____, Françoise Le Barbier, and Marie-Claire Bergère. *China from the 1911 Revolution to Liberation*. New York: Random House, 1977.

Chomsky, Noam. *Necessary Illusions: Thought Control in Democratic Societies*. Toronto: Anansi, 1991.

_____. *Rethinking Camelot: JFK, the Vietnam War and US Political Culture*. Montreal: Black Rose Books, 1993.

Clapp, Jennifer A. "Interpreting Agricultural Performance in Guinea under Structural Adjustment." *Canadian Journal of African Studies*, 27,2 (1993): 196-217.

Clarence-Smith, W.G. "The Myth of Uneconomic Imperialism: The Portuguese in Angola, 1836-1926." *Journal of Southern African Studies*, 5,2 (1979): 165-80.

_____. *The Third Portuguese Empire, 1825-1975: A Study in Economic Imperialism*. Manchester, England: Manchester University Press, 1985.

Cleveland, William L. *A History of the Modern Middle East*. Boulder, Col.: Westview Press, 1994.

Cohen, W.I. and A. Iriye. *The Great Powers in East Asia, 1953-1960*. New York: Columbia University Press, 1990.

Colby, Gerard, with Charlotte Dennett. *Thy Will Be Done: The Conquest of the*

*Amazon: Nelson Rockefeller and the Evangelism in the Age of Oil.* New York: Harper Collins, 1995.

Colby, William. *Honourable Men: My Life in the* CIA. New York: Simon and Schuster, 1978.

Cole, Juan R.I. and Nikki R. Keddie, eds. *Shi'ism and Social Protest.* New Haven, Conn.: Yale University Press, 1986.

Comarin, Elio. *L'Etat du Tiers Monde.* La Découverte/Comité Français.

Comaroff, John L. "Democracy, Fried Chicken and the Atomic Bomb: A Brief Reflection on the 'New' South Africa." *Cultural Survival Quarterly,* Summer/Fall 1994: 34-9.

Constable, Pamela and Arturo Valenzuela. *A Nation of Enemies: Chile under Pinochet.* New York: Norton, 1991.

Coquery-Vidrovitch, Catherine. *Africa: Endurance and Change South of the Sahara.* Berkeley: University of California Press, 1988.

Corradi, Juan E. *The Fitful Republic: Economy, Society and Politics in Argentina.* Boulder, Col.: Westview Press, 1985.

Corradi, Juan E., Patricia Weiss Fagan, and Manuel Antonio Garreton, eds. *Fear at the Edge: State Terror and Resistance in Latin America.* Berkeley: University of California Press, 1992.

Cottam, Richard W. "The Iranian Revolution." In Cole and Keddie, eds., *Shi'ism and Social Protest*: 55-87.

Cowen, M. and R.W. Shenton. "The Origin and Course of Fabian Colonialism." *Journal of Historical Sociology,* 4,2 (1991): 143-74.

_____. *Doctrines of Development.* London: Routledge, 1996.

Cribb, Robert and Colin Brown. *Modern Indonesia: A History since 1945.* Harlow, England: Longman, 1995.

Cumings, Bruce. *The Origins of the Korean War: Liberation and the Emergence of Separate Regimes, 1945-1947.* Princeton, N.J.: Princeton University Press, 1981.

_____. "The Abortive Abertura: South Korea in the Light of Latin American Experience." *New Left Review,* 173 (January-February 1989): 5-32.

_____. *The Origins of the Korean War: The Roaring of the Cataract, 1947-1950.* Princeton, N.J.: Princeton University Press, 1990.

_____. *The Two Koreas: On the Road to Unification?* New York: Foreign Policy Association, Fall 1990.

_____. "Illusion, Critique, and Responsibility: The 'Revolution of '89' in West and East," in *The Crisis of Leninism and the Decline of the Left: The Revolutions of 1989,* ed. Daniel Chirot. Seattle: University of Washington Press, 1991: 100-28.

Dalloz, Jacques. *The War in Indo-China, 1945-54.* Dublin: Gill and Macmillan, 1990.

Dalton, Dennis. *Mahatma Gandhi: Nonviolent Power in Action.* New York: Columbia University Press, 1993.

David, Steven R. "Why the Third World Still Matters." *International Security,* 17,3 (Winter 1992/93): 127-59.

Davidson, Basil. *The Black Man's Burden: Africa and the Curse of the Nation State.* New York: Random House, 1992.

Davidson, Basil. "Africa: The Politics of Failure," in *Socialist Register 1992,* ed. Miliband and Panitch: 212-26.

Davidson, Basil. *Modern Africa: A Social and Political History*. Harlow, England: Longman, 1994.

Davies, Mike. "Who Killed Los Angeles? Part Two: The Verdict is Given." *New Left Review*, 199 (May-June 1993): 29-54.

Deschamps, Hubert. *L'Union Française: Histoire, Institutions, Realités*. Paris: Berger-Levrault, 1952.

De Folin, Jacques. *Indochine, 1940-1955: La Fin D'Une Rêve*. Paris: Perrin, 1993.

De Gouvea Neto, Raul. "The Role of Transnational Companies in the Brazilian Defence Tripod." *Journal of Latin American Studies*, 23,3 (1991): 573-97.

De Kadt, Emanuel and Gavin Williams. *Sociology and Development*. London: Tavistock, 1974.

Devillers, Philippe and Jean Lacoutre. *End of a War: Indochina, 1954*. New York: Praeger, 1969.

Dietz, James L. "The Debt Cycle and Restructuring in Latin America." *Latin American Perspectives*, 16,1,60 (Winter 1989): 13-30.

Dinh, Q. "Vietnam's Policy Reforms and Its Future." *Journal of Contemporary Asia*, 23,1 (1993): 532-53.

Divine, Robert A. "Vietnam Reconsidered." *Diplomatic History*, 12,1 (Winter 1988): 79-93.

Dominguez, Jorge I. "Cuba since 1959," in *Latin America since 1930: Mexico, Central America and the Caribbean*, vol.7, *The Cambridge History of Latin America*, ed. Leslie Bethell. Cambridge: Cambridge University Press, 1990: 457-508.

Dominguez, J.I., R.A. Pastor, and R.D. Worrell, eds. *Democracy in the Caribbean*. Baltimore, Md.: Johns Hopkins University Press, 1993.

Dore, Liz and John Weeks. "The Changing Faces of Imperialism." NACLA *Report on the Americas*, 30,2 (September/October 1996): 10-15.

Duiker, W.J. *The Communist Road to Power in Vietnam*. Boulder, Col.: Westview Press, 1981.

Dulles, John Foster. "Policy for Security and Peace." *Foreign Affairs*, 32,1 (October 1954): 353-64.

————. *War or Peace*. New York: Macmillan, 1950.

Dunkerley, James. *Political Suicide in Latin America*. London: Verso, 1992.

Dunn, John. *Modern Revolutions: An Introduction to the Analysis of a Political Phenomenon*. Cambridge: University of Cambridge Press, 1972.

Dupuy, A. *Haiti in the World Economy: Class, Race and Underdevelopment since 1700*. Boulder, Col.: Westview Press, 1989.

Eastman, Lloyd E. *Family, Fields and Ancestors: Constancy and Change in China's Social and Economic History, 1550-1949*. New York: Oxford University Press, 1988.

Eayrs, James. *Indochina: Roots of Complicity*. Toronto: University of Toronto Press, 1983.

Eckert, Carter J. *Offspring of Empire: The Koch'ang Kims and the Colonial Origins of Korean Nationalism*. Seattle: University of Washington Press, 1991.

Eckstein, Susan Eva. *Back from the Future: Cuba under Castro*. Princeton, N.J.: Princeton University Press, 1994.

Ehrlich, Avishal. "The Gulf War and the New World Order," in *Socialist Register 1992*, ed. Miliband and Panitch: 227-38.

Ehsani, Kaveh. "'Tilt but Don't Spill': Iran's Development and Reconstruction Dilemma." *Middle East Report*, 24,6,191 (November-December 1994): 16-21.

Einaudi, Jean-Luc. *La bataille de Paris: 17 Octobre 1961*. Paris: Seuil, 1991.

Engelhardt, Tom. *The End of Victory Culture: Cold War America and the Disillusioning of a Generation*. New York: Basic Books, 1995.

Eralp, Atila, "Turkey in the Changing Postwar Political Order: Strategies of Development and Westernization," in *Developmentalism and Beyond*, ed. Oncu, Keyder, and Ibrahim: 204-29.

Escobar, Arturo. *Encountering Development: The Making of the Third World*. Princeton, N.J.: Princeton University Press, 1995.

_____ and Sonia E. Alvarez. "Introduction: Theory and Protest in Latin America Today," in *The Making of Social Movements in Latin America: Identity, Strategy and Democracy*, ed. Arturo Escobar and Sonia E. Alvarez. Boulder, Col.: Westview Press, 1992: 1-15.

Esposito, John. *The Islamic Threat: Myth or Reality?* New York: Oxford University Press, 1992.

Evans, Grant and Kelvin Rowley. *Red Brotherhood at War*. London: Verso, 1990.

Evans, Peter. *Dependent Development: The Alliance of Multinational, State, and Local Capital in Brazil*. Princeton, N.J.: Princeton University Press, 1979.

Fairbank, John K. *The United States and China*. Cambridge, Mass.: Harvard University Press, 1976.

_____ and Albert Feuerwerker, eds. *Republican China, 1912-1949*, vol. 13, Part 2, *The Cambridge History of China*. Cambridge: Cambridge University Press, 1986.

Fandy, Mamoun. "Egypt's Islamic Group: Regional Revenge?" *The Middle East Journal*, 48,4 (Autumn 1994): 607-25.

Ferguson, James. *Papa Doc, Baby Doc: Haiti and the Duvaliers*. Oxford: Basil Blackwell, 1987.

Field, Robert Michael. "China's Industrial Performance since 1978." *China Quarterly*, September 1992: 577-607.

Fieldhouse, D.K. *Black Africa 1945-1980*. London: Allen and Unwin, 1986.

Finnigan, William. *A Complicated War: The Harrowing of Mozambique*. Berkeley: University of California Press, 1992.

Fiori, José Luiz. "Cardoso among the Technopols." NACLA *Report on the Americas*, 27,6 (May/June 1995): 17-22.

Fitch, Robert and Mary Oppenheimer. *Ghana: End of an Illusion*. New York: Monthly Review Press, 1966.

Fitzgerald, Frances. *Fire in the Lake: The Vietnamese and the Americans in Vietnam*. New York: Vintage Books, 1972.

Flower, Ken. *Serving Secretly: An Intelligence Chief on Record: Rhodesia into Zimbabwe*. London: Murray, 1987.

Frank, André Gunder. *Capitalism and Underdevelopment in Latin America: Historical Studies of Chile and Brazil*. New York: Monthly Review Press, 1967.

_____ . "Latin American Development Theories Revised: A Participant Review." *Latin American Perspectives*, 73,19,2 (Spring 1992): 125-39.

Frankel, Francine R. *India's Political Economy, 1947-1977: The Gradual Revolution*. Princeton, N.J.: Princeton University Press, 1978.

Frelick, Bill. "Haitians at Sea: Asylum Denied." NACLA *Report on the Americas*, 26,1 (July 1992): 34-8.

Freund, Bill. *The Making of Contemporary Africa: The Development of African Society since 1800*. Bloomington: Indiana University Press, 1984.

Friedman, Edward, "The Innovator," in *Mao Tse-Tung in the Scales of History*, ed. Dick Wilson. Cambridge: Cambridge University Press, 1977: 300-20.

Friedmann, Harriet. "The Political Economy of Food: The Rise and Fall of the Postwar International Food Order." *American Journal of Sociology*, 88 (Supplement, 1982): 248-86.

_____. "Distance and Durability: Shaky Foundations of the World Food Economy." *Third World Quarterly*, 13,2 (1992): 371-83.

_____. "The Political Economy of Food: A Global Crisis." *New Left Review*, 197 (January/February 1993): 29-57.

Frings, Viviane. "Cambodia after Decollectivization (1989-1992)." *Journal of Contemporary Asia*, 24,1 (1994): 49-66.

Furtado, Celso. *Development and Underdevelopment: A Structural View of the Problems of Developed and Underdeveloped Countries*. Berkeley: University of California Press, 1964.

Gendzier, Irene L. *Managing Political Change: Social Scientists and the Third World*. Boulder, Col.: Westview Press, 1985.

George, Susan. *A Fate Worse than Debt: A Radical New Analysis of the Third World Debt Crisis*. Harmondsworth, England: Penguin Books, 1988.

_____. *The Debt Boomerang: How Third World Debt Harms Us All*. Boulder, Col.: Westview Press, 1992.

_____ and Fabrizio Sabelli. *Faith and Credit: The World Bank's Secular Empire*. London: Penguin Books, 1994.

Ghai, Dharam, ed. *The IMF and the South: The Social Impact of Crisis and Adjustment*. London: Zed Books, 1991.

Ghassan, Salamé. "Torn between the Atlantic and the Mediterranean: Europe and the Middle East in the Post-Cold War Era." *The Middle East Journal*, 48,2 (Spring 1994): 231-49.

Gibbon, Peter. "The World Bank and Agrarian Poverty, 1973-91." *Journal of Modern African Studies*, 30,2 (June 1992): 193-220.

Gifford, Prosser and Wm. Roger Louis, eds. *The Transfer of Power in Africa: Decolonization, 1940-1960*. New Haven, Conn.: Yale University Press, 1982.

_____, eds. *Decolonization and African Independence: The Transfers of Power, 1960-1980*. New Haven, Conn.: Yale University Press, 1988.

Gilbert, Alan. *Latin America*. London: Routledge, 1990.

Gillebaud, Jean-Claud and Raymond Depardon. *Return to Vietnam*. London: Verso, 1994.

Gleijeses, Piero. "Ships in the Night: The CIA, the White House and the Bay of Pigs." *Journal of Latin American Studies*, 27,1 (February 1995): 1-42.

_____. "Cuba's First Venture into Africa: Algeria, 1961-1965." *Journal of Latin American Studies*, 28,1 (February 1996): 159-95.

Goldman, Merle. *Sowing the Seeds of Democracy in China: Political Reform in the Deng Xiaoping Era*. Cambridge, Mass.: Harvard University Press, 1994.

Goldrich, Daniel and David V. Carruthers. "Sustainable Development in Mexico?

The International Politics of Crisis or Opportunity." *Latin American Perspectives*, 72,19,1 (Winter 1992): 97-122.

Goldsworthy, David. *Colonial Issues in British Politics, 1945-1961: From "Colonial Development" to "Winds of Change."* Oxford: Oxford University Press, 1971.

Golub, Stephen S. "The Political Economy of the Latin American Debt Crisis." *Latin American Research Review*, 26,1 (1991): 175-215.

Goncharov, Sergei N., John W. Lewis, and Xue Litai. *Uncertain Partners: Stalin, Mao and the Korean War*. Stanford, Cal.: Stanford University Press, 1993.

Goode, James. "Reforming Iran during the Kennedy Years." *Diplomatic History*, 15,1 (1991): 13-29.

Goodman, David S.G. *Deng Xiaoping and the Chinese Revolution: A Political Biography*. London: Routledge, 1994.

Gordon, David C. *The Passing of French Algeria*. London: Oxford University Press, 1966.

Gosse, Van. *Where the Boys Are: Cuba, Cold War America and the Making of a New Left*. London: Verso, 1994.

Gowan, Peter. "The Gulf War, Iraq and Western Liberalism." *New Left Review*, 187 (May/June 1991): 29-70.

Graf, William. "Sustainable Ideologies and Interests: Beyond Brundtland." *Third World Quarterly*, 13,2 (1992): 553-9.

Green, Daniel. "Ghana's 'Adjusted' Democracy." *Review of African Political Economy*, 66 (1995): 577-85.

Green, Duncan. "Chile: The First Latin American Tiger?" NACLA *Report on the Americas*, 28,1 (July/August 1994): 12-16.

Greenfield, Gerard. "The Development of Capitalism in Vietnam," in *Socialist Register 1994*, ed. Ralph Miliband and Leo Panitch. London: Merlin Press, 1994: 202-34.

Grimal, Henri. *La Décolonisation de 1939 à nos jours*. Paris: Éditions Complexe, 1985.

Grimshaw, Anna, ed. *The C.L.R. James Reader*. Oxford: Blackwell, 1992.

Guillebaid, Jean-Claude. *Return to Vietnam*. London: Routledge, 1994.

Guillén, Arturo. "Crisis, the Burden of Foreign Debt, and Structural Dependence." *Latin American Perspectives*, 16,1,60 (Winter 1989): 31-51.

Gulalp, Haldun. "Islamist Party Poised for National Power in Turkey." *Middle East Report*, 25,194/5 (May-June/July-August 1995): 54-6.

Habel, Janette. *Cuba: The Revolution in Peril*. London: Verso, 1991.

Halberstram, David. *The Best and the Brightest*. New York: Random House, 1972.

Hall, Stuart. "Negotiating Caribbean Identities." *New Left Review*, 209 (January/February 1995): 3-14.

Halliday, Fred. *The Making of the Second Cold War*. London: Verso, 1986.

————. *Cold War, Third World: An Essay in Soviet-American Relations*. London: Century Hutchinson, 1989.

————. "An Elusive Normalization: Western Europe and the Iranian Revolution." *The Middle East Journal*, 48,2 (Spring 1994): 309-26.

————. *Islam and the Myth of Confrontation: Religion and Politics in the Middle East*. London: I.B. Taurus, 1995.

Halliday, Jon and Bruce Cumings. *Korea: The Unknown War*. London: Viking, 1988.

Hamilton, Nora and Timothy F. Harding, eds. *Modern Mexico: State Economy, and Social Conflict*, vol. 1, *Latin American Perspectives Readers*, Beverly Hills, Cal.: Sage, 1986.

Hamilton, Nora and Eun Mee Kim. "Economic and Political Liberalisation in South Korea and Mexico." *Third World Quarterly*, 14,1 (1993): 109-35.

Hane, Mikiso. *Eastern Phoenix: Japan since 1945*. Boulder, Col.: Westview Press, 1996.

Hanlon, Joseph. *Mozambique: Who Calls the Shots?* London: James Currey, 1993.

Harbeson, John W. and Donald Rothchild, eds. *Africa in World Politics: Post-War Challenges*. Boulder, Col.: Westview Press, 1995.

Hargreaves, J.D. *Decolonization in Africa*. New York: Longman, 1988.

Harris, Nigel. *The End of the Third World: Newly Industrializing Countries and the Decline of an Ideology*. Harmondsworth, England: Penguin Books, 1987.

Harrison, Paul. *Inside the Third World*. Harmondsworth, England: Penguin Books, 1987.

Hawthorn, Geoffrey. "The Difficulties of Governance Now Are Dauntingly Stupendous." *London Review of Books*, 18,14 (July 18, 1996): 6-7.

Hecht, Susanna B. "Love and Death in Brazil." *New Left Review*, 204 (March/April 1994): 129-37.

Hellinger, Douglas. "US Aid Policy in Africa: No Room for Democracy." *Review of African Political Economy*, 55 (1992): 84-5.

Hemery, Daniel. *Ho Chi Minh: De L'Indochine au Vietnam*. Paris: Gallimard, 1990.

Henderson, Gregory. *Korea: The Politics of the Vortex*. Boston: Harvard University Press, 1968.

Hennessy, Alastair. *Intellectuals in the Twentieth-Century Caribbean*. 2 vols. London: Macmillan, 1992.

Henwood, Doug. "Global Economic Integration: The Missing Middle East." *Middle East Report*, 184,23,5 (September-October 1993): 7-8.

Hernandez, Luis and Laura Carlsen. "Political Storms of 1994." NACLA *Report on the Americas*, 27,1 (July/August 1994): 18-21.

Herring, George. *The Longest War: The United States and Vietnam, 1950-1975*. New York: John Wiley and Sons, 1979.

Hill, Hal. *The Indonesian Economy since 1966: Southeast Asia's Emerging Giant*. Cambridge: Cambridge University Press, 1996.

Hill, Polly. *Development Economics on Trial: The Anthropological Case for a Prosecution*. Cambridge: Cambridge University Press, 1986.

Hinnebusch, Ramond A. "Class, State and the Reversal of Egypt's Agrarian Reform." *Middle East Report*, 184,23,5 (September-October 1993): 21-3.

Hinton, William. *Hundred Day War: The Cultural Revolution at Tsinghua University*. New York: Monthly Review Press, 1972.

————. *Fanshen: The Continuing Revolution in a Chinese Village*. New York: Random House, 1983.

Hiro, Dilip. *Iran under the Ayatollahs*. London: Routledge and Kegan Paul, 1985.

————. *Islamic Fundamentalism*. London: Paladin, 1988.

————. *Desert Shield to Desert Storm: The Second Gulf War*. London: Paladin, 1992.

_____. *Between Marx and Muhammad: The Changing Face of Central Asia.* London: Harper Collins, 1994.

Hobsbawm, Eric. *The Age of Empire, 1875-1914.* New York: Pantheon Books, 1987.

_____. "The Crisis of Today's Ideologies." *New Left Review,* 192 (March/April 1992): 55-64.

_____. *Age of Extremes: The Short Twentieth Century, 1914-1991.* London: Penguin Books, 1994.

_____. *Nations and Nationalism since 1780: Programme, Myth and Reality.* Cambridge: Cambridge University Press, 1992.

_____ and Terence Ranger, eds. *The Invention of Tradition.* Cambridge: Cambridge University Press, 1983.

Hodgkin, Thomas. *African Political Parties: An Introductory Guide.* Harmondsworth, England: Penguin Books, 1965.

Holland, R.F., ed. *Emergencies and Disorder in the European Empires after 1945.* London: Cass, 1994.

Holland, R.F. *European Decolonization, 1918-1981: An Introductory Survey.* London: Macmillan, 1985.

Hopwood, Derek. *Egypt: Politics and Society, 1945-1984.* 2nd ed. London: Routledge, Chapman and Hall, 1985.

Hsu, Immanuel C.Y. *China without Mao: The Search for a New Order.* Oxford: Oxford University Press, 1990.

_____. *The Rise of Modern China.* New York: Oxford University Press, 1995.

Huntington, Samuel P. *Political Order in Changing Societies.* New Haven, Conn.: Yale University Press, 1968.

_____. "The Clash of Civilizations?" *Foreign Affairs,* 72,3 (1993): 22-49.

_____. "Why International Primacy Matters." *International Security,* 17,4 (Spring 1993): 68-83.

Hutchful, Eboe. "A Tale of Two Regimes: Imperialism, the Military and Class in Ghana." *Review of African Political Economy,* 14 (January-April 1979): 36-55.

_____. *The IMF and Ghana: The Confidential Record.* London: Zed Books, 1987.

Hutton, Will. *The State We're In.* London: Jonathan Cape, 1995.

Ienaga, Saburo. *The Pacific War, 1931-1945.* New York: Random House, 1978.

Hwang, Eui-Gak. *The Korean Economies: A Comparison of North and South.* Oxford: Oxford University Press, 1993.

Ibrahim, Saad Eddin, "Egypt's Landed Bourgeoisie," in *Developmentalism and Beyond,* ed. Oncu, Keyder, and Ibrahim: 19-43.

Iliffe, John. *Africans: The History of a Continent.* Cambridge: Cambridge University Press, 1995.

Iriye, A. *The Great Powers in East Asia, 1953-1960.* New York: Columbia University Press, 1990.

Irving, R.E.M. *The French Indochina War: French and American Policy, 1945-1954.* London: Croom Helm, 1975.

Isaacs, A.R. *Without Honor: Defeat in Vietnam and Cambodia.* Baltimore, Md.: Johns Hopkins University Press, 1983.

Jabber, Paul. *Not By War Alone.* Berkeley: University of California Press, 1981.

Jalal, Ayesha. "Towards the Baghdad Pact: South Asia and Middle East Defence in the Cold War, 1947-1955." *International History Review,* 11,3 (August 1989): 409-612.

_____. *The State of Martial Rule: The Origins of Pakistan's Political Economy*. Cambridge: Cambridge University Press, 1990.

Jamal, Vali and John Weeks. *Africa Misunderstood or Whatever Happened to the Rural-Urban Gap?* Houndmills, England: Macmillan, 1993.

James, C.L.R. *Nkrumah and the Ghana Revolution*. London: Allison and Busby, 1982.

Janvry, Alain de. *The Agrarian Question and Reformism in Latin America*. Baltimore, Md.: Johns Hopkins University Press, 1981.

Joffé, E.G.H. "Relations between the Middle East and the West." *The Middle East Journal*, 48,2 (Spring 1994): 250-67.

Johnson, R.W. *How Long Will South Africa Survive?* London: Macmillan, 1977.

Kahin, Audrey R. and George McT. Kahin. *Subversion as Foreign Policy: The Secret Eisenhower and Dulles Debacle in Indonesia*. New York: New Press, 1995.

Kahin, George McT. *Nationalism and Revolution in Indonesia*. Ithaca, N.Y.: Cornell University Press, 1952.

_____. *The Asian-African Conference: Bandung, Indonesia, April 1955*. Ithaca, N.Y.: Cornell University Press, 1955.

Kahler, Miles. *Decolonization in Britain and France: The Domestic Consequences of International Relations*. Princeton, N.J.: Princeton University Press, 1984.

Kamrava, Mehran. *Revolution in Iran: The Roots of Turmoil*. London: Routledge, 1990.

_____. *Politics and Society in the Third World*. London: Routledge, 1993.

Karol, K.S. *Guerillas in Power: The Course of the Cuban Revolution*. New York: Hill and Wang, 1970.

_____. *The Second Chinese Revolution*. New York: Hill and Wang, 1974.

Kataoka, Tetsuya. *The Price of a Constitution: The Origin of Japan's Postwar Politics*. New York: Crane Russak, 1991.

Kaufman, Michael. *Jamaica under Manley: Dilemmas of Socialism and Democracy*. Toronto: Between the Lines, 1985.

Kay, Cristóbal. *Latin American Theories of Development and Underdevelopment*. London: Routledge, 1989.

_____. "For a Renewal of Development Studies: Latin American Theories and Neoliberalism in the Era of Structural Adjustment." *Third World Quarterly*, 14,4 (1993): 691-702.

Kay, Geoffrey. *Development and Underdevelopment: A Marxist Analysis*. London: Macmillan, 1975.

Keck, Margaret E. "Brazil's PT: Socialism as Radical Democracy." NACLA *Report on the Americas*, 25,5 (May 1992): 24-9.

Keddie, Nikki R. *Roots of Revolution: An Interpretive History of Modern Iran*. New Haven, Conn.: Yale University Press, 1981.

_____. *Iran and the Muslim World: Resistance and Revolution*. Basingstoke, England: Macmillan, 1995.

Keegan, William. *The Spectre of Capitalism: The Future of the World Economy after the Fall of Communism*. London: Vintage Books, 1993.

Keen, Benjamin. *A History of Latin America*, vol. 2. Boston: Houghton Mifflin, 1996.

Kelliher, Daniel. *Peasant Power in China: The Era of Rural Reform, 1979-1989*. New Haven, Conn.: Yale University Press, 1992.

Kemp, Tom. *Industrialization in the Non-Western World*. 2nd ed. London: Longman, 1989.

Kennedy, Paul. *The Rise and Fall of the Great Powers: Economic Change and Military Conflict from 1500 to 2000*. New York: Random House, 1987.

_____. *Preparing for the Twenty-First Century*. Toronto: HarperCollins, 1993.

Kepel, Gilles. *The Prophet and Pharaoh: Muslim Extremism in Egypt*. London: Zed Books, 1985.

Kesselman, Mark. "Order or Movement? The Literature of Political Development as Ideology." *World Politics*, 26 (October 1973-July 1974): 139-54.

Keyder, Caglar. *State and Class in Turkey: A Study in Capitalist Development*. London: Verso, 1987.

Keyder, Caglar and Ayse Oncu. "Introduction: Comparing Egypt and Turkey," in *Developmentalism and Beyond*, ed. Oncu, Keyder, and Ibrahim: 1-18.

Khanh, H.K. *Vietnamese Communism, 1925-1945*. Ithaca, N.Y.: Cornell University Press, 1982.

Kiely, Ray. "Development Theory and Industrialization: Beyond the Impasse." *Journal of Contemporary Asia*, 24,2 (1994): 133-59.

Kiernan, Ben. *How Pol Pot Came to Power*. London: Verso, 1985.

Kiernan, Ben. "William Shawcross: Declining Cambodia." *Bulletin of Concerned Asian Scholars*, 18,1 (1986): 56-63.

Kiernan, Ben. *The Pol Pot Regime: Race, Power, and Genocide in Cambodia under the Khmer Rouge, 1975-79*. New Haven, Conn.: Yale University Press, 1996.

Kiernan, Ben and C. Boua, eds. *Peasants and Politics in Kampuchea, 1942-1981*. London: Zed Books, 1982.

Kiernan, V.G. *Marxism and Imperialism*. London: Edward Arnold, 1974.

Kihl, Young W. *Politics and Policies in a Divided Korea*. Boulder, Col.: Westview Press, 1984.

Kim, Byoung-Lo Philo. *Two Koreas in Development*. New Brunswick, N.J.: Transaction Books, 1992.

Kim, Ipyong J. *Communist Politics in North Korea*. New York: Praeger, 1975.

Kitching, Gavin. *Class and Economic Change in Kenya: The Making of an African Petite Bourgeoisie, 1905-1970*. New Haven, Conn.: Yale University Press, 1980.

_____. *Development and Underdevelopment in Historical Perspective: Populism, Nationalism and Industrialization*. London: Methuen, 1982.

Klare, Michael T. "Deadly Convergence: The Perils of the Arms Trade." *World Policy Journal*, 6,1 (Winter 1988-89): 141-68.

_____. "U.S. Military Policy in the Post-Cold War World," in *Socialist Register 1992*, ed. Miliband and Panitch: 131-42.

Kneen, Brewster. *Invisible Giant: Cargill and Its Transnational Strategies*. London: Pluto Press, 1995.

Kolko, Gabriel. *Confronting the Third World: United States Foreign Policy, 1945-1980*. New York: Random House, 1988.

_____. *The Politics of War: The World and United States Foreign Policy, 1943-1945*. New York: Random House, 1990.

_____. *Anatomy of War: Vietnam, the United States and the Modern Historical Experience*. New York: New Press, 1994.

Kolko, Joyce. *Restructuring the World Economy*. New York: Random House, 1988.

Kueh, Y.Y. "Foreign Investment and Economic Change in China." *China Quarterly*, September 1992: 637-90.

Kurkcu, Ertugrul. "The Crisis of the Turkish State." *Middle East Report*, 26,2 (1996): 2-7.

Kuttner, Robert. *The End of Laissez-Faire: National Purpose and the Global Economy after the Cold War*. New York: Knopf, 1991.

Labelle, Micheline. *Ideologie de couleur et classes sociales en Haiti*. Montréal: Les Presses de l'Université de Montréal, 1989.

La Botz, Dan. *Democracy in Mexico: Peasant Rebellion and Political Reform*. Boston: South End Press, 1995.

Lacey, Terry. *Violence and Politics in Jamaica, 1960-1970*. Manchester, England: Manchester University Press, 1977.

Laclau, Ernesto. "Feudalism and Capitalism in Latin America." *New Left Review*, 67 (1971): 19-38.

Lacoste, Yves. *Les Pays Sous-Développés*. Paris: PUF, 1979.

Lacoutre, Jean. *De Gaulle*, vol. 2, *The Ruler, 1945-1970*. London: Collins Harvill, 1991.

Lacoutre, Jean. *Ho Chi Minh*. Harmondsworth, England: Penguin Books, 1968.

LaFeber, Walter. *Inevitable Revolutions: The United States in Central America*. New York: Norton, 1984.

Laffey, John. *Civilization and Its Discontented*. Montreal: Black Rose Books, 1993.

Laguerre, Michel. *The Military and Society in Haiti*. Basingstoke, England: Macmillan, 1993.

Landau, Saul. *The Dangerous Doctrine: National Security and U.S. Foreign Policy*. Boulder, Col.: Westview Press, 1988.

Lardy, Nicholas R. "Economic Recovery and the First Five-Year Plan," in *The People's Republic*, Part I, "The Emergence of Revolutionary China, 1949-1965," vol. 14, *The Cambridge History of China*, ed. Roderick MacFarquhar and John K. Fairbank. Cambridge: Cambridge University Press, 1987: 144-84.

Lairson, Thomas D. and Skidmore, David. *International Political Economy: The Struggle for Power and Wealth*. Fort Worth, Tex.: Harcourt, Brace, 1993.

Larrain, Jorge. *Theories of Development: Capitalism, Colonialism and Dependency*. Cambridge: Cambridge University Press, 1989.

Latin American Bureau, ed. *The Poverty Brokers: The IMF and Latin America*. London: LAB, 1983.

Laurell, Ana Cristina. "Democracy in Mexico: Will the First Be the Last?" *New Left Review*, 194 (July/August 1992): 33-53.

Lawrence, Peter and Seddon, David. "What Price Economic Reform?" *Review of African Political Economy*, 47 (1990): 3-7.

Leacock, Ruth. *Requiem for a Revolution: The United States and Brazil, 1961-1969*. Kent, Ohio: Kent State University Press, 1990.

Leffler, Melvyn P. *A Preponderance of Power: National Security, the Truman Administration, and the Cold War*. Stanford, Cal.: Stanford University Press, 1992.

Lehmann, David. *Democracy and Development in Latin America: Economics, Politics and Religion in the Post-War Period*. Cambridge: Polity Press, 1990.

L'Heriteau, M.-F. *Le Fonds Monetaire International et le Pays du Tiers Monde*. Paris: PUF, 1986.

LeoGrande, William M. "From Reagan to Bush: The Transition in US Policy towards Latin America." *Journal of Latin American Studies*, 24 (1992): 595-621.

————. "Washington et l'Écueil Haitien." *Le Monde Diplomatique*, 487 (Octobre 1994): 7-8.

Lerner, Daniel. *The Passing of Traditional Society: Modernizing the Middle East*. Toronto: Collier-Macmillan, 1964.

Levant, Victor. *Quiet Complicity: Canadian Involvement in the Vietnam War*. Toronto: Between the Lines, 1986.

Lewis, Gordon K. *The Growth of the Modern West Indies*. New York: Monthly Review Press, 1993.

Leys, Colin. *Underdevelopment in Kenya*. London: Heinemann, 1975.

————. "The 'Overdeveloped' Post-Colonial State: A Re-evaluation." *Review of African Political Economy*, 3 (January-April 1976): 39-48.

————. "Underdevelopment and Dependency: Critical Notes." *Journal of Contemporary Asia*, 7,1 (1977): 92-107.

————. "Confronting the African Tragedy." *New Left Review*, 204 (March/April 1994): 33-47.

————. *The Rise and Fall of Development Theory*. London: James Currey, 1996.

Libby, Ronald T. "The United States and Jamaica: Playing the American Card." *Latin American Perspectives*, 65,17,1 (Winter 1990): 86-109.

Link, Perry. "Plant Less, Produce More, Harvest Less." *London Review of Books*, 18,14 (July 18, 1996): 3-5.

Lockhart, Greg. *Nation in Arms: The Origins of the People's Army of Vietnam*. Sydney, Australia: Allen and Unwin, 1989.

Louis, W.R. *The British Empire in the Middle East, 1945-1951: Arab Nationalism, the United States and Postwar Imperialism*. Oxford: Oxford University Press, 1985.

Louis, W.R. *Imperialism at Bay: The United States and the Decolonization of the British Empire, 1941-1945*. Oxford: Oxford University Press, 1978.

Lowe, Lisa. *Critical Terrains: French and British Orientalisms*. Ithaca, N.Y., and London: Cornell University Press, 1992.

Lowe, Peter. *The Origins of the Korean War*. London: Longman, 1986.

Loxley, John. "Structural Adjustment Programmes in Africa: Ghana and Zambia." *Review of African Political Economy*, 47 (1990): 8-27.

Loxley, John and Bonnie K. Campbell, eds. *Structural Adjustment in Africa*. London: Macmillan, 1989.

Lucas, Scott. *Britain and Suez: The Lion's Last Roar*. Manchester, England: Manchester University Press, 1996.

Lundahl, Mats. "Underdevelopment in Haiti: Some Recent Contributions." *Journal of Latin American Studies*, 24 (1992): 411-29.

Lundestad, Geir. *East, West, North, South: Major Developments in International Politics, 1945-1990*. Oslo: Norwegian University Press, 1991.

Macaulay, Nicholas. "Karachi Slays Me." *Index on Censorship*, 3 (1995): 8-12.

MacEwan, Arthur. "Globalization and Stagnation," in *Socialist Register 1994*. London: Merlin Press, 1994: 130-43.

Mallon, Florencia E. "Indian Communities, Political Cultures and the State in

Latin America, 1780-1990." *Journal of Latin American Studies*, 24 (Quincentenary Supplement, 1992): 35-53.

Manguel, Alberto. "Memory and Forgetting." *Index on Censorship*, 25,5 (September/October 1996): 123-31.

Maniruzzaman, Talukdar. "Bangladesh," in *The Cambridge Encyclopedia of India, Pakistan, Bangladesh, Sri Lanka, Nepal, Bhutan and the Maldives*, ed. Francis Robinson. Cambridge: Cambridge University Press, 1989: 216-22.

Manley, Michael. *Jamaica: Struggle on the Periphery*. London: Writers and Readers Publishing, 1982.

Mann, Michael. "As the Twentieth Century Ages." *New Left Review*, 214 (November/December 1995): 104-24.

Manning, Michael. *Jamaica: Struggle on the Periphery*. London: Writers and Readers, 1992.

Manning, Patrick. *Francophone Sub-Saharan Africa, 1880-1985*. Cambridge: Cambridge University Press, 1988.

Marable, Manning. *African and Caribbean Politics*. London: Verso, 1987.

Marchak, M. Patricia. *The Integrated Circus: The New Right and the Restructuring of Global Markets*. Kingston and Montreal: McGill-Queen's University Press, 1993.

Martin, Marie Alexandrine. *Le Mal Cambodgien*. Paris: Hachette, 1989.

Martinez, Osvaldo. "Debt and Foreign Capital: The Origin of the Crisis." *Latin American Perspectives*, 76,20,1 (Winter 1993): 64-82.

Mason, E.S. "Stages of Economic Growth Revisited," in *Models and Methodology*, vol. 1, *Economics in the Long View: Essays in Honour of W.W. Rostow*, ed. C.P. Kindleberger and Guido di Tella. New York: New York University Press, 1982.

McCormack, Gavin. "Kim Country: Hard Times in North Korea." *New Left Review*, 198 (March/April 1993): 21-48.

McCormick, Thomas J. *America's Half-Century: United States Foreign Policy in the Cold War and After*. Baltimore, Md.: Johns Hopkins University Press, 1995.

McCoy, Alfred W. *The Politics of Heroin: CIA Complicity in the Global Drug Trade*. New York: Lawrence Hill, 1991.

McMahon, Robert. *Colonialism and Cold War: The United States and the Struggle for Indonesian Independence, 1945-49*. Ithaca, N.Y.: Cornell University Press, 1981.

————. *The Cold War on the Periphery: The United States, India and Pakistan*. New York: Columbia University Press, 1994.

Mehmet, Ozay. *Westernizing the Third World: The Eurocentricity of Economic Development Theories*. London: Routledge, 1995.

Mehta, Ved. *Rajiv Gandhi and Rama's Kingdom*. New Haven, Conn.: Yale University Press, 1994.

Meisner, Maurice. *Mao's China and After: A History of the People's Republic*. New York: Free Press, 1986.

Merrick, Thomas W. "The Population of Latin America, 1930-1990," in *Latin America since 1930: Economy and Society*, vol. 6, *The Cambridge History of Latin America*, ed. Leslie Bethell. Cambridge: Cambridge University Press, 1994: 3-31.

Mesler, Bill. "The Ghosts of Kwangyu: U.S./Korean Partnership in Repression." *Covert Action Quarterly*, 56 (Spring 1996): 53-7.

Meyer, Michael C. and William L. Sherman. *The Course of Mexican History*. 4th ed. New York: Oxford University Press, 1991.

Midré, Georges. "Bread or Solidarity? Argentine Social Policies, 1983-1990." *Journal of Latin American Studies*, 24 (1992): 343-73.

Milani, Mohsen M. *The Making of Iran's Islamic Revolution: From Monarchy to Islamic Republic*. Boulder, Col.: Westview Press, 1994.

Miliband, Ralph and Leo Panitch, eds. *Socialist Register 1992*. London: Merlin Press, 1992.

Miller, Norman and Rodger Yeager. *Kenya: The Quest for Prosperity*. Boulder, Col.: Westview Press, 1994.

Moghadam, Valentine M., ed. *Gender and National Identity: Women and Politics in Muslim Societies*. London: Zed Books, 1994.

Monroe, Trevor. *The Cold War and the Jamaican Left, 1950-55: Reopening the Files*. Kingston, Jamaica: Kingston Publishers, 1992.

Moore, Barrington. *The Social Origins of Dictatorship and Democracy*. Boston: Beacon Press, 1966.

Moody, Kim. "NAFTA and the Corporate Redesign of North America." *Latin American Perspectives*, 84,22,1 (Winter 1995): 95-116.

Morley, Morris. *Imperial State and Revolution: The United States and Cuba, 1952-1956*. New York: Cambridge University Press, 1987.

Moughrabi, Fouad. "The Media and the Polls: Domesticating the Body Politic." *Middle East Report*, January/February 1993: 38-40.

Munck, Ronaldo. *Politics and Dependency in the Third World*. London: Zed Books, 1984.

Munson, Henry J. *Islam and Revolution in the Middle East*. New Haven, Conn.: Yale University Press, 1988.

Nak-chung, Paik. "South Korea: Unification and the Democratic Challenge." *New Left Review*, 197 (January/February 1993): 67-84.

Nettleford, Rex, ed. *Jamaica in Independence: Essays on the Early Years*. Kingston, Jamaica: Heinemann, 1991.

Newman, R.P. *Owen Lattimore and the 'Loss' of China*. Berkeley: University of California Press, 1991.

Nicholls, David. *From Dessalines to Duvalier: Race, Colour and National Independence in Haiti*. Cambridge: Cambridge University Press, 1989.

Ninh, Bao. *The Sorrow of War*. London: Secker and Warburg, 1994.

Nolan, Peter. "Assessing Economic Growth in the Asian NICs." *Journal of Contemporary Asia*, 20, 1 (1990): 41-63.

Noman, Omar. *The Political Economy of Pakistan, 1947-85*. London: Kegan Paul, 1988.

————. "Pakistan and General Zia: Era and Legacy." *Third World Quarterly*, 11,1 (January 1989): 28-55.

Nordas, Hildegunn K. "South African Manufacturing Industries-Catching Up or Falling Behind?" *Journal of Development Studies*, 32,5 (June 1996): 715-33.

Nouschi, André. *La France et le Monde Arabe*. Paris: Vuibert, 1994.

Novick, Peter. *That Noble Dream: The 'Objectivity Question' and the American Historical Profession*. Cambridge: Cambridge University Press, 1988.

Nun, José. "Democracy and Modernization, Thirty Years Later." *Latin American Perspectives*, 79,20,4 (Fall 1993): 7-27.

Nye, Joseph S., Jr. *Bound to Lead: The Changing Nature of American Power.* New York: Basic Books, 1990.

O'Brien, Donal Cruise. "Modernization, Order, and the Erosion of a Democratic Ideal: American Political Science, 1960-70." *Journal of Development Studies*, 8,4 (July 1972): 351-71.

O'Brien, Philip and Paul Cammack, eds. *Generals in Retreat: The Crisis of Military Rule in Latin America.* Manchester, England: Manchester University Press, 1985.

O'Donnell, Guillermo. "Reflections on the Patterns of Change in the Bureaucratic-Authoritarian State." *Latin American Research Review*, 12,1 (1978): 3-38.

O'Meara, Dan. *Forty Lost Years: The National Party, the Crisis of Apartheid, and the Politics of the South African State, 1948-1993.* Johannesburg, South Africa: Ravan Press, 1996.

Oncu, Ayse. "Street Politics," in *Society and Politics in Egypt and Turkey*, ed. Oncu, Keyder, and Ibrahim, 1994.

Oncu, Ayse, Caglar Keyder, and Saad Eddin Ibrahim, eds. *Developmentalism and Beyond: Society and Politics in Egypt and Turkey.* Cairo: American University in Cairo Press, 1994.

Oppenheim, Lois Hecht. *Politics in Chile: Democracy, Authoritarianism and the Search for Development.* Boulder, Col.: Westview Press, 1993.

Osborne, Milton. *Sihanouk: Prince of Light, Prince of Darkness.* London: Allen and Unwin, 1994.

Otero, Geraldo. "Mexico's Political Future(s) in a Globalizing World Economy." *Canadian Review of Sociology and Anthropology*, 32,3 (August 1995): 315-39.

Ovendale, Richie, ed. *The Foreign Policy of the British Labour Governments, 1945-1951.* Leicester, England: Leicester University Press, 1984.

Owen, Roger. *State, Power and Politics in the Making of the Modern Middle East.* London: Routledge, 1992.

————. "A New Post-War System? The Middle East in a Realigned World." *Middle East Report*, 184,23,5 (September-October 1993): 2-6.

Oviedo, Rodolfo M. "Are We or Aren't We?" NACLA *Report on the Americas*, 25,4 (February 1992): 19.

Oxhorn, Philip. "The Popular Sector—Response to an Authoritarian Regime: Shantytown Organizations since the Military Coup." *Latin American Perspectives*, 67,18,1 (Winter 1991): 66-91.

Panton, David. *Jamaica's Michael Manley: The Great Transformation (1972-92).* Kingston, Jamaica: Kingston Publishers, 1993.

Parfitt, Trevor. "Lies, Damned Lies and Statistics: World Bank and ECA Structural Adjustment Controversy." *Review of African Political Economy*, 47 (1990): 128-41.

Park, Jae Kyu and Jung Gun Kim, eds. *The Politics of North Korea.* Boulder, Col.: Westview Press, 1979.

Parry, J.H., Philip Sherlock, and A. Manigot. *A Short History of the West Indies.* London: Macmillan, 1987.

Pastor, Manuel. "Latin America, the Debt crisis, and the International Monetary Fund." *Latin American Perspectives*, 16,1,60 (Winter 1989): 19-110.

Payer, Cheryl. *The World Bank: A Critical Analysis*. New York: Monthly Review Press, 1982.

_____. *The Debt Trap: The* IMF *and the Third World*. Harmondsworth, England: Penguin Books, 1984.

Payne, Anthony. *Politics in Jamaica*. London: Hurst, 1988.

_____. "The 'New' Manley and the New Political Economy of Jamaica." *Third World Quarterly*, 13,3 (1992): 463-73.

_____. "Liberal Economics Versus Electoral Politics in Jamaica," in Modern Caribbean Politics, ed. Anthony Payne and Paul Sutton. Baltimore, Md.: Johns Hopkins University Press, 1993.

Pearce, Jenny. *Under the Eagle*. Boston: South End Press, 1982.

Peemans, Jean-Philippe. "Imperial Hangovers: Belgium—The Economics of Decolonization." *Journal of Contemporary History*, 15,2 (April, 1980): 257-86.

Pereira, Anthony W. "Economic Underdevelopment, Democracy and Civil Society: The North-East Brazil Case." *Third World Quarterly*, 14,2 (1993): 365-79.

Petras, James. "Building a Popular Army in Argentina." *New Left Review*, 71 (January-February 1972): 45-50.

_____. "The New Class Basis of Chilean Politics." *New Left Review*, 172 (November-December 1988): 67-81.

_____ and Morris Morley. *U.S. Hegemony under Seige: Class, Politics and Development in Latin America*. London: Verso, 1990.

_____ and Steve Vieux. "Twentieth-Century Neoliberals: Inheritors of the Exploits of Columbus." *Latin American Perspectives*, 74,19,3 (Summer 1992): 25-46.

_____ and F.I. Leiva, with Henry Veltmeyer. *Democracy and Poverty in Chile: The Limits to Electoral Politics*. Boulder, Col.: Westview Press, 1994.

Phillips, Anne. *The Enigma of Colonialism: British Policy in West Africa*. London: James Currey, 1989.

Pilger, John. "On Her Majesty's Bloody Service." *New Statesman and Society*, 7,296 (1994): 16-18.

Pipes, Daniel. "Fundamental Questions about Muslims." *Wall Street Journal*, Oct. 30 1992, A11, cited in *Journal of Palestine Studies*, 25,2 (Winter 1996): 201-2.

Pomonti, Jean-Claude and Hugues Tertrais. *Viêtnam, Communistes et Dragons*. Paris: Le Monde Éditions, 1994.

Porter, A.N. and A.J. Stockwell. *British Imperial Policy and Decolonization, 1938-64*, vol. 2, *1951-64*. Basingstoke, England: Macmillan, 1989.

Porter, Bernard. *The Lion's Share: A Short History of British Imperialism, 1850-1983*. London: Longman, 1984.

Porter, Gareth. "The Politics of 'Renovation' in Vietnam." *Problems of Communism*, 39 (May-June 1990): 72-88.

_____. "The Transformation of Vietnam's World-view: From Two Camps to Interdependence." *Contemporary Southeast Asia*, 12,1 (June 1990): 1-19.

Post, Ken. *Revolution, Socialism and Nationalism in Viet Nam: An Interrupted Revolution*. 3 vols. Belmont, Mass.: Wadsworth, 1989.

Poulton, Robin and Michael Harris. *Putting People First: Voluntary Agencies and Third World Development*. London: Macmillan, 1989.

Prince, Rod. *Haiti: Family Business*. London: Latin American Bureau, 1985.

Quirk, Robert E. *Fidel Castro*. New York: Norton, 1994.

Rabe, Stephen G. *Eisenhower and Latin America: The Foreign Policy of Anticommunism*. Chapel Hill: University of North Carolina Press, 1988.

Ramirez, Miguel D. *Mexico's Economic Crisis: Its Origins and Consequences*. New York: Praeger, 1989.

Ravenhill, J. "The North-South Balance of Power." *International Affairs*, 66,4 (1990): 731-48.

Reed, David, ed. *Structural Adjustment and the Environment*. Boulder, Col.: Westview Press, 1992.

Regaud, Nicolas. *La Cambodge dans la Tourmente: Le Troisième Conflict indochinois, 1978-1991*. Paris: Harmattan, 1992.

Reporters Sans Frontières. *Le drame Algérien: Un Peuple en Otage*. Paris: Éd. La Découverte, 1994.

Ruedy, John. *Modern Algeria: The Origins and Development of a Nation*. Bloomington: Indiana University Press, 1992.

Reynolds, David. *Brittania Overruled: British Policy and World Power in the Twentieth Century*. London: Longman, 1991.

Richards, Alan and John Waterbury. *A Political Economy of the Middle East: State, Class, and Economic Development*. Boulder, Col.: Westview Press, 1990.

Riddell, Barry. "Things Fall Apart Again: Structural Adjustment Programmes in Sub-Saharan Africa." *Journal of Modern African Studies*, 30,1 (1992): 53-68.

Rioux, Jean-Pierre. *The Fourth Republic, 1944-1958*. Cambridge: Cambridge University Press, 1989.

Robertson, B.A. "Islam and Europe: An Enigma or a Myth?" *The Middle East Journal*, 48,2 (Spring 1994): 288-308.

Robison, Richard. *The Rise of Capitalism in Indonesia*. Sydney, Australia: Allen and Unwin, 1986.

Rock, David. *Argentina, 1516-1987: From Spanish Colonization to Alfonsin*. Berkeley: University of California Press, 1987.

————. "Argentina, 1930-46," in *Argentina since Independence*, ed Leslie Bethell. Cambridge: Cambridge University Press, 1993.

Rooney, David. *Kwame Nkrumah: The Political Kingdom in the Third World*. New York: St. Martin's Press, 1988.

Rothermund, Dietmar. *An Economic History of India: From Pre-Colonial Times to 1991*. London: Routledge, 1993.

Roxborough, Ian. *Theories of Underdevelopment*. Houndmills, England: Macmillan, 1979.

Ruiz, R.E. *Cuba: The Making of a Revolution*. New York: Norton, 1970.

Ruscio, Alain. *La Décolonisation Tragique: Une Histoire de la Décolonisation Française, 1945-1962.* Paris: Messidor, 1987.

Ruscio, Alain. *La Guerre Française D'Indochine*. Paris: Éditions Complexe, 1992.

Sadowski, Yahya. "The New Orientalism and the Democracy Debate." *Middle East Report*, 183 (July-August 1993): 14-21.

Sader, Emir and Ken Silverstein. *Without Fear of Being Happy: Lula, the Workers Party and Brazil*. London: Verso, 1991.

Said, Edward W. *Orientalism: Western Conceptions of the Orient*. London: Penguin
    Books, 1978.
————. "Orientalism Reconsidered." *Race and Class*, 2 (Autumn 1985): 1-15.
————. *Culture and Imperialism*. Toronto: Random House, 1993.
Salamé, Ghassan. "Torn between the Atlantic and the Mediterranean: Europe and
    the Middle East in the Post-Cold War Era." *The Middle East Journal*,
    48,2 (Spring 1994): 226-49.
Sarkar, Sumit. *Modern India, 1885-1947*. Delhi: Macmillan (India), 1983.
Salisbury, Harrison. *The New Emperors: China in the Era of Mao and Deng*. New
    York: Avon, 1993.
Salomon, Jean-Jacques and André Lebeau. *Mirages of Development: Science and
    Technology for the Third Worlds*. Boulder, Col.: Lynne Rienner, 1993.
Sandbrook, Richard, with Judith Barker. *The Politics of Africa's Economic Stagna-
    tion*. Cambridge: Cambridge University Press, 1985.
————. *The Politics of Africa's Economic Recovery*. Cambridge: Cambridge Uni-
    versity Press, 1994.
Sarlo, Beatriz. "Argentina under Menem: The Aesthetics of Domination." NACLA
    *Report on the Americas*, 27,2 (September/October 1994): 33-7.
Schell, Orville. *To Get Rich Is Glorious: China in the Eighties*. London: Robin Clark,
    1986.
———— and Todd Lappin. "China Plays the Market." *The Nation*, 255,20
    (December 14, 1992): 727-43.
Schneider, Ronald M. *"Order and Progress": A Political History of Brazil*. Boulder,
    Col.: Westview Press, 1991.
Schram, Stuart P. *The Political Thought of Mao Tse-tung*. New York: Praeger, 1963.
————. *Mao Tse-tung*. Harmondsworth, England: Penguin Books, 1967.
Schurmann, Franz. *Ideology and Organization in Communist China*. Berkeley:
    University of California Press, 1970.
————. *The Logic of World Power: An Inquiry into the Origins, Currents, and
    Contradictions of World Politics*. New York: Random House, 1974.
————. and Orvill Schell, eds. *Republican China: Nationalism, War and the Rise
    of Communism, 1911-1949*. New York: Vintage Books, 1967.
Scott, Peter Dale. "The United States and the Overthrow of Sukarno, 1965-1967."
    *Pacific Affairs*, 58 (Summer 1985).
Seabrook, Jeremy. *Victims of Development: Resistance and Alternatives*. London:
    Verso, 1993.
Sender, John and Sheila Smith. *The Development of Capitalism in Africa*. London:
    Methuen, 1986.
Shawcross, William. "Tragedy in Cambodia." *New York Review of Books*, Nov. 14,
    1996: 41-6.
Sheehan, Neil. *After the War Was Over: Hanoi and Saigon*. New York: Vintage
    Books, 1991.
Shumway, Nicolas. *The Invention of Argentina*. Berkeley: University of California
    Press, 1991.
Sigmund, Paul E. *The Overthrow of Allende and the Politics of Chile, 1964-1976*.
    Pittsburg, Penn.: University of Pittsburg Press, 1976.
Silva, Patricio. "Technocrats and Politics in Chile: From the Chicago Boys to the
    CIEPLAN Monks." *Journal of Latin American Studies*, 22 (1990):
    385-412.

Simmie, Scott and Bob Nixon. *Tiananmen Square*. Vancouver: Douglas and McIntyre, 1989.

Singer, H.W. and Surya Sharma, eds. *Economic Development and World Debt*. Basingstoke, England: Macmillan, 1989.

Skocpol, Theda. *States and Social Revolutions: A Comparative Analysis of France, Russia and China*. New York: Cambridge University Press, 1979.

Smil, Vaclav. *China's Environmental Crisis*. London: M.E. Sharpe, 1993.

Smith, Gavin. *Livelihood and Resistance: Peasants and the Politics of Land in Peru*. Berkeley: University of California Press, 1989.

Smith, Peter H. "Mexico since 1946: Dynamics of an Authoritarian Regime," in *Mexico since Independence*, ed. Leslie Bethell. Cambridge: Cambridge University Press, 1991: 321-96.

Smith, R.B. *An International History of the Vietnam War*. 3 vols. London: Macmillan, 1983-91.

Smith, William C. "Reflections on the Political Economy of Authoritarian Rule and Capitalist Reorganization in Contemporary Argentina," in *Generals in Retreat*, ed. O'Brien and Cammack.

Sobham, Salma. "National Identity, Fundamentalism and the Women's Movement in Bangladesh," in *Gender and National Identity*, ed. Moghadam: 63-80.

Spear, Percival. *Modern India*. Ann Arbor: University of Michigan Press, 1961.

Spence, Jonathan D. *In Search of Modern China*. New York: Norton, 1990.

————. *Chinese Roundabout: Essays in History and Culture*. New York: Norton, 1992.

Spooner, Mary Helen. *Soldiers in a Narrow Land: The Pinochet Regime in Chile*. Berkeley: University of California Press, 1994.

Spurr, David. *The Rhetoric of Empire: Colonial Discourse in Journalism, Travel Writing and Imperial Administration*. Durham, N.C.: Duke University Press, 1993.

Staniland, Martin. *American Intellectuals and African Nationalists, 1955-1970*. New Haven, Conn.: Yale University Press, 1991.

Stairs, Denis. *The Diplomacy of Constraint: Canada, the Korean War and the United States*. Toronto: University of Toronto Press, 1974.

Starn, Orin. "'I Dreamed of Foxes and Hawks': Reflections on Peasant Protest, New Social Movements, and the Rondas Campesinas of Northern Peru," in *The Making of Social Movements in Latin America: Identity, Strategy and Democracy*, ed. Arturo Escobar and Sonia E. Alvarez. Boulder, Col.: Westview Press, 1992: 112-33.

Stavrianos, L.S. *Global Rift: The Third World Comes of Age*. New York: William Morrow, 1981.

Stearns, Monteagle. *Entangled Allies: US Policy toward Greece, Turkey and Cyprus*. New York: Council on Foreign Relations Press, 1992.

Stephens, Evelyne H. and John D. Stephens. *Democratic Socialism in Jamaica: The Political Movement and Social Transformation in Dependent Capitalism*. Princeton, N.J.: Princeton University Press, 1986.

Stephens, Robert. *Nasser*. London: Penguin Books, 1971.

Sprinker, Michael, ed. *Edward Said: A Critical Reader*. Cambridge: Blackwell, 1992.

Stockwell, S.E. "Political Strategies of British Business during Decolonization:

The Case of Gold Coast/Ghana, 1945-57." *Journal of Imperial and Commonwealth History*, 23,2 (1995): 277-300.

Stone, Carl. *Class, State, and Democracy in Jamaica*. New York: Praeger, 1986.

————. "Power, Policy and Politics in Independent Jamaica," in *Jamaica in Independence: Essays on the Early Years*, ed. Rex Nettleford. Kingston, Jamaica: Heinemann, 1989.

Stone, I.F. *The Hidden History of the Korean War*. New York: Monthly Review Press, 1952.

Stork, Joe and Laura Flanders. "Power Structure and the American Media." *Middle East Report*, January/February 1993: 2-7.

Strange, Susan. *States and Markets*. London: Pinter Publishers, 1994.

Stubbs, Richard. *Hearts and Minds in Guerilla Warfare: The Malayan Emergency, 1948-1960*. Singapore: Oxford University Press, 1989.

Stueck, William, "The March to the Yalu: The Perspective from Washington," in *Child of Conflict: The Korean-American Relationship, 1943-1953*, ed. Bruce Cumings. Seattle: University of Washington Press, 1983: 195-237.

Sutton, John L. and Geoffrey Kemp. "Arms to Developing Countries, 1945-1965." *Adelphi Papers*, 28 (October 1966): 1-45.

Sutton, Paul, ed. *Dual Legacies in the Contemporary Caribbean: Continuing Aspects of British and French Domination*. London: Frank Cass, 1986.

Swift, Jamie and Tomlinson, Brian, eds. *Conflicts of Interest: Canada and the Third World*. Toronto: Between the Lines, 1991.

Swainson, Nicola. "The Rise of a National Bourgeoisie in Kenya." *Review of African Political Economy*, 8 (January-April 1977): 39-55.

Tarock, Adam. "Civilisational Conflict? Fighting the Enemy under a New Banner." *Third World Quarterly*, 16,1 (1995): 5-17.

Tavares, Ricardo. "Land and Democracy: Considering the Agrarian Question." NACLA *Report on the Americas*, 28,6 (May/June 1995).

Temu, Arnold and Bonaventure Swai. *Historians and Africanist History: A Critique*. London, Zed Books, 1981.

Teubal, Miguel. "Internationalization of Capital and Agroindustrial Complexes: Their Impact on Latin American Agriculture." *Latin American Perspectives*, 14,3 (Summer 1987): 316-64.

Thakur, Ramesh. "Restoring India's Economic Health." *Third World Quarterly*, 14,1 (1993): 137-57.

Thakur, Ramesh. *The Government and Politics of India*. Basingstoke, England: Macmillan, 1995.

Thomas, Clive Y. *The Rise of the Authoritarian State in Peripheral Societies*. New York: Monthly Review Press, 1984.

Thorne, Christopher. "After the Europeans: American Designs for the Remaking of Southeast Asia." *Diplomatic History*, 12,2 (Spring 1988): 201-8.

Throup, David. *Economic and Social Origins of Mau Mau, 1945-53*. London: James Currey, 1988.

Timerman, Jacobo. *Chile: Death in the South*. New York: Knopf, 1987.

Tironi, Eugenio. *Pinochet: La Dictature Néo-Liberal*. Paris: Éditions L'Harmattan, 1987.

Tohidi, Nayereh, "Modernity, Islamization and Women in Iran," in *Gender and National Identity*, ed. Moghadam: 110-47.

Tomlinson, B.R. *The Political Economy of the Raj, 1914-1947: The Economics of Decolonization in India*. London: Macmillan, 1979.

Tordoff, William. *Government and Politics in Africa*. Basingstoke, England: Macmillan, 1993.

Trimberger, Ellen Kay. *Revolution from Above: Military Bureaucrats and Development in Japan, Turkey, Egypt, and Peru*. New Brunswick, N.J.: Transaction Books, 1978.

Tripp, C., ed. *Contemporary Egypt: Through Egyptian Eyes*. London: Routledge, 1993.

Turshen, Merideth. "US Aid and AIDS in Africa." *Review of African Political Economy*, 55 (1992): 95-101.

Vanaik, Achin. "Reflections on Communalism and Nationalism in India." *New Left Review*, 196 (November/December 1992).

Vatikiotis, Michael R. *Indonesia under Suharto: Order, Development and Pressure for Change*. 2nd ed. New York: Routledge, 1994.

Vatikiotis, P.J. *The History of Modern Egypt: From Muhammad Ali to Mubarak*. Rev. ed. London: Weidenfeld and Nicholson, 1991.

Vergara, Pilar. "Changes in the Economic Functions of the Chilean State under the Military Regime," in *Military Rule in Chile: Dictatorship and Oppositions*, ed. J. Samuel Valenzuela and Arturo Valenzuela. Baltimore, Md.: Johns Hopkins University Press, 1986.

Vickery, Michael. *Kampuchea: Politics, Economics and Society*. London: Pinter, 1986.

Vines, Alex. *Renamo: Terrorism in Mozambique*. London, James Currey, 1991.

Vivian, Jessica. "NGOs and Sustainable Development in Zimbabwe: No Magic Bullets." *Development and Change*, 25 (1994): 167-93.

Wallace, Elizabeth. *The British Caribbean: From the Decline of Colonialism to the End of Federation*. Toronto: University of Toronto Press, 1977.

Waterbury, John. *The Egypt of Nasser and Sadat: The Political Economy of Two Regimes*. Princeton, N.J.: Princeton University Press, 1983.

Watkins, Kevin. "Agriculture and Food Security in the GATT Uruguay Round." *Review of African Political Economy*, 50 (1991): 38-50.

_____. *Fixing the Rules*. London: Catholic Institute of International Affairs, 1992.

Welch, Cliff. "Rivalry and Unification: Mobilizing Rural Workers in Sao Paulo on the Eve of the Brazilian Golpe of 1964." *Journal of Latin American Studies*, 27,1 (February 1995): 161-87.

Wesseling, H.L. "Post Imperial Holland." *Journal of Contemporary History*, 15,1 (January 1980): 125-42.

Widner, Jennifer A. *The Rise of a Party-State in Kenya: From 'Harambee!' to 'Nyayo!'*. Berkeley: University of California Press, 1992.

Wiener, Jon. *Professors, Politics and Pop*. London: Verso, 1991.

Wilber, Charles K., ed. *The Political Economy of Development and Underdevelopment*. New York: Random House, 1988.

Wilentz, Amy. *The Rainy Season: Haiti since Duvalier*. London: Jonathan Cape, 1989.

Williams, Raymond. *Keywords: A Vocabulary of Culture and Society*. Rev. ed. Glasgow: Fontana, 1983.

Wilson, Rodney. "The Economic Relations of the Middle East: Toward Europe or within the Region." *The Middle East Journal*, 48,2 (Spring 1994): 268-87.

Winn, Peter. *Americas: The Changing Face of Latin America and the Caribbean*. New York: Pantheon Books, 1992.

Wittner, Lawrence S. *Cold War America*. New York: Praeger, 1974.

Wolfe, Alan, ed., *America at Century's End*. Berkeley: University of California Press, 1991.

Wolpert, Stanley. *A New History of India*. New York: Oxford University Press, 1992.

_____. *Zulfi Bhutto of Pakistan: His Life and Times*. Oxford: Oxford University Press, 1994.

Wood, Robert E. *From Marshall Plan to Debt Crisis: Foreign Aid and Development Choices in the World Economy*. Berkeley: University of California Press, 1986.

Worsley, Peter. *The Three Worlds: Culture and World Development*. London: Weidenfeld and Nicolson, 1984.

Yapp, M.E. *The Near East since the First World War*. Harlow, England: Longman, 1991.

Yergin, Daniel. *Shattered Peace: The Origins of the Cold War and the National Security State*. Boston: Houghton Mifflin, 1977.

_____. *The Prize: The Epic Quest for Oil, Money, and Power*. New York: Simon and Schuster, 1991.

Young, Crawford. *The Colonial State in Comparative Perspective*. New Haven, Conn.: Yale University Press, 1994.

Young, Marilyn. *The Vietnam Wars, 1945-1990*. New York: HarperCollins, York, 1991.

Zasloff, Joseph J. and MacAlister Brown. *Communist Indochina and U.S. Foreign Policy: Postwar Realities*. Boulder, Col.: Westview Press, 1978.

Zhou, Kate Xiao. *How the Farmers Changed China: Power to the People*. Boulder, Col.: Westview Press, 1996.

Zimbalist, Andrew. "Teetering on the Brink: Cuba's Current Economic and Political Crisis." *Journal of Latin American Studies*, 24 (1992): 407-18.

Zins, Max Jean. *Histoire Politique de l'Inde Indépendante*. Paris: PUF, 1992.

Zubaida, Sami. *Islam, the People and the State: Essays on Political Ideas and Movements in the Middle East*. New York: Routledge, 1989.

Zubaida, Sami. "Turkish Islam and National Identity." *Middle East Report*, 26,2 (1996): 10-15.

# Government Documents and Official Publications

Amnesty International. *The 1993 Report on Human Rights around the World*. Almeda, Cal.: Hunter House, 1993.

_____. *Power and Impunity: Human Rights under the New Order*. New York, 1994.

Canada-Americas Policy Alternatives (CAPA). *Focus on Corruption: Report on Canada's Sixth Year in the OAS*. CAPA Occasional Paper. Toronto, June 1996.

German, Tony and Judith Randel. "Eradicating Poverty: The Achievable Alternative," in *The Reality of Aid 1996*, ed. Randle and German: 4-12.

Helleiner, Gerald K., ed. *Africa and the I.M.F.* Washington, D.C.: IMF, 1986.

International Monetary Fund (IMF). *Annual Report, 1992*. Washington, 1993.

Kim, Il-Song. *Answers to the Questions Raised by the Costa Rica-Korean Association of Friendship and Culture*. Pyongyang, North Korea: Foreign Languages Publishing House, 1975.

Patel, I.G., ed. *Policies for African Development: From the 1980s to the 1990s*. Washington, D.C.: IMF, 1992.

Randle, Judith and Tony German, eds. *The Reality of Aid 1996: An Independent Review of International Aid*. London: Earthscan Publications, 1996.

South Commission. *The Challenge to the South: The Report of the South Commission*. Oxford: Oxford University Press, 1990.

Stockholm International Peace Research Institute (SIPRI). *SIPRI Yearbook, 1996: Armaments, Disarmament and International Security*. New York: Oxford University Press, 1996.

Tomlinson, Brian. "Canadian Aid Performance," in *The Reality of Aid 1996*, ed. Randle and German: 101-7.

United Nations Development Programme (UNDP). *Human Development Report 1990*. New York: Oxford University Press, 1990.

_____. *Human Development Report 1996*. New York: Oxford University Press, 1996.

UNICEF. *The State of the World's Children*. New York, 1989.

United States, State Department. *The United States Policy in the Korean Crisis*. Far Eastern Series. Washington, D.C.: U.S. Government Printing Office, 1950.

Van Hees, Ted, Sasja Bokkerink, Pettermann, and Pepijn Nicolas. "Another Reality of Debt: The Role of the Creditor," in *The Reality of Aid 1996*, ed. Randle and German: 28-31.

World Bank. *Awakening the Market: Viet Nam's Economic Transition*. Washington, D.C., 1992.

_____. *Caribbean Region: Current Economic Situation, Regional Issues and Capital Flows*. Country Study. Washington, D.C., 1992.

_____. *Indonesia: Sustaining Development*. Country Study. Washington, D.C., 1994.

_____. *Trends in Developing Economies*. Washington, D.C.: IBRD, 1995.

_____. *World Development Report, 1985: International Capital and Economic Development Indicators*. New York: Oxford University Press, 1985.

_____. *World Development Report, 1995: Workers in an Integrating World*. Oxford: Oxford University Press, 1995.

_____. *World Development Report, 1996: From Plan to Market*. Oxford: Oxford University Press, 1996.

_____. *World Tables 1993*. Baltimore, Md.: Johns Hopkins University Press, 1993.

World Commission on Environment and Development (Gro Brundtland, chair). *Our Common Future*. Oxford: Oxford University Press, 1987.

# Works of Reference

Brown, Lester R. et al. *State of the World 1995: A Worldwatch Institute Report on Progress toward a Sustainable Society*. New York: Norton, 1995.

East, Roger, ed. *Keesing's Record of World Events, 1990-95*. London: Longman, 1990-95.

Europa Editions Limited. *Africa South of the Sahara 1991*. London: Europa Publications, 1990.

_____. *The Europa World Yearbook 1995*. 2 vols. London: Europa Publications, 1995.

Keyfitz, Nathan and Wilhelm Flieger. *World Population Growth and Ageing: Demographic Trends in the Late Twentieth Century*. Chicago: University of Chicago Press, 1990.

Kurian, George Thomas. *Encyclopedia of the Third World*. 3rd ed. New York: Facts on File, 1987.

Le Monde. *L'Histoire au Jour le Jour, 1944-1991*. Paris, 1992.

# Index